Flourishing and Floundering Financially in Emerging Adulthood

EMERGING ADULTHOOD SERIES

Series Editor
Larry J. Nelson

Books in the Series

Emerging Adults' Religiousness and Spirituality: Meaning-Making in an Age of Transition
Edited by Carolyn McNamara Barry and Mona M. Abo-Zena

Flourishing in Emerging Adulthood: Positive Development during the Third Decade of Life
Edited by Laura M. Padilla-Walker and Larry J. Nelson

The Marriage Paradox: Why Emerging Adults Love Marriage Yet Push It Aside
Brian J. Willoughby and Spencer L. James

The Life Story, Domains of Identity, and Personality Development in Emerging Adulthood: Integrating Narrative and Traditional Approaches
Michael W. Pratt and M. Kyle Matsuba

The Romantic Lives of Emerging Adults: Getting From I to We
Varda Konstam

Leaving Care and the Transition to Adulthood: International Contributions to Theory, Research, and Practice
Edited by Varda R. Mann-Feder and Martin Goyette

Young Adult Development at the School-to-Work Transition: International Pathways and Processes
Edited by E. Anne Marshall and Jennifer E. Symonds

The Experience of Emerging Adulthood among Street-Involved Youth
Doug Magnuson, Mikael Jansson, and Cecilia Benoit

Sexuality in Emerging Adulthood
Edited by Elizabeth M. Morgan and Manfred H. M. van Dulmen

Generation Disaster: Coming of Age Post-9/11
Karla Vermeulen

Cultivating Student Success: A Multifaceted Approach to Working with Emerging Adults in Higher Education
Tisha A. Duncan and Allison A. Buskirk-Cohen

A New Lens on Emerging Adulthood: Fluidity as the Path to Settling Down
Shmuel Shulman

Flourishing as a Scholar: Research Methods for the Study of Emerging Adulthood
Edited by Angela Sorgente, Rimantas Vosylis, Shannon Claxton, and Joseph Schwab

Flourishing and Floundering Financially in Emerging Adulthood: A Handbook
Edited by Ashley B. LeBaron-Black, Heather Kelley, and Angela Sorgente

Flourishing and Floundering Financially in Emerging Adulthood

A Handbook

Edited by
Ashley B. LeBaron-Black
Heather Kelley
and
Angela Sorgente

OXFORD
UNIVERSITY PRESS

OXFORD
UNIVERSITY PRESS

Oxford University Press is a department of the University of Oxford.
It furthers the University's objective of excellence in research, scholarship,
and education by publishing worldwide. Oxford is a registered trade mark of
Oxford University Press in the UK and in certain other countries.

Published in the United States of America by Oxford University Press
198 Madison Avenue, New York, NY 10016, United States of America.

Library of Congress Cataloging-in-Publication Data
Names: Lebaron-Black, Ashley, editor. | Kelley, Heather Howell, editor. |
Sorgente, Angela, editor.
Title: Flourishing and floundering financially in emerging adulthood :
a handbook / edited by Ashley B. LeBaron-Black, Heather
Kelley and Angela Sorgente.
Description: New York, NY : Oxford University Press, [2025] |
Series: Emerging adulthood series |
Includes bibliographical references and index.
Identifiers: LCCN 2024040455 (print) | LCCN 2024040456 (ebook) |
ISBN 9780197699126 (paperback) | ISBN 9780197699140
(epub) | ISBN 9780197699157
Subjects: LCSH: Financial literacy. | Finance, Personal. |
Young adults–Finance, Personal.
Classification: LCC HG179 .F558 2025 (print) | LCC HG179
(ebook) | DDC 332.024–dc23/eng/20241226
LC record available at https://lccn.loc.gov/2024040455
LC ebook record available at https://lccn.loc.gov/2024040456

DOI: 10.1093/9780197699157.001.0001

Printed by Integrated Books International, United States of America

MIX
Paper
FSC FSC® C183721

Contents

PART II. FINANCIAL CONSIDERATIONS IN EMERGING ADULTHOOD

PART III. SOCIODEMOGRAPHIC CHARACTERISTICS AND EMERGING ADULTS' FINANCIAL LITERACY

Acknowledgments

A huge thank-you to the brilliant authors of all 20 chapters. They are world-renowned experts in their fields, and we are in awe of and deeply honored by their contributions to this book. Another huge thank-you to the incredibly generous reviewers of all 20 chapters, who are also world-renowned experts in their fields. Unfortunately, in academia, review work is almost entirely uncompensated, and the system relies heavily on gifts of time and expertise given by those selflessly motivated by the generation of knowledge for the benefit of society. Our reviewers' insights and suggestions were invaluable to helping each chapter fulfill its potential. In alphabetical order, our expert reviewers were Dr. Shikha Bhatia, Dr. Brenda Cude, Dr. Jeff Dew, Dr. Anne Fletcher, Dr. Gabriela Fonseca, Dr. Daniel Gray, Ellie Hansen, Dr. Rona Hart, Dr. Jeff Hill, Dr. Jae Min Lee, Dr. Sunwoo Lee, Dr. Lijun Li, Paula Lopez, Dr. Mandeep Mahendru, Dr. Johanna Peetz, Dr. Cliff Robb, Matthew Saxey, Dr. Aleissa Sconti, Dr. Giulia Sesini, and Dr. Maja Zupančič. Thank you to Dr. Larry Nelson, who generously invited us to contribute this volume to his prestigious emerging adulthood book series. Thank you to Oxford University Press for taking a chance on three junior scholars. Last of all, thank you to our husbands, mentors, and others who have supported us in this enormous endeavor.

Sincerely,
Ashley, Heather, and Angela

Contributors

Kathryn A. Carroll is an Associate Professor in the Department of Nutrition and Family Sciences at the University of Central Arkansas (UCA). Her research interests are in consumer decision-making, with a focus on food and financial choices. Kathryn is also a faculty affiliate of the Arkansas Center for Research in Economics, and an active volunteer with the IRS-VITA program in Central Arkansas. At UCA, she teaches undergraduate and graduate courses in personal finance. Kathryn earned her PhD in Consumer Behavior and Family Economics at the University of Wisconsin-Madison, and an MS in Ag and Applied Economics at the University of Delaware.

Alexander Chan, PhD, is the mental health specialist for the University of Maryland Extension. His Extension program development has focused on stigma reduction, mental health of farmers, and the opioid crisis in rural Maryland. Dr. Chan is also a Licensed Marriage and Family Therapist in Maryland, New York, and Washington, D.C.

Swarn Chatterjee, PhD, Bluerock Professor of Financial Planning, serves as the Department Head for Financial Planning, Housing and Consumer Economics at the University of Georgia. His research focuses on evaluation of financial socialization on young adults' financial and subjective well-being; and identification of factors that improve financial decision-making among transitioning young adults. Dr. Chatterjee serves as an Associate Editor for the *Journal of Financial Counseling and Planning, Financial Services Review,* and the *Journal of Financial Service Professionals.* He received his PhD in Consumer Economics with a Specialization in Personal Financial Planning from Texas Tech University.

Laura Colautti is a psychologist and research fellow in the Department of Psychology at Università Cattolica del Sacro Cuore, Milan, Italy. She earned a PhD in Psychology by investigating decision-making under value-based conditions and the relationships with executive functions in typical older adults and patients with Parkinson's disease. She previously attended a postgraduate program in clinical neuropsychology of adults and older adults. Her main research interests concern the cognitive mechanisms underlying decision-making and other complex cognitive processes.

Sharon M. Danes is Professor Emeritus of the Family Social Science Department at the University of Minnesota. Dr. Danes authored the *Family Financial Socialization Theory.* Her research focus emphasizes the intersection of economic and social decision-making. That research and her consultations incorporate both implicit and explicit socialization, teaching children about money, couple relational processes associated with finances, and financial behavior relating to overall well-being.

Phuc Dang is a second-year student in Purdue University's Social Psychology

PhD program. During his undergraduate studies, his research interests focused on financial socialization, cultural values, and social exclusion. As he pursues graduate training, he continues to explore some of these interests, in addition to developing his expertise in pro-social behavior and agreeableness under the guidance of Dr. William Graziano.

Kayla Dutton is an alumna of the University of Wisconsin—Madison, where she earned her BS in Personal Financial Planning. Throughout her undergraduate studies, she exhibited a dedication to exploring the impacts between socioeconomic conditions and financial well-being, particularly in navigating volatile financial landscapes. Since graduating, Kayla has honed her expertise in financial forecasting and portfolio management, leveraging her academic foundation to provide strategic insights and ensure the health and resilience of portfolios under her stewardship.

Pamela Dysart is a PhD student at the University of Minnesota in the Family Social Science Department. Her research interests focus on death, dying, grief, and loss. She has engaged in the community as an AmeriCorps VISTA and Peace Corps Volunteer and worked with middle school students on financial literacy education. Pamela has her MSW, taught English as a Second Language to Community College students, and has been working in both clinical and community settings throughout her career.

Nusroon Fatiha is a doctoral candidate in the Department of Family Social Science at the University of Minnesota. Her driving force is to serve minoritized couples, families, and communities as a collaborative family scholar, amplifying their expressed hopes rather than imposing assumed needs. Stemming from community priorities, her work envisions social change, well-being, and empowerment through research resonating with marginalized visions. With three book chapters and five peer-reviewed articles, Fatiha exemplifies a commitment to elevating underrepresented voices through collaborative scholarship.

Mihaela Friedlmeier, PhD, is an Associate Professor of Psychology at Grand Valley State University, USA. Her primary scholarly interests lie in the area of intergenerational relationships throughout the lifespan, particularly focusing on the relationships between adolescents, emerging adults, and their parents across different cultures. She asserts that parent–child relationships are essential for a child's development, emphasizing that parents serve as primary socialization agents.

Valeria A. Giannella holds an MSc in Psychology of Groups, Communities and Organizations. A PhD, she is now Assistant Professor at the Politecnico di Milano. She has been conducting research on gender differences in the economic, organizational, and professional fields. She is a member of the European Association of Social Psychology and the Society for Personality and Social Psychology. She collaborates with many companies as a consultant for well-being and gender equity.

Emily Hales is a Senior Financial Aid Processor at Kaplan North America. Emily completed her master's degree in Human Development and Family Studies at Utah State University. During her graduate studies, Emily was interested in student loan issues and wrote her thesis on how financial well-being and other factors may relate to student loan use. After graduating, Emily began working as a financial aid processor for Kaplan North America, where she manages student accounts daily. She reviews student aid eligibility including student loan use and helps award student aid in the most beneficial manner for students.

Paola Iannello, PhD, is an Associate Professor in General Psychology at the Università del Sacro Cuore. Her research interests focus on the cognitive processes underlying reasoning and decision-making, with a specific focus on the role that individual differences play within financial domain. She is the coordinator of the LIFE working group (Interdisciplinary Laboratory for Economic Education), whose activities are aimed at researching and empowering financial decision-making processes.

Heather Kelley is a researcher at Utah State University's Institute for Disability, Research, Policy and Practice. Her research interests focus on understanding various factors that influence relational well-being in families and strengths-based approaches to understanding mental health concerns. She has published over 45 peer-reviewed journal articles. She is a mixed-methods researcher with strengths in both qualitative and quantitative methodologies and teaches graduate-level mixed-methods courses.

Jinhee Kim is a Professor and Associate Dean at the University of Maryland Extension and the Department of Family Science at the University of Maryland, College Park. Her research centers on financial socialization, stress, family relationships, financial well-being, and health outcomes. Dr. Kim has led extensive community-based projects, including initiatives on financial literacy, relationship and financial education, and responses to the rural opioid crisis.

Kyoung Tae Kim, PhD, is an Associate Professor and Graduate Program Coordinator in the Department of Consumer Sciences at the University of Alabama, where he teaches in the CFP Board–registered undergraduate and master's programs. His research interests include household finance, financial planning, and financial literacy. He has published over 70 peer-reviewed research articles, including in the *International Journal of Consumer Studies, Journal of Consumer Affairs, Journal of Economic Psychology*, and *Journal of Family and Economic Issues.*

Margherita Lanz, PhD, is a full Professor of Psychometrics in the Department of Psychology at Università Cattolica del Sacro Cuore, Milan. Her main research topics concern research methods, emerging adulthood, family, financial well-being. She is member of the editorial board of *Emerging Adulthood Journal* and *TPM* (*Testing, Psychometrics, Methodology in Applied Psychology*) *Journal.*

Ashley B. LeBaron-Black is an Assistant Professor of Family Life at Brigham Young University in Provo, Utah. She received her PhD in Family Studies and Human Development from the University of Arizona. Ashley teaches family theory (at the undergraduate and graduate levels), family finance, and close relationships. Her research focus is family finance, including finances in couple relationships and financial socialization. Ashley has published over 60 peer-reviewed articles and is an Associate Editor for the *Journal of Family and Economic Issues.* She is Chair of the Family Financial Wellbeing Focus Group for the National Council on Family Relations.

Sunwoo T. Lee is an Assistant Professor in the School of Administrative Studies at York University, Canada. She earned her BS in Consumer Sciences and Business Administration, and her MS in Consumer Sciences from Seoul National University, followed by a PhD in Consumer Sciences from the Ohio State University. Dr. Lee's research explores the intricate dynamics of household economics, financial behaviors, and the multifaceted processes underlying financial decision-making. Her work delves into the connection between personal characteristics and financial choices, contributing insights to both academia and practical applications in finance.

Yoon G. Lee, PhD, is a Professor in the Department of Human Development and Family Studies at Utah State University. She specializes in teaching and researching family economic and financial issues, including household debt, saving, and credit use decisions and relevant financial education and policy issues. Her research projects in the family finance area focus on types of debt, financial stressors, financial behaviors, and financial well-being. She is also interested in research related to family-owned businesses. She currently investigates how couple-owned family businesses balance business and family demands and how this is related to their business success.

Žan Lep is an Assistant Professor in Social Psychology at the Department of Psychology, Faculty of Arts, University of Ljubljana, and a Research Associate in the Centre for Applied Epistemology, Educational Research Institute, Slovenia. He holds a PhD in Developmental Psychological Studies. In his research, he focuses on the motivational and cognitive underpinnings of behavior and decision-making broadly related to civic participation, politics, money, and health. He enjoys working in interdisciplinary teams across various (inter)national projects and collaborations.

Xiaomin Li is an Assistant Professor at the Department of Applied Social Sciences, The Hong Kong Polytechnic University. Dr. Li's research interests are broadly how family members navigate challenging conditions and obtain desirable outcomes in personal mental health, couple relationships, and children/adolescents development. At present, Dr. Li is studying how financial literacy benefits individuals, couples, and families in the short and long term. Dr. Li also studies how to facilitate financial literacy, especially among young adults who are striving for economic independence and among women who are significantly more disadvantaged in finance than men.

Favian Ray Lininger is a student of Kansas State University on the brink of completing his bachelor's degree in Personal Financial Planning. He spent his college career building and maintaining the communities in the dorms (which earned him K-State's Student of the Year award), within the PFP department at K-State and in his current and prior workplaces.

Sonya Lutter, PhD, is a Certified Financial Planner™, and a professional and licensed marriage and family therapist. She serves as the inaugural Director of Financial Health and Wellness with Texas Tech University's School of Financial Planning, where she leads curriculum and continuing education opportunities in the areas of financial psychology, financial therapy, and financial behavior. In addition, Dr. Lutter is the owner of ENLITE, where she helps bridge the gap between mental health and financial planning.

Megan McCoy, PhD, is an Assistant Professor in Kansas State University's Personal Financial Planning program. She is a licensed marriage and family therapist, an accredited financial counselor, and was the first certified financial therapist. Dr. McCoy's research is focused on the intersection between financial and overall well-being. She serves on the Financial Therapy Association's Board of Directors and is co-editor of *Financial Planning Review*. For her work, Dr. McCoy has received grants from FPA, FP of Canada, NEFE, and the CFP Board, and she has been featured in major media outlets like *The Today Show*, *TIMES*, *The Wall Street Journal*, and NPR.

Oana Negru-Subtirica, PhD, is an Associate Professor at the Department of Psychology, Babes-Bolyai University, Romania, leading the Self and Identity Development Lab. She researches intentionality and agency through identity, motivation, and goals. Her work investigates personal and social factors that contribute to self and identity formation in multiple life domains, with a curious eye on cultural and digital components. She uses quantitative, qualitative, and mixed methodologies to capture life in all its complexity. She coordinates large-scale longitudinal and applied identity and personality formation studies financed through the European Commission, ERSTE Foundation, Jacobs Foundation, and UEFISCDI.

Julia A. Nuckols is a doctoral researcher, working on her PhD that investigates how the COVID-19 pandemic affected the financial and social well-being of adolescents and young adults. Her main research focus is on themes relating to life-course transitions, financial well-being, agency, and social issues among young people. Nuckols is completing her PhD in affiliation with the DigiConsumers research consortium, a multidisciplinary research project focusing on the financial and digital skills of young people ages 13–25.

Nilton Porto is an Associate Professor of Consumer Finance in the College of Health Sciences at the University of Rhode Island. His research interests include financial decision-making, consumer behavior, financial education, and financial well-being. He is a research affiliate for the Center for Financial Security, a faculty affiliate for the Social Policy Institute, Washington University in St. Louis, and a former visiting scholar at FINRA. His research has received support from the NEFE, NIFA, and Real Jobs RI. Nilton earned his PhD in Household Economics from the University of Wisconsin—Madison and his MBA from Case Western Reserve University.

Mette Ranta, PhD, is an Associate Professor at the University of Helsinki and currently works as a Senior Specialist at the Ministry of Justice, Finland, in implementing a national financial literacy strategy for Finland. Dr. Ranta is a member of the Strategic Research Council–funded DigiConsumers research consortium, a multidisciplinary research project for identifying solutions to improve the financial and digital skills of young people between the ages of 13 and 25, especially in digital environments.

Emanuela E. Rinaldi holds a MSc in Economic Psychology and a PhD in

Sociology. She is now Associate Professor at University of Milan-Bicocca. For years, she has been conducting research on financial culture and education and on gender differences in economic socialization. She is the Scientific Director of the research and training program called Objective EFFE. Female Empowerment for a More Equal Future; a member of the steering committee of various bodies, including RN-N10 of the European Sociological Association, European Association for Economic Education–Italy, National Observatory of Economic Education; and a member of the Center for Interdisciplinary Studies in Economics, Psychology and Social Sciences.

Cliff A. Robb, PhD, is a Professor and Chair of the Department of Consumer Science at the University of Wisconsin—Madison. His research explores financial decision-making, college student financial behavior, and financial well-being. His work has been widely published in numerous journals, and he serves on several editorial boards. He earned his doctorate in Consumer Economics and Personal Financial Planning from the University of Missouri in 2007. He also holds a master's in Consumer Economics from the University of Alabama and a bachelor's in psychology from the University of the South.

Matteo Robba is a postdoctoral researcher in the Department of Economic and Business Education at the University of Mannheim. He obtained his PhD in Psychology from Universitá Cattolica del Sacro Cuore, Milan, Italy. His research focuses on behavioral economics and the influence of psychological characteristics on financial decision-making and consumption behavior.

Ashlyn Rollins-Koons, CFP®, is a financial advisor in Northern California and a PhD in Personal Financial Planning at Kansas State University. Ashlyn's research interests are behavioral finance, financial technology, housing, and family financial socialization.

Matthew T. Saxey is a doctoral student (majoring in Human Development and Family Science) and Presidential Graduate Research Fellow at Auburn University. He is passionate about researching how to help individuals, couples, and families achieve financial well-being. He has authored several peer-reviewed articles, book chapters, and lay audience–focused blog posts in seeking to help individuals, couples, and families flourish financially and relationally. He also loves instructing undergraduate students about social science research methods, quantitative data management, and family finance.

Alyssa Scott received her master's degree in the Couple and Family Therapy Program in the Department of Human Development and Family Science at the University of Rhode Island.

Joyce Serido is Professor Emerita of the College of Education and Human Development (CEHD) at the University of Minnesota—Twin Cities. Dr. Serido is a leading expert in financial behavior at the intersection of family processes and personal well-being, with a particular focus on youth and young adults. She has authored or co-authored over 70 scholarly articles in refereed journals exploring the connection between financial parenting, financial behavior, well-being, and young adult self-reliance. Since 2012, Dr. Serido has served as a principal investigator for the Arizona Pathways to Life Success for University

Students (APLUS) project, a multiuniversity research initiative of the first longitudinal, multidisciplinary study of young adults' financial behaviors.

Soyeon Shim is the Elizabeth Holloway Schar Dean and Ted Kellner Bascom Professor in the School of Human Ecology at the University of Wisconsin—Madison. Dr. Shim is internationally recognized as a consumer science researcher, with more than 120 scholarly papers in high-impact consumer and business journals internationally. She has built a global community of researchers in the consumer financial behavior field. In acknowledgment of her scholarship, Dr. Shim was named the Ted Keller Bascom Professor. As the Elizabeth Holloway Schar Dean of the School of Human Ecology at UW—Madison, she was honored as one of Wisconsin's 35 Most Influential Asian Americans in 2022.

Catherine Solheim is a Professor in the Department of Family Social Science, College of Education and Human Development, at the University of Minnesota. Her research centers on the ways in which race, culture, socioeconomic status, and immigration experiences intersect with U.S. economic systems to offer opportunities or barriers for family financial well-being and wealth creation. She is currently collaborating with a nonprofit organization to develop culturally attuned financial coaching materials for refugee adolescents and adults. She teaches an undergraduate course on family resources and economic justice in multicultural America and graduate courses on family conceptual frameworks and theorizing. She has led 14 learning-abroad courses in Thailand and supported eight graduate students in 2-month global internships, working on projects with Thai nongovernmental organizations.

Angela Sorgente, PhD, is an Assistant Professor of Psychometrics in the Department of Psychology at Università Cattolica del Sacro Cuore, Milan, Italy. Her main research interest is financial well-being's conceptualization and measurement, and she has developed the Multidimensional Subjective Financial Well-being Scale (MSFWBS) to measure emerging adults' financial well-being. She also has an interest in quantitative methodology and teaches classes in research methods and statistical software.

Rimantas Vosylis is a full Professor at the Institute of Psychology, Mykolas Romeris University, Lithuania. With a passion for studying human development, Dr. Vosylis has dedicated most of his scholarly career to investigating how family economic circumstances shape the psychosocial developmental trajectories and broader experiences of adolescence and emerging adulthood. Dr. Vosylis's scholarly career began with his doctoral thesis, where he examined the connections between the pathways that individuals take toward adult social roles and the typical experiences of emerging adulthood. Over the years, his research interests have evolved to a more specialized focus on personal and family financial issues during emerging adulthood, identity development, and academic motivation. In his two recent personal projects, Dr. Vosylis explored the formation of financial capabilities and the role of parental financial support in shaping the experiences of those navigating emerging adulthood.

Jing Jian Xiao is a Professor at the University of Rhode Island. Dr. Xiao conducts research and teaches courses in consumer finance in the Department of Human Development and Family Science at the University of Rhode Island, USA. He also serves as the editor-in-chief of the *Journal of Financial Counseling and Planning.*

Introduction to the Handbook

Ashley B. LeBaron-Black[1], *Heather Kelley*[2], *and Angela Sorgente*[3]

Purpose of the Handbook

Today's financial world is more complex and daunting than ever. Some of these challenges include disruptions to many economic systems caused by the COVID-19 pandemic; wild fluctuations in the stock market; highly uncertain job markets; high levels of inflation; rising costs of housing, groceries, and other basic necessities; easy access to information that generates misinformation or information overload, leading to financial paralysis; ever-looming unexpected events such as economic crisis; and wars that have strongly affected the global market. Considering these global economic challenges, many governments and organizations have developed increased interest in preparing people to operate within that complexity. One group that is uniquely vulnerable and requires specific attention is emerging adults (approximately ages 18–30). As the vast literature has documented, emerging adults throughout the world are struggling financially (Sinha et al., 2018; Terriquez & Gurantz, 2015).

The financial domain is a key aspect of the transition to adulthood for several reasons. First, financial independence and financial well-being are primary goals for many emerging adults and are viewed as markers of adulthood (Arnett, 2000; Arnett et al., 2014). However, financial independence has become increasingly out-of-reach for emerging adults. For example, in the United States, more than half of emerging adults live with their parents out of financial necessity (Pew Research Center, 2020) and student loan debt has reached unprecedented levels (Bartholomae & Fox, 2021). Perhaps because of the developmental importance of financial well-being, these

[1] School of Family Life, Brigham Young University, USA
[2] Institute for Disability Research, Policy, and Practice, Utah State University, USA
[3] Department of Psychology, Università Cattolica del Sacro Cuore, Milan, Italy

Ashley B. LeBaron-Black, Heather Kelley, and Angela Sorgente, *Introduction to the Handbook*. In: *Flourishing and Floundering Financially in Emerging Adulthood*. Edited by: Ashley B. LeBaron-Black, Heather Kelley, and Angela Sorgente, Oxford University Press. © Oxford University Press (2025). DOI: 10.1093/9780197699157.003.0001

financial struggles can be detrimental to emerging adults' physical and mental health (Eisenberg et al., 2001; Serido & Deenanath, 2016) and are associated with delayed marriage and parenthood (Badger et al., 2006; Carroll et al., 2009). In short, emerging adults' financial well-being affects other facets of life and can have developmental consequences.

Second, various national and international scientific reports have stressed the problematic lack of financial literacy among emerging adults (Babiarz & Robb, 2014; LeBaron & Kelley, 2021; OECD, 2020a). Scholars have repeatedly called for better financial socialization and financial education of children and adolescents in preparation for a financially flourishing emerging adulthood (LeBaron & Kelley, 2021). Efforts must also be made to help current emerging adults increase their financial knowledge and improve their financial behaviors.

Third, financial knowledge, attitudes, and behaviors developed during emerging adulthood persist into adulthood (Angrisani et al., 2020). In other words, financial wellness in emerging adulthood sets the stage for financial well-being for decades to come. Current efforts to improve emerging adults' financial literacy will foster a future in which people will be able to navigate financial uncertainty and complexity. Given the importance of financial socialization from one generation to another, we can assume that efforts to help current children, adolescents, and emerging adults will have positive spillover effects on future generations.

Taken together, these reasons highlight the need for an evidence-based, application-centered handbook that could offer insight to researchers, educators, clinicians, and parents about how to help emerging adults flourish rather than flounder financially—and give emerging adults themselves the tools to improve their own financial situation.

Overview of Part I

Given the wide scope of the financial domain, we organized this book around the core construct of *financial literacy*. This is because the Organisation for Economic Co-operation and Development (OECD)—an international organization that works to establish evidence-based international standards and find solutions to social, economic, and environmental challenges—believes that financial literacy has become a long-term policy priority in many countries and economies, and is recognized as an important complement to prudent regulation, financial inclusion, and the like. In the *Recommendation of the Council on Financial Literacy* that the OECD published in 2020 (OECD, 2020b), financial literacy is defined as a "combination of financial awareness, knowledge, skills, attitudes and behaviours necessary to make sound financial decisions and ultimately achieve individual financial well-being" (p. 6). As made clear in this definition, financial literacy is a process more than a state. The combination of many elements is necessary to flourish financially.

The financial literacy process we have described applies to all people, regardless of age (OECD, 2020a). At the same time, we believe it is important to recognize that each of the constructs listed here can look different according to the stage of life in which one is living. For example, during the transition to adulthood, financial well-being is more strongly related to peer comparison and perception of one's financial future than it is during other stages of life (Norvilitis et al., 2003; Sorgente & Lanz, 2019). Given this context, we have decided to dedicate the first part of our book to how each element included in the definition of financial literacy (i.e., financial awareness and knowledge, financial skills, financial attitudes, financial behavior, financial decisions, and financial well-being) operates in emerging adulthood. Each of these elements is discussed in one chapter. Additionally, even though there is agreement in recognizing the importance of the different elements included in the OECD definition of financial literacy, not all theoretical models addressing emerging adults' financial literacy have related these elements in the same way. Given the complexity of financial literacy, we dedicated the first chapter of the book to reviewing prominent definitions and models of financial literacy in emerging adulthood (see Chapter 1).

Individuals need to have some knowledge related to finances (e.g., the meaning of inflation and interest), both an objective mastery of such topics (i.e., objective financial knowledge) as well as the individual's subjective perception of their knowledge related to finances (i.e., financial awareness or subjective financial knowledge) (see Chapter 2). When there is a mismatch between one's objective and subjective financial knowledge, this is often termed as financial overconfidence (when subjective perceptions are higher than objective knowledge) or financial underconfidence (when objective knowledge is higher than individuals' perceptions of their knowledge); both overconfidence and underconfidence can be problematic (Angrisani & Casanova, 2021; Aristei & Gallo, 2021).

Individuals also need to have some financial competencies, or more specifically, healthy financial skills (i.e., qualities, characteristics, or abilities that influence one's ability to apply their financial knowledge in decision-making and behaviors; see Chapter 3), financial attitudes (i.e., thoughts or feelings about money that are not easily modifiable and that guide financial behaviors; see Chapter 4), and financial management behaviors (e.g., budgeting, saving, investing, and credit/debt management; see Chapter 5). These competencies allow people to make conscious, well-informed financial decisions (see Chapter 6) and avoid bias caused by cognitive and neurological mechanisms that underlie financial decisions (e.g., impulsivity).

When the facets of this process are optimized, individuals can achieve financial well-being (see Chapter 7). Financial well-being can be defined as a positive, beneficial financial condition that includes both an objective and a subjective side (Sorgente & Lanz, 2017). Objective financial well-being refers to material resources such as income and assets (e.g., house, car) as well as debts. Subjective financial well-being corresponds to the individual's emotional and cognitive evaluation of their own financial condition. Furthermore, there is an ongoing debate about whether financial well-being (see Chapter 7) and financial stress/anxiety (see Chapter 8) are two different sides of the same coin or separate constructs (Brzozowski & Spotton Visano, 2020; Sorgente et al., 2023). Thus, we included a chapter about financial stress/anxiety to complement the chapter about financial well-being.

Overview of Part II

While the OECD definition is an important starting point as it is internationally recognized as the lens from which to study financial issues, it is important to note that emerging adulthood is unique compared to other developmental stages. Thus, emerging adults face unique financial circumstances that are important to address in this book. Specifically, during the transition to adulthood, there is the struggle to reach different markers of adulthood such as completion of education, securing full-time employment, leaving the parental home, achieving financial independence, finding a stable partner, and eventually having children (Billari & Liefbroer, 2010). Each of these markers includes some financial challenges.

For example, many emerging adults decide to attend post-secondary education. From a financial point of view, this is often an investment in increased earning potential but increasingly also involves student loans (see Chapter 9). These factors can have long-lasting financial effects. Additionally, finding a stable, full-time job that meets financial needs is currently difficult for many emerging adults because the job market can be unstable and uncertain. The financial implications of this instability, and other evolving career considerations for emerging adults, will be discussed (see Chapter 10).

Leaving the parental house is a marker of adulthood that in the past coincided with financial independence from parents. Nowadays, emerging adults struggle to be truly independent from parents. This process of financial differentiation, which is not just physical but also psychological, will be discussed primarily in three chapters. One chapter is specific to financial independence (see Chapter 11), focusing on how reliance on parents for financial aid impacts the financial well-being of emerging adults and the differing paths emerging adults take to become financially self-reliant. Another chapter is specific to financial identity (see Chapter 12), defined as the response to this question: "Who am I from a financial point of view?" To be able to answer that question, emerging adults often explore alternative money management styles than the one presented by parents and commit to the style they believe is right for them. Discussed in a third chapter is the common mismatch in emerging adulthood between low income and high consumption and how this further impedes emerging adults' struggle for financial independence from parents and often involves taking on debt (see Chapter 13).

Finally, in order to truly become adults, many cultures dictate that emerging adults create a family of their own. Partnership and family formation decisions are often tied to financial factors, and partners influence one another's finances. Thus, many emerging adults experience bidirectional influences between their finances and the formation and quality of their romantic relationships (see Chapter 14).

Overview of Part III

We believe that the first 14 chapters will offer a fairly comprehensive overview of the financial life of emerging adults and what may lead to financial flourishing or floundering. At the same time, we recognize that emerging adults come from diverse backgrounds and experience diverse circumstances that profoundly influence their financial literacy and transition to adulthood. In order to address such diversity, this section of the book will focus on the main sociodemographic characteristics that generate diversity in emerging adults' financial experiences: socioeconomic vulnerability, including inequitable access to financial systems, products, and services (see Chapter 15); gender, as literature indicates that women report lower levels of financial literacy and well-being than men (see Chapter 16); and cultural and racial considerations, as culture can influence all elements of financial literacy and some emerging adults must navigate racial inequities in the process (see Chapter 17). In addition to these three chapters being specifically dedicated to sociodemographic considerations, we recognize the importance of diversity, equity, and inclusion across all the topics discussed in this book. As such, many of the chapters include some level of discussion about how sociodemographic characteristics relate to the topic at hand.

Overview of Part IV

Finally, we will conclude the book with a section about how to help emerging adults who are floundering financially to move toward flourishing. Literature suggests that the two most common ways in which individuals improve their financial literacy are from parent financial socialization (see Chapter 18) and from experts who offer financial education programs (e.g., college, work, the military, or free access resources; see Chapter 19). These chapters will discuss how financial learning during childhood and adolescence impacts emerging adults' financial literacy as well as ongoing possibilities for financial learning during emerging adulthood.

The book's concluding chapter (see Chapter 20) will provide a summary of the current state of research on financial literacy during emerging adulthood and directions for future research, education, and practice. In particular, the chapter begins by summarizing and integrating the content of the previous 19 chapters. Based on these findings, the main methodological limitations of the literature on emerging adults' financial literacy are presented and suggestions for future studies offered. Finally, the author explains why the concept of financial literacy should be replaced by the concept of financial capability that better captures ability-opportunity aspects, which several other chapters (e.g., Chapter 1 and Chapter 15) also discussed. Specifically, Chapter 20 also proposes a model (financial capability systems theory) that can serve as a theoretical framework for future studies on emerging adults' financial literacy.

Conclusion

As all three editors are family finance researchers, educators, and emerging adults ourselves, we believe in the importance of this book. We hope this handbook is useful for researchers, educators, and clinicians interested in the financial life of emerging adults. Our goal is to provide in one book most of the evidence-based knowledge existing on this topic. We also hope this handbook is useful for parents and emerging adults themselves. Some chapters include information and/or tips specifically for emerging adults based on the reviewed research, and some chapters include brief narratives from real emerging adults on the topic. Wherever you are in the world and whatever your relationship to finances in emerging adulthood, we hope you enjoy this book.

PART I

EMERGING ADULTS' FINANCIAL LITERACY

Chapter 1
Models of Emerging Adults' Financial Literacy

Žan Lep[1]

Introduction

The financial landscape is becoming increasingly complex, and individuals are becoming more active and responsible for their financial planning and decisions (Aren & Dinç Aydemir, 2014). Further complicated by the recent turmoil caused by health emergencies and conflicts that impacted the global economy, rising inflation and interest rates, and a widening income gap for some portions of the population (e.g., Nolan et al., 2019), successful management of personal finances is becoming increasingly important. Mounting evidence from around the globe suggests, however, that many people from the general population lack the knowledge (see Chapter 2) and skills (see Chapter 3) needed to make informed judgments and engage in financial behavior (see Chapters 5 and 6) that would be in their long-term interest (Atkinson & Messy, 2012; Lusardi & Mitchell, 2011). In other words, they lack the financial literacy needed to actively participate in the economy.

While financial literacy is an important skill for everyone (Lusardi, 2015), it is especially important for emerging adults (Lusardi & Mitchell, 2011; Shim et al., 2010). This is mainly because people in this developmental period are forming life-long financial decisions and acquiring skills they will use throughout their adult life. While attainment of financial independence (see Chapter 11) is one of the key markers of entering adulthood (Arnett, 2015), many emerging adults remain at least partially financially dependent on their parents, lack experience with managing money, and are only starting to enter the economic market as employees (see Chapter 10). Thus, financial literacy can help them flourish, while a lack of financial literacy can cause them to flounder.

[1] Department of Psychology, Faculty of Arts, University of Ljubljana and Centre for Applied Epistemology, Educational Research Institute, Slovenia

Žan Lep, *Models of Emerging Adults' Financial Literacy.* In: *Flourishing and Floundering Financially in Emerging Adulthood.* Edited by: Ashley B. LeBaron-Black, Heather Kelley, and Angela Sorgente, Oxford University Press.
 DOI: 10.1093/9780197699157.003.0002

The importance of financial education (see Chapter 19) and, in turn, the financial literacy that results from this process has been recognized since the early 1990s by researchers and international organizations such as the Organisation for Economic Co-operation and Development (OECD) as one of the important factors of successful financial functioning (Świecka, 2019). The importance of financial literacy is further supported by empirical studies showing that higher degrees of financial literacy were linked, for example, with higher net worth of individuals (van Rooij et al., 2012), higher savings for retirement (Lusardi & Mitchell, 2011), more and better investing (Guiso & Viviano, 2015; van Rooij et al., 2011), less impulsive buying (Potrich & Viera, 2018), and higher financial satisfaction (Xiao et al., 2014). On the other hand, lower financial literacy can result in poor financial decisions and behaviors (see Chapters 5 and 6; Breitbach & Walstad, 2016; Mandell, 2008).

Thus, the evaluation of financial literacy was included in a range of international studies, including OECD's Programme for International Student Assessment (PISA), that aim to inform policy planning and interventions on an international level. The problem is, however, that there are many approaches to defining financial literacy, which hinders comparability across studies. Still, different operationalizations and models have more convergence than differences. They differ mostly in terms of their breadth—how many aspects they include—and focus—whether they consider financial literacy to be a state (a quantity than can be measured) or a process (an everchanging interplay of various factors that lead to different outcomes in different situations). In this chapter, we first provide a brief narrative review of theoretical definitions and models of financial literacy, including their commonalities as well as their shortcomings in terms of application to emerging adults. Then, we discuss some of the process-oriented models and how they relate to determinants and outcomes for emerging adults. The aim of this chapter is not to provide an exhaustive review of all the definitions and theoretical models of financial literacy (for such reviews, see, e.g., Aren & Dinç Aydemir, 2014; Hung et al., 2009; Remund, 2010), but to synthesize the definitions that could be used in future studies of and practical work with emerging adults.

Theoretical Definitions and Models of Financial Literacy

The definitions of financial literacy generally fall into two categories: The definitions in the first group refer to it as an ability, while in the second, financial literacy is closely linked with financial knowledge. Specifically, financial literacy can be defined as an ability to make informed judgments and effective decisions regarding money (Bernheim & Garrett, 2003; Gale & Levine, 2010;

Noctor et al., 1992). This definition considers different skills, contexts, and domains of decision-making that should be in the best interest of the person in both the short and long term (Mandell, 2009). Alternatively, financial literacy can be considered an ability to process economic information and make informed financial decisions (Lusardi & Mitchell, 2014), or a measurement of a person's understanding of financial concepts (Kartini et al., 2020).

On the other hand, a much larger group of researchers base their definitions on (financial) knowledge. They stress, however, that knowledge is not sufficient for financial literacy. At minimum, financial literacy has two aspects: financial understanding—knowledge—and financial application—the ability to apply this knowledge (Huston, 2010) or the way this knowledge is used in a given financial context (Delgadillo, 2014) or decision-making process (Lusardi & Mitchell, 2014). Broadening the scope, financial literacy may consist of either three or four aspects. The three aspects are financial knowledge (see Chapter 2), financial attitudes (see Chapter 4), and financial behavior (see Chapter 5) (Agarwalla et al., 2013; Atkinson & Messy, 2012; Firli, 2017), and the fourth (sometimes included) aspect is financial ability (Hung et al., 2009) or financial skills (see Chapter 3) (OECD/INFE, 2012; Świecka, 2019).

Perhaps the most used definition of financial literacy is the one proposed by the OECD, stating that financial literacy is a "combination of financial awareness, knowledge, skills, attitudes, and behaviours necessary to make sound financial decisions and ultimately achieve individual financial well-being" (Atkinson & Messy, 2012, p. 12). Similarly, within the PISA framework for its 2021 wave, financial literacy is defined as "knowledge and understanding of financial concepts and risks, as well as the skills and attitudes to apply such knowledge and understanding in order to make *effective decisions across a range of financial contexts, to improve the financial well-being of individuals and society, and to enable participation in economic life*" (OECD, 2019, p. 18).

It is evident that many of the definitions presented here focus on a common set of components. Because these definitions serve as foundations for many operationalizations used in empirical studies, we discuss these key components in the following sections to establish a basic understanding of the construct. More detailed descriptions of each of the components and how they relate to financial flourishing and floundering are available in subsequent chapters of this volume.

Financial Knowledge and Skills

Financial knowledge (see Chapter 2) is a central concept in most extant definitions of financial literacy (see Hung et al., 2009). It includes the understanding of financial concepts and mechanisms such as inflation, interest, and investment, and of the purposes of financial products (e.g., credit cards, loans). Financial knowledge can be further divided into conceptual, procedural, and applied knowledge, and comprises knowledge regarding saving and spending, planning and budgeting, and informed decision-making (i.e., knowing where to look for information and what the consequences of financial actions could be; APEC, 2014).

When financial knowledge is applied in different economic decisions (e.g., evaluations, choices), these could be considered financial skills (see Chapter 3; Świecka, 2019). Financial skills span a broad range of skills that can be beneficial in the areas of earning, managing, and investing money as well as understanding the cost of borrowing (APEC, 2014). For example, these skills include the use of financial knowledge, understanding how to manage an expected or an unpredictable situation or problem (Świecka, 2019), but also any other skill that is needed for making healthy financial decisions, even if not from the financial domain (e.g., reading comprehension, executive functioning, numeracy; see Chapter 3). On a more rudimentary level, these skills include a range of cognitive processes applied to financial context, for example, comparing and contrasting, evaluating, judging, and deciding (OECD, 2019). In addition, mathematical skills such as numeracy and mathematical literacy are important when calculating percentages or thinking about numbers (Hung et al., 2009). It is crucial, however, to distinguish between financial literacy and concepts that are related to it but broader in nature. Numeracy, for instance, shares some features with financial literacy as they both benefit from easy manipulation of numbers. But because numeracy could also be applied to a range of other (including more basic) situations, it is not inherently linked to financial literacy (see Box 1.1).

Box 1.1 Financial Literacy and Related Concepts

Sometimes, financial literacy is used interchangeably with financial education, financial knowledge, financial sophistication, or financial capability (see Aren & Dinç Aydemir, 2014). This terminological overlap hinders comparability and integration of findings from different authors and across disciplines such as psychology, sociology, and economics.

There is some conceptual justification for the use of different terms, however, as they overlap in terms of content. For example, the OECD Expert Subgroup on the Measurement of Financial Literacy considers financial literacy and financial capability as interchangeable (Kempson et al., 2017). On the other hand, others (e.g., Xiao, 2016) consider financial capability to be a combination of financial literacy and behavior (for an alternative view about the relationship between financial literacy and capability, see Chapter 20). Similarly, the relation between components of financial literacy and financial literacy as a whole is sometimes unclear, for example, the relationship between financial literacy and numeracy discussed in this chapter (see also Hung et al., 2009). It is thus important to consider the different definitions and specific meanings being used when reading about financial literacy.

Finally, both researchers and practitioners should be wary of using the terms "financial literacy" and "financial education" interchangeably. Financial education is a process that leads to financial literacy and can thus not be part of the construct itself (Aren & Dinç Aydemir, 2014).

Financial Attitudes

While both financial knowledge and skills are central to financial literacy, mere possession of them is not enough if they fail to translate into healthy financial behavior. In this process, a range of noncognitive psychological characteristics may benefit emerging adults' financial literacy and other outcomes. These traits are commonly labeled "financial attitudes" (see Chapter 4) and represent individuals' tendency toward financial practice or an inclination to undertake the behavior (APEC, 2014). Their role in positive financial outcomes, however, is not clear-cut in different theoretical operationalizations, and they impact financial literacy and behavior in multiple ways. Within the PISA framework, for example, financial attitudes have a dual role in financial literacy: They are considered both a goal of financial education and—in turn—also as instrumental in building financial knowledge and skills (OECD, 2019). Moreover, some research suggests that positive financial attitudes are crucial for the translation of financial literacy into healthy financial behaviors (Fernandes et al., 2014).

In extant literature, the term "financial attitudes" includes a range of traits that might not be considered attitudes in the traditional sense (i.e., as evaluative judgments that have cognitive, affective, and behavioral components; Maio et al., 2018), but rather fall within a broader set of self-perceptions and personal traits. These include financial self-efficacy or a confidence to deal with financial situations, future orientation and control, proneness to risk taking, consideration of the well-being of others, sense of self-worth, and passion toward self-development (APEC, 2014; Warmath & Zimmerman,

2019). Likewise, some individuals might be more motivated to seek financial information and learn about finances than others. This could increase both their financial knowledge and skills because motivation is paramount for engagement in financial behaviors such as saving (Lep et al., 2021; Otto, 2013).

Another form of beliefs about money that falls under the broader category of financial attitudes is money scripts (Lawson et al., 2015). They are underlying assumptions and beliefs about money that form early in life and are passed down through generations both within families and wider society (Klontz & Klontz, 2009). The four categories include money avoidance, money worship, considering money as a status symbol, and money vigilance. While these scripts are not necessarily true or beneficial, money scripts still have the capacity to influence financial behavior throughout one's life and may lead to better or worse financial outcomes (Klontz & Britt, 2012; Lawson et al., 2015). For example, an individual who sees money as a means to attain happiness (money worship) might spiral into a never-ending and self-reinforcing pattern of hard work, earning, and spending, but never reaching the desired endpoint. This might then be associated with negative psychological and behavioral outcomes such as anxiety, lower life satisfaction, gambling, and dishonesty (see Lawson et al., 2015). As money scripts are rooted in impressionable financial experience in childhood, they may be unconscious, and particular attention is paid to them in financial therapy.

Financial Behavior

In terms of financial literacy, financial behavior can be considered either a decision-making process (see Chapter 6) or engagement in healthy financial behaviors (see Chapter 5). In both cases, the focus is on the application, rather than the replication of knowledge in real-life situations. To be considered "literate," individuals' financial decisions should be aimed at satisfying their needs (Świecka, 2019) or lead to favorable outcomes such as financial well-being (see Chapter 7). The types of financial behaviors characteristic of a financially literate person include, among others, habits of saving, budgeting, and prioritization; making responsible choices; and various forms of entrepreneurial and asset management behaviors (such as investing and assessing financial opportunities). All of those are considered to lead to favorable financial outcomes. This is supported by literature linking financial literacy with, for example, saving and retirement planning (Lusardi & Mitchell, 2011; van Rooij et al., 2012). Additionally, a financial literacy toolbox also includes charitable behavior and a focus on effort (APEC, 2014).

It is also important to consider that financial behaviors should be applied in various contexts in various stages of the lifespan. A financially literate emerging adult will learn and apply their financial knowledge throughout their adult life. And while financial decisions in childhood or adolescence are relatively simple and carry little risk, these decisions become increasingly complex as emerging adults gain financial independence (see Chapter 11), gain employment (see Chapter 10), and consider lifelong financial decisions (e.g., obtaining a loan or a mortgage, setting up an investment plan or retirement savings account), making financial literacy all the more important in this developmental period.

Integrating and Modeling the Components of Financial Literacy

As the research in the field of financial literacy has gained traction since the turn of the millennium, there have been some efforts to integrate various definitions of financial literacy into a composite definition. This would enable insight into its mechanisms and the relationships between the components and provide a clear distinction between financial literacy and related concepts. Based on a review of extant definitions, Hung et al. (2009) have proposed a conceptual model of financial literacy, which they define as "knowledge of basic economic and financial concepts, as well as the ability to use that knowledge and other financial skills to manage financial resources effectively for a lifetime of financial well-being" (Hung et al., 2009, p. 12). In this model, financial knowledge (see Chapter 2) is perceived as a basis of financial literacy and is predictive of financial skills (see Chapter 3), perceived knowledge (see Chapter 2), and financial behavior (see Chapter 5), which all rely on an adequate level of knowledge. Both financial skills and perceived knowledge, in turn, influence the behavior, and financial behavior strengthens both the knowledge and perception of knowledge.

Özkale and Özdemir Erdoğan (2022) developed the colosseum model based on a review of selected studies, including those dealing with concepts related to financial literacy. They expanded the scope of financial literacy by including the affecting factors, that is, variables that influence all three components of financial literacy but are not themselves part of it. These can further be divided into personal and environmental factors. The former comprise various perceptions, emotions, cognitive biases, needs, motivations, and self-confidence, while the latter refer to financial socialization and the wider financial setting (e.g., legislation, the economic system). The authors posit that the addition of affecting factors might make the model more applicable.

For example, they propose that the model could be used in education to foster youth financial literacy and, in turn, their flourishing. While this model aims to be an overarching one, it offers little empirical insight into the mechanisms of financial literacy beyond the need to consider a range of predictors if we were to understand its development.

The issue with many of the models of financial literacy is that they are conceptual in nature, which has two important implications. First, because they have not been empirically tested, the directionality between the (correlated) constructs is unclear. This hinders our understanding of how various components of financial literacy are, in fact, related or how they impact each other. Second, because financial literacy is considered a multifaceted construct, it is hard to operationalize and, in turn, measure empirically. Often, this leads the researchers to resort to questionable shortcuts (see Box 1.2).

Box 1.2 Measuring Financial Literacy

The approaches to measuring financial literacy (and instruments) are not standardized in extant literature (Bajaj & Kaur, 2022; Potrich et al., 2016). In most studies, financial literacy is considered equivalent to financial knowledge for the purpose of measuring, which seems insufficient given both theoretical and empirical evidence to its multifaceted nature. Financial knowledge is measured either as self-assessment or as performance on a financial knowledge test (Hung et al., 2009). The drawback of self-assessment as a measuring approach lies in the fact that people tend to overestimate their financial knowledge, while performance on knowledge tests might overestimate financial literacy as most scales only tap into comparably simple financial concepts and behaviors (for a review, see Aren & Dinç Aydemir, 2014; Hung et al., 2009; Huston, 2010; Vieira et al., 2019).

A better option might thus be to measure different aspects of the construct (e.g., knowledge, attitudes, skills, behaviors) separately as it is done in process-oriented models of financial literacy, or compute a composite score of financial literacy. Such an approach was used in the PISA studies, for example, where a financial literacy index was computed as a sum of responses to different types of questions (i.e., multiple-choice questions, Likert-type scales, binary response questions) measuring the three components of financial literacy. Alternatively, Potrich and colleagues (2016) relied on a combined index of financial literacy based on standardized scores derived from factor analysis. Studies using a composite score, however, are rare, perhaps because the resulting index is conceptually more difficult to grasp.

In sum, various approaches to measuring financial literacy may yield theoretically questionable results while hindering comparability and standardization across studies, which makes the issue of financial literacy measurement an important topic to consider in further research.

Regarding the first issue, some efforts have been made in testing different models using confirmatory factor analysis and structural equation modeling. For example, Jorgensen and Savla (2010) found that financial knowledge has an effect on financial attitudes that, in turn, were predictive of better financial behavior. Dewi et al. (2020) supported a model in which financial awareness and financial experience contribute to subjective financial knowledge and financial skills. These two factors influence financial capability that then contributes to higher financial goals, better financial behaviors, and better financial decisions. Considering different theoretical definitions of financial literacy, Potrich et al. (2016) tested three models of financial literacy. In the first, financial knowledge and attitudes preceded financial behavior, with knowledge having a more positive influence on financial behavior compared to financial attitudes. The second model was built on the theoretical definitions proposed by OECD, Agarwalla and colleagues (2013), and Atkinson and Messy (2012). It considered financial literacy to be a second-order construct influenced by the measures of financial knowledge, financial attitudes, and financial behavior. Finally, the third model considered financial literacy as a "unique" and indivisible construct comprising the three aspects into a single (latent) measure. In a series of studies conducted with university students, the authors found most support for the first model in which financial knowledge and attitudes impact financial behavior. In contrast, Bajaj and Kaur (2022) found support for a measurement model of financial literacy as a second-order latent structure comprising financial knowledge, financial attitudes, and financial behavior, which were significantly intercorrelated. While both studies offer some insight into the mechanisms of financial literacy, they were conducted using nonrepresentative samples (from different countries). Thus, little can be inferred about the replicability of the models, which calls for further empirical examinations.

Process-Oriented Models of Financial Literacy

The core definitions of financial literacy conceptualize it as a state, that is, a construct that can be developed but that represents an outcome in and of itself. The models described in the previous section extend the scope of inquiry by including some additional psychological variables. In doing this, they offer more insight into how financial literacy is "built" and developed and come closer to the process-oriented models of financial literacy. Still, while such models are valuable, they lack consideration of the context in which financial literacy is developed. Research shows, however, that there are significant differences in financial literacy between people of different genders (see Chapter 16), socioeconomic statuses (see Chapter 15), races (see Chapter 17), and other backgrounds.

Moreover, the traditional research focus on the outcomes (be it financial literacy or financial behavior) and exploration of individual and sociodemographic differences in different aspects of financial literacy lacks consideration of the process explaining these differences and various contexts in which financial literacy is developed. These contexts include families, peer groups, schools, and wider communities. While conceptualizing financial literacy as a state seems practical in terms of measurement and evaluation—this goal is especially present in studies focusing on outcomes of education (such as PISA) or for comparing levels of literacy across countries—such an approach also has several drawbacks. As the financial landscape is constantly evolving and the nature of many financial concepts is changeable (e.g., interest rates, inflation), a financially literate person must adapt to these changes to remain literate. Moreover, defining financial literacy as a state is less informative for policy planning because it offers little insight into the interplay of different aspects and into the process of its development, both of which are needed in crafting effective policy interventions.

Thus, some researchers have explored financial literacy as a process, looking into socioeconomic, relational, and psychological antecedents of financial literacy, and have explored its impact on various outcomes. As a result, the scope of interest has shifted from financial literacy itself to an overarching process of its development: financial socialization (see Chapter 18). In the following paragraphs, we will present two such models that have been developed specifically for emerging adults and have been particularly influential in the field.

The first model of financial socialization was developed by Gudmunson and Danes (2011) through an iterative process. First, they conducted a literature review on financial literacy, which they operationalized as the "ability to interpret, communicate, compute, develop independent judgments, and take actions resulting from those processes in order to thrive in our complex financial world" (Danes & Haberman, 2007, p. 49). Their focus was on the importance of personal dispositions and processes that improve financial behavior. Their resulting model of financial socialization is based on Ward's (1974) definition of socialization, which focuses on knowledge, skills, and attitudes, but instead of skills, they use the term "capabilities" (Gudmunson & Danes, 2011). The model is divided into two parts. First, family socialization processes involve personal and family characteristics that influence interactions and relationships within a family and purposive financial socialization. These two factors influence financial socialization outcomes, specifically emerging adults' financial attitudes, knowledge, and capabilities, which, in turn, influence their financial behavior and financial well-being.

In a second model of financial socialization, researchers (Shim et al., 2010) were guided by the theory of consumer socialization (Moschis, 1987) and the theory of planned behavior (Ajzen, 2012). Their hierarchical model of financial socialization processes explains the pathways to financial socialization outcomes (i.e., healthy financial behavior, financial satisfaction, and financial relationship with parents) using four levels of constructs that consider different contexts of socialization. In the model, parental financial behavior, family context (parental socioeconomic status [SES]), direct parental teaching, high school work experience, and high school financial education (collectively labeled anticipatory financial socialization) predict cognitive financial learning outcomes (i.e., financial knowledge and adoption of parents as financial role models). These variables then shape financial attitudes (i.e., perception of parental subjective norms, perceived behavioral control in the financial domain, and financial attitudes), which, in turn, influence the financial socialization outcomes (financial relationship with parents, financial satisfaction, healthy financial behaviors).

This model of financial socialization has also been tested (and supported with minor adjustments) in the cultural settings of Austria and Slovenia (Sirsch et al., 2020) and has been extended to account for not only emerging adult outcomes but also parental outcomes such as financial management satisfaction, parent–child financial relationship satisfaction, and financial well-being (e.g., Zupančič et al., 2023). While both models deal with the process of financial socialization, it is evident they include concepts linked with or comprising financial literacy (i.e., financial education, financial knowledge, financial attitudes, financial behavior). Thus, these models could be useful in financial literacy-related policy planning and in working with emerging adults because they offer a wide range of variables that could be targeted through financial education or other measures. While the generalization of the models might be limited as both were developed using emerging adult samples, this developmental focus is not surprising. Individuals in this developmental period are encountered with more complex and demanding financial situations as they strive toward gaining financial independence (see Chapter 11), while also forming financial habits that will influence their financial functioning throughout adulthood (Shim et al., 2010).

Cross-Cultural and Individual Considerations in Financial Literacy Research

It is important to note that the empirical models presented in this chapter—even if tested in different countries—draw on samples of (mostly) university students that are not always representative of emerging adults. In order for the models to inform effective policy planning aimed at fueling the financial flourishing of emerging adults, future studies should explore financial literacy in more representative samples and among emerging adults from groups that, for various reasons, face bigger challenges in their attainment of financial literacy and are more prone to financial floundering. These might include, but are not limited to, emerging adults from lower socioeconomic backgrounds, immigrants, less educated or unemployed emerging adults, emerging adults with disabilities, and minorities (see Chapters 15, 16, and 17; see Breitbach & Walstad, 2016, for a review). Members of all these groups might have less access to both financial education and financial products, making it harder for them to gain financial knowledge and skills. Furthermore, their unique experiences and circumstances might influence their financial attitudes (e.g., money scripts). Thus, we should not solely study higher-SES emerging adults and assume the same models apply to lower-SES emerging adults.

Similarly, in exploring financial literacy in international environments, researchers should be careful in making generalizations. While some models were tested and validated in different countries with varying economic contexts (and other approaches such as the PISA framework were developed specifically for international testing), the meaning of financial literacy and its outcomes might vary significantly across societies and economic systems. The differences are especially stark when considering non-WEIRD (i.e., non-Western, Educated, Industrialized, Rich, Democratic) countries, societies undergoing rapid economic development, developing countries, or post-socialist countries (e.g., Kovács & Terták, 2019; Thomas & Spataro, 2018). In each of these, the range of financial products and their importance might differ significantly from the capitalistic West (e.g., the investment markets are less developed, young people have less or no access to credit cards), making it harder to use the same measures to assess financial literacy. Still, research from around the globe paints a worrisome picture of emerging adults' financial literacy and financial well-being (e.g., Garg & Singh, 2018; Totenhagen et al., 2015). Therefore, a valuable approach might perhaps be to focus on the outcomes of financial literacy such as financial behavior (if possible, decontextualized) (see Chapter 5) and financial well-being (see Chapter 7) that are important globally, regardless of the content of financial knowledge.

Conclusion

From a practical perspective, financial literacy is not an end goal policymakers (and individuals) strive toward (Gudmunson & Danes, 2011; Mandell, 2008). Rather, we can consider it as a means leading to better financial socialization outcomes such as healthy financial behavior (see Chapter 5; Breitbach & Walstad, 2016) and financial well-being, which is becoming an increasingly important topic in recent research in the area (see Chapter 7; Sorgente & Lanz, 2017). Financial literacy and its components, however, are directly associated with financial behavior and financial well-being (both objective and subjective financial well-being; LeBaron & Kelley, 2021), making it an important domain of research interest. Moreover, as financial well-being is the culmination of most financial education (see Chapter 19) and socialization (see Chapter 18) endeavors, acquiring financial literacy in emerging adulthood is paramount for financial flourishing throughout adult life.

To be effective in improving the financial literacy of emerging adults, we must employ effective policy interventions and targeted financial education programs. To date, however, not all financial literacy education programs for youth have been effective (Totenhagen et al., 2015). As Totenhagen and colleagues point out, this might partly be attributed to suboptimal delivery methods and lack of specificity of target populations. On the other hand, as we have established in this chapter, the field of financial literacy lacks common definitions and operationalizations, which might also thwart the efforts of such programs. The lack of theoretical consensus might further result in measures that could be improved on in terms of their validity (Kunovskaya et al., 2014; LeBaron & Kelley, 2021) and content, as they presently rely heavily on financial knowledge. Moreover, as the financial landscape is becoming more complex and is ever-changing, the content of measures (and policy/education programs) should also reflect these changes. Finally, models of financial literacy should be tested and adapted to emerging adults who strive to thrive in diverse economic settings.

Chapter 2
Objective and Subjective Financial Knowledge among Emerging Adults

Sunwoo T. Lee[1] *and Kyoung Tae Kim*[2]

Introduction

Defined as the life stage between adolescence and full-fledged adulthood, emerging adulthood is marked by a unique set of challenges, with one of the most pressing being the need to manage their own finances. Over the past few decades, the financial landscape facing emerging adults has grown increasingly complex, and financial knowledge has received significant attention as a key factor associated with positive financial decisions throughout one's life. While financial knowledge may not provide a complete explanation for all behaviors, it is undeniable that the relationships between financial understanding and crucial financial actions are very strong (see Chapters 5 and 6). Findings from previous empirical studies have consistently shown that financial knowledge is positively associated with savings (Jacobs-Lawson & Hershey, 2005; Kim & Yuh, 2018), wealth accumulation (Letkiewicz & Fox, 2014; Lusardi et al., 2017), stock market participation (van Rooij et al., 2011, 2012), and retirement planning (Agnew et al., 2013; van Rooij et al., 2012). In the United States, financial knowledge has been assessed in various household-level national datasets, including but not limited to the American Life Panel (ALP), Health and Retirement Study (HRS), National Financial Capability Study (NFCS), National Longitudinal Survey of Youth (NLSY), Survey of Consumer Finances (SCF), and Understanding America Study (UAS). These datasets have prompted researchers to actively analyze financial knowledge from various angles.

Financial knowledge is typically examined in two major aspects: (1) objective financial knowledge and (2) subjective financial knowledge.

[1] School of Administrative Studies, York University, Canada
[2] Department of Consumer Sciences, University of Alabama, USA

Sunwoo T. Lee and Kyoung Tae Kim, *Objective and Subjective Financial Knowledge among Emerging Adults*. In: *Flourishing and Floundering Financially in Emerging Adulthood*. Edited by: Ashley B. LeBaron-Black, Heather Kelley, and Angela Sorgente, Oxford University Press. © Oxford University Press (2025). DOI: 10.1093/9780197699157.003.0003

Objective financial knowledge pertains to an individual's factual comprehension of financial concepts and principles. It is often assessed through standardized tests, such as the Big Three financial knowledge questions, which cover fundamental personal finance topics like (1) interest rates, (2) inflation, and (3) risk diversification (Lusardi & Mitchell, 2011). These questions have been widely used by many researchers (Lusardi & Mitchell, 2014). On the other hand, subjective financial knowledge measures one's self-assessed or perceived level of financial knowledge. It is usually assessed through self-report surveys where individuals rate their own financial knowledge. For example, many available secondary datasets ask respondents to answer questions like "On a scale from 1 to 7, where 1 means very low and 7 means very high, how would you assess your overall financial knowledge?" The Organisation for Economic Co-operation and Development's (OECD's) definition of financial knowledge focuses on the objective understanding of personal finance, while the OECD uses the term "financial awareness" to refer to the self-perception people have of their financial knowledge. Thus, the OECD's definition of financial knowledge aligns with objective financial knowledge, and financial awareness is comparable to subjective financial knowledge. We choose to use the subjective versus objective dichotomy, as it is more commonly employed in the academic literature.

In addition to objective and subjective financial knowledge, some researchers have analyzed the differences between these two knowledge indices because an individual's objective financial knowledge may not always align with their perception of their knowledge. This disconnect has often been referred to in previous studies as *overconfidence in financial knowledge* when objective financial knowledge exceeds subjective perception, and *underconfidence in financial knowledge* when perceived knowledge surpasses objective knowledge. Previous studies documented the detrimental effect overconfidence in financial knowledge has on the financial management of individuals (e.g., Carlsson Hauff & Nilsson, 2020; Lee & Kim, 2020; Richardson et al., 2022), while underconfidence in financial knowledge was not found to necessarily cause financial misbehaviors or even lead to better financial practices (e.g., Heo et al., 2021; Lee & Hanna, 2022; Porto & Xiao, 2016). Thus, this chapter will mainly focus on the overconfidence aspect of emerging adults.

The chapter is structured as follows: Section 1 provides an overview of financial knowledge levels among emerging adults and discusses the importance of delving into the financial knowledge of this demographic. Common predictors and outcomes of financial knowledge are also examined in this section. Section 2 presents a systematic review aimed at providing a more systematic assessment of emerging adults' objective and subjective financial knowledge, with a particular emphasis on the disparities between these two measures. The methods section outlines the process of selecting research articles, and we review a total of 73 selected articles from two perspectives: first, by focusing on the comparison of objective and subjective measures of financial knowledge, and second, by highlighting studies that directly observe disparities within these two aspects of financial knowledge. The conclusion section offers insights into potential future research directions and discusses implications for various stakeholders interested in this subject matter.

Section 1: Financial Knowledge Landscape of Emerging Adults

Significance of Financial Knowledge for Emerging Adults

The financial knowledge of emerging adults is paramount for their financial well-being (see Chapter 7). Emerging adults are transitioning from adolescence to adulthood (Arnett, 2014). It is essential to note that their status lies between dependence and independence (see Chapter 11). Some rely on family support for living and educational expenses, while others are entering or fully engaged in the labor market, earning income, and accumulating assets (see Chapter 10). Certain emerging adults continue to engage in basic financial activities from adolescence, while others face new financial decisions, taking on responsibility for their own financial affairs. To study this transitional phase effectively, it is necessary to employ approaches that can discern the specific characteristics of this developmental stage (Sorgente & Lanz, 2017).

Unfortunately, emerging adults are vulnerable to various challenges due to their lack of financial capability. The OECD (2020) reported that emerging adults between the ages of 18–29 consistently had the worst financial knowledge and attitude scores compared to other age groups, which could exacerbate the difficulties they experience. Sinha et al. (2018) reported that many U.S. emerging adults lack the necessary financial skills or knowledge. The study showed that more than half were categorized as either financially precarious (32%) or financially at-risk (36%).

Another reason why the financial knowledge of emerging adults is important is because developing sound financial knowledge during emerging adulthood lays the foundation for a lifetime of financial well-being (see Chapter 7). The financial decisions made during this period can significantly impact an individual's immediate and long-term financial future (see Chapters 5 and 6; Robb, 2011). Emerging adulthood is also crucial because individuals have the opportunity to gain substantial financial experience and receive financial education both at post-secondary institutions and in the workplace (see Chapter 19). Their chance to flourish financially in the future could be improved dramatically based on their decisions during emerging adulthood.

Finally, a large segment of emerging adults was severely affected by the 2008 financial crisis (Sironi, 2018) and again by the ongoing economic crisis driven by the COVID-19 pandemic (Birmingham et al., 2023; Reyes-Portillo et al., 2022). Previous studies have documented that large-scale financial shocks disproportionately affect certain populations, with financially vulnerable groups suffering the most (Kim et al., 2017). Discussing the financial knowledge of emerging adults is a timely issue, given the challenging economic conditions they face in the post-pandemic era. This is crucial not only to secure the financial stability of emerging adults but also for their mental health. The impact of COVID-19 on anxiety and depressive symptoms was stronger for those experiencing financial distress (LeBaron-Black et al., 2022).

Emerging adults must possess sound and acceptable financial attitudes grounded in robust financial knowledge to effectively navigate and attain financial well-being within the intricate financial landscape they encounter (Totenhagen et al., 2015). The level of financial knowledge they possess, along with the discrepancy between objective and subjective assessments of that knowledge, can have far-reaching and significant consequences as they venture into unfamiliar financial domains and throughout their entire lives.

Assessing Financial Knowledge of Emerging Adults: Tools, Methods, and Comparisons

As mentioned earlier, the Big Three financial knowledge questions, developed by Lusardi and Mitchell (2011), have served as a benchmark for measuring objective financial knowledge in numerous studies (Lusardi & Mitchell, 2014). These Big Three questions assess understanding of three key concepts (interest rates, inflation, and risk diversification). They have been expanded to the Big Five financial knowledge questions, which include two additional concepts: mortgage payments and asset pricing. Both sets of questions, Big Three and Big Five, have been frequently utilized by researchers due to the extensive literature and the advantage of achieving high comparability of statistics across various U.S. national datasets (e.g., HRS, SCF, NFCS, NLSY), as well as international surveys (Li, 2020; Lusardi, 2019).

In their recent study, Lusardi and Mitchell (2017) further developed and introduced more sophisticated instruments for measuring objective financial knowledge, consisting of 13 questions that assess both basic and advanced financial topics. Studies employing these questions, based on the Big Three framework, to gauge objective financial knowledge generally found that emerging adults tend to have lower levels of objective financial knowledge compared to older age groups (Boisclair et al., 2017; Henager & Cude, 2016; Kadoya & Khan, 2020). Furthermore, among Americans ages 25–34, individuals who are younger, belong to racial/ethnic minority groups, are women, have lower incomes, and possess lower levels of education tend to exhibit lower levels of objective financial knowledge (see Chapters 15, 16, and 17; de Bassa Scheresberg, 2013). Similar results were also reported in a study by Lusardi et al. (2010), which focused on Americans between the ages of 23 and 28.

However, a few researchers have raised concerns about the validity and reliability of the Big Three and Big Five financial knowledge questions, highlighting their narrow scope of topics and lack of real-world relevance (Hastings et al.,2013; Knoll & Houts, 2012; Kunovskaya et al., 2014; Li, 2020). Kunovskaya and colleagues argued, based on classical test theory and the Rasch model, that it is questionable whether the Big Three-based measures are superior to others in assessing an individual's factual understanding of financial concepts. As a result, researchers have been developing alternative measures of objective financial knowledge. For instance, Knoll and Houts created a psychometrically sound 20-item scale based on item response theory, and their findings indicated that younger adults had lower objective financial knowledge compared to older individuals.

Conversely, a predominant approach in the existing literature on subjective financial knowledge focuses on the following single-item measure, "On a scale from 1 to 7, where 1 means very low and 7 means very high, how would you assess your overall financial knowledge?" This question has been included in many U.S. datasets (e.g., NFCS, SCF) and has been utilized in numerous empirical studies as a means of measuring subjective financial knowledge (e.g., Allgood & Walstad, 2016; Babiarz & Robb, 2014; Tang & Baker, 2016; Tokar Asaad, 2015). Allgood and Walstad (2013) conducted subsample analysis of Americans by age group and found that subjective financial knowledge was lowest among the 18–29 age group and highest among individuals aged 60 and over, on average.

Despite the widespread use of this single-item measure by many researchers, alternative measures have also been developed due to challenges regarding the validity and reliability of using a single item. For example, numerous researchers adapted Flynn and Goldsmith's (1999) five-item measure of subjective knowledge to estimate financial knowledge (e.g., Goldsmith & Goldsmith, 2006; Larson et al., 2016; Lim et al., 2018; Perry & Morris, 2005). Carlsson Hauff and Nilsson (2020) used five items to gauge the subjective financial knowledge of university students, with respondents rating how certain they were about their answers to each of the Big Five financial knowledge questions.

As of now, various assessment tools have been developed by researchers, with many adapted to estimate the objective and subjective financial knowledge of emerging adults. While a brief discussion of literature in this section demonstrated the overall lack of financial knowledge among emerging adults, we present a systematic review of literature in the next section for a more comprehensive understanding of their objective and subjective financial knowledge, as well as the difference between the two indices.

Section 2: Systematic Review of Emerging Adults' Financial Knowledge

This section includes a description of our systematic review procedure, a review of research related to the objective and subjective financial knowledge of (1) the overall population and (2) emerging adults, as well as a brief discussion on the discrepancy between objective and subjective financial knowledge. We reviewed articles that conducted empirical analyses on financial knowledge and differentiated between the objective and subjective aspects of financial knowledge. This section demonstrates how the two aspects of financial knowledge—or the discrepancy between them—are associated differently with appropriate financial behaviors that emerging adults should practice. We provide implications for educators, practitioners, or policymakers interested in improving the financial well-being of emerging adults.

Search Procedures

The analysis utilized the EBSCOhost and SCOPUS databases. The search was restricted to articles published in academic journals in English between 2000 and 2022. The keywords employed in the search (connected by the Boolean operator OR) included "subjective financial knowledge," "subjective financial literacy," "perceived financial knowledge," "perceived financial literacy," "objective financial knowledge," "objective financial literacy," "financial self-efficacy," "financial overconfidence," "financial knowledge overconfidence," and "financial literacy overconfidence."

Following the initial search, we identified 186 articles from EBSCOhost and 238 articles from SCOPUS. The first screening phase involved assessing the article titles to determine if the primary topic of the article was related to individuals' financial knowledge. After this initial screening, we identified 52 articles from EBSCOhost and 86 articles from SCOPUS. Duplicate documents from the two database sources were eliminated, resulting in a total of 109 articles for our final review. The final screening process involved reading the full texts of these articles and evaluating them based on two criteria: (1) whether they distinguished and examined the concepts of objective (actual) and subjective (perceived) financial knowledge in their empirical analysis, or (2) whether they specifically estimated and examined the discrepancy between objective and subjective financial knowledge. Given that the primary objective of this section is to showcase studies focusing on differences in the objective and subjective aspects of financial knowledge among emerging adults, we excluded articles that examined only one of these aspects, whether it be objective or subjective financial knowledge. The final number of articles included for bibliometric analysis totaled 73. Figure 2.1 provides a summary of our selection procedure.

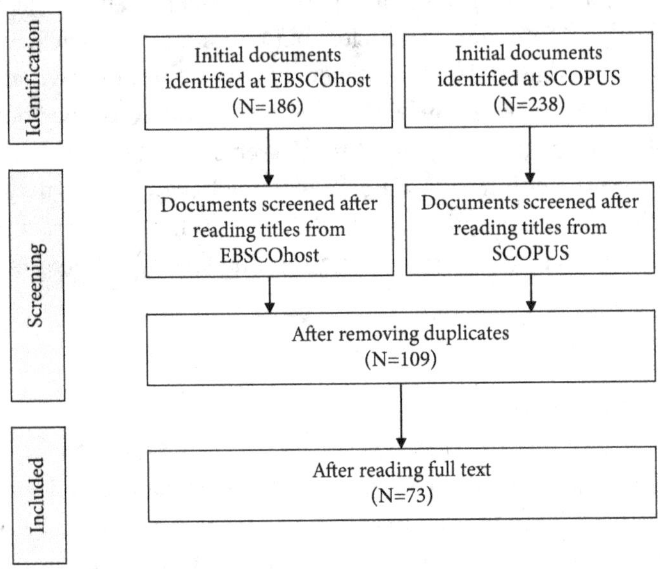

Figure 2.1 Procedure of Selection

Note. Figure adapted from PRISMA's flow chart for systematic reviews (Moher et al., 2010).

Research on the Objective and Subjective Financial Knowledge of the Overall Population

We conducted a review of 73 articles published in academic journals, all of which examined both objective and subjective financial knowledge or overconfidence in financial knowledge. The most frequently utilized secondary survey dataset was the National Financial Capability Study (NFCS), commissioned by the Financial Industry Regulatory Authority (FINRA) Investor Education Foundation in the United States (12%). Other datasets included the Survey of Consumer Finances (SCF), collected and distributed by the Federal Reserve Board (7%), and the Canadian Financial Capability Survey (CFCS) from the Statistics Canada Research Data Centre (4%). Additionally, secondary datasets from government agencies in various countries, such as China, South Korea, and Türkiye, were also employed. Approximately 44% of the studies relied on primary survey data, with 58% of these surveys conducted in the United States. Surveys were also conducted in other countries, including Australia, China, Germany, Hungary, Iran, Poland, Sweden, and Vietnam. The empirical evidence indicates that concerns regarding the discrepancy between the objective level of financial knowledge and subjective assessments of knowledge are not limited to specific countries.

Most of the studies (75%) investigated associated variables with financial knowledge as an independent variable. These studies examined its relationship to financial behavior (see Chapter 5), satisfaction, and well-being (see Chapter 7). The domain of financial behaviors examined was broad and included, but was not limited to, credit management (see Chapter 13), investment, savings, spending, retirement, and seeking financial advice. Comparatively fewer studies explored the impact of various predictors on the financial knowledge of emerging adults. However, prior research on the general population has demonstrated that age is a crucial factor to consider when evaluating financial knowledge. It has been documented that age and the level of financial knowledge follow an inverse U-shaped pattern, with emerging adults exhibiting lower levels of financial knowledge compared to older working-age populations, and lower levels again in old age with deteriorating cognitive ability (Boisclair et al., 2017; Kadoya & Khan, 2020). Since we are examining a specific age group of emerging adults, we initially aimed to explore the relationship between age and financial knowledge levels and assess how empirical studies demonstrated age differences not only between emerging adults and other age groups but also within the emerging adult population. Table 2.1 provides a summary of the impact of age on one's financial knowledge level from selected studies.

Table 2.1 Relationship between Age and Financial Knowledge, Selected Studies

Studies	Population	Objective Financial Knowledge (OFK)	Subjective Financial Knowledge (SFK)	Overconfidence in Financial Knowledge
Cude et al. (2019)	Iranian investors	No significant relation to basic literacy but 61-year-olds or older had lower advanced literacy than 18- to 30-year-olds.	N/A	Not significant
García et al. (2022)	Spain	N/A	N/A	Age negatively related to two measures of overconfidence.
Gerrans (2021)	Australian university students	Age positively related to basic and advanced literacy.	Age positively related to self-assessed investment and superannuation knowledge.	Age positively related to being underconfident (believing they have fewer correct responses) compared to calibrated (correct number of correct responses). No significant relation to overconfidence (believing they have more correct responses).
Gerrans & Heaney (2019)	Australian university students	Age positively related to basic and advanced literacy.	Age positively related to self-assessed investment and super-annuation knowledge.	Age negatively related to basic confidence (no. of predicted minus no. of actual correct answers). No significant relation to advanced confidence.

Khan et al. (2017)	Canada	N/A	N/A	Compared to reference group (35–44 years old), younger group (18–24 years old) underestimated, but older group (45 and older) overestimated, their financial knowledge.
Lee & Kim (2022)	U.S.	Age positively related to objective financial knowledge.	Age positively related to subjective financial knowledge.	Age positively related to overconfidence.
O'Conner (2019)	U.S.	Age positively related to objective financial knowledge.	Age negatively related to subjective financial knowledge.	N/A
Rothwell & Wu (2019)	Canada	Age positively related to objective financial knowledge.	Age positively related to subjective financial knowledge.	N/A
Xiao & Porto (2017)	U.S.	Age positively related to objective financial knowledge.	Age positively related to subjective financial knowledge.	N/A
Xiao et al. (2022)	China	N/A	Not significant	Not significant

Most of the studies found a positive relationship between age and objective financial knowledge (e.g., Gerrans, 2021; Gerrans & Heaney, 2019; Lee & Kim, 2022; O'Connor, 2019; Rothwell & Wu, 2019; Xiao & Porto, 2017). Age also had a positive correlation with subjective financial knowledge in the majority of studies (e.g., Gerrans, 2021; Gerrans & Heaney, 2019; Lee & Kim, 2022; Rothwell & Wu, 2019; Xiao & Porto, 2017). In summary, both objective and subjective financial knowledge tend to increase with age, with a few exceptions such as the study by O'Connor, which found that age has a negative effect on subjective financial knowledge, and the study by Xiao et al. (2022), which found a statistically nonsignificant relationship between age and subjective financial knowledge. The positive relationship between age and objective financial knowledge could be attributed to the accumulation of knowledge, personal financial experiences, and the general improvement of cognitive abilities over time. For instance, Henager and Cude (2016), who documented age differences in correct answers by topics, found that the correct answer rate for the inflation question among the youngest age group was approximately half (37.3%) of that among the oldest age group (81.1%), suggesting disparities in familiarity with specific topics based on one's life stage. Furthermore, the positive effect observed not only on objective but also on subjective financial knowledge suggests that individuals generally perceive their objective financial knowledge accurately to a certain degree. However, there may be some groups experiencing disparities, which will be further discussed in the next section. Emerging adults are likely to have relatively lower objective and subjective financial knowledge compared to older age groups (Gerrans, 2021; Gerrans & Heaney, 2019; Lee & Kim, 2022; Rothwell & Wu, 2019; Xiao & Porto, 2017), placing them in a vulnerable position.

Research on the Objective and Subjective Financial Knowledge of Emerging Adults

Next, we conducted a more in-depth review of studies that specifically focused on the analytical sample of emerging adults. A summary of the selected studies can be found in Table 2.2. Approximately 72% of the 18 selected studies primarily targeted university students. University students have garnered attention from researchers because they represent emerging adults in the transitional phase from financial dependence to independence (see Chapter 9). They begin to manage their day-to-day finances independently, moving away from the financial support of their parents or legal guardians (see Chapter 11). Some studies also restricted their analysis to

Table 2.2 Summary of Selected Studies about Objective and Subjective Financial Knowledge of Emerging Adults

Studies	Population	Measurement of OFK	Measurement of SFK	Key Findings
Ali & Talha (2022)	Pakistani university students	5 items	6 items	Both objective and subjective financial knowledge had positive effect on financial well-being and financial management behaviors.
Britt et al. (2015)	U.S. university students	6 items	1 item	Financial counseling had a positive effect on subjective financial knowledge but did not have a consistent and significant effect on objective financial knowledge.
Carlsson Hauff & Nilsson (2020)	Swedish emerging adults (ages 24–29)	5 items	5 items	N/A
Gerrans (2021)	Australian university students	Basic: 4 items Advanced: 4 items Post-survey: 13 items	2 items	After completing a semester-long personal finance course, objective and subjective financial literacy improved. Students retained objective and subjective financial literacy for a few years despite some decays.
Gerrans & Heaney (2019)	Australian university students	Basic: 4 items Advanced: 4 items Applied: 13 items	2 items	After completing a semester-long personal finance course, objective and subjective financial literacy improved.

continued

Table 2.2 *continued*

Studies	Population	Measurement of OFK	Measurement of SFK	Key Findings
Henager & Cude (2016)	U.S. analysis by age group	5 items	1 item	The odds ratio for objective financial knowledge on financial behaviors increased with each age group. The odds ratio for subjective financial knowledge (confidence) on financial behaviors decreased with each age group up to age 44.
Kim et al. (2019)	U.S. millennials (18–34 years old)	5 items	1 item	Millennials have lower-than-average objective financial knowledge but similar-to-average subjective financial knowledge compared to all U.S. adults. Both financial knowledge indices were positively related to appropriate short-term and long-term financial behaviors.
Lee & Kim (2020)	U.S. millennials (18–34 years old)	6 items	1 item	OFK was negatively related to costly credit management behaviors, but SFK was mostly related positively to inappropriate credit management behaviors.
Liu & Zhang (2021)	Chinese college students	5 items	1 item	Both OFK and SFK had a negative impact on risky credit behaviors, while the effect of SFK was greater than OFK. The strength of correlation increased when finance-related stress levels increased.

McCannon et al. (2016)	U.S. university students	16 items	16 items*	OFK was not related to one's trust in investing.
Rabbani et al. (2022)	U.S. university students	28 items	1 item	Based on three dimensions of financial knowledge (objective, subjective, comparative), the study classified subjects into three groups. They exhibited significant difference in financial well-being, risk tolerance, and education.
Richardson et al. (2022)	Australian university students	5 items	1 item	Overconfidence in financial knowledge leads to inaccuracy in retirement need projection, but the relation is mitigated by objective financial knowledge.
Salas-Velasco (2022)	Spanish final-year undergraduate students	6 items	3 items*	Financial education intervention had positive impact on both OFK and SFK. OFK mediated the relation between financial education and SFK.
Sconti (2022)	Italian high school students (Gen Z)	3 items	1 item	Both traditional in-person and digital Web-based financial education programs had a positive effect on financial literacy.
Smith & Barboza (2014)	U.S. university students	3 items	12 items*	The likelihood of holding low credit card debt and student loans increased with the self-reported financial knowledge transferred from parents, and OFK reduced the overall debt holding.

continued

Table 2.2 *continued*

Studies	Population	Measurement of OFK	Measurement of SFK	Key Findings
Tenney et al. (2021)	U.S. university students (during and after college)	15 items	1 item	Positive correlation between OFK and SFK was found. First-year students were less likely, senior students were more likely to perceive themselves as financially literate compared to 5 years after university.
Totenhagen et al. (2019)	U.S. university students (during and after college)	15 items	1 item	Positive correlation between SFK and relationship satisfaction was found, but not between OFK and relationship satisfaction.
Xiao et al. (2011)	U.S. university students	8 items	2 items	SFK has stronger correlation to preventing risky credit management behaviors than OFK.

Note. *McCannon et al. (2016)'s SFK variable is vastly different from other studies. The study asked respondents how confident they feel about the accuracy of their responses to objective financial knowledge questions. Salas-Velasco (2022) labeled the variable as perceived financial self-efficacy while it did measure subjective financial knowledge to some extent. Smith and Barboza (2014) labeled the category of items as self-reported financial knowledge and financial experience. The authors considered 5 out of 12 items they used to be more related to financial experiences.

specific age groups. For example, Carlsson Hauff and Nilsson (2020) conducted their analysis on Swedish emerging adults between the ages of 24–29. Kim et al. (2019) and Lee and Kim (2020) explored the financial knowledge of U.S. millennials, and Sconti (2022) focused on Italian Generation Z. In the majority of these studies, the Big 5 questions proposed by Lusardi and Mitchell (2007, 2011) were used to measure objective financial knowledge, sometimes with slight modifications. Subjective financial knowledge was typically estimated using a single item that asked respondents to assess how knowledgeable they believed themselves to be financially.

As emerging adults are a group of individuals experiencing the transition from adolescence to adulthood and gradually entering the labor market (see Chapter 10), the research topics tended to focus on financial domains that have a crucial impact during this phase. Researchers have explored the effects of financial knowledge on various financial behaviors (see Chapter 5) and found significant relationships. For instance, Henager and Cude (2016) and Kim et al. (2019) utilized comprehensive measures of appropriate financial behaviors and observed a positive effect of financial knowledge. Interestingly, Henager and Cude documented differences in the strength of the correlation between financial knowledge and financial behaviors among different age groups, indicating that this dynamic changes as individuals age. Subjective financial knowledge was found to be more strongly connected to long- and short-term financial behaviors than objective financial knowledge among emerging adults in comparison to older adults.

Other studies have focused on specific domains of financial behaviors, and one domain that has garnered considerable attention from researchers is credit management behaviors (Lee & Kim, 2020; Liu & Zhang, 2021; Smith & Barboza, 2014; Xiao et al., 2011). Emerging adults often encounter financial burdens such as student loans as they pursue post-secondary education (see Chapter 9), and they may also misuse or overuse credit due to financial constraints and mismanagement (see Chapter 13). According to the cited studies, higher financial knowledge generally leads to better credit management. However, the relationship between financial knowledge and credit behaviors varies depending on how financial literacy is assessed. Studies by Liu and Zhang as well as Xiao et al. found that subjective financial knowledge had a stronger preventive effect on risky credit management behaviors. In contrast, Lee and Kim found that objective financial knowledge among millennials was negatively related to costly credit management behaviors, while subjective financial knowledge was positively correlated with inappropriate behaviors. Both Lee and Kim as well as Smith and Barboza focused on this discrepancy between objective and subjective aspects of financial knowledge, which they labeled as overconfidence in financial knowledge.

Another aspect that researchers have focused on is the effect of financial education on financial knowledge (see Chapter 19; e.g., Gerrans, 2021; Gerrans & Heaney, 2019; Salas-Velasco, 2022; Sconti, 2022). The cited studies have found financial education to be an effective intervention for improving the understanding of financial matters among emerging adults. Upon completing a finance course or a financial education module, university students saw improvements in both objective and subjective financial knowledge (Gerrans, 2021; Gerrans & Heaney, 2019; Salas-Velasco, 2022), and students retained this financial knowledge for a few years, despite some decay over time (Gerrans, 2021). The study by Sconti found that both traditional in-person and digital Web-based financial education programs were effective for emerging adults. This is an important finding because young people are more familiar with the digital environment, and Web-based financial education proves to be an effective and powerful tool. This suggests that there are diverse avenues through which financial educators can reach emerging adults.

Research on the Discrepancy between Objective and Subjective Financial Knowledge of Emerging Adults

Out of the 73 articles, 34 articles (42%) examined the discrepancy between objective and subjective financial knowledge. Most studies examining why there is a discrepancy and who exhibits such characteristics share a common interest in the two-fold dimensions of financial knowledge. The majority of these studies labeled the difference, specifically when subjective assessment surpasses objective financial knowledge, as overconfidence in financial knowledge. However, a few studies used different terminologies such as financial literacy miscalibration (Nejad & Javid, 2018) and financial knowledge gap (Khan et al., 2017).

Table 2.3 presents a summary of selected studies that specifically focused on overconfidence in financial knowledge among emerging adults. Many of these studies used the numerical difference between subjective and objective knowledge scales to measure overconfidence (Carlsson Hauff & Nilsson, 2020; Lee & Kim, 2020; Richardson et al., 2022). Lee and Kim defined overconfidence as having above-average (or median) subjective knowledge and below-average (or median) objective knowledge, a commonly used estimation by previous authors (e.g., Lee & Hanna, 2022; Porto & Xiao, 2016; Robb et al., 2015). Other studies assessed overconfidence

Table 2.3 Summary of Selected Studies about Financial Knowledge Overconfidence of Emerging Adults

Studies	Population	Measurement of Overconfidence	Key Findings
Carlsson Hauff & Nilsson (2020)	Swedish emerging adults (ages 24–29)	Numerical difference between SFK and OFK scales	People with overconfidence in financial knowledge had greater debt than those who did not.
Gerrans (2021)	Australian university students	Overconfident: Predicted correct number > Actual correct number Underconfident: Predicted correct number < Actual correct number Calibrated: Predicted correct number = Actual correct number	Little to no significant correlation between the completion of financial education and overconfidence.
Gerrans & Heaney (2019)	Australian university students	Overconfident: Predicted correct number > Actual correct number Underconfident: Predicted correct number < Actual correct number	No statistically significant correlation between the completion of financial education and overconfidence. Females were underconfident than males. Age was negatively correlated to basic overconfidence.
Lee & Kim (2020)	U.S. millennials (18–34 years old)	(1) Numerical difference between SFK and OFK; (2) residual from OLS of OFK on SFK; (3) binary indicator of having lower than median OFK and higher than median SFK	Millennials who are overconfident in financial knowledge were more likely to participate in costly credit management behaviors.
McCannon et al. (2016)	U.S. university students	Sum of confidence points for incorrect OFK questions	People with overconfidence in financial knowledge were more likely to make greater contributions to investment game, and more likely to trust investment.
Richardson et al. (2022)	Australian university students	Numerical difference between SFK and OFK scales	Overconfidence in financial knowledge leads to inaccuracy in retirement needs projection, but the relation is mitigated by objective financial knowledge.

by examining respondents' predicted confidence in each of the questions. The studies by Gerrans, as well as Gerrans and Heaney, compared the number of questions that respondents believed they answered correctly with the number of questions they actually answered correctly. McCannon et al. (2016) estimated overconfidence by adding up each confidence point for objective financial knowledge questions that respondents got wrong.

In the psychological literature, overconfidence has been defined in three ways: overestimation, overplacement, and overprecision (Moore & Healy, 2008). *Overestimation* occurs when an individual believes that their performance or abilities are better than they actually are. *Overplacement* refers to the belief that one's abilities or performance is superior to those of others. *Overprecision* refers to excessive confidence in the accuracy of one's own beliefs, predictions, or estimates. These researchers used the combination of overestimation, overplacement, and overprecision (Moore & Healy, 2008) to measure overconfidence in the financial knowledge of younger adults.

Several interesting findings were reported by studies that focused on this topic. The discrepancy between objective and subjective financial knowledge is generally found to have a negative impact on emerging adults' financial management. Specifically, Carlsson Hauff and Nilsson (2020) found that Swedish emerging adults with overconfidence in financial knowledge had greater debt than those who were not overconfident. Lee and Kim (2020) documented that millennials in the United States engaged in inappropriate credit card management if they were overconfident. Respondents were more likely to make minimum payments, pay late or over-limit fees, and use credit cards for cash advances. In addition, Richardson et al. (2022) found that Australian university students with overconfidence exhibited inaccuracy in retirement needs projection. As noted earlier, because emerging adults are at the stage of initiating independent financial management (see Chapter 11), inappropriate financial behaviors could adversely affect their chances of financial flourishing (see Chapter 5).

Unfortunately, the financial education modules carried out either directly or indirectly by researchers were not found to be effective in reducing the degree of overconfidence among emerging adults, according to three studies that used a measure of overconfidence. The studies by Gerrans (2021) and Gerrans and Heaney (2019) shed light on this by examining the outcome of a semester-long personal finance course. The overconfidence levels right after and 3 years after the completion of the unit did not significantly improve. On the other hand, the study by Sconti (2022), while it did not explicitly measure overconfidence, asserted that real and perceived financial knowledge improved and became more aligned after financial education.

Conclusion

This chapter provides a systematic review of the financial knowledge of emerging adults. It explores various pieces of evidence demonstrating the lack of financial knowledge among this population. It also highlights that if their levels of objective and subjective financial knowledge are not aligned, it can have a detrimental impact on their financial well-being (see Chapter 7). These findings have important implications for various interested parties.

First, as mentioned earlier, financial educators should be aware that emerging adults generally have a relatively lower level of objective financial knowledge and may experience a mismatch between their actual and perceived financial knowledge (i.e., overconfidence). Studies on emerging adults have shown that financial knowledge is a key factor affecting financial outcomes (e.g., Henager & Cude, 2016; Kim et al., 2019; Lee & Kim, 2020; Liu & Zhang, 2021; Smith & Barboza, 2014; Xiao et al., 2011; Zhu, 2018). The need to improve objective financial knowledge is evident, and research has found that financial education is an effective means of enhancing emerging adults' understanding of financial issues (see Chapter 19; e.g., Gerrans, 2021; Gerrans & Heaney, 2019; Salas-Velasco, 2022; Sconti, 2022). Global surveys have also documented the prevalence of financial illiteracy worldwide (Klapper & Lusardi, 2019; Mitchell & Lusardi, 2015). To enhance individuals' financial knowledge, both the United States federal and state governments have invested substantial efforts in financial education across all 50 states and the District of Columbia, although the degree of enforcement varies across states (Council for Economic Education, 2022).

However, studies have also shown that financial education programs could be further improved to better meet the specific needs of emerging adults. Despite efforts in the public domain, such as state-required education, the review in this chapter documents that the education programs tested in empirical analyses so far have not been successful in reducing the degree of overconfidence among emerging adults (e.g., Gerrans, 2021; Gerrans & Heaney, 2019). Ineffective financial education could potentially widen the gap between the two aspects of financial knowledge and lead to detrimental long-term outcomes. Therefore, financial educators should invest their resources in developing programs that minimize this discrepancy. This can be achieved by allowing students to objectively assess their knowledge, identifying their areas of strength and weakness, and providing tailored education modules to meet their specific needs.

Furthermore, at-home education also plays a crucial role, and parents or guardians can serve as the most approachable source of financial education (Shim et al., 2010). As parents, they should make an effort to gradually introduce their children to the financial aspects of the family and help them understand the role of finances in daily life, enabling them to gain real-life experiences. Financial socialization is a useful and effective way for children to acquire basic financial knowledge (see Chapter 18; Jorgensen & Savla, 2010; LeBaron & Kelley, 2021). While doing so, parents should be aware that both objective and subjective financial knowledge can significantly impact a person's life. By ensuring that their children are well prepared with knowledge of financial matters and a realistic perception of their own knowledge as they leave the nest, parents can enhance the likelihood of their financial flourishing.

The findings of this chapter are also crucial for policymakers. The Financial Literacy and Education Commission (FLEC) under the Department of the Treasury has emphasized the need for all stakeholders to work together in the mission of educating and empowering U.S. households toward financial independence. This requires a united front at the state or country level to implement regulations and allocate resources. It is imperative that policymakers understand the overall lack of financial knowledge among the younger generation and how this could have severe consequences for the financial stability of households. These insights should be carefully incorporated into policies.

Financial practitioners should also be prepared for emerging adult clients who may not possess a full understanding of financial issues, especially given the potential for overconfidence. As many studies cited in Tables 2.2 and 2.3 have focused on the credit management of emerging adults, financial practitioners need to provide assistance to those who are struggling with debt management and lack financial knowledge to address the situation on their own (see Chapter 13).

The review in this chapter also revealed a general lack of studies focusing on overconfidence specifically among emerging adults. The financial situation at this early stage of life can have a continuous and significant impact on their future. Acquiring financial knowledge would enable them to make optimal financial decisions and develop appropriate financial habits. Therefore, there is a need for researchers to further examine the implications for emerging adults. Additionally, many studies have treated financial knowledge or overconfidence as independent variables rather than dependent variables in their empirical models. While the effect of financial knowledge on financial behaviors is well documented (see Chapter 5), more attention should be given to how to improve the level of financial knowledge, for instance, through more effective financial education (see Chapter 19), and what factors can bridge the gap between objective and subjective financial knowledge.

Furthermore, emerging adults have undergone significant life changes due to the COVID-19 pandemic. It is highly likely that they have exhibited different behaviors between the pre- and post-pandemic periods. Understanding how emerging adults who lacked financial knowledge or exhibited overconfidence in financial knowledge fared during the pandemic could provide valuable insights. In essence, further investigation of financial knowledge is still needed, as it serves as the cornerstone for emerging adults to progress toward financial flourishing rather than floundering.

Chapter 3
Emerging Adults' Financial Skills

Ashlyn Rollins-Koons[1], *Megan McCoy*[1], *and Favian Ray Lininger*[1]

Introduction

Emerging adults face a multitude of new financial challenges and decisions (see Chapter 6). They may start student loan payments for the first time (see Chapter 9), begin managing their paychecks more thoughtfully, move toward financial independence (see Chapter 11), or develop a financial identity (see Chapter 12). Handling these financial behaviors and transitions requires many financial skills. Financial skills are defined as the attributes that impact one's ability to apply financial knowledge to their decision-making and behaviors. These are characteristics that *predispose* some individuals to select healthier financial behaviors (see Chapter 5). This chapter will review the literature on the financial skills that lead to financial flourishing—numeracy, reading ability, and executive functioning—and suggest methods of improving and developing these skills for emerging adults.

Numeracy

Numeracy, or the ability to understand and work with numbers, is a critical financial skill. Numeracy is the "ability to access, use, interpret and communicate mathematical information and ideas, to engage in and manage the mathematical demands of a range of situations in adult life" (Jonas, 2018, p. 12). The level of proficiency an emerging adult has with numbers influences their ability to save, invest, and enact other financial behaviors (see Chapter 5).

[1] Department of Personal Financial Planning, Kansas State University, USA

Ashlyn Rollins-Koons, Megan McCoy, and Favian Ray Lininger, *Emerging Adults' Financial Skills*. In: *Flourishing and Floundering Financially in Emerging Adulthood*. Edited by: Ashley B. LeBaron-Black, Heather Kelley, and Angela Sorgente, Oxford University Press. © Oxford University Press (2025). DOI: 10.1093/9780197699157.003.0004

Numeracy encompasses elements of intelligence, critical thinking, and problem-solving abilities (Jonas, 2018). Without these abilities, an emerging adult's chances of successfully navigating the many new financial challenges of adulthood dwindle. Floundering math scores across American high schools may be indicative of a lack of numeracy skills (U.S. Department of Education, 2019). This is not to say that all emerging adults must be expert mathematicians. Instead, a strong basis in applied mathematics and an understanding of how it relates to financial concepts—such as compound interest or tax brackets—can go a long way toward being able to flourish.

Influence on Behaviors, Opportunities, and Well-Being

Strong numeracy skills—or the lack thereof—can affect the opportunities available to emerging adults. More jobs are becoming dependent on individuals having high numeracy abilities to learn the skills necessary to succeed in these careers (Windisch, 2015). Those who lack these skills may find their roles redundant or even replaced with technology (Smits, 2007; Windisch, 2015). Having numeracy skills can improve employment opportunities even for those with less formal education (Lane & Conlon, 2016). Gainful employment is important for an emerging adult's financial flourishing (see Chapter 10), especially as many face rising housing costs and student loan burdens (see Chapter 9).

In addition to career development, numeracy can also help people make rational choices in their finances (Garcia-Retamero et al., 2019). For example, individuals with high numeracy tend to spend more time evaluating the options available to them and are more skilled in decision-making (see Chapter 6; Ashby, 2017). Highly numerate individuals may also ask more questions about their financial alternatives, such as fees or interest rates, which allows them to make financially beneficial decisions (Estrada-Mejia et al., 2016).

There is also an argument that numeracy is a contributing factor in many activities that are not obviously related to finances but can have a financial impact (Barton, 2006). For example, shopping requires the ability to estimate sales tax, add item prices together, understand store credit card offers, and recall budget limits (see Chapter 13). Even hobbies, such as gardening or do-it-yourself projects, require numeracy skills (Barton, 2006). A lack of these skills can easily result in overspending or running out of money for essentials, which could prevent an emerging adult from flourishing. Many emerging adults may not feel confident with numeracy, as discussed in Box 3.1.

Box 3.1

To gather an emerging adult's perspective on the concepts described here, Favian Lininger, an undergraduate personal financial planning student at Kansas State University, shared his thoughts and experiences with the many financial skills covered in this chapter. We have edited this interview transcript for length and clarity.

FAVIAN: I did take note that a lot of this chapter, in my eyes, is guided by the idea of "productive disposition." This starts from a very young age when children start asking themselves questions like "Am I smart?" or "Am I dumb?" When it comes to financial literacy, I think about how my loved ones along with their friends hated school, especially math, which led to them calling themselves "dumb" and dreading the subject whenever it came up in school. Their unproductive disposition toward math was "I'm too dumb, so I'm going to avoid it," and I feel that for some of them, their disposition carried over to other subjects, beyond school even, taming their curiosity and perseverance to learn. I believe the first thing that needs to be addressed is the individual's disposition and how it impacts their ability to learn about finances.

ASHLYN: This dichotomy of "I'm bad at school or not bad at school" or "I'm good at math or bad at math"—it's not necessarily a real dichotomy, but we hear it so often, and it sounds like you have observed it.

FAVIAN: I don't want to say that I'm smart because I don't think it's that black and white. But like, growing up, my parents and older sister would call me smart. Both my mom and older sister never did enjoy school. Which might be why they would ask me things like "What's wrong with the WiFi?" or "How do I work this app or TV?" They would feel that they weren't competent enough to worry about or think about these things. My father loved math growing up and had a much more positive outlook on school, sometimes going as far as to say that he missed [school]. Despite that, it would still be difficult to talk to him about retirement, credit scores, or budgeting in general. That's something they would put on me, being the "smart kid." So, because I was their son/brother who happened to be "smart," they'd just hand it off to me in the hopes that I could fix their financial life.

How to Improve Numeracy

One major concern for numeracy skill development is that some emerging adults are not able to apply the mathematical skills learned through formal schooling in their day-to-day lives (Tout & Gal, 2015). Part of this could be a result of the gap in how mathematical concepts are presented to children versus how they operate in the "real world" (see Box 3.2). In school, children engage with straightforward questions with one right answer, whereas everyday mathematics may not have one right answer (see Box 3.3). This could include a variety of activities such as:

- Deciding how much to contribute to a retirement account
- Filling out a W-4 for withholding taxes
- Calculating compound interest on investment returns
- Choosing a life insurance policy

Box 3.2

FAVIAN: Math in school is frustrating because, as you said, real life is hardly as straightforward as a "yes" or "no," or solving for X. The most relevant stuff isn't going to be straightforward, and it's not a matter of being super-smart or dumb. Going back to what you're saying about being partially correct and partially incorrect, that's something that isn't even hinted at in school or math class, especially at a young age. I remember one time in high school my pre-calc teacher decided to take things into his own hands and show us some basic budgeting/personal finance tools. That was the only time that had ever happened during high school.

MEGAN: Oh, gosh! I just had a flashback to middle school people saying, "Oh, I'm never going to use the Pythagorean theorem again, like, why do we have to learn this?" But that insertion of financial tips into numeracy courses—math courses—can help people see the real-life connections from the theory to what they'll need in life to succeed.

Education courses should consider ways to connect mathematical concepts with real-world applications. This is especially important when considering the debilitating effects of an exponential growth bias. Practically, this bias results in individuals underestimating how fast the balance of their debt will grow and overestimating how their savings will grow (Stango & Zinman, 2009). As a result, individuals may rely more on borrowing, especially using short-term loans. There is some evidence that financial literacy and exponential growth bias are negatively related (Almenberg & Gerdes, 2012). Goda et al.'s (2019) findings that households with a better understanding of exponential growth were less likely to use payday loans help illustrate the relationship between financial literacy, exponential growth bias, and financial behaviors.

Box 3.3

MEGAN: This makes me reflect on the importance of numeracy as a foundational financial skill. I started thinking about how so much in math early on is very black and white, right or wrong, whereas if you're reading a story for reading comprehension assessments, there's interpretation. There's more gray. So, you can get partial credit or positive reinforcement even when you don't get the question completely right. So, maybe this might have implications for how we teach math. Maybe instead of focusing on marking answers [as] right or wrong, we develop ways to help students reflect on what they did get right and have opportunities to redo problems to get them right. The goal is discovering your problem-solving abilities after a mistake, rather than getting it right instantly.

FAVIAN: Yeah, it's really unfair. I know for a fact that most people can [flourish financially]. [But] I guess that's why [financial] professionals have their jobs. Sometimes it's not just a matter of not believing that you can do it. It's just time-consuming, and people have other things to worry about, but when it comes to something like saving for retirement, there's no one else that can do that for you. Their "smart son" can't do that for them. So, that's why it's hard to talk to them about this because they just don't think they can do it or should do it, or they have other priorities right now, which is fair. There are lots of other variables, but being able to give themselves a chance is where it starts, and that's where they struggle.

Numeracy may also be enhanced by improving how information is presented to emerging adults. In one experiment, undergraduate students were presented with a probability question that used either a simple form using frequency data (e.g., 100 out of 200 students) or a complex form using percentages or fractions (Johnson & Tubau, 2013). After they solved the problem, they were given a numeracy test. Regardless of numeracy level, students struggled more with complex problems and if irrelevant information was presented in the problem. Presenting information, especially information coming from financial institutions, in an accessible format could be one avenue for improving comprehension and financial decision-making. This can be accomplished:

- Removing extraneous information
- Keeping problems concise
- Displaying problems in a variety of formats (e.g., word, graphics, audio)
- Avoiding phrases or colloquialisms that would be unfamiliar to non-native speakers

Another interesting solution to improving numeracy abilities is through gamification or game-based learning. Harvard Business Publishing (n.d.) has software that allows students from a variety of disciplines to engage with simulations that test their ability to use the concepts learned in class in "real-world" scenarios. Similar gamification can occur with younger age groups. Singh et al. (2021) tested whether a card game—*Math Zap*—could potentially improve numeracy skills. The researchers found that the card game improved a child's ability to think quickly and compute mathematical outputs. Teachers and parents may be able to use innovative learning techniques to increase the enjoyment associated with learning numerical concepts (see Chapters 18 and 19).

While socialization and educational opportunities exist to teach children numerical skills, there is a need to develop these skills as an emerging adult. Financial professionals, for example, work with individuals from varying backgrounds and with varying levels of numerical skills. Risk assessments are a common tool that advisors use to evaluate their clients' investment objectives. Perhaps there is an opportunity in the financial planning world for advisors to use their expertise to evaluate their clients' numerical literacy and determine how they can improve their clients' skills in these areas (Sages & Grable, 2010). Clients who develop this skill may have a greater willingness to save and plan for their financial future (Brounen et al., 2015; Garcia-Retamero et al., 2019). Moreover, financial professionals may benefit their clients by taking time to clearly explain the financial ratios they use and the basics behind mathematical concepts, such as compound interest or future and present value.

Reading Ability

Although numeracy may seem an obvious financial skill to facilitate financial capability, reading ability may seem less applicable. Yet, research has found that "children and young people who have good reading skills are four times as likely to have good financial skills compared with their peers who have poor reading skills" (Teravainen-Goff & Clark, 2019, p. 1). This may be surprising to those who assume that some people are naturally gifted at math and others at reading. We have heard from many students the quote "I am just not good at math." However, research does not support this claim. In a large-scale study of adolescent twins, results suggested that individuals were gifted in reading *and* math, or neither (Davis et al., 2014). There are some hypotheses regarding this fallacy. Some argue that the siloed nature of elementary schools creates a false dichotomy between coursework; students see math and reading as distinct, so they do not recognize how the skills overlap (Taylor & Taylor, 2022). Or perhaps students' identities as good or bad at math or reading develop early in their education based on their comparison group, which creates a self-fulfilling prophecy throughout their lives (Bishop, 2012). Further debate on why people appear to believe they can only be good at math or reading is beyond the scope of this chapter. What is within the scope of this chapter is to explore how reading ability is another key ingredient that connects to financial behaviors (see Chapter 5), opportunities, and well-being (see Chapter 7).

Influence on Behaviors, Opportunities, and Well-Being

Teravainen-Goff and Clark (2019) authored one of the few articles that have explored the influence of reading ability on financial behaviors, opportunities, and well-being. The authors described how reading ability is related to general academic motivations or a positive attitude toward school/education. They also suggested that reading ability has a direct relationship with perseverance and a willingness to engage with problems. As discussed in Box 3.4, these core characteristics (e.g., academic motivation, positive attitude toward education, perseverance) also enable one to flourish in numeracy, financial education courses, and to have higher financial literacy and better financial behaviors. Furthermore, early reading ability is a primary contributing factor to confidence and self-worth in children, thus creating a self-identity as intelligent and capable.

Box 3.4

FAVIAN: I'm pretty happy to see that the research kind of supports that there's a relationship between reading and financial capability because I feel that reading is a much more relevant activity. That's something that we engage in more often than math problems.

MEGAN: Yes! This week I had students in my undergraduate course ask me what the best credit card to get is. I told them that I can't answer that for them and sent them a bunch of websites to read about the best credit cards. For them to make a financial decision, they had to read a ton of material and critically think about that reading.

FAVIAN: I also thought it was interesting to examine how reading capability factors into this, like when the chapter discusses the research by Teravainen-Goff and Clark (2019) who found that reading capability had a strong correlation with financial capability, perseverance, and a positive outlook on school. When it comes to personal finances, most just find a way to get by, but when it comes to finding a way to flourish, to go beyond paycheck-to-paycheck living, it can seem impossible.

Research also suggests that having the ability to read allows one to comprehend financial documents (Mania & Tröster, 2017). Through the ability to comprehend financial documents, one can compare financial products, read the fine print for credit cards, and even be able to better understand one's eligibility for employment benefits, tax deductions, and investment strategies (Mania & Tröster). Furthermore, reading ability is linked to the development of critical thinking skills (Elder & Paul, 2004). In other words, one's reading ability will translate into better financial decision-making because one will be able to make more informed decisions.

As discussed in Box 3.5, reading ability may have the unexpected benefit of improving our future time perspective because it may help us become more empathetic of our future selves (Schroeder, 2021). fMRI scans found that people perceive their present selves differently than strangers but their future selves the same as strangers (Ersner-Hershfield et al., 2009). "From a financial perspective, we mentally treat saving money for our future selves as if we were giving money to our boss or a Starbucks barista. No wonder we struggle with saving for retirement" (Schroeder, 2021, p. 1). Reading makes us immerse ourselves in the characters we are reading about, increasing our empathy, and making those characters feel less like strangers. This may be a transferable skill to make ourselves more empathetic to our future selves and to make our future selves feel like less of a stranger.

Box 3.5

MEGAN: Okay, I want to selfishly switch topics to something that I included that I found fascinating but does not have a lot of research support. It was the idea that reading also makes us more empathetic and that may help us be more empathetic for our future selves [referencing the fMRI study by Schroeder (2021)].

FAVIAN: Yeah, when I first read that, I kind of thought it was reaching.

MEGAN: Well, honestly it might be! (*All laughing*)

FAVIAN: There's something that has a stronger correlation than the idea of being able to empathize with your future self that explains why it's so hard to save. For my parents, and many other people, there's no way they're ever going to think about future retirement because they live paycheck to paycheck, which to me is worth considering more in-depth. There is the case where someone is financially stable and making good money where I think this is more relevant, but it can still be hard. I remember watching this podcast with Simply Nailogical [created by YouTuber Cristine Rotenberg], and she talked about why she started working out and why some people fall out of it. She mentioned how doing it for someone else or to look good for someone else can get someone started but won't last for long. One of the things that she thinks kept her in her regimen was doing it for herself, so in that sense, there's some self-compassion or empathy, like "I love me so I'm doing this for me" type of thinking. The struggle with some financial skills is that it's for our future selves or "strangers" like you referenced from the fMRI research, so I can see the connection for some cases.

ASHLYN: I can see how that ties into the idea. You have to see your future self as you, to make the sacrifices today for that future self.

FAVIAN: Yeah. And that's why forming a buddy system, or talking about spirituality, the idea of fellowship. That sense of community can keep you on track with goals.

How to Improve Reading Ability

"Reading is among the most highly complex skills that school children are called upon to master, and it is influenced by a variety of perceptual, linguistic, and cognitive abilities" (Braze et al., 2007, p. 226). Due to the complexity of skills related to reading ability, there are numerous ways to foster reading ability at different developmental stages. For example, in early childhood, parents can aid in the development of reading ability by speaking to their child often because children who are spoken to more frequently will have better linguistic understanding (i.e., knowledge of different words), which aids in reading ability. Similarly, in studies of emerging adulthood, research suggests that reading for enjoyment (Mol & Bus, 2011) can build vocabulary and promote reading development.

More research is needed, but if the connection between reading ability and financial skills is due to the ability to empathize with characters and project onto our future selves, then one other way to develop reading ability is to not be too meticulous about the content areas of reading, but just attempt to devour multiple types of content regularly. Emerging adults would benefit from creating a reading checklist or a reading goal that encourages regular reading using the medium they enjoy the most regarding topics they are passionate about or in which they are interested. It also can be powerful to enlist a friend to share their passions with, whether it is creating a book club or simply sharing what they had learned about in their most recent read. Increasing one's reading ability is also related to the next underlying financial skill, executive functioning, because developing stronger executive functioning can also aid in reading ability (Butterfuss & Kendeou, 2018).

Executive Functioning

The final contributing factor related to emerging adults' financial skills covered in this chapter is executive functioning. Executive functioning describes an important aspect of our prefrontal cortex, the part of our brain that deals with our working memory, cognitive flexibility, self-control, and future orientation (Drever et al., 2015). Executive functioning is a skill in many areas of life, but it is also a financial skill critical to an emerging adult's ability to flourish. For example, working memory is our ability to receive information and make appropriate decisions based on our experiences with similar information (see Chapter 6; Drever et al., 2015), and after filing a few tax returns, an emerging adult may be able to use their previous knowledge to adjust to tax law changes. Cognitive flexibility is our ability to come up with multiple creative solutions to problems (e.g., determining whether to pay debts off by the largest balance or largest interest rates). Future orientation directly impacts our ability to pay attention to the present while also projecting to hypothesize the consequences of our actions (e.g., saving today will allow for a vacation next summer). Self-control is key to our ability to stay calm and be in charge of our emotions, thoughts, and behaviors through decreasing physiological arousal with logic and remaining in control of our impulses (e.g., not overspending when upset; Drever et al., 2015).

Influence on Behaviors, Opportunities, and Well-Being

There is preliminary evidence that supports executive functioning's role in financial management. Studies have found that participants with prefrontal cortex damage make less favorable financial decisions (Moretti et al., 2009) and are more likely to make riskier financial decisions (Clark et al., 2008) than individuals with a healthy prefrontal cortex (see Chapter 6). Even when individuals have a healthy prefrontal cortex, if they become emotionally aroused (e.g., angry or stressed), they are more likely to make worse financial decisions (Sanfey et al., 2003). Moffitt et al. (2011) found that early parent and teacher scoring of a child's self-control was linked to saving rates, investment behaviors, retirement account ownership, credit score ratings, and overall financial well-being later in life. Dare et al. (2022) found that executive functioning was directly related to participants' self-rating of current financial stress and expected future financial security.

Spinella et al. (2007) also found a link between self-rated executive functioning questionnaires and financial management behaviors (see Chapter 5). More specifically, low ratings on self-reported executive functioning were found to be linked to credit card debt, lower income, the disorganization of financial documents, and more difficulty delaying gratification or delay discounting (i.e., preferring smaller, immediate rewards over larger, more delayed responses). The components of executive functioning often work together. Drever et al. (2015) describe how working memory keeps our savings goals in the forefront of our mind, while our self-control system allows us to forego certain purchases to continue saving for that goal, and our cognitive flexibility allows us to adjust savings plans based on life events along the way. The result is that individuals struggling with executive functioning may have difficulty with the following financial behaviors:

- Starting and/or completing budgets
- Prioritizing different debts to pay off
- Following directions or a sequence of steps needed to complete a financial task

- Keeping track of their financial accounts
- Managing their time, which may result in late payments
- Restricting impulsive and compulsive purchases for future financial goals

How to Improve Executive Functioning

Most executive functioning development occurs early in life, but as discussed in Box 3.6, the prefrontal cortex is not fully formed until late adolescence or even early adulthood (some argue development continues until the third decade of life; Johnson et al., 2009; see Chapter 6). Some of an individual's executive functioning development is based on genetics, but there are environmental and socialization influences as well (Drever et al., 2015). Despite the rapid development of executive functioning early in life, it is never too late to build this component of our brain structure.

Box 3.6

FAVIAN: I started thinking about the fact that I am older compared to my peers. I'm a junior [in college], but I'm 23. So, I would joke around with my younger friends saying, "You ain't thinking with that prefrontal cortex."

MEGAN: (*Laughing*) That probably is partially true. There's new research that shows that development goes all [the way] into your late twenties. So, your prefrontal cortex may be a bit more developed than some of your younger friends.

FAVIAN: There are some things that I know for a fact my friends are way better at than [me] when it comes to priorities and self-control. Reading through this section, I started thinking about how there's a lot for me to improve on when it comes to executive functioning. It's not going to just stem from my prefrontal cortex, it's something that I have to personally put in the work and effort [for]. I would ask my friends because they would have these beautiful calendars that would give me a whole lot of anxiety at the same time, "How do you do this? How do you literally plan out your life on a daily basis?" But it's just like you said, Dr. McCoy, it's just practice. It's something you can practice.

Diamond and Lee (2011) found that diverse interventions and activities have been shown to improve executive functions. Although results are strongest in children, adults with attention deficit/hyperactivity disorder (ADHD), and those with neurological impairments, all of the following activities may strengthen an individual's executive functioning:

- *Computer training.* Computer games have been developed to help develop executive functioning. For example, *CogMed*© is a computer game that helps children develop their executive function through fun activities. The game increases difficulty with right answers to scaffold growth but also decreases difficulty with wrong answers to prevent frustration.
- *Exercise.* Almost all exercise helps with executive functioning because it requires some level of following directions, task switching, self-control, and working memory (Guiney & Machado, 2013). Aerobics, team sports, and yoga are the most effective (Diamond & Lee, 2011). Traditional martial arts provide additional support for executive functioning development because it emphasizes self-control, discipline, and character development.
- *School curricula.* There have been school curriculum programs that have received empirical support in the development of executive functioning. One such is *Tools of the Mind*, which emphasizes the importance of social pretend play for children to develop skills in remembering their own and others' roles and flexibly adjusting as their friends improvise (Parkinson, 2015).

Taken together, it appears that structured tasks that require following directions, confidence, exercise, self-esteem, and emotion regulation foster the development of the prefrontal cortex and, therefore, our executive functioning.

We would be remiss to end this section on executive functioning's role in finances without a conversation about how financial socialization practices within the family will improve executive functioning and financial management behaviors (see Chapter 18). Caregivers who provide experiential learning opportunities related to money (e.g., allowance, opening accounts) with kind and supportive oversight can provide the pathway toward a stronger future orientation, working memory, and organization skills needed to manage one's finances (Drever et al., 2015). In addition, the caregiver models the self-control needed to pursue future financial goals rather than succumbing to instant gratification purchases, which provides the foundational skills needed to develop their children's executive functioning that is linked to financial well-being.

Diversity, Equity, and Inclusion Issues Related to Financial Skills

Individuals from different cultures, racial/ethnic groups, genders, and socioeconomic backgrounds often have experienced differences in the development of their financial skills (see Chapters 15, 16, and 17). Different cultures, for example, assign different expectations and definitions to numeracy. While some cultures may see numeracy as skills learned throughout one's formal education, others perceive it as a capability necessary in adulthood (Tout & Gal, 2015). In general, countries whose populations more often engage with and use numeracy in day-to-day life also have higher numeracy scores (Jonas, 2018). However, interestingly, Jonas (2018) found that the United States falls well below the average numeracy score across OECD countries despite having the second-highest engagement score. Likewise, Japan has one of the lowest engagement scores but the highest numeracy scores (Jonas, 2018). This may indicate that there are other, stronger reasons (e.g., employment or education) than how much a country relies on numeracy engagement to explain who flounders and who flourishes financially (Jonas, 2018). Although numeracy levels may significantly vary across cultures and countries, the impact of financial literacy on well-being tends to hold steady (see Chapter 7). Bruin and Slovic (2021) found that in high-income and low-income countries (as classified by the World Bank), those with low numeracy were more likely to be some of the poorest individuals who struggled to live on their income. These studies illustrate that countries define and value numeracy differently, but low numeracy skills can have negative financial well-being implications worldwide.

Just as numeracy can be defined and emphasized differently depending on the country, reading ability can vary dramatically. Students in the United States tend to be moderately better at reading text than students in other countries, but in terms of integrating contextual information and background knowledge, U.S. students appear to be deficient (Reardon et al., 2012). This variation between literacy proficiency and reading comprehension is due, in part, to differences based on socioeconomic backgrounds, which show how reading ability has a gulf due to the wealth gap (see Chapters 15 and 17). This gap has numerous catalysts, such as not having the financial means to acquire reading material for home or stress impacting parents' ability to engage in activities that promote children's reading skills (Guo & Harris, 2000). There are gaps between White and Asian students' and Black and Hispanic students' reading abilities as well (Reardon et al., 2012). Bilingual households may experience obstacles in terms of reading ability. This may make it even more essential to provide opportunities for all students to read stories and content that focuses on characters both like and unlike them, to learn about similarities and differences in the human experience.

Executive functioning performance has been linked to socioeconomic status (SES), race, ethnicity, and disability (Grissom & Reyes, 2019). Researchers posit that lower SES creates stress on parents, reducing their ability to meet children's nutritional and physical needs, enact consistent discipline, and provide positive involvement. This reduced capacity of the parents can lead to higher levels of stress that will negatively impact their children's executive functioning (Raver et al., 2013; Vernon-Feagans et al., 2016). This is in line with the family stress model (Masarik & Conger, 2017), which says that economic hardships are related to child and adolescent maladjustment because financial stress can cause interparental relationship problems and disrupted parenting.

As discussed in Box 3.7, the link between executive functioning and race/ethnicity is due to confounding variables such as the unjust racial/ethnic wealth gap, racism, or testing flaws (Grissom & Reyes, 2019). First, there is a well-documented racial/ethnic wealth gap that shows wealth being skewed to White households due to "centuries of racialized, exploitative social and legal structures—policies that set the foundation for a skewed distribution of land, labor, political power, and resource ownership by race" (Santos et al., 2019, p. 2; see Chapters 15 and 17). Second, stress negatively impacts our executive functioning performance (see Chapter 8). Racism is a stressor event, and research has found that marginalized groups may have poorer performance on executive functioning tasks due to racial discrimination (Thames et al., 2014). Finally, research has suggested that other factors, such as linguistic ability and acculturation, influence executive functioning task performance, potentially explaining why some researchers (e.g., Roberts et al., 2020) found large differences in executive functioning among racial/ethnic groups. In summary, differences in executive functioning by race/ethnicity are not due to differences in inherent abilities, but rather the aforementioned factors.

Box 3.7

FAVIAN: I am aware that systemic racism plays a role in how well-off a generation is. That's something worth bringing up and talking about. In terms of my personal experiences, as someone who isn't a minority in the slightest sense, a mere straight White male, I just couldn't share any experience that would show issues comparable to what my friends in those minority groups faced themselves.

MEGAN: I think that harkens back to the power of your sense of identity underlying financial skills and how if you're not in certain groups where reading ability is predicated on the dominant or privileged group's language or values, it can create another hurdle to having that identity as capable at numeracy or reading. For instance, there has been research on many standardized tests having inherent biases that privilege some groups over others in using language that is more "White" or Eurocentric.

FAVIAN: I [am] excited for what ChatGPT can offer in terms of helping anybody increase their executive functioning, like being able to understand Old English written [long] ago. [I have] the ability to ask ChatGPT, "Hey, break this down for me. What does this actually mean?" And when it did, I was like, "Okay, I'm able to understand what I'm reading now. I'm actually learning right now." I don't know how OpenAI, which is the company that is behind ChatGPT, is addressing bias when they're training these AIs, like what you said about White language. I do see ChatGPT kind of reducing the amount of bias when it comes to political ideologies and even reading ability. I see it leveling the playing field by so much because everybody is going to have easier access to knowledge including financial planning that can be broken down and explained in a way that is encouraging, not intimidating. I could see it having no problem giving you those first initial steps.

Conclusion

Throughout this chapter, we have shared Favian's reflections and experiences with developing financial skills and observing how others are affected by a lack of financial capability, perceived or real, which coincided with many of the research findings explored in this chapter. His reflections also highlighted the link between financial skills and financial well-being (see Chapter 7). Numeracy predominantly affects emerging adults' financial well-being in terms of job market opportunities (see Chapter 10) and rational financial decision-making (see Chapter 6). Strong reading abilities enable emerging adults to find creative solutions to problems and persevere through difficult situations. Executive functioning can apply to many facets of an emerging adult's life such as family, career, personal goals, and personal finances.

Developing these skills likely requires interventions throughout life, but the earlier these efforts start, the better. For example, whether emerging adults are oriented toward the future could be a result of their financial socialization as children (see Chapter 18). Parental encouragement and whether a parent gives their child a savings education can influence how future-oriented they are (Bucciol & Luca, 2019; Webley & Nyhus, 2013). Educators should continue to implement the innovative techniques outlined in this chapter to improve these skills throughout childhood (see Chapter 19). Financial professionals are in a unique position to reach emerging adults and boost their financial well-being by improving their financial skills.

There is a need for future research to provide empirical evidence to better understand (1) what factors influence the development of these financial skills, and (2) what interventions can most effectively improve numeracy, reading abilities, and executive functioning. Researchers should explore the aforementioned financial skills, and also what other financial skills have been overlooked that would facilitate financial literacy. There may be psychological characteristics that predispose some to be more competent in certain financial skills. For example, the Big Five personality traits have been shown to correspond with a variety of financial behaviors—such as conscientious individuals being more likely to save for retirement (Asebedo et al., 2019). These relationships may also exist between personality and financial skills. What we do know is that financial skills can also affect emerging adults' health, social interactions, and even their opinions of themselves. Likely, one cannot truly achieve financial flourishing and overall well-being in life without strong financial skills in the areas of numeracy, reading abilities, and executive functioning.

Chapter 4
Emerging Adults' Financial Attitudes

Sonya Lutter[1] *and Matthew T. Saxey*[2]

Introduction

In general, attitudes are firmly held thoughts or feelings. *Financial* attitudes are thoughts or feelings about money that are not easily modifiable and that guide financial behaviors. Attitudes are typically formed through direct experience and through observations (Cherry, 2023). Emerging adults experience many financial adjustments during this developmental time period. For example, entering college or the workforce might lead to emerging adults having increased hands-on involvement with their money management (see Chapters 9 and 10). As such, financial attitudes can shift quickly and vastly as these financially related experiences are ongoing. Development of financial attitudes such as "the opportunity cost of not having $100 jeans now means I can save money for my future" creates habits that foster financial flourishing; in contrast, financial attitudes such as "credit cards are meant to provide comfort now" create habits that could lead to financial floundering.

In an attempt to formally measure financial attitudes, Beutler and Gudmunson (2012) examined the unique financial attitudes among a sample of adolescents (the average age of respondents was 16.5 years old—slightly younger than emerging adulthood). Attitudes held by these adolescents included contrasting financial entitlement (e.g., believing it is a parent's job to pay for one's needs and wants and provide extra spending money) and financial conscientiousness (e.g., exhibiting caution when spending parents' money) attitudes (Beutler & Gudmunson, 2012). Because of how closely this sample was to entering emerging adulthood, financial attitudes like these two might carry over into emerging adulthood and, ultimately, impact emerging

[1] School of Financial Planning, Texas Tech University, USA
[2] Department of Human Development and Family Science, Auburn University, USA

Sonya Lutter and Matthew T. Saxey, *Emerging Adults' Financial Attitudes*. In: *Flourishing and Floundering Financially in Emerging Adulthood*. Edited by: Ashley B. LeBaron-Black, Heather Kelley, and Angela Sorgente, Oxford University Press. © Oxford University Press (2025). DOI: 10.1093/9780197699157.003.0005

adults' financial behaviors (see Chapter 5; e.g., Jorgensen et al., 2017; Riaz et al., 2022). Throughout this chapter, we will give several more examples of financial attitudes emerging adults might espouse.

Given that emerging adulthood is a period of significant changes in personal, social, and economic circumstances (e.g., it is a time of major decisions around employment, education, and financial management), it is no surprise that we see a peak in the financial consequences of attitudes during this stage. Emerging adults are creating narratives about the way in which they watched important adults in their life manage money to guide how they use money (see Chapter 18). They are also basing their financial behaviors off the attitudes they form from observing what their friends are doing. Ultimately, financial attitudes can promote financial flourishing or floundering during emerging adulthood, depending on *what is consistently done* based on the observations being made that inform financial attitudes.

To deepen our understanding of financial attitudes among this transitioning population, we requested feedback on financial attitudes from emerging adults via the first author's LinkedIn account. After explaining what financial attitudes are, the first author asked questions about emerging adults' earliest memories concerning money; what common money-related phrases (e.g., enjoy now, pay later) are heard from parents or friends, on social or mass media, or in school; one's family financial motto; how one's financial attitudes might evolve over the next 5–10 years; confidence in money management; and financial satisfaction. In response to our questions, one respondent brought to life the theoretical idea that emerging adults' financial attitudes can be connected to behavior:

> I was surprised by how often memories about my parents' divorce came up and how that impacted my view of money. It gave me an attitude of "money can be taken away at any time. And at any time, you might have to take an extra job (maybe an undesirable job) to pay the bills."

To provide qualitative insight into our discussion of financial attitudes, additional quotes from emerging adults are included throughout this chapter. Furthermore, the peer-reviewed literature is somewhat scant related to emerging adults' financial attitudes, so in addition to the available literature and data, we drew on our own experience as researchers (both authors), a practitioner (first author), and an emerging adult (second author). Combined, this experience has taught us that financial attitudes matter. For instance, financial attitudes (e.g., beliefs about tracking monthly expenses), and associated financial behaviors (see Chapter 5; e.g., tracking monthly expenses), are especially salient during this period because of their long-term effects on financial outcomes, such as consistent budgeting, savings, and wealth accumulation

(Shim et al., 2010, 2015). In the following sections of this chapter, we discuss the influence of family of origin experiences, individual demographic characteristics, and social influences that might impact emerging adults' financial attitudes.

Familial Factors Influencing the Formation of Financial Attitudes

Money scripts might be considered one precursor to financial attitudes. Money scripts are early developmental money memories, often subconscious, that develop into beliefs and behaviors toward money in adulthood (Klontz & Klontz, 2009). Examples of money scripts include the following: "rich people are greedy," "money buys freedom," "money is what gives life meaning," "money should be saved, not spent," and "there will never be enough money" (Klontz et al., 2011). Other scholarship supports the theoretical idea that financial attitudes, even subconscious financial attitudes like money scripts, can lead to financial behavior (see Chapter 5; Klontz & Britt, 2012). Put simply, parental influence plays a crucial role in shaping the money scripts and financial attitudes of emerging adults. That is, parents act as financial role models—whether they know it or not—and provide verbal instruction for their children, and parents' attitudes toward money evidenced in their financial behaviors and their communication about money can impact their children's financial attitudes, and, in turn, their financial behaviors and financial well-being (see Chapter 18; for a recent review, see LeBaron & Kelley, 2021).

For example, when emerging adults can look to their parents as financial role models (i.e., parents show robust financial behavior), their emerging adult children tend to report better attitudes toward money management (e.g., agreeing that credit cards should be paid in full each month) and, in turn, better financial behaviors (e.g., spending within a budget; Shim et al., 2010). Additionally, emerging adults who grew up in households with parents who saved regularly are more likely to save compared to those who did not have parents who prioritized savings (e.g., Tang, 2017). In contrast, a young person who grew up in a financially stable household may be more comfortable taking on debt or spending money on non-essentials (Borden et al., 2008), but a young person who watched adults struggle to find stable employment may prioritize job security and financial planning. In essence, individuals who experience financial stress or debt early in life may develop more cautious attitudes toward spending and borrowing (see Chapter 13).

Where families live might also play a role in transmitting financial attitudes. For instance, compared to emerging adults living in other regions of the

United States, those living in the Northeast tend to value security and, thus, have financial attitudes that prioritize high financial achievement and view money as a source and symbol of power (Jorgensen et al., 2017). Therefore, it is possible that because of the prominent role families can play in impacting emerging adults' financial attitudes (Gudmunson & Danes, 2011; LeBaron & Kelley, 2021), the geographic environments that families find themselves in might also impact what financial attitudes are valued more over others and, eventually, transmitted to emerging adult children.

When asked to describe their family financial motto, emerging adults from our LinkedIn survey responded with topics very much tied to family financial socialization. One emerging adult, a son of a financial planner, reported that their family financial motto follows the words of Albert Einstein: "Compound interest is the eighth wonder of the world." This emerging adult recalled his first money memory where he began discussing Roth IRAs with his father to "save as much as I could in order to let compound interest do the work." His father's work focused on life-centered financial planning, which framed his other family motto of "Do what brings you joy." Seen in these quotations, family financial attitudes can lead to financial behaviors that may, ultimately, lead to greater meaning found in life in general. Together, these data suggest that family of origin experiences might impact emerging adults' financial attitudes.

Individual Demographic Factors Influencing the Formation of Financial Attitudes

In addition to the prominent influence of family of origin experiences on emerging adults' financial attitudes, previous scholarship and our LinkedIn survey data suggest that individual demographic characteristics can also play a role in shaping emerging adults' financial attitudes. The next three subsections outline three of these individual demographic characteristics that can impact emerging adults' financial attitudes—gender (see Chapter 16), socioeconomic status (see Chapter 15), and educational attainment along with associated debt accumulation (see Chapter 9).

Gender

Men, in general, report higher perceived control of their economic destiny than women (Robson & Peetz, 2020). As additional evidence for gender differences, it is repeatedly reported that men have higher levels of financial literacy (e.g., Lusardi & Mitchell, 2011) and financial confidence than women (e.g., Tang, 2022). Even after accounting for gender gaps in objective financial knowledge, women report being less confident in their financial knowledge and abilities than men (see Chapter 2; Angrisani & Casanova, 2021; Chen & Volpe, 1998; Morris et al., 2022). A study by Robson and Peetz (2020) indicated that these differences are explained, in part, by the underlying gender differences in perceived economic control and by other psychological characteristics. Additionally, adult women ages 25–75 tending to report more discomfort with having debt (Almenberg et al., 2021) may also lead to decreased feelings of financial control for women bound by debt repayments. Because there appear to be gender differences in constructs adjacent to financial attitudes—in control over one's economic destiny (Robson & Peetz, 2020), financial confidence in financial knowledge and abilities (Angrisani & Casanova, 2021; Chen & Volpe, 1998; Morris et al., 2022), financial literacy (Lusardi & Mitchell, 2011), and comfort with debt (Almenberg et al., 2021)—we suspect that it is possible there may also be gender differences in financial attitudes of emerging adults, which future research might profitably explore.

Gender differences in financial attitudes from family financial socialization were also somewhat evident in our LinkedIn survey data. A male emerging adult reported, "My earliest memory about money is my dad and I having a savings talk about allowance: 50% would go to savings and 10% would go to tithing." Other men involved in our LinkedIn survey reported similar messaging about the importance of saving from their fathers. A female emerging adult cited the following as her earliest memory of messages, and parental action, surrounding savings:

> When I was a kid, my mom used to give my brothers and I dimes to motivate us to behave, do our chores, etc. I was always a "saver," so I ended up saving something like $5 worth of dimes. One day, I knocked over a planter in front of our house, and my mom punished me by taking away all my dimes. At first, I was pretty upset about it, but when I looked around at the grocery store later that week, I realized how little my dimes were actually worth. After the planter incident, my mom wasn't able to motivate me to do extra chores with dimes any more, because it wasn't worth it to me.

The emerging adult men emphasized savings messages from fathers especially; however, a particularly negative experience for this emerging adult woman appeared to taint the message of saving from her mother. Accordingly, future research might explore gender differences in how parents financially socialize their children and how parent financial socialization from same-gender parents might impact emerging adults' financial attitudes.

The previous quotation was from a respondent who grew up in a wealthy family in a not-so-wealthy town. Although, as a child, she was taught to avoid talking about money, now, as an emerging adult, she sees financial secrecy as unhealthy. She said:

> I think when I was younger, I came off as very spoiled and insensitive to my peers (e.g., "if you hate your phone so much, why don't you ask your parents to buy you a new one"). . . . Of course, this is a super-privileged perspective, but I think that if my parents were more transparent about money, I would have realized why I didn't "fit in" with a lot of the people my age. I'm definitely the opposite of my parents—I love talking about money because I want to help people make the most out of what they earn. I've had friends approach me [for] . . . all types of financial questions. As long as they approach me, I like being able to give good advice.

While this respondent reports being very open to talking about money, she added an important caveat, *as long as they approach me*. This caveat appears to reflect a subconscious attachment to retaining some level of privacy about financial matters, though not to the extent of her parents. That is, even though the financial attitude of currently loving to talk about money appears to be evident, this emerging adult woman appears to continue to latch onto parent financial socialization in her current financial attitudes.

The influence of gender (see Chapter 16), and associated financial gender differences (e.g., Lusardi & Mitchell, 2011; Robson & Peetz, 2020), might not be a focus of most financial education programs (see Chapter 19). However, financial education programs for emerging adults might consider modifying curriculum to especially emphasize improved financial self-efficacy and literacy for women to narrow the gap of financial literacy and financial confidence across gender. Put another way, like sex education programs that may separate participants by gender, it is also possible that financial education programs would benefit from tailoring content by gender during the formative years of emerging adulthood. Future research, however, should explore whether gender-specific financial education tailored toward emerging adults' financial attitudes might be valuable.

Socioeconomic Status

Income might also be a predictor of financial attitudes among emerging adults (see Chapter 15; e.g., Jorgensen et al., 2017). For instance, low-income individuals—perhaps, in part, due to exposure to financial hardships—might espouse financial attitudes such as distrust in financial institutions, a belief that bank account fees are too high or unpredictable, or that avoiding a bank provides more privacy (FDIC, 2021). Consequently, low-income individuals and families might be less likely to use compound interest—a benefit that may come with bank and investment accounts—to their advantage. In this way, a low socioeconomic status (SES) and associated financial attitudes about financial institutions could be disadvantageous for emerging adults. Conversely, high-income individuals might have more positive financial attitudes because they often have greater access to financial resources and more exposure to positive financial role models. Indeed, emerging adults from high-SES backgrounds tend to have a greater understanding of financial matters—potentially due to financial socialization from their parents, including previous parent-facilitated financial experiences (see Chapter 18; Lusardi et al., 2010). Therefore, it appears that an emerging adult's high SES can also contribute to their financial attitudes.

Depending on how parents react to emerging adults' curiosity regarding family SES (e.g., an emerging adult's questions related to family SES during college funding applications), emerging adults may acquire financial attitudes like "money is a taboo topic that should not be discussed openly." This theme was expressed by some, though not all, of the emerging adults who provided input about their financial attitudes. A respondent who grew up wealthier than her friends reported anxiety about losing her financial status. Her parents explicitly taught her not to ask about or talk about money with others, which likely contributed to her financial anxiety. She said:

> One or two emergencies will knock me out. I'm terrified of medical debt and the systems in our country that consistently keep people poor. I'm also anxious about the climate disaster and other pressing issues that will have an effect on my finances in the long term. I feel like it's impossible to know how much money I'll need for retirement, or if it's even going to be possible for me to retire, or if I'll even live long enough to retire.

Despite her privileged family SES and her possible current savings behavior, the likelihood of her financial anxiety becoming reality is probably low, though the financial anxiety, likely stemming from her parents' "money is taboo" financial attitude, remains a strong contributor to her feelings about money. We find it striking that a high SES could lead to more favorable financial attitudes for emerging adults, but parents' lack of discussion of their family's high SES could potentially lead to less favorable financial attitudes like financial anxiety (see Chapter 8). In essence, high SES might provide emerging adults with unique advantages, but SES may not be a panacea for financial attitudes that might lead to emerging adults' financial flourishing in the long term.

As mentioned previously, a low SES might place emerging adults at risk for less favorable financial attitudes. However, one emerging adult's response leads us to believe that emerging adults can be resilient even in the context of a low SES. One emerging adult from our survey shared the following:

> Growing up and even still today, my parents' financial attitudes have been generally very negative. They talked a lot about finances but only because they were always worried about them. . . . I feel like our family motto really was "money doesn't grow on trees." To some extent, I do agree that money doesn't grow on trees. . . . However, I feel like the phrase implies that we have no control over our financial situation and that we might not be where we would like to be financially simply because money doesn't just come to us. I think that it's important to remember our own responsibility in creating a healthy financial situation for ourselves. Sure, there are some things that we cannot control, but there are many things that we can do and that is what we should be focusing on.

We completely agree with this emerging adult's perspective, which is also in line with the peer-reviewed literature (e.g., Dew et al., 2020). This resilient emerging adult further reflected on the development of their own financial attitudes:

> As I have gotten older, I have realized that being "rich" isn't about the salary you are making each year Rather, it's about having the discipline to live within your means and truly understand what brings you happiness. I've come to understand that for the most part, I am in control of my financial situation and financial future. It feels empowering but at times overwhelming.

In short, these survey data and previous findings lead us to believe that SES can impact emerging adults' financial attitudes in nuanced ways. As such, future scholarship might explore what predicts more favorable financial attitudes for emerging adults in the context of a low-SES background and what predicts less favorable financial attitudes for emerging adults even in the context of a high-SES background to provide further understanding of how practitioners might help emerging adults from various socioeconomic backgrounds develop productive financial attitudes.

Educational Attainment and Debt Accumulation

Emerging adults, especially young emerging adults in the United States, are stressed about finances (see Chapter 8). The American Psychological Association (APA, 2022) found that among U.S. emerging adults ages 18–25, 82% report money is a significant source of stress in their lives. One potential reason for this financial stress could stem from the financial resources required to obtain higher education (see Chapter 9; e.g., Britt et al., 2017), which we describe next. The income gap by educational attainment is evident, especially in the United States. For example, recent data from the National Center for Education Statistics (2023) suggest that the median annual earnings for those who have completed high school or a high school equivalent was about $40,000. The median annual earnings for those with a bachelor's degree, however, was over $60,000, and the median annual earnings for those with a master's degree or higher was around $75,000 (National Center for Education Statistics, 2023). Accordingly, emerging adults may receive messages from their parents, peers, and others that to earn greater income, greater education is often required. Thus, financial attitudes like "higher education is important" and "higher education will translate to greater income" might be common.

Nevertheless, the financial resources required to gain higher education are sometimes left out of these conversations. Many emerging adults might find themselves following through with "higher education will translate to greater income" financial attitudes—even if that means accumulating student loan debt. For instance, around 34% of emerging adults have student loan debt, and the average amount of student loan debt in the United States for those age 25–34 is about $33,000 (see Chapter 9; Hanson, 2023). As emerging adults continue on with financial attitudes like "higher education will translate to greater income," they might also seek graduate education (e.g., a master's degree). However, the average federal student loan debt for those with graduate education is about $107,000 (Hanson, 2023). While student loans can provide the opportunity to gain higher education, incurring large amounts of debt for this education—especially during the years of emerging adulthood—could lead to financial attitudes ranging from "going into debt for something crucial might be necessary" to "it is okay to go into debt for something I want." Coupled with these experiences with student loans are, especially in the United States, somewhat pervasive messages about debt.

As we write this chapter, the national debt in the United States is $33.7 trillion—and counting. Although this national debt level should be part of a nuanced discussion that might be best suited for conversations outside this chapter, the United States on a national level might provide implicit messages that going into debt is "okay" and even "necessary." Experiences related to the U.S. national debt and student loan debt, and associated financial attitudes, might translate to other experiences with debt such as purchasing a car or using credit cards (see Chapter 13). For example, the average emerging adult ages 18–25 has around $3,000 in credit card debt (Capital One, 2023), and financial behaviors with credit cards might be related to education. That is, about 1 in 4 student loan borrowers also have credit card debt that is related to their education (Hanson, 2023). Specific to auto loan debt, emerging adults have approximately $24 billion in auto loans (Jones et al., 2023).

In essence, using student loans to finance education could lead to financial attitudes like "going into to debt for things I want is okay" that might then lead to incurring other debt, such as credit card debt and auto loan debt, that is somewhat pervasive in the United States. These messages about debt, however, do not often include the differentiation between "good debt" like mortgages (i.e., going into debt while also investing in an appreciating asset) and "bad debt" like credit card debt (i.e., debt that sometimes has interest rates of 20% or higher). As such, emerging adults might have financial attitudes related to educational attainment that lead to incurring debt, which could be to their long-term financial detriment (see Chapters 9 and 13).

For instance, emerging adults might hope for programs that emphasize student loan forgiveness like the Public Student Loan Forgiveness program. As such, emerging adults might follow through with a "going into debt for something crucial might be necessary" financial attitude, especially if they believe the debt can be forgiven later. However, if emerging adults follow through with incurring student loan debt that likely stemmed from their financial attitudes, they will almost certainly end up being responsible for paying their student loans, and associated interest, because only about 3.3% of Public Service Loan Forgiveness applications have been approved since the program began (Hanson, 2023). In this way, educational attainment and debt-related experiences, and commensurate financial attitudes, can lead to financial decisions in emerging adulthood that can lead to financial floundering for years to come. At the same time, gaining higher education might also promote financial flourishing in terms of higher income later on, too. In short, it would be difficult for us to ignore the impact of educational attainment and debt-related experiences on emerging adults' financial attitudes.

During their education, one emerging adult reported the negative messaging from a professor about their financial future:

> My professor painted a gloomy picture that we are all screwed, that Social Security won't last, and we probably won't be able to retire.

College students who receive such messaging, on top of everyday financial stress (see Chapter 8), are also likely to develop negative financial attitudes, such as low financial self-efficacy or external locus of control. Despite potentially having negative financial attitudes, like low financial self-efficacy, emerging adults' college experiences might require better financial attitudes for financial flourishing. That is, having low financial self-efficacy is associated with worse financial behaviors among emerging adults, but better financial self-efficacy can lead to better financial behaviors in general (see Chapter 5; Okamoto et al., 2023) and debt-specific financial behaviors (see Chapter 13; Saxey et al., 2023). In some countries such as the United States, college students often receive a lump sum allocation of financial aid—whether student loans, grants, or scholarships—that is intended to last an entire semester. However, depending on an emerging adult's financial self-efficacy and commensurate financial behaviors (Okamoto et al., 2023; Saxey et al., 2023), these funds may or may not last throughout the semester, which could again impact their debt-related behaviors (e.g., credit card behavior) that likely stemmed from financial attitudes like financial self-efficacy. These experiences and exposures to financial events inform their financial attitudes that may follow them into adulthood and continue to influence how they manage their finances and make financial decisions.

Students who are unable to live off their lump sum allocation or other financial funding tend to be under especially high financial stress (see Chapter 8). These students are more likely to drop out of college and start earning income (see Chapter 10; Britt et al., 2017), albeit often at a reduced rate than what they could have earned with a college degree (see Chapter 9; National Center for Education Statistics, 2023). Young people who are college-age but not currently enrolled in college may have different financial attitudes than college students. Research on this population is limited; however, we hypothesize that financial independence (see Chapter 11) is even more important among the non-college goers who are generally reliant on the income they generate versus the supplements of student loans, grants, and the like that college students often anticipate. In these ways, educational attainment and debt-related experiences can impact emerging adults' financial attitudes, which could lead to financial flourishing in some ways and financial floundering in others.

Social Factors Influencing the Development of Financial Attitudes

The influence of peer behavior appears to also be predictive of emerging adults' financial behaviors as they search to establish their own identities and look to others for guidance on how to behave (see Chapter 18; LeBaron-Black et al., 2023; Serido et al., 2015). The impact of peer influence is notable among emerging adults—for instance, people might be more likely to save money if they believe that saving is a normative behavior among their peers or if they receive social support for saving. Similarly, emerging adults may be more likely to engage in risky financial behaviors, such as taking on debt, if they perceive that such behaviors are normative or socially acceptable within their peer group. Indeed, social pressure can perpetuate materialistic financial attitudes and lead to financial anxiety among emerging adults.

The emergence of social media has transformed the way we can access and share information, including financial information. Emerging adults turn to social media platforms for financial advice and guidance, which provides exposure to diverse perspectives. In turn, this information—whether accurate or not—has the potential to shape financial attitudes. Due to the personal stories shared on social media, the potential positive financial benefits of social media use include an increased desire to save for future consumption and to hold socially responsible attitudes toward money, such as donating to charitable causes. Additionally, social media can facilitate financial behavior change through social influence and social comparison (e.g., Yanto et al., 2021).

Conversely, social media can lead to financial anxiety and stress among individuals, particularly when they are exposed to images of peers engaging in expensive or luxurious activities (Foster, 2022). Social media can perpetuate unrealistic financial expectations, leading to individuals feeling inadequate or unsuccessful if they do not meet these expectations (see Chapters 8, 10, and 13). Repeated messages geared toward missed financial opportunities can leave emerging adults feeling down or depressed about their financial situation, as evidenced by the next emerging adult's response:

> I get a lot of messages from social media, everything from debt is dumb, to crypto, NFTs, options, etc. There is a lot of negativity in mass media about younger people being poorer than the generations before them and not being able to afford housing. There's also negativity surrounding inflation and social security.

Thus, while social media provides a platform for financial education and awareness, it also presents new challenges in terms of its influence on individuals' financial attitudes and behaviors, particularly among emerging adults. An emerging adult who provided feedback for this chapter was aware of the unrealistic expectations portrayed on social media. She said it's common to see the attitude "Invest $100 and earn a million" on social media. "This isn't an exact phrase but more of an attitude I see a lot on social media. People are always saying that it's easy to get big returns and that it doesn't require much effort or education."

The influence of peers and social media on the financial attitudes of emerging adults highlights the importance of considering social context when designing interventions to promote financial well-being. By understanding the social norms that shape emerging adults' financial attitudes and behaviors, researchers and policymakers can develop more targeted interventions that are more likely to be effective in promoting flourishing financial outcomes.

Promoting Financial Attitudes That Can Create Financial Flourishing

Engendering positive financial attitudes among emerging adults is crucial. As we have outlined in this chapter, individuals with high levels of financial self-efficacy are more likely to engage in positive financial behaviors, such as saving and investing, and are less likely to engage in negative financial behaviors, such as overspending and debt accumulation (Farrell et al., 2016; Shim et al., 2010). Promoting positive financial attitudes such as financial self-efficacy, therefore, can encourage financial flourishing and limit financial floundering. Indeed, longitudinal data suggest that as emerging adults improve their financial self-efficacy and general financial attitudes (e.g., beliefs about engaging in financial behaviors), they are also likely to improve their financial behaviors (see Chapter 5; Shim et al., 2015). As such, we provide recommendations for policy to aid efforts to improve emerging adults' financial attitudes.

Two primary policy recommendations emerged from this chapter. First, gender-based education programming may more effectively encourage positive financial attitudes. In some countries, physical education and sex education typically separate genders as children age. The same process for school-based financial education could provide the necessary targeted communication based on different lived experiences. Second, we believe that intervening with positive peer-based social programming would likely encourage positive financial attitudes for emerging adults. There is a mix of positively and negatively framed messaging on social media as noted by the emerging adults who provided feedback for this chapter. This population turns to social media for guidance on big and small financial issues, so getting accurate information from social media is paramount to their financial success. Training peer ambassadors to promote accurate and positively framed financial information on social media could aid in the development of positive financial attitudes.

As this chapter has shown, financial attitudes matter. That is, financial attitudes likely influence financial behavior (see Chapter 5; Klontz & Britt, 2012; Okamoto et al., 2023; Saxey et al., 2023; Shim et al., 2010, 2015), which might impact emerging adults' financial floundering or financial flourishing trajectories throughout emerging adulthood. Financial attitudes can be a product of emerging adults' family of origin experiences, individual demographic characteristics (e.g., gender, SES, educational attainment, debt accumulation), and social influences (e.g., social media, peers). It is our hope that this chapter provided a general overview of a few salient factors that may impact emerging adults' financial attitudes while also highlighting the need for future research that aims to understand emerging adults' financial attitudes so that researchers, practitioners, educators, and policymakers alike can help emerging adults flourish financially.

Chapter 5
Financial Behavior among Emerging Adults

Cliff A. Robb[1] *and Kayla M. Dutton*[1]

Introduction

Financial behavior is inherently complex, and it is common to see studies address behavior in the context of numerous other factors such as financial knowledge (see Chapter 2), attitudes (see Chapter 4), and socialization (see Chapter 18). This handbook appropriately contextualizes the fact that behaviors do not occur independent of these other factors. Instead, behaviors are built and reinforced over time as individuals make spending, saving, and borrowing decisions both large and small (see Chapter 6). Many of these critical factors are addressed in other chapters of this volume. For the purpose of this chapter, we will be simplifying things to emphasize observed and reported behaviors among emerging adults. It is important to distinguish between these two distinct data categories—observations versus reports. Whereas direct observation of behavior provides powerful insights, the research process is often reliant on self-reports. Self-reports can be limiting due to biases or flaws in the reporting, but in many cases, these self-reports can illuminate specific vulnerabilities or perspectives of individuals who are living the experience.

Broadly, we can consider any aspect of money management as falling within the category of financial behavior. From this perspective, understanding financial behavior can feel overwhelming. Based on a review of the literature, we hone in on the financial behaviors that are most studied, resulting in the following broad categories: budgeting (or cash flow management), saving/investing, and credit/debt management. For many of these categories, there are additional subdimensions of interest. For example, saving behavior may be considered not only in the context of short-term needs or emergency

[1] Department of Consumer Science, University of Wisconsin—-Madison, USA

Cliff A. Robb and Kayla M. Dutton, *Financial Behavior among Emerging Adults*. In: *Flourishing and Floundering Financially in Emerging Adulthood*. Edited by: Ashley B. LeBaron-Black, Heather Kelley, and Angela Sorgente, Oxford University Press. © Oxford University Press (2025). DOI: 10.1093/9780197699157.003.0006

saving, but it may also be analyzed in the context of retirement planning or other longer-term goals. Similarly, debt can be divided into different categories based on the purpose or structure of the loan (see Chapter 13). This can be further complicated by the actual measurement of any given behavior. It is not uncommon to see binary measurement of financial behaviors, such as whether someone owns a credit card or not. In other cases, variables may be categorical, or they may be continuous (or ordinal) and provide insight into the extent to which people engage in a behavior (e.g., magnitude of debt, how consistent people are when it comes to saving, or how attentive they are when it comes to constructing or following a budget).

For each of the core behaviors previously identified, we consider how different patterns of behavior are related to flourishing or floundering among emerging adults. Understanding the behaviors of emerging adults can be particularly important when considering long-term well-being (see Chapter 7), as research suggests financial patterns established at a younger age tend to persist for many years (Shim et al., 2010). The remainder of the chapter will consider each of these behaviors in turn. A careful analysis of measurement and prior findings will be provided. In addition, we hope to provide some insight into the current behavior of emerging adults in the United States based on a recent, nationally representative sample of adults. The National Financial Capability Study (NFCS) provides rich data on financial behavior and well-being for adults in the United States. The state-by-state NFCS has surveyed over 25,000 adults every 3 years since 2009. This chapter uses data from the 2021 wave of the NFCS, looking at the subsample of over 4,000 emerging adults (ages 18–29). To learn more about the financial capability of Americans by year, please visit https://finrafoundation.org/knowledge-we-gain-share/nfcs/about-nfcs. Whereas there are certainly many differences in terms of institutional frameworks and observed financial behavior from country to country, the sample of U.S. respondents used here provides a good starting point for understanding broader trends in developed economies with similar institutional structures. Data collected by the Organisation for Economic Cooperation and Development (OECD) suggested that emerging adults (18–29) demonstrated generally lower financial knowledge (see Chapter 2) and less prudent financial behavior compared to other adults (OECD, 2020).

Budgeting

One critical determinant of consumers' financial well-being is the degree to which they make a plan around the flow of dollars (i.e., budget; Zhang et al., 2022). In many cases, consumers do not adhere to a strict budgeting strategy. Rather, many consumers may track income and expenses more loosely, and they may lack a specific plan to guide financial decisions that is at the heart of strong budgeting. General income and expense tracking without a guiding plan can be a less effective strategy for improving financial well-being. Tracking of income and expenditures can be useful for establishing a solid understanding of one's financial condition and may serve as an important pre-cursor to creating a budget. With modern technology, budgeting and tracking are easier than ever. When connected to a bank account, many apps will allow consumers to easily track spending and will produce monthly statements that further divide spending into key expenditure categories. This can improve transparency and help emerging adults better understand where they are spending. This can facilitate better budgeting. We used data from the NFCS to explore utilization of applications and websites to facilitate financial decisions, including for budgeting purposes. Roughly 56% of emerging adults indicated they did so at least some of the time, with 17% of respondents reporting frequent use. This is nearly double the rate at which other adults frequently use applications or websites (9.6%).

Research from a nationally representative survey of U.S. households indicated that a "desire to avoid overspending one's income" was one of the most common reasons that consumers listed for adopting a budget (Zhang et al., 2022, p. 73). Arnett (2004) highlighted the increased financial responsibility that often comes with the transition to adulthood, and other research notes that the transition to adulthood and establishment of financial independence is taking longer for recent generations (see Chapter 11; Pew Research Center, 2012). Evidence suggests that making ends meet is a real challenge for many emerging adults in the United States (NFCS, 2021). When asked the question "In a typical month, how difficult is it for you to cover your expenses and pay all your bills," 58% of emerging adults answered either very difficult (14%) or somewhat difficult (44%), compared to roughly 38% of adults 30 and older. There is also evidence that a significant proportion of emerging adults struggle to stay on budget, as only about 36% reported spending less than their income. The remainder of the sample reported spending more than their income (29%) or about equal to their income (35%). Additionally, about 31% of the sample of emerging adults reported overdrawing their checking account occasionally. This suggests that a significant proportion of emerging adults are struggling financially, further highlighting the critical importance of budgeting for emerging adult consumers and also pointing to possible challenges related to resource constraints (see Chapter 13). For budgeting tips, see Box 5.1.

Box 5.1 Budgeting Tips for Emerging Adults

The best strategy when it comes to budgeting and tracking finances is to find a method that works for you. There are numerous options to choose from, including mobile applications (like Mint, YNAB, or GoodBudget), online banking programs, spreadsheets, or even just good old paper and pen. The key is to establish a clear spending plan, or budget, and then work on being consistent in tracking and reviewing expenditures to be sure you are staying on track. Being proactive and engaged can make a world of difference.

Savings

Individuals' saving behavior has implications for their own financial security and wealth accumulation as well as broader impacts on micro- and macroeconomic growth. Overall evidence from the U.S. population suggests that adequate savings is a challenge for many households regardless of age, with average savings rates currently below 4% of personal disposable income (BEA, September 2023). Emerging adults face a host of challenges when it comes to savings. Emerging adults may have real resource challenges related to their more recent entry into the workforce (e.g., lower income than older workers with more experience; see Chapter 10), and they may have thin credit files resulting in limited credit (see Chapter 13). To add to these challenges, emerging adults may have questions around the proper amount to save as well as the actual mechanics of saving (e.g., what types of savings accounts or products should they be seeking). Any discussion of saving behavior must acknowledge the general need for some short-term liquidity as well as long-term financial security. Critically, saving at a young age is often vital to long-term financial security because starting earlier in life maximizes the timeline available for asset appreciation and interest compounding. It is also important to acknowledge the importance of good habit formation, such as allocating a percentage of each paycheck to savings (Loibl et al., 2011). Individuals who delay saving behaviors not only forfeit possible interest compounding due to their shorter time horizon but also risk running into mental accounting issues like perceived income loss (whereby later savings activity makes their take-home pay appear smaller in comparison to previous payments; Thaler & Benartzi, 2004).

Saving behavior has received a significant amount of attention from economists and other researchers. Often, studies are limited to measures that indicate whether or not saving is occurring. In considering the why of saving behavior, many of our existing policy approaches rely on assumptions detailed in the life-cycle income hypothesis (LCIH) developed by Ando and Modigliani (1963). Theoretically, individuals are thought to demand relatively smooth (or even) consumption over their lifetime, and the main challenge is managing the relatively uneven lifetime income flow. Under this model, emerging adults may engage in heavier borrowing (in essence, relying on their larger expected future income to repay this debt) because more active saving will be possible during their peak earning years (see Chapter 13). These savings can, in turn, be allocated toward paying down earlier debts and preparing for future retirement income needs.

As previously noted, saving behavior can be further divided into different categories based on time horizon or intentions. Short-term saving behavior is often addressed in the form of emergency savings (de Bassa Scheresberg, 2013). Access to adequate emergency funds is a strong signal of financial stability. Unfortunately, evidence from the most recent NFCS (2021) indicates that only about 42% of emerging adults reported having an emergency fund equal to 3 months' worth of expenses. This is further complicated by the fact that 14% of respondents indicated that it was very difficult to meet their monthly payments or expenses, with another 44% indicating this was somewhat difficult. As a final measure of financial security, we analyzed emergency saving behavior, controlling for self-reported income volatility. Income volatility may be rooted in a variety of factors, including but not limited to switching jobs, fluctuation of work hours, or unexpected circumstances. Recent years have also seen the emergence of more informal work arrangements, sometimes referred to as the "gig economy." Whereas gig work might be conceptualized as a means of smoothing income due to its flexibility, evidence suggests that a substantial proportion of gig workers indicate that this work actually increases their income volatility (see Chapter 10; Federal Reserve, 2020). Unfortunately, those emerging adults who reported having more volatile incomes were also less likely to report having an adequate emergency fund, as seen in Table 5.1. Taken together, these findings provide a concerning picture in terms of emerging adults' financial security.

In terms of long-term savings, the behavior of most Americans is heavily influenced by the availability of employer plans. Emerging adults may be at a particular disadvantage because many entry-level jobs may not provide strong benefits like qualified retirement plans to facilitate long-term savings. Even when plans are available, evidence suggests that emerging adults may

Table 5.1 Comparison of Mean Income Volatility Based on Emergency Fund Holdings among Emerging Adults

	Emergency Fund	No Emergency Fund	*p*-value
Income Volatility	1.68	1.83	.002

Note. Income volatility is a self-reported measure ranging from 1 (highly stable income) to 3 (highly volatile income) and an increase in mean scores is associated with greater volatility. The *p*-value column indicates a significant mean difference (based on a *t*-test) in income volatility for emerging adults with an emergency fund versus those with no emergency fund.

not be saving enough as they often fail to exceed the minimum contribution amount (Nkoutchou & Eiselen, 2012). Based on 2021 NFCS data, 51% of emerging adults indicated that they did not have access to a retirement plan through their employer, and another 13% indicated not knowing whether they had access to a plan. Among those who did report having access to a qualified plan, 74% reported participating. It is important to note that the NFCS data did not provide details on the amount being saved. Overall, these statistics raise concerns about emerging adults' longer-term financial stability as many among this population lack access to or fail to take advantage of opportunities available to them. For saving tips, see Box 5.2.

Box 5.2 Savings Tips for Emerging Adults

When it comes to savings, time is one of the most important factors to consider. If you make some income (whether it is doing chores for neighbors or taking on your first job with an income statement), it is a good idea to get in the habit of saving a portion of your earnings. Even a small amount of savings can make a big impact over the long run.

Aside from holdings in qualified retirement plans or other advantaged accounts, it is important to consider how emerging adults make decisions related to investments. As with budgeting, technology has made it easier for individuals to access investment products because many applications offer low- to no-cost trading. Trading platforms like Robinhood have explicitly courted emerging adult investors by simplifying the process, and evidence suggests that a large percentage of their users are first-time investors (Barber et al., 2021). The simplicity of these platforms may appeal to new investors, but it also raises serious questions about whether those new investors are being given the proper information to make wise investment decisions.

These platforms often engage in a strategy of gamification, which can result in increased trading or an emphasis on more limited data in making choices among investments. What is clear is that there is demand for these platforms. Data from the NFCS indicate that among emerging adults (ages 18–34) who reported owning stocks, 78% reported using a mobile application for trading, compared to just 15% of those age 55 and older (Lin et al., 2022).

Despite the advances offered by technology, recent data from the NFCS indicate that only about one-third (33%) of emerging adults have investments in stocks, bonds, mutual funds, or other securities (excluding any holdings in qualified retirement plans). It should be noted that a majority of American adults do not have individual investment holdings outside of retirement plans, and the proportion of older Americans holding these assets is only around 40% (Lin et al., 2022). Additionally, the proportion of emerging adults identifying as investors seems to be increasing, as only about 23% of emerging adults indicated having nonretirement investments in 2015 (Lin et al., 2022). Other notable behavioral differences include a higher tolerance for risk among young investors, with 24% of younger investors (18–34) indicating a willingness to take substantial financial risk, compared to only 13% of 35- to 53-year-olds and 3% of those 55 or older. A much higher proportion of emerging adults reported that they have invested in cryptocurrencies (53% of emerging adults ages 18–34, compared to 33% of adults ages 35–54 and 7% of adults ages 55 and older) as well (Lin et al., 2022).

These data present a challenging picture in terms of long-term financial security and well-being (or flourishing; see Chapter 7). Although emerging adults have a longer investment time horizon, indicating they should be able to bear a greater deal of risk in their investments, they still might be placing themselves in a difficult position over the long run if they invest heavily in less stable options (like cryptocurrency or individual companies). Survey evidence suggests that emerging adults are not only more prone to engage in risky investment behavior but also are more likely to believe that they will outperform the market when compared to older investors (Lin et al., 2022). Prior research has indicated that less experienced investors are more inclined to significant investor biases, resulting in them chasing returns and purchasing stocks that are overvalued (Greenwood & Nagel, 2009). Emerging adults of today are also engaging in different forms of social communication, and evidence suggests that social media play a strong role in investment decisions and trading behavior (Shanmugham & Rayma, 2012). Poor investment decisions early in one's life can have a severe impact on financial flourishing in the long run, as one of the key advantages young investors have over older investors is time horizon. For investing tips, see Box 5.3.

Box 5.3 Investment Tips for Emerging Adults

All investments carry some degree of risk (here defined as a risk of loss because your investments may lose value). It is important to understand the costs and risks involved in the decision. Whereas many young investors tend to think in terms of individual companies, there are many alternatives in the market like index funds that allow for easier diversification (or risk spreading) and a diversified portfolio, even if individuals are only investing small dollar amounts. An index fund is a type of mutual fund or exchange-traded fund (ETF) with a portfolio constructed to match or track the components of a financial market index, such as the Standard and Poor's 500 (S&P 500) Index (Fernando, 2023).

Credit and Debt Management

As discussed previously, the LCIH provides a theoretical framework for borrowing behavior (Modigliani, 1986). It is common to see borrowing at an early age to facilitate some degree of income smoothing (see Chapter 13). Theoretically, the magnitude of borrowing should be directly related to future income expectations because, logically, those who anticipate earning more in the near future can afford more debt in the present. Credit and debt markets are a bit more complex, and evidence suggests that consumers often borrow in ways that are not necessarily the most efficient. To better understand the credit and debt management behavior of emerging adults, it is helpful to start by considering the different types of debt that are typically available to them.

Before moving directly into the market for consumer credit, which encompasses a plethora of products and services, it is worth considering more informal pathways utilized by emerging adults. It is increasingly common to see emerging adults maintain some level of financial dependence into their early to mid-twenties (see Chapter 11). Looking at the NFCS sample, more than a quarter (26%) of respondents reported living with their parents at the time of the survey. We have highlighted the significant financial strain for many emerging adults previously, as many find it challenging to meet their financial obligations. This financial stress (see Chapter 8) is often shared by parents who may feel the inclination to help their children. Lowe and Arnett (2020) highlight evidence of a rise in parental concern regarding the ability of their children to become financially independent. They note that whereas about 37% of parents were "not at all concerned," a majority were "somewhat concerned" (43%) or "very concerned" (20%; Lowe & Arnett). The authors further highlight that this can impact relationships, with a significant percentage of respondents articulating a rise in conflict between parents and their children based on emerging adults' monetary challenges.

Credit Cards

Moving to the financial markets, one of the most common ways that consumers first begin to access credit is through obtaining a credit card. The history of credit markets is interesting but beyond the scope of this chapter (for a brief review, see Robb, 2022, or Durkin et al., 2014, for a more detailed exploration). Trend data suggest that possession of credit cards has grown over time, with between 70–80% of adults indicating that they own a credit card at the present time, as compared to about 65% in the 1980s (FRB NY, 2020; Durkin, 2000).

Looking at the emerging adult sample drawn from the NFCS, credit card ownership is consistent with data from the broader population: Roughly 70% indicated owning at least one credit card. Among credit card holders, 61% of emerging adults reported that they paid their credit cards off in full during the previous year (classifying them as nonrevolvers). Among the same sample, about 48% reported sometimes making only the minimum payment on their card(s). These findings indicate some degree of strain among a significant portion of emerging adults because paying only the minimum payment adds significantly to the overall cost of borrowing by extending the payback period. Overreliance on credit and maintaining a revolving balance can both have a significant negative impact on one's finances and can limit financial growth and well-being (see Chapter 13). In considering other measures of financial strain with respect to credit cards, emerging adults in the NFCS sample also reported instances of late fees and over-the-limit charges and using credit cards for a cash advance. Late fees were the most common issue, with about 27% of respondents reporting these over a 12-month period, followed by cash advances (24%) and over-the-limit fees (20%). These data point to a significant portion of emerging adults demonstrating negative behaviors that can result in financial floundering. For credit card tips, see Box 5.4.

Box 5.4 Borrowing Tips for Emerging Adults

A credit card can be an effective tool for developing a credit history, but it is not a necessity. Emerging adults should be discerning when shopping for a credit card and should apply for a credit card that offers a reasonable limit (i.e., an amount that you would be comfortable paying back). By using the card for small, regular purchases and paying the balance in full each month, younger consumers can establish a history of steady debt repayment while also avoiding high interest rates associated with a revolving balance.

Student Loan Debt

Even though not all emerging adults choose to pursue an advanced degree after graduation from high school, student loan debt remains one of the largest categories of consumer debt in terms of dollars borrowed (second only to mortgage debt) in the United States (see Chapter 9). Recent estimates from the United States indicate that there is about $1.75 trillion in outstanding student loan debt (federal and private; Hahn, 2023). This debt has grown substantially over the past several decades. According to the Education Data Initiative, the average federal student loan debt is $37,574 per borrower and increases to close to $40,000 per borrower when private student loan debt is included (Hanson, 2023). From a more global perspective, whereas many countries provide support to minimize tuition costs, others face challenges similar to those in the United States. Countries like Finland, Scotland, Sweden, and Germany offer relatively low- or no-cost tuition models, minimizing the need for debt. Other countries like the United Kingdom, Australia, and Canada have similar borrowing trends as the United States, though there are differences in repayment structures and the number of students reliant on loans, which may make this debt feel less like a societal concern.

It should be noted that much of this increase in borrowing is driven by the rising costs of obtaining an education. To make education a possibility, many U.S. students rely on student loans to cover tuition and other living expenses. Evidence suggests that the rising cost of obtaining a degree is beginning to impact enrollment decisions, with some students seeking alternative options and current students borrowing more to attend than previous cohorts (Bleemer et al., 2017). There are still many students who feel that higher education is the best choice despite the rising costs. This is partially because education debt is often framed as "good" debt or reasonable, considering how it can assist in skill development and future earnings. Recent trends of relatively stagnant wage growth, coupled with rising costs, incite real questions about the efficacy of higher education for many consumers who are heavily reliant on loans (see Chapter 9).

Debt of this magnitude can have a significant impact on consumers, and evidence indicates that it can influence decisions around degree completion, employment, marriage, and timing of home purchases (Addo, 2014; Bleemer et al., 2017; Haughwout et al., 2015; Robb, 2017; Robb et al., 2011, 2020). These are not trivial impacts, and they suggest that student loan debt can have adverse impacts on the financial stability of emerging adults at a crucial time in their development (see Chapter 9). Prior research has further highlighted that student loan debt is the most likely category of consumer debt to become delinquent (FRB NY, 2018). To further explore the significance of this issue, it is worth noting the number of emerging adults who are directly impacted. Census data suggest that just under half of all Americans have some level of advanced degree, including associate degrees (U.S. Census Bureau, 2022).

The emerging adult sample from the NFCS is a bit skewed in favor of higher education attainment, with 58% reporting an associate degree or higher. About 57% of our emerging adult sample indicated having no student loans at the present time, with the remainder reporting loans for either themselves (33%) or a spouse (9%). From a financial planning standpoint, it is worth noting that a little more than half of the respondents (52%) reported having tried to estimate the future monthly payments when their loans were taken out. For many individuals, this student loan debt is not necessarily a burden, though we can explore other aspects of behavior to ascertain to what extent emerging adults are facing challenges due to their student loan debt. Several measures related to financial challenges associated with student loan debt are available in the NFCS data. Notably, a majority (52%) of those with student loan debt reported being concerned that they will not be able to repay their loans. About a quarter (26%) of respondents reported being late on their student loan debt payments at least once, with more than half of that group indicating being late multiple times. For student loan tips, see Box 5.5.

Box 5.5 Student Loan Tips for Emerging Adults

Student loans, when used properly, can be an effective tool to help pay for higher education. Emerging adults should be thoughtful and estimate actual need before borrowing. Since the process of taking out loans is incremental (semester to semester), it can be easy to lose track of exactly how much is really being borrowed. For those who choose to use student loans, there can be a lot of stress with regard to paying them back. You should consider factors related to possible earnings after college (often related to your major) and whether the investment makes sense over possible alternatives. Some links are provided below to help you explore repayment plans and potential forgiveness programs:

https://studentaid.gov/manage-loans/repayment/plans
https://studentaid.gov/manage-loans/forgiveness-cancellation

Medical Debt

Increasingly, emerging adults in the United States are grappling with another category of debt: medical debt. Rising healthcare costs, coupled with a complicated system of insurance and supports, create unique challenges for emerging adults. Although emerging adults are generally estimated as being healthier than older adults, a significant number of them will have to deal with the heavy costs associated with necessary emergency care or chronic health concerns, including disability. It should be noted that medical debt is an almost uniquely American phenomenon. Most other developed countries have systems that limit out-of-pocket costs for their citizens.

Evidence from the NFCS does provide some insight into the challenge of medical debt for emerging adults in the United States. About 27% of emerging adult survey respondents reported having unpaid medical bills (compared to about 21% of survey respondents ages 30 and older). This is a concerning statistic because it provides evidence of another strain on the financial resources of emerging adults. The NFCS data also provide details on several concerning behaviors that are driven by financial constraints among the emerging adult population. Specifically, roughly one-fifth (21%) of emerging adults indicated not filling a prescription due to its cost, and about one-quarter (24.5%) indicated forgoing a medical test, treatment, or follow-up recommended by a doctor due to the cost. Perhaps most concerning, nearly one-third (30.5%) of emerging adults reported having a medical problem but not seeing a doctor due to the cost. These figures point to a disturbing trend among a segment of the population, as delaying preventative procedures or recommended care due to cost concerns may ultimately lead to more severe medical problems in the long run, resulting in higher costs being borne by those consumers.

Summary

Emerging adults face an increasingly complex financial environment, and their behavior can have significant long-term consequences. Behaviors in emerging adulthood set the tone for future decisions, as these actions establish habits or carry consequences that can persist for many years. In this chapter, we have articulated a few critical areas for consideration and have developed a current picture of how emerging adults are doing in terms of their financial security. Several concerning trends stand out with regard to the rising costs of education, healthcare, and cost of living in general. These rising costs, coupled with a trend of relatively flat wage growth (see Chapter 10), can result in heavier borrowing (see Chapter 13) and less capacity for saving and investing. Prior research has articulated the importance of behavior in considering financial well-being (see Chapter 7; Sherraden, 2013), but it is clear that additional institutional factors can be influential, as will be made clear in other chapters.

Chapter 6

Emerging Adults' Financial Decisions: A Neurocognitive Perspective

Matteo Robba[1,2], Laura Colautti[2], and Paola Iannello[2]

Introduction

Emerging adulthood includes the years during which the most significant events of life are most likely to occur, and, therefore, the period when the most significant decisions are made (Tanner, 2006). Some of these significant decisions relate to emerging adults' own finances. Indeed, emerging adults' financial choices are crucial because those decisions heavily impact their future (Oehler et al., 2018). Hence, it is fundamental for them to make "good" financial choices. However, understanding what constitutes a good decision is not always straightforward and clear. Good decisions don't necessarily have to be the "absolute best" choice, but rather, those that lead to desirable or positive outcomes, considering individuals' goals and specific circumstances. Moreover, each person defines their own unique objectives, making it impossible to establish a "golden standard" for judging how good a decision is; the only relevant benchmark is based on the person themself. It follows that, rather than being the "perfect" one, a good decision can be defined as an informed and responsible decision, that is, a decision made with awareness and understanding of the available options, potential outcomes, and relevant information. Indeed, the level of awareness with which we make our financial decisions (e.g., taking the time to evaluate options and considering the long-term implications) makes all the difference. Consequently, when it comes to adults managing their own finances, the decisional process can be quite complex, and, if possible, it is even more complex for emerging adults.

[1] Department of Economic and Business Education, University of Mannheim, Mannheim, Germany
[2] Department of Psychology, Università Cattolica del Sacro Cuore, Milan, Italy

Matteo Robba, Laura Colautti, and Paola Iannello, *Emerging Adults' Financial Decisions: A Neurocognitive Perspective.* In: *Flourishing and Floundering Financially in Emerging Adulthood.* Edited by: Ashley B. LeBaron-Black et al., Oxford University Press. © Oxford University Press (2025). DOI: 10.1093/9780197699157.003.0007

Today, emerging adults are facing new challenges in comparison with prior generations due to a climate of economic and financial uncertainty. In addition to that, younger generations are currently struggling with a noninclusive labor market, which is characterized by limited job opportunities and lower wages for the new workforce. Taken together with demographic decline (i.e., the progressive decrease in births and aging of the population in many countries) and increasing life expectancy, this phenomenon has contributed to form an environment in which it is not easy to get financial security in retirement, thus requiring emerging adults to take particular care of their future financial well-being by making impactful financial decisions early in life (Bloom et al., 2007; OECD, 2019).

Furthermore, technological progress is radically changing the financial world. Consumers are now able to check and manage their finances online and through mobile devices. Likewise, brokerage platforms allow retail investors to operate in financial markets at every moment of the day, even without any intermediaries. Individuals now have access to powerful and complex financial instruments that require high levels of financial sophistication. Thus, financially illiterate individuals face more risk of misbehaviors and suboptimal decision-making. This might be especially true for emerging adults, who report generally lower financial literacy than older adults (see Chapter 2; Kim et al., 2019; Lusardi et al., 2010).

Emerging adults also show peculiar psychological characteristics that might negatively affect their decision-making capabilities. For instance, literature reports that adolescents and emerging adults are more prone to sensation seeking and assume risk-seeking behaviors (Josef et al., 2016; Mata et al., 2016; Steinberg et al., 2008). Though risk tolerance is a key determinant in investment decision-making (Keller & Siegrist, 2006; Robba et al., 2024a, 2024b), individuals lacking financial literacy may engage in risky investment or trading behaviors without proper competencies.

Likewise, literature reports a strong association between age and self-control (Moffit et al., 2011; Steinberg et al., 2009). Indeed, the younger individuals are, the harder it is for them to exercise control over impulsive responses (Oliva et al., 2019). Those lacking self-control tend to be more present-biased and prefer immediate rewards over greater but distant future outcomes (Ottaviani & Vandone, 2011; Xiao & Porto, 2019). Also, time perspective plays a key role in financial decision-making because individuals are often asked to delay gratification (i.e., spending in the present) to increase their future wealth. Thus, self-control is a factor that might have a significant role in emerging adults' financial behaviors.

Finally, evidence shows that emerging adults tend to overestimate their financial knowledge and skills (see Chapter 2; Lusardi & Mitchell, 2014). Self-confidence is essential in motivating individuals to reach their goals because it represents the link between knowledge and action (Bandura, 1977, 1982). However, excessive trust in one's own financial competence might drive individuals to financial misbehaviors or ineffective decision-making (Barber & Odean, 2000; Robba et al., 2024c). This might be especially true for emerging adults, who usually show higher confidence despite their lower levels of financial sophistication (Lusardi & Mitchell, 2014).

The present chapter aims to present a comprehensive framework of the main individual characteristics and abilities that can (positively or negatively) affect financial decision-making, namely, impulsivity and self-control, sensation seeking and risk attitude, and overconfidence. Moreover, to better understand how these features support financial decisional processes, a focus on the cognitive and neural aspects of such characteristics is provided. The final part of the chapter encompasses practical implications and provides possible suggestions aimed at supporting good decisional processes in emerging adults.

Individual Characteristics That Influence Financial Decision-Making

Individual differences can affect how people make financial decisions by shaping attitudes, beliefs, and preferences regarding money management, and saving and investing behaviors (Brown & Taylor, 2014; Gathergood, 2012; Sekścińska & Rudzinska-Wojciechowska, 2020). Given the sensitivity of the transition between adolescence and adulthood, some specific individual characteristics seem to play a significant role in influencing both the process and the outcome of emerging adults' financial decision-making. The tendency to make decisions quickly and without thinking hard about the consequences in the long term (i.e., impulsivity and present bias), the propensity for risky choices (i.e., risk attitudes), and the level of subjective confidence in the accuracy of one's abilities and competences (i.e., (over)confidence) are among the characteristics that most impact emerging adults' financial decisions, thus influencing their flourishing or floundering within this specific domain of life (e.g., Carlsson Hauff & Nilsson, 2020; Ma & Yao, 2023; Reardon et al., 2018). Each characteristic that will be taken into consideration throughout the chapter may have an impact, which could be either helpful or harmful, on emerging adults' developmental trajectories. These individual characteristics—shaping the financial decision-making process—may either enable emerging adults to close the gap between where they are currently and where they aim to be in their future (i.e., flourishing) or make them incapable of mindfully deciding about their future (i.e., floundering).

Impulsivity and Self-Control

An individual characteristic that can affect financial decisions is impulsivity (Frigerio et al., 2020). It can be defined as a propensity for acting quickly and recklessly without either considering possible consequences or considering temporal elements characterizing the contingent situation (Colombo et al., 2020; Moeller et al., 2001). In this way, it can affect the decision-making process, with impulsive individuals preferring immediate rewarding outcomes and discounting delayed but more optimal outcomes. Conversely, the opposite tendency (i.e., self-control) is characterized by preferring delayed and greater outcomes. Self-control can be defined as a set of "top-down" processes to voluntarily target personal resources and resist possible urges in order to achieve goals that are relevant for the individual. Self-control implies high-level cognitive mechanisms and encompasses mental operations used to inhibit impulsive behaviors and accomplish personal purposes from a long term perspective (Gillebaart & De Ridder, 2018; Rey-Ares et al., 2021). Accordingly, such an ability shows some conceptual overlap with inhibition and can be viewed as the opposite of impulsivity (Antonietti et al., 2023; Frigerio et al., 2020; Strömbäck et al., 2017). Self-control is related to the concept of executive functions (Duckworth & Kern, 2011), which comprises a wide set of goal-oriented abilities such as cognitive flexibility, working memory, inhibitory control, planning, and monitoring (Cristofori et al., 2019). Consistently, executive functions are assumed to be crucial for sustaining an optimal decisional process across the lifespan, preventing excessively risky choices that may lead to negative consequences (for a scoping review, see Colautti et al., 2022). However, it is well established that such abilities continue to develop until around 20 years old, when the frontal lobe—which plays a key role in executive functions—reaches its neuroanatomical maturation (Pharo et al., 2011; Tervo-Clemmens et al., 2022; Toga et al., 2006).

Several studies have pointed out the importance of self-control in financial decision-making (e.g., Strömbäck et al., 2017). Higher levels of self-control seem to be related to greater savings and wealth accumulation (Choi et al., 2011; Liu et al., 2019). Likewise, it is associated with financial market participation (Robba et al., 2024b; Sekścińska et al., 2021). On the contrary, a lack of self-control is related to behaviors that can reflect a difficulty in resisting (or inhibiting) the urge to gratify immediate consequences, such as indebtment and excessive debt burden (Frigerio et al., 2020). Impulsive individuals are not only more prone to hold debts (Achtziger et al., 2015) but are also more likely to make use of consumer credit (Ottaviani & Vandone, 2011). This tendency may imply negative consequences that can limit the prospects of growth and development for emerging adults, sometimes marking their financial future inexorably. Accumulating debts beyond one's ability to repay them during this phase of life might indeed have repercussions throughout their future lifespan (see Chapter 13). Debt burden can become overwhelming, impacting various life aspects, including mental health and overall well-being.

A recent study (Rey-Ares et al., 2021) considering a sample of Spanish emerging adults found that self-control was linked to positive financial attitudes and behaviors. Specifically, those with higher self-control were more likely to have long-term financial purposes and to plan for their expenses. Furthermore, they were more likely to invest in stock markets and hold savings accounts and less likely to have personal loans. Similarly, studies reported that emerging adults with self-control issues were more prone to engage in compulsive buying behaviors and had higher credit card debt (Ma & Yao, 2023; Peltier et al., 2016).

Emerging adults might be further at risk of debt holding. Due to their lower financial sophistication and greater impulsive tendencies, together with the ease of getting consumer credits, they might be more likely to engage in compulsive buying behaviors and credit consumption (see Chapter 13). Promoting cognitive control in everyday life decision-making seems necessary to help individuals make optimal choices, especially for emerging adults.

To better explain possible mechanisms underlying individual choices connoted by immediate gratifications or delaying rewards, in the last decades, several studies have focused on understanding the neural mechanisms related to decision-making. According to evidence from neuroimaging studies, the decisional process involving possible rewards (or losses) encompasses different cortical and subcortical structures in which a pivotal role is played by the dopaminergic pathways and the cortico-basal ganglia circuits (Kraemer et al., 2020). In this way, dopamine is essential to motivation, reward processing and reward-predicting cues, reinforcement learning, as well as cognitive control functions (i.e., executive functions; for reviews, see Colautti et al., 2023 and Ott & Nieder, 2019). From an anatomic point of view, the prefrontal cortex (PFC) and the subcortical structures belonging to basal ganglia (e.g., caudate, putamen, globus pallidus, nucleus accumbens, substantia nigra, and subthalamic nucleus) are crucial (Haber, 2016). In detail, choice options implying the possibility to receive immediate rewards mainly activate a network composed of paralimbic structures, such as the ventral striatum, lateral and medial orbitofrontal cortex (OFC), and ventromedial PFC (vmPFC; McClure et al., 2004). Such structures are assumed to be involved in the anticipation and judgment of which option is the most preferable for the decision-maker, considering both rewards and costs (as they are involved in the mental operations that assign the so-called subjective value to different options; Peters & Büchel, 2011). Consistently, a greater resting-state functional connectivity intensity within such a network is positively associated with higher discounting rates (i.e., the longer the reward delay when making a choice, the lower its value is perceived, reducing the probability the decision-maker will choose it among other options). Thus, a higher discount rate is possibly influenced by reward sensitivity and encourages impulsive responses (Li et al., 2013). Choices connoted by a preference toward higher but delayed rewards (i.e., rewards distant in time) seem to mostly engage a network that is also involved in cognitive-control processes, encompassing frontoparietal areas, such as lateral OFC, dorsolateral PFC (dlPFC), and posterior parietal cortex (Li et al., 2013; McClure et al., 2004; Menon & D'Esposito, 2022). Accordingly, studies that used stimulation methods showed that the inhibition of dlPFC can lead individuals to display more impulsive behaviors, specifically, making faster decisions and preferring immediate rewards. On the contrary, the enhancement of dlPFC can support choices characterized by a more reflective approach and delayed rewards (Colombo et al., 2020; Zhang et al., 2022). Similarly, greater activation in the lateral OFC is connected to a less discounting tendency (Boettiger et al., 2007).

Moreover, confirming previous evidence, the activation of the ventral striatum and vmPFC may be linked to individual differences in discounting reward, which is strictly linked to impulsivity (Moreira & Barbosa, 2019). Thus, individuals who display the tendency to discount delayed options present a higher activation in such structures for immediate rewards rather than delayed ones, while the difference in activation is smaller for individuals who present the opposite tendency (Cooper et al., 2013). Also, characteristics of the decisional situation, such as the difficulty in choosing between options (i.e., decision conflict), can affect responses. When the choice options present similar values, deciding is seen to be more difficult than when the value of options is markedly different. In such situations, the degree of conflict is related to the activity in prefrontal control regions, mainly in the anterior cingulate cortex (which is involved in monitoring the ongoing behavior, signaling error occurrences, and response conflict) and lateral PFC (which sustains inhibition and other executive-function abilities; Cai & Liu, 2004; Hoffman et al., 2008; McClure et al., 2004; Panikratova et al., 2020; Peters & Büchel, 2011).

From a cognitive point of view, such neuroimaging data are in line with the assumption that two main processes—which respectively encompass affective and cognitive dimensions—occur in decision-making when it implies reward processing (Colautti et al., 2022; Kalenscher et al., 2006), including financial decisions. The former process—concerning affective aspects, such as emotion elicited by possible consequences—involves lower-level automatic mechanisms; the latter implies higher-level abilities underlying cognitive control and other executive functions, including economical reasoning and future-oriented planning (Kalenscher et al., 2006). So, according to data available to make a decision, the individual's characteristics, and cognitive functioning, a decision can be based mainly on: (1) cognitive reasoning, by processing information and elaborating a goal-directed and future-oriented response, or (2) the affective dimension, relying on the decision-maker's intuitions and the contingent emotional state elicited by the situation (Colautti et al., 2022). In this way, together with other individual characteristics (e.g., risk attitudes), it is suggested that differences in neural developmental trajectories until early adulthood may contribute to the tendency toward risky behaviors in emerging adults, where subcortical regions involved in reward processing present an early development relative to PFC regions involved in cognitive control and inhibition (Casey et al., 2008; Pharo et al., 2011). Thus, in emotionally salient situations, such as decision-making implying monetary gains, the decisional process may be biased by affective aspects that may overcome the inhibitory mechanisms in suppressing risky choices; this is common during adolescence, which is just before emerging adulthood (Casey et al., 2008).

Sensation Seeking and Risk Attitudes

As previously reported, an individual characteristic that covers a relevant role in financial decision-making is risk attitude. Indeed, financial risk tolerance is strictly related with financial market participation and asset allocation, as risk-prone individuals are more likely to hold riskier portfolios (Keller & Siegrist, 2006; Nguyen et al., 2017; Robba et al., 2024c). Likewise, risk attitudes are associated with trading behaviors; indeed, risk-tolerant investors generally trade more frequently (Hoffmann et al., 2015).

Literature on risk attitudes in financial domains has focused mainly on demographic differences such as gender and age (Fisher & Yao, 2017; Mata et al., 2016), although some attention has been spent on biological drivers of risk tolerance. A key determinant of risk-taking behaviors is sensation seeking, namely, a personal characteristic that drives one toward the search for novel, varied, and intense experiences (Zuckerman, 1979). As reported by Levenson (1990), sensation seeking is a biological need for stimuli that often results in risk-taking behaviors.

It seems that sensation seeking might play a relevant role in financial domains. Literature reports a strong association between sensation seeking and financial risk tolerance (Rabbani et al., 2020; Zabel et al., 2009). Thus, sensation seeking might affect investment decisions and behaviors (Grinblatt & Keloharju, 2009; Lee et al., 2019). However, while risk tolerance, when accompanied by careful considerations, can be considered a characteristic associated with financial decisions that align with an individual's life goals, the tendency for sensation seeking is mostly associated with dysfunctional decision-making processes and outcomes (Reardon et al., 2018). In other words, a willingness to take calculated risks, along with thoughtful evaluation, can lead to functional decisions that contribute to the individual's life objectives. On the contrary, a strong inclination toward seeking sensations or thrills may result in dysfunctional outcomes, meaning decisions that might not align with the person's best interest or long-term financial well-being. Among other results, it turned out that sensation seeking plays a role in gambling behaviors. Various studies (e.g., Barrault & Varescon, 2013; Reardon et al., 2018) have reported that this personal characteristic is involved in pathological gambling among emerging adults.

Sensation seeking has also been linked to other problematic financial behaviors in emerging adults such as overspending, excessive use of credit, and trouble in paying bills (Worthy et al., 2010). Because sensation seeking is generally higher among adolescents and emerging adults and tends to decrease with age (Roth et al., 2005; Steinberg et al., 2008; Zuckerman et al., 1978), the role it might play in emerging adults' financial behaviors and decisions should be further investigated.

To better understand why some individuals are more likely to display higher levels of sensation seeking than others, it is worth mentioning that neurobiological elements correspond with this trait, especially neurotransmitter systems (Roberti, 2004). Specifically, biological systems involving dopaminergic and serotonergic activity are associated with sensation-seeking traits recorded from self-report instruments (Netter et al., 1996). Moreover, to highlight the importance of dopamine in individual traits related to decision-making under risk, it has been noted that people with high sensation-seeking scores present an increased release of dopamine in dopaminergic systems where stressful situations occur (Piazza et al., 1993) and a greater reactivity for intense stimuli (Zuckerman, 2005). In this direction, it has been seen that high sensation seekers display a stronger neural response to high-arousal stimuli than lower sensation seekers in those areas that support arousal and reinforcement, such as the insula and the posterior medial OFC, while they present a lower activation in those areas linked to behavioral monitoring, emotional regulation, and decision-making, such as anterior cingulate and anterior medial OFC (Joseph et al., 2009). Moreover, a recent study (Xu et al., 2019) investigated feedback-related negativity (FRN)—which is assumed to underlie anterior cingulate cortex activity (Gehring & Willoughby, 2002)—in participants with high and low sensation seeking to explore individual processing in assigning values to outcomes (Gehring & Willoughby, 2002; Luck, 2014). Results highlighted that low sensation seekers display higher FRN after outcomes characterized by large loss magnitude rather than by small ones, while high sensation seekers presented no FRN changes after a large or small loss magnitude.

These results highlight the presence of differences in neural responses in individuals with high and low sensation-seeking traits. Specifically, the former seems to present a tendency toward arousal by itself, overriding the content or the valence (positive or negative) of the situation that caused arousal (Joseph et al., 2009) and possibly biasing the evaluation of the contingent situation and the decisional process required. This can explain how this characteristic tends to dominate in directing choices and personal behaviors, especially under situations connoted by uncertainty of the possible consequences. In such situations, high sensation seeking may result in a reduced sensitivity to negative outcomes (i.e., considering more the possible positive outcomes and disregarding the negative ones), which can affect the decisional process and lead to engaging in higher-risk behaviors (Xu et al., 2019).

Overconfidence

In many everyday decisions, the information required to make a choice is incomplete and individuals have to make judgments based on limited information (e.g., in investment decision-making or planning). In such cases, the level of confidence that an individual has in their own abilities can be critical to the decision-making process (Fernandez-Vargas et al., 2021; Iannello & Colautti, 2023). Whereas confidence can be considered as the subjective perception derived from the metacognitive process involved in the evaluation of performance (Molenberghs et al., 2016), which reflects the probability that a choice can be functional (Fernandez-Vargas et al., 2021), overconfidence can be conceptualized as an excessive confidence (or trust) in one's own decision-making capacities despite a lack of appropriate skills, which can lead to detrimental consequences, especially in medical or financial fields (Iannello & Colautti, 2023; Molenberghs et al., 2016). Accordingly, higher levels of confidence (i.e., overconfidence) can also be linked to lower performance on tasks that require making a decision (Pennycook et al., 2017) and to a lower-quality metacognitive process (Molenberghs et al., 2016). Indeed, overconfidence can lead individuals to make decisions too quickly, without fully considering all available information and weighing the potential risks of different options (Fischhoff et al., 1977).

Overconfidence has been thoroughly investigated in the financial domain, especially for investment decision-making (e.g., Yeh & Ling, 2022). Confidence is a key motivator for action. For instance, greater confidence in one's own financial capabilities is associated with retirement planning (Parker et al., 2012), market participation (Robba et al., 2024b), and holding riskier portfolios (Cupák et al., 2021). However, sometimes individuals are excessively confident in their capabilities (see Chapter 2).

Concerning financial domains, evidence shows that overconfident individuals are more likely to participate in the stock market (Xia et al., 2014; Yeh & Ling, 2022). Although investing is a way to increase wealth, it also requires adequate skills and knowledge. Thus, overconfident investors might be more subject to nonoptimal decision-making. For instance, overconfidence has been associated with low portfolio diversification (Broekema & Kramer, 2021). Moreover, various studies reported that excessive confidence may be associated with the tendency to engage in more speculative investment strategies such as trading activity (Deaves et al., 2009; Grinblatt & Keloharju, 2009).

Besides negative investment decision-making, literature supports the idea that overconfidence may lead to other risky financial behaviors (see Chapter 2). Indeed, individuals overestimating their competencies could be less likely to plan for their future (Lee & Hanna, 2020, 2022) and to seek financial advice (Kramer, 2016). Furthermore, a recent study (Carlsson Hauff & Nilsson, 2020) involving a sample of Swedish college students found that overconfident individuals tended to borrow higher amounts of money.

Emerging adults are generally more subject to overconfidence in their self-perceived performance than older adults (Korreck et al., 2013). This may be due to the developmental changes that occur during emerging adulthood, such as increased autonomy and identity exploration, which can lead to a sense of invincibility and overconfidence. Indeed, nowadays technology allows individuals to easily participate autonomously in capital markets. Emerging adults could be attracted by the persistent presence of exchange and trading services advertisements on social media, thus deciding to invest their money despite a lack of adequate financial skills and knowledge (see Chapter 5). Financial education programs (see Chapter 19) can help alleviate this phenomenon by making emerging adults more aware of their actual capabilities and limitations.

Concerning possible neural mechanisms underlying such an individual characteristic, an fMRI study, in which participants underwent a task involving high-level inferential cognitive processes, revealed differential activation patterns comparing responses characterized by low or high confidence (Molenberghs et al., 2016). Specifically, low levels of confidence activated structures also connected to metacognition (Fleming & Dolan, 2012; Yuki et al., 2019) such as dorsal medial and anterior PFC and midcingulate cortex, as well as lateral OFC, which is assumed to be involved in negative reward prediction and processing of nonreward or punishing stimuli (Kringelbach & Rolls, 2004; Rolls, 2019). Conversely, high levels of confidence resulted in an increased activity of the striatum (mainly in the caudate), which is linked to reward processing and stimulus–action–reward association (Haruno & Kawato, 2006; Schultz et al., 2008), and in structures exploited in action preparation and execution such as the postcentral gyrus, precentral gyrus, and supplementary motor area (Molenberghs et al., 2016). Such activations can suggest that overconfidence may contribute to a strong link between the motor response and the pleasant experience involved. Indeed, the link with striatum can be consistent with a higher response speed detected in conditions characterized by overconfidence (Muller et al., 2020).

Conclusion

From youth to old age, everyone must continually make financial decisions that have a great impact on one's life. Additionally, nowadays, individuals are being asked at the onset of adulthood to make critical financial decisions that will have consequences for their entire life, such as saving and planning for retirement. Hence, it is fundamental to focus on the financial decision-making of emerging adults in order to understand those specific elements that may impact both the decision-making process and the quality of the outcome. Within a conceptualization of decision-making as a complex process in which several elements come into play (Colautti et al., 2022; Iannello & Colautti, 2023), the present contribution provides a neurocognitive framework to gain an understanding of the main neural and cognitive mechanisms that affect emerging adults' financial decision-making. By investigating those mechanisms, we can gain insights into why some emerging adults may be more susceptible to financial mistakes and mismanagement (ultimately, financial floundering) than others. As emerging adults face important financial decisions related to education (see Chapter 9), employment (see Chapter 10), and housing, just to name a few, insights concerning cognitive and neural correlates of financial decision-making could have significant implications for emerging adults' long-term financial stability and success (i.e., financial flourishing). Specifically, it is worth considering how differences in neurocognitive development until early adulthood (i.e., earlier development of subcortical structures processing rewards than PFC regions supporting inhibitory mechanisms and cognitive control), together with individual characteristics, may contribute to risky financial decisions. Hence, emerging adults might be led to make emotionally salient choices by following the affective aspects, rather than by implementing an exhaustive cognitive process. From this, some considerations follow.

First of all, it appears important for emerging adults approaching financial decisions—and for practitioners who work with them—to know the critical cognitive mechanisms related to the individual characteristics that can lead to dysfunctional choices, such as the tendency toward making reckless decisions, the propensity for risky choices, and the personal beliefs about one's own ability to make a financial decision. Such knowledge is pivotal for increasing individuals' awareness, which is the first step to promote changes in attitudes and behaviors when they are suboptimal, especially within interventions aimed at enhancing financial decision-making (Antonietti et al., 2016).

Several implications for emerging adults, educators, practitioners, financial institutions, and policymakers can be outlined (also see Box 6.1). For emerging adults, understanding the variables involved in an optimal decisional process can contribute to paying more attention to how they deal with the most critical decisional steps, giving meaning to emotions they feel elicited by the contingent situation, and thus supporting—at least in part—less impulsive behaviors and avoiding mistakes. For educators and practitioners, such knowledge can support the design of effective interventions aimed at fostering good financial decisions through a metacognitive approach that emphasizes the importance of reflecting on and being aware of the mental processes involved during the decisional process. In this way, it might be easier for emerging adults to identify possible dysfunctional mechanisms and correct them strategically (Antonietti et al., 2016). Accordingly, for practitioners, it appears crucial to assess such characteristics, both to provide useful insight for the individuals concerning their functioning and to design effective interventions for those more prone to make suboptimal decisions. Specifically, the most common assessment methods encompass behavioral tasks and self-report tools (Dang et al., 2020). It is important to carefully choose the tools to use according to the purposes of the intervention. In fact, behavioral tasks are generally characterized by the presence of monetary gains and losses, and the decision-maker is required to choose between various options that are safer or riskier in terms of potential economic outcomes. To make a decision, cognitive processes such as estimating values and costs, evaluating the outcome, and feedback processing are highlighted (Rangel et al., 2008). These tasks record participants' performance rather than their related perception (which self-report measures record) and enable controlling other individual aspects that could bias results, especially if participants present a low awareness. Conversely, self-report instruments are usually preferred over behavioral tasks when investigating individual beliefs and attitudes related to decision-making because they require the respondents to reflect on their behaviors in real-life situations. On the other hand, while behavioral tasks can have low ecological validity as responses recorded doing a specific task may show differences from how the person would behave in external settings, self-report tools might be biased by social desirability, providing only an indirect measure of psychological characteristics (Cyders & Coskunpinar, 2011).

Box 6.1

Emerging adults are required to make financial decisions that will heavily impact their future financial well-being. Hence, understanding the specific neurocognitive functioning and individual characteristics shaping emerging adults' decision-making is crucial to promote functional financial decisions and behaviors. Financial decision-making is not only a matter of objective financial capabilities, but also various psychological characteristics that come into play, influencing the final outcome. For this reason, some tips for designing effective financial education programs for emerging adults follow:

- Programs specifically designed for emerging adults should help them to become more aware of the future consequences of their present financial behaviors and enhance the adoption of forward-looking perspectives to set better financial goals for their future.
- Besides theoretical aspects, such initiatives should also include practical exercises and role play to help emerging adults understand the variables involved in a functional decisional process and to pay more attention to how they deal with the most critical decisional steps.
- Educators and practitioners should also foster financial decisions through a metacognitive approach, making emerging adults more aware of the mental processes involved during the decisional process. This awareness could make it

easier for emerging adults to identify possible dysfunctional mechanisms and correct them strategically.

- To reduce the gap between objective and perceived financial capabilities, financial education programs should not merely transfer information but should make emerging adults more aware of their actual knowledge and skills.

Moreover, implications derived can also be useful for financial institutions because understanding the neurocognitive mechanisms involved in emerging adult decisions can support the development of services that are specifically tailored to the target's needs. For instance, behavioral economics principles could be used to design services that discourage impulsive spending and promote saving behaviors. Furthermore, this understanding can be used by policymakers to develop ad hoc educational programs that prompt individuals to analyze how they make a decision, paying attention to the cognitive mechanisms involved and detecting those that can be dysfunctional. Thus, continued investigation in this field is essential for advancing our comprehension of this topic and promoting financial flourishing for emerging adults.

Chapter 7
Emerging Adults' Financial Well-Being: Conceptualization and Measurement

Angela Sorgente[1] *and Margherita Lanz*[1]

Introduction

The current chapter focuses on the final outcome of the financial literacy process: financial well-being (FWB). This construct has received overwhelming attention in the last decades, as demonstrated by the numerous recent FWB-related academic publications in the form of systematic reviews (Bashir & Qureshi, 2023a, 2023b; Brüggen et al., 2017; Ghazali et al., 2020; Gonçalves et al., 2021; Kaur et al., 2021; Kaur & Singh, 2022; Mahendru et al., 2022b; Nanda & Banerjee, 2021; She et al., 2023; Sorgente et al., 2022; Sorgente & Lanz, 2017; Wilmarth, 2021), special issues (e.g., Kabadayi & O'Connor, 2019; Lanz & Serido, 2020), and books (e.g., Sharma et al., 2023). Furthermore, there has been an explosion of FWB publications in grey literature as well (Riitsalu et al., 2023), with many policymakers and financial sector institutions recently publishing FWB reports (e.g., CFPB, 2015; Comerton-Forde et al., 2020; UNCDF, 2021; UNSGSA, 2021).

Thus, the current chapter has three main aims. First, we summarize and simplify the FWB-related literature in order to define this construct and highlight important changes that have occurred in the study of FWB in the last decades. Second, we demonstrate how the conceptualization and measurement of FWB should be adjusted when this construct is applied to the emerging adult population. Finally, we clarify why one FWB model cannot fit all emerging adults because the meaning that emerging adults attribute to FWB is shaped by the culture they belong to and the socioeconomic conditions of the country they live in. We conclude the chapter with three suggestions to help emerging adults flourish financially.

[1] Department of Psychology, Università Cattolica del Sacro Cuore, Milan, Italy

Angela Sorgente and Margherita Lanz, *Emerging Adults' Financial Well-Being: Conceptualization and Measurement.* In: *Flourishing and Floundering Financially in Emerging Adulthood.* Edited by: Ashley B. LeBaron-Black et al., Oxford University Press. © Oxford University Press (2025). DOI: 10.1093/9780197699157.003.0008

Definition of Financial Well-Being: A Conceptualization in Progress

Financial well-being (FWB) is an "emerging concept that addresses the financial side of individuals' and families' ability to thrive in society" (UNSGSA, 2021, p. 3). Scholars from psychology, economics, and social sciences have proposed different definitions of FWB (see Riitsalu & van Raaij, 2022, and Riitsalu et al., 2023, for a detailed list). We here refer to the definition proposed by Aubrey et al. (2022) because it aligns with the typical definition of general well-being as encompassing hedonic and eudaimonic components (Keyes et al., 2002), while being more specific to one's financial situation. Aubrey et al. (2022) define FWB as a "positive psychological state characterized by a sense of contentment about one's personal financial situation and by a positive perception of one's financial situation as able to actively meet one's current needs and future aspirations" (p. 3).

To help readers understand the complexity of this construct, we map five major changes in the conceptualization of FWB over the last decades: (1) from objective to subjective, (2) from economics to psychology, (3) from a unidimensional to multidimensional construct, (4) from present to future, and (5) from offstage to onstage.

From Objective to Subjective Financial Well-Being

Originally, FWB was synonymous with income, as income was considered the financial factor that makes people happy (Sorgente & Lanz, 2017). People with higher levels of income were expected to be happier than people with lower levels of income (Easterlin, 1973). Things changed when Easterlin (1974) published his paradox, empirically demonstrating that happiness does not increase as a country's income rises. People nowadays hold the notion that a positive financial condition is something that goes beyond a high income (Sorgente & Lanz, 2017). Similarly, scholars (e.g., Brüggen et al., 2017; Mahendru et al., 2022a) agree that FWB has both an objective and a subjective side, and the latter cannot be reduced to the former. Objective financial well-being (OFWB) refers to material resources such as income, savings, and assets (e.g., house, car) (Mahendru et al., 2022b). Subjective financial well-being (SFWB) corresponds to the individual's emotional and cognitive evaluation (i.e., perceptions) of their financial condition (Sorgente & Lanz, 2017). These perceptions are entirely personal and subjective (Brüggen et al., 2017; She et al., 2023), implying that individuals may experience certain levels of SFWB regardless of their OFWB (e.g., people with similar income may experience different levels of SFWB depending on their personal characteristics, values, reference group). While all scholars now agree that *both* the objective and subjective sides are relevant for the study of FWB, the investigation of the subjective side has become more prominent. Most of the "recent conceptualisations of the term FWB identify and embrace this subjective aspect" (Kaur & Singh, 2022, p. 2), as done, for example, by Aubrey et al. (2022)'s definition reported beforehand here. Similarly, Bashir and Qureshi (2023a) stated that their systematic review of literature "revealed that compared to objective and a combination of objective and subjective measures of financial well-being, the extant literature on financial well-being is dominated by subjective measures. This might be because subjective measures . . . provide a more holistic view of financial well-being by capturing the perceived feelings of individuals about their financial situation" (p. 41).

From Economics to Psychology

This attention to the subjective side of FWB led to a second change in FWB's literature. While originally economists were the *only* experts of this construct, once the subjective side of FWB was recognized, psychologists started to apply their expertise about the subjective side of well-being (see concepts like subjective well-being or psychological well-being) to the study of FWB. This gave rise to a drastic increase in the number of studies on FWB published by psychologists. For example, in a review collecting studies about emerging adults' FWB (Sorgente & Lanz, 2017), 43.18% (19 out of 44) of the studies were categorized in the discipline of psychology. Nowadays, scholars recognize that both economics and psychology—together with sociology, marketing, and consumer finance—have contributed to the development of the FWB discipline (Mahendru et al., 2022b).

From a Unidimensional to Multidimensional Construct

The first change in FWB's literature (from objective to subjective) was also a precursor to the third change we identified: FWB shifting from a unidimensional to a multidimensional construct. The increase of study on the subjective side of FWB has raised awareness that SFWB itself is a complex construct that cannot be reduced to just one dimension (Comerton-Forde et al., 2018). A more dated conceptualization of SFWB defined this construct as satisfaction with one's present financial condition (e.g., Shim et al., 2009).

Consequently, the assessment of this construct was obtained through unidimensional measurement scales (e.g., Prawitz et al., 2006; Shim et al., 2009). Now, SFWB's definitions as well as developed assessment tools recognize the complex nature of SFWB by conceptualizing and/or measuring different dimensions of this construct. A literature review conducted by Aubrey et al. (2022) found that, across several conceptualizations of the SFWB (e.g., Brüggen et al., 2017; CFPB, 2015; Kempson & Poppe, 2018; Muir et al., 2017; Netemeyer et al., 2018; Sorgente & Lanz, 2019), seven distinct dimensions of this construct have been proposed: income adequacy (i.e., having access to an income seen as adequate to meet one's needs), life enjoyment (i.e., perception of being able to enjoy life thanks to one's financial condition), temporal (i.e., perception of one's future financial condition as positive), relativity (i.e., perception of having a good financial condition compared to others' condition), control (i.e., perception of being able to plan and manage one's finances), cognitive evaluation (i.e., perception of one's financial situation as satisfactory), and emotional evaluation (i.e., experience of pleasurable emotions in relation to one's financial condition not tainted by negative emotions, such as stress or anxiety).

From Present to Future

The temporal dimension of the seven-dimension model proposed by Aubrey et al. (2022) represents another important change in FWB conceptualization. When FWB was synonymous with income, only the present financial condition (i.e., the current level of income) was taken into consideration (Easterlin, 1973). Once the subjective perception of one's financial condition was recognized as being equally important as income, some researchers suggested that the perception of one's future financial condition could influence present happiness as well. In particular, the first study suggesting that SFWB also has a future dimension was Norvilitis et al. (2003). Nowadays, most of the FWB definitions (see, e.g., Brüggen et al., 2017; CFPB, 2015; Salignac et al., 2020) take into consideration this future perception; similarly, instruments aiming to assess individuals' FWB include a dimension assessing perceptions of the future (Netemeyer et al., 2018; Sorgente & Lanz, 2019). Nowadays, scholars agree that future expectations about one's financial condition can contribute, together with the evaluation of one's current situation, to present financial satisfaction and general well-being (Aubrey et al., 2022). Furthermore, literature suggests that, for emerging adults specifically, future financial perception may have an even bigger impact on present general well-being than present financial perception does (Iannello et al., 2021).

From Offstage to Onstage

Finally, the last change we identified in FWB's literature was a drastic shift from an offstage position to an onstage position. Although FWB has always been studied, its core relevance for people's lives has been fully recognized only in the last two decades. In particular, the 2008 economic recession was a reminder of the huge impact that finances have on individuals' well-being. According to Brüggen et al. (2017), after the 2008 crisis, the financial health of citizens became a topic of increasing importance for companies, policy-makers, and regulators. Different systematic reviews (e.g., Bashir & Qureshi, 2023a; Brüggen et al., 2017; Sorgente & Lanz, 2017) collecting studies on FWB have indeed found that most of the published studies are dated 2009 or later. If the financial dimension of well-being moved from an offstage position to an onstage position in 2008, more recent events have contributed to FWB remaining onstage, including the COVID-19 pandemic (OECD, 2021); the consequent increase in poverty and inequality in many parts of the world (Bashir & Qureshi, 2023a); and the digitalization of open banking, which disrupted the role of traditional banks (Comerton-Forde et al., 2020; Money and Pensions Service, 2019).

We believe that the next trend in the conceptualization and operationalization of FWB will be the adaptation of this construct to specific stages of life. As highlighted by Wilmarth (2021, p. 126), "There is still a gap in the literature in using comprehensive financial and economic well-being measures with age specific components, and if the antecedents change with age. Moving into the next decade, continuing to have age specific investigations on financial and economic well-being measures would help to expand the body of knowledge for both researchers and practitioners." In other words, we may expect that, in the future, FWB conceptualizations will shift from being referred to as one-size-fits-all to being adapted to specific developmental stages.

Financial Well-Being during Emerging Adulthood

Originally, the relation between age and FWB was investigated only through quantitative studies with the aim of verifying whether individuals' age predicted the FWB *level* they reported. Most of these studies (Delaney et al., 2006; Hansen et al., 2008; Plagnol & Easterlin, 2008; Vera-Toscano et al., 2006) found that satisfaction with one's financial condition (i.e., SFWB) increases with age and is surprisingly high at old age despite low levels of income (i.e., OFWB) after retirement (see George, 1992 for an overview).

Nowadays, the scientific community is calling for qualitative studies with the aim of verifying if the *meaning* of FWB changes with age (Wilmarth, 2021). If we are not sure that the meaning of FWB is the same across ages, comparing levels of FWB across age groups may generate misleading results. Recently, some scholars (e.g., Riitsalu et al., 2023; Salignac et al., 2020) have conducted qualitative studies to investigate whether the meaning and components (or dimensions) of FWB change over the life-course. These studies found that FWB has different meanings at different ages and indeed concluded that "financial wellbeing must be understood within a life-course framework—this includes the stage people are at in the life-course (early childhood, childhood, adolescence, young adulthood, adulthood, older adulthood)" (Salignac et al., 2020, p. 1586).

A Financial Well-Being Definition Adapted to Emerging Adults

To the best of our knowledge, there are only two qualitative studies that have investigated whether the meaning of FWB changes with age: The first was conducted in Australia with 72 participants (Salignac et al., 2020) and the second one in Europe with 47 participants (Riitsalu et al., 2023). Both studies concluded that the conceptualization of FWB of young people is different from people of other age groups.

In particular, Salignac et al. (2020) found that, across all age groups, FWB had three dimensions: (1) *meeting expenses and having some money left over* (i.e., having an adequate income to meet basic needs, pay off debts, cover unexpected expenses, and have some money left), (2) *being in control of one's finances* (i.e., feeling and acting in control now and in the future), and (3) *feeling financially secure* (i.e., not having to worry much about money and having a sense of satisfaction with one's financial situation). Interestingly, despite these dimensions being the same across age groups, "the importance and meaning of the dimensions of financial wellbeing changed over the life-course and in response to different life-course stages" (Salignac et al., 2020, p. 1592). In particular, many young people (i.e., people ages 18–25 years) described increases in their expenses as they became independent from their parents (see Chapter 11). Young people had financial goals and priorities associated with their age and life-course stage such as finding independent housing, traveling, and buying a car, which were all considered important for personal growth in spite of their high expense. For young people, this increase in expenses did not necessarily mean a decrease in FWB but could instead represent a financial achievement needed to complete the transition to adulthood. In other words, while for other age groups, the dimension *meeting expenses and having some money left over* was more related to saving money, emerging adults were more focused on making extraordinary purchases they perceived as necessary to becoming adults.

Even more significant differences across age groups were found in Riitsalu et al. (2023)'s study. In particular, Riitsalu et al. compared the definitions of FWB provided by three age groups: 17–23, 26–47, and 55–64 years old. Interestingly, they found that these three age groups shared only the meaning they attributed to *present* FWB, while they had different perceptions of FWB component(s) related to the *future*. Specifically, Riitsalu et al. (2023) found that across all age groups, participants attributed FWB to have a present dimension and interpreted it in the same way: Present-related FWB consists of perceived ability to maintain one's current lifestyle. This entails making ends meet without stress and feeling secure about one's personal or household finances.

Specific to differences in the perception of future-related element(s) of FWB, Riitsalu et al. (2023) found that future-related FWB conceptualization of individuals ages 17–23 was more complex than that of other age groups. Among the respondents belonging to the two older groups (26–47 and 55–64 years old), only *one* future-related component of FWB was described: financial freedom or independence. Those ages 26–47 saw this as having the freedom to choose how to earn and spend money without being forced into certain choices by their financial situation. For individuals ages 55–64, financial independence was understood as not needing financial support from anyone through the final years of life, including being able to cover one's own funeral costs. Instead, respondents ages 17–23 differentiated *two* FWB components when referring to their future. The first one was the perception of being on the right track to achieve a desired lifestyle; this dimension was not present in the other age groups. As reported by Riitsalu et al. (2023, p. 10), this difference "might be related to their life stage—youth were only starting to manage and plan their own finances, build their careers, and find their desired lifestyle, while middle-aged [i.e., ages 26–47] and older individuals [i.e., ages 55–64] have already come to the mid-point of this journey and established their standard of living. It is also possible that they are simply more realistic about their opportunities than the youth."

The second future-related FWB component reported by the 17- to 23-year-old group was financial freedom. Financial freedom meant something different to young people than it did for older individuals. Youth interpreted financial freedom as earning sufficient passive income and not having to work in the traditional way that previous generations saw as the default option. This is similar to the principles of the FIRE (Financial Independence, Retire Early) movement (Taylor & Davies, 2021). Some of them explicitly stated the arguments that the FIRE philosophy prioritizes (e.g., frugality, reduced consumption, and extreme saving in order to earn passive income and enjoy free time). In summary, Riitsalu et al. (2023) concluded that FWB for individuals ages 17–23 consists of three dimensions (two which are future-oriented): maintaining current lifestyle, achieving a desired lifestyle, and achieving financial freedom.

Results from Salignac et al. (2020) and Riitsalu et al. (2023) can be complemented with those of Rea et al. (2019), who conducted a qualitative study with 31 U.S. college-educated emerging adults (23–30 years old) aiming to investigate the definition that they attributed to FWB. Distinct from Salignac et al. (2020) and Riitsalu et al. (2023), Rea and colleagues' study did not compare young respondents with participants from other age groups. However, its results clearly show that emerging adults' definition of FWB is strongly related to their stage of life (e.g., independence from parents) and, consequently, different from a definition applicable to other age groups. Indeed, Rea et al. (p. 261) found that emerging adults interpret FWB as an "ability to balance taking care of their money for stability and freedom to live independently from their parents, with feeling unconstrained by their finances."

Overall, these three qualitative studies (Rea et al., 2019; Riitsalu et al., 2023; Salignac et al., 2020) investigated, with slightly different aims, how FWB is conceptualized by emerging adults. Findings from these studies seem to agree in recognizing that emerging adults evaluate their FWB through both a present and a future perspective. When referring to their present, emerging adults consider FWB as "having an adequate income" (Salignac et al., 2020, p. 1597) as well as the ability of "taking care of their money" (Rea et al., 2019, p. 261) in order to "meet basic needs" (Salignac et al., 2020, p. 1597) and "keeping the current lifestyle" (Riitsalu et al., 2023, p. 7). This is accompanied by emerging adults' perception of "feeling financially secure" (Salignac et al., 2020, p. 1597) and "feeling unconstrained by their finances" (Rea et al., 2019, p. 261). When referring to their future, emerging adults consider FWB as the condition of "feeling and acting in control" of their future financial condition (Salignac et al., 2020, p. 1597) so that their future condition can allow the achievement of their "desired lifestyle" (Riitsalu et al., 2023, p. 10) and "being able to afford in the future anything one desires" (Riitsalu et al., 2023, p. 10). Both present and future FWB are connected to the issue of financial independence from parents (see Chapter 11). For example, in the present, more expenses (e.g., buying a house) are justifiable if they result in independence from parents (Salignac et al., 2020). Similarly, a positive perception of future FWB implies the ability "to live independently from their parents" (Rea et al., 2019, p. 263).

The evidence that emerging adults conceptualize FWB differently from people of other age groups has relevant implications. First, as suggested by Riitsalu et al. (2023, p. 11), "communication from financial sector and financial education initiatives should target the specificities of age groups in their efforts to increase FWB" (see Chapter 19). Second, the measurement of FWB in samples of emerging adults should happen using instruments able to map the specifics of this construct during the transition to adulthood (Sorgente & Lanz, 2019).

A Financial Well-Being Measure Adapted to Emerging Adults

Recently, a systematic review of the studies investigating emerging adults' FWB (Sorgente & Lanz, 2017) reported a lack of instruments specifically developed and validated to assess emerging adults' FWB. While the literature is still scarce from this point of view, it is important to offer some guidelines about how to assess both OFWB and SFWB when the target population consists of emerging adults.

The OFWB of *adult* respondents is usually assessed through ratios in the areas of liquidity, savings, asset allocation, inflation protection, tax burden, housing expenses, and credit (Greninger et al., 1996). Many of these elements do not yet apply to *emerging adults* who are still developing their role as financial individuals in society. According to Sorgente and Lanz (2017), when emerging adults' OFWB is assessed, measures both of income (e.g., annual earnings) and debts (e.g., credit card debt) are needed, and those must be complemented with indicators that recognize the transition to adulthood these individuals are undergoing. For example, it should be assessed (1) whether subjects own a savings account (see Chapter 5; Friedline et al., 2014), as many young individuals do not; (2) whether they receive any financial support from and/or live with parents (see Chapter 11; Solis & Durband, 2015); as well as (3) whether they have a job and how stable it is (see Chapter 10; Clarkberg, 1999). Furthermore, when emerging adults are students, OFWB can be also assessed by evaluating the presence of student loans, scholarships, and grants (see Chapter 9; Solis & Durband, 2015). Finally, a future perspective can be applied to OFWB, too. For example, Chan et al. (2012) assessed the "anticipated income" of a sample of college students, where participants were asked to estimate their income after graduation.

Regarding SFWB, different validated scales are available to assess the SFWB of *adult* respondents (see Aubrey et al., 2022), while only two SFWB scales have been specifically developed for emerging adults. They are the Student Financial Well-Being Scale (Norvilitis et al., 2003) and the Multidimensional Subjective Financial Well-Being Scale (MSFWBS; Sorgente & Lanz, 2019).

The Student Financial Well-Being Scale (Norvilitis et al., 2003) comprises eight items evaluated on a scale from 1 (strongly agree) to 5 (strongly disagree). The scale is composed of two subscales: current financial concern (six items) and future expectation (two items). The strengths of this scale are that it is a brief instrument and that it can map two important dimensions of SFWB: the present and the future dimensions. On the other hand, this instrument has some weaknesses. First, it only targets a specific subgroup of emerging adults (i.e., students). Second, having many items referring to debts and student loans, it is applicable only in some cultural contexts. Student loans and debt are quite common among emerging adults in the United States, where the scale was developed. In other countries, debts and loans are less common among emerging adults (Guille, 2002), making this scale less applicable.

The second validated instrument developed to assess the SFWB of emerging adults is the MSFWBS (Sorgente & Lanz, 2019). It is composed of 25 items evaluated on a 5-point scale (1 = absolutely false; 5 = absolutely true). This scale measures five different dimensions of emerging adults' SFWB: (1) emerging adults' general evaluation of their financial condition (*cognitive* dimension), (2) emerging adults' perception of their ability to manage material resources (*behavioral* dimension), (3) emerging adults' evaluation of the sufficiency of their material resources (*materialistic* dimension), (4) emerging adults' evaluation of their financial condition when compared with peers' (*relational* dimension), and (5) emerging adults' expectations about their future financial situation (*temporal* dimension). The strength of this instrument is its ability to map most of the seven FWB dimensions identified by the literature review of Aubrey et al. (2022). Furthermore, this instrument is not specific to students and can be administered to any emerging adult. Finally, this instrument was originally developed in Italy (Sorgente & Lanz, 2019), but it has been successively adapted and validated in Austria, Canada, Finland, Portugal, Romania, Slovenia, and Turkey (Sorgente et al., 2024).

One weakness of this instrument is its relatively high number of items. Furthermore, initial evidence suggests that this instrument may not be applicable in non-Western countries. In a recent cross-cultural study (Sorgente et al., 2024), the five-factor structure of the MSFWBS was not replicated in India. This stresses the importance of considering the country in which emerging adults live when we are interested in the conceptualization and/or measurement of FWB.

One Financial Well-Being Model Fits All Emerging Adults?

Literature suggests that theoretical models of FWB should be adjusted not only in light of individuals' stage of life, but also in light of the culture individuals belong to and the socioeconomic conditions of the country they live in (Riitsalu & van Raaij, 2022). Regarding *cultural factors*, for example, a systematic review of studies conducted in Malaysia (Ghazali et al., 2020) demonstrated that some psychological factors that usually affect SFWB in individualistic cultures (e.g., self-esteem) were not influential in Malaysia, whereas culture-specific factors (e.g., the Islamic practice called *wasatiyyah*; Ramlee et al., 2019) did influence SFWB. Similarly, other authors stressed that FWB is related to the *socioeconomic conditions* of the country in which individuals live. Recently, Mahendru and colleagues (Mahendru, 2021; Mahendru et al., 2022a) argued that there is a need to build new theoretical models of FWB specifically suited to developing countries' situations. In particular, Mahendru (2021) stated that the "majority of the work studying financial well-being has been undertaken in the developed countries" (p. 1), but "the diverse socioeconomic, environmental conditions create disagreement on a single definition [of FWB] for developed and developing countries, thereby calling for separate conceptualization for developing countries" (p. 10).

The idea that conceptualization and measurement of FWB should be adapted to the culture and socioeconomic conditions of the country emerging adults live in is consistent with findings from Sorgente et al. (2024). As stated above, the five-factor model of the MSFWBS was not confirmed in India; this may be due to India being the most different country in terms of both culture and socioeconomic conditions from the other countries taken into consideration in the cross-national study (i.e., Austria, Canada, Finland, Italy, Portugal, Romania, Slovenia, and Turkey). In particular, India has a collectivistic culture (Chadda & Deb, 2013) and is classified as a developing economy (United Nations, 2014). Previous studies (e.g., Telzer et al., 2010) have demonstrated that individuals from *collectivistic countries* could have a completely different conception of money, especially when it comes to relating with other people. In particular, Telzer et al. (2010)—in a study in which they observed participants' neural reward activity while participants made decisions to contribute money to their family and themselves—found that, whereas White participants showed more reward activity when gaining cash for themselves,

Latino participants showed more reward activity when contributing to their family. Similarly, the relevance that financial independence from parents has for emerging adults changes across cultures (see Chapter 11). While in individualistic cultures being economically independent from parents is a marker of adulthood (Arnett, 2001), in collectivistic cultures, such as China (Nelson et al., 2004) and India (Seiter & Nelson, 2011), being an adult may mean being able to economically support one's parents.

Furthermore, the misfit of MSFWBS in India may also be due to the socioeconomic circumstances of the place where emerging adults live. As stressed by Mahendru et al. (2022a), what it means to thrive financially in *developing countries* may be specific to those countries. For example, in developing countries, people may evaluate their FWB by considering how much their quality of life is improving because in these countries there are very large differences in quality of economic life among citizens. In contrast, in developed countries in which the quality of life among citizens is generally sufficient, it is harder to obtain differences in objective financial circumstances that strongly affect subjective evaluations of one's quality of life.

The evidence collected by Sorgente et al. (2024) seems to confirm that both the conceptualization and measurement of emerging adults' FWB should be adapted to the country the emerging adults live in. If they live in an individualistic and economically developed country, it is very likely that the five-factor model of FWB (Sorgente & Lanz, 2019) will work well to conceptualize and measure emerging adults' FWB. Scholars are invited to administer the 25-item MSFWBS and confirm its five-factor model through a confirmatory factor analysis. If the emerging adults live in a collectivistic and/or economically developing country, we advise scholars that it is unlikely the MSFWBS will be able to accurately assess how emerging adults experience their financial condition. Unfortunately, literature is still scarce regarding how emerging adults living in collectivistic and/or economically developing countries conceptualize their FWB and, consequently, how to properly measure it. Many scholars have indeed stressed that future research on FWB should target developing countries.

In particular, regarding the *conceptualization* of FWB, Mahendru and colleagues (Mahendru, 2021; Mahendru et al., 2022a) argued that there is a need to build new theoretical models of FWB specifically suited to developing countries' situations. Mahendru (2021) stated that the "majority of the work studying financial well-being has been undertaken in the developed countries" (p. 1), but "the diverse socioeconomic, environmental conditions create disagreement on a single definition [of FWB] for developed and developing countries, thereby calling for separate conceptualization for developing countries" (p. 10). Similarly, regarding the *measurement* of FWB, Bashir and

Qureshi (2023a)'s systematic review of literature found that all scales measuring FWB "have been developed and tested in developed countries alone. This reduces the utility of using them in developing nations and also makes cross-country comparisons difficult" (p. 12). We fully agree with these calls for future studies on FWB in developing countries in order to understand how cultural and socioeconomic factors shape the meaning emerging adults attribute to their FWB. In particular, scholars need to first conduct qualitative studies (e.g., Mahendru et al., 2022a) to understand how individuals living in collectivistic and developing countries conceptualize subjective experiences of their finances. Based on these findings, a new *conceptualization* of FWB and new questionnaires (*measurement*) should be developed to properly operationalize FWB for these populations.

How to Help Emerging Adults Flourish Financially

We hope this chapter has highlighted how FWB is a complex and multidimensional construct and why, when studying it in emerging adulthood, scholars and practitioners should consider the unique factors of this stage of life as well as the cultural and socioeconomic factors of the country emerging adults live in (see Chapter 17). We are happy to end this chapter with three suggestions to help emerging adults flourish financially.

First, as reported in the introduction of this book, the Organisation for Economic Co-operation and Development (OECD, 2020) considers FWB as the final outcome of a dynamic, complex process called "financial literacy," which entails different elements like financial awareness, knowledge, skills, attitudes, behaviors, and decisions (see Chapter 1). In other words, according to OECD (2020), in order to flourish financially, individuals (including emerging adults) need to have a high level of financial knowledge and be aware of their actual level of knowledge (see Chapter 2), possess financial skills like numeracy (see Chapter 3), have positive financial attitudes like recognizing the importance of saving (see Chapter 4), enact healthy financial behaviors like the action of saving money (see Chapter 5), and make adequate financial decisions such as those based on self-control rather than impulsivity (see Chapter 6). In sum, emerging adults need to be financially competent in order to financially flourish. We refer the readers to the cited chapters for more details on the matter.

Second, it is important to recognize that FWB is a multidimensional construct. This may help both practitioners (see Box 7.1) and emerging adults themselves (see Box 7.2) understand how to improve emerging adults' FWB. In particular, because FWB encompasses many facets, practitioners should design multidimensional interventions to help their clients' FWB flourish. Similarly, emerging adults themselves should consider each dimension of their FWB and evaluate which aspects they are currently struggling with and should be more careful about.

Box 7.1 For Practitioners

Financial well-being is seen as the ultimate outcome of financial education. As this chapter has demonstrated, emerging adults' conceptualization of financial well-being is different from that of older people, and because of that, practitioners should design financial education programs, interventions, and services that take into consideration the unique factors of this stage of life. For example:

1. Financial well-being is a multidimensional construct, and its dimensions can assume a different meaning during emerging adulthood. For example, the dimension related to the future is particularly important for emerging adults. Make sure to design a service that covers all these dimensions.
2. If you are evaluating the efficacy of your financial intervention by assessing emerging adults' financial well-being before and after the intervention, make sure to adopt an instrument that has been validated on a sample of emerging adults and that accounts for the culture and socioeconomic conditions in your specific country.
3. As younger people, differently from older ones, have aspirations for financial freedom in the FIRE (Financial Independence Retire Early) sense, financial education programs should help emerging adults learn about investing, sustainable development goals, and green finance.

Box 7.2 For Emerging Adults

Are you dissatisfied with your financial condition? According to Sorgente and Lanz's (2019) model, your subjective perception of your financial condition (i.e., subjective

continued

Box 7.2 *continued*

financial well-being) may depend on five different factors. Reflect on the following questions to understand which factor(s) is influencing your perception, and then work on it:

1. Are you satisfied with your financial condition and how it makes you feel (e.g., security vs. worry)?
2. Are you satisfied with the way you manage your money?
3. Are you satisfied with the way in which your economic resources allow you to meet your needs?
4. Are you satisfied with your financial possibilities when you compare them with those of your peers?
5. Are you satisfied with how you are getting ready for the financial challenges you will likely face in the future?

Finally, we suggest that scholars, practitioners, emerging adults, and parents place appropriate value on money. Literature indeed suggests that money may not be sufficient to buy happiness. In particular, increases in individual income (i.e., OFWB) do not necessarily lead to happiness because materialistic individuals tend to be unhappier (Diener & Biswas-Diener, 2002; Ng & Diener, 2014). Increases in OFWB do not necessarily lead to increases in SFWB, as seen in research demonstrating that individuals with the same income may experience different levels of SFWB, depending on their benchmark (e.g., materialistic expectations, peer comparison; Brüggen et al., 2017; Sorgente & Lanz, 2019). Furthermore, Killingsworth et al. (2023) recently found that, for the least happy 20% of the population, an increase in income generates an increase of happiness only when income is lower than $60,000. Then, the increase of happiness flattened somewhere between $60,000 and $90,000. Put simply, for individuals who are not in poverty, people who are originally unhappy cannot become happy only via money. Individuals (including emerging adults) need to cultivate happiness in other domains of their life (e.g., friends, family, work, hobbies, attitude). We could say to emerging adults, "Money does not buy happiness. Money can only help you to better enjoy what you are cultivating outside the financial domain."

Chapter 8
Emerging Adults' Financial Stress and Financial Anxiety

Jinhee Kim[1], Swarn Chatterjee[2], and Alexander Chan[3]

Introduction

Money is one of the top stressors for many people. An American Psychological Association (APA) study found that 72% of Americans feel stressed about money at least some of the time. During difficult economic times, some people face more financial challenges than others (APA, 2015). A financial stressor is defined as a circumstance in which a person's financial needs exceed their financial ability to meet them (Lazarus & Folkman, 1984). Financial stressors can lead to the experience of financial stress, which has been defined as the negative subjective reaction or negative emotional condition an individual has regarding their finances (Falconier & Epstein, 2011; Ismail & Zaki, 2019). Financial stress is a feeling or reaction caused by financial circumstances, rather than the financial circumstance itself. Reactions to stressors are not always negative. For example, data from recent economic crises (e.g., the Great Recession, COVID-19) show that some couples, given adequate social support and effective coping skills, can emerge from financial crises with increased commitment and relationship satisfaction (Dew et al., 2018; Kelley et al., 2023; LeBaron et al., 2020). However, the focus of this chapter will be on the disadvantageous outcomes of financial stress. This literature provides insights into the proper support and resources that help individuals deal with financial stress.

Financial stress may be experienced by both lower- and higher-resource individuals. Any individual experiencing financial stress may suffer severe adverse outcomes. Studies have found that adverse mental health outcomes

[1] Department of Family Science, University of Maryland, USA
[2] Department of Financial Planning, Housing, and Consumer Economics, University of Georgia, USA
[3] University of Maryland Extension, University of Maryland, USA

Jinhee Kim, Swarn Chatterjee, and Alexander Chan, *Emerging Adults' Financial Stress and Financial Anxiety.* In: *Flourishing and Floundering Financially in Emerging Adulthood.* Edited by: Ashley B. LeBaron-Black, Heather Kelley, and Angela Sorgente, Oxford University Press. © Oxford University Press (2025). DOI: 10.1093/9780197699157.003.0009

as a result of financial stress are particularly common among low-income individuals, those with limited access to resources, and marginalized racial and ethnic groups (see Chapters 15 and 17; Qian & Fan, 2021; Williams et al., 1997). Other studies document a positive relationship between financial stress, depression, and other negative mental health outcomes; generally, the relationship is stronger among those with low income or wealth (Bøe et al., 2017; Guan et al., 2022; Northern et al., 2010). In this context, the wealth effect, described as the outcome of changes in the amount left over after subtracting one's liabilities from assets, is more of a psychological concept where a negative change in wealth is associated with an adverse effect on individuals' perception of their financial well-being (Brulé & Suter, 2019). On the other hand, an income effect is characterized as the effect of the perception of an individual's income (i.e., amount earned over a specific period) relative to their immediate reference group. Individuals are more likely to feel financially stressed when their income is lower than the income of their immediate reference group of neighbors, friends, colleagues, and relatives (Ferrer-i-Carbonell, 2005).

Financial stress has been linked to several negative mental health– and physical health–related outcomes such as depression, increased blood pressure, and even suicidal thoughts (Bridges & Disney, 2010; Chen et al., 2022; Drentea & Reynolds, 2012; Friedline et al., 2017; Sweet et al., 2013). Financial stress has also been associated with increased general anxiety and financial anxiety of individuals (Archuleta et al., 2013; Cooke et al., 2004; Greenglass & Mara, 2012; Hall et al., 2009; Jessop et al., 2005; Northern et al., 2010). The term "financial anxiety" has been introduced to describe anxious feelings or worries related to finances (Archuleta et al., 2013). Financial anxiety includes feelings of worry, uneasiness, or distress that may arise from experiencing financial stress associated with income or job loss, high debt burden, or unexpected expenses. However, financial anxiety is distinct from financial stress in that it can occur in the absence of financial stressors. Prior research establishes financial anxiety as an overall anxious avoidant response to financial stimuli (Shapiro & Burchell, 2012). In sum, financial stress is generally tied to financial stressors, whereas financial anxiety encapsulates an individual's overall psychological and physiological response to external or internal stimuli (e.g., thoughts about financial matters; Lee et al., 2023). Financial anxiety can result in physical symptoms like headaches, difficulty sleeping, and irritability, as well as emotional symptoms like feelings of hopelessness and depression (Sweet et al., 2013).

Emerging adulthood is an important developmental phase that individuals go through between adolescence and adulthood, encompassing a period from the late teens to late twenties (Arnett, 2000). This period is characterized by exploration, identity formation, and developments in multiple areas, including education (see Chapter 9), career (see Chapter 10), and relationships (see Chapter 14; Arnett, 2000). The quantity and intensity of life transitions can lead to higher levels of stress and other mental health concerns for some emerging adults (Archuleta et al., 2013; Chatterjee et al., 2021a; Matud et al., 2020). In the transitional period of financial independence (see Chapter 11), several studies indicate that emerging adults experience high levels of financial stress (Andrews & Wilding, 2004; Bøe et al., 2017; Eagan et al., 2016; Guan et al., 2022; Sweet et al., 2013; Tran et al., 2018). Previous studies document that financial stress experienced by emerging adults has been associated with poor academic performance, suicidal thoughts, financial anxiety, and adverse or languishing mental health status (Andrews & Wilding, 2004; Borden et al., 2008; Britt et al., 2015; Roberts et al., 1999). Bialik and Fry (2019) found that although emerging adults in 2016 were better educated than earlier generations, they also carried more student loan debt than previous generational cohorts. Moreover, emerging adults from racial and ethnic minority backgrounds carry a disproportionately higher student loan debt burden (Holzer & Baum, 2017). Overall, financial debt burden, including student loan debt and credit card debt, has been negatively associated with emerging adults' mental health in the past literature (see Chapters 9 and 13; Archuleta et al., 2013; Kim & Chatterjee, 2021; Liu et al., 2023).

De Bassa Scheresberg (2013) found that many emerging adults had lower levels of financial literacy (see Chapter 2) and were more likely to make poor financial choices (see Chapter 6) that could result in financial stress and negative outcomes related to their well-being. McCloud and Bann (2019) found that financial stress was negatively associated with the mental health of emerging adults. Additionally, in prior literature, mental health–related issues such as anxiety and depression have been found to be predictors and outcomes of financial strain (Choung et al., 2022; Drentea & Lavrakas, 2000). Financial stress and anxiety among emerging adults are a growing concern and can have a significant impact on their workplace productivity, academic success, and overall well-being (Kim et al., 2006; Shim et al., 2009). However, managing financial stress successfully with capabilities could promote increased growth in couple relationships (Dew et al., 2018; Kelley et al., 2023; LeBaron et al., 2020). Financial capabilities such as financial management behavior (see Chapter 5) could mediate the effects of financial stress on mental health and well-being (Rahman et al., 2021). It is possible to help emerging adults increase their financial capabilities to address their financial stress. Therefore, it is important to further study the financial stress and financial anxiety of emerging adults to ensure their well-being and promote financial resiliency.

The remainder of this chapter explores various factors associated with financial stress and financial anxiety and how these factors are connected to financial attitudes (see Chapter 4), behavior (see Chapter 5), and the financial and overall well-being of emerging adults (see Chapter 7). Implications for future research and practice are also discussed.

Predictors of Financial Stress and Financial Anxiety

Financial Literacy

"Financial literacy," the ability to understand and apply financial concepts effectively, is a critical determinant of financial health (see Chapter 1; Lusardi et al., 2010). Many emerging adults lack the financial literacy necessary to make informed financial decisions (see Chapter 6) and successfully manage their finances (see Chapter 5). A lack of financial literacy can lead to poor money management practices, higher debt burden (see Chapter 13), and inadequate savings, all of which contribute to poor financial health (Lusardi & Mitchell, 2014; Lyons et al., 2006).

Financial literacy is negatively associated with financial stress and financial anxiety among emerging adults (Lusardi et al., 2010), which means that emerging adults with lower levels of financial literacy, who often carry higher levels of debt, are more likely to experience adverse mental health concerns such as financial stress and anxiety (Archuleta et al., 2013; Callendar & De Gayardon, 2021). Social comparison, or the process of comparing oneself financially to others, can heighten financial stress and anxiety, particularly when individuals perceive that their financial situation is inferior to that of their peers (see Chapters 4, 10, and 13; Serido et al., 2013). Additionally, cultural expectations related to financial success, independence, and consumerism can create pressure for emerging adults to achieve certain financial milestones (see Chapters 11 and 13; Chatterjee et al., 2021a), further exacerbating financial stress and anxiety.

Financial Attitudes

"Financial attitudes" can be described as beliefs, feelings, and principles that individuals have toward money and financial resources (see Chapter 4; Shim et al., 2010). Financial attitudes play an important role in shaping how emerging adults manage their finances (see Chapter 5) and cope with financial stress. In previous studies, financial attitudes and behaviors were associated with financial well-being (see Chapter 7; Kim, 2004). Serido et al. (2020) found in their study that emerging adults' financial worry about having adequate financial resources to meet their needs was positively associated with having higher levels of financial stress and anxiety. Several other studies have investigated the relationship between financial attitudes and financial stress among emerging adults. A study of first-year college students at a large U.S. land-grant university by Shim et al. (2010) found that undesirable financial attitudes, such as financial distrust and perceived lack of confidence about managing money, were associated with higher levels of financial stress. Similarly, a study of college students at a large Midwestern public land-grant university by Britt et al. (2015) found that financial attitudes such as financial satisfaction were significantly associated with financial stress. A study by Hira and Mugenda (1999) continues to support existing literature by showing that financial attitudes, such as financial locus of control, mediated the relationship between financial stress and depression among respondents. Additionally, Prawitz et al. (2006) found that financial attitudes were significant predictors of financial stress for both males and females, but the association was stronger for females, and the association between financial attitudes and financial stress was also stronger for minority racial and ethnic groups (Kim et al., 2017).

Employment status, income, financial socialization in childhood, closeness to mother, and parental resources were positively associated with financial health and financial behavior in emerging adulthood (Kim & Chatterjee, 2013, Kim et al., 2012; Shim et al., 2010; Xiao et al., 2014). Emerging adults' higher levels of financial resources were associated with holding positive financial attitudes (Kim & Chatterjee, 2013).

Financial Self-Efficacy, Financial Behavior, and Financial Stress in Emerging Adulthood

"Financial self-efficacy" refers to individuals' belief in their ability to manage their finances effectively (see Chapter 4; Bandura, 1977, 2006; Chatterjee et al., 2011). Emerging adults with high financial self-efficacy tend to engage in more responsible financial behaviors (Serido et al., 2020). Shim et al. (2019) found that individuals who had lower levels of financial self-efficacy were more likely to perceive stress in their ability to pay off their debt. Similarly, financial knowledge, or individuals' understanding of financial concepts and principles (see Chapter 2), is positively associated with better financial management practices (Lusardi et al., 2010). Emerging adults with higher financial knowledge are more likely to make informed financial decisions, save more, and avoid debt (Chen & Volpe, 1998).

"Financial behaviors" include the decisions that individuals make in managing their finances, such as budgeting, saving, investing, and borrowing (see Chapter 5; Shim et al., 2010). Emerging adults who engage in negative financial behaviors are more likely to experience financial stress and poor financial well-being (Serido et al., 2020). Studies have shown that irresponsible financial behaviors, such as overspending, carrying credit card balances, and failing to plan for financial goals, can lead to financial stress and financial insecurity (see Chapter 13; Klontz et al., 2012). Similarly, in a study using a national sample of emerging adults ages 17–21 from 2005, Kim and Chatterjee (2013) found that higher levels of credit card debt were associated with higher levels of financial stress and anxiety. Serido et al. (2014) used the National Longitudinal Study of Adolescent Health and found that respondents experiencing financial strain were more likely to engage in alcohol misuse as a coping strategy.

Family of Origin Influences

Family of origin also plays an important role in emerging adults' financial behaviors. Parental financial socialization, or the process through which parents transmit financial knowledge, attitudes, and behaviors to their children, plays an important role in the development of financial behaviors of emerging adults (see Chapter 18; Gudmunson & Danes, 2011; Kim & Chatterjee, 2013). Emerging adults who lack financial literacy, or those who may not have experienced adequate financial socialization in their childhood, are more likely to avoid positive financial behaviors as they navigate their financial independence. LeBaron-Black et al. (2022a) found that financial socialization by modeling parental behavior was associated directly with the financial behaviors and satisfaction of emerging adults and was associated indirectly with other financial outcomes. Financial socialization from child–parent conversations and discussions did not have significant direct or indirect associations with emerging adults' financial behaviors or outcomes.

Finally, LeBaron-Black et al. (2022b) found that financial socialization was negatively associated with anxiety and depression among emerging adults and was positively associated with emerging adults' life satisfaction. Moreover, those emerging adults who received better financial socialization were more likely to have an internal locus of control, which reduced their likelihood of experiencing anxiety or depression.

Outcomes of Financial Stress in Emerging Adults

Theorized Mechanisms Linking Financial Strain and Mental Health Outcomes

Past studies have found three primary mechanisms that link debt and other forms of financial stressors to adverse mental health outcomes (Guan et al., 2022). The first mechanism is through social causation (Guan et al., 2022). The social causation theory posits that individuals from households with low financial resources (income and wealth) were more likely to experience greater income and economic uncertainty, utilize unhealthy coping mechanisms, and experience adverse physical health, mental health, and food security outcomes (Kim et al., 2016; Lund & Cois, 2018; Reading & Reynolds, 2001). The second mechanism through which financial stressors may affect well-being is adverse psychological outcomes. Previous studies have shown that debt burden was associated with adverse mental health outcomes for individuals, especially if the individual perceived the debt burden as stressful (Asebedo & Wilmarth, 2017; Bridges & Disney, 2010; Kim & Chatterjee, 2021). The third mechanism through which financial stressors can lead to adverse health-related outcomes is social selection. The social selection theory posits that individuals who are depressed or have a floundering mental health status are more likely to experience financial stress, which, in turn, may further affect their mental and physical well-being (Lund & Cois, 2018; Lund et al., 2010).

Financial Stress and Health and Well-Being

"Financial well-being" has been defined as a construct that encompasses an individual's perception of their financial situation, financial satisfaction, financial security, and financial stability (see Chapter 7; Brüggen et al., 2017). Robb and Chy (2023) found that "financial stress" was negatively associated with financial well-being of emerging adults. Conversely, responsible financial behaviors, such as saving regularly, paying bills on time, and avoiding high-cost debt, are associated with better financial well-being (see Chapter 5; Hira & Mugenda, 1999; Lown et al., 2015; Kim & Chatterjee, 2013).

Past studies have also found that financial stress was associated with negative outcomes, including symptoms of depression and diminished perception of well-being among emerging adults (Friedline et al., 2017). Moreover, emerging adult men are more likely to experience mental health concerns related to debt burden and are more likely to engage in substance misuse such as smoking and binge drinking (Qian & Fan, 2021) in response to these stressors. Additionally, emerging adults with poor financial health are more likely to experience barriers to accessing credit and healthcare, and have increased risk of experiencing negative health outcomes due to lack of financial resources (Pollack & Lynch, 2009; Woolf et al., 2015).

Financial stressors associated with emerging adulthood are conceivably connected with survival (i.e., shelter, resource scarcity), and thus may activate stress response systems such as fight-or-flight (Cannon, 1932). LeBaron-Black et al. (2022c) found that financial distress experienced during the COVID-19 pandemic partially mediated the association between COVID-19-related stress and anxiety among emerging adults and fully mediated the association between COVID-19-related stress and depression.

Mental Health and Financial Stressors among Emerging Adults

Financial stressors and mental health share a bidirectional relationship. Financial stressors predict adverse mental health concerns (Drentea & Lavrakas, 2000), and individuals with anxiety or depression are more likely to report financial strain, miscalibrate their retirement planning horizon, and have difficulty paying bills (Choung et al., 2022; Drentea & Lavrakas, 2000). Thus, financial stressors and mental health have the potential to create a self-reinforcing spiral of negative outcomes, especially when negative coping strategies are employed.

Mental health concerns can adversely affect an individual's ability to work, thus compromising their income-earning capacity and financial stability (see Chapter 10). According to Richardson and colleagues' (2013) meta-analysis, 78.5% of studies reported that being in debt was related to poor health outcomes. Financial stressors, including carrying debt, can bring along many health-related concerns, such as being unable to afford healthcare and certain prescriptions, being unable to keep doctors' appointments, depression, suicide attempts, and a variety of other mental health–related issues. Consequently, these challenges can result in higher debt levels, reduced savings, and increased overall financial strain. Another study found that emerging adults with mental health concerns were more likely to have lower incomes, higher levels of debt, and lower financial satisfaction than their peers without mental health concerns (Narendorf & Palmer, 2016).

Individuals experiencing adverse mental health outcomes are less likely to be able to maintain stable employment (Paul & Moser, 2009). According to the Paul and Moser study, mental health concerns such as anxiety and depression can impair cognitive functioning, which may affect job performance and reduce work productivity. As a result, individuals with poor mental health may experience job loss, reduced work hours, and lower earnings compared to those without mental health concerns. Additionally, individuals with mental health concerns may incur additional costs associated with seeking treatment and care. These expenses can be significant financial stressors for emerging adults who are already experiencing high levels of financial stress and anxiety.

Effects of Financial Stress on Mental Health and Relationship Functioning

Overall, financial stress has been linked to negative health outcomes, such as financial anxiety and depression, which, in turn, can impair an individual's ability to work and function productively (Kim et al., 2006; Kim & Garman, 2004; Zhang & Chatterjee, 2023). Chronic financial stress has been associated with mental health concerns such as languishing or floundering mentally (Knoesen & Naude, 2018). Past research has shown that financial stress was also associated with a higher risk of suicide among emerging adults during periods of greater social isolation amid prevailing economic- and health-related uncertainty, such as during the COVID-19 pandemic (Chen et al., 2022).

Debt is linked to a higher incidence of arguments over money and is negatively associated with relationship satisfaction (Chatterjee et al., 2021b). Past research has also found that effective financial communication can moderate the association between financial stress and negative relationship outcomes (Wikle et al., 2021). Additionally, financial stress and anxiety may lead to social isolation because emerging adults may feel embarrassed or ashamed of their financial struggles and withdraw from social interactions (Falconier et al., 2015; Serido et al., 2013).

Coping with Financial Stress and Anxiety

Regardless of the source of anxiety, chronic experiences of anxiety place emerging adults at a higher risk of depression (Riggs & Han, 2009). Understanding how emerging adults cope with stress can inform educational approaches to reducing the effects of chronic financial stressors. Past literature has identified several coping mechanisms that emerging adults use to cope with stress. Approach and avoidance are two strategies commonly used to characterize a person's response to a stressful situation (Roth & Cohen, 1986). People are not uniformly approachers or avoiders; it is common for an individual to apply both approach and avoidance strategies to the same problem. Emerging adults who report greater sensitivity to negative emotions tend to use more avoidant coping strategies. This also includes a reliance on others to help them manage negative feelings, rather than employing strategies that directly address the stressor (Jenzer et al., 2019). With respect to financial approach and avoidance, the experience of financial scarcity is positively related to financial avoidance (Hilbert et al., 2022). Furthermore, avoidance is also positively related to financial scarcity. In other words, scarcity generates anxiety, which individuals may respond to by using avoidant strategies. These avoidant coping mechanisms may lead to poorer financial choices or a lack of action to directly address the problem (Hilbert et al., 2022).

Jenzer et al. (2019) found that avoidant coping tends to decline during emerging adulthood, but that emerging adults are not necessarily replacing avoidant strategies with more adaptive or approach-based coping strategies. Research also shows that those individuals who switch from approach- (e.g., problem solving, eliciting social support, cognitive reframing) to avoidance-based coping show increases in depressive symptoms (Herman-Stabl et al., 1995). This suggests that educational interventions to reduce avoidance-based coping with financial stressors are relevant and may curb the onset of depressive symptoms in emerging adulthood.

Implications

Several associations between financial stress, financial anxiety, and overall well-being have been discussed in this chapter. Some studies have shown the effectiveness of providing emerging adults access to behavioral, cognitive, and mindfulness-related intervention programs in promoting their overall well-being (Regehr et al., 2013). Perreault et al. (2017) suggest that providing individuals easier access to mental health–related services in communities can help in the management and promotion of mental health and well-being within communities. Cobb (1976) has also suggested the importance of providing greater social support for alleviating stress in communities. In this regard, Goetz et al. (2011) found that providing peer financial education within college campuses provided an effective intervention resulting in positive outcomes for college students.

Stein et al. (2013) found that symptoms associated with financial anxiety, and the related risk of depression, are reduced when emerging adults employ education and communication strategies to help manage their finances. Furthermore, research has suggested that financial education may help to improve financial attitudes and reduce financial stress (Friedline et al., 2017; Short et al., 2019). Serido et al. (2010) found that emerging adults who employed budgeting and investing as coping strategies to manage their financial anxiety reported better psychological well-being. Roy and Andrews (2008) also suggest that providing greater financial education can help emerging adults improve their financial self-efficacy and confidence in managing their finances, which, in turn, can help in reducing their perceived financial stress. Other studies have also found that emerging adults with good financial health report better physical and mental health outcomes (Kim & Chatterjee, 2021; Shim et al., 2009). Furthermore, having a strong sense of financial control and stability can lead to increased feelings of confidence, security, and overall well-being (Fan et al., 2022). Overall, education has the potential to promote approach-based coping techniques as replacements for the avoidant strategies that many emerging adults employ with respect to financial management (Kim et al., 2017). For example, financial education (see Chapter 19) could help people with knowledge (see Chapter 2) and skills (see Chapter 3), which can help alleviate the impacts of financial stressors and prevent future financial crises.

Addressing the existing financial disparities among women (see Chapter 16), racial and ethnic minorities (see Chapter 17), and other underserved populations (see Chapter 15) is critical to reducing financial stress and anxiety and thus promoting financial health and well-being among all emerging adults (Fry, 2014). Financial education programs (see Chapter 19) can provide emerging adults with the knowledge (see Chapter 2) and skills (see Chapter 3) necessary to make informed financial decisions (see Chapter 6) and manage their finances effectively (see Chapter 5; Lyons et al., 2006). A study by Mandell and Klein (2009) found that financial education programs significantly improved financial attitudes (see Chapter 4) and reduced financial stress among emerging adults.

Research has shown that providing access to financial counseling and therapy services can help emerging adults develop communication and conflict resolution skills to navigate financial stress in their personal relationships (see Chapter 14; Goetz et al., 2011). Finally, fostering healthy coping mechanisms, such as engaging in physical activity, practicing mindfulness, or seeking social support, can help emerging adults manage financial stress and protect their mental health (Heckman et al., 2014).

Some researchers suggest that helping individuals and families that are experiencing financial crises to develop positive meanings about their situation, such as mental reframing, staying positive, and focusing on gratitude, could help them better cope with financial stressors (Kelley et al., 2023;

LeBaron et al., 2020). Understanding resilience factors and coping strategies is critical in creating support and resources for financially distressed emerging adults. However, without appropriate management, emerging adults' financial crises could lead to accumulated financial strains and long-term adverse health outcomes (Ferraro & Shippee, 2009).

While addressing the financial stress and anxiety of emerging adults is valuable, addressing emerging adults' underlying mental health is also important. If stress is left unattended for an extended period of time, it can have harmful effects on short- and long-term decision-making processes, including financial ones. Providing emerging adults with access to professional help and developing a comprehensive approach that encompasses financial, emotional, and mental well-being are crucial for promoting positive outcomes among emerging adults. However, more evaluative research is needed to examine whether interventions that build financial management skills and competencies across time can help emerging adults manage stress and anxiety. For example, although research has shown that providing access to financial counseling and therapy services can help emerging adults develop communication and conflict resolution skills to navigate financial stress in their personal relationships (Goetz et al., 2011), more research is needed to understand the extent to which financial counseling and therapy-related services can be effective in developing greater resiliency among emerging adults across time.

There is also a need for future research that examines the pathways through which emerging adults' financial stress affects their financial management (see Chapter 5) and long-term decisions (see Chapter 6) such as education (see Chapter 9), career (see Chapter 10), relationships (see Chapter 14), and independence (see Chapter 11). It is likely that simply teaching financial literacy may not be sufficient if emerging adults are overwhelmed by stress and anxiety because their emotions can compromise their ability to apply their knowledge effectively. Adopting a holistic approach that combines financial management education with stress management and coping strategies holds promise.

Studies have shown that incorporating mindfulness-related stress reduction strategies through cognitive–behavioral therapy (a type of psychological treatment; Beck, 2011) is effective in reducing stress and anxiety and in improving emotional regulation and life satisfaction for high school females and college students (Dvořáková et al., 2017; Shahidi et al., 2017). It is possible that incorporating similar mindfulness skills or cognitive–behavioral techniques into financial education programs could help emerging adults develop the skills to manage negative emotions and regulate stress effectively.

By simultaneously addressing financial stress and anxiety management, individuals may be better equipped to make informed financial decisions, practice self-control, and prioritize long-term goals regarding their financial well-being.

Conclusion

Emerging adults experience high levels of financial stress that can lead to adverse mental and physical issues. Notably, financial stress is disproportionately high among underprivileged groups such as low-income emerging adults (see Chapter 15), first-generation college students, and racial and ethnic minority emerging adults (see Chapter 17). Financial literacy, financial self-efficacy, high debt burdens, income, and other factors contribute to financial stress. Financial stressors can have long-term impacts on the health and well-being of emerging adults by interfering with their education (see Chapter 9), career choices (see Chapter 10), relationship formation (see Chapter 14), and financial and residential independence (see Chapter 11). Financial stress is also associated with anxiety, financial anxiety, and other mental health concerns. Conversely, anxiety and financial anxiety can negatively affect the coping and management of individuals, leading to higher levels of financial stress. If a person's response to stress and anxiety relies on avoidance, financial problems are more likely. Additionally, anxiety has been negatively associated with self-control. A lack of self-control is associated with impulse buying, with a focus on the present rather than on delayed gratification (see Chapter 6). Effective interventions may include an integrative approach to addressing financial capability and literacy that includes helping emerging adults manage negative emotions such as stress and anxiety. It is critical to provide financial assistance and economic opportunities for those who experience high levels of financial stress with inadequate support systems.

PART II

FINANCIAL CONSIDERATIONS IN EMERGING ADULTHOOD

Chapter 9
College and Student Loans in Emerging Adulthood

Yoon G. Lee[1] *and Emily Hales*[2]

Introduction

One of the first financial decisions an emerging adult makes is if they should pursue a college education. Emerging adults might consider where the school is and what programs are offered, but they also need to be aware of the price tag. More individuals are choosing to attend college, whether to earn a degree or progress in their career and be more competitive in the job market (see Chapter 10), all while college costs in the United States continue to rise (Baggett & Cole, 2022; Baker et al., 2017; Cho et al., 2015; Johnson et al., 2016). This one decision, almost forced upon emerging adults, becomes debt they will be paying off for decades, and the student loan debt will go on to impact an individual's financial well-being (see Chapter 7), stress (see Chapter 8), and financial goals (Baker & Montalto, 2019; Cherney et al., 2020; Dynarski, 2016; Elliott & Lewis, 2015; Kim & Chatterjee, 2019; Kim et al., 2021; Lee et al., 2018; Walsemann et al., 2015).

As the cost of secondary education rises, student loans have become an issue around the globe. Many other countries are also experiencing some version of a student loan crisis, with student loan debt in the United Kingdom at almost $260 billion, Canada at $40 billion, and Australia borrowers sharing over $74 billion (Bolton, 2023; Ey, 2023; Wong, 2023). Yet these numbers pale in comparison to the United States student loan debt total of over $1.7 trillion, including federal and private loans (Hahn & Tarver, 2023). Because student loan debt is significantly higher in the United States than in other countries, understanding the characteristics and impacts of student loans in the United States could provide crucial insight to educating emerging adults and suggest

[1] Department of Human Development and Family Studies, Utah State University, USA
[2] Kaplan North America, USA

Yoon G. Lee and Emily Hales, *College and Student Loans in Emerging Adulthood*. In: *Flourishing and Floundering Financially in Emerging Adulthood*. Edited by: Ashley B. LeBaron-Black, Heather Kelley, and Angela Sorgente, Oxford University Press. © Oxford University Press (2025). DOI: 10.1093/9780197699157.003.0010

important implications for financial practitioners and emerging adults in the United States and other countries.

This chapter first reviews background information on why a college education is valuable and prevalent, and why student loans are in crisis in the United States. This chapter also reviews the literature about student loans across generations and the role of financial literacy and education in student loan decisions. The chapter further reviews the research on what sociodemographic factors are associated with student loan decisions and how holding student debt is associated with the financial well-being of borrowers in general. Finally, the chapter suggests important key points for financial practitioners and emerging adults.

Literature Review

College Education and Human Capital Investments

A college education is something many Americans strive for in their life (Hanson, 2024g; U.S. Bureau of Labor Statistics, 2020). This could be because formal education increases an individual's human capital (Rothstein & Rouse, 2011; Stark & Poppler, 2016). Human capital can be defined as the skills and knowledge that individuals possess which allow them to become more valuable in their workplace (Becker, 1993; Crook et al., 2011; Schultz, 1961; Ueda, 2019). Research has shown that human capital can influence personal income and growth in employment, health, and other life areas (Kenton, 2023; Mincer, 1958). Thus, many emerging adults are willing to pay for higher formal education in hopes of increasing their human capital in specific career fields and professions (see Chapter 10; Hess et al., 1994).

A study found that those who attended college received greater returns in terms of their wages (Carneiro et al., 2010). Median earnings are 84% higher for college-graduates than those who did not receive education after high school (Association of Public Land-Grant Universities, 2023). Despite the issues brought by student loans, the more student loan debt an individual had when graduating from college, the more likely they were to get higher-paying jobs or full-time employment (Luong, 2010), and emerging adults with a college education tended to report higher rate of homeownership than those without a college education (Dynarski, 2016).

However, taking out student loans is not always the best option. A study found that the more student loan debt an individual carried for their education, the less likely they are to continue to a graduate degree (Fox et al., 2017).

According to a recent statistic, about 40% of student loan borrowers did not complete a college degree (Greenberg, 2022). Furthermore, individuals without a degree were more likely to be unemployed than those with a degree (Bouchrika, 2023; Gladieux & Perna, 2005). Thus, when an emerging adult takes out a student loan, future and current employment opportunities should be thoroughly considered.

The Student Loan Crisis in the United States

The demand for a college degree in the workplace is growing (see Chapter 10), yet many individuals cannot afford to earn a degree without taking on tens of thousands of dollars of student loan debt (Akers & Chingos, 2014; Baker et al., 2017; Cho et al., 2015; Johnson et al., 2016). For example, the average cost of attendance at a public four-year institution in the United States is about $26,027 per year, or a total of $104,108 over 4 years (Hanson, 2024b). The average cost of attendance at a private, nonprofit university is about $55,840 per year, or a total of $223,360 over 4 years (Hanson, 2024b). However, most students take longer than 4 years to earn their undergraduate degree, and these statistics do not include room/board, school materials, and other living expenses.

The United States is infamous for their student loan debt crisis, which is shared among 43.6 million student loan borrowers in 2023 (Federal Reserve Bank of New York, 2023; Hahn & Tarver, 2023). As of the end of 2022, the average student loan borrower held about $37,574 of student loan debt (Welding, 2023). Student loans may seem necessary to achieve a college degree, yet student loans are influencing individuals' lives in dramatic ways. Committing to student loan debt may not feel as overwhelming as other debts due to the role student loans play in earning a college education. However, student loans are a type of debt that individuals carry for decades and can add to one's financial stress and burden (Britt et al., 2017).

Outside of the United States, student loan debt looks different because many countries have implemented strategies to reduce tuition costs and improve student loan programs. Many other countries offer government-funded post-secondary education, such as Denmark, Brazil, Germany, Finland, Ireland, Norway, and Poland (Kirkham, 2018; Value Colleges, 2020). In these countries, colleges are funded by the government through taxes and other resources. Even in countries where college is not government-funded, student loan options and payment plans are more straightforward. For example, Australia has implemented a unique version of the income-based repayment plan for all student loan borrowers (Dickler, 2018; Kirkham, 2018). This universal income-based repayment plan does not require payments until graduates make at least $40,000 per year, and student loan payments are automatically taken from an individual's bank account, making payments more convenient and reducing student loan default rates (Dickler, 2018).

In the United States, there are several options for student loans and payment plans. Different ideas have been proposed to handle this increasing student debt, such as adjusted payment plans, loan consolidation techniques, expanded public employee loan forgiveness, and even massive student loan forgiveness for all borrowers. The income-based repayment plan allows student loan payments to be adjusted to consume 10% of discretionary income (Federal Student Aid, 2024a; Mueller & Yannelis, 2019). While the United States has numerous payment plan options for student loan borrowers, certain plans can only apply toward specific loan types or specific occupations. Some may argue that the United States still forgives some student loan debt. However, this is often after an individual carries the debt for 20–25 years or through a public service loan forgiveness program (Consumer Financial Protection Bureau, 2023). While various parties attempt to find a more permanent solution to the student loan debt crisis, student loan debt is affecting both new and old borrowers, even throughout their post-education lives.

Another student loan problem in the United States is college dropout rates. While some individuals with a college degree can find a job with higher income, other individuals drop out from college and end up with lower income and struggle to pay their student loan debt (Bouchrika, 2023). Approximately, 39% of college students drop out of college every year (Hanson, 2024e). Those who drop out of college make 35% less than those who hold a bachelor's degree, and they are 20% more likely to be unemployed (Hanson, 2024e). These higher dropout rates and lower college graduation rates may have been caused by the costs of a college education in the United States, which are continually increasing. The costs are significantly more than those in many other countries such as Canada, Japan, South Korea, and other European countries (Hanson, 2024a). All of these factors combine to form a large problem. Student loan research has been conducted for years; however, in the last couple of decades, personal finance professionals have started to focus more on this fast-growing issue (Dillon & Carey, 2009; Fry, 2012; Kim et al., 2012; Redd, 2001; Scott-Clayton, 2018). Researchers in the field of personal finance have sought to understand the impact of student loans and found that student loan debt influences numerous financial and personal aspects of an individual's life. This can include lower net worth, poor mental health, delayed home buying, increased financial distress, and decreased financial well-being (Britt et al., 2017; Elliott & Lewis, 2015; Mountain et al., 2020; Walsemann et al., 2015). While research has revealed some of the significant impacts that student loans may have on an individual, there are still many questions surrounding student loan use and behaviors, especially among emerging adults who are taking out student loans to fund their college education.

Student Loan Repayment and Default in the United States

Student loans are accumulated during formal education and often have a deferment period while the individual is still in school. When individuals take out a student loan, they are usually offered a certain amount per school year, and they can decide how much of the loan they need (Federal Student Aid, 2024b). If there is any tuition or fees on the student's account when they take out the loan, this is paid off using the loan. If there is any funding remaining after tuition and other costs are paid, the student may receive the remainder of the loan in cash. Students can decide whether to return the excess loan funds, reducing their total student loan liability, or they can keep this refund and apply it toward "educational expenses," which can include housing, groceries, and other cost-of-living expenses the student may incur while at school (Delisle & Holt, 2015).

Previous study has found that emerging adults entering college generally are unable to pay for tuition without taking out student loans, and they also rely on advice from guidance counselors, parents, and friends when making these decisions (Griffiths, 2022; Hawkins, 2017; Johnson et al., 2016). Because they rely so heavily on this advice, emerging adults often do not know much about the loans they will need to repay (Johnson et al., 2016; Kyaw, 2020). Another study indicated that only about 20% of students tried to calculate their student loan payments and almost half of all students had no idea how much they would be paying on their student loans after graduation (Andruska et al., 2014; Montalto et al., 2019). Students may be most concerned with completing their education now, pushing off the concerns of student loan repayment until after graduating from college.

Once an individual takes out a student loan, federal student loans allow a 6-month grace period from either graduation or leaving a program before payments begin (Federal Student Aid, 2024c). Student loans are a long-term debt, with most repayment plans lasting 10 years (Federal Student Aid,

2024d). Because of this lengthy period, it becomes important to develop positive repayment habits to maintain a positive standing on one's student loans. Previous studies indicated that completing one's degree and being employed were strong predictors of student loan repayment, but family income was not a significant predictor (Hillman, 2014; Lochner et al., 2013).

Many student loan borrowers adjust their repayment plan during the repayment period, often extending loan periods, and some will proceed to default on their loans. Aside from formal repayment, student loans are nearly impossible to remove, with student loan forgiveness reserved for public service positions having strict requirements and very little chance of student loans being removed if the borrower later files a bankruptcy petition (Austin, 2013). Every year, 4 million federal student loans enter default, and 1 out of every 10 Americans has defaulted on a student loan (Hanson, 2024e). Default begins after the borrower has been delinquent for 270 days, meaning they have not made a payment on their student loans in 9 months (Federal Student Aid, 2024e; Montalto et al., 2019). When individuals default on their student loans, they are in danger of wage garnishment, tax withholdings, and poor credit reporting (National Consumer Law Center, 2023).

With so many student loan borrowers defaulting on their loans, it is important for researchers to understand what characteristics may influence student loan repayment behavior. Minority students and males were more likely to default on their student loans, even though it took females longer to pay off their student loan debt (Montalto et al., 2019). Those who come from low-income families and borrowers who attended proprietary schools and 2-year colleges were more likely to default on paying their student loans (Dynarski, 1994; Miller, 2019). Student loan default rates spiked during the Great Recession; however, the introduction of the Income-Based Repayment Plan in 2009 has since helped to reduce student loan default rates (Mueller & Yannelis, 2019).

Student Loans across Generations

In research, differences in student loan borrowings can often be found across generations such as baby boomers (those born from 1946 to 1964), Generation X (1965–1980), millennials (1981–1997), and the up-and-coming Generation Z (1998–2012) (Fry, 2016). The baby boomer generation saw the creation of the federal student loan program in 1958, as part of the National Defense Education Act (New America, 2020). Before this program was established, individuals questioned the concept of taking on debt to fund education, similar to taking on a mortgage to buy a home (Overs, 1957). Within the next few decades, student loan debt had become a national issue, with an increase in student loan defaults and requests for student loan discharge through bankruptcy prompting concerns about the federal program and its structure (Kirkpatrick, 1968).

In the late 1980s, when Generation Xers were emerging adults, student loan research was already examining the growing debt crisis and its consequences, such as excessive debt, student loan default, and student loan repayment (Cronin & Simmons, 1987; Greene, 1989; Hansen, 1987; Hansen & Rhodes, 1988). The average student graduated with almost $7,000 in student loan debt ($13,500 in today's dollars), and anxiety around the student loan debt crisis grew over time for Generation Xers (Wilkerson, 1987). Generation X also experienced slow wage increases and accelerated college tuition costs (similar to what millennials contended with), which pushed many to take on student loans (Draut & Silva, 2004).

In the last 20 years, student loan debt has increased by more than a trillion dollars (Hanson, 2024d; Welding, 2024). Most college students during this time have been millennials (30.3%), with Generation Z now in the process of gaining their college education (Hanson, 2023). The millennial generation has taken on greater amounts of debt in student loans and other debts (Mountain et al. 2020), and the financial burden of student loans could delay the homeownership timing among millennials with student loan debt (Mountain et al., 2020). Fry (2014) found that the average age of student loan holders was about 31 after the Great Recession, indicating that student loan debt now impacts millennials who graduated from college in the 2010s and are now trying to move onto the next stage of life and build families. Generation Z will continue to see a growth in the student loan debt crisis, much like millennials. Without some kind of intervention or program assistance, the student loan crisis will simply pass on to the next generation (Draut & Silva, 2004; Fry, 2012; Hanson, 2023).

Financial Literacy, Financial Education, and Student Loan Decisions

Financial literacy (see Chapter 1), financial education (see Chapter 19), and other factors could play a role in the acquisition of student loans (Hales, 2021; Mandell, 2008; Sabri, 2011). Many colleges offer financial assistance and have offices dedicated to assisting students in financial aid. However, some college students decide to take out student loans when other resources such as scholarships, grants, or work-study programs are available. Darolia (2016) noted that information on student loans was not enough to help students in this important decision-making. Taking out student loans is a valuable investment in human capital, but it is important that emerging adults understand what other resources available, what types of the loans they are taking out, and how much they really need to borrow (Griffiths, 2022; Hawkins, 2017; Johnson et al., 2016).

Previous studies have found that among emerging adults who had general financial education that focused on budgeting, money management, or wise use of credit, many chose to take out student loans (Booij et al., 2012; Johnson et al., 2016). Markle (2019) stated that those who had received financial education were more likely to see student loans as a financial strategy and investment. This means that general financial education available for students in high school or college (see Chapter 19) might not have a great impact on their student loan decisions; however, financial literacy that measures financial knowledge (see Chapter 2) and capability could influence their decisions. Financial literacy can be developed with the help of financial education targeted specifically at the consequences of taking out student loans.

In the last few decades, research on financial literacy has increased as researchers attempt to understand the development and implementation of personal financial literacy. In the literature, financial literacy is often used interchangeably with financial knowledge (see Chapter 2; Avard et al., 2005; Bowen, 2002; Lusardi & Mitchell, 2007). Several studies have examined the association between financial knowledge and financial decisions (see Chapter 6; Avard et al., 2005; Bowen, 2002; Cordero et al., 2020; Kaiser & Menkhoff, 2017; Lusardi et al., 2010). The literature also indicates that the greater an individual's financial literacy, the more likely they are to participate in positive financial behaviors (see Chapter 5; Lusardi & Mitchell, 2007; Xiao et al., 2020).

The decision to take on student loan debt can be made even more overwhelming when emerging adults do not have enough financial knowledge and financial literacy necessary to make the best financial decisions regarding their education and future. Enhancing financial literacy could change an emerging adult's student loan decision. For example, equipping emerging adults and their families with knowledge and facts on student loans could be helpful for those considering applying for student loans (see Box 9.1). In-depth financial education that explains the long-term consequences of debt and interest should be required before a student is permitted to take out a student loan.

Box 9.1 For Practitioners

Literature indicates that those with higher objective financial knowledge (see Chapter 2) may be more inclined to consider whether to borrow student loans more carefully and may seek out other resources to pay for college. Equipping emerging adults and their families with knowledge and facts on student loans could be helpful for those considering applying for student loans. Based on the reviewed literature, we present a set of potential questions that can be used by financial practitioners to gauge knowledge of federal student loans when working with emerging adults.

1. **Besides student loans, other forms of financial assistance for college include . . .**
   a) university/college/department scholarships
   b) third-party scholarships (i.e., company scholarships, online scholarships, etc.)
   c) federal, state, or university grants
   d) government work-study programs
   e) working while in school
   f) tuition reimbursement from employers
   g) all of the above
2. **What is the term for when student loan interest charges are delayed for 6 months after leaving school?**
   a) Direct PLUS Loan
   b) Direct Subsidized Loan
   c) Direct Unsubsidized Loan
   d) Direct Consolidation Loan
3. **What is the recommended maximum amount of student loans a student could take out before graduating?**
   a) the amount needed to cover schooling and living expenses
   b) as much as you need to complete your schooling
   c) 3 times the amount of your anticipated annual income
   d) anticipated first-year starting annual income
4. **How long is the standard repayment plan for federal student loans?**
   a) 10 years
   b) 15 years
   c) 20 years
   d) 30 years

continued

Box 9.1 *continued*

5. **Suppose you are offered a $1,000 unsubsidized loan and a $2,000 subsidized loan. Which loan will accumulate more interest by the time you graduate from college?**
   a) the $2,000 subsidized loan because $2,000 is greater than $1,000
   b) the $1,000 unsubsidized loan because unsubsidized loans start accumulating interest while you are in college and subsidized loans do not accumulate interest until after you graduate
   c) the $1,000 unsubsidized loan because $1,000 is a lot of money
   d) the $2,000 subsidized loan because subsidized loans start collecting interest while you are in college and unsubsidized loans do not accumulate interest until after you graduate

The answers for the five questions are as follows: 1 = g, 2 = b, 3 = d, 4 = a, 5 = b.

Sociodemographic Differences in Student Loan Decisions

In the literature, sociodemographic factors that may have influenced student loan decisions and behaviors include gender (see Chapter 16), race/ethnicity (see Chapter 17), marital status (see Chapter 14), education, and income (Beiser, 2003; Karolyi, 2016; Looney & Yannelis, 2015; Min & Taylor, 2018). These characteristics can play a role in financial opportunity, financial inclusion (see Chapter 15), and financial education (see Chapter 19), which would influence student loan decisions and outcomes (Karolyi, 2016; Williamson, 2010). Furthermore, an individual's personal background such as risk tolerance (see Chapter 6) or attitude toward credit usage (see Chapters 4 and 13) can affect decisions such as the pursuit of higher education and student loan use (Looney & Yannelis, 2015; Luong, 2010; Lusardi, 2008; Miller, 2017; Min & Taylor, 2018). This section provides previous research related to the association between some sociodemographic factors and student loan decisions.

Gender differences in financial behaviors are frequently examined in research (see Chapter 16). In 2021, women accounted for 58% of the undergraduate student population; however, more than two-thirds of student loan debt holders were females (Hanson, 2024c; National Center for Education Statistics, 2023). This could be due to the gender wage gap that awaits females on the other side of a college education. Luckily, the income disparity does not seem to affect whether females attend college or not, and it seems that the pursuit of higher education is seen as an important investment in human capital regardless of gender (Bartholomae et al., 2019).

The use of student loans becomes tricky when considering race/ethnicity (see Chapter 17) as it plays two roles. On one hand, student loans allow some minority individuals to have opportunities that they might not be able to afford otherwise. The use of student loans increased enrollment and college completion rates among Black students (Gordon, 2022; Jackson & Reynolds, 2013). On the other hand, Black students were found to take on greater amounts of student loan debt and were in repayment for a longer time period than White students (Addo et al., 2016; Baker et al., 2017; Scott-Clayton & Li, 2016). Previous studies have noted that while student loans could close the racial gap in college participation, it increased the racial disparities seen in income, homeownership, and other financial behaviors after college graduation (Addo et al., 2016; Jackson & Reynolds, 2013; Scott-Clayton & Li, 2016).

When it comes to gaining a college education, family income (see Chapter 15) is a large factor. Those with less access to financial resources may struggle to attend school and take on greater debt burdens (Baker & Montalto, 2019; Fry, 2012). College students from high-income families were more likely to adjust and reduce their student loan borrowing (Mangrum, 2022). Students from high-income families may receive more family support or have other financial resources that reduce their need to borrow (see Chapter 13; Delisle & Holt, 2015; Mangrum, 2022). However, individuals from low-income families tend to have lower financial literacy (see Chapter 15; Goyal & Kumar, 2020; Grohmann, 2018), and they were more likely to borrow student loans given their relative lack of personal financial resources to fund their college education (Baker et al., 2017; Looney, 2021; Luna-Torres et al., 2018).

Student Loans and Financial Well-Being

Student loans are not necessarily considered a positive financial decision for emerging adults, even though they can be seen as a human capital investment (Christie & Munro, 2003; Fox et al., 2017; Rothstein & Rouse, 2011). Holding a student loan has been found to be negatively associated with financial well-being (see Chapter 7; Aboagye & Jung, 2018; Fry, 2014; Henager & Wilmarth, 2018). Holding a student loan has been found to influence financial well-being in both direct and indirect ways, and these relationships can become complicated and intertwined (Baggett & Cole, 2022; Montalto et al., 2019). In fact, any amount of student loan debt can decrease financial well-being, even if students are not borrowing more than the amount recommended by the government, and more student loan debt is associated with floundering (Elliott & Lewis, 2015; Gutter & Copur, 2011). Previous studies noted that individuals with student loan debt tended to have less net worth, home equity, investments, and accumulated assets than those with no student loan debt (Elliott & Lewis, 2015; Luong, 2010; Mountain et al., 2020).

While holding student loans can impact any individual's financial well-being, there are groups that are impacted even more by this debt burden, and such debt burden will decrease the financial well-being of certain sociodemographic groups. For example, student loan debt burden has negatively impacted the mental health of Black and Latino/Latina/Latinx emerging adults (Deckard et al., 2022). Black and Latino/Latina/Latinx borrowers carry a disproportionate student loan debt burden and are struggling more financially with the student debt burden than White student loan borrowers (Department of Financial Protection and Innovation, 2023; Looney, 2021). Nonetheless, individuals from low-income families can often increase their financial well-being and flourish as they receive more formal education (Cherney et al., 2020).

Discussion

Student loan debt is a seemingly never-ending topic of conversation among financial professionals, policymakers, and even the average individual considering attending college. The conversation can often feel like less of a decision on whether to take out a student loan and more of a discussion of when and how much. For many emerging adults, student loans are necessary to achieve higher education and may seem like the "best" option or solution. However, it is crucial for professionals to share alternative financial opportunities and resources for those who may be planning for college in the future. Specifically, financial educators can do their best to provide individuals and families with as much information as possible about student loans and other resources for college.

Equipping students with more financial knowledge (see Chapter 2) and helping them apply such knowledge could help emerging adults make effective student loan decisions. It may be crucial for school-based financial education programs prior to college to provide substantial student loan information (Fernandes et al., 2014; Mandell, 2008). Furthermore, requiring more detailed student loan entrance counseling would help students understand the complicated nature of student loans. While the Federal Student Aid website states that entrance counseling can help an individual learn more about how their loan works, the website also states that this version of student loan education only takes about 30 minutes and may be completed in one sitting (Federal Student Aid, 2024f). Policymakers should seek to expand student loan education opportunities and courses in high schools, colleges, and communities to increase financia literacy rates (see Chapter 19).

Conclusion

Student loan education is critical for emerging adults because they are in the life-cycle stage where gaining a college education has become a societal expectation and a requirement for many entry-level job positions (see Chapter 10), but most emerging adults do not yet have the resources to fund the expenses of college. Without proper financial literacy and student loan education, individuals in this life-cycle stage may easily bite off more than they can chew. Offering high-quality financial education programs (see Chapter 19) and helping students build student loan financial literacy (e.g., asking questions regarding available resources, different loan types, loan terms, interest rates, and how to handle loan repayment) are vital for emerging adults in the United States and other countries with high rates of student loan debt. In addition, improved policies regarding college costs and tuition rates, student loan programs, scholarships, and grant opportunities are needed.

Chapter 10
Career Considerations in Emerging Adulthood

Julia A. Nuckols[1] *and Mette Ranta*[2]

Introduction

There are many ways young professionals today are being described, ranging from one end to another—be it lazy and entitled or driven, ambitious, and socially responsible (Harrington et al., 2015). Even though making zealous assumptions about an entire generational cohort is generally inadvisable because they are often misleading, there are some characteristics scholars have found to be true of emerging adults today. From a perspective focusing strictly on changes in work and career culture, scholars have noted that there has been a shift from traditional, long-term careers to more flexible and dynamic career trajectories (Harrington & Hall, 2007). Additionally, studies have shown that emerging adults today have high expectations for work–life balance, promising career development, job security, and career satisfaction. However, emerging adults have also shown to have lower expectations of obtaining job security (De Hauw & De Vos, 2010). Finally, in the era of globalization, social mobility has never been so present (Lent & Brown, 2020).

These are some of the examples of how emerging adults today experience work–life differently compared to their preceding generations. In this chapter, we will explore these changes as well as the risks for floundering and the opportunities for flourishing that emerging adults face as they make the transition to work–life in an ever-connected world and a rapidly changing work culture. First, we shall take a comprehensive look at the pressures emerging adults experience in today's world in terms of pressures to succeed, post-graduation plans and financial concerns, and self-esteem. Second, we

[1] Department of Social Sciences and Philosophy, University of Jyväskylä, Finland
[2] Department of Education, University of Helsinki, Finland

Julia A. Nuckols, and Mette Ranta, *Career Considerations in Emerging Adulthood*. In: *Flourishing and Floundering Financially in Emerging Adulthood*. Edited by: Ashley B. LeBaron-Black, Heather Kelley, and Angela Sorgente, Oxford University Press. © Oxford University Press (2025). DOI: 10.1093/9780197699157.003.0011

will discuss the role of social media and its ubiquitous presence in the context of emerging adulthood, particularly in terms of how social media corresponds with both career opportunities as well as career-related challenges.

This gives us natural momentum into the third topic of interest, which focuses on the professional skill requirements placed on emerging adults in today's world, which largely revolve around globalism and digitalization. Due to the outstanding relevance of digital skills in the modern context, we discuss digital skill requirements as a stand-alone section. In our last section prior to our concluding remarks, we will discuss emerging adults' career development and financial well-being particularly in times of amplified uncertainty. In light of the recent COVID-19 pandemic, which shocked the global economy and caused rapid changes in the composure of working life and labor markets, it is important to understand the extent of these amplified career and financial uncertainties experienced by emerging adults. Throughout the text, we provide comments from emerging adults on graduating and finding work collected in a focus group study by a Finnish university (Nuckols et al., 2023b), as well as practical advice for emerging adults, parents, and educators.

Sources of Stress for Emerging Adults Entering the Workforce

Higher education is a time in a young person's life that is considered both the embodiment of youth and endless opportunities and a time when more serious commitments and decisions should be made. These pressures would undoubtedly make individuals prone to states of stress and possibly even more strenuous mental health concerns such as anxiety and depression (see Chapters 8 and 9). Indeed, a study by the American College Health Association (2014) found that general anxiety was the most common mental health concern reported among college students. Additionally, studies have found rising trends in reported anxiety and depression among college students (Gallagher, 2015; Mahmoud et al., 2012). Considering global statistics indicating a rise in both anxiety and depressive symptoms among emerging adults, looking into the possible factors influencing this trend from an occupational perspective is necessary.

One study focusing on the stressors in modern college environments found 10 sources of stress among students in modern U.S. college environments (Beiter et al., 2015). These sources included academic performance, pressure to succeed, post-graduation plans, financial concerns (see Chapters 8 and 9), and self-esteem. Other sources (i.e., stressors that are not attached to college experiences alone but relate to overall well-being) included quality of sleep, relationship with friends, relationship with family, overall health, and body image. Beiter and colleagues' research also found that many of these stressors were related to experienced symptoms of anxiety, depression, and stress. What seems telling of these findings is that they encompass a rather comprehensive scope in many important areas of a young person's life, which understandably would be overwhelming if one had to think and feel pressure or concern over all of the mentioned areas. Other postulated causes behind these stressors are rising academic pressures, inaccessibility to higher education (see Chapter 9), and mental health services on campus, changing male-to-female ratios (in the sense the women are more likely to seek help; therefore, more cases of mental distress are reported among their gender), technology (e.g., internet addiction and problematic internet use), and lifestyle. Moving away from one's parental home to study may introduce new lifestyle choices that are less likely to support both mental and physical health, therefore contributing to weakened mental health and increased risk for floundering (Flatt, 2013).

Overall, most of the stressors mentioned are not exclusive to the academic environment alone but are potential stressors after education as well and are perhaps telling of the overall pressures emerging adults are experiencing in the modern era. Out of the aforementioned, the particular areas of interest in this chapter are the pressure to succeed, post-graduation plans, financial concerns, and self-esteem.

Pressure to Succeed

Starting from the pressure to succeed, we must first disclose that in the context of the research conducted by Beiter et al. (2015), it primarily refers to the academic context, ergo the social and institutional pressures experienced by students enrolled in higher education. However, career pressures are just as relevant in emerging adulthood, particularly when graduating and entering the labor market, that is, the school-to-work transition (Saks, 2018; Steiner et al., 2022). In fact, therein lies a bridge between the pressures to succeed in education and in one's work (or obtaining work) (Doherty, 2021; Garcia-Aracil et al., 2021). After all, research has found that positive perceptions of goals, achievements, and competencies in academia tend to cater to better feelings of confidence when transitioning from education to work and flourishing in careers (Doherty, 2021). However, the school-to-work transition has become more dynamic and complex (Akkermans et al., 2021). The transition from education to work is also frequently linked with uncertainty, increased individualization, and the attainment of independence (Wilska, 2004).

For those not graduating from higher education, such as those in trade professions or entrepreneurship/freelancing, there are different challenges and opportunities to consider (Carnevale & Hanson, 2015). Trade professions typically entail better job security (Tanzi, 2023), but as seen during the COVID-19 pandemic, there were those who had to remain essential workers and be at risk for infection (e.g., mechanics, retailers) (Reid et al., 2021) or be furloughed (e.g., service industry) (Li et al., 2023). Freelance work or entrepreneurship, on the other hand, entails more freedoms but also more risk and heightened individual responsibility (Fowle, 2019). What makes trade professions and graduating from them particularly lucrative in terms of employment is the emphasis on training prior to graduation, ensuring these professionals already have the necessary work experience before entering the labor markets (Zimmermann et al., 2013). Essentially, many prominent factors play a role in the development of emerging adults, which certainly come with their own personal, social, societal, and institutional expectations (Arnett, 2015). Becoming a successful citizen in today's complex and ever-changing financial and career landscape requires strong efficacious financial responsibility and risk management.

Post-Graduation Plans and Financial Concerns

Post-graduation plans surely have a presence in the life of emerging adults even before degree obtainment, as career trajectories are initially set into motion through training and education. As Pisarik et al. (2017) found in their study of college students, there were two primary concerns regarding life after graduation: never finding work or not finding work that they would be satisfied with. This also segues into the issues of financial concerns, as the monetary aspect of choosing jobs surely plays a role in pursuing one's career interests. These concerns were found to be heavily influenced by the experienced pressures stemming from the expectations of parents, educational institutions, peer pressure, or the graduates themselves (Pisarik et al.). Basically, emerging adults early on in their adult lives may feel immense pressure to not only flourish in school alone to better their career outcomes, but also pressure to succeed in choosing and finding work that satisfies the expectations they feel the need to fulfill as well as their financial needs. This may lead to a perfect storm in which general uncertainty about one's future and ambitions is met with the immense need to make ideal decisions (Doherty, 2021).

As seen in financial crises such as the 2008 market crisis, when the risk in failing to satisfy these work expectations and financial needs was greater, issues in this area of emerging adulthood have been found to increase stress (see Chapter 8), maladaptive behaviors, and risks to flounder (Ranta, 2013).

Self-Esteem

Self-esteem is a relatively difficult variable to discuss concisely because it encompasses so many complex and subjective meanings that reflect one's perception, emotional evaluations, and the acceptance of self (Patel et al., 2018). If we were to examine self-esteem purely from the topic of career considerations in emerging adulthood, we could start again from an educational setting. For instance, a study by Salmela-Aro and Nurmi (2007) found that high overall self-esteem during university studies predicted positive career outcomes 10 years later, such as more stable employment, high salary, high levels of work engagement, and job satisfaction. While self-esteem is a very human characteristic, the modern era challenges our self-esteem due to platforms in which we constantly compare ourselves with others, namely, social media.

Social Media as a Tapestry of Opportunity or Lack Thereof

In the dawn of social media, most individuals intended to use social media platforms to cater to personal relationships already present in their lives, only adding a new layer of communication and means of networking with their more immediate circle (Kross et al., 2021). Now, however, the presence of social media has become nearly omnipotent, being a necessity in order to belong to the current zeitgeist. Social media has brought us new routines in interaction such as following and liking the content of others, and as a result of this rapid expansion, a stark normalization in the phenomenon of promoting and branding oneself (Whitmer, 2019). With the more casual forms of self-promotion and branding being something as simple as sizing up and posting catered content to keep up with peers, to going as far as individuals making their livelihoods off self-promotion by being influencers, therein also lies the professional realms of self-promotion, with platforms such as LinkedIn being established for that sole purpose (Minor-Cooley & Parks-Yancy, 2020; Whitmer, 2019).

LinkedIn began much like other social media platforms, with the intent to facilitate online connectivity between one's former and present colleagues and keep up with their professional lives (Minor-Cooley & Parks-Yancy, 2020)—something comparable to an online catalogue of one's professional network, with the added features of recruitment and advertising. In many cases, young people are implored to create LinkedIn profiles, if nothing else when approaching their graduation and being prepared to enter the labor markets as fresh professionals. Social media has also revolutionized the way businesses market themselves, providing a platform to reach audiences across the globe instantaneously. However, this is a two-way street, as audiences now have more direct access to correspond with businesses and organizations around the world (Icha, 2015). Then again, the robust possibilities to utilize social media and digital tools come with not only the pressures to be productive and readily able to use them in the professional context, but they also have the potential to distract and lower productivity (Marsh et al., 2022).

In addition to advantages and opportunities for flourishing seen in the culture of social media, such as expansion of one's network, the ability to form meaningful relationships with others, and the ability to express oneself and further facilitate individual identities (Davis et al., 2020), researchers have also identified the potential downsides and disadvantages of social media, including issues such as social comparisons (see Chapters 4, 8, and 13), decreased life satisfaction, and depression (Braghieri et al., 2022). Particularly from a perspective of self-esteem, scholars believe that social comparison, particularly when feelings of inferiority emerge, leads to decreased self-esteem (Braghieri et al., 2022). Van Dijck (2013) found that the majority of emerging adults make both upward (i.e., feeling inspired) and downward (i.e., feeling superior to someone) comparisons with others in their social media use. The upward comparisons, in particular, drove the participants to feel envious, inferior, ungrateful, and less satisfied with their own lives. Another study found that social media facilitates ability-related social comparisons, which, in turn, leads to decreased performance-oriented self-esteem (Brandenberg et al., 2019). In other words, social media has the potential to challenge very particular skill-and-ability related feelings of confidence, beyond just one's overall self-esteem.

If we consider the example of LinkedIn solely due to the fact that it brands itself as a social media platform of professionalism and networking, many have lately found its gritty, hustle culture–invoking environment to be so off-putting that it has lost credibility as a professional networking site. If anything, it has shifted away from its initial resume-sharing and networking agenda into a hub for professionals to brag about and announce their major career developments (Kelley, 2022). It has also become relatively commonplace for young professionals to post about their graduation and job seeking in hopes of connecting with recruiters. While doing so could bring forth great opportunity, therein lies an issue with the constantly growing competition of said posts (this dichotomy between opportunity and competition is also expressed in Box 10.1). While that alone is not an issue, it does raise questions about what kind of recruitment and job-seeking culture social media platforms such as LinkedIn are cultivating among young impressionable adults, who may already be susceptible to comparative thinking among their peers (see Box 10.2).

Box 10.1

Finnish IT student, male, last year of studies, on increasing working opportunities:

"I'd say with opportunities there is also the flipside of more competition, that you have to be ready to continue learning and expanding your skill sets in order to stay competitive."

Box 10.2 Tips for Emerging Adults

In a time when we are more prone than ever before to be made aware of the flourishing of others via social media, the pressure to succeed from peers and those around us is unavoidable. What is more, being so connected and globalized, we are drenched in a liminal space of endless opportunity but also difficult choices. Under these circumstances, it is important to ground yourself with the comforting notion that the paths we take in our own development are ours alone and that the stories we hear and the visuals we see are all catered to give the most positive imagery. Instead of focusing on the progress of others, it is important to recognize our own journeys and their wonderfully complex and ever-changing trajectories, while being brave enough to be mindful of the opportunities and capabilities we have in making our own way through life.

On a more optimistic note, however, social media (and the internet overall) provides great insight into current trends in the labor market, from what career pathways would seem most promising at the time to the more nuanced and detailed aspects of what skills are currently favorable as well as how to obtain them (Antenucci et al., 2014; Dogruer et al., 2011). While there are elements to social media that may be less ideal for our well-being, the ubiquitous presence of current information and tools to be utilized thanks to these modern digital developments is but a few clicks away, giving modern day emerging adults pools of information that were previously non-existent. Another aspect to consider is the new challenge to the work–life balance, as on one hand social media makes it possible to communicate with friends and family, while at work, work-related social media may also bleed into one's time outside of work, creating a headspace that is always at least a little bit at work (Sharma & Sudhesh, 2018).

Professional Skill Requirements in Modern Labor Markets

An important element in the school-to-work transition is the process of becoming capable and adequate as an employable candidate. Studies have shown that even though graduates of higher education typically enjoy favorable employment rates (see Chapter 9), much of it is dependent on their choices of field, as well as the skills they acquire via education (Chevalier, 2011; Jacob & Klein, 2019). When considering confidence in finding work post-graduation, the role of acquired skills via education is a factor (see Box 10.3; McIlveen et al., 2013). As an example, studies have shown that those with a degree from the field of humanities are less likely to feel that they have acquired practical and applicable work skills; thus, their perceived competency decreased when looking for work after education (Suorsa & Sainio, 2020).

Box 10.3 Tips for Emerging Adults

After graduating, it may be difficult to begin to apply for jobs, especially without relevant experience in the field—a challenge many face. However, the degree you obtained has given you much more that you can include in your job application apart from the title of the position you seek; try looking deeper into what you have learned during your training and how to put that into words that match the current desired skills in your field. Is it critical thinking? The ability to find important information? Teamwork skills? The degree you get in education goes beyond the content you learn; you also accumulate other important working skills in the process.

Very often, one might come across the term "information society." It is a term used to describe the modern day of highly prevalent technological and informational innovations and the strong digital presence across all walks of life, including work (Tynjälä et al., 2006). The characteristics of work in this information society were outlined by Tynjälä et al. as follows: the development of information and communication technology, globalization, continual change, complexity and uncertainty, networking, teamwork, projects, symbolic-analytic work, person-to-person services, and routine production services. Since the publication of the study by Tynjälä et al. in 2006, many of these characteristics can only be assumed to have become even more relevant as much of the technological aspects of life have only grown more prominent, especially in Western societies. In career research, it has been found that policymakers, employers, and researchers put a strong emphasis on higher education graduates' marketable skills and believe they should be improved on (Asonitou, 2015). Furthermore, lifelong learning is discussed as a concept, fulfilling the increasing and changing demands in modern work (Asonitou, 2015). This begs two questions: First, what are the particular skills that are deemed important for graduates when finding work after education? Second, what is the role of higher educational institutions in improving the working skills of graduates before they leave their academic institutions?

The characteristics outlined by Tynjälä et al. (2006) found that these important skills include computer skills, media literacy, problem solving, learning skills, language skills, abstract thinking, social skills, and punctuality. A study by Humburg et al. (2013), on the other hand, found that the most important skills for graduates in finding work were professional expertise, interpersonal skills, commercial/entrepreneurial skills, innovative/creative skills, strategic/organizational skills, and general academic skills. This international study utilized responses from more than 900 employers from 12 European countries and complemented the findings via focus group interviews with both employers and relevant stakeholders. Out of the aforementioned, general academic skills scored the lowest in terms of importance, highlighting that the skills acquired in academia alone may not be sufficient for modern-day work demands (Humburg et al., 2013). Of course, much of this depends on one's degree choice as well as the profession one is looking to enter post-graduation. Professional expertise and interpersonal skills, however, were considered most valuable from the perspective of employers. Professional expertise is surely one skill that is natural to gain via education, although it requires conscious effort from the student as well, in order to not only gain but also be able to apply the acquired knowledge (as also indicated by Humburg and colleagues).

Much overlap can be found between both aforementioned studies. Furthermore, one can expand their understanding of skills by looking at the aspects of skills as well. The information society is believed to particularly demand professional expertise, a valuable, key skill as previously mentioned. This professional expertise includes but is not limited to having specific knowledge and the ability to apply abstract thinking (as also noted by Tynjälä et al., 2006), as well as general analytical thinking skills (Humburg et al., 2013). The previously noted importance of flexibility was also noted as a result of growing uncertainties in the modern era. This involves aspects such as the capability to learn new things, to invest in improving employability skills, and to cope with changes (again, as determined by Tynjälä et al. and Humburg et al.).

It is also believed that graduates should be more flexible in the sense that they should be more willing and ready to accept available opportunities in the job market, even if they are not their first choice of employment (Alpaydin & Kultur, 2022; Yorke & Harvey, 2005). With the growing trend of information technology becoming more prominent, graduates are expected to apply creative and information and communications technology (ICT) skills, as well as the ability to implement them in their working life. With the globalization and mobilization of human resources, the demand for communication and teamwork skills, language skills, and self-management skills is on the rise. Tynjälä et al. (2006) also found that graduates firmly believe that social and teamwork skills are particularly important to succeeding in finding work. Finally, Humburg et al. (2013) found that there is more demand for entrepreneurial skills and capabilities among modern-day graduates. This comes with the need to be able to identify risks for floundering and opportunities for flourishing in branding oneself.

As for the role of higher educational institutions and how they prepare their students for job seeking and working, the general emphasis is placed on garnering expert-level knowledge in a specific area and how to apply said knowledge, as well as general academic skills such as knowing how to find needed information and to process it critically (Humburg et al., 2013). Students themselves feel that mastery of domain knowledge and theoretical knowledge are the most pronounced set of skills they gained from higher education, while actual work skills were garnered the most from actual work (Tynjälä et al., 2006). Students stated that the uselessness of certain courses and the lack of certain courses were the main deficiencies of higher education in terms of preparing them for working life (Tynjälä et al.).

Thinking of how educational institutions can, in practice, improve the working skills of graduates is not a simple task due to the stark differences of graduate labor markets in terms of country, degree, and even—in some cultures—the reputation of a school (Alpaydin & Kultur, 2022). For instance, the prevalence of how much emphasis is placed on vocational and practical training during one's studies not only depends on one's degree structure, but also one's country, as some countries put more emphasis in general on internship and training-based learning before graduation (Alpaydin & Kultur). On a pragmatic note, it could be argued that institutes of higher education not only should find ways to prepare students for working life from the perspective of skills, but also from the perspective of how to find work in practice. Many schools already provide various career services and other activities such as a résumé or curriculum vitae (CV) workshops to prepare students for life post-graduation.

One practical implication that educators should be more inclined to focus on would be understanding as comprehensively as possible the current labor market demands and, even further, what the labor market demands are for specific fields. By mediating and better understanding what the current skills in demand are, educational institutions can better implement practices that leave graduates feeling more confident in their acquired knowledge and skills (Mañé & Corbella, 2017). Furthermore, some suggest that higher educational institutions could better monitor the skill sets of their students to ensure that their current knowledge and abilities match the prevailing labor market trends (Řihová, 2016). Finally, many believe that higher educational institutions should be more inclined to work together with businesses to both mediate and facilitate better employment options for their students (Alpaydin & Kultur, 2022). However, as labor market shifts and employability are inherently complicated, a valid criticism against putting too much responsibility onto higher educational institutions prevails, as they alone cannot be held accountable for graduate employability (as Alpaydin and Kultur note). Due to the undeniable presence and imperativeness of digital skills and the overall digitalization of basic societal functions, the digital skill requirements and skill levels of emerging adults today warrant their own section, in which we will briefly explore just *how* skilled our modern-day emerging adults are and what could be improved on for their sake.

Finally, the sudden emergence of highly developed artificial intelligence (AI) has raised concerns regarding its implications for labor market trends, especially in terms of emerging adults who have not yet built well-established careers. Particularly due to AI's expected rapid development, these changes may be sudden and unexpected. A study by Holm and Lorenz (2022) projected that while AI has the power to replace jobs and decrease employee autonomy, it also can be a valuable tool to facilitate learning and increase productivity. For this reason, educators should also encourage their students to learn how to best utilize AI to their advantage. Meanwhile, educators, emerging adults, researchers, and policymakers alike should be well aware of the projected development of AI and anticipate what labor market shifts could follow from these developments.

Digital Skills of Emerging Adults Today

In the era of widespread technology, with many emerging adults having grown up around digital tools and technological innovations, a misappropriate generalization is often made that emerging adults are by default tech-savvy and naturally adept at using technology (Bennett & Maton, 2010; Helsper, 2008; Sibide, 2015). With ICT skills and digital literacy being in ever-growing demand in modern-day professions, it is important to also look beyond the assumption that young people's tech skills are a given. While the use of digital devices such as smartphones or tablets is ubiquitous among all, actual ICT skills may not be as sophisticated as is generally assumed (Bennett & Maton, 2010; Correa, 2016). Some believe that the assumption that modern emerging adults are automatically versed in ICT skills only perpetuates inequalities and risks, as the need to teach them the required skills required today are easily overlooked or the risks of over-engagement with technology are ignored (Hakkarainen et al., 2015; Helsper & Smahel, 2020; Livingstone et al., 2023).

While access to technology has never been so abundant, therein lies the question of what technology is being used for and what practical skills are gained from doing so. For instance, while communicating through digital platforms and the internet is nearly always present in the lives of young people, their actual knowledge of more archaic and complex internet functions is less known (Bennett & Maton, 2010; Kennedy et al., 2009). It would be no longer feasible to discuss technology skills as a sum of all ICT-related skills and abilities; research has found that while often emerging adults are proficient in certain areas of technology-based activities, they may have gaps in knowledge that may be relevant in a professional setting (Thrupp, 2008). For instance, those keen on playing video games may be very proficient in gaming-related technology, while others may be well versed in the use of content creation and digital visual tools. However, neither guarantees proficiency in very common digital tools used in professional spaces (i.e., Microsoft Excel).

One study conducted by the Organisation for Economic Co-operation and Development (OECD) found that among U.S. millennials, up to 19% struggled with a task involving sorting email responses to a party invitation into pre-determined folders between those who could attend and those who could not (Sibide, 2015). Furthermore, 39% were able to sort emails but not able to locate information in a spreadsheet and email it. Respectively, 34% were able to locate information in a spreadsheet and email it. The highest-ranking 8% were able to use a reservation system to book a meeting room. This is relatively surprising given how many middle-skilled jobs require technology skills, with the demands only growing further (Sibide, 2015).

This strengthens the discussion on how young people's digital skills cannot be taken for granted but instead should be strengthened when possible and emphasized in order to improve the default skill level of emerging adults entering the labor market. However, a comforting notion is that young people so accustomed to using digital devices would surely be readily prepared to learn and adapt professionally practical technological skills as well. One global event that truly served as a catalyst to widespread technology use in all age cohorts was the COVID-19 pandemic, which promptly pushed individuals to learn and adapt to a more digitized way of living, be it social or occupational. People worldwide were suddenly driven to utilize digital devices, either for remote work, everyday endeavors, or to fulfill their social needs in a time of deep isolation. While the pandemic gave way to new digital means of living, to the point that some are reluctant to return to office spaces for work, it also elicited many elements of uncertainty in the lives of emerging adults.

Emerging Adults' Career Development and Financial Well-Being during Societal Uncertainty

Emerging adults' flourishing in psychological developmental tasks, such as the transition from education to work, largely influences their levels of general well-being (Lent et al., 1999; Ranta et al., 2013). That is, emerging adults who make the transition from being a student to being an employee in work life, for example, are generally happier and more satisfied with their life in comparison to emerging adults feeling "in-between" (Arnett, 2015). The process of career development significantly impacts emerging adults' financial well-being. It plays a crucial role in protecting them from immediate financial problems, especially when there are limited economic resources available (Kuhn & Ploj, 2020). Additionally, it aids in their advancement toward achieving higher occupational status and increased earnings over time (Steffy et al., 1989). However, due to the fact that careers are evermore unstructured, a flourishing school-to-work transition is not about acquiring necessary skills and long-term employment but about seeing it as an adaptive transition (Akkermans et al., 2021; Fang & Saks, 2022). Furthermore, financial well-being is defined not only by objective resources but also as a reflection of personal success expectations (see Chapter 7; Burcher, 2017). Therefore, it is likely that perceptions of financial well-being differ according to contextual circumstances, personal factors, and demographic factors (e.g., age, gender, career stage).

An example of these contextual circumstances is changes in the macroeconomic environment (e.g., financial crises or economic downturns), as shown in a recent extensive review by She and colleagues (2022). For example, during the Great Recession of 2008, emerging adults ages 18–24 were the population most affected by the crisis due to a highest increase in unemployment and reduced employment prospects (Aassve et al., 2013). In terms of other societal crises, the impact of the COVID-19 pandemic on emerging adults worldwide has been both deep and disproportionate mainly due to the restrictions set to slow the spread of the virus, which affected the everyday life of emerging adults especially (see Box 10.4). Emerging adults were more likely to experience job loss, financial insecurity, and mental health problems due to the global pandemic than older-age cohorts (Eurofound et al., 2021). Employment disruptions, such as job loss and income loss, also influence immediate and future financial and general well-being, as shown in a recent cross-national study on how emerging adults have perceived the impact of the pandemic (Li et al., 2023).

Box 10.4

Swedish medical graduate, female, on how COVID-19 disrupted her initial plans in gaining work experience in a specific field of medicine:

"I was hoping to do an internship in a different area of medicine, but then I was suddenly moved into working with COVID-19 patients, which wasn't at all what I was interested in. So that was quite disappointing."

In addition to the fact that more research is needed to understand how emerging adults' financial well-being (see Chapter 7) relates to these contextual factors (She et al., 2022), the subjective perceptions on how young people experience these factors as affecting their financial well-being and the career life domain are also a critical issue. Individuals, in general, perceive these situations differently according to various personal factors, such as personality.

For example, in a COVID-19 related study, it was found that emerging adults' predisposition to avoid difficult situations and tasks, portraying a tendency to see the current situation as out of their own control, was related to being concerned about how the pandemic will affect their mental health, economic situation, and career and education life domains (Ranta et al., 2020). Mental health strain caused by the lack of social contacts and social support during the pandemic has been significant for emerging adults in terms of their education, work, and relationship formation at this critical life stage. For example, a recent study using data collected from emerging adults in Finland, Sweden, and the United Kingdom showed that experiencing loneliness during the pandemic played a significant role in increasing income and career concerns in all three countries (Nuckols et al., 2023a).

Living and life-course development from a crisis-to-crisis perspective, as some may put it, and the uncertainty emerging adults face not only in the career life domain but also in the midst of global insecurity, topped off with the demands emerging adults set upon themselves, pose a challenge for emerging adults' mental health. As many demands are made on emerging adults in the career life domain today, an ability to "bounce back" is crucial. Resilience (see Chapter 8) refers to successful adaptation and competence despite significant risk or adversity that may affect the achievement of major developmental tasks (Masten & Powell, 2003), such as the transition from education to work and from financial dependence to financial independence (see Chapter 11). In fact, resilience is not simply avoiding negative outcomes in challenging times but the individual's ability to identify, optimize, and analyze one's strengths to overcome such challenges (Hussong et al., 2021). However, research has also shown how psychosocial adaptation to cope with social change does not necessarily buffer pandemic-related changes in emerging adults' domain-specific satisfaction such as financial well-being (Recksiedler & Landberg, 2021). No matter how resilient emerging adults are, in extreme conditions such as the COVID-19 pandemic, resilience may be insufficient in overcoming the societal crisis's actual and perceived impact and for emerging adults to withstand extreme hardship and uncertainty (especially for minoritized groups; see Box 10.5).

Box 10.5

While diversity and inclusion have always been important, with social mobility at its peak and in the era of globalization, it is becoming increasingly relevant for educational institutions, employers, and policymakers to implement systems that support inclusivity and promote equal opportunity for all individuals regardless of their backgrounds. Particularly in the age of information technology, the ability to adapt to an ever-diversifying world has never been more applicable.

Conclusion

The purpose of this chapter has been to explore the career considerations of present-day emerging adults and the affiliated themes relevant to their career trajectories, these being an integral part of emerging adults' immediate and future financial well-being (see Chapter 7). The overall changes in generational trends related to career life, such as developmental transitions taking place at a later age, technology, and gender roles, significantly influence emerging adults' career and financial development today. This was accompanied by a look at the risks that floundering modern-day emerging adults face as they navigate their career trajectories in a world that is rapidly changing culturally, societally, and digitally.

While emerging adults are seemingly living in a world more connected than ever with ever-expanding opportunities, our review of the research also found that issues involving stress and anxiety have become increasingly present even before transitioning from education to work (see Chapter 8; Gallagher, 2015; Mahmoud et al., 2012). While there are many reasons for emerging adults to experience additional stress in this area of life, we found pressure to succeed, post-graduation plans, financial concerns, and self-esteem to be the most relevant, particularly in terms of the career-related topics we explored in this chapter.

In terms of social media, many studies have found that there are both ample opportunities associated with social media, as well as increasingly concerning mental health implications. Never-ending flourishing stories and the pressure to live up to them, to have something to post about, have undoubtedly added an entirely new layer of peer pressure (Brandenberg et al., 2019; Kelley, 2022). Contemporary scholars have found that themes relevant to a modern information society include the rapid development of information and communication technology, globalization, continual change, complexity and uncertainty, networking, teamwork, projects, symbolic-analytic work, person-to-person services, and routine production (Tynjälä et al., 2006). Interestingly, this coincides with the work values found among emerging adults such as those relating to flexibility and heightened social mobility. As for skills, our information society is believed to have increased demand in skills relating to linguistics, computers, media literacy, and professional expertise, among others (Humburg et al., 2013; Tynjälä et al., 2006). With this increased demand for specific skills, experts believe that educational institutions, as well as services that support career development, should be more inclined to cater to these skill requirements (Alpaydin & Kultur, 2022; Asonitou, 2015). This was found to be particularly important in the context of digital skills because while it is easy to assume that emerging adults today have been more exposed to digital devices throughout their young lives, many still lack the specific skills needed to remain professionally sufficient (Bennett & Maton, 2010). This adds incentive to improve the professional digital skills of emerging adults instead of assuming that they are naturally adept.

Ascribe these elements to a cohort already amid a developmental stage characterized by uncertainty, such as in terms of career development and gaining financial independence (see Chapter 11) (Arnett, 2015), and then add a sudden global crisis that elicits a multitude of uncertainty relating to both mental and physical health. The COVID-19 pandemic was undoubtedly challenging for emerging adults, with issues involving job and income loss, compromised well-being, mental health problems, and general financial and career uncertainty (Eurofound et al., 2021; Li et al., 2023; Nuckols et al., 2023a, 2023b; Ranta et al., 2020). Currently, emerging adults are facing increased uncertainty due to wars (e.g., the Russian invasion of Ukraine and subsequent war, the Hamas attack on Israel and ensuing war, the civil war in Sudan and Myanmar, to name a few conflicts), as well as the climate crisis and continuing inflation, sadly creating life-course trajectories that mean they are living from one crisis to another. This invokes a practical question: How can we improve the resilience and adaptation abilities of emerging adults when struck with sudden societal crises that demand more flexibility and fortitude than they can afford?

This chapter paints a picture of increased opportunity, complexity, flexibility, but also uncertainty. Today, we are more prone than ever to be bombarded with information about the world around us, including the flourishing of others, the demands of society, and the rapidly changing, acute situations of global crises. In a way, one could say that while the global world around us has become smaller and more accessible, the scope of the risks for floundering in this world has only grown, with issues and implications beyond our physical, immediate personal circles becoming increasingly closer to us. It is a time when individuals, institutions, and societies have to swiftly adapt to a rapidly changing, uncertain world.

Chapter 11
Navigating Financial Self-Sufficiency

The Role of Parental Financial Support in Emerging Adults' Financial and General Well-Being and Development

Rimantas Vosylis[1] *and Oana Negru-Subtirica*[2]

Introduction

Societal changes in the 21st century have substantially altered how adolescents mature into adults. Developmental transitions in modern post-industrial societies now look vastly different compared to the relatively straightforward trajectories to adulthood of half a century ago (Arnett, 2014; Billari & Liefbroer, 2010; Corijn & Klijzing, 2001; Fussell & Furstenberg Jr., 2013). Most notably, in many societies, more young people seek tertiary education (see Chapter 9) and spend considerably more time studying (Quintini et al., 2007). More so, before settling into a stable career, many try multiple jobs (see Chapter 10; Arnett, 2014; Fussell & Furstenberg Jr., 2013). As a result, the milestones central to reaching adulthood, like having a stable job or having children, now occur later in life (Billari & Liefbroer, 2010; Corijn & Klijzing, 2001).

Engagement in tertiary education and extended transition to stable employment have driven many parents to provide extensive financial support to their emerging adult children (18–29 years old) (Cobb-Clark & Gørgens, 2014; Fingerman et al., 2009, 2016). These changes imply that the path toward financial self-sufficiency for emerging adults has become lengthier and diversified (Fingerman et al., 2009, 2016). While some may achieve financial self-reliance quickly, many achieve it gradually and remain partially reliant on their parents until their early thirties (Bea & Yi, 2019). Not surprisingly, due to these changes, the significance of adult role transitions in becoming an adult

[1] Institute of Psychology, Mykolas Romeris University, Lithuania
[2] Department of Psychology, Babes-Bolyai University, Romania

Rimantas Vosylis and Oana Negru-Subtirica, *Navigating Financial Self-Sufficiency*. In: *Flourishing and Floundering Financially in Emerging Adulthood*. Edited by: Ashley B. LeBaron-Black, Heather Kelley, and Angela Sorgente, Oxford University Press. © Oxford University Press (2025). DOI: 10.1093/9780197699157.003.0012

has substantially diminished; in other words, relatively few emerging adults consider role changes, such as getting married, as important for a person to be considered an adult. Instead, the centrality of financial self-sufficiency in reaching adulthood has become a new norm (Nelson & Luster, 2015).

Against this background, the role of financial assistance from parents in shaping well-being and developmental processes during emerging adulthood has received considerable attention from researchers. The current chapter explores the pathways linking parental financial support to emerging adults' financial and general well-being and development.

Extending the Nest: The Increasing Role of Parental Financial Support

Estimating the extent of parental financial support for emerging adult children from different cohorts is challenging due to factors such as data scarcity for earlier generations, contemporary parents having fewer children, and the need to account for inflation (Schoeni & Ross, 2013). Complicating things further, parental financial support can also take a variety of forms, broadly categorized into *direct* (e.g., direct financial transfers, monetary gifts, monthly allowances) and *indirect* financial support (e.g., allowing an emerging adult child to reside in the parental home, covering various life expenses). Despite these challenges, studies indicate that over half of recent emerging adult generations receive parental financial assistance (Johnson & Ridgeway, 2023; Wightman et al., 2013).

The increase of emerging adults relying on parental financial support is most evident in the indirect indicators of extended support, such as the timing of leaving parental homes, which has undergone significant changes and reversals in recent decades. From 1960 to the late 1980s, young people in the United States, Canada, and many European countries left their parental homes increasingly earlier. However, since the early 1990s, the trend has reversed, with the mean age for leaving home rising, suggesting a higher percentage of emerging adults relying at least on indirect financial support (for a review, see Seiffge-Krenke, 2013). One study also indicated that the proportion of emerging adults receiving direct financial support from parents in the United States has increased by roughly 20% in recent generations (Wightman et al., 2013).

For recent generations of emerging adults in the United States, studies estimate that over half of 18- to 29-year-olds receive at least some parental financial support. For instance, Manzoni (2018), using nationally representative data, found that during 2001–2002, about 41% of adults ages

18–24 lived with their parents, while an additional 46% received financial support despite not residing with their parents. Although these percentages decreased in a follow-up 8 years later (when participants were 25–29 years of age), a significant proportion still lacked financial self-sufficiency, with only around 39% living independently. Similarly, Johnson and Ridgeway (2023), using another dataset representative of the U.S. emerging adult population, reported that approximately 60% of emerging adults (ages 17–27 in this study) received some form of financial support. Overall, findings highlight that younger and many older emerging adults rely on parental financial support.

Undoubtedly, the percentage of financially dependent emerging adults varies across cultural contexts (e.g., Fingerman et al., 2016). However, when it comes to economically developed societies, the main variation seems to relate to the *form* of support rather than the *level* of support. A recent international study analyzing 2015 data from 18 European countries indicated a clear inverse relation between direct financial support (financial transfers) and indirect support (residing with parents) indicators on the country level (Van Herreweghe & Van Lancker, 2021). In Northern European countries, such as Sweden and Denmark, where most emerging adults tend to leave their parental homes early, a larger percentage of emerging adults receive direct financial support. Conversely, direct parental financial support is less common in Southern European countries like Spain, Italy, or the Balkans, where many emerging adults continue to live with their parents. With few exceptions, the remaining European countries cluster in a way reflecting the following trend: The frequency of financial transfers becomes lower as the percentage of emerging adults living with parents is higher at the country level. In sum, while extended financial support is prevalent across most developed societies, cultural preferences dictate the type of support parents choose to provide (see also Mudrazija, 2014).

Notably, beyond the figures representing average tendencies in parental financial support patterns, there exists a concerning trend of increasing diversification and inequality in the amount of support provided to emerging adult children by their parents. Many studies emphasize that the amount of parental financial assistance emerging adults receive varies greatly within the populations and their social strata (Manzoni, 2018; Schoeni & Ross, 2013). Nevertheless, others show an evident diversification, according to which emerging adults can be grouped into four trajectories (Bea & Yi, 2019).

The first of the four trajectories, labeled as "consistently independent," characterizes emerging adults who transition to financial self-sufficiency remarkably early (i.e., they receive little financial help for paying bills and tuition for education during the early years of emerging adulthood, but some continue living in parental homes). The second trajectory, labeled as "quickly independent," characterizes emerging adults who rely on their family for housing during the early years of emerging adulthood, with a smaller reliance on familial support for bills and tuition. The key characteristic of this group is that parental support decreases rapidly by ages 20–21. The third group, labeled "gradually independent," characterizes those who show a steady progression toward independence. These emerging adults receive familial support for bills, housing, and tuition, but reliance decreases steadily over time, and by ages 26–27, nearly all are financially self-sufficient. The last group, "consistently supported," relies on familial assistance for bills, housing, and tuition throughout emerging adulthood. These findings indicate that many emerging adults receive sufficient funds from their parents, helping them to postpone entering the workforce for extended periods. Nevertheless, others receive minimal or no support at all. Considering such diversity, the role of parents' financial assistance in shaping emerging adults' well-being and development has received considerable attention from researchers, with findings offering a mixed picture.

Cushioning the Transition: Parental Financial Support and the Financial Well-Being of Emerging Adults

A body of research examining the implications of prolonged parental financial assistance has delved into its effects on emerging adults' subjective financial well-being (Johnson & Ridgeway, 2023; Serido et al., 2018; Vosylis & Klimstra, 2022). So far, this line of research has indicated that protracted parental financial support plays a protective role against the economic challenges and pressures that many emerging adults face during the transition to stable employment and income (see Chapter 10). Importantly, this finding is supported by both cross-sectional and longitudinal investigations, with the latter showing that the effects of parental financial support are both short- and long-term.

Studies using longitudinal data and cross-lagged panel models show that extended parental financial support predicts relative increases (rank-order changes, i.e., increases or decreases in relation to other study participants) in emerging adults' subjective financial well-being (see Chapter 7) and decreases in financial stress (see Chapter 8). One short-term longitudinal study with first-year Lithuanian college students showed that higher levels of parental financial support predicted a relative increase in satisfaction with their present personal financial situation over a 4-month period (Vosylis &

Klimstra, 2022). An investigation using two waves of the U.S.-based National Longitudinal Study of Adolescent to Adult Health (Add Health) data found that higher levels of financial support predicted a relative decrease in financial stress over a 5-year period (Serido et al., 2018). Moreover, a third investigation using the U.S.-based Panel Study of Income Dynamics study data found that parental financial assistance was associated with a relative decrease in financial worries over a 2-year period (Johnson & Ridgeway, 2023).

The findings of a longitudinal study conducted in the United States that examined variations in how emerging adults transition to financial self-sufficiency using group-based trajectory models further support these results (Bea & Yi, 2019). This study, which identified the previously introduced financial independence trajectories, also found that individuals assigned to each trajectory differed in their levels of financial security in their late twenties. The *consistently independent* and *quickly independent* emerging adults exhibited the highest levels of financial insecurity in their late twenties. Conversely, *gradually independent* and *consistently supported* emerging adults, who relied on parental financial support for the longest time, were more likely to be financially secure later in emerging adulthood. Importantly, differences in financial security within and across groups were only slightly attenuated after controlling for employment status. This suggests that the timing of parental financial support cessation may have long-lasting effects on emerging adults' financial security, regardless of their employment status.

Cross-sectional associations also indicate that emerging adults without parental financial assistance experience higher levels of financial stress (see Chapter 8; Johnson & Ridgeway, 2023). Interestingly, however, they also show that the timing of reaching financial self-sufficiency may moderate these associations. The study found that younger emerging adults without parental financial support experience increased financial worries, while among older emerging adults, increased financial worries were more evident for those who were still financially supported by their parents, compared to those who were financially independent (Johnson & Ridgeway, 2023). These findings highlight that the positive role of parental financial support in financial flourishing may apply mostly during the early years (roughly 18–24 years of age) of emerging adulthood. When parental support is discontinued during the early years of emerging adulthood, emerging adults may be forced to take on low-paying, part-time jobs, which can have negative effects on their financial flourishing, possibly leading to extended financial stress. In later years of emerging adulthood (roughly 25–29 years of age), when emerging adults have moved into stable employment with higher incomes, the reduction of parental support may actually be correlated with increased financial flourishing.

In this respect, the financial well-being of emerging adults who continue to receive parental financial support until the end of their twenties or even later may be relatively lower than that of those who rely on employment-related income.

The studies that show a clear directionality of effects and the presence of short- and long-term impacts (Johnson & Ridgeway, 2023; Serido et al., 2018; Vosylis & Klimstra, 2022) also imply that the mechanisms linking parental financial support to emerging adults' financial well-being are likely multifaceted. While these mechanisms have not yet been explored directly in the existing research, the studies we review suggest a few possible mechanisms. One likely mechanism connects extended parental financial support to the offspring's financial well-being (see Chapter 7) via prolonged education and better job prospects (see Chapter 10). The second links financial support to financial well-being via student debt (see Chapter 9).

It is generally assumed that by providing continuous financial support, parents can offer their emerging adult children the resources necessary to engage in extended academic pursuits, which may potentially lead to higher-paying occupations and higher financial well-being later in life (Fletcher & Allgood, 2022; Manzoni, 2018; Swartz, 2008). One study conducted in the United States reports that the more direct financial support (monetary transfers) emerging adults receive, the higher their subsequent occupational status is later in life (Manzoni, 2018). Another longitudinal study with young Australian emerging adults (those who just finished secondary education) found that those who moved out of their parents' home early and lacked financial support were more likely to enter full-time employment earlier, limiting their ability to pursue further education (Cobb-Clark & Gørgens, 2014). The same study also showed that emerging adults who stayed in the parental home and enjoyed extended support were less likely to engage in part-time work, allowing more time to focus on education. These findings were supported by another study conducted in the United States, which reported that parental financial aid increased offspring's college graduation prospects (Hamilton, 2013). In summary, parental financial support for their emerging adult children may work as a protective mechanism for allowing them to fully and successfully engage in university studies and thoroughly prepare educationally for higher-paying jobs after graduation.

An earlier discussed study on trajectories to financial self-sufficiency also found that among "consistently independent" emerging adults, fewer received some tertiary education, and even a smaller percentage completed a 4-year degree than in other trajectories. In contrast, among the *gradually independent* and *consistently supported* trajectories, more emerging adults finished college or higher-level education (Bea & Yi, 2019). Dropping out of college has also been directly linked to students' inability to afford their education, especially in contexts where tertiary education costs are high and little government support is available (see Chapter 9). In particular, findings from a study conducted in the United States (Terriquez & Gurantz, 2015) show that students struggling with the financial burden of education tend to have a higher likelihood of leaving college prematurely, as the financial pressure can be immense for those who cannot rely on family support to manage education-related expenses.

Another potential mechanism linking parental financial assistance to emerging adults' financial well-being relates to student loans. Noteworthy, this mechanism may primarily apply to emerging adults pursuing tertiary education in the United States, where student loan debt has significantly increased in recent decades (see Chapter 9; e.g., Webber & Burns, 2021). Overall, student loan debt has a strong and consistent negative effect on the subjective financial well-being of emerging adults. This effect is unrelated to the emerging adults' educational stage, as it was found during their first year of college, near the end of college, and in the initial years following graduation (Cherney et al., 2020). Studies also indicate that students from higher-income and college-educated families tend to have lower student loan debt compared to their less advantaged counterparts (Houle, 2014). Such findings suggest that higher-income families are more likely to cover their children's college and university tuition costs, thus reducing the latter's debt burden. As many emerging adults from lower- and middle-income families struggle to afford tertiary education, they also face higher debt risk than their higher-income counterparts.

The Socioeconomic Divide: The Role of Parental Socioeconomic Status in Financial Support for Emerging Adult Children

The reviewed findings unequivocally show that prolonged parental financial support shields emerging adults from many potential financial difficulties that arise as they transition into financially self-sufficient adults. Considering that parents' ability to provide prolonged financial assistance to their children partly depends on their own financial condition, it has been suggested that (the lack of) parental financial support during emerging adulthood may even play a significant role in reproducing economic inequalities within families (see Chapter 15; Swartz, 2008; Swartz & O'Brien, 2016).

The association between parental socioeconomic status (SES) and the extent of financial support provided to adult children has been consistently demonstrated across studies (Manzoni, 2018; Schoeni & Ross, 2013; Swartz et al., 2011). Research in the United States indicates that emerging adults (18- to 34-year-olds) from families within the top income quartile receive nearly 3 times as much assistance as those from the bottom two quartiles (Schoeni & Ross, 2013). Notable socioeconomic disparities have also been observed in emerging adults' financial independence trajectories and the support patterns they receive throughout their life-course. As indicated by their parents' educational attainment, emerging adults from higher socioeconomic backgrounds were more likely to experience extended support during their transition to adulthood. These individuals typically followed trajectories characterized by a gradual transition to financial self-sufficiency or a prolonged reliance on parental financial assistance (Bea & Yi, 2019).

The considerable differences in financial support accessible to emerging adults from various social strata are not exclusive to the U.S. context and have also been observed in other countries. Research conducted with Australian emerging adults indicated that young individuals from socioeconomically disadvantaged families tended to attain self-sufficiency earlier, as they no longer lived with their parents or received parental financial support (Cobb-Clark & Gørgens, 2014). In several European countries, higher parental socioeconomic status correlated with an increased likelihood of parental financial assistance (Majamaa, 2013; Van Herreweghe & Van Lancker, 2021).

Interestingly, the association between parental SES and financial support for emerging adults is stronger for direct financial assistance, such as the amount of transferred money, and considerably weaker for indirect support. For instance, Swartz et al. (2011) observed that parents from all income groups were inclined to provide at least some financial help for living expenses to their emerging adult children, suggesting that parental SES differences documented in other studies likely relate to the amount of money parents directly provide. Similarly, some studies report that co-residence is linked to parental SES but in the opposite direction of direct support, in other words, parents with lower education levels were more likely to live with an adult child (Fingerman et al., 2016). In sum, financial transfers are more affected by parental SES than co-residence, indicating that lower-income parents are willing to assist their children financially but find it more cost-effective to support their emerging adult children through co-residence rather than providing direct financial support (Cobb-Clark & Gørgens, 2014).

As higher-income parents provide more substantial amounts of direct financial support, one might expect financial support to mediate the connection between parental SES and their offspring's financial flourishing as they reach adulthood. Indeed, some studies demonstrate that emerging adults' occupational success is linked to parental financial support (Manzoni, 2018). However, such findings are not consistent. For instance, one study showed that the disparities in the subjective financial well-being of emerging adults based on their parents' income (see Chapter 15) tend to diminish over time (Cherney et al., 2020). In other words, for those from less privileged families, distancing themselves from their family's financial circumstances and building their financial resources improved their financial well-being. Conversely, those from more privileged families experienced a decline in their financial well-being as they became more independent from their parents (Cherney et al.). Considering these findings, more research is needed to understand how parents' capacities to support their emerging adult children financially perpetuate inequality in the next generation. The relation between parental SES and the financial support provided to their emerging adult children is not as straightforward as it may initially seem, as both higher- and lower-SES parents tend to support their children, though in different ways.

Parental Financial Support and Emerging Adults' Psychosocial Development

Parental financial support during emerging adulthood contributes to emerging adults' financial flourishing and allows extended education enrollment that may lead to better job prospects. Nevertheless, its effect on emerging adults' psychosocial development is, somewhat surprisingly, largely unfavorable. In particular, the findings reviewed in this section suggest that sustained parental financial support seemingly slows down desirable developmental changes expected to occur as individuals mature into full-fledged adults.

Building on Arnett's seminal research on criteria for adulthood, which consistently found that "achieving financial independence from parents" was ranked among the top three markers necessary for adulthood by emerging adults (Arnett, 1994, 1997, 1998, 2003), early investigations delved into the relation between emerging adults' self-perceived adult status and financial self-sufficiency. Echoing Arnett's work, a U.S.-based cross-sectional study involving 25- to 26-year-olds found that those not relying on parental financial support were more likely to self-identify as adults compared to their counterparts who did (Shanahan et al., 2005). Another U.S.-based longitudinal study of 19- to 21-year-olds indicated that individuals who assumed greater financial responsibilities (such as paying rent or financially supporting themselves and their families) over a 2-year period were more likely to perceive themselves as adults compared to those with fewer financial obligations (Benson & Furstenberg, 2006). Expanding on these findings, another study with Lithuanian students reported a positive cross-sectional association between financial dependence and feelings of being neither an adolescent nor an adult, indicating that emerging adults still relying on parents for financial assistance were less likely to self-identify as adults (Vosylis & Klimstra, 2022). Unsurprisingly, similar observations have been reported in another U.S. study involving parents; those who provided more substantial financial support to their emerging adult children were less likely to view their offspring as full-fledged adults (Padilla-Walker et al., 2012).

Another line of research showed that the maturation-decelerating effects of parental financial support extend beyond perceived adult status, shaping many other life domains. For instance, one U.S.-based study found that parental financial support for education increased the likelihood of college graduation but was also associated with lower grade point averages (Hamilton, 2013). At the same time, another U.S.-based study found that emerging adults who received minimal financial assistance from their parents had a more developed sense of occupational identity (Padilla-Walker et al., 2012). Such findings suggest that students relying on parents for financial support may have lesser interest in their academic ability and invest less effort in their educational pursuits and the development of their occupational career goals.

While financially dependent emerging adults do not necessarily perceive themselves as less capable of taking responsibility for their actions (Johnson & Ridgeway, 2023), reliance on parental financial support was linked to less favorable outcomes regarding risky and rule-breaking behaviors. A cross-sectional study conducted in the United States showed that compared to those who were entirely financially dependent on parents (i.e., did not have any income from employment), emerging adults who received minimal parental financial assistance engaged in fewer drinking and binge drinking behaviors (Padilla-Walker et al., 2012). Moreover, a longitudinal study conducted in the Netherlands indicated that reaching financial self-sufficiency was associated with a decreased likelihood of engaging in adolescent-like delinquent behaviors, and this effect held irrespective of the educational and employment status or living arrangements of emerging adults (Hill et al., 2017).

Studies have also demonstrated a longitudinal connection between parental financial support and self-evaluations beyond self-perceived adulthood. For instance, one U.S.-based study found a relative decrease in self-esteem associated with extended financial dependence (Johnson, 2013). Another study with U.S. emerging adults showed that parental financial support corresponded with a relative decline in general self-efficacy (Mortimer et al., 2016). Additionally, several studies, one from the United States (Johnson, 2013) and one from South Korea (Oh & Lee, 2023), found a positive relation between parental financial support and depressive symptoms. Interestingly, deviating from the generally negative associations with well-being in emerging adults, a South Korean study reported a positive relationship between parental financial support and life satisfaction (Oh & Lee, 2023). However, this finding is not entirely unexpected or likely to be specific to a certain cultural context, given that life satisfaction is a global person-based criteria assessment of one's quality of life (Shin & Johnson, 1978) and can involve an evaluation of one's financial situation.

Noteworthy is that studies targeting a broader range of parental financial support indicators, such as housing assistance, suggest that the disadvantageous effects of parental financial support on the well-being and developmental outcomes of emerging adults primarily apply to direct financial support. For instance, Mortimer et al. (2016) found that diminished self-efficacy in emerging adults was linked solely to direct financial support, not co-residence. Similarly, a study examining the relation between parental financial support and delinquent behaviors found negligible effects related to residential status (Hill et al., 2017). Therefore, it is plausible that direct and indirect support may carry different implications during emerging adulthood.

The Dynamics of Parent–Child Relationships in the Context of Prolonged Parental Financial Support

The general life task that emerging adults from industrialized societies face as they transition to full adulthood can be described as "learning to stand alone" (Arnett, 1998, 2014). This task involves a transition from dependence to independence in the context of emerging adults' relationships with their parents (Tanner, 2006). According to recentering theory (Tanner, 2006), this transformation involves a three-stage process. The first stage sees individuals at the boundary of adolescence and emerging adulthood, largely dependent on their families, sharing legal responsibility for their actions. The second stage, typically during emerging adulthood, is marked by exploratory involvement in education (see Chapter 9), occupations (see Chapter 10), and relationships (see Chapter 14). In this stage, emerging adults move from complete to semi-dependence, striving for autonomy but still requiring parental support and renegotiating power dynamics within their parent–child relationships.

During the semi-dependence stage, parents and emerging adult children face the challenge of determining the extent of autonomy and freedom the latter should have in their life choices. Simultaneously, they must decide to what extent emerging adults should heed parental advice, particularly considering that many parents continue to provide financial support. As emerging adults' identity stabilizes (see Chapter 12) and they acquire resources for a self-sufficient life, they reach the third stage, where family boundaries become clearer.

Supporting this theory, a recent comprehensive review of existing studies showed that the onset of emerging adulthood marks a significant shift in the dynamics between an individual and their family (Oliveira et al., 2020). Specifically, parent–child relationships tend to evolve toward enhanced mutuality during emerging adulthood, improved communication, heightened reciprocity, increased equality, improved closeness, and reduced turmoil. These positive changes are, however, accompanied by a downward trend in the frequency of family communication and the intensity of emotional bonds with parents. While these transformations are partly triggered by the fact that many emerging adults move out of the parental home during this period, they are also shaped by how much financial support parents still offer their children, which often regulates the level of control parents can exercise in their children's lives (Padilla-Walker et al., 2012).

Providing evidence that finances are important in the dynamics of parent–child relationships, studies in the United States investigating how parents and emerging adult children view their relationships show that emerging adults' occupational career prospects and family money issues are the two most frequently discussed topics in conversations between emerging adults and their parents (Bartoszuk et al., 2021). These topics are also perceived to be central by both emerging adults and their parents, and they are those on which parents and their children disagree most.

A study in the United States also showed that parental concerns about their children's transition to self-sufficiency significantly increase the likelihood of financial conflicts in their relationship (Lowe & Arnett, 2019). While a study in South Korea also showed that higher levels of parental financial support were correlated with increased pressure stemming from parents' career expectations, which was, in turn, associated with heightened symptoms of depression in emerging adults (Oh & Lee, 2023). These studies show that extended reliance on parental assistance may inadvertently lead to emerging adults failing to meet their and their parents' expectations regarding their transition to successful employment (see also Johnson, 2013), potentially resulting in their poorer well-being, and this effect may not be culturally dependent.

The level of financial support that parents provide also shapes the level of control they have in their children's lives. Among first-year U.S. college students, parental financial support was linked to parental overinvolvement in the lives of children (Lowe et al., 2015). A higher level of parental control in multiple domains of life was also associated with higher dependence on parental financial support among emerging adults from the United States (Padilla-Walker et al., 2012). These findings illustrate that it is likely prolonged parental financial support can undermine emerging adults' efforts as they seek to establish themselves as independent, self-sufficient, and responsible individuals (see Chapter 12). Considering that controlling parenting has many detrimental effects on emerging adults' psychological functioning (e.g., Costa et al., 2015; Soenens et al., 2005), the unfavorable effects of parental financial support on emerging adults' developmental progression and well-being may be at least partly linked to the higher level of parental control.

Directions for Future Research

Before attempting to draw conclusions that summarize the reviewed studies, it is worth reflecting on the limitations that apply to this line of research. The complexity and limitations of existing research on parental financial support for emerging adult children's financial and general well-being provide multiple avenues for future research.

First, most studies addressing the links between parental financial support and developmental outcomes are either cross-sectional or use relatively short-term longitudinal designs that rarely extend beyond emerging adulthood. Therefore, the potential long-term implications of parental financial support later in life remain largely unstudied. In this respect, it is unclear if the unfavorable effects of prolonged parental financial support are limited to emerging adulthood or extend beyond established adulthood. Future studies should rely on long-term designs extending beyond emerging adulthood and measure both psychosocial developmental and financial outcomes in relation to financial support received from parents.

Second, parental financial support has been mainly measured through direct financial assistance, meaning how much money parents give to their emerging adult children. Nevertheless, existing research shows that parental financial support extends beyond direct support and includes multiple types of indirect support. These forms may be especially culturally specific (see Chapter 17) and dependent on family SES (see Chapter 15). Future research should chart these alternative forms of support in specific cultural contexts and investigate their effects on emerging adult children's financial well-being and developmental progression.

Third, the mechanisms that are at play in the associations between parental financial support and financial and general flourishing and floundering are yet relatively understudied. While we discussed a few most likely mechanisms, additional ones may also be important. For example, one mechanism that may explain the link between financial support and the financial well-being (see Chapter 7) of emerging adults is that financial support from parents can protect emerging adult children from potential financial stress (see Chapter 8) during the extended transition to stable employment (see Chapter 10) as emerging adults usually try multiple jobs before settling on a steady career. Another mechanism may involve the development of financial capabilities. In particular, the links between the level and form of parental financial support and the formation of financial capabilities have not yet been sufficiently studied. It may be that parental financial support has a positive role in financial flourishing during the early years and a more negative role in later years of emerging adulthood because emerging adults in their early twenties may not have the financial skills (see Chapter 3) and knowledge (see Chapter 2) necessary to manage their money effectively. This can make it difficult for them to transition to financial independence without the support of their parents and can lead to financial stress. On the other hand, emerging adults who receive full or partial parental financial support for longer periods may have more time to develop the financial skills and knowledge they need to be financially independent. Both of these mechanisms are certainly worth further study.

Conclusion

In this chapter, we discussed the role of parental financial support in the financial and general well-being and development of emerging adults. We first reviewed the increasing role of parental financial support in contemporary societies. Findings of the existing studies clearly reveal that around half of emerging adults in the United States and other Western industrialized societies rely at least on partial parental financial support. We also highlighted the diversity of the transition to financial self-sufficiency, with some emerging adults reaching financial self-sufficiency early, whereas others remain financially dependent on their parents well into their thirties. This diversity has implications for how we understand the consequences of extended parental financial support.

We also discussed the culturally shaped nature of parental financial support. We stressed that in economically developed societies the main variation in parental financial support seems to relate to the form of support rather than the level of support. For example, parents in some cultures may prefer to provide direct financial assistance, such as money transfers, while parents in other cultures may prefer to provide indirect support, such as co-residence. In this respect, we stressed that the cultural context and type of support that parents prefer need to be considered to understand how extended parental support can shape the financial and general well-being of emerging adults.

Third, we also examined how parental financial support shapes the financial well-being of emerging adults (see Chapter 7). Based on existing cross-sectional and longitudinal evidence, we uncovered the positive longitudinal effects of parental financial support on emerging adults' financial flourishing and floundering. Considering that longitudinal effects are both short- and long-term, we also stressed that these effects are likely indirect and can be explained through mechanisms involving the length of the educational period, varying job prospects (see Chapter 10), student loan debt (see Chapter 9), and potentially other factors that need to be examined further.

Fourth, we tackled the socioeconomic divide, discussing the role of parental SES (see Chapter 15) in the type of financial support they can provide to their emerging adult children. We pointed out that while higher-SES families can and do provide more direct financial help to their children, families of lower-SES also offer indirect financial help to their offspring. While we additionally show that levels of financial support can explain the link between parental SES and a child's financial well-being during emerging adulthood, we stressed that the effect of parental investments on offspring's financial wellness may be less visible as the offspring enters full adulthood. In this respect, we underscored that the efforts of emerging adults themselves may play an increasingly important role in their financial flourishing as they become financially self-sufficient adults.

Fifth, we investigated how parental financial support shapes emerging adults' developmental changes. We highlighted that extended parental financial support, paradoxically, has mostly unfavorable effects on emerging adults' psychosocial development. Existing findings suggest that sustained parental financial support slows down desirable developmental changes expected to occur as individuals mature into full-fledged adults. More so, we emphasized that parent–child relationships and, in particular, the level of parental control may also mediate the effects of parental financial support on emerging adults' developmental progression. Considering the favorable effects of extended parental financial support on financial well-being and the unfavorable effects on developmental progression, we concluded that parental financial support should not be viewed as something that is either positive or negative. Instead, extended versus short-term support likely puts emerging adults on different life paths, both of which have their own merits and drawbacks.

Financial independence from parents is a cornerstone for entering established adulthood. Nevertheless, contemporary societies set high educational and occupational standards for many emerging adults (see Chapters 9 and 10), which financially bind them to their families for extended periods of time. This prolonged parental financial support is both a blessing (e.g., children have the time and space to engage in educational and vocational exploration, they can focus on completing their tertiary education) and a curse (e.g., continued parental financial support into late emerging adulthood may hinder the development of their children's capacities for autonomy). Parents around the world strive to offer their emerging adult children the type of financial support that is most accessible and acceptable in their socioeconomic strata (see Chapter 15) and cultural context (see Chapter 17). Therefore, parental financial support is a long-term manifestation of parent–child relationships marked by intergenerational care. Parents offer their children the chance for a better future by cushioning their emerging adult years through direct and indirect financial support, hence helping them navigate toward financial self-sufficiency.

Chapter 12
Emerging Adults' Financial Identity

Joyce Serido[1], Mette Ranta[2,], and Soyeon Shim[3]*

Introduction

The Danish philosopher Soren Kierkegaard is credited with saying, "Life can only be understood backwards; but it must be lived forwards." Indeed, the individual life narrative emerges from a life-long process of adapting to changing life demands in order to foster personal development and well-being (Baltes & Baltes, 1990). The transition to adulthood signals a major developmental shift, with individuals making life choices that will shape the trajectory of their adult life. Although finances play an important role in the choices people make, which subsequently affect the life outcomes of such choices, research often focuses on descriptive analyses of their choice behaviors at a given time, rather than considering such impact in a developmental context over time. Yet, if we were to reflect on where we are, who we are, and how we arrived here, the connection between finances and the choices we made in life reveals itself. In this chapter, we focus on the formation of the financial self in emerging adulthood, which we refer to as "financial identity."

Emerging adulthood is a time of exploration and identity development. Individuals explore their identity in a variety of domains. We contend that the formation of financial identity during emerging adulthood is an important domain for understanding the transitional pathways to adulthood (Serido et al., 2020). In the process, emerging adults become aware that many of the demands and obligations of adult life involve finances. Whether (and whom) to marry (see Chapter 14), what career to pursue (see Chapter 10), choosing to attend college (see Chapter 9), even when (or if) to move out of the parental home (see Chapter 11) or become a parent themselves, are

[1] Family Social Science, University of Minnesota, USA
[2] Department of Education, University of Helsinki, Finland
[3] School of Human Ecology, University of Wisconsin—Madison, USA
* Funding from the Finnish Strategic Research Council [# 352545] was used to support Dr. Mette Ranta's time writing this chapter.

Joyce Serido, Mette Ranta, and Soyeon Shim, *Emerging Adults' Financial Identity*. In: *Flourishing and Floundering Financially in Emerging Adulthood*. Edited by: Ashley B. LeBaron-Black, Heather Kelley, and Angela Sorgente, Oxford University Press. DOI: 10.1093/9780197699157.003.0013

choices that shape the individual life pathway. The effects of each choice serve as guideposts in the pathway to adult self-sufficiency, that is, making and taking responsibility for one's own actions across multiple life domains (Arnett, 2000; Erikson, 1950, 1968). To answer the question "Who am I from a financial point of view?," this chapter begins with a description of identity formation, why we study identity, how it develops and changes, and its multidimensional nature. We then focus on the role of financial independence in emerging adult development (see Chapter 11), including conceptualizations, in association with decision-making and change. We demonstrate how financial identity in general, and financial decision-making styles in particular, contribute to a dynamic person-centered journey to financial independence (see Chapter 11) and well-being (see Chapter 7). Where possible, we provide examples drawn from interviews conducted with some of the emerging adult participants in our studies. We conclude the chapter with suggestions for advancing our understanding of the processes that promote financial well-being and independence among emerging adults.

Identity Formation

In the classic work of developmental psychologist and psychoanalyst Erik Erikson (1950, 1968), identity has been conceptualized as a process of individual differentiation and reconciliation. As such, the individual becomes increasingly aware of the demands of the external world and strives to create a personal identity, a coherent understanding of the self in the context of the external world. Identity encompasses one's goals (see, e.g., Box 12.1), values, and beliefs as well as one's connections to aspects of groups with which one is affiliated. Although initially conceived of as an adolescent developmental task, Erikson (1950, 1968) emphasized that identity formation continues to develop throughout the life span as an ongoing process of psychodynamic responses to sociohistorical circumstances. In other words, individuals continue to make meaning of changing life circumstances. Erickson (1950, 1968) has suggested that a fully formed identity—defined as a state in which an individual has made commitments to personally meaningful values and beliefs after a period of exploration—is an essential aspect of human development. In this sense, a fully formed identity serves as a guiding force or compass for the choices one makes and the opportunities one pursues. In subsequent study, Adams and Marshall (1996) outlined several self-regulatory functions of identity, including facilitating self-understanding, providing meaning and direction through commitments, values, and goals, offering a sense of personal control, and guiding investment in future-oriented endeavors.

Box 12.1

What are your financial goals, say, 5 years from now? "I guess helping my parents financially. I am on my own, but they help me out when I need it, so I think I would like to give back. Hopefully I will be financially well enough to give back. Not only to make myself comfortable but continue to make them comfortable. I guess that is one of my goals, you could say."

—"Rosie," Latina, age 23

"I would love to just kind of cut ties for a year, buy a decent motorcycle, get some camping gear, and just go as far as I can in a year. Like either go across the country, if I get that far then go up to Alaska, if I get that far then take a ferry to Russia [and] go through Europe. I would love to just do that for a year, and in the course of that year try to find a place that I really enjoyed being, that I could see myself spending the next 4 or 5 years and then set up shop there."

—"Mark," White man, age 20

Why Study Identity Formation in Emerging Adults?

Interest in the study of identity formation is growing across disciplines (Galliher et al., 2017), demonstrating that a well-developed identity may serve as a guide for emerging adults in navigating the increasing complexity and uncertainty of contemporary life. A distinctive, coherent, and continuous sense of self has been associated with the practice of prosocial behaviors (e.g., internalization of values, spirituality; Padilla-Walker et al., 2008), higher-quality romantic relationships (Barry et al., 2009), attainment of financial independence (Butterbaugh et al., 2020), and greater health and well-being (Ritchie et al., 2013). Based on the assertion that one's identity is correlated with one's life outcomes in various ways, we turn our focus to the formation of domain-specific identities—self-perceptions in different aspects of daily life—and explore the ways in which financial identity may be correlated with one's life outcomes. If these arguments are valid, then the formation of a financial identity would seem to be a salient domain-specific context during the transition to adulthood, given the increasing expectations of self-sufficiency and independence that occur during this stage of life (Mortimer et al., 2016; Ranta et al., 2012; Serido et al., 2020).

The Study of Domain-Specific Identity Formation

From a life-span perspective, identity is often construed as a global sense of self or personal identity. However, in light of the fact that specific life concerns become salient at different developmental stages and across different contexts (e.g., culture, geography), identity researchers have provided evidence on the formation of domain-specific identities at different life stages (Vosylis et al., 2018), as well as reconsideration and revision of one's personal identity in response to changing circumstances and social roles (Crocetti et al., 2013; Luyckx et al., 2006). For example, the transition to full-time career work remains an important context for identity formation during emerging adulthood (see Chapter 10), attributable in part to the lengthening transition to adulthood. Several studies have shown that identity exploration in the area of work contributes to positive career and life outcomes (e.g., Laughland-Booy et al., 2017; Luyckx et al., 2014; Stringer & Kerpelman, 2010). Furthermore, educational identity development, an important adolescent context (e.g., Negru-Subtirica et al., 2017), continues to play an important role in post-industrial societies (Aronson et al., 2015; Luyckx et al., 2008), with many emerging adults enrolling in higher education to secure more stable career employment (see Chapter 9).

Although a robust literature demonstrates that identity progresses toward commitment both within and across domains (McLean et al., 2016; Syed & McLean, 2015) and that commitment within each domain contributes positively to a global identity (Vosylis et al., 2018), there is a need to examine identity formation at the intersection of multiple identity contexts (Crocetti et al., 2018; Galliher et al., 2017; Mancini et al., 2015). That is, identity formation must be understood within the lived experiences of the individual, including the influences of sociodemographic, cultural, and individual factors. One example of how multiple influences shape the formation of career identity comes from Mancini et al. (2015). In this study of Asian American college students, the researchers identified differences in the ways that culture (e.g., individualistic vs. collectivist; acculturation vs. differentiation) influences career identity. Although there are several methods of assessing content identity and multiple process models of identity formation, there is some consensus that identity formation is a complex and shifting collection of interrelated, domain-specific identities (see, e.g., Box 12.2; Crocetti et al., 2018; Negru-Subtirica et al., 2017).

Box 12.2

"I grew up in [country] and because of the poor education offered there, we decided to move to America. And my parents' education was high . . . so my mom didn't have to work. They went to college in [country], but their education wasn't accepted according to the curriculum in the United States, so they are now only considered high school graduates here."

—"Astra," immigrant woman, age 22

The Role of Financial Independence in Emerging Adult Development

Although adult status has been historically defined as achieving adult social roles (e.g., completion of education, full-time career work, leaving the parental home, marriage, and parenthood) for contemporary emerging adults these milestones are less likely to occur in sequential order, if they occur at all (Settersten & Ray, 2010), due to changing social norms and labor market opportunities. Because the pathways to achieving observable markers of adulthood are more dynamic and diverse, Arnett (2000) argued that a subjective component is essential in defining adult status in contemporary society. Consequently, the transition from adolescent dependence to adult independence is better understood as accepting responsibility for oneself, making independent decisions, and becoming financially independent (see, e.g., Box 12.3; Arnett, 2000).

Box 12.3

Do you consider yourself an adult?

"Yes and no. Adult in an economic perspective, no. I can't support myself right now. I can't live on my own, I live with roommates and obviously get a lot of help from my parents. Emotionally, yes. I am mature and can rationalize decisions, I can think about consequences, think about [the] future. Just the way I behave, yes, but not economically."

—"Lisha," Black woman, age 19

Much of the literature examining the role of finances in emerging adult development has focused on achieving financial independence from parents (see Chapter 11), defined as a subjective feeling of being able to financially support oneself. For example, a majority of survey studies of emerging adults and older adolescents endorse establishing financial independence from parents as a precursor to adult status (Arnett, 1998, 2000; Galambos et al., 2005). When asked to describe a time when they felt like an adult, acquiring financial responsibilities (e.g., paying my own bills) was an often cited example (Lowe et al., 2013). Indeed, emerging adults who receive more parental financial support may be less likely to perceive themselves as an adult (Padilla-Walker et al., 2008, 2012) and more likely to report lower levels of well-being (Kirkpatrick Johnson, 2013; Mortimer et al., 2016).

Because learning how to navigate the financial domain is an essential component of self-sufficiency (Arnett, 2000; Serido et al., 2020), the study of financial identity as a domain-specific component of identity development in the transition to adulthood is a timely and important topic.

Conceptualization, Structure, and Measurement of Financial Identity

The concept of financial identity originated in the consumer finance literature and was formalized as an outcome of computerized credit assessment. Specifically, the use of sophisticated credit scoring programs, such as Fair Isaac's FICO algorithm, measured individual credit worthiness (Lauer, 2010). From the perspective of financial institutions, financial identity offered a form of "moral accounting" (Lauer, 2010, p. 696) to determine who could borrow money and on what terms. In other words, financial identity in this case served as an objective indicator of one's ability to repay borrowed money and had little to do with one's subjective feeling regarding their financial self. In fact, the reality is that people's financial lives, including their experiences with and understanding of the financial system, are much more complex than what a credit score can capture. Because money, credit, and consumption play a central role in emerging adult financial independence, Barber et al. (2011) launched a line of inquiry on the formation of the financial self, that is, the study of the role of financial values and beliefs in developing agentic functioning in the domain of finances.

In conceptualizing financial identity, Barber et al. (2011) drew on Erikson's (1950, 1968) theory of identity formation and Marcia's (1966) operationalization of Erickson's theory of identity resolution. The proposed structure operationalizes the dimensions of *exploration*, or the sense that one has questioned and considered the range of alternatives to identities provided by significant others or society, and *commitment* to a set of values and beliefs. By crossing these two dimensions as applied to the financial domain, four types of identity status can be described that vary in strength of exploration and commitment, as seen in Box 12.4.

Box 12.4 Conceptualization of Financial Identity

Exploring means actively searching for information regarding financial beliefs, values, and practices; in contrast, *accepting* means relying on established options and proven practices. *Committing* means deciding which options best fit the individual and applying those options in different settings; in contrast, *unconcerned* means a lack of attachment or interest in the options. Crossing these two dimensions results in four typologies of financial identity:

- Achievement: high exploration and high commitment
- Moratorium: high exploration and low commitment
- Foreclosure: low exploration and high commitment
- Diffusion: low exploration and low commitment

The researchers developed and pilot-tested a new measure, modifying 12 items (3 items for each status), from the Adams et al. (1979) Extended Objective Measure of Ego Identity Status (EOM-EIS) by inserting target content about financial management, use of credit, or spending in place of the domains contained in the original measure.

The Barber et al. (2011) study sought to determine if the concept of financial identity status, using this new measure, could be useful in understanding how emerging adults differ with respect to their engagement with credit, debt, and budgeting, and how those issues are integrated into their views of themselves. After confirming that the measure was comparable across a sample of college students from the United States and Australia, the researchers found that all four statuses were related to indicators of emerging adults' financial behavior (see Chapter 5) and well-being (see Chapter 7). Notably, higher levels of achieved and foreclosed financial identity generally were associated with more positive outcomes, while moratorium financial identity was associated with more negative outcomes. Although higher diffused status was associated with more negative financial behavior, the association with well-being was not significant. The authors speculated that as first-year students, many may not be directly responsible for finances or aware of the implications of their behaviors.

Bosch et al. (2016) expanded on this work using data collected from college students enrolled at a university in the United States in their first and fourth years of college to assess change in status and to investigate potential antecedents of financial identity status. The findings suggest that although financial identity status remained relatively stable during the college years, there was some evidence of a shift from higher exploration to higher commitment from the first to fourth year of college. The study also added to the robust body of literature on the important influence of family financial socialization (see Chapter 18) received by individuals not just on their future financial well-being but also on their relational, mental, and physical well-being (see LeBaron & Kelley, 2021, for a recent review). Specifically, early parental communication about finances contributed to higher achieved identity status in the fourth year of college, whereas higher parental socioeconomic status and compliance to parental expectations contributed to higher foreclosure in the fourth year of college. For example quotations from emerging adults and tips about the influence of parents on financial identity, see Box 12.5.

Box 12.5 Financial Identity

Tip: Parents and practitioners can help promote financial self-sufficiency by pointing out the relevance of financial management practices in the everyday contexts of family life and encouraging emerging adult children to apply these practices.

"I think mostly she's [Mom has] been a really good role model. I mean, I always watched her balance her checkbook when I was little. Even before I really understood it, I knew, 'Oh, you have to keep track of your money and you know, you're not spending more than you have.' And my mom's the one who told us you know, 'You should never have a balance on a credit card.'"

—"Minerva," Latina, age 24

Tip: Be cautious about setting expectations without providing a rationale to avoid compliance without understanding.

"And so, you know, they [parents] would tell me 'It's your money, but it seems like you're wasting it just to go out for a meal.' But then I think it sort of gradually changed, like my parents would eventually be like, 'You're not going out as much, you have more money to do more fun things.'"

—"Lindy," White woman, age 24

Tip: Understand that family background influences emerging adults' value and meaning of money.

"If you're asking me compared to Americans, then yes, it is different the way we were raised and how allowance was, there was no such thing as allowance. For us, if it was needed, they considered buying it for us, and if it was not, we were to live without it. I rarely see them spend money on themselves."

—"Astra," immigrant woman, age 22

"Yeah, my mom would sit down 3 or 4 times a year and just go over all my bank statements and my Fidelity account, which is where I put all of my money to save things like that, so she shows me where I spent my money and kind of where I'm wasting mine, too, when I spend money. . . . I think that they did a really good job holding me accountable for all my finances, like if I spent money, you know that was stuff that I would have to pay off that my parents wouldn't do for me."

—"Jason," White man, age 24

Sorgente et al. (2020) conducted a multinational validation study of emerging adults in three countries (i.e., United States, Italy, Lithuania) to assess the validity of the measure. After minor rewording of one compound sentence (i.e., "I've never really questioned my views about saving and spending. If it's right for my parents, it must be right for me"), the measure was found to be valid and reliable. A subsequent study on the associations between family financial socialization and emerging adult outcomes, including the Financial Identity Scale (FIS), was conducted by Vosylis and Erentaitė (2020). In this study of Lithuanian emerging adults, the researchers found that while common practices exhibited some degree of cultural variability (e.g., norms around saving) as well as differing associations by type of outcome (e.g., FIS, financial behavior, financial anxiety), financial socialization factors strongly influenced financial identity statuses, and, in turn, financial identity statuses influenced both financial behavior and financial anxiety. Taken together, the literature suggests that financial identity may represent a process of internalization of selected family values into emerging adults' financial style.

Financial Identity and Financial Decision-Making Styles

The FIS provides an assessment of an individual's endorsement of each of the four identity status types. Although individuals may endorse one identity status type more strongly than another, there is likely to be considerable variation in the strength of each endorsement and the pattern of endorsement across the four types (Waterman, 1999). That is, the combination of endorsement of each status might be a better indication of how one approaches problem solving or, in our case, how emerging adults make financial decisions. Building on the identity status model (Marcia, 1966), Berzonsky (1989) proposed the concept of "identity style" to explain how individuals make decisions on a daily basis. This work provided evidence of three distinct problem-solving approaches: *informational*, which refers to a proactive, open-minded, and flexible approach to addressing life choices; *normative*, which refers to adhering to the expectations and norms established by others (including cultural as well as familial guidelines); and *diffuse-avoidant*, which refers to procrastination and attempting not to deal with important life decisions.

Applying this framework to the financial domain, Shim et al. (2013) identified three *financial identity styles* (see Box 12.6) using cluster analysis of the four identity statuses as reported by a sample of U.S. college students. In the first cluster, labeled *pathfinder*, achieved financial identity status scored highest (i.e., achieved a style that emerged from reflection and experience), similar to the informational identity-processing style. In the second cluster, labeled *follower*, foreclosed financial identity scored highest (i.e., the students adopted their parents' financial management style), similar to the normative identity-processing style. The third cluster, labeled *drifter*, scored high on moratorium (i.e., still exploring) and diffused (i.e., not particularly concerned about money) and low on achieved and foreclosed, most closely resembling the diffused-avoidant identity-processing style. In examining the role of financial socialization factors on these three styles, pathfinders reported higher levels of parental direct teaching and communication, while followers reported higher levels of parental role modeling. In addition, pathfinders, compared to followers and drifters, reported higher levels of self-agency, actively seeking out financial knowledge and information on their own. This work further emphasizes the important role of family financial socialization in promoting emerging adults' financial decision-making skills as well as underscoring the value of and the need for self-directed financial learning opportunities (see Chapter 18; Serido, 2021).

Box 12.6 Financial Identity Styles

Pathfinders are actively engaged in learning about financial matters. They seek information from multiple sources and explore different approaches to managing their finances. They think before making financial choices and are flexible when it comes to making financial decisions. Here are some questions for pathfinders to consider when making financial choices:

- What are the downsides of this decision?
- Is there a more efficient/effective way to think about my choices?
- Should I talk to someone with professional knowledge or experience before making a decision?
- Will this choice be good for me in the short term, long term, or both?

Followers often adopt the financial practices of their parents or other influential people in their lives without questioning or fully understanding how these practices contribute to financial choices. While following the practices of positive role models is a good approach, seeking additional information and evaluating options in the context of current circumstances may lead to more informed decision-making. Here are some questions for followers to consider when making financial choices:

- Am I doing this because it is expected of me?
- Will this choice teach me more about managing my finances?
- What additional information should I seek before making this decision?
- What other choices do I have?

Drifters show little interest in financial topics. They may reject the financial practices of their parents and other role models but do not have a consistent approach of their own. They may be reluctant about making financial decisions and consequently make choices without a lot of thought. Drifters may not understand that financial choices today impact their future. Here are some questions for drifters to consider when making financial choices:

- Do I understand that my financial choices affect not only my financial well-being but my physical and mental health as well?
- What information and knowledge do I need to make choices that benefit me?
- Who can make learning about financial matters easier to understand?

Financial Identity: Longitudinally and as a Person-Centered Process

Whereas financial identity statuses provide a glimpse into financial identity at a moment in life, and financial identity style suggests an approach to making financial decisions, neither fully addresses Erikson's (1950, 1968) conceptualization of identity as a dynamic process. However, there have been a few attempts to address this gap using longitudinal data to focus on the process of financial identity development.

In the first study, Vosylis et al. (2022) framed their investigation of identity formation in a three-factor model (Crocetti et al., 2008). According to this model, identity development involves two iterative cycles (i.e., formation and evaluation) that encompass three core processes. As adapted to the financial domain, the first process is commitment to a decision-making approach to managing personal finances; the second is the in-depth exploration and active reflection of current financial management practices; and the third is a reconsideration of one's current approach and alternatives as a result of dissatisfaction (e.g., with one's current approach and/or financial circumstances). The data, collected from Lithuanian college students 3 times over 20 months, provided support for the model. In addition, emerging adults who were dissatisfied with their current money management practices and in the process of exploring alternatives (high reconsideration) decreased their commitment to their current practices over time, while those who were satisfied decreased their reconsideration over time. The longitudinal approach also emphasizes that while financial identity is instrumental in promoting positive financial behaviors (see Chapter 5) and financial well-being (see Chapter 7), current financial circumstances must be taken into account (see Box 12.7). Given high levels of financial instability among emerging adults, this is an important consideration for understanding both identity formation and well-being among this demographic.

Box 12.7 Just-in-Time Financial Coaching

Financial circumstances influence financial identity and prompt individuals to seek out alternatives. Emerging adults may be open to receiving practical guidelines and information from colleagues and peers, particularly information to help them make more informed financial choices. Encourage emerging adults to seek additional information from a variety of sources, vetting the information through accredited financial sources, including financial professionals. Here are some questions that may pique emerging adults' interest in learning more about finances:

- Is it better to pay off debt or save for a house?
- What is a reasonable amount of money to have on hand for emergencies?
- How do you budget when you have seasonal income or multiple freelance jobs?
- Is investing in bitcoin safe?
- What are good investments?

To study the relation between financial identity and self-perception of adult status, Serido et al. (2022) used a unique longitudinal dataset from a cohort of college students in the United States collected at four time points over an 8-year period (2008–2016). This study expands on the understanding of financial identity formation by conducting a rigorous longitudinal and person-centered analysis. Authors adopted a person-centered analysis as they were able to classify emerging adults into three financial identity profiles (Shim et al., 2013) based on the scores they reported for the four financial identity statuses (Barber et al., 2011; Sorgente et al., 2020). Authors also adopted a longitudinal approach as they aimed to assess movement between profiles over time and to determine the direction of the association between financial identity and emerging adults' perception of adult status. The key finding of the study was empirical directional evidence of financial identity as a predictor of adult status and not the reverse. Erikson (1950, 1968) has stated that there is nothing static or unchangeable about any identity commitments. The Serido et al. (2022) study provided evidence that emerging adults do transition into and out of financial identity profiles; however, it appears that they commit more strongly to a certain financial identity profile over time, and this, in turn, may contribute to achieving adult self-sufficiency. Although financial identity may function as a guiding motivational force in promoting self-sufficiency, stable employment and the income it generates are likely to play an important part in becoming self-sufficient (see Chapter 10; Mortimer et al., 2016). Moreover, it is worth emphasizing that the influence of systemic, cultural, and structural factors (see Chapters 15 and 17) also plays an important part in achieving adult self-sufficiency. Understanding how these external factors shape financial identity and progress toward adult self-sufficiency remain unanswered.

Where Do We Go from Here?

Becoming a self-sufficient adult, a challenging developmental journey in the best of times, has become increasingly problematic in the aftermath of the COVID-19 pandemic. Unstable financial circumstances, lack of work-relevant skills (see Chapter 10), and a limited professional network render many emerging adults vulnerable to the long-term effects of the pandemic (British Academy, 2021; Kalleberg, 2020). In this context, further research on financial identity as part of the process by which emerging adults gain a sense of financial well-being (see Chapter 7), and how parents and professionals can aid in this process (see Chapters 18 and 19), is warranted. In setting an agenda for future research and practice, we offer the following suggestions based on our review of the literature.

As a starting point, there is an urgent need for qualitative studies to investigate how emerging adults see themselves within the financial domain. This is an often ignored area when investigating the life choices and diverse pathways to adulthood experienced by emerging adults. This is especially important because little is known about the influences of culture, class, and race (see Chapters 15 and 17) on what money means in defining self-sufficiency or financial well-being. Similarly, the limited research conducted with emerging adult samples outside the United States suggests that social norms and government policies play a role in the timing and formation of financial identity. Cross-national and international studies—including of youth not in employment, education, or training—may be of special importance in a post-pandemic reality. Although focusing on the formation of financial identity and its association with emerging adults' financial well-being makes sense for achieving adult self-sufficiency, investigating these processes and associations in adolescence may provide insights on early antecedents of financial identity. Longitudinal studies with older samples would be useful in understanding the stability and/or fluctuation of one's financial identity and its impact on the quality of life over time. Finally, studies that consider intersecting identities would yield insights on how financial identity influences or is influenced by other domain-specific identities (e.g., career; see Chapter 10) and the association with one's overall sense of self.

Conclusion

Erikson (1950, 1968) established the foundation for the study of identity as "an appreciation of the underlying interrelationships of a myriad of psychodynamic responses to sociohistorical circumstances" (Waterman, 1999, p. 186). Since then, a robust literature has emerged to demonstrate that a well-developed identity serves to guide and stabilize individuals as they navigate the demands of modern living (for reviews, see Côté & Levine, 2002, and Kroger & Marcia, 2011). In this chapter, we focus on the contribution of financial identity to our understanding of the formation of a well-developed emerging adult self in an era of social, economic, and political transformation.

Chapter 13
Emerging Adults' Consumption and Borrowing Behavior

Jing Jian Xiao, PhD[1] and Alyssa Scott, MS[1]

Introduction

The age range of emerging adults was originally defined as 18–25 (Arnett, 2000), which is the age range for a typical undergraduate student in college. In recent years, researchers expanded the age range of emerging adulthood to 18–29 or even 18–35 (Kadic-Maglajlic et al., 2019). In this chapter, following the definition provided by the Society for the Study of Emerging Adulthood (https://www.ssea.org/), we define emerging adults as those ages 18–29. For people within this age range, if they do not attend college or other training schools (see Chapter 9), they may either (1) find a job (see Chapter 10), becoming financially independent (see Chapter 11), or (2) engage in other activities, most likely supported by their parents. As of 2020, 40% of all 18- to 24-year-olds in the United States were enrolled in a post-secondary degree program (National Center for Education Statistics, n.d.). According to the U.S. Bureau of Labor Statistics (2023), among the 28,804,000 18- to 24-year-old nonstudents, 17,167,000 (60% of this population) were employed, 1,462,000 (5%) were unemployed (i.e., unemployed but looking for jobs), and 10,174,000 (35%) were not in the labor force (i.e., not looking for jobs, such as those in unpaid caregiving roles).

The purpose of this chapter is to review the research literature on the consumption and borrowing behaviors of emerging adults. "Consumption behavior" refers to activities in which consumers spend money to purchase and use products and services from the market, and "borrowing behavior" means activities in which consumers obtain funds from financial institutions and other sources, with or without interest, for a certain time period that will

[1] Department of Human Development and Family Science, University of Rhode Island, USA

Jing Jian Xiao and Alyssa Scott, *Emerging Adults' Consumption and Borrowing Behavior*. In: *Flourishing and Floundering Financially in Emerging Adulthood*. Edited by: Ashley B. LeBaron-Black, Heather Kelley, and Angela Sorgente, Oxford University Press. © Oxford University Press (2025). DOI: 10.1093/9780197699157.003.0014

be repaid (Xiao, 2015). We believe it is important to investigate consumption and borrowing behaviors during emerging adulthood because they are related to emerging adults' financial well-being (see Chapter 7), financial capability, and financial independence (see Chapter 11).

Consumption is an important indicator of consumer financial well-being. In consumer economics, major indicators of economic well-being include income, expenditure, debt, and savings. Income is the available resource, expenditure is a direct measure of consumption, debt is for financing current consumption, and savings is for future consumption. Debt (i.e., the consequence of borrowing) is an indicator that has a complicated relationship with consumer financial well-being (Xiao, 2015). Generally speaking, consumption is positively related to quality of life, where a higher level of consumption refers to higher life quality, which is evidenced by many measures of quality of life such as the human development index annually reported by the United Nations, of which income is a component (UNDP, 2022). However, borrowing is not straightforward for consumer financial well-being. Credit access can be good for consumers who need funds for current consumption and to build credit history, but too many debts may cause financial burdens (see Chapter 8) and lead to bankruptcy (Xiao & Yao, 2022). For emerging adults, consumption behavior and borrowing behavior may affect their financial well-being (see Chapter 7) directly. When emerging adults become financially independent (see Chapter 11), they have full responsibility for paying their living expenses. If they have insufficient economic resources, they may borrow from various sources. The purpose of borrowing is to transfer future resources to cover current expenses. In that sense, borrowing is a channel for emerging adults to have a certain standard of living.

Consumption and borrowing behaviors are also important indicators of financial capability. Financial capability refers to the ability to apply appropriate financial knowledge (see Chapter 2), perform desirable financial behaviors (see Chapter 5), and take financial opportunities for achieving financial well-being (Xiao et al., 2022). Emerging adults' financial literacy level is low (Lusardi et al., 2010), and they are starting to learn how to perform desirable financial behaviors, especially borrowing behaviors (Xiao et al., 2009).

Finally, performing desirable consumption and borrowing behaviors is critical for the financial independence of the young (Cui et al., 2019; Xiao et al., 2014). Their consumption patterns and borrowing purposes are different depending on their work (see Chapter 10) and school (see Chapter 9) statuses (Shim et al., 2009, 2010), and desirable financial behavior (see Chapter 5) may help emerging adults reach financial independence (see Chapter 11) sooner.

The rest of this chapter is organized as follows. In the following two sections, the literature on emerging adults' consumption and borrowing behaviors, respectively, will be reviewed. Then, future research directions on emerging adults' consumption and borrowing behaviors will be discussed. The final section concludes with a call-out box including implications for practitioners.

Consumption Behavior of Emerging Adults

Overview

The direct measure of consumption is expenditure. Based on the most recent estimate, in the United States, the average annual expenditure for all consumer units (i.e., individuals or families) in 2021 was $66,928. Overall, housing accounted for the highest share (33.8%) of the expenditures, followed by transportation (16.4%), food (12.4%), and personal insurance and pensions (e.g., worker-contributed retirement savings) (11.8%) (Bureau of Labor Statistics, 2022).

The consumption patterns of emerging adults are different from those of older age groups. According to economists, consumer spending is "hump-shaped" over the life cycle: Spending ramps up in early adulthood, peaks around middle age (40–50), and then declines with age (Attanasio & Weber, 1995; Fernández-Villaverde & Krueger, 2007). The pattern is verified with recent research. With data of 32 years (1983–2012) of U.S. consumer expenditure surveys, researchers have found that middle-aged households, on average, spend around $60,000 (measured in 2012 dollars) per year, about $21,000 more than the average spending for younger households ($38,500) and about $13,000 more than the average spending for older households ($47,200) (Nie & Gautam, 2020). In other words, the average consumption of younger households (i.e., the head of household ages 18–29) is 64% of the middle-aged households (i.e., head ages 30–60).

Researchers also found age differences in terms of consumption amounts and shares. In terms of consumption amounts, young households are the lowest in four categories (rent, household goods and services, health, and food) but greater than older households in two categories (transportation and leisure, and education and communication). In terms of consumption shares (i.e., a specific item consumption/total consumption), young households are the lowest in three categories (rent, household goods and services, and health), highest in two categories (transportation and leisure, and education and communication), and almost the same in one category (food) among the three age groups (Nie & Gautam, 2020). The information is informative for public policymaking regarding young people's consumption.

Desirable Consumption Behaviors

Consumption behaviors can be categorized into desirable and undesirable behaviors. Desirable consumption behaviors include smart shopping behavior, ethical consumption behavior, and socially responsible consumption behavior (Xiao, 2015). In recent years, researchers have started to use the term "sustainable consumption behavior" for desirable behavior because its definition covers a broad range of good behaviors. Sustainable consumption behavior is defined as any consumer act that directly or indirectly contributes to consumer welfare and environmental protection (Xiao, 2022). It is associated with life satisfaction (Xiao, 2021; Xiao & Li, 2011). Sustainable consumption behavior may contribute to emerging adults' general well-being. Data from a sample of U.S. college students ages 23–26 showed that reduced consumption, an indicator of sustainable consumption, is positively associated with subjective well-being (Helm et al., 2019).

Several studies have identified factors contributing to sustainable consumption behaviors (Annunziata et al., 2019; Helm et al., 2019; Kadic-Maglajlic et al., 2019; Kreuzer et al., 2019; LeBaron-Black et al., 2023). Research indicated a low literacy level about sustainable consumption among emerging adults. Data from a sample of emerging adults ages 18–26 in Italy demonstrated that sustainability labels such as Rainforest Alliance certification and Libera Terra have never been noted by large percentages of respondents. Moreover, the degree of understanding of these labels is generally low (Annunziata et al., 2019). Researchers in Germany have conducted mixed-method research based on the cube model (Geiger et al., 2018) to identify patterns and barriers of sustainable consumption among emerging adults ages 22–23 and found that emerging adults primarily consider the acquisition and less so the phases of use and disposal during their realized sustainable consumption behavior. The main barriers identified are high price, lack of information, as well as knowledge and abilities (Kreuzer et al., 2019).

Researchers in Slovenia and Croatia, using data from emerging adults ages 18–35, showed that pro-environmental/pro-social engagements (conscious attention, enthused participation, and social connection) are significant predictors of pro-environmental/pro-social consumption behavior

(Kadic-Maglajlic et al., 2019). Data from the United States indicated that parental and employment influences are positively associated with responsible spending behaviors, while peer and media influences are negatively associated with responsible spending behaviors among emerging adults (LeBaron-Black et al., 2023).

In sum, existing research has identified several factors associated with sustainable consumption behavior among emerging adults. However, most of these studies on emerging adults' sustainable consumption are based on samples collected in a specific region of a specific country. Larger-scale studies on sustainable consumption behavior are limited and should be encouraged.

Undesirable Consumption Behavior

Undesirable consumption behavior refers to acts that may hurt consumer well-being such as conspicuous consumption, compulsive buying, unethical consumption, overspending, and impulsive buying (Xiao, 2015). In this chapter, we focus on two of them: "conspicuous consumption" and "compulsive buying."

When individuals engage in conspicuous consumption, they aim to demonstrate their social status by purchasing and using certain visible goods and services (Sun et al., 2012; Veblen, 1899). Buying and using luxury goods are considered conspicuous consumption. Research shows that several psychological factors such as competitiveness, narcissistic rivalry, and dark traits—each discussed more below—influence the conspicuous consumption of emerging adults (Barrera & Ponce, 2021; Niesiobędzka & Konaszewski, 2022; Zhu et al., 2022). Using data of college students in Chile, researchers found that competitiveness is associated with conspicuous consumption in new luxury brands in clothing, perfume, and smartphone categories (Barrera & Ponce, 2021). Among emerging adults in Poland, researchers showed that narcissistic rivalry directly affects propensity for conspicuous consumption and narcissistic admiration is related to self-verified activity on Facebook, implying that Facebook usage in this manner increases the display of expensive, glamorous products as external signals of status (Niesiobędzka & Konaszewski, 2022). Data from Chinese college students showed that men report more conspicuous consumption for the purpose of interpersonal mediation (i.e., facilitating communication and perpetuating relationships via consumption) and ostentation (i.e., seeking praise or envy or fulfilling psychological needs by buying expensive products), while women report more conspicuous consumption for the purpose of materialistic hedonism (i.e., acquiring information and pleasure through consumption) (Zhu et al., 2022).

Country differences in conspicuous consumption have begun to be explored. Researchers have examined differences in luxury fashion brand value perceptions, a measure of conspicuous consumption, between German and Chinese emerging adults ages 18–25. They found that Chinese emerging adults have higher sociosymbolic, hedonic, and functional as well as higher price value perceptions of luxury fashion compared to their German peers (Faschan et al., 2020). However, no research has explored the consequences of conspicuous consumption, which may be a direction for future research.

Compulsive buying is considered a psychological disorder that forces consumers to buy things they do not need (O'Guinn & Faber, 1989; Wang & Xiao, 2009). There may be gender differences in compulsive buying. Among a sample of college students ages 18–24, researchers in the United Kingdom categorized consumers into four types: noncompulsive, noncompulsive with occasional tendency, mildly compulsive, and severely compulsive. Their results suggest that while both genders experience occasional compulsive buying urges and have the potential to progress into a more serious condition, its development into a problematic disorder is more prevalent in women (Maccarrone-Eaglen & Schofield, 2020).

Research shows that social and psychological factors are associated with compulsive buying (see Chapter 6). Data from a sample of emerging adults with a mean age of 20 in Malaysia demonstrated that excessive use of social network sites is positively related to online compulsive buying behavior (She et al., 2021). Another study conducted among college students in Malaysia showed that the power prestige and anxiety dimensions of a money attitude scale have significant effects on compulsive buying via materialism (Ong et al., 2021). Using data from a sample of young people ages 16–25 in Malaysia, researchers found that there are positive relationships between heavy social networking and financial social comparison (see Chapters 4, 8, and 10), financial social comparison and materialism, as well as materialism and online compulsive buying (Pahlevan Sharif et al., 2022). Data from an online survey of emerging adults in the United States showed that young, materialistic consumers are at high risk of developing depression; moreover, obsessive–compulsive tendencies and impaired self-esteem resulting from this depression may facilitate and fuel compulsive buying addiction (Darrat et al., 2023). Factors identified by these studies may be used to develop intervention tools to help reduce compulsive buying behavior among emerging adults.

Borrowing Behaviors of Emerging Adults

Overview

From a life-cycle perspective, for emerging adults, borrowing is a new financial behavior to learn because the legal age for signing a contract is 18 years old in the United States and many other countries. When emerging adults find their first formal job and start their career, they usually get low, entry-level pay that may not be able to maintain a standard of living matching that of their parents (see Chapter 5). Then, the emerging adult may need to borrow like other age groups in an economy where credit markets are well developed (Xiao & Yao, 2022). Also, many emerging adults begin to borrow when they are in college to meet their consumption and human capital investment needs (Shim et al., 2009).

U.S. statistics show that emerging adults hold various types of debts and face serious debt problems. As of September 2022, student loan borrowers in the United States owed a collective $1.76 trillion in federal and private student loan debt, according to the Federal Reserve (see Chapter 9). If we look at the class of 2020, 55% graduated with student debt, with an average debt of $28,400 (Helhoski et al., 2023). According to the Federal Reserve Bank of New York, auto loan debt is the third-largest debt category following mortgages and student loans. Overall, Americans owe $1.52 trillion in auto loan debt, with Americans younger than 50 taking out $38.5 billion in auto debt monthly. When compared with $22.4 billion by those 50 and older, younger adults are accumulating more auto loan debt (Jones, 2022). According to Bolognesi et al. (2022), 43% of Americans ages 18–37 used payday lenders, pawnshops, and the like in 2018, which increased from only 26% for the same age group in 2009. Nearly 20% of emerging adults ages 18–24 in the United States with a credit record have debt in collections (Martinchek et al., 2022).

This objective condition of emerging adults nowadays has implications for their concerns and attitude toward debts (see Chapter 4). For example, a qualitative study based on a sample of U.S. emerging adults ages 22–25 indicated that while most respondents are open to taking on debt at the time of post-secondary enrollment, their later inability to meet the demands of their debt leads to frustration and anxiety (see Chapter 8) (Napolitano et al., 2022). Furthermore, emerging adults may have critical attitudes toward loan products. Qualitative interviews among emerging adults ages 18–25 in Hong Kong showed four themes: A personal loan is a modern way of solving a debt problem; personal loan advertisements encourage materialism and overspending; personal loan advertisements are misleading; and emerging adults do not see personal loan advertisements as affecting them (Fan & Chan, 2019). Emerging adults' borrowing behavior may thus be due to the new consumer culture regarding credit. Focus group research demonstrated that middle- and upper-middle-class Danish emerging adults are likely to borrow for consumption because of the changing meanings and categories of money, credit, and debt in the contemporary consumer culture about credit (Hohnen et al., 2020).

Research on the borrowing behavior trends of emerging adults is limited. In a dated study, Houle (2014a) examined cohort changes in terms of emerging adult indebtedness in the 1970s, 1980s, and 2000s with data from the U.S. National Longitudinal Survey of Youth (NLSY). He showed that debt burdens (i.e., debt relative to economic resources) have increased substantially across the three cohorts of study; emerging adult debt portfolios have shifted toward non-collateralized (i.e., unsecured) and student loan debt over time (see Chapters 8 and 9); and cohort changes in debt have occurred unequally across social class lines (see Chapter 15) (Houle, 2014a). This kind of trend research should be encouraged with more recent data.

The prominent role that borrowing behavior has in the lives of emerging adults calls for the investigation of the predictors and outcomes of this behavior, which will be reviewed in the following sections.

Factors Associated with Borrowing Behavior

Borrowing behavior is affected by many factors. Emerging adults' socio demographic factors may affect their borrowing behavior. With data from the U.S. Transition to Adulthood and Panel Study of Income Dynamics, researchers showed that demographics such as age, gender (see Chapter 16), race (see Chapter 17), and work status (see Chapter 10) are associated with the debt burden of emerging adults (Kim et al., 2012). Racial differences (see Chapter 17) were also found to be an important factor in other studies. Using data from the 1997 NLSY cohort, researchers found that Black emerging adults have substantially more debt than their White counterparts. This difference is partially explained by differences in wealth, family background, post-secondary educational differences, and family contributions to college (Addo et al., 2016).

Having debt may also be related to life-cycle stage, including the unique stage of emerging adulthood. With data from a national panel in Finland, researchers showed that debt problems are highly common in emerging adulthood and increase after young adults leave their parental home, especially among those who began to live on their own at a young age.

Debt problems also tend to increase after one becomes a parent. On the other hand, steady employment is associated with a lower level of debt problems (Oksanen et al., 2016). Debt problems are more serious among low-income emerging adults (see Chapter 15). Data from a sample of 18- to 35-year-old Finns showed that many higher-income parents had safeguarded their indebted adult children by means of financial support. Chronic welfare users are particularly likely to receive parental financial support (Majamaa & Rantala, 2019).

Factors beyond sociodemographic characteristics can also affect emerging adults' borrowing behavior. Different studies have found that financial knowledge (see Chapter 2), financial literacy (see Chapter 1), and financial attitude (see Chapter 4) are all associated with borrowing behavior. For example, researchers in Sweden found that, compared with an overall mortgage amount, explicit information about future monthly payments reduces the tendency to take on too much debt (Carlsson-Hauff & Nilsson, 2020). Financial literacy may also affect emerging adults' borrowing behavior. Using a sample of students from a land grant university in the United States, researchers showed that students who score low in financial literacy are more likely to underestimate future student loan payments, while high financial literacy reduces the probability of significant payment underestimation (Artavanis & Karra, 2020). Finally, for financial attitude, data from a sample of Swedish emerging adults ages 18–30 in experimental research showed that the likelihood of borrowing is strongly suppressed by a negative attitude toward borrowing (Gärling et al., 2020).

Parental characteristics may affect emerging adults' borrowing behavior as well. Using data from the NLSY, a researcher found that the relationship between parents' income and student loan debt is nonlinear, such that emerging adults from middle-income families have a higher risk for debt than those from low- and high-income families (Houle, 2014b). Closeness to their mother, communication with her, and parental resources are negatively associated with young adults' borrowing behavior (Kim et al., 2012). However, parents may not teach children about borrowing behavior. With data from a sample of Polish emerging adults, researchers found no association between parents' financial socialization (see Chapter 18) and debt literacy (Cwynar et al., 2019). Future research is needed to explore why.

Overall, existent research has identified both individual characteristics and parental factors associated with emerging adults' borrowing behaviors. In addition, emerging adults' borrowing behavior results in life outcomes in both financial and other life domains.

Outcomes of Borrowing Behaviors

Debt holding may reduce financial well-being (see Chapter 7) and delay the homeownership of emerging adults. With panel data from U.S. college students, researchers showed that student debt becomes negatively associated with financial well-being over time (Cherney et al., 2020). Furthermore, data from the 1997 NLSY demonstrate a negative association between debt and homeownership in some models (Houle & Berger, 2015). Debt holding may also increase economic hardship and financial stress for emerging adults (see Chapter 8). With data from the U.S. National Financial Capability Study, a researcher found that student loan debt is positively related to all indicators of financial stress and hardship (Zhan, 2022).

Besides negative financial outcomes, borrowing may also result in negative outcomes in mental health among emerging adults. In particular, debt holding may increase mental stress (see Chapter 8; Kim & Chatterjee, 2021; Oksanen et al., 2018; Qian & Fan, 2021; Zhang & Kim, 2019). Using five biannual waves from the U.S. Transition to Adulthood, researchers showed that increases of $1,000 in student loan and credit card debt result in 6% and 4% higher odds of distress, respectively (Zhang & Kim, 2019). Additionally, data from the Panel Study of Income Dynamics and its Transition to Adulthood supplement showed that amount of revolving debt is negatively associated with emerging adults' mental health (Kim & Chatterjee, 2021). Data collected in three samples of emerging adults from Finland and the United States demonstrated that problem gambling is associated with consumer debt, which is further associated with debt problems. Subsequently, both consumer debt and debt problems are associated with psychological distress (Oksanen et al., 2018). Gender differences may also be found in the way that debt is associated with mental and other problems. Data from the 1997 NLSY showed that student loans have more negative effects on young men than young women, in terms of mental health problems, smoking, and heavy drinking (Qian & Fan, 2021).

Finally, research suggests that borrowing behavior may also affect interpersonal relationships, both romantic (see Chapter 14) and parent–child. Regarding the former, borrowing behavior affects the quality of a romantic relationship and timing of marriage (Addo, 2014; Addo et al., 2019; Saxey et al., 2023). Data from a sample of U.S. emerging adults showed that credit score is indirectly, positively associated with the quality of a romantic relationship via a positive association with financial self-efficacy and a negative association with financial deception (Saxey et al., 2023). Data from the 1997

NLSY cohort indicated that credit card debt is positively associated with co-habitation for men and women, and that women with education loan debt are more likely than women without such debt to delay marriage and transition into co-habitation (Addo, 2014). This trend of delaying marriage due to borrowing has become even more obvious recently. Using data from the 1977 and 1979 NLSY, researchers showed that in the 1997 cohort, student loan debt among college-attending emerging adults is associated with delays in marriage, although the same association was not found in the 1979 cohort (Addo et al., 2019).

Regarding the parent–child relationship, borrowing may cause a "boomerang" effect in that emerging adults continue living with their parents (Dettling & Hsu, 2018; Houle & Warner, 2017). Data from the 1997 NLSY showed that student loan debt is not associated with boomeranging in the complete sample. However, the association differs by race, such that the link between student debt and returning home is stronger for Black than for White youth (Houle & Warner, 2017). Debt holding may leave Black emerging adults with no other choice but to live with their parents. Using panel data derived from credit reports, researchers documented an association between debt characteristics and subsequent entry into parental co-residence and its duration (Dettling & Hsu, 2018).

In sum, evidence suggests that borrowing behaviors have pervasive consequences in both financial and other life domains such as financial well-being (see Chapter 7), mental health (see Chapter 8), and relationship qualities (see Chapter 14). Further study of borrowing behaviors will help improve emerging adults' quality of life in multiple dimensions.

Future Research Directions

Theory

A conceptual framework of emerging adults with regard to consumption and borrowing behaviors would be a useful development. Theoretically, emerging adults are in the life-cycle stage of transitioning from financial dependence on parents to financial independence (see Chapter 11). In addition, from a perspective of life-cycle stages, by this age they have learned how to purchase goods and services. However, they are just starting to learn how to borrow because in the United States and many other countries, 18 is the legal age to sign contracts including many loan contracts. Emerging adults may have learned from their parents about the concept of saving (see Chapter 18); those with part-time jobs may start to save, while often only those with full-time jobs with benefits will start serious long-term savings such as saving for retirement. No conceptual framework exists (1) to describe what consumption and borrowing behaviors are appropriate for emerging adults' life-cycle stage and (2) to help them achieve financial flourishing and general well-being. We encourage scholars to develop theoretical frameworks to address these important issues.

Contents

Better-documented descriptions of emerging adults' consumption and borrowing behavior would be helpful for the field. There is some research that describes emerging adults' consumption and borrowing behaviors and compares them with those of older age groups, but it is limited. Indeed, systematic research on this topic is limited, too.

Factors associated with emerging adults' consumption behaviors should be expanded. In this chapter, research on two types of consumption behaviors, desirable and undesirable consumption behaviors, is reviewed. Sustainable consumption behavior is a set of desirable consumption behaviors that benefit both environmental protection and social justice. Research on this topic has recently emerged but needs to be expanded, especially among emerging adults because they will soon become mainstream consumers. Research on undesirable consumption behaviors such as conspicuous consumption and compulsory consumption behavior should also be expanded.

As for the borrowing behaviors of emerging adults, existing research has mainly focused on student loan debts (see Chapter 9). Emerging adults also borrow with other types of loans (see Chapter 5). Additionally, factors influencing borrowing behavior related to different types of loans may vary among emerging adults from different backgrounds (see Chapters 15 and 17). Systematic research on the borrowing behaviors with regard to all types of debts needs to be conducted to understand this important behavior and help emerging adults financially flourish.

The outcomes of emerging adults' consumption and borrowing behaviors should also be better examined. Consumption is an important indicator of financial well-being (Xiao, 2015). However, little is known about which consumption categories are more important to emerging adults' financial and general well-being. Also, further research is needed to examine the consequences of desirable and undesirable consumption behaviors of emerging adults on their own well-being and the well-being of society. Debt is a complicated indicator of financial well-being because it needs to be measured in terms of ratio or in another indirect way. Having credit access is beneficial if emerging adults need money, but it is undesirable if people borrow too much to manage their debts (Xiao & Yao, 2022). Also, more research should be conducted to examine which types of debts are more harmful for emerging adults and ought to be avoided, and which borrowing behaviors are desirable (or undesirable) and ought to be encouraged (or avoided) to help emerging adults achieve financial flourishing and general well-being.

Methodologies

Research on the consumption and borrowing behavior of emerging adults includes both quantitative and qualitative methodologies with data from different countries. Both types of methodologies should be encouraged in future research. For descriptive studies, we hope more scholars will describe the consumption and borrowing of emerging adults using national and international data. To explore unique factors associated with, and outcomes of, the specific consumption and borrowing behaviors of emerging adults, experimental and survey studies could be used. To explore nuanced and emerging consumption and borrowing behaviors, qualitative research could be utilized. Future research might also apply machine learning methodologies and unconventional data sources to study the consumption and borrowing behaviors of emerging adults.

Furthermore, the trends of emerging adults' consumption and borrowing behavior should be more thoroughly researched. In this chapter, only one trend analysis of emerging adults' indebtedness is cited (Houle, 2014a). More recent studies like this on both the consumption and borrowing behaviors of emerging adults are needed. Long-term trend analyses would be helpful for understanding changes in emerging adults' consumption and borrowing behaviors over time. Relevant datasets from the United States are available, such as the NLSY and Panel Study of Income Dynamics (and its supplement, Transition to Adulthood), and should be used to update trend research. Relevant data from other countries should be identified and used for international comparisons.

Conclusion

Consumption is an important indicator of emerging adults' financial well-being (see Chapter 7). Borrowing is a means to obtain funds to finance current consumption when one's current income is inadequate (see Chapter 5). Consumption behavior and borrowing behaviors are important components of financial capability to help emerging adults achieve financial flourishing and avoid financial floundering. Research shows that factors associated with consumption and borrowing behaviors are diverse and include emerging adults' personal characteristics as well as environmental factors such as their family and parental characteristics (see Chapters 15 through 18). Emerging adults have learned basic life skills in spending but have just started to learn skills in borrowing. To help emerging adults flourish financially, desirable consumption and borrowing behaviors should be encouraged and undesirable behaviors should be discouraged. Information presented in this chapter has implications for practitioners who work with emerging adults, as presented in Box 13.1.

Box 13.1 Key Points for Practitioners

- Practitioners should be aware of the behavioral differences of emerging adults in terms of family backgrounds and provide the differentiated services they need.
- Practitioners should encourage emerging adults to engage in sustainable consumption behaviors that benefit both environmental protection and social justice.
- Practitioners should discourage emerging adults from performing undesirable consumption behaviors such as conspicuous consumption and compulsive buying.
- Practitioners should educate emerging adults on how to manage their debts. They need to tell young people that the major responsibility of a borrower is to repay the debt back after a planned time period.
- Practitioners should inform emerging adults on how to avoid high-cost debts (such as payday loans) and how to maintain a lifestyle by relying on increasing income and reducing expenses instead of borrowing.

Chapter 14
Finances and Romantic Relationships in Emerging Adulthood

Xiaomin Li[1]

Introduction

Money has been referred to as a taboo topic, and most people would prefer to talk about their sexual life before initiating a conversation on finances (Romo, 2011). Yet, money permeates almost every aspect of couples' daily lives, regardless of whether they are dating, cohabiting, or married. Salient questions include but are not limited to: Who should pay for the night out? Whose name should be on the rental lease? Who should be responsible for groceries or utility bills? How should the mortgage loan be split?

Because emerging adults are often pursuing economic independence (see Chapter 11) and establishing a committed and loving partnership at the same time, finances and romantic partnerships during emerging adulthood can be especially intertwined. Specifically, emerging adults may learn how to handle money by observing how their romantic partners handle money (Serido et al., 2015). Due to the explorative nature of this developmental stage, emerging adults may be open to a variety of opportunities and a myriad of vulnerabilities when navigating the world of money in relationships (Kutin et al., 2019, 2022). Some emerging adults manage to flourish financially and relationally at the same time, yet others may unfortunately fall and get trapped in financial difficulties and relational distress (Li et al., 2022; Saxey et al., 2022c). This chapter explores the connections between finances and romantic partnerships during emerging adulthood and—in turn—informs future research and practice.

[1] Department of Applied Social Sciences, The Hong Kong Polytechnic University, Hong Kong SAR

Xiaomin Li, *Finances and Romantic Relationships in Emerging Adulthood*. In: *Flourishing and Floundering Financially in Emerging Adulthood*. Edited by: Ashley B. LeBaron-Black, Heather Kelley, and Angela Sorgente, Oxford University Press. © Oxford University Press (2025). DOI: 10.1093/9780197699157.003.0015

Defining Finances and Romantic Relationships

"Finances" refers to the ownership and management of money by either one partner or both in a romantic partnership. The "ownership of money" includes more objective constructs (e.g., income, saving amount, or debt) and more subjective constructs (e.g., the satisfaction of or worries about one's financial situation). The objective constructs are linked to the comfort of living (e.g., whether one can afford food, housing, transportation, or medication; Conger et al., 2010). Whereas some scholarship indicates that objective constructs (e.g., credit score) might be linked to romantic relationship well-being (Saxey et al., 2023b), subjective constructs tend to be more proximal and salient to psychological and relational well-being (Conger et al., 2010; Shrum et al., 2022). The "management of money" includes behaviors, beliefs, and feelings surrounding the use of money (e.g., spending, budgeting, saving, investing; see Chapter 5). Interpartner communication around money is included as another facet of the management of money mainly because the economic interdependence between two partners renders financial discussions as inevitable and crucial (Eickmeyer et al., 2023; Hiekel et al., 2014; Präg et al., 2019). However, these financial communications may not unfold as smoothly and openly as desired (Papp, 2018; Papp et al., 2009; Saxey et al., 2022b).

"Romantic relationships" include the formation and quality of relationships. "Formation of romantic relationships" refers primarily to the formation of marriage because marriage—as compared to other types of relationships (e.g., cohabitation and civil unions)—carries unique financial benefits and liabilities (Widiss, 2016). For financial benefits, getting married can result in benefits at both the state and federal levels (e.g., tax, employment, and medication; Widiss, 2016). For financial liabilities, high wedding expenses are common across Western and Eastern societies today; as of 2022, the average wedding costs 30,000 USD in the United States (Nerdwallet, 2023) and 48,970 USD (or 384,366 HKD) in Hong Kong SAR (ESDlife, 2022). Getting married may also mean that the two spouses pool together their income and impose personal debt onto each other (Addo, 2014; Eickmeyer et al., 2023; Smock et al., 2005). Thus, the formation of marriage requires a meticulous consideration of finances.

The "quality of romantic relationships" can be understood either as a subjective and global evaluation (Fincham & Bradbury, 1987) or as a combination of positive and negative aspects (Cooper et al., 2017; Totenhagen et al., 2013). The positive aspects include satisfaction (i.e., relational outcomes as compared to experiences or expectations), maintenance (i.e., exerted efforts to encourage the continuation, stability, and health of the relationship), and commitment (i.e., intention to stay in the relationship) (Cooper et al., 2017; Totenhagen et al., 2013). The negative aspects include conflict and ambivalence. Integrating prior literature, the quality of romantic relationships is defined as a broad concept that encompasses indicators of happiness and stability of romantic relationships.

Everything Is Here Except for Money: Finances Predict Romantic Relationships

Prior researchers have investigated the associations between finances and romantic relationships (e.g., Eickmeyer et al., 2023; Li et al., 2022). In this section, studies that identified finances as possible precedents of romantic relationships are reviewed. Importantly, many reviewed studies in this and the next two sections are cross-sectional in nature (a note is included if a particular study was based on a longitudinal design), and the directionality in these cross-sectional studies is more theoretically speculated than empirically supported. Furthermore, in line with the overall introduction here, emerging adults are those who are 18–29 years old. Yet in this chapter, some reviewed studies include participants who are in their mid-thirties (a note is included if this is the case). Even though the mid-thirties goes beyond the defined age range of emerging adulthood, findings on individuals in their mid-thirties may still be informative for emerging adults today because—according to theories and empirical studies—individuals in their mid-thirties (as with their counterparts who are 18–29 years old) are still striving for the sense of growing up and being an adult (Arnett, 2007; Li et al., 2019). Notably, studies that included those who were, on average, in their mid-thirties were based on the same dyadic, longitudinal dataset on a nationally representative sample of U.S. newlywed couples—Couple Relationships and Transition Experiences (CREATE; James et al., 2022). When reviewing these studies using the CREATE dataset, a note will be included.

Finances Predict Relationship Formation

The ownership and management of money by either partner or both may predict emerging adults' decision to get married. Smock et al. (2005) conducted semi-structured interviews with 115 individuals ages 18–36 years old who were either currently cohabiting or had recently cohabited. They identified a lack of money as a major barrier to getting married. Notably, gendered patterns were identified in Smock et al.'s (2005) study, and participants found it especially difficult to turn a cohabiting relationship into marriage when men could not financially support their partner and kids.

More recently, Addo (2014) and Li et al. (2022) collected longitudinal data from a large sample of emerging adults. Addo (2014) analyzed data from 7,669 emerging adults ages 20–29 years old. For female emerging adults, having large amounts of credit card debt (see Chapter 13) and educational loans (see Chapter 9) was associated with an increased likelihood of cohabiting and a decreased likelihood of getting married (Addo, 2014). For male emerging adults, however, only a large amount of credit card debt was associated with an increased likelihood of co-habiting (Addo, 2014). Interestingly, the ownership of money is also relevant to the choice to co-habit. For example, emerging adults with the least total assets were also most likely to remain single (rather than co-habiting; Addo, 2014). Furthermore, for today's emerging adults, moving in together means some extent of economic integration, and 40 % of emerging adults in co-habiting relationships reported a complete money pooling (e.g., one partner managing all family money and giving the other a share, or two partners pooling all money together and each taking out their needed shares; Eickmeyer et al., 2023).

Li et al. (2022) analyzed data from 2,084 emerging adults from 2008 (when participants were 19 years old, on average) to 2016 (when participants were 27 years old, on average). Emerging adults who demonstrated healthy financial behaviors (e.g., spending within a budget, saving regularly, and making an investment for long-term goals; see Chapter 5) during college years were generally satisfied with their financial situation during the college-to-work transition (Li et al., 2022). Five years after college, these emerging adults also experienced fewer financial obstacles when pursuing goals, including getting married (Li et al., 2022).

Summary

Getting married today is a privilege that is disproportionately experienced by emerging adults in better financial situations (Addo, 2014; Li et al., 2022; Smock et al., 2005). For emerging adults who lack money or the skills to manage money (see Chapter 3), cohabitation or remaining single may be their alternatives (Addo, 2014).

Finances Predict the Quality of Romantic Relationships

The ownership and management of money by either partner or both in a relationship can be predictive of the quality of emerging adults' romantic relationships. Specific to the roles played by the ownership of money, the well-cited family process model (or family stress model) proposed that economic distress and poverty (see Chapter 15) may trigger relational problems such as hostility, withdrawal, and low stability (Conger et al., 2010). Using cross-sectional, dyadic data from 419 cohabiting emerging adult couples and 432 married emerging adult couples, Hardie and Lucas (2010) found that economic hardships (e.g., being evicted for not paying the full rent or mortgage, having gas or electricity shut off) were related to more frequent conflicts between romantic partners. Yet, receiving money from other family members was related to fewer conflicts between partners, though this finding was found among co-habiting couples only (Hardie & Lucas, 2010).

Specific to the roles played in the management of money, studies have been conducted on emerging adults' own financial behaviors (see Chapter 5) and their perceptions of their partner's money management. Using CREATE data at Wave 2 and Wave 3, Saxey et al. (2022c) found that 57.7% of couples in which both partners were good at budgeting and saving were more satisfied with their romantic relationships than the 11.8% of couples in which neither partner could spend within a budget, pay down bills, or save regularly.

Yet—as compared to emerging adults' own financial behaviors—the perceptions and evaluations of their partner's money management were even more predictive of emerging adults' relationship quality. Specifically, Li et al. (2019) analyzed data from 208 emerging adults from 2010 (when participants were 21–24 years old) to 2016 (when participants were 26–31 years old). Including emerging adults' own financial behaviors and their evaluation of their partner's money management (e.g., how often did your partner track their expenses?) using the same model, Li et al. (2019) found that only the evaluation of their partner's money management predicted romantic relationship quality 3 years later. More recently, Li et al. (2023a) drew Wave 1, 2, and 3 data from CREATE, which replicated the findings in Li et al. (2019).

As an explanation for their findings, Li et al. (2019, 2023a) proposed that—when evaluating the quality of romantic relationships and therefore deciding whether to remain committed to them—emerging adults may emphasize their own outcomes (e.g., whether and to what extent their partner has financially impacted them) more than their partner's outcomes (e.g., how their own financial behaviors may impact their partner). If emerging adults identified any costs in the relationship (e.g., a partner holding onto money too tightly or a partner spending beyond budget; Li et al., 2019, 2020, 2023a), they reported low relationship quality.

Regarding how the perception of a partner's money management may predict romantic relationship quality, some researchers further investigated whether it is more relationally detrimental for someone to perceive their partner as a "tightwad" rather than a "spendthrift" (or vice versa). Tightwads experience pain when spending money and thus spend less than they ideally would. Spendthrifts, conversely, spend more than they ideally would (Rick et al., 2011). In a survey study of 257 men and 258 women who were, on average, in their mid-forties, regarding the partner as a spendthrift was associated with more conflicts between two partners, but regarding the partner as a tightwad was not related to interpartner conflicts (Britt et al., 2017). Such findings make sense because tightwads, in a separate study, were associated with higher saving amounts and less credit debt, whereas spendthrifts often struggled financially (Rick et al., 2008).

However, among younger couples and at Wave 3 of the CREATE project, perceiving their partner as a tightwad and perceiving their partner as a spendthrift were both associated with diminished relationship satisfaction and commitment (Kelley et al., 2022). Yet, fewer statistically significant pathways were found for perceiving the partner as a tightwad than for perceiving the partner as a spendthrift (6 vs. 10; Kelley et al., 2022). For why perceiving the partner as a tightwad was relationally harmful to younger couples (vs. middle-aged individuals in romantic relationships), two possible explanations are proposed here.

For Explanation 1, the discussion again refers to Li et al.'s (2020, 2022) statement on emerging adults' emphasis on personal outcomes in couple relationships. Today's emerging adults need to avoid overspending (see Chapter 13) so that they can have adequate money for a better financial future (Li et al., 2019, 2022); however, incurring some discretionary expenditures on leisure activities and unnecessary items is required for emerging adults to be accepted in their peer group (see Chapter 4; Williams & Page, 2011). When perceiving one's partner as a tightwad who is too controlling or frugal with money, emerging adults may feel that their needs have been ignored and their lives have been interfered with, which may lead to lower reports of relationship quality.

For Explanation 2, there are possible relational benefits to a partner spending some money on joint leisure activities (e.g., eating out, shopping, going to see a movie). Drawing data from Waves 2, 3, and 4 of the CREATE project, Totenhagen et al. (2023) found that (at least among couples that had adequate income to cover these expenses) the couple spending money on shared leisure activities predicted higher relationship quality in the 2 years that followed. If either partner is a tightwad, the couple's ability to enjoy the relational benefits that money can provide may be reduced, which may then harm their relationship.

That said, emerging adults need to carefully weigh money saving/earning and money spending in their relationship depending on the ownership of money. Overall, neither being tightwads nor being spendthrifts can be beneficial for relationship quality (Kelley et al., 2022). Yet, couples who live on a very tight budget (i.e., with an annual household income of 15,000 USD or less) may need to stick to a frugal lifestyle and work out economic adversities first (Totenhagen et al., 2023). Otherwise, the expenditures on shared leisure activities may further exacerbate the detrimental effects of financial distress on the quality of their relationship quality (Totenhagen et al., 2023).

Studies on Romantic Partners' Co-Management of Household Financial Issues

As noted earlier, money is an inevitable issue in couple relationships, and it is a "must" for both partners to work on household financial issues together (Rea et al., 2016). Using qualitative data collected via open-ended survey questions and from 24 emerging adults in committed relationships (i.e., engaged, co-habiting, or married), Rea et al. (2016) identified household financial issues that came up very early—for example, within the first 2 years of dating—in romantic relationships (e.g., how to pay for bills or debts, having joint or separate accounts, spending and saving as a team). Through a thematic analysis, Rea et al. (2016) also found that open discussion is not only a useful tool for handling family financial issues, but it is also a method to stay connected with one's partner.

Using quantitative data from 1,950 emerging adults in romantic relationships, Saxey et al. (2022a, 2022b) replicated and extended the qualitative findings from Rea et al. (2016). Emerging adults who can openly talk about household financial issues (e.g., budget, big purchases, income, taxes) with their partner reported high relationship quality and rarely argued with their partner about money (Saxey et al., 2022a). Conversely, emerging adults who were less honest with their partner about money (e.g., hiding cash, purchases, and financial statements from each other) were also less likely to report a high-quality relationship (Saxey et al., 2022b). Furthermore, the earlier emerging adult partners initiated money-related conversations in relationships (e.g., soon after meeting each other), the more likely the two partners engaged in open communication on household financial issues (Saxey et al., 2022a).

Summary

The ownership and management of money can be predictors of emerging adults' romantic relationship quality (Hardie & Lucas, 2010; Li et al., 2019,

2023). Specific to the management of money, emerging adults—along with their own healthy financial behaviors (see Chapter 5)—need to openly communicate on family financial issues with their partner to maintain the quality of their romantic relationship (Saxey et al., 2022a, 2022b).

Couples Can't Win with Money Unless They Are a Good Team: Romantic Relationships Predict Finances

Researchers have found supportive evidence for a high-quality romantic relationship as a possible precedent of the ownership of money and healthy and collaborative money management among emerging adults. Using cross-sectional data from 1,950 emerging adults in romantic relationships, LeBaron-Black et al. (2022) specified relationship quality as the predictor for financial distress (see Chapter 8) in their model and found a medium-sized negative effect on this pathway. Using cross-sectional data from 517 emerging adults in romantic relationships, Eickmeyer et al. (2023) specified commitment as the predictor for income pooling. Those who reported more love and dedication in the relationship were more likely to completely pool their money together (Eickmeyer et al., 2023).

The directionality in the associations from romantic relationship quality to finances has been supported by longitudinal research. Using Wave 3 and Wave 4 data from the CREATE project and conducting a relatively stringent cross-lagged panel analysis, Saxey et al. (2023a) found that higher relationship satisfaction predicted more open communication on family financial issues a year later. Yet, communication on family financial issues did not predict marital satisfaction a year later (Saxey et al., 2023a). In another study using dyadic, longitudinal data—albeit based on middle-aged (vs. emerging adult) couples and not using a cross-lagged panel model to account for possible bidirectionalities—Dew et al. (2021) found that higher relationship satisfaction predicted healthier financial behaviors (see Chapter 5) as a couple and, in turn, fewer financial worries (see Chapter 8).

To explain why romantic relationship quality may also predict finances, the reader is referred to Dew et al.'s (2021) and Eickmeyer et al.'s (2023) statements that putting personal money into a shared family account, spending within budget, and openly discussing with one's partner family purchases all constitute substantial investments in the relationship. For example, instead of keeping hard-earned money secret for personal use, an individual would openly discuss with their partner how to use this money and then decide to contribute the money toward the shared financial goal of a down payment on a house. In this scenario, the individual has foregone personal pleasure for a better future with their partner, which is somewhat expected if the individual is in a happy and committed romantic relationship. The efforts to manage family money in a healthy and collaborative way then pay off, as demonstrated by prior researchers' findings that higher relationship quality was related to fewer economic worries (LeBaron-Black et al., 2022). Conversely, individuals who experience high relational distress or anticipate a breakup soon may hide personal cash from their partner and begin to spend family money (Dew et al., 2022; Zagorsky et al., 2005).

Summary

When investigating associations between finances and romantic relationships, researchers typically assume finances as precedents for romantic relationships (as reviewed in the prior section "Everything Is Here Except for Money"). Yet as suggested by couples and finances theory (CFT; Archuleta & Burr, 2015) and longitudinal studies (Dew et al., 2021; Saxey et al., 2023a), the associations between finances and romantic relationships can be circular and reciprocal.

It's Not Just about the Money: Constructs That Cannot Be Overlooked When Considering Finances and Romantic Partnerships

When it comes to money in relationships, there may be many emotionally charged moments. For example, the more financially dependent partner usually feels guilty about spending, even when spending money on family groceries (Xu et al., 2020). Additionally, couples can display a lot of anger and depression when arguing with each other about money (Papp et al., 2009). Why are partners so vulnerable to money? In our society, money not only puts food on the table, clothes on our back, and a roof overhead. Money also carries substantial psychological meanings and reflects each partner's self-worth, shame, and fears (Shapiro, 2007; Tang, 2010). Thus, in romantic relationships, partners may use money as a source of love or security (Mikulincer & Shaver, 2008). Partners may also regard money as a source of influence and privilege (Kutin, 2019, 2022). Thus, when investigating the links between finances and emerging adults' romantic partnerships, constructs related to the psychological meanings of money (see Chapter 4) should be considered.

Attachment Orientations, Finances, and Romantic Relationships in Emerging Adulthood

Attachment orientations reflect internal working models of the self (i.e., whether individuals view themselves as valued and able to elicit others' support) and others (i.e., whether other people are trustworthy and helpful; Bowlby, 1973). Attachment orientations are formed during the early years of life and remain relatively stable (Mikulincer & Shaver, 2012). Even when individuals grow up and enter romantic partnerships, the attachment orientations formed during early childhood may still impact how emerging adults emotionally attach to their partner (i.e., romantic attachment orientations; Mikulincer & Shaver, 2012). Insecure attachment orientations are characterized by high attachment anxiety (i.e., viewing the self as unlovable yet the other as reliable) and/or high attachment avoidance (i.e., viewing the self as lovable yet the other as unreliable) (Mikulincer & Shaver, 2009).

As to why attachment orientations should be highlighted in finances and romantic relationships, emerging adults who rate higher on attachment insecurity lack stable emotional ties with others and may instead fill social voids with money (Mikulincer & Shaver, 2008). For example, those with attachment avoidance may want to impress others with the possession of wealth or expensive items, and those with attachment anxiety may want to please others by giving expensive gifts (Mikulincer & Shaver, 2008). However, using money to supplement the lack of secure emotional ties does not bode well economically or relationally. Using cross-sectional data from 635 emerging adults in romantic relationships and then couples from Waves 1–3 from the CREATE project, Li et al. (2020, 2023a, respectively) found that high attachment anxiety and high attachment avoidance were related to less healthy financial behaviors among emerging adults. High attachment anxiety and high attachment avoidance were also related to emerging adults' perception of their partner's money mismanagement, which was especially detrimental to romantic relationship quality (e.g., regarding their partner as a tightwad or spendthrift) (Li et al., 2020, 2023a).

Summary

"Buying love with money" is a myth (Mikulincer & Shaver, 2008). If emerging adults want to flourish both relationally and financially, healing attachment injuries from early years (if any) may help them navigate the world of money in romantic relationships.

Power, Finances, and Romantic Relationships in Emerging Adulthood

Power is one's capability to change their partner and to resist their partner's attempts to change them (Miller et al., 2022). In romantic relationships, power can be both a blessing and a curse. If power is equally distributed, the two partners can show mutual respect, which benefits romantic relationships (LeBaron et al., 2019). When power is disproportionately held by one partner or if partners constantly fight with each other for power, then unilateral bullying or mutual aggression can occur (Li et al., 2023b; Mallory et al., 2016).

For good or for bad, the ownership and management of money go hand in hand with power in emerging adults' romantic relationships. Using Wave 2, Wave 3, and Wave 4 data from the CREATE project, Li et al. (2023b) found that both partners' healthy financial behaviors (see Chapter 5) predicted the equal distribution of relationship power. However, money may also be a tool of control and manipulation in emerging adults' romantic relationships.

In emerging adults' romantic relationships, economic abuse (i.e., behaviors to control the partner's ability to acquire, use, and maintain economic resources) is not rare (Christy et al., 2022). There are multiple turning points when emerging adults become especially vulnerable to economic abuse: the onset of the relationship, moving in with the partner, and getting married (Kutin et al., 2019, 2022). Based on interviews with 24 emerging adults and 24 practitioners who worked with emerging adults, economic abuse may take place in multiple ways (e.g., the abuser signing the victim's name on the official paperwork for a large amount of debt without letting the victim know, the abuser persuading the victim to relinquish control over money; Kutin, 2019, 2022). These actions of economic abuse relegate victims into a loop of "doom": a cycle of economic hardships and power losses (Christy et al., 2022) as the abuser minimizes the victim's economic worth and financial sufficiency, therefore justifying the abuser's limiting the victim's ability to make decisions because the victim is now viewed as limited in their financial contributions to the family unit (Christy et al., 2022).

Notably, with regard to power and money in romantic relationships, women may be more disadvantaged than men (e.g., earning less money, taking charge of trivial but not major family financial decisions) and at a higher risk of being economically abused (see Chapter 16; Clarke et al., 2005; Hoff & Lee, 2021; Kutin, 2019). As stated by practitioners who worked with emerging adults on economic abuse issues, the male entitlement privilege still prevails even among today's emerging adults: "I'll do as I please. You'll do as I say." "He's the breadwinner most often. Sometimes they won't work and they will take the woman's money" (Kutin et al., 2019, p. 120). Because it is difficult for emerging adults to create equal romantic partnerships in a cultural context where patriarchal hierarchy is pervasive, the whole society—including educators, policymakers, and individuals—needs to make joint efforts to challenge systematic inequalities related to power and money (Kutin et al., 2019).

Summary

Money is a source and symbol of power in emerging adults' romantic relationships. With the presence of healthy and collaborative financial management (e.g., each partner spending within budget, the two partners working out financial challenges as a team), money opens up avenues for equal and high-quality partnerships (LeBaron et al., 2019; Li et al., 2023b). Yet if one partner insists on taking advantage of the other, exploitation and manipulation take place (Christy et al., 2022; Kutin, 2019, 2022).

Conclusion

Collectively, finances and romances are intertwined and reciprocal among emerging adults. Emerging adults who possess adequate financial resources and manage money well—by themselves and with their partner—are more likely to form and maintain a satisfying and stable couple relationship. A happy and committed romantic partnership can, in turn, promote the ownership and healthy management of money. To achieve this upward spiral, the psychological meanings assigned to money should be considered. Instead of using money as a tool to fill one's own emotional void or to control one's partner, emerging adults should work toward equal partnership and secure financial and romantic relationships. The key points in this chapter for researchers, emerging adults, and practitioners may be found in Box 14.1, Box 14.2, and Box 14.3, respectively.

Box 14.1 Key Points for Researchers

Despite all the progress that prior researchers have made, a lot of questions await further investigation, and some of them are listed below:

- The ownership and management of money by either partner or both are dynamic, as are the formation (vs. dissolution) and quality of relationships.

continued

Box 14.1 *continued*

> Thus, future researchers should consider tracking and depicting couples' developmental paths in money and relationships across time. In addition to investigating the differences at the *between-couple* level (e.g., as compared to those with less money, those with more money were happier in romantic relationships), researchers might also investigate the changes at the *within-couple* level (e.g., if one couple gets more money over time, does their relationship satisfaction increase across time, too?).

As readers may already recognize, inequities exist in finances and romantic relationships. In fact, identities including gender (see Chapter 16), socioeconomic status (see Chapter 15), race, and ethnicity (see Chapter 17) may work jointly (vs. uniquely) to create diverse experiences related to money ownership, money management, and their associations with romantic relationship formation and quality. Researchers should consider taking an intersectional perspective to unpack these nuances and diversities.

Box 14.2 Key Points for Emerging Adults

A general message regarding how to navigate finances in romantic relationships is "use money, love people" versus "love money, use people." Certainly, money is valuable, and people who do not care about money are usually those who already have it. Yet, success in finance *should not* be obtained at the cost of one's partner or family. Instead, working on one's romantic relationship is likely to lead to financial flourishing. Specific suggestions on how to obtain the desired outcomes on both counts follow:

- Emerging adults themselves need to learn healthy money management skills (see Chapter 3).
- Emerging adults need to have open conversations on family financial issues early on in their romantic relationships (e.g., at least before moving in together and signing their names on a lease/mortgage and utility bills) and frequently. When initiating these conversations, the two partners should also discuss what money means to them and to each other (see Chapters 4 and 12).
- When handling money (e.g., saving, investing, and spending), two partners should prioritize shared goals and learn to forego some immediate personal

enjoyment. When doing so, it is important to achieve some level of fairness; the situation of one partner constantly sacrificing their wants and needs for the other's should be avoided.

Box 14.3 Key Points for Practitioners

In each study reviewed here, researchers have proposed how their empirical findings might inform practice. These points are summarized below:

- The importance of financial education cannot be emphasized enough, especially for those who are disadvantaged and underserved (e.g., women, low-income populations, and people of color; see Chapter 19). Disadvantaged and underserved populations face barriers to earning money and receiving training in money management (see Chapters 15, 16, and 17). In addition to providing social welfare and benefits, teaching people how to handle financial issues is just as important for empowerment.
- When working with couples who are struggling with money in their relationship, practitioners should go beyond the manifested issues (e.g., one partner's spending behaviors and debt) to help the two partners reflect on their own emotional needs and how these emotional needs may be linked to the couple's money problems. Practitioners should also help both partners share their own feelings about money and better understand each other's vulnerable feelings related to it.
- Financial sectors and societies generally should also shoulder the responsibility to protect emerging adults. For example, if the finance and retail sectors carefully checked the loan applications many emerging adults submit versus banking on their naiveté, then the risk of economic abuse (e.g., one partner applying for credit cards in the other's name) could be reduced. Furthermore, policymakers might consider implementing more stringent regulations on lending services, which could prevent emerging adults from racking up large debt (see Chapter 13).

PART III

SOCIODEMOGRAPHIC CHARACTERISTICS AND EMERGING ADULTS' FINANCIAL LITERACY

Chapter 15
Socioeconomic Vulnerability of Emerging Adults in the United States

Catherine Solheim[1], Nusroon Fatiha[1], and Pamela Dysart[1]

Introduction

This chapter focuses on the financial literacy (see Chapter 1), financial capability, and overall financial well-being (see Chapter 7) of socioeconomically vulnerable emerging adults in U.S. society. A recent systematic review by Xiao et al. (2022) identified multiple ways that family finance scholars have conceptualized financial literacy, including behavior, knowledge, knowledge-behavior, outcome, and ability-opportunity. Xiao and co-authors (2022) aligned the ability-opportunity conceptualization of financial literacy with the field of social work, making it seem tangential to the financial education discipline. However, the ability/access-opportunity aspect of finances is especially pertinent to the financial well-being of socioeconomically vulnerable emerging adults (see Chapter 1). A myopic focus that only examines an individual's knowledge (see Chapter 2), skills (see Chapter 3), behavior (see Chapter 5), and demographic characteristics (see Chapters 16 and 17) without considering access and opportunity, specifically the lack thereof, can perpetuate the "Horatio Alger" myth, also referred to as the "American Dream," which assumes that the U.S. financial system is a level playing field for all (see Box 15.1).

> **Box 15.1**
>
> Horatio Alger was an author whose 1868 novel portrays the classic "rags to riches" narrative that is often called the "American Dream." The message that has persisted
>
> *continued*

[1] Department of Family Social Science, University of Minnesota, USA

Catherine Solheim, Nusroon Fatiha, and Pamela Dysart, *Socioeconomic Vulnerability of Emerging Adults in the United States*. In: *Flourishing and Floundering Financially in Emerging Adulthood*. Edited by: Ashley B. LeBaron-Black et al., Oxford University Press. © Oxford University Press (2025). DOI: 10.1093/9780197699157.003.0016

Box 15.1 *continued*

for more than a century is that people should persevere in the midst of adversity through hard work and moral and ethical strength. What people fail to recognize, however, is that Alger's main characters were young White males and, although downtrodden in low-paying menial jobs, they had privilege because their social identity aligned with dominant White U.S. culture.

The American Dream myth has led us to embrace the idea that if people work hard enough and exercise constraint to improve their financial knowledge, skills, and behaviors, they will eventually achieve their goals of financial success and well-being. The myth has also led financial professionals to employ education approaches and intervention strategies that predominantly work for privileged people from the dominant White U.S. culture who do not face the same barriers that limit their ability to succeed through knowledge and hard work. Recently, Kim and Xiao (2021) acknowledged that although research on financial capability has proliferated in recent years, racial/ethnic differences, a critical dimension of marginalized social identities, remain understudied (see Box 15.2).

Box 15.2

The *Unequal Opportunity Race* (https://youtu.be/vX_Vzl-r8NY?si=b5_mxUrLsGAuNahD) is a 4-minute animated YouTube video that illustrates various aspects of structural discrimination that can block the progress of minoritized populations from building wealth. Produced by the African American Policy Forum in 2010; conceived and written by Kimberlé Crenshaw and Luke Harris (2021); animation by Erica Pinto.

There is an emerging body of family finance research that considers social identity factors such as education level, income, racial/ethnic identification, immigration status, and generation, suggesting that the discipline is beginning to pay attention to marginalized social identities (e.g., Emmons & Noeth, 2013; Smeeding, 2016; Williams et al., 2016). However, conclusions in these studies still discuss social identity factors as individual characteristics (e.g., race, ability, gender expression, ethnicity). Missing is a discussion about how an individual's social identity intersects with macro-level financial systems to create inequities in financial access and opportunity.

When the 1996 welfare policy reform created new realities for families, social work scholars drew important attention to ways that systemic barriers prohibited individuals from developing wealth-building assets that are critical to move people out of poverty (Sherraden, 1991, 2010). Family financial research that is more recent supports the use of an ability-opportunity approach that examines knowledge, behavior, skills, and *access and opportunity* to understand financial literacy — or what these scholars have termed "financial capability" — a concept that includes both individual capabilities (e.g., knowledge, skills, and behaviors) and macro-system constraints (e.g., systemic racism in financial services, housing disparities; see Chapters 1 and 20). Sherraden (2010), Hamilton & Darity (2017), Hanks et al. (2018), Al-Bahrani et al. (2019), Hong et al. (2022), and Sun et al. (2022) support an argument that the poor economic decisions and economic hardships of socioeconomically vulnerable people cannot be solely attributed to their lack of financial literacy (i.e., knowledge and skills). Although their research questions and methods differ, the scholars reached similar conclusions, namely, that these individuals' exclusion from or limited access to financial systems influences financial decisions (see Chapter 6) and behaviors (see Chapter 5) more than does their level of financial literacy. Examination of an individual's financial literacy without considering their financial environments and their experiences within those environments leads to inaccurate conclusions (Hong et al., 2022).

Therefore, recognizing that financial education (see Chapter 19) alone will not close the wealth gap, it is our contention that there needs to be a more complex approach to understand and support socioeconomically vulnerable emerging adults' financial capability development. The approach should address financial knowledge, skills, and behaviors *and* inclusive, equitable access to financial systems that offer a variety of opportunities, depending on the emerging adult's intersecting social identity.

Intersectionality highlights the ways in which dimensions of one's social identity such as race, ethnicity, class, sexual orientation, and gender expression are interdependent with one another and create interlocking systems of oppression and disadvantage that create barriers to financial flourishing in the lives of emerging adults (Crenshaw, 2017). Our intention for this chapter is to use an intersectional lens to examine selected aspects of the financial realities of socioeconomically vulnerable emerging adults and the families who launch them into adulthood.

Emerging Adulthood for Socioeconomically Vulnerable Individuals

Arnett (2000), credited with identifying emerging adulthood developmental tasks including becoming financially independent from parents, raised concern that emerging adult research is typically framed from an individualistic, White perspective (Arnett, 2003). Therefore, he examined the fit of emerging adulthood conceptualization for minoritized emerging adults, specifically African Americans, Latine, and Asian Americans. Results from Arnett's (2003) study showed that financial independence (see Chapter 11) and becoming self-sufficient was a salient task for emerging adults across these three groups with some important differences. Minoritized participants were more likely to indicate that men (57% Asian Americans, 70% African Americans and Latine, vs. 29% Whites) and women (49% Asian Americans, 60% African Americans and Latine, vs. 30% Whites) should become capable of supporting a family financially during the emerging adulthood stage.

There was a similar pattern for role transition tasks. For example, more minoritized emerging adults emphasized becoming employed full-time (43% African Americans, 50% Latine, and 35% Asian Americans) than did Whites (19%) as a criterion for adulthood. Perhaps most interesting in Arnett's (2003) study was that African American (59%) and Latine (54%) participants were much more likely than Asian Americans and Whites to perceive that they had already accomplished most tasks associated with adulthood, such as confirming one's identity (see Chapter 12) and investing in goals for the future. Arnett suggested that this difference might be due to their lower socio-economic status (SES) and the greater likelihood of becoming parents in emerging adulthood for African American and Latine participants compared to the other two groups (Fuligni et al., 1999; Phinney, 2000). Arnett (2003) concluded that results reflected the high value of family obligations and perhaps a more collectivist versus individualistic worldview in minoritized communities (see Box 15.3). One could conclude that many minoritized emerging adults, who research shows enter more quickly into adulthood and parenting roles than their White counterparts, do not experience a similar "emerging adulthood phase" in which to gradually become financially independent and develop their financial capabilities. Rather they are thrust quickly into the work world with an expectation of earning money to support themselves, perhaps a partner and child, and extended family members.

Box 15.3

People with collectivist worldviews prioritize harmony among group members and group well-being over individual well-being when using and making decisions about resources. In contrast, people with individualist worldviews prioritize personal independence and individual well-being over group well-being when using and making decisions about resources.

Arnett's (2003) examination of racial and/ethnic differences in emerging adulthood suggests that intersecting social identity factors such as SES, race, culture, and family circumstances are critical influences on tasks like the development of financial capability associated with emerging adult development (see Chapter 17).

Financial Realities of Socioeconomically Vulnerable Emerging Adults and Their Families

An overview of the statistical realities of socioeconomically vulnerable emerging adults and their families provides a baseline for understanding their financial well-being (see Chapter 7). Briefly, 15% of Black and 19% of Latine emerging adults were more likely to be considered financially vulnerable than their White (11%) and Asian American (8%) peers (Geron et al., 2020). Minoritized individuals were more likely to come from lower income house holds and have fewer assets than their White counterparts, limiting their access to financial resources and opportunities (Levine & Ritter, 2022). Minoritized individuals face significant barriers including systemic racism and bias in the college admissions process and limited access to financial aid (Levine & Ritter, 2022). Discrimination and bias in employment create significant barriers to career advancement, which limits opportunities for higher-paying jobs (Sullivan et al., 2015). A 2020 Financial Health Network and GenForward report (Geron et al., 2020) found that Black (31%) and Latine (28%) emerging adults experienced levels of debt that were difficult to manage. The intersections among limited access to family financial assets, systemic barriers to higher education (see Chapter 9), jobs, career advancement (see Chapter 10), and debt (see Chapter 13) create significant barriers to financial stability and wealth building, leaving already socioeconomically vulnerable emerging adults floundering in a cycle of financial vulnerability that is difficult to break.

Multisystemic and Interdependent Financial Realities That Contribute to Financial Literacy and Socioeconomic Vulnerability in Emerging Adults

In the following section, we attempt to highlight the ways in which differences in emerging adults' financial realities may contribute to their financial literacy and socioeconomic vulnerability, namely, credit health, education access, student loan debt (see Chapter 9), employment opportunities (see Chapter 10), asset accumulation and wealth, and home ownership.

Existing research documents differences in financial literacy among Whites and minoritized individuals (Kim & Xiao, 2021; Lusardi & Mitchell, 2023; van Rooij et al., 2012). Using 2018 U.S. National Financial Capabilities Studies data (FINRA), Kim and Xiao (2021) found that Whites had higher levels of financial literacy than minoritized individuals did after controlling for socioeconomic factors. Age, income, banking status, and unexpected income drops contributed significantly to financial literacy differences between Whites and Blacks and Whites and Hispanics, leading them to conclude that there are important factors that represent "still unexplained gaps attributed by unobservable characteristics, for example, financial experience or social exclusion among minority groups" (p. 392).

Credit Health

A recent Urban Institute report highlighted racial differences in emerging adults' credit health (see Chapter 13). Minoritized emerging adults are more likely than their White peers to have past-due credit card debt (6.4% vs. 3.6%) and be delinquent in their car/store loans (9.1% vs. 4.7%), and medical or student debt repayment (see Chapter 5). Minoritized emerging adult borrowers were more likely than their White peers to be involved in debt collections (24.8% vs. 17.3% respectively; Martinchek et al., 2022). Race, education, gender, and asset differences were also evident in a Consumer Financial Protection Board study of Buy Now, Pay Later (BNPL), zero interest, installment loans, a borrowing option used by consumers who may be struggling with accumulated debt (Shupe et al., 2023). If used with caution, BNPL is not necessarily a bad option for consumers (Rathner, 2023). However, these loans still represent debt, and consumers must have sufficient cash flow to pay the installments when due.

A recent study by Shupe and colleagues (2023) found that the most likely BNPL borrowers were Black, Hispanic, female, had high school versus college degrees, and annual household incomes between $20,000 and $50,000. Being a renter (22%) versus owning a home (15%) and identifying as Black (26%) versus White (16%), or Hispanic (24%) versus non-Hispanic (15%), increased BNPL use. Furthermore, BNPL borrowers were younger (under age 35; 22%) versus older (over age 65; 10%). BNPL borrowers had access to traditional credit; however, minoritized borrowers held twice as much credit card debt than their White counterparts. Shupe et al. (2023) suggested that the BNPL option was more attractive to these borrowers than using their credit cards because they would likely pay between 19–23% interest on their credit card balances due to having subprime credit scores. Moreover, the zero interest, four-installment BNPL loan did not add to their high-interest debt burden. An interesting note was that the correlation of low household income ($20,000–$50,000) with higher likelihood of BNPL use may be influenced by an underlying systemic reason; they speculated that this relationship could be related to "supply factors such as where BNPL is advertised or the share of applicants approved in this income group" (Shupe et al., 2023, p. 7).

Education

Education is a key factor that influences financial capability and emerging adults' opportunities to earn income, build wealth, and achieve financial well-being (see Chapter 7) in adulthood. However, educational inequality is a growing concern for all students and disproportionately limits opportunities for underserved students. The U.S. education system has a long history of systemic racism that disproportionately affects minoritized students compared to their White peers. Racially biased education funding perpetuates economic inequality for historically marginalized communities, a practice known as "educational redlining" (Welbeck & Kaufman, 2020).

In recent years, colleges and universities realized significant growth in U.S.-based post-secondary enrollment including minoritized and first-generation students. These students, who typically have fewer financial resources, need to rely on financial aid to cover their tuition and living costs (Markle,

2019). However, as the student demographic profile changed to include more minoritized and first-generation students, colleges and universities raised tuition rates to address their financial challenges, and, simultaneously, state and federal funding for higher education infrastructure decreased. As a result, these students increasingly turned to loans to finance their education (see Chapter 9; NCES, 2017).

Research documents that student loans are necessary for minoritized and socioeconomically vulnerable students to bridge the gap between their limited family resources and rising college costs (Perry et al., 2021). Many families take out student loans to finance their children and grandchildren's education, encouraged by policies such as Parent PLUS Loans, which institutions actively market to parents of their enrollees (Saunders et al., 2016). However, having student debt is increasingly becoming a marker of relative disadvantage as more people attend college. Those with student debt are often those who financed their education on their own, indicating that their families were unable to pay for their tuition (Perry et al., 2021). In this way, the racial and generational wealth gap often leads to a spiral effect where students from historically marginalized groups struggle to repay their student loans (Havens, 2021).

Student Loan Debt

Race

Although the amount of student loan debt (see Chapter 9) for all graduates has grown significantly and outpaced inflation (Long, 2022), students from marginalized racial/ethnic groups — including Black, Latine, Native American, and other minoritized communities — are disproportionately affected (Campbell, 2018; Havens, 2021). They are statistically more likely to come from families without generational wealth, which increases their likelihood of being low-income and, in turn, more reliant on borrowing loans for post-secondary education (see Chapter 9; Jones, 2015).

Eighty percent (80%) of Black students graduate with debt compared to 64% of White students (Shapiro et al., 2013). A recent survey showed that this higher level of debt often leads to financial constraints that force Black students to drop out of undergraduate studies to earn a steady income to support themselves and their families (Shapiro et al., 2013). Black (28%) and Latine (28%) emerging adults compared with White (18%) and Asian American (14%) emerging adults reported that their debt delayed their education (Geron et al., 2020).

In this cyclic relationship between education and student loans, students from minoritized backgrounds are amassing higher debt while receiving partial or incomplete education (see Chapter 9). Debt exacerbates their disadvantage in the financial and employment arenas compared to their more educated and better-resourced White male peers.

Other Disadvantaged Social Locations

Students from disadvantaged backgrounds have high student loan default rates, including nearly half of first-generation college attendees from low-income families, 82% of those in Alternative Eligibility programs without a high school credential, and over a third of students with disabilities (Campbell, 2018). Gender and sex assigned at birth are other factors affecting emerging adults' financial vulnerability. LGBTQ+ students assume $16,000 more educational loan debt, on average, than their cisgender heterosexual peers do, often due to lower levels of financial assistance from family members (Hsueh et al., 2020). Parents' refusal to cooperate with federal aid application forces these minority group students to take on higher debt through private student loans or credit cards (Flynn et al., 2023). Women hold 67% of America's student loan debt (see Chapter 9), with Black women incurring the highest balances (Williams et al., 2023). Furthermore, across all racial groups, research shows that women experience greater stress from student loan repayment pressures (Miller, 2017). This financial strain shapes life decisions, as loans prompt women to delay home purchases, accept less desirable jobs, and reduce retirement savings (Miller, 2017).

Despite the barriers and extraordinary challenges, minoritized emerging adults strive to achieve success and financial stability through gaining post-secondary degrees (Taylor & Cantwell, 2019). Over time, however, systemic injustice perpetrated within higher education systems contributes to a generational wealth gap and the financial disenfranchisement of minoritized emerging adults (Havens, 2021; Welbeck & Kaufman, 2020).

Employment

Getting a well-paying job with good benefits is a key factor of emerging adults' ability to achieve financial well-being (see Chapter 10; Bonnie et al., 2017). However, in the cycle of economic inequality historically, individuals from some minoritized groups have been subject to discrimination while seeking employment (Wanberg, 2012), which affects the accessibility of work-related benefits such as decent wages and health insurance (Bonnie et al., 2017; Gemelas et al., 2021). Of the workers occupying some of the highest-paying

U.S. jobs, such as professional and managerial positions, 52% are Asian, 42% are White, 31% are Black, and 23% are Hispanic workers. In contrast, of the workers in low-paying service occupations, 24% are Black and 25% are Hispanic (U.S. Bureau of Labor Statistics, 2019). These minoritized racial/ethnic groups experience stress from minimal benefits such as no paid sick leave or job security (Shierholz, 2014).

Women must attain higher education levels than men to qualify for comparable salaries post-graduation (see Chapter 16). Research has documented that women need a master's degree to earn wages on a par with the associate degree earnings of male peers (Williams et al., 2023). Disabled individuals face significant employment and pay disparities, despite similar qualifications. On average, they earn $12,700 less annually and have nearly double the unemployment rate (9.2% in 2017) of their able-bodied counterparts (Campbell, 2018). In addition to income disparities, gender and sexual minorities confront workplace discrimination, exacerbating delays in student debt repayment (Flynn et al., 2023).

The recent trend toward work in the "gig" economy (see Chapter 10) contributes to existing socioeconomic and racial disparity in the workforce (Ajunwa, 2020). Gig work jobs are typically part-time positions or contract employment with place and schedule flexibility. However, this work arrangement lacks benefits, predictability, and job security, which disproportionately affects minority and immigrant workers with no advanced degrees.

Homeownership

Although homeownership is a cornerstone asset that contributes significantly to financial well-being (Kochhar et al., 2011), owning a home is challenging for socioeconomically vulnerable individuals and families (NCRC, 2019). Black individuals with a college degree have lower rates of homeownership than do White individuals without a high school diploma. This results partially because Blacks have more student debt burden than their White counterparts do (see Chapter 9), regardless of their post-graduation income. Research from the Federal Reserve Bank of St. Louis showed that White graduates often receive financial support such as wealth transfers from their families to help them buy homes. Conversely, Black graduates tend to use their income to provide financial support to their families after college, which often compromises their ability to repay student loans (Perry et al., 2021). These differential patterns of intergenerational transfers by race — older to younger for White graduates and younger to older for Black graduates — result in a higher likelihood that White individuals compared to Black individuals will invest in home ownership after college.

Discriminatory lending practices, redlining, and limited access to credit have historically hindered African American homeownership (Bhutta et al., 2020; Boen et al., 2020). Relative to White borrowers, mortgage application denial was more common for Blacks (Wheeler & Olson, 2015). If approved, they historically held higher interest rates (Cheng et al., 2015). Consequently, it is only in recent years that we have seen an increase in African American homeownership. Still, these families are more likely to have high-risk mortgages, leaving them more vulnerable to foreclosure and housing market fluctuations (Hanks et al., 2018; Shapiro et al., 2013). This was evident when the 2008 Great Recession stripped away half of African American family wealth and 67% of Latine family wealth due to the dominant role of home equity in their wealth portfolios and the prevalence of predatory high-risk loans in communities of color (Shapiro et al., 2013). However, even with the struggles to achieve homeownership, it plays a crucial role in the wealth of Black families, accounting for 53% of their wealth compared to 39% for White families (Shapiro et al., 2013). A provocative article by Friedline and colleagues (2023) explicates credit scores, a key factor in determining if one qualifies for a home mortgage, a "carceral practice" (p. 1) that should be abolished to create a more just and inclusive financial system.

There is a lack of reliable data on sexual orientations and gender identities of homeowners and borrowers. However, the 2023 Census Bureau's Household Pulse Survey found that LGBTQ+ individuals, who are younger than the non-LBBTQ+ population (51% under 35 compared with 23% who are straight and cisgender), face significant discrimination in the housing market, resulting in lower homeownership among this group of emerging adults (Visalli et al., 2023).

Although the homeownership gender gap is narrowing, major barriers persist, especially for younger women. Choi (2023) reported that women's overall lower incomes counteract their higher levels of education, creating a barrier to home buying. Millennial and Gen Z women have less financial knowledge (see Chapter 2) and confidence than their male peers; they also lack trusted advisors to support them in the home-buying process. Choi (2023) concludes that although we see promising social shifts for emerging adult women, knowledge access and economic disadvantages continue to block the pathway to homeownership equity.

Intergenerational Transfer of Wealth

Research demonstrates that wealth is a critical indicator of well-being and a significant predictor of an individual's lifetime financial prospects. It plays a defining role in determining upward economic mobility (Levy, 2022). Unfortunately, the distribution of wealth is uneven across families, and the number of households with no wealth or negative wealth is on the rise (Levy, 2022). According to data from the Survey of Consumer Finances, the median net worth for a typical white family in 2022 was $285,000 compared to $44,900 for a typical Black family (Aladangady et al., 2023). Moreover, the intergenerational transmission of this wealth gap disproportionately affects minoritized emerging adults' ability to build wealth (Aliprantis et al., 2022). Although most Americans do not inherit much or any money, emerging adult African Americans were much less likely to inherit compared to White Americans (7% vs. 36%, respectively) (Shapiro et al., 2013). Moreover, African American emerging adults prioritize intergenerationally transmitted wealth for emergency savings rather than asset-building strategies such as financing higher education or buying a home (Shapiro et al., 2013).

Systemic Financial Barriers

Although it is necessary to deconstruct a specific area of an emerging adult's financial reality into single components such as education, debt, employment, and the like, in order to discuss them one at a time, they do not exist or operate in isolation. For example, an emerging adult of color's educational trajectory is affected by their family of origin, by the higher education system, and by financial aid and lending infrastructures. Education, in turn, affects employment opportunities that shape one's ability to earn adequate income, to save money, and to build assets, including home ownership. Degree completion and employment are markers of success; however, asset accumulation and wealth building may be significantly hampered by student loan debt that negatively and disproportionately affects minoritized emerging adults.

Additionally, it is important to be aware of the role that systemic barriers play in emerging adults' financial capability. Discriminatory laws (e.g., Jim Crow laws), policies (e.g., redlining), and financial institutions (e.g., predatory lending) have perpetuated the wealth gap between minoritized and White families. Although some may be a part of our history, their lingering effects still exist (see Chapter 17; Geron et al., 2020; Sullivan et al., 2015). Others — such as unequal access to education, job opportunities, and homeownership — are contemporary systemic barriers that create inequities in maintaining financial stability and building wealth that are perpetuated across generations (Darity & Hamilton, 2012; Mehrotra et al., 2022). Obstacles stemming from one's immigration status, language barriers, and cultural dissimilarities also hinder accessibility of mainstream financial services and limit opportunities for families and emerging adults belonging to minoritized populations (Aliprantis et al., 2022; Geron et al., 2020). These limitations perpetuate intergenerational poverty for socioeconomically vulnerable families; their emerging adults inherit this legacy and continue to experience financial vulnerability into their adult lives (van Meeter et al., 2022).

Recent research examined how individuals were able to persist in their pursuit of financial goals, despite the financial barriers they experienced. Hong and colleagues (2022) focused on the role of psychological self-sufficiency (PSS), in addition to the variables included in Sherraden's (2010) financial capability model, in supporting people's attainment of financial goals. PSS theory posits that there is a "process-oriented progression from financial knowledge and skills through perceived financial barriers and financial hope to enhance the financial attitude and financial behavior aspects of financial literacy" (p. 691). A central premise is that people make choices that align with their identities (see Chapter 12) and are congruent with their evaluation of whether their future is possible. Their identities and motivations are interdependent with culture, experience, SES, race, ethnicity, and neighborhood; they struggle to be motivated to pursue their goals because it requires them to overcome experiences of marginalization and exclusion from mainstream opportunities and resources (Fisher et al., 2017). Psychological barriers such as lack of hope and control over life circumstances negatively affect individuals' financial capability (Buckland, 2010; Hong et al., 2018; Kempson et al., 2004). Without a sense of hope, people are unable to imagine a way to pursue their financial goals. Hope emerges through developing their strengths and feeling empowered despite barriers such as financial exclusion and discrimination. Hong et al.'s (2018) findings revealed that financial hope mediates the relationship between perceived financial barriers and financial attitudes (see Chapter 4) and behaviors (see Chapter 5). They concluded that a comprehensive conceptualization of financial capability must include reflection on systemic barriers and development of empowerment practices to overcome them, which activates individual agency and capacity to strive for financial goals. Moreover, empowerment activates collective action that, in turn, creates demand for systems to change. It is important to note that this does not mean we should not continue to work to eliminate the barriers that discriminate against and exclude people from the financial mainstream. Rather, it points to acknowledging that they exist and helping individuals develop effective strategies to overcome them. It is also important to provide inclusive and easy access to financial products and services, specifically emergency savings, financial institution services, affordable credit, and technological tools that facilitate product and service delivery, especially with historically excluded communities (Sun et al., 2022).

Financial Education

Ongoing financial socialization (see Chapter 18) and effective financial education (see Chapter 19) are critical investments and should be accessible across the lifespan (Sun et al., 2022). To provide effective financial education to minoritized emerging adults, it is important for financial educators and coaches to pay careful attention to the existence of "systematic bias" in both content and delivery of financial education (Al-Bahrani et al., 2019, p. 594). Al-Bahrani et al. studied racial differences in financial education effectiveness and concluded that although their findings supported the trend that financial education (see Chapter 19) in recent years increased financial knowledge (see Chapter 2), it was "advancing Whites at a greater rate than minorities" (p. 594), thus contributing to wealth disparities rather than reducing them. They speculated that this might be due to educators' focus on enrollment in but not completion of financial education courses. Program completion might depend on whether educators sought target audience input when they developed the program. Neglecting to tailor programs to participants' realities may result in ineffective curricula and increased attrition rates, particularly in predominantly minoritized communities (Al-Bahrani et al., 2019).

It is also critical that financial educators are aware of their personal biases, specifically their privilege, if they are members of dominant White U.S. society. Financial systems, services, and products were designed by and for them; it is critical that White financial educators be aware of this privilege, so they don't assume that minoritized clients or learners will have experiences similar to their own with financial institutions, and so forth. Optimally, curricula and coaching would be developed and delivered by or with cultural and community insiders who know the obstacles their communities have faced historically and now. This will allow them to identify the systemic barriers that participants may encounter, co-develop strategies to overcome those barriers, and provide culturally attuned examples of financial ideas that fit the values and experiences of minoritized emerging adults' experiences.

Moving from Floundering to Flourishing

Can we agree that the Horatio Alger myth (see Box 15.1) sets unrealistic expectations? Can we also agree that even if we develop emerging adults' financial knowledge (see Chapter 2) and skills (see Chapter 3) and change their behaviors (see Chapter 5), many will still face deep-seated systemic barriers that differentially affect their ability to build wealth? If the answers are "yes" to these two questions, then we can collectively work to reduce and even eliminate barriers that hinder socioeconomically vulnerable emerging adults' ability to build wealth and achieve financial well-being (see Chapter 7). The good news is that there is movement from floundering to flourishing. Increasingly, reports highlight innovative solutions from think tanks and nonprofit organizations such as the Center for Financial Inclusion, the Brookings Foundation, the Aspen Institute, Prosperity Now, and the Urban Institute, and government agencies such as the Federal Reserve and the Consumer Financial Protection Bureau (Hanks et al., 2018). Here, we report on initiatives that could help vulnerable and floundering emerging adults to flourish financially.

Student Loan Debt Repayment

Advocates have suggested promising programs and practices for financial aid awards and loan repayment. Levine and Ritter (2022) proposed including total net worth in the financial aid assessment process to lower expected contributions toward children's education from their families. They also proposed income-driven repayment (IDR) programs that would reduce loan payments to a percentage of the borrower's disposable income (Levine & Ritter, 2022). Overall, advocates argue that we need comprehensive solutions to promote equity in higher education:

> Means-tested grant and loan aid that promote access and completion at high-quality educational institutions; rigorous oversight of institutions that participate in federal programs; progressive, well-designed, and well-administered income-based repayment plans that insulate borrowers whose education doesn't

pay off; and targeted relief to borrowers who can clearly demonstrate that their loans impose significant economic hardship. (Looney, 2022, pp. 2–3)

Baby Bonds and Child Savings Accounts

Baby bonds invest in children's futures to reduce racial wealth disparities. The government sets aside money for children at birth and invests it. At adulthood, an individual can invest these funds in wealth-building assets such as a home, college education, or a small business (Brown et al., 2023; Hamilton & Darity, 2010; Markoff et al., 2022).

Nonprofit organizations offer child savings account programs (CSAs), currently in 36 states with about 1 million enrollees (Thiemann, 2021). Similar to baby bonds, they aim to reduce racial disparities by helping low-income families invest in long-term savings for their children from birth, often with an end-goal of financing post-secondary education when the child reaches age 18. Participants receive a typical $50 initial deposit and are encouraged to save regularly through incentives such as savings matches, deposit bonuses, and prize-linked savings (Thiemann, 2021).

Community Cultural Capital, Whole-Family Learning, and Financial Wellness at Work

Barbara Robles (2014) one of the authors of *The Color of Wealth: The Story Behind the U.S. Racial Wealth Divide*, champions the idea that financial educators must understand and leverage cultural capital and support whole-family learning to be effective in culturally diverse communities. Cultural capital refers to "cultural knowledge, skills, abilities, and contacts possessed by socially marginalized groups that often go unrecognized and unacknowledged" (Yosso, 2005, p. 69). Likewise, socioeconomically vulnerable families and their emerging adults who disproportionately come from communities of color can access their cultural wealth to achieve financial well-being. Rather than focusing on problems, challenges, and deficits, a community cultural wealth approach to financial education leverages the values, traditions, strengths, and capitals in diverse communities (Solheim et al., 2021).

Whole-family learning involves the entire family and even entire communities in the financial education endeavor; it is not just for adults (Robles, 2014). This culturally aligned model reduces stigma, confusion, or shame about sensitive financial topics. It also builds on the collective cultural worldview of most minoritized communities by activating Yosso's (2005) familial and social capitals to enhance learning. Educators must develop their understanding of cultural landscapes to harness cultural wealth and deliver culturally attuned financial education with multicultural family systems.

Financial educators should also consider infusing empowerment in their programs. This will encourage disenfranchised emerging adults to reflect on their experiences and develop psychological self-sufficiency or hope, which, in turn, can motivate them to pursue their financial goals (Hong et al., 2022). Empowerment in the context of community cultural wealth (Yosso, 2005) and whole-family learning (Robles, 2014) will enable emerging adults to collectively activate and leverage their cultural capital to create innovative ways to achieve their financial goals.

Conclusion

As we have discussed in this chapter, emerging adults face a myriad of individual challenges as they journey from financial dependence to financial independence (see Chapter 11). Socioeconomically vulnerable emerging adults from minoritized backgrounds face additional systemic obstacles that make their journey more challenging. To support all emerging adults to achieve financial capability (see Chapter 20), we must work to ease their burden, eliminate structural impediments, and facilitate access to opportunities to achieve financial well-being (see Chapter 7) in adulthood. We must support policies that create financial equity and inclusion for all families. This includes measures that deal with income and wealth inequality and advanced access to a high standard of education that is affordable and does not lead to unmanageable student loan debt (see Chapter 9). We must increase the availability of safe and affordable housing and healthcare, and deal with bias and discrimination in the workplace.

Financial educators must consider socioeconomically vulnerable emerging adults' financial realities through critical, intersectional lenses to provide effective, culturally responsive education (see Chapter 17). They must challenge the status quo and seek changes in existing discriminatory systems that create barriers to financial opportunity and well-being, especially in minoritized communities (Daniels et al., 2021). We need to equip individuals and families with financial knowledge (see Chapter 2), skills (see Chapter 3), and behaviors (see Chapter 5) they need to navigate our complex financial systems. Additionally, we can tackle persistent discriminatory systems and build a more just and equitable society where everyone has the chance to flourish financially and realize their full potential.

Chapter 16
Gender and Finances in Emerging Adulthood: Sex, Gender, and Inequalities

Emanuela E. Rinaldi[1] *and Valeria A. Giannella*[2]

Introduction

The terms "sex" and "gender" are sometimes used interchangeably. Although for many people their sex and gender coincide, for some these terms indicate two distinct concepts. According to the World Health Organization (n.d.), sex refers to characteristics that are biologically and physiologically defined, whereas gender refers to the characteristic of boys, men, girls, and women (and other gender identities) that are socially constructed. In detail, sex (labeled "female" or "male") is usually based on a chromosomal typing that occurs before birth, individuals' genitalia, and/or the type of gametes (i.e., sperm cells or egg cells) produced by their reproductive organs. Sex is the assumed biological category into which individuals are placed, regardless of their gender identification. Gender, instead, is a social construct referring to norms, roles, and behaviors associated with being a man, woman, girl, or boy, as well as the genders' relationship with each other.

Gender identity is one's personal sense of self and how an individual conceptualizes one's own gender. Although gender is not binary (Richards et al., 2017), "women" and "men" are the two categories most widely studied in the literature about the role that financial knowledge (see Chapter 2), financial attitudes (see Chapter 4), and financial behaviors (see Chapter 5) play in adolescence, emerging adulthood, and adulthood (e.g., Bottazzi & Lusardi, 2020; Chen & Volpe, 2002; Cupák et al., 2021; Gonçalves et al., 2021; Goyal & Kumar, 2021; Terriquez & Gurantz, 2015), and these two will be the focus

[1] Department of Business and Law, Università degli studi di Milano-Bicocca, Italy
[2] Department of Management Engineering, Politecnico di Milano, Italy

Emanuela E. Rinaldi and Valeria A. Giannella, *Gender and Finances in Emerging Adulthood: Sex, Gender, and Inequalities*. In: *Flourishing and Floundering Financially in Emerging Adulthood*. Edited by: Ashley B. LeBaron-Black et al., Oxford University Press. © Oxford University Press (2025). DOI: 10.1093/9780197699157.003.0017

of our chapter. In most societies over the course of history, gender has been used as a category that ruled people's access to different power resources such as money, preventing women from accessing money and managing it autonomously (Graeber, 2012; Simmel, 1900/1989). Nowadays as well, in capitalist societies, gender is considered a hierarchical variable in that it produces significant inequalities that intersect with other sociodemographic variables—such as ethnicity (see Chapter 17), disability, and age, among others—to produce economic disparities (see Chapter 15) such as different levels of income and financial well-being, making women the disadvantaged gender (Chancel et al., 2022; World Economic Forum, 2022; World Health Organization, 2006).

Some readers may assume that, in most contemporary modern countries, women and men have the same rights to access money, open a bank account, access credit, and take a paying job, and that these are all socially acceptable behaviors. However, we must bear in mind that women's right to access credit or open a bank account was the object of heated struggle even in recent times. Throughout history (see, e.g., Graeber, 2012, pp. 165–210; Johnson, 1994), including after the Industrial Revolution, it was not easy for middle-class women to secure the right to manage money. It was not until 1974, for example, that the United States passed the Equal Credit Opportunity Act; until that time, banks required all single, widowed, or divorced women to be accompanied by a man to co-sign any credit application, and required married women to have their husband co-sign, regardless of the women's income (*The Guardian*, n.d.). Even nowadays, studies about financial inclusion show that women have less access to money than their male counterparts (Morsy & Youssef, 2017; World Economic Forum, 2022). Understanding the role that money plays in gendered trajectories in emerging adulthood is thus crucial to shedding more light on how these inequalities are built, reinforced, or reduced, as they strongly affect the flourishing or floundering of individuals' financial independence (see Chapter 11) and ultimately their financial well-being (see Chapter 7) as they transition to adulthood.

Doing Gender with Money

According to the "doing gender" perspective (West & Zimmerman, 1987, 2009), the fact that gender expectations are social constructs means that they change over time and from society to society. In other words, gender is not something that individuals possess but instead something that they "do," that they continuously act out (Hollander, 2013). Family, media, peers, schools, and other socialization agents all contribute to shaping these expectations and norms. It is not easy for individuals alone, through their agentic power (i.e., their ability to act independently of the constraining power of social structures), to bring about change in terms of modifying or diverging from such norms (Bandelj et al., 2021; Campbell, 2009; McKenzie, 2023). In capitalist societies, several cultural norms related to gender have to do with the division of labor and its economic and noneconomic rewards (e.g., raising children or performing domestic labor; Rossi, 2018; Zelizer, 1994, 1997). On the basis of this evidence, several authors have argued that money—with its uses, the restrictions on using it, and the social meanings attached to it—plays a significant role in doing gender in capitalist society (Deutsch et al., 2003; McKenzie, 2023; Zelizer, 2005) and in shaping young women's and men's transition to adulthood and expectations about their future (Bandelj et al., 2017, 2021; Rossi, 2018).

The extent to which the perception of money in emerging adulthood is affected by gender was found to change across several countries (Crocetti et al., 2015; García-Mendoza et al., 2022). For example, young women may perceive emerging adulthood as a more unstructured period when they must face a difficult balance between family life and work life, and may decide to give up one of them, especially in a country with a high level of gender-stereotyped roles, like Italy (Leccardi, 2007). On the one hand, young women strive to realize themselves in the workplace due to a combination of extrinsic motivation (such as the need for two sources of income within the family unit) and intrinsic drive (such as the need to establish financial independence from one's family of origin [see Chapter 11] or the desire to find fulfilling work). On the other hand, most Italian young people still endorse a traditional view of family roles that put the responsibilities of caring for children and home primarily on women (Crocetti et al., 2015).

Also, whereas in the past women may have been more able to rely on their husband's income when married and on their husband's pensions as they aged (and consequently, they may have anchored their expectations about their transition to adulthood and to old age in traditional stereotypes around women's dependence on men for financial resources; Dwyer et al., 2013), with increasing divorce rates in a number of countries as well as lower marriage rates (OECD, 2019), these gendered expectations may not be fulfilled any more (Agarwalla et al., 2015).

As stated in the introduction of this book, the financial domain is a key aspect of the transition to adulthood because financial independence (see Chapter 11) is a primary goal for many emerging adults and is viewed as a marker of adulthood (Arnett, 2000, 2014). However, on a societal level, access to paid work (see Chapter 10; Blossfeld et al., 2015; Matsumoto & Elder, 2010) and the ability to build financial independence are much more difficult for young women than they are for young men. Internationally, although bank account ownership does continue to grow for women, there continue to be inequalities globally: Only 65% of women hold a bank account compared to 72% of men. Similarly, access to digital technology (i.e., a mobile phone and/or the internet) tends to be lower among women, poorer adults, the less educated, and other traditionally disadvantaged groups (Demirgüç-Kunt et al., 2020). Women also have lower participation in the risky asset market because of lower self-confidence, despite their education and financial literacy (Cupák et al., 2018). Women also face unique challenges in experiencing financial stability due to their lower lifetime incomes as compared to men due to longer career breaks caused by taking off time from work to raise children (PWC, 2023). In some countries, women have different financial needs than men because they are more likely to spend a portion of their retirement years as widows (Bucher-Koenen et al., 2017; Streeter, 2020). In addition, women are less likely than men to devise retirement plans, which makes them less prepared to face financial hardship as they age (Lusardi & Mitchell, 2006). On the whole, adult women face several difficulties in the job, financial, and technological markets, the roots of which start in earlier stages of their life.

When looking at the financial career from adolescence to adulthood, international data show that, even nowadays, girls and women (compared to boys and men) have a higher probability of being engaged in unpaid or underpaid work, living in extreme poverty, and experiencing conditions of food insecurity, with some of these disparities exacerbated during the pandemic (UN Women, 2019; PWC, 2023). Across the OECD, on average, the gender wage gap (measured from median earnings for full-time workers) in 2022 stood at 12%; even if women now tend to have similar or better qualifications than men, they often work in lower-paying jobs (see Chapter 15; OECD, 2022) and suffer the so-called motherhood penalty (i.e., the loss in lifetime earnings experienced by women raising children) in several countries (PWC, 2023). This disparity is wider among mothers, immigrant women, and women of color. Although there are promising results in reducing the gender pay gap for countries and companies that have implemented a pay-transparency policy (Bennedsen et al., 2023), this gap is still a significant factor that shapes women's paths to financial well-being (see Chapter 7) and independence (see Chapter 11) during the course of their lives. According to the World Economic Forum (2022), the most salient factors contributing to gender-based wealth inequity are gender pay gaps, unequal career progression trajectories, life events, and financial literacy. We will focus our attention on the gender gap in financial knowledge (see Chapter 2), attitudes (see Chapter 4), and behaviors (see Chapter 5) among emerging adults.

Gender Differences in Financial Literacy

Gender Differences in Emerging Adults' Financial Knowledge

There are several risks associated with low financial literacy during the transition to adulthood for both men and women: higher likelihood of payday borrowing, higher risk of suffering economic abuse in relationships (see Chapter 14), and higher rates of credit delinquency (Harvey, 2019; Kutin et al., 2019; Preston & Wright, 2019). Furthermore, the new generations are facing a less obvious pathway into employment (see Chapter 10), family formation (see Chapter 14), and property ownership than past generations, thus making the transition to adulthood itself more unpredictable from the financial point of view as well (Serido et al., 2013; Walther & Plug, 2006). However, researchers have documented a paucity of interventions aimed at improving emerging adults' financial well-being (She et al., 2023). At the same time, a gender gap in financial knowledge levels has been found among emerging adults in several economies, from developing countries to industrialized ones, with women performing worse than men and emerging adults performing worse than adults (e.g., Ali et al., 2021; Atkinson & Messy, 2012; Bucher-Koenen et al., 2017; Chobhthaigh, 2019; Davoli & Rodríguez-Planas, 2022; Hasler & Lusardi, 2017; Lusardi & Mitchell, 2006; OECD, 2020).

More specifically, several studies have found a gender gap in emerging adults' financial knowledge, with women having less knowledge than men (see Chapter 2; Chen & Volpe, 2002; García Mata, 2021; Marinucci et al., 2024). Emerging adult women are less likely than emerging adult men to answer financial education questions correctly, and the gap is present not only overall but also within each topic (e.g., knowing what inflation is or how to calculate compound interest), and the gap is present across countries with different income levels (e.g., United States, Switzerland, and Finland; see, for instance, Lusardi, 2019). Emerging adult women are also more likely to admit that they do not know the answers to specific questions, demonstrating excessive insecurity. Even in Finland, which is a relatively gender-equal society, a study found that 27% of women, compared to 44% of men, answered all financial education questions correctly, and 18% of women gave at least one "don't know" answer, compared to less than 10% of men (Kalmi & Ruuskanen, 2017). However, no gender gap in financial knowledge was found among emerging adults studying finance at universities in Italy (Bongini et al., 2015), and evidence worldwide among college students generally (i.e., regardless of their field of study) is mixed (Agasisti et al., 2023; Falahati & Paim, 2011; Jorgensen & Savla, 2010). On the whole, most of the studies evidence significant gender differences in financial knowledge, at the disadvantage of females, but there may be some specific clusters (such as among college students who take courses in finance or economics) who show no disadvantage and need to be studied more in depth.

When it comes to the causes of the gender gap in financial knowledge (see Chapter 2), there is no single explanation that can satisfactorily address gender differences (or the lack thereof). Some have argued that the gender gap may depend on the language used in related surveys, as finance is considered primarily a male domain (Boggio et al., 2015), or it may depend on the measurement of financial knowledge (Palladino, 2022). Yet, this explanation does not seem satisfactory when gender gaps are not found in countries such as Spain or among adolescents, and when they are, conversely, observed in countries such as Italy, where the same measurement and language are used, such as in the OECD-PISA case (Rinaldi et al., 2022). Gender differences in noncognitive factors like self-rated confidence in knowledge about financial matters (which is lower for women in several age groups; see Chapter 4; Arellano et al., 2018; Cupák et al., 2018) explain only a small part of the gap, while a larger part may be due to varying socioeconomic environments across countries (Davoli & Rodríguez-Planas, 2022) and across regions with matrilineal or patrilineal cultural environments (Filipiak & Walle, 2015).

According to other studies, the gender gap in financial knowledge is largely explained by disparities in the factors or processes that lead to knowledge, rather than by variations in the demographic and socioeconomic traits of men and women (Barboza et al., 2016; Bottazzi & Lusardi, 2020; Driva et al., 2016; Preston & Wright, 2019; Salas-Velasco, 2022); hence, the gender disparity in financial knowledge may be caused by unrecognized psychological and behavioral characteristics as well as cultural and societal conventions and stereotypical beliefs. In rural areas, for example, where the gender gap in financial knowledge is wider, the low scores may be attributed to the tradition of young men assuming responsibility for family finances, which could make women less inclined to acquire financial knowledge or exercise prudence in their financial behavior (Agarwalla et al., 2015). However, this gap is found to exist even in Iceland, a nation at the forefront of gender equality according to the World Economic Forum (Gudjonsson et al., 2022).

Family has been identified as one of the main sources of financial socialization (see Chapter 18; Agnew et al., 2018; Gudmunson & Danes, 2011), and research about childhood suggests that financial socialization based on gender begins at an early age through the financial attitudes of parents toward their children, with parents in several countries giving more pocket money to boys than to girls (ISTAT, 2011; Wilson, 2022). Some authors (Agnew & Cameron-Agnew, 2015; Arellano et al., 2018; Fonseca et al., 2012; Rinaldi et al., 2022) indicate that children may acquire their financial knowledge differently while growing up. "As boys and girls grow up, they may be exposed to different opportunities to learn and improve their financial competencies, such as different access to labor and financial markets, and therefore they may develop different levels of financial knowledge and different financial strategies in adulthood over time" (OECD, 2014, p. 81).

Agnew and Cameron-Agnew's study (2015) demonstrated the impact of the home—in particular, financial conversations at home—on children and adolescents' financial knowledge levels: On average, boys had their first financial discussion at a younger age than girls, and this difference held true for students from different socioeconomic backgrounds. Even after controlling for other factors such as socioeconomic position, the age of the child when the family had its first financial chat affected the financial knowledge levels of young men in college. Stereotypical societal expectations and perceptions regarding the need for men to be more financially literate than women may exist, with these influences possibly beginning in the home at a relatively young age (Agnew & Cameron-Agnew, 2015) and being reinforced during adolescence (Bottazzi & Lusardi, 2020; Driva et al., 2016).

In their study among U.S. college students—though they did not find significant gender differences in financial knowledge—Jorgensen and Savla showed an interaction effect between gender and implicit/explicit[1] parent financial socialization on financial knowledge, attitudes, and behavior: men who thought they learned only implicitly about finances from their parents had a significantly higher financial knowledge score than men and women who believed they also learned explicitly, whereas this was not found to be true for women. On the contrary, women who perceived having learned both implicitly and explicitly about finances from their parents had a significantly higher financial behavior score than those who perceived having learned

[1] The implicit/explicit variable was studied with this question: "How would you describe how finances were communicated in your family?" Implicit only = "We didn't talk much about finances, but I learned from their examples." Explicit = "My parents explicitly taught me about finance (e.g., credit cards, debt, budgeting, and saving)." The authors assumed that students who learned explicitly from their parents about finance also learned from their parents' examples (Jorgensen & Savla, 2010, p. 470).

only implicitly (Jorgensen & Savla, 2010). This finding points to the need to focus on gendered parent financial socialization to reduce the gender gap in financial literacy, for example, by being more explicit in teaching finance and financial information seeking, as suggested by a recent study on young Malaysian adults (Pahlevan Sharif et al., 2020).

According to some authors, the gendered division of labor within households, with men typically being more responsible for money matters, can mean that young women—by virtue of viewing their mothers as role models—are less motivated to invest in learning about finance, thus explaining part of their lower financial knowledge levels (Agarwalla et al., 2015; Preston & Wright, 2019). In their study about the source of the gender gap, Preston and Wright (2019) compared adolescents (15–19 years old), younger emerging adults (20–24 years old), and older emerging adults (25–29 years old) using nationally representative data in Australia. They found that those who still live at home at older ages have financial knowledge rates that are 10% lower if male and 17% lower if female, but having a mother who was employed when the respondent was 14 years old was an important factor that improved the financial knowledge of female adolescents and emerging adults, thus reducing the gap. In sum, the financial knowledge gender gap among emerging adults is far from being satisfactorily explained, and further research is needed to clarify countries' cultural differences. The issues that accompany the gender gap—explained in the previous paragraphs—need to be addressed urgently in order to not exacerbate the gender inequalities in financial, occupational, and social inclusion.

Gender Differences in Emerging Adults' Financial Attitudes

We also see gender differences in emerging adults' financial attitudes—the set of perceptions, meanings, and values attributed to money (see Chapter 4; Yamauchi & Templer, 1982). As has been amply demonstrated in the literature, money is not a neutral element but is charged with values and meanings based on how people examine their everyday lives (Tang, 1992). Financial attitudes can be related to one's striving for status and power, improving one's self-esteem (Lindgren, 1980), seeking security, and satisfying one's needs (Knight, 1968).

The impact of gender on attitudes toward money has been previously analyzed by Scott (1976). In this seminal work, emerging adult men saw money as closely related to identity, esteem, and power, whereas emerging adult women saw money as a means to obtain possessions and experiences. Subsequent studies have provided evidence for gender differences in attitudes toward money in general (Sesini et al., 2023) and among emerging adults specifically (Bapat, 2020). Emerging adult men report more confidence (see Chapter 4) and thus independence of action and take more risks (Charness & Gneezy, 2012). Their identity, self-esteem, and sense of power are inextricably linked to money (see Chapter 13). Rudmin (1990), in his work on motivations for ownership, confirms that for men money is power and that women, in contrast, view money more in a relational aspect and for specific social purposes. Furthermore, women tend to seek present gratification through spending (see Chapter 13), be more interested in bargain hunting, and be more oriented toward security in management. Personal possessions also acquire different meanings for men and women: Men are more likely to view their possessions from a functional and self-oriented point of view, while women tend to view possessions on a symbolic and other-oriented level (Dittmar, 1989). Jacobson (1980) concluded that risk is more culturally valued and has a higher value for men. Furthermore, emerging adult men tend to see money as a status symbol and use it to gain power and influence others, whereas emerging adult women score higher in terms of financial planning and tend to be more security-conscious (Amagir et al., 2020; Edwards et al., 2007).

Moving from the symbolic meanings attached to money and consumption to financial attitudes, studies show that financial education (see Chapter 19) makes a difference in the confidence (i.e., self-efficacy; see Chapter 4) emerging adults have in their own money management (Danes & Haberman, 2007). Just as with financial knowledge, to a large extent, financial attitudes can be attributed to one's parent financial socialization (see Chapter 18); for example, discussing money matters with parents is strongly correlated with positive attitudes toward money, and participating in family financial decisions is positively correlated with financial planning (Amagi et al., 2020; Jorgensen & Savla, 2010; Shim et al., 2013). The observed gender differences in attitudes toward money may be attributable to gender-based socialization during childhood and the gender roles enacted by parents, as discussed previously in this chapter. As children develop, their perceptions of money, including what is appropriate for their particular gender, may be reinforced by the family's financial activities and attitudes (West & Zimmerman, 2009).

Gender Differences in Emerging Adults' Financial Behaviors

The literature also highlights gender differences in financial behaviors (see Chapter 5) during emerging adulthood. For example, compared to male students, female students were more likely to have a written budget, planned their spending, and kept their receipts well organized in order to save regularly (Hayhoe et al., 2000; Henry et al., 2001). However, the literature is somewhat contradictory on the description of emerging adult women's behavior, as some studies have indicated that they are more likely to take risks in using credit cards than men (Lyons, 2008). These inconsistencies can be explained simply by the fact that, in reality, gender differences in this area are only the result of gender stereotypes in relation to money and its use, and not from an objective biological difference between men and women, as discussed more in the following section.

In light of this evidence, we can identify financial education (see Chapter 19)—to the extent that it is free of stereotypes—as a concrete possibility to enhance healthy financial behavior among emerging adults. For example, Borden et al. (2008) demonstrated the effects of a basic financial skills seminar on emerging adults. Participants in this seminar reported significant changes in their intentions to limit their use of credit cards and manage their finances in more beneficial ways, using different types of savings/investment vehicles, increasing the number of effective financial behaviors, and decreasing the number of risky financial behaviors. Indeed, for people without financial experience, financial education programs have been identified as key to improving financial literacy and promoting personal financial responsibility (Kaiser et al., 2022; Lusardi, 2019). Furthermore, enhancing female financial literacy could make girls feel more confident about managing money and asking for higher income, and reduce their probability of falling victim to economic violence (see Chapter 14).

The Role of Gender Stereotypes

Thus far, researchers have been unable to fully explain gender differences in financial knowledge (see Chapter 2), attitudes (see Chapter 4), and behaviors (see Chapter 5). Let's now focus on a key element of gender socialization anticipated in the previous discussion: stereotypes. In a recent review, Sesini and colleagues (2023) advanced the idea that stereotypical beliefs and gender role prescriptions related to money may play an important role in explaining such differences. The literature has shown that women's unfamiliarity with financial topics is correlated with girls' tendency to avoid competitive contexts (Niederle & Vesterlund, 2010) because they lack the confidence to engage in tasks that are outside a gender-specific domain (Coffman, 2014). For example, finance is considered primarily a male domain (see Boggio et al., 2015), so many women are somewhat uncomfortable with financial contexts and topics.

Driva and colleagues (2016) suggest that gender differences in financial matters are due to gender-based expectations: Boys who perform better than girls in financial knowledge also think that returns on financial knowledge are higher for males than for females and that males are more likely to deal with financial matters at work. This is because stereotypes are cultural products that provide an image associated with a certain social category (Ashmore et al., 1981). They are beliefs that are both descriptive and prescriptive. Stereotypes do not describe reality as it objectively is (Judd & Park, 1993) but rather describe what is culturally conveyed about a certain social category (Cialdini & Trost, 1998). Despite being distorted images, stereotypes unfortunately have a strong influence on people's cognitive functioning, motivation, and behavior (Ellemers, 2018).

As for gender, the stereotype content model (Fiske et al., 2002) clarifies the specific content of stereotypical beliefs about what is associated with men versus women: We expect women to be warm, affectionate, and caring (i.e., expressive), whereas we expect men to be competent, dominant, and combative (i.e., instrumental). Cross-cultural studies have confirmed that these stereotypical images, especially those related to women, are consistent across different cultural contexts (Kosakowska-Berezecka et al., 2023). Thus, more or less consciously, women can construct their identity around stereotypical images of the groups to which they belong. This phenomenon is called "stereotype internalization" or "stereotype embodiment" in the literature (e.g., Aarntzen et al., 2023). It may enhance the "doing gender" process mentioned earlier. One example of this phenomenon in emerging adulthood is in relation to career choices. These can often unconsciously trace gender stereotypes. For this reason, we find very few girls enrolled in STEM disciplines despite the fact that there are no scientifically documented gender differences in logical-mathematical abilities, and therefore girls are equally well suited to STEM subjects as boys (Makarova et al., 2019). Because in several countries STEM majors still get the most lucrative jobs, women's educational choices may turn into "bad" choices from an earnings perspective (Simon et al., 2017).

Sesini et al. (2023) suggest that stereotypic beliefs on gender and money operate on two levels: direct discrimination and stereotype embodiment. On the one hand, due to the persistence of stereotypic gender beliefs related to money in today's society, women can experience direct discrimination and face, for instance, limited access to financial education as shown in the review of the literature on financial knowledge. Moreover, studies conducted in different cultural contexts show a persistent effect of gender stereotypes on the gender pay gap, on leadership positions in the financial industry, and on activities in high finance (e.g., Capelle-Blancard & Reberioux, 2021; Tinghög et al., 2021; Williams et al., 2010). As for stereotype embodiment, women can assume and internalize stereotypical beliefs about gender and money (Hentschel et al., 2019). Indeed, women's behavior can be negatively influenced by the activation of money-related stereotypes. Women are aware of the existence of stereotypes that see them as less capable than men of handling money, and this awareness may preclude their *a priori* effectiveness or interest in financial matters. Therefore, the internalization and acceptance of stereotypes may prevent women from effectively managing money (see Chapter 5) and using financial knowledge, while increasing their anxiety (see Chapter 8) and ambivalence on the topic.

Even if stereotypical beliefs can explain a lot about the complicated relationship between gender and money, little research has been done in analyzing the specific content of stereotypical beliefs related to gender and money and how they can actually affect the differences observed in knowledge, attitudes, and behaviors. Broadening this research topic might give rise to new, effective intervention tools with the aim of reducing the gender gap in financial well-being for emerging adults. For example, a recent study (Manzi et al., under review) conducted on a nationally representative sample of Italians explored the effects of stereotypical beliefs related to gender and money and tested the effects of these beliefs on women's attitudes toward money (see Chapter 4) at both implicit and explicit levels. This study shows that gender stereotypes limit and condition women, leading them to manage money differently. These results also suggest that effective financial communication against stereotypes seems to be crucial. Indeed, financial promotional messages often use terminology that is stereotypically masculine, invoking metaphors and dimensions related to spheres that are considered culturally masculine (Prast et al., 2018); this study instead showed that promotional messages constructed with concepts and metaphors that do not confirm the stereotype, thus being counter-stereotypical, can better suit female spheres and be more effective and attractive to women. Thus, gender differences in money are also determined by psychological dispositions and gender norms acquired during early socialization and become, for this reason, fixed, stable, and consistent characteristics throughout life (LeBaron & Kelley, 2021. It is for this reason that when young female adults identify strongly with their gender, then they are more concerned about money than their male peers (Bandelj et al., 2021); gender and money intersect with each other.

Ultimately, this body of research has not only demonstrated that stereotypes are one of the main obstacles women face in accessing the financial world, it has also shown that modifying and changing stereotypical beliefs can greatly improve women's attitudes toward financial matters, thus decreasing the gender gap in financial literacy.

Key points in this chapter for practitioners and researchers can be found in Box 16.1 and Box 16.2, respectively.

Box 16.1 Key Points for Practitioners

When it comes to money matters, there are some differences between emerging adult women and men that should be accounted for by practitioners.

- Emerging adult women have lower financial literacy than emerging adult men, and this may hold true for college and university students specifically. You may need to put in more effort to give financial information (or teach how to find reliable information) to women rather than men.
- In certain countries, gender differences in financial literacy are found at age 15, and some argue that gendered patterns of financial socialization (see Chapter 18) are found during childhood. The cause of this gender gap is not clear yet, but it is crucial to act at an early stage to prevent the widening of the gender gap during the transition to adulthood.
- Women tend to live longer than men in most countries and face the final years of their lives alone as widows. Therefore, it is crucial to help them to learn how to manage money autonomously earlier in life, such as during emerging adulthood.
- Gender stereotypes may influence the attitudes of people working in banks and other financial institutions, who may unintentionally discriminate against female customers simply because they are stereotypically less good at handling money. Thus, practitioners working in these spheres should take intentional steps to counteract any such discrimination.

Box 16.2 Key Points for Researchers

- Future research should better investigate the effects of gender prescriptions in emerging adults and whether changing gender stereotypes can improve emerging adult women's financial knowledge, attitudes, and behaviors.
- Given that gender in most research about financial literacy is considered as binary ("male" and "female"), there is a need to further investigate how gender diversity interacts with building financial literacy, financial independence, and thus the financial flourishing or floundering of emerging adults.

Chapter 17
Cultural and Racial Considerations in Financial Literacy

Mihaela Friedlmeier[1] *and Phuc Dang*[2]

Introduction

The primary aim of this chapter is to describe and discuss characteristics of financial literacy in countries around the world, with particular focus on challenges and opportunities encountered by emerging adults. The chapter focuses on similarities and differences in financial literacy based on national and international studies. Although there is limited published research outside the Western world, we will base our discussion on existing empirical work as well as findings from global surveys (e.g., Organisation for Economic Co-operation and Development [OECD], Standard & Poor's Global Financial Literacy Surveys). Measures of financial literacy used in large-scale surveys often cannot be meaningfully used in non-Western cultural contexts, making such comparisons less useful. We finish the chapter with suggestions for future research, improved policies, and practical recommendations for individuals, communities, and entire nations. As Lusardi (2010) put it,

> Financial literacy is an essential piece of knowledge that every student should have. . . . Just as reading and writing became skills that enabled people to succeed in modern economies, today it is impossible to succeed without being able to "read and write" financially. (p. 1)

[1] Psychology Department, Grand Valley State University, USA
[2] Department of Psychological Sciences, Purdue University, USA

Mihaela Friedlmeier and Phuc Dang, *Cultural and Racial Considerations in Financial Literacy.* In: *Flourishing and Floundering Financially in Emerging Adulthood.* Edited by: Ashley B. LeBaron-Black, Heather Kelley, and Angela Sorgente, Oxford University Press. © Oxford University Press (2025). DOI: 10.1093/9780197699157.003.0018

Global Perspectives on Financial Literacy in Emerging Adults

The impact of culture on economic outcomes has received attention from various disciplines in the past. While culture is a notoriously difficult term to define, with hundreds of definitions available (Kroeber & Kluckhohn, 1952), the one provided by Guiso et al. (2016) fits our current purpose well: "those customary beliefs and values that ethnic, religious, and social groups transmit fairly unchanged from generation to generation" (p. 1). For instance, Banfield (1958) and Putnam (1993) were among the first to connect culture to economic outcomes. They argued that differences in economic performance across Italian regions originate from the free city-states' experience during the late Middle Ages that encouraged stronger civic and cooperative behavior, a cultural trait still present in parts of current Italian society (Guiso et al., 2016).

The impact of culture has been examined more extensively in recent decades, with studies showing that various aspects of national cultures impact the effectiveness of institutions (Licht et al., 2007), economic development (Guiso et al., 2016), and household financial behavior (Haliassos et al., 2017). While existing work on financial literacy has focused primarily on sociodemographic indicators such as gender (see Chapter 16; Cupák et al., 2018a; Fonseca et al., 2012), age (Xiao et al., 2015), and education (Lusardi, 2012), less is known about the link between culture and financial literacy levels.

Financial Literacy and Cultural Dimensions at the Country and Individual Levels

More recently, Ahunov and Van Hove (2020) combined the 2014 Standard & Poor's Global Financial Literacy survey with Hofstede's cultural dimensions for a sample of 92 countries across all continents. The first set of findings showed strong differences across countries with regard to financial literacy: While in Denmark and Norway 73% of the population was financially literate, only 13% and 14% of Yemen and Albania, respectively, were financially literate. They also showed that economic variables such as GDP per capita or national cognitive scores failed to explain much of the variation (Ahunov & Van Hove, 2020). At the same time, differences in cultural variables have a much more significant impact; for instance, power distance (i.e., the extent to which the less powerful members of organizations and institutions expect that power is distributed unequally) and individualism (i.e., whether individuals are integrated into groups) helped to explain variation in financial literacy across countries. Hofstede (2011) explained that in high power-distance societies "less powerful members of organizations and institutions (like the family) accept and expect that power is distributed unequally" (p. 9); consequently, countries that are high in power distance will tend to be lower in financial literacy because people delegate their financial decisions to particular members of the family, such as the household head. In India, for instance, a country that scores high on power distance, Agarwalla et al. (2015) found that urban young people living with families have low financial literacy, explained by the tradition of the head of a joint family in India making all the key financial decisions. This is also somewhat reflected in the experiences of emerging adults illustrated in Box 17.1 and Box 17.2. In individualistic cultures, more people prefer to manage their financial affairs themselves (Ahunov & Van Hove, 2020); thus, they are more likely to be financially literate (Hsu, 2016). Because in individualistic societies demand for complex financial products is high, people are more likely to invest in financial literacy in order to be able to make sound decisions (Ahunov & Van Hove, 2020).

Box 17.1

"Growing up in a middle-class household with my father as the sole breadwinner, I observed his prudent approach towards materialistic expenses. Our spending focus was broad when it came to essential needs but remarkably conservative on unnecessary expenditures. This habit, perhaps crucially, shielded our family from financial instability, eliminating the need to seek financial assistance from others. Despite this frugal mindset, we led a satisfying lifestyle, successfully fulfilling all our desires. This upbringing naturally instilled a strong inclination towards saving in me. Witnessing my father's financial prudence empowered me to make rational decisions about money from the moment I started earning. The disciplined approach to spending and the emphasis on saving have become foundational elements in my own financial journey."

—Female, 21, India

Box 17.2

"My dad runs a business through [which] I got an idea about investment and how someone make[s] money through that. I saw how he use[d] to invest and sell the products after that, through which he made profits, that is how I did learn

continued

Box 17.2 *continued*

about earnings. On the other side, my mother was a teacher when I was a child and I saw her saving, and I did ask her about what you would do about this money, so with her answers I did learn the importance of saving."

—Female, 21, India

In another recent study, De Beckker and colleagues (2020) examined the effect of national culture on adult financial literacy levels across 12 countries (i.e., 24,512 individuals from Belgium, Canada, Croatia, Estonia, Hong Kong, Jordan, Latvia, Malaysia, the Netherlands, New Zealand, Thailand, and the United Kingdom, ages 18 and above). The data used to explore the influence of culture on financial literacy across countries originate from the 2015 OECD/INFE international survey on adult financial literacy competencies (OECD, 2016). Different from many previous studies, they examined individual sociodemographic characteristics and captured the effect of culture by employing Hofstede's cultural dimensions of uncertainty avoidance (i.e., feeling at ease in unstructured situations) and individualism. While other cross-country studies used aggregated financial literacy data (e.g., Ahunov & Van Hove, 2020), De Beckker et al. (2020) used individual-level observations, enabling them to disentangle the link between culture and financial literacy. They found that individuals tend to be more financially literate in countries with a culture of high uncertainty avoidance (e.g., Belgium, Croatia, Jordan, Latvia), and are less financially literate in countries with a culture that promotes individualism (e.g., Canada, United Kingdom). Those who live in cultures oriented toward uncertainty avoidance may invest more in financial literacy to make it easier to deal with unexpected financial events (De Beckker et al., 2020). These findings are consistent with some previous literature showing that more individualistic people tend to show overconfidence in their financial capabilities, which seemingly led to seeking less financial advice (De Beckker et al., 2020). At the same time, this stands in contrast with the arguments and findings from Ahunov and Van Hove (2020) that showed a positive link between individualism and financial literacy. Further studies are needed in order to shed more light on aspects of national culture and the link to financial literacy, especially with regard to individualism as evidence points to different directions of influence.

Financial Literacy and Country of Ancestry

Another interesting line of research integrated the epidemiological approach (Fernandez, 2008). Davoli and Rodriguez-Planas (2020) demonstrated an association between adults' financial literacy in the United States and the financial literacy level in their self-reported country of ancestry. They relied on a sample of over 6,000 adults from the National Longitudinal Survey of Youth born (mostly) in the United States between 1957–1961 and 1980–1984 who identified with 26 different countries of ancestry. Davoli and Rodriguez-Planas argued that adults living in the United States but who identify with different countries of ancestry are influenced by "customary beliefs and values that ethnic, religious, and social groups transmit fairly unchanged from generation to generation" (Guiso et al., 2016, p. 1). They found that respondents from countries of ancestry that emphasize patience, long-term orientation, and risk aversion (e.g., Germany, the Netherlands, Denmark) exhibited significantly higher financial literacy in the United States.

A Developmental Perspective on Financial Literacy in Different Cultures

Thus far, we have discussed how cultural variables of different countries and nations are linked to various aspects of financial literacy. Beyond that, however, it is essential to note that such differences in macro-systems contribute to different models of the transition to adulthood (Arnett, 2015). Emerging adulthood is a developmental time frame when parent–child individuation occurs in many life domains (e.g., religion, relationships; Arnett, 2016). Financially, emerging adults around the world remain widely dependent on their parents, who pay the bills and remain the gatekeepers of their offsprings' finances (see Chapter 11; Schoeni & Ross, 2005; Shim et al., 2010). Across cultures, parents are the first and the most important socialization agents, and that includes the financial domain (see Chapter 18). However, parents are not the only socialization agents; with increasing age especially, children in different cultures are exposed to varying degrees of financial education provided in schools as well as working opportunities. Financial socialization is defined as the "process of acquiring and developing values, attitudes, standards, norms, knowledge, and behaviors that contribute to financial viability and individual well-being" (Danes, 1994, p. 128), and this can happen through explicit teaching, but also through implicit modeling and other financial practices within the family and the broader culture, as illustrated in Box 17.3 (Norvilitis & MacLean, 2010; Serido et al., 2015). In the next sections, we will discuss aspects pertaining to financial literacy specific to different world regions, with a particular focus on a variety of financial socialization efforts (e.g., via family, national or school financial curriculum, job and training opportunities) directly or indirectly impacting emerging adults.

Box 17.3

"Growing up, my parents never taught me about finances or how to manage my money. Myself, I did not produce questions about this either. It simply wasn't a topic that would be discussed in our family. We wouldn't be motivated with money either, as my parents believe in intrinsic motivation. However, of course getting older, I realized that finance management is very important, and I learned from my own mistakes or discussed it with a few very close friends. I then took it upon myself to pass on what I learned to my little sister, [who] is eight years younger than me. She now regularly comes to me for questions involving financial topics."

—Female, 30, Luxembourg, half-Spanish

Financial Literacy in Northern, Western, and Eastern Europe

Northern Europe

Generally speaking, financial literacy is moderately high among European countries, with Northern Europe scoring the highest, followed by Western Europe and, finally, Eastern Europe. Different from the rest of Europe, the Nordic region is rather culturally cohesive and the school systems are quite similar. The social and economic system ("the Nordic model") is known for combining economic efficiency with social equality. In the school curricula of these countries, financial education (see Chapter 19) is emphasized at all grade levels and across a variety of disciplines (e.g., social science, mathematics, and home economics). Based on Standard & Poor's Ratings Services Global Financial Literacy Survey from 2014, Denmark, Norway, and Sweden were the leading countries and Finland scored eighth in financial literacy out of 140 participating countries (Klapper et al., 2015). Using the same data, Batsaikhan and Demertzis (2018) found that in Denmark and Sweden, the countries with the highest financial literacy scores, almost all adults reported that they saved money from monthly paychecks. In Denmark, Norway, and Sweden, both numeracy skills and financial literacy were high, while Finland came in slightly behind them.

In Finland, many studies about financial literacy have included emerging adults. For instance, a longitudinal study by Ranta and Salmela-Aro (2018) demonstrated the importance of financial self-efficacy (see Chapter 4) for financial behavior (see Chapter 5) and well-being (see Chapter 7) among emerging adults ages 24–27 years old. An important finding in a related study by Ranta et al. (2019) was that financial confidence was linked to emerging adults' well-being as measured by life satisfaction and the manifestation of depressive symptoms. In a qualitative study of Finnish emerging adults ages 26–35 years who held bank mortgages, Lehtinen (2017) showed that they were systematic, cautious, and economical in managing their finances. Overall, results from the Nordic region demonstrate that efficient digitalization and coordinated activity and cooperation between the public, private, and third sector have a positive impact on citizens' financial literacy, including emerging adults (Raijas, 2021). Financial education provided in school seems to be of particular relevance here and, likely, of long-term impact leading into emerging adulthood.

Western Europe

Among Western European countries, Germany, Austria, Switzerland, and the Netherlands are leaders in financial literacy and financial confidence (OECD, 2020). In 2012, the OECD added a module about financial literacy as part of its Programme for International Student Assessment (PISA) project investigating the financial literacy of youth (i.e., 15-year-old students) around the world. Results showed that Dutch students scored above the OECD average (OECD, 2020). Interestingly, only 50% of respondents in Switzerland were able to correctly answer the three widely used questions developed by Lusardi and Mitchell on the topics of saving, interest, and inflation (Lusardi, 2019). A consistent pattern in Switzerland, as in some other Western European countries, is that financial literacy varies widely among different population groups: lower among women (see Chapter 16), low-income and less-educated households (see Chapter 15), and households with a migrant background that are non-native speakers. Switzerland is characterized by a high level of cultural and institutional heterogeneity; therefore, it would be important to understand how financial literacy among households is correlated with not just socioeconomic but also cultural background. A study conducted by Brown and colleagues (2018) compared secondary school students along the German–French language border within Switzerland and showed that Swiss students in the French-speaking region scored lower on a financial knowledge test than those in the German-speaking region, interpreting their findings through the lens of cultural differences. While certainly an interesting study, culture was not measured in any explicit way, just implied. It is likely that schools in different regions of Switzerland approach financial education differently, and also that parents in the French- versus German-speaking regions engage differently with their children when it comes to money, and these differences are reflected in emerging adults' financial literacy scores. However, very little research focused these differences at the family level.

Eastern Europe

Across various dimensions of financial literacy (see Chapter 1)—knowledge (see Chapter 2), confidence, and attitudes (see Chapter 4)—Eastern Europe fares, on average, worse than Western Europe (Cwynar, 2021). Perhaps not surprisingly, there is large heterogeneity in financial literacy among these countries. For instance, considering the OECD data (OECD, 2016, 2020), the financial knowledge scores range from 31% (Romania) to 68% (Latvia). Except for Bulgaria and Romania, the European Union (EU) member countries display higher financial literacy compared to nonmember countries (Cwynar, 2021). The case of Romania is particularly interesting, especially because it is an EU member, and it is more developed than many other Eastern European countries. To some extent, the low financial literacy rates can be explained by comparatively low financial inclusion rates (World Bank, 2018). Due to negative experiences caused by repeated banking crises in the last two decades, Romanian citizens may have become reluctant to use financial intermediaries (Beckmann, 2013).

Different from Western Europe, one interesting finding about Eastern European countries is the lack of gender differences in financial knowledge scores. This may be explained by common experiences shared by these countries for more than 40 years following the Second World War: Bucher-Koenen et al. (2017) speculated that the lack of a gender gap in financial literacy in former Eastern European socialist countries may be a result of egalitarianism as to social gender roles in these states. Even though not directly documented, it is to be expected that such patterns influence children's socialization at the family level and beyond, with ramifications into emerging adulthood.

Further empirical studies in Eastern European countries suggest that the link between age and financial literacy follows a different pattern from the one found in many developed Western countries (see the review of Stolper & Walter, 2017), with emerging adults scoring similarly in financial literacy tests compared to middle-age individuals. This may be explained by younger generations understanding current financial challenges in the society better than older generations that perhaps are still somewhat rooted in the past, centralized economy. Despite exposure to a different type of economy post-Communism, Damian et al. (2020) showed that financial behaviors (see Chapter 5) of Romanian emerging adults are predicted by parents' healthy financial behaviors (from the perspective of emerging adults). They also showed that financial satisfaction was predicted by high socioeconomic status (see Chapter 15), perhaps not surprising for a country still struggling after the transition to a market economy. In Romania, Beckmann (2013) found that the peak in financial literacy occurs faster than in other highly industrialized countries, and the youngest group displays a relatively high level of financial literacy. This was also reflected in the examples mentioned by Romanian emerging adults in Box 17.4 and Box 17.5. Financial socialization within the family (see Chapter 18) may follow different rules and expectations depending on the cultural context. In support of that, Sirsch et al. (2020) showed that parental financial socialization among Slovene emerging adults has a more influential role than among Austrian emerging adults, with Slovene students being more likely to live with their parents and needing more financial support from them. Further studies are needed in order to better understand the influence of various socialization agents on emerging adults in countries and cultures that have been through more major social, economic, and political transitions compared to more stable environments.

Box 17.4

"I remember when I was little, my mother would always make sure that I understood the value of money in order for me to become a free-from-vanity person. In order to do so, she made me work at our family's clothing shop, and at the beginning of the day I used to negotiate the percentage I will get from the total amount I would sell in that day. By doing so, I was more eager to [be] involve[d in] the business and help customers buy more so I will receive more at the end of the day. Now I understand that money does not grow on trees, and work and devotion are necessary. Also, I am not ashamed to negotiate a fair price for one piece of clothing."

—Female, 19, Romania

Box 17.5

"When I was young, my dad would always make sure I was present at his business meetings. After several meetings, I was fascinated and wanted to know more. Also, I knew that I would like to follow in my father's footsteps and pursue a career as an

continued

Box 17.5 *continued*

entrepreneur. After a while I learned how money works and developed my negotiation skills, which help me to this day. As a result, I can say with confidence that I am always one step ahead in any financial matters that would occur to me, and I can set apart the feelings and emotions when [it] comes to money, no matter the circumstances, so that it won't affect my mental health."

—Male, 19, Romania

Financial Literacy and Racial Differences in the United States

The Unites States is a multicultural society, is ethnically diverse, and is generally characterized by a very high level of individualism, even when compared to other Western cultures (Triandis, 1995). At the individual level, self-enhancement motivations are dominant, with a strong focus on three distinct values: hedonism, achievement, and power (Schwartz, 2012). Such macro-system cultural orientations have an impact on cultural norms and expectations at every level of society, including the family, the school system, and training and job opportunities. As already mentioned, the United States is ethnically diverse, with 18.5% of the population identifying as Hispanic or Latino, 13.4% Black, and 5.9% Asian (see Chapter 15; Statista, 2022. In spite of this, few studies have specifically linked aspects of cultural or ethnic differences to financial literacy; instead, most literature in the United States has focused on the relationship between socioeconomic status and financial well-being and/or literacy. Consequently, this section is organized around existing studies about wealth disparities in the United States, influence within the family, school curriculum, and unique challenges faced by the different ethnicities, with a particular focus on emerging adults and youth in general.

Racial inequality in wealth in the United States is an issue that the government, researchers, and the general public have been discussing persistently for the past several decades (see Chapter 15; Campbell & Kaufman, 2006; Kochhar & Fry, 2014; McKernan et al., 2014; Shapiro et al., 2014). The racial wealth gap in 2016 was still as large as it was in the 1950s and 1960s (Schularick et al., 2018), and non-White households were more critically impacted by the 2008 financial crisis compared to White households (Schularick et al., 2018; Wolff, 2017). Because wealth is often an indicator of financial well-being, many studies have examined the root cause of these wealth disparities (McKernan et al., 2014; Shapiro et al., 2014). One of the factors that has been identified as a determinant of household wealth is financial knowledge (van Rooij et al., 2012). Factors such as discrimination, wealth disparity, labor force instability, and a history of less exposure to financial markets and financial information may impact financial socialization practices (Gutter et al., 2014). Lower levels of financial literacy and wellness among some minority groups (i.e., Latinos and Blacks) may adversely impact how financial socialization (see Chapter 18) is transferred in these households, which consequently affects people of all ages, including emerging adults. Blacks, in particular, consistently demonstrate lower levels of financial literacy and well-being than other races (Yakoboski et al., 2019), and this often translates into a lack of, or limited, information and skills to model positive financial behaviors to their children (Sherraden, 2013). Quantitative and qualitative studies in this area are needed in order to understand and improve the financial literacy of youth in these groups.

Beyond financial socialization provided within the family, schools play an important role. Over the past several decades, the number of states offering financial education in high school has been increasing (see Chapter 19). However, the year that mandatory financial education was implemented and the content and type of mandatory education differ among the states. Not all of the states have made this a requirement, even though high school financial education could have a crucial impact in the long run. For instance, Bernheim et al. (2001) documented a difference in subsequent asset accumulation by the time individuals reach middle age due to their exposure to state-mandated high school financial education or not. Brown et al. (2016) also found evidence of the positive effect that high school financial education had on debt behaviors after graduation between ages 19–29. The significance of the state variable in these analyses suggests state-specific policies' potential effect and suggests ways in which a local network could influence racial/ethnic disparities. Other explanations for the racial gap in financial literacy could be related to differences in general academic achievement, especially math (see Chapter 3). For instance, using data from the 2018 National Financial Capability Study, Lee and Kim (2022) found a positive relationship between mathematical ability and financial knowledge, which contributed substantially to the racial/ethnic gap. Improving access to better education for all would lead to better outcomes, including higher financial literacy in emerging adults.

Multiple scholars have assessed U.S. college students' financial literacy. In Jorgensen and Savla's (2010) research, college students from six states scored, on average, about 58% on the financial knowledge questions. Norvilitis et al. (2006) and Robb (2011) identified the positive influence of college students' financial knowledge (see Chapter 2) on their credit card behaviors (see Chapter 13). Based on their study of 1,511 U.S. college students, Serido et al. (2013) concluded that objective financial knowledge was not sufficient to result in responsible financial behaviors (see Chapter 5), suggesting that financial skills (see Chapter 3) are also necessary. In a study using data from the 2014 National Student Financial Wellness Survey of undergraduate students (5.0% of the sample consisted of Blacks, 5.6% Hispanic or Latino, 5.6% Asians), White et al. (2021) aimed to test how the types of financial socialization messages given by parents to their children vary by race and how the relationships between particular financial socialization messages and financial outcomes vary by race (see Chapter 18). For all racial/ethnic groups, having received an investing message from one's parents was significantly associated with higher financial management scores (see Chapter 5), higher financial optimism, and lower financial stress (see Chapter 8). Of all groups, Hispanic students were least likely to receive the investment message. Immigration factors such as noncitizenship could impact investment messages provided by Hispanic parents. White and Asian students were more likely to report receiving messages related to savings and banking than their Black peers, suggesting a lack of trust in traditional banks among Black parents. These findings are, in part, reflected in the experiences shared by emerging adults in Box 17.6, Box 17.7, and Box 17.8.

Box 17.6

"I receive an allowance from my parents and learn about investing through their financial advisor. I learned additional finance information in a high school personal finance elective that emphasized paying off credit cards and how to build a good credit score."

—Female, 20, United States, White

Box 17.7

"My mom used to have fake money, and my siblings and I would play candy store. We used the money to buy things from our kitchen and my dad would have us count out the total amount of money and calculate how much change we should get back. This helped me recognize the difference between coins as well as the value of a dollar."

—Female, 24, United States, Black

Box 17.8

"My parents were immigrants and wanted to give me a good life, so they were fairly secretive about financial matters. Even then, I noticed a lot of their conscientious and organized habits and, thanks to their vigilance, I've found myself doing the same: paying bills on time and budgeting appropriately."

—Male, 22, United States, Asian

Because much of the U.S.-based research on finances in emerging adulthood has been conducted on White college students (LeBaron & Kelley, 2021) and much of this handbook already highlights that perspective, we focus in this chapter on the unique financial literacy experiences of Black, Hispanic, and Asian U.S. emerging adults.

Financial Literacy of Black American Emerging Adults

After Hispanics, Blacks represent the largest ethnic minority group in the United States. From the studies that explored interrace differences, the consensus is that Blacks show lower outcomes in various aspects of financial capability compared to not only Whites but also other ethnic groups (Anong, 2016; Lee & Hanna, 2012). Across all life stages, Blacks are less financially literate than Whites (Lusardi et al., 2010; Mandell, 2008; Robb & James, 2009). For instance, compared to Whites, 15% of Black emerging adults ages 23–28 participating in the 2007–2008 National Longitudinal Survey of Youth (NLSY) scored 3% lower on the interest question, 19% lower on the inflation question, and 12% lower on the investment diversification question. Some of these racial gaps may be explained, in part, by parental education (Mandell, 2008) as well as issues of discrimination, financial inclusion, wealth-based opportunities, and so on (see Chapter 15).

Racial disparities in financial literacy translate into disparities in financial outcomes (Anong, 2016). The Black–White wealth gap has widened since the Great Recession; White median wealth was $192,500 in 2007 compared to $19,200 for Blacks, whereas in 2013 the median wealth of Whites was $141,900 compared to $11,000 for Blacks (Kochbar & Fry, 2014). This wealth gap is driven by income, college education, homeownership (primarily), unemployment, and intergenerational transfers (see Chapter 15). Black households have disproportionately experienced discrimination with traditional financial services as it relates to their savings and banking needs (Hunter, 2019), which has led to a historical and present distrust of banks for many of these households.

Although few studies have addressed the financial literacy of and related challenges faced by Black emerging adults, from the information provided here, we can draw the conclusion that financial outcomes are poor and changes at all levels of society are needed (e.g., better education and access to resources and opportunities for both parents and their children).

Financial Literacy of Hispanic American Emerging Adults

According to the 2020 U.S. Census data, Hispanics represent the largest minority group in the United States. There is very limited literature on the financial literacy of Hispanics, especially studies focusing on emerging adults. In this limited literature, Hispanics have been shown to engage in less optimal and mainstream financial behaviors (Al-Bahrani et al., 2019; Porto, 2016). At the core of this issue is a generally disadvantaged foundation of financial literacy, which is likely to perpetuate throughout generations, especially considering financial socialization processes (Gudmunson & Danes, 2011).

Similar to Blacks, a common problem Hispanics experience is insufficient access to mainstream financial resources such as banking (Kim et al., 2019). Areas densely populated by Hispanics and other minority populations have far less access to such resources in addition to having easier access to more predatory services (i.e., pawnshops, cash services; Kim et al.). According to a report by the Federal Deposit Insurance Corporation (2016), 57% of unbanked households utilized such alternative services, whereas only 21% of banked households utilized alternative services.

Research suggests that citizenship status is an important consideration for financial literacy within immigrants for a variety of reasons. In certain immigrant populations, the extent of acculturation has been described as a barrier in outcomes such as income and financial literacy (Sharpe & Abdel-Ghany, 2006), meaning that those who have resided within the United States for longer periods of time and have deepened their roots are likely to differ in such outcomes. Research has also shown English proficiency to be an important factor in financial outcomes (Campbell & Kaufman, 2006), a relationship likely strongly intertwined with citizenship status and acculturation.

As shown earlier in the chapter, financial behaviors (see Chapter 5) are often influenced by cultural factors. For example, we learn from previous works that Hispanics tend to prioritize the needs of both their family and extended family over their own (Gallo et al., 2009), a cultural motivation that likely impacts a wide variety of financial aspects (e.g., distribution of financial resources). The barriers experienced by Hispanic emerging adults have been shown to result in, or at least be related to, a disparity in both financial literacy and success (Porto, 2016). These preexisting disadvantages are likely to be expressed in the financial socialization process (see Chapter 18). What could have been positives of direct financial teaching from and observed learning of parents may instead result in negative outcomes as the parents themselves find difficulty navigating a system in which they are not fully included.

Although the studies mentioned here have not specifically focused on emerging adults, we can easily understand how the described cultural norms regarding family dynamics, the limited access to financial resources, along with the language barriers, may lead cumulatively to long-term effects in emerging adulthood and beyond. For future research and policy initiatives, it is particularly important to pay mind to the risk factors that might transfer between generations. Policies must be informed by such research and be considerate of the specific needs of Hispanic Americans as a distinct but diverse population with a distinct but diverse culture.

Financial Literacy of Asian American Emerging Adults

Relative to Black and Hispanic populations in the United States, there seems to be even less research on Asians' financial literacy, let alone the financial literacy of Asian emerging adults. Frequently discussed both in the media and literature is the dominant status of Asians in terms of both financial success and academic success (Yao, 2016). More specifically, the 2020 U.S. Census has shown Asians to be highly educated and to generally earn substantially higher salaries than other groups. According to the Pew Research Center, Asians earn a median annual income of $85,800, $24,000 higher than the median income of all households, in addition to half of Asians over 25 having earned a bachelor's degree compared to 33% among all American households (Budiman & Ruiz, 2021). However, these general findings fail to capture the nuances of financial literacy and success that exist within such a diverse group, a problem also found within the literature on Blacks and Hispanics. The Asian population in the United States is highly heterogeneous and comprises several different subgroups (e.g., Chinese, Japanese, Korean, Vietnamese, Filipino). The diverse nature of these cultures requires a deeper examination to accurately understand the mechanisms producing such positive financial outcomes.

Li et al. (2021) suggest that an important distinction between each subgroup of Asian immigrants is related to their country of origin. The industrialized nature of East Asian nations like Japan, China, and Korea versus the more unstable and less wealthy conditions of other Asian nations has shown to produce contrasting outcomes between Asian immigrants in the United States (Li et al., 2021). In other words, researchers have argued that the motives in immigration are different between these two groups. There is obviously a difference between escaping poverty and dangerous living conditions and seeking opportunities to further your career and education. Considering the sparse literature on the direct financial socialization experiences of Asian emerging adults in the United States, it would be helpful to have more insight into the values and attitudes around finances or financial parenting.

Future efforts for both researchers and policymakers should be similar to the suggestions made previously for literature on Hispanic emerging adults. Ideally, future studies should consider how Asian emerging adults as a group compare to other minority groups, their immigrant predecessors, and how specific groups differ from one another. More culture-specific models are warranted.

Financial Literacy in Asia

There is a great deal of diversity among Asian countries when it comes to population, income, the Human Development Index (HDI), education, and culture. Based on the information from the S&P Global Financial Literacy Survey, Israel received the highest score (68), while countries from South Asia such as Afghanistan (14) received the lowest (Klapper & Lusardi, 2019). Most countries in East and Southeast Asia integrated financial education (see Chapter 19) into school curricula (OECD, 2019). For instance, schools in Japan strongly promote saving behavior (OECD, 2019). Financial literacy research has been conducted with college students in countries such as Thailand, Indonesia, and Malaysia, showing positive influences on financial behavior and well-being (e.g., Rafinda & Gal, 2020, Indonesia; Yew et al., 2017, Malaysia). Different from East and Southeast Asia, most countries in South Asia do not have national strategies for financial education, and financial literacy scores are generally low (e.g., 14 for Afghanistan and Bangladesh).

There is also an extensive body of financial literacy research conducted in India with some literature reviews available (e.g., Naidu, 2017), studies focused on adult women (Baluja, 2016), and some studies that examined the potential effects of financial literacy on financial behaviors (see Chapter 5), such as financial planning (e.g., Agarwal et al., 2015). One study with adults conducted in Lebanon and Turkey found that financial literacy increases with education, both in terms of years of education as well as quality of the education (Karakurum-Ozdemir et al., 2019).

Russia is a transcontinental country located in East Europe and North Asia. There have been intense efforts in recent years to provide training and education to students, teachers, and parents, efforts initiated and conducted by several entities, such as the Bank of Russia as well as a large number of universities (OECD, 2016, 2019). However, academic research about financial literacy in the Russian context is limited.

Overall, challenges and needs associated with financial literacy among emerging adults in Asian countries are very diverse, and efforts should reflect the level of socioeconomic development and quality of life in each country (Xiao, 2021).

Financial Literacy in Africa

Financial literacy is generally low across African countries, with about 80% of the adult population of sub-Saharan Africa not using formal financial services due to access and infrastructural barriers or other socioeconomic challenges (e.g., Demirgüç-Kunt & Klapper, 2012). South Africa was the only African country to participate in the OECD/INFE International Survey of Adult Financial Literacy Competencies (OECD, 2016, 2018), receiving the lowest financial knowledge score among the 30 participating countries. No African country participated in any of the optional PISA financial literacy data collection (OECD, 2020). Important to mention is that measures of objective financial concepts used in such global assessments are not ideal to use in the African context, which relies on predominantly informal markets such as mobile money (Anong et al., 2021). Therefore, assessments developed specifically for the African context and reflecting the financial experiences of citizens are essential in order to help with designing and implementing effective national strategies for their less formal and less developed markets. Likely due to a lack of financial and logistical resources, there are limited data commissioned by governments or other institutions in Africa. There are, however, some exceptions, such as the FinScope National Surveys (FinMark Trust, 2021), with data collected in 23 African countries sponsored by FinMark Trust, a research organization established in 2002 (Anong et al., 2021). A few studies have used FinScope National Survey data to assess financial literacy in African countries. For instance, using principal component analysis to construct a composite score of financial literacy, Nanziri and Leibbrandt (2018) found that South Africans who were Black, women, youth, low-income, less educated, and those located in the Eastern Cape province scored below the average. It is apparent from this survey that emerging adults fall under the age groups with low financial literacy scores.

Efforts from within Africa such as FinScope National Survey demonstrate that researchers are essential partners in helping with securing funding for such national assessments, which are important for developing effective national financial education strategies (Anong et al., 2021). Such strategies would benefit institutions, economies, and individuals of all ages, including emerging adults, whether attending college or not.

Financial Literacy in Central America and the Caribbean

When it comes to financial literacy efforts in Central America and the Caribbean (CAC), a variety of strategies, national policies, programs, and initiatives are being used, some of these being more effectively implemented in some regions (i.e., Trinidad and Tobago) than others (e.g., El Salvador). Generally, few of these initiatives target young people, and little is known about financial literacy rates specifically for emerging adults. Economic growth has been positive in the CAC countries in recent years. Inflow of money by migrants working in the United States (e.g., $38.5 billion to Mexico alone, the third highest remittance amount for any country in the world according to the World Bank, 2020) contributes to supporting education costs and other human capital needs. According to Standard & Poor's Global Financial Literacy (2015), the financial literacy rates for adults in CAC countries ranged from 18% in Haiti to 35% in Costa Rica and the Dominican Republic. As large percentages of the population in these regions are under persistent financial stress (see Chapter 8) and face unique social and economic challenges (e.g., sizable unbanked populations, poverty, unemployment), financial literacy may matter in even more significant ways in developing countries (Bel & Eberlein, 2015). Across CAC countries, special attention is given to financial inclusion, understood as expanding public access to and usage of tailored financial services. The success of such programs varies widely across these countries, and it is unclear to what extent emerging adults are included in these efforts; therefore, more information is strongly needed.

Financial Literacy in South America

Very low levels of financial literacy in South America are widely documented in various studies, often tangled with political and economic unrest. Many argue that little can be expected from financial literacy initiatives while inequalities still persist with deep structural roots (Rivero, 2021).

Across many Latin American countries, financial education initiatives (see Chapter 19) are aimed at young people in secondary school. While this may be advantageous, it is difficult to evaluate the real impact of such programs because little official data have been published (Rivero, 2021). According to the results of the PISA tests of financial capabilities in the participating South American countries (i.e., Brazil, Chile, Colombia, and Peru), the results are well below the OECD average (OECD, 2017). Moreover, access to and the general quality of education in the region are low, with South American students performing poorly in reading, mathematics, and science, and massive dropout rates in secondary school are a concern. Little attention is given to the effect of family on young people's financial learning (Rivero, 2021). An additional challenge is connected to digitization and the digital divide related not only to the lack of digital skills but also to difficulties in connecting to the internet and/or the inability to access smartphones. With help from more research focusing on a greater variety of financial socialization efforts, we could better understand cultural specifics associated with financial literacy in South American emerging adults.

Financial Literacy in Australia and New Zealand

Over the past two decades, there has been a major increase in efforts across many levels to improve the financial literacy of the general population in Australia and New Zealand, both countries being now seen as leaders in national financial literacy policy. In 2011, the Australian Security and Investments Commission (ASIC) released its first National Financial Literacy Strategy identifying financial literacy as a critical skill for consumers and investors, recognizing the significant disparities in knowledge (see Chapter 2) and understanding of financial matters across different groups in the community, and highlighting the individual and societal benefits of improved financial literacy (ASIC, 2011). At the same time, the strategy focused on educating the next generations through the formal education system (see Chapter 19) and on improving research (ASIC, 2014). Unique and innovative strategies have been introduced in New Zealand, such as Building Wealthy Lives (Commission for Financial Capability, 2015) that includes five distinct activity streams around financial literacy and well-being: (1) "Talk," encouraging everyone to talk about money; (2) "Learn," to promote optimal financial learning throughout life; (3) "Plan," to ensure everyone has a current financial plan and is prepared for the unexpected; (4) "Debt smart," to encourage people to make smart use of debt; and (5) "Save/invest," to inspire everyone to be saving and investing. Globally, Australia has a high financial literacy, ranking in the top 10 of the Standard & Poor's Ratings Services Global Financial Literacy Survey (Klapper et al., 2015). Additionally, 15-year-old students in Australia ranked fifth in the OECD and 6 points above the OECD average in the 2018 OECD Program for International Student Assessment (PISA), with girls outperforming boys (OECD, 2020).

Similar to other countries, financial literacy among the young is lower in Australia and New Zealand compared to older age groups. For example, the 2014 ANZ Survey found that emerging adults ages 18–25 had lower scores on most aspects of financial literacy, especially with regard to keeping track of finances, planning ahead, and choosing suitable financial products (ANZ, 2015). Student debt is of particular concern for many young Australians (see Chapter 9), the same survey finding that less financial knowledge is associated with a reliance on debt, risky financial behaviors, more use of credit cards, living beyond their means, and holding more destructive beliefs about money (ANZ, 2015).

Only recently, more attention has been given to the Indigenous (Aborigines and Torres Strait Islanders in Australia, Māoris and Pasifikas in New Zealand). Interestingly, financial diaries of Māoris identified cultural values connected to financial behaviors. More specifically, Houkamau and Sibley (2017) found that the Māori value positive family relationships, with the family seen as a form of future financial security, leading to saving behaviors for planned or unplanned family needs. At the same time, saving or keeping it for oneself or immediate family led to guilt, making money management culturally challenging for Māori (Houkamau et al., 2019).

Overall, based on the results presented here, we can conclude that efforts to improve financial literacy have been successful, and emerging adults seem to have benefited from them. Empirical evidence from studies done with Indigenous populations brings additional and very important insights.

Suggestions, Conclusions, and Future Outlook

Around the world, financial literacy plays an important role in consumer financial decision-making (see Chapters 5 and 6). Financially literate individuals are more likely to save (Brounen et al., 2016), are less prone to over-indebtedness (Huston, 2012), and participate more often in financial markets (van Rooij et al., 2011). As a result, financially literate individuals accumulate more net wealth throughout their life (van Rooij et al., 2012), which may, in turn, lead to broader economic development (Lusardi & Mitchell, 2014).

As demonstrated by previously mentioned studies (e.g., Ahunov & Van Hove, 2020; De Beckker et al., 2020), certain aspects of national culture matter (sometimes more than the standard economic variables such as GDP, per capita income, or economic growth indicators), and some determinants of financial literacy are deeply rooted in a country's culture and therefore difficult to change in the short term. This tells us that programs aimed at increasing financial literacy should be tailored to a society's culture, and the effect of financial literacy initiatives will depend partly on the cultural aspects of the society. Future international financial literacy research should include analyzing how variation in cultural subgroups has an impact on financial literacy levels (De Becker et al., 2020). For example, with increasing migration in recent years, and given that immigrants all have their own cultural attitudes, linguistic backgrounds, skills, and knowledge (Bove & Elia, 2017), immigration patterns could advance our understanding of financial literacy trends and prevalent financial literacy levels across countries (De Beckker et al., 2020).

For certain parts of the world such as Latin America, addressing the gender gap issue with regard to access to education and resources is of crucial importance. In many Latin American countries (e.g., Ecuador, Argentina, Paraguay), women have access to mainly lower-paid or part-time jobs due to limited childcare options, and they are not given the opportunity to participate in the economy more formally. Financial education efforts (see Chapter 19) need to address such pervasive societal inequalities based on class as well as gender (see Chapters 15 and 16; Rivero, 2021).

Research also tells us that in Eastern Europe financial education strategy prioritization should differ from Western Europe (Cwynar, 2021). Specifically, in these former socialist countries discussed in this chapter, women and emerging adults do not seem to be as vulnerable as they are in the West. Finally, considering the strong heterogeneity in that region and presumably strong influence of associated cultural factors on financial literacy and financial behavior, financial education strategies should be designed and implemented with cultural differences in mind.

Based on the existing financial education programs mandated by the U.S. federal and state governments (see Chapter 19; Council for Economic Education, 2018), we can conclude that in-depth and intensive education provided to *all* groups (starting with parents) may help close the gap between ethnic groups; also, there is a strong need to provide resources to encourage communities to offer tailored financial education programs especially to Blacks and Hispanics. As Kim and Xiao (2021) demonstrated in their research, financial education was the only contributing factor to reduce the Black–White gap in financial capability. Additionally, income, banking status, and unexpected income drop were important contributors to explain the gap between Black and White respondents as well as between Hispanic and White respondents across all financial measures (see Chapter 15; Kim & Xiao, 2021). Methodologically speaking, there are overall few studies specifically focusing on the financial issues that Blacks face, and they are often combined with other ethnic minorities and compared with Whites, which is likely an inaccurate generalization across distinct groups. That is, Blacks and Hispanics, for example, are not just "non-White" but include their own unique groups that may be as different from each other as they are from Whites, not to mention within-group variation. We also note that comparing all other racial groups to Whites may perpetuate White supremacy.

As we have learned from national literacy strategies in New Zealand (Commission for Financial Capability, 2015), sending a strong message that encourages learning and talking about money as a country leads to very positive outcomes at the family and individual level. Similar programs are needed in other parts of the world. At the same time, sensitivity to cultural beliefs of subgroups of people (e.g., Māoris) has to be taken into account as well.

For practitioners and educators who work with families, it is important to recognize that the foundation for financial well-being is established at home (see Chapter 18). To become financially self-reliant (see Chapter 11), children need opportunities to put their financial knowledge (see Chapter 2) and skills (see Chapter 3) into practice, make financial choices (see Chapter 6), and reflect on their choices (Serido et al., 2013). Good financial decisions emerge from the intersection of financial knowledge and skills and the thoughtful use of available resources. Content knowledge alone cannot change financial practices; opportunities to practice knowledge and understand consequences are important. As Gudmunson and Danes (2011) pointed out, people make financial choices based on relevant information available to them in real-life situations. As such, much of the literature and the implications of positive financial parenting in promoting positive outcomes from early childhood to emerging adulthood may reflect a majority bias. Thus, future research is needed to examine financial socialization norms and values across diverse samples, including racial/ethnic minority and immigrant families. Particularly, the role of parents as models is greatly understudied outside Western cultures.

Broadly speaking, financial educators, practitioners, and policymakers should make an increased effort to integrate parental involvement when designing financial education programs. For instance, financial communication with parents can be framed as a part of homework for students. At the same time, financial practitioners are encouraged to provide workshops to teach parents how to communicate and educate their children on financial matters at home, especially those parents with less than college education levels, in order to improve their own financial literacy. Policymakers should advocate parent–child interaction on financial matters by affirming that such interaction is healthy and beneficial for individuals' subjective financial well-being (see Chapter 7).

From the gathered literature and based on the foundation already set by literacy and socialization researchers, academics and policymakers are given a difficult task in being considerate of the numerous factors influencing financial literacy from a global perspective. It has become clear that both improving and understanding financial literacy require knowledge of circumstance-specific information and tailoring of both research and policy toward such needs. Priority should be given to developing comprehensive profiles of target populations, detriments within these communities related to financial literacy, and personalization of policy and research to gain a clear and accurate understanding of the current circumstances of each community.

PART IV

HOW TO IMPROVE EMERGING ADULTS' FINANCIAL LITERACY

Chapter 18
Financial Socialization and Emerging Adults' Financial Outcomes

Matthew T. Saxey[1], *Ashley B. LeBaron-Black*[2], *and Heather Kelley*[3]

Introduction

As adolescents enter emerging adulthood, they are often confronted with financial transitions such as navigating the removal or adjustment of parental financial support (see Chapter 11), learning how to pay bills on time, learning—sometimes by painful experience—what they can and cannot afford to spend money on in a given month; the list could go on and on. Despite these formidable financial transitions, adolescents (Program for International Student Assessment, 2018) tend to have low financial literacy. As adolescents with low financial literacy enter emerging adulthood, recent estimates suggest that approximately 82% of U.S. emerging adults ages 18–25 report that money is a significant source of stress in their lives (see Chapter 8; American Psychological Association, 2022). Financial education programs (see Chapter 19) might be one potential solution to help improve the financial literacy, financial behaviors (see Chapter 5), and financial well-being (see Chapter 7) of emerging adults, but meta-analytic evidence suggests that financial education interventions explain a minuscule amount of the variance in financial behaviors (i.e., 0.1%; Fernandes et al., 2014). As such, particularly over the last decade, many scholars interested in promoting emerging adults' financial well-being have examined the role that parents play in engendering financial flourishing, or floundering, for their emerging adult children.

Although a focus on how parents financially socialize their emerging adult children poses its own challenges (e.g., emerging adults may not internalize financial messages from their parents well; Rea et al., 2019), a wealth of

[1] Department of Human Development and Family Science, Auburn University, USA
[2] School of Family Life, Brigham Young University, USA
[3] Institute for Disability Research, Policy, and Practice, Utah State University, USA

Matthew T. Saxey, Ashley B. LeBaron-Black, and Heather Kelley, *Financial Socialization and Emerging Adults' Financial Outcomes*. In: *Flourishing and Floundering Financially in Emerging Adulthood*. Ashley B. LeBaron-Black et al., Oxford University Press. © Oxford University Press (2025). DOI: 10.1093/9780197699157.003.0019

evidence suggests that parents play a primary role in shaping their emerging adult children's financial behaviors and well-being (see Chapter 1; for reviews, see Gudmunson & Danes, 2011; Gudmunson et al., 2016; LeBaron & Kelley, 2021; Serido & Deenanath, 2016)—for better or for worse. Because parents play a salient role in the financial socialization of emerging adults, most of this chapter focuses on reviewing recent scholarship about how parents impact their emerging adult children's financial well-being through financial socialization. After reviewing parent financial socialization scholarship, we briefly review scholarship about other salient financial socialization agents, which is followed by a discussion of diversity, equity, and inclusion. Finally, specific implications for researchers, practitioners, and emerging adults are identified.

The Intergenerational Transmission of Financial Flourishing and Floundering

Financial socialization is defined as the "process of acquiring and developing values, attitudes, standards, norms, knowledge, and behaviors that contribute to . . . financial viability and individual wellbeing" (Danes, 1994, p. 128). A primary goal of this financial socialization as it pertains to parents, according to Gudmunson and Danes' (2011) theory (see Chapter 1), is to promote positive financial behaviors and financial well-being for their children. Positive financial behaviors (see Chapter 5) are exhibited by a "pattern of action over time such as earning, saving, spending, and gifting," which can promote financial well-being (Gudmunson & Danes, 2011, p. 650; LeBaron & Kelley, 2021). Although an entire chapter in this volume has been devoted to financial well-being in emerging adulthood (see Chapter 7), financial well-being can parsimoniously be defined in terms of subjective financial well-being (i.e., satisfaction with and emotions toward one's financial situation) and objective financial well-being (i.e., level of income, debt, expenses, assets, savings, insurance, education; Sorgente & Lanz, 2017).

Over the last decade, several reviews have adeptly provided an overview of financial socialization scholarship (Gudmunson & Danes, 2011; Gudmunson et al., 2016; Serido & Deenanath, 2016), even particularly related to financial socialization scholarship in one of the leading scholarly journals in this area (LeBaron & Kelley, 2021). Nonetheless, these reviews have not delineated recent *quantitative* financial socialization scholarship primarily through the lens of *qualitative*, theoretical advances regarding the financial socialization of emerging adults. Although qualitative research typically does not generalize to a population of study, it "may offer a type of validity or depth of truth that is difficult [to] access in other ways" (Marks, 2015, p. 504). As such, framing the previous quantitative scholarship on financial socialization of emerging adults through the insights that have been gained through qualitative inquiry provides unique direction for researchers, practitioners, parents, and emerging adults alike.

In addition to identifying *what* financial information can best help emerging adults flourish financially (Jorgensen et al., 2019; LeBaron, 2019; LeBaron et al., 2018a, 2018b, 2018c; Loderup et al., 2021; Solheim et al., 2011), recent qualitative scholarship has revealed three primary financial socialization methods of *how* parents can impact emerging adults' financial well-being (LeBaron et al., 2019, 2020b; Rosa et al., 2018). The next three sections of this chapter detail each primary method of parent financial socialization and how these methods tend to impact emerging adults. As the coming pages will show, parents tend to intergenerationally transmit financial flourishing or floundering to their emerging adults. These descriptions are primarily based on findings from U.S. samples, however, which limits the generalizability of these findings and provides an important call for more financial socialization scholarship outside the United States.

We Don't Talk About That: Parent–Child Financial Discussion

Although financial socialization is an ongoing process before, throughout, and beyond emerging adulthood, previous scholarship typically focuses on the role of parent financial socialization in childhood and adolescence—and how that socialization impacts emerging adults financially later on. The first primary method of parent financial socialization derived from qualitative scholarship is parent–child financial discussion (LeBaron et al., 2020b). Although finances can be a taboo topic of discussion in families (e.g., with one study about this topic starting their title with "We Don't Talk About That"; White et al., 2021a, p. 328), researchers often view parent–child financial discussion as an essential aspect of preparing emerging adults for financial flourishing (e.g., Serido et al., 2010).

Qualitative scholarship with emerging adults over the last decade has revealed what emerging adults did, and did not, appreciate about parent–child financial discussion. Parent–child financial discussion can help prepare children and adolescents for emerging adulthood through both *parent*-initiated discussions and *child*-initiated discussions (LeBaron et al., 2020b). Furthermore, these discussions can be useful as planned discussions or discussions that occur spontaneously (LeBaron et al., 2018a). In essence, the principle from emerging adults' recollections is perhaps easier said than done: "Money should be openly discussed" (Solheim et al., 2011, p. 106). Helpful discussion topics include but are not limited to openness about previous financial mistakes, credit scores, major financial decisions (e.g., buying a car or a house), specific budgeting practices, and retirement accounts (LeBaron et al., 2020b). Despite this hope for open financial communication in the home, some emerging adults have never seen their parents' budget—or heard them talk about it—which did not appear to help prepare these individuals financially for emerging adulthood (LeBaron et al., 2018b). Although parents might sometimes avoid discussing money to protect their children from things like "unnecessary worry," one emerging adult noted that "everyone in the family knew exactly what was happening" despite their parents' avoidance of financial discussions (Solheim et al., 2011, p. 107).

The quantitative evidence tells a similar story. As parents engage in healthy parent–child financial communication (e.g., frequent, open discussion), their emerging adult children report better financial management behaviors (see Chapter 5; Jorgensen et al., 2017; LeBaron et al., 2020a; Serido et al., 2010; Shim et al., 2015; Vosylis & Erentaitė, 2020), less financial stress and financial anxiety (see Chapter 8; Serido et al., 2010; Vosylis & Erentaitė, 2020), better financial self-efficacy (see Chapter 4; Shim et al., 2015), and more financial knowledge (see Chapter 2; Jorgensen & Savla, 2010). Indeed, even during emerging adulthood, as parent–child communication increases in quality (e.g., less financial conflict), this increase in quality communication predicts an increase in emerging adults' healthy financial behavior and financial self-efficacy (Shim et al., 2015). Parent–child discussion even shows benefits in adolescence, which can help prepare children for emerging adulthood. For example, better parent–child communication about their adolescent donating money (e.g., to a charitable organization) was positively connected with adolescents' saving behaviors (Kim et al., 2011).

Despite the evidence engendering the importance of parent–child financial discussion, a recent study of a diverse sample of 4,182 U.S. emerging adults found that when accounting for the other two primary methods of financial socialization (i.e., parent financial modeling and experiential learning), open parent–child financial discussion in childhood and adolescence was not associated with emerging adults' later financial behaviors, financial self-efficacy, financial distress, financial satisfaction, or financial independence (LeBaron-Black et al., 2023a). This new evidence casts doubt on the assumption that, relative to other financial socialization methods, open parent–child financial discussion is the most important method of financial socialization for emerging adults' financial well-being; this finding merits further research, however. Perhaps parent–child financial discussion is primarily helpful as a tool to engage in or enhance the other methods of socialization. While parent–child financial discussion appears to help emerging adults flourish financially, qualitative and quantitative evidence suggests that if parents avoid openness about money with their children, adolescents, and emerging adults, their children might not be as well prepared financially for emerging adulthood.

Because That Is What My Parents Did: Parent Financial Modeling

The second primary method of financial socialization concerns not just what parents say to their children but *what their actions implicitly say* (i.e., parent financial modeling; Rosa et al., 2018). In the words of Hira (2012), "[A] teacher who does not model what they set out to teach cannot be very effective" (p. 505). If parents want to help prepare their children financially for emerging adulthood, according to recent scholarship, they should *practice* what they hope their emerging adult children will do. Indeed, qualitative evidence suggests that parents' financial actions, especially how they managed money, can speak just as loudly as their words (LeBaron et al., 2018a; Rosa et al., 2018; Solheim et al., 2011).

Quantitative scholarship has revealed that parents' healthy financial behaviors are associated with their emerging adult children reporting healthy financial behaviors (see Chapter 5; Damian et al., 2020; LeBaron-Black et al., 2023a; Lep et al., 2022; Serido et al., 2015; Shim et al., 2010, 2015; Sirsch et al., 2020) and higher satisfaction with their financial situation (Allsop et al., 2021; Damian et al., 2020; LeBaron-Black et al., 2023a; Shim et al., 2010). From a deficit perspective, however, if parents reported financial distress (see Chapter 8) when their children were adolescents, this parental financial distress predicted their emerging adult children's higher financial distress and lower financial satisfaction 5 years later (Allsop et al., 2021). Emerging adults with parents who argued about finances were also more likely to have at least $500 USD in credit card debt (Hancock et al., 2013). Put simply, what emerging adults witness their parents *do*—not just what they say—can lead to children financially flourishing or floundering in emerging adulthood.

Although emerging adults appear to be likely to follow in their parents' financial footsteps, there is some qualitative evidence that suggests emerging adults can choose to do what it takes to thrive financially *because of* their parents' bad financial example (Rosa et al., 2018; Solheim et al., 2011). With a sample of over 4,000 U.S. emerging adults, scholars recently quantitatively tested whether emerging adults could compensate for their parents' bad financial example. These authors found that emerging adults who reported having parents who were a good financial example *and that they followed in their parents' footsteps* were the best off financially (i.e., in terms of financial satisfaction and financial distress; LeBaron-Black et al., 2024a). However, emerging adults who reported having a bad example of parent financial modeling but chose to learn from their parents' bad financial example in emerging adulthood also were better off financially (i.e., in terms of financial satisfaction, distress, and independence) than their emerging adult peers who did not report managing their finances well—regardless of whether their parents did or did not manage their finances well. Together, these findings give life to the words of Ralph Waldo Emerson, "Your actions speak so loudly, I cannot hear what you are saying" (Rosa et al., 2018, p. 54).

Teaching an Emerging Adult to Fish: Experiential Learning of Finances

If emerging adults are given a fish, financially speaking, they might be fed for a day. If emerging adults are taught how to fish, financially speaking, they might be fed for a lifetime. This timeless principle undergirds the third primary method of financial socialization: experiential learning, which entails providing children and adolescents with their own experiences with managing finances (LeBaron et al., 2019). Out of the three primary methods of financial socialization, experiential learning of finances seems to have the most limited literature. Qualitative research suggests that emerging adults wished they had more opportunities to manage their own finances in childhood and adolescence (LeBaron et al., 2018b), and quantitative scholarship might illustrate why.

For example, maintaining a savings account and having one's spending monitored in childhood were associated with more responsibility for managing money (see Chapter 11) and less financial worry (see Chapter 8), respectively, in emerging adulthood (Kim & Chatterjee, 2013). Likewise, having been given experiences to learn with finances in childhood and adolescence (e.g., allotting a certain amount of income to savings) is associated with better financial self-efficacy (see Chapter 4), financial management behaviors (see Chapter 5), and financial satisfaction and less financial distress in emerging adulthood (LeBaron-Black et al., 2023a). Providing children and adolescents with financial experiences of their own (e.g., receiving an allowance) might help lessen financial anxiety (see Chapter 8) before entering into emerging adulthood (Kim et al., 2011). Although further research with this financial socialization method is needed, these findings suggest that providing children and adolescents with financial experiences of their own can help prepare them financially for emerging adulthood.

Parent Financial Socialization in Emerging Adulthood

While much of the available research focuses on the impact of parent financial socialization in childhood and adolescence on emerging adults' financial outcomes, parents' financial socialization efforts can persist as children transition into emerging adulthood (Serido et al., 2020a; Shim et al., 2015). Serido and colleagues (2020a) analyzed three waves of data from a cohort of U.S. college students ($N = 922$). They found that from the first year of college to 2 years after college (i.e., 6 years later), both explicit (i.e., deliberate teaching) and implicit (i.e., parent financial modeling) financial parenting declined, though the decline in implicit parenting was more gradual than the decline in explicit parenting. In investigating whether this decline in financial parenting was driven by a decrease in proximity, the authors found no difference between students who remained at home and the students who moved away from home, suggesting that this decline is representative of a global shift in responsibility as adolescents age into emerging adulthood (see Chapter 11). However, they also noted that the small-to-medium effect sizes of change suggest that parental financial socialization continues well into emerging adulthood.

Sorgente and colleagues (2024) also found that earlier conflictual parent–emerging adult financial communication was longitudinally associated with less frequent positive parent–emerging adult financial communication later in emerging adulthood. This finding suggests the way parents and emerging adults communicate about finances might be an indication of how their financial communication changes over time. These longitudinal findings open the door to a promising area of future scholarship—that is, understanding how parent financial socialization might developmentally change *during* emerging adulthood.

Other Financial Socialization Agents: Romantic Partners, Peers, Media, and Employment

Several studies comparing the influence of parents to the influence of other financial socialization agents have found that parents are, by far, the strongest influence on emerging adults' financial learning (Clarke et al., 2005; Jorgensen & Savla, 2010; Pinto et al., 2005; Serido et al., 2020b; Shim et al., 2010; Sohn et al., 2012). However, these other agents have measurable, meaningful influence and should continue to be considered in research and practice—especially when emerging adults have received low-quality financial socialization from parents and could benefit from compensatory financial socialization from other sources. We will briefly discuss the influence of four other agents: romantic partners, peers, media, and employment.

As individuals become increasingly independent from parents during adolescence and emerging adulthood (see Chapter 11), romantic partners and peers gradually replace some of their parents' influence, including in the area of financial socialization (Curran et al., 2018; Serido et al., 2015). Romantic partners' healthy financial behaviors are positively associated with emerging adults' healthy financial attitudes and behaviors (see Chapter 14; Serido et al., 2015), suggesting that partners' financial well-being tends to match—whether both partners are healthy or both partners are unhealthy. However, the stronger the financial influence of peers and media, the less healthy emerging adults' financial behaviors tend to be (LeBaron-Black et al., 2023b), suggesting that peer and media financial socialization may be harmful—especially in encouraging irresponsible, comparison-driven spending (see Chapters 4, 8, 10, and 13).

Financial learning from employment, on the other hand, is associated with greater financial knowledge (Shim et al., 2010) and more responsible spending behaviors (LeBaron-Black et al., 2023b). Through employment, emerging adults might learn lessons like "$20 is two and a half hours of work," suggesting that earning income through employment can intensify emerging adults' attention to their financial situation (Loderup et al., 2021, p. 82). Overall, emerging adults seem to receive healthy financial influence from employment and unhealthy financial influence from peers and media. Furthermore, financial socialization from romantic partners seems to have a similar (though much smaller) effect as financial socialization from parents: When the socialization received is high-quality, emerging adults benefit, and when the socialization received is low-quality, emerging adults suffer (see Chapter 14). Parents' and romantic partners' financial examples tend to rub off on emerging adults, for better or for worse.

Diversity, Equity, and Inclusion in Financial Socialization Scholarship

Recent findings suggest that incorporating diversity, equity, and inclusion (DEI) in furthering financial socialization scholarship would be valuable. For instance, although previous scholarship reveals that sex (male/female) may (e.g., Jorgensen & Savla, 2010) or may not (e.g., LeBaron et al., 2020a) play a role in understanding how parent financial socialization might impact emerging adults financially (see Chapter 16), other financial socialization scholarship about the LBGTQ+ community provides further insight. Relative to cisgender individuals, transgender and gender-diverse college students reported receiving worse parent financial socialization, lower financial optimism, lower financial self-efficacy, and more financial strain (White et al., 2022).

Furthermore, other evidence suggests that race/ethnicity—and potentially associated cultural norms and familial expectations—might play a role in financial socialization and financial outcomes for emerging adults (see Chapters 15 and 17). For instance, Black and Hispanic families typically discuss finances less (White et al., 2021a), and Black and Hispanic emerging adults might have received fewer messages about saving and investing from their parents (White et al., 2021b). These findings are important because they highlight gender and racial/ethnic minorities that might have disadvantages in how they were financially socialized. In advancing financial socialization scholarship, researchers should explore whether or not the answers to their research questions might vary depending on gender identity and race/ethnicity.

Conclusion

Parents play an important role in setting their children up for financial flourishing or floundering in emerging adulthood. Financial socialization during childhood and adolescence through open discussions regarding finances, modeling financial behaviors, and providing children with opportunities for experiential learning with money impact emerging adults' financial behaviors (see Chapter 5) and well-being (see Chapter 7). Furthermore, while both explicit and implicit parental financial socialization persist into emerging adulthood, peers, romantic partners (see Chapter 14), and employment also begin playing an important socializing role during this time. Continued research on financial socialization and emerging adults' financial outcomes that investigates differences by gender (see Chapter 16), socioeconomic status (see Chapter 15), and race/ethnicity (see Chapter 17) is needed. Key points on this chapter for researchers, practitioners, and emerging adults may be found in Box 18.1, Box 18.2, and Box 18.3, respectively.

Box 18.1 Key Points for Researchers

- In future quantitative scholarship, researchers should consider analyzing the answers to their research questions with moderation by gender identity and race/ethnicity or multiple group models that can examine possible differences across these groups. Doing so might help us understand gender and racial/ethnic minorities better so that we can create more targeted education and interventions.
- For those interested in measuring parent financial socialization retrospectively through parent–child discussion, parental modeling, and experiential learning of finances for emerging adults, LeBaron-Black et al. (2022) have recently developed reliable and valid measures for these three constructs. As they put it, "[A] study (and, on a larger scale, a field) is only as good as its measures" (LeBaron-Black et al., 2022, p. 943). Short versions of these same scales are also forthcoming (LeBaron-Black et al., 2024b). To accurately capture such constructs in consistent ways across studies, we suggest using these new scales.
- Of the three primary methods of parent financial socialization, experiential learning of finances has received the least scholarly attention. As such, future research should continue to examine the correlates of emerging adults having received hands-on experiences with finances.

Box 18.2 Key Points for Practitioners

- When counseling or educating emerging adult clients, it might be common to focus on what their parents explicitly taught them about money. We agree that parent–child financial discussions can help emerging adults. However, parents' example and what experiences they provided when the emerging adult was a child and adolescent can be powerful in understanding emerging adults' financial attitudes, beliefs, and behaviors.
- Although emerging adults are likely to follow in their parents' financial footsteps, it is crucial to help emerging adults understand that they can intentionally

compensate for their parents' bad financial example, lower their financial distress, and raise their satisfaction with their financial situation. Put another way, emerging adults are not doomed to become their parents. Sharing this information can provide financial hope that can lead to change.

- In the words of LeBaron et al. (2018b), "[A] 10-year-old makes $50 mistakes, a 20-year-old makes $5,000 mistakes, and a 30-year-old makes $50,000 mistakes" (p. 230). Encouraging parents to provide children and adolescents with financial experiences so that they can make (less costly) mistakes—and learn from them—is pivotal.
- We suggest encouraging parents to teach children about finances through *all three* financial socialization methods. Parent–child discussion after an experiential learning opportunity, for example, might be more illustrative than discussion alone.

Box 18.3 Key Points for Emerging Adults

- Understanding what one's parents explicitly taught about money, what their financial example taught, and what experiences they provided with money can help emerging adults understand why they do what they do—and think the way they do—financially. Such knowledge can help emerging adults understand how they can improve financially.
- Whether parents prepared their child financially for emerging adulthood well or not, becoming more financially educated can pay current, and future, dividends. Online and in-person financial education resources or conversations with parents and other trusted adults might be great places to start in becoming financially educated (see Chapter 19).

Chapter 19
Financial Education of Emerging Adults

Nilton Porto[1] and Kathryn A. Carroll[2]

Introduction

In the 2021 National Financial Capability Study (NFCS), 5,606 emerging adults (ages 18–30) in the United States were asked a series of questions related to their financial experiences, attitudes, habits, and behaviors to evaluate their financial capability (Lin et al., 2022). Among these questions, emerging adults were asked if they had been offered financial education and, if so, whether they had participated in the training. A total of 2,270 (40% of emerging adults) answered they were offered financial education in either high school or college, at work, or in the military. Just over 26%, or 1,491 emerging adult respondents, participated in financial education, sometimes receiving training from more than one venue.

A lack of financial education among emerging adults can also be seen globally. The Organisation for Economic Co-operation and Development (OECD) recognized the importance of financial literacy and launched the International Network on Financial Education (INFE) in 2008 to develop research and policies to foster financial literacy across its members. In their data collection, patterns of low levels of financial literacy and minimum access to financial education emerged. For instance, only 25% of the emerging adult respondents answered five or more financial knowledge questions correctly out of seven in a survey of six Commonwealth of Independent States (OECD, 2019). At the time of the most recent Programme for International Student Assessment (PISA) survey, 11 OECD countries had developed national strategies for financial education, from embedding it in school curricula in Canada to websites in Latvia and contests in Russia.

[1] Department of Human Development and Family Science, University of Rhode Island, USA
[2] Department of Nutrition and Family Sciences, University of Central Arkansas, USA

Nilton Porto and Kathryn A. Carroll, *Financial Education of Emerging Adults*. In: *Flourishing and Floundering Financially in Emerging Adulthood*. Edited by: Ashley B. LeBaron-Black, Heather Kelley, and Angela Sorgente, Oxford University Press. © Oxford University Press (2025). DOI: 10.1093/9780197699157.003.0020

Financial knowledge (see Chapter 2) can be acquired from many sources including family, friends, social media, online searches, paid advice/counseling, and others (see Chapter 18). In this chapter, we will focus on financial education as a source to improve the financial literacy (see Chapter 1) of emerging adults. Financial literacy is a "combination of the awareness, knowledge, skills, attitudes, and behaviors necessary to make sound financial decisions and ultimately achieve individual financial well-being" (Atkinson & Messy, 2012, p. 14).

The OECD (2005) defines financial education as

> the process by which financial consumers and investors improve their understanding of financial products, concepts, and risks and, through information, instruction, and/or objective advice, develop the skills and confidence to become more aware of financial risks and opportunities, to make informed choices, to know where to go for help, and to take other effective actions to improve their financial well-being.

Based on this approach, we consider financial education that is delivered formally and professionally either online or in-person from a reputable source and/or an expert educator. Financial education can be an online course, a series of educational videos and readings, a class delivered by an instructor, or a combination of different methods. Using a randomized control trial in Italy, Sconti (2022) found that both traditional classroom delivery and digital learn-by-playing delivery methods of financial education had positive effects on financial knowledge, but only the traditional approach effect persisted in the long run.

While there have been disputes about the costs and benefits of financial education, more recent research has provided strong evidence that it matters in a positive way (Lusardi, 2019). A recent meta-analysis concluded that financial education has positive treatment effects, and it is cost-effective like other forms of education (Kaiser et al., 2022). Mandates to avoid selection issues also matter when judging the effects of financial education. Harvey (2019) showed that state mandates reduced the likelihood and frequency that young consumers use payday lending. Also using state mandates in a quasi-experimental design, Urban et al. (2020) discovered that financial education requirements improved credit scores and reduced defaults of 18- to 21-year-olds. As of October 2023, 23 U.S. states require a semester-long personal finance class in high school prior to graduation, while another 22 states have active legislation to include financial education in their curriculum.[1] Across

[1] For updated tracking of state requirements and active personal finance bills, check Next Gen Personal Finance at https://www.ngpf.org/bill-tracker.

the globe, compulsory financial education in secondary school is infrequent, with the highest levels found in Australia, Belgium, and the Czech Republic (Cordero et al., 2022).

Both the quality and quantity of financial education are relevant components to downstream financial benefits. Porto and Xiao (2021) found that both the quality and dosage of financial education matter for emerging adults. When more hours of education were in place and students perceived the training as high-quality, emerging adults performed more desirable financial behaviors (see Chapter 5) and felt more capable of managing their own finances (see Chapter 4).

Knowledge (see Chapter 2) and behaviors (see Chapter 5) are the two most often cited benefits of financial education. However, there is also research that indirectly connects financial education with financial satisfaction and financial well-being (see Chapter 7). Using a mediation analysis, researchers suggested that financial education has multiple benefits to financial well-being via elements of financial capability (Xiao & Porto, 2017). Positive financial practices/behaviors (potentially from financial education and/or financial socialization) have been linked with higher financial well-being of emerging adults (Burcher et al., 2021). Similarly, higher levels of financial literacy (e.g., financial knowledge) are associated with financial well-being (Philippas & Avdoulas, 2020).

The following sections review four possible sources of financial education for emerging adults: college, work, the military, and on their own. For each venue, we will discuss benefits, challenges, and current trends. While most of the chapter will focus on the experience of U.S. emerging adults due to more data availability, examples and research from across the globe will be included when available. At the end of this chapter, needs and areas for improvement and advancement in current financial education programming and dissemination will be discussed.

Four Sources of Financial Education for Emerging Adults

Financial Education in College

Emerging adults attending college are likely experiencing first-time financial independence or semi-independence from their families, a potentially key period to learn how to manage their own finances (see Chapter 11). However, college enrollment has been dropping in the last decade, and not all emerging adults will attend college in the United States (see Chapter 9; Hanson, 2022).

Historically, home economics departments across land grant universities in the United States have been at the forefront of offering some form of financial education (Xiao, 2022). This has often taken the form of budget classes or outreach programs from extension specialists.

When financial education is delivered to college students, we see benefits on financial knowledge, financial confidence (subjective financial knowledge), and financial behaviors (see Chapters 2 and 5; Porto & Xiao, 2021; Urban et al., 2020). Using experimental designs, researchers have found that financial education delivered in online videos increased subjective and objective financial knowledge (Brugiavini et al., 2020), fostered financial confidence and positive financial behaviors (Atlas et al., 2018), and improved financial satisfaction (Gerrans & Heaney, 2019).

There are no clear statistics on the number of colleges that offer financial education classes and their enrollment in either the United States or globally. Financial literacy courses have been included as options in business schools in China (Tan et al., 2022), as a course unit in Australia (Gerrans & Heaney, 2019), and as both a compulsory module in the Department of Family and Consumer Sciences and as an elective course for students from other departments in Indonesia (Johan et al., 2021).

While college can be an ideal time for many emerging adults to receive financial education, it misses important financial decisions made before attendance. High schoolers and their families will not just have to decide if college is the next step but also how to finance the education, both financial decisions with long-term implications (see Chapter 9). In fact, financial education requirements in high school have been shown to help incoming freshmen to acquire low-cost financing (Stoddard & Urban, 2020). Additionally, high school graduates who decide not to continue their studies will not have the opportunity to take a college-level personal finance course.

Financial Education at Work

One of the earliest studies in the field found that household savings increase when employers offer financial education at the workplace (Bernheim & Garrett, 2003). A few years later, Bayer et al. (2009) confirmed these findings by showing that frequent retirement seminars increased participation and contributions to retirement savings. Workplace financial education has also been shown to improve financial satisfaction (Garman et al., 1999), financial knowledge (see Chapter 2; Edmiston & Fisher, 2006), and financial behaviors (see Chapter 5) such as budgeting and use of financial institutions

(Toosi et al., 2020). More recently, Clark (2023) reviewed20 years of research on the effectiveness of financial education in the workplace concerning saving for retirement, claiming pension and benefits, and the timing of retirement. While Clark cautioned about the generalizability of the findings due to selection issues and sampling, the review finds positive impacts on delivering financial education to new hires, using midcareer informational nudges, and even offering seminars to workers nearing retirement.

While this chapter focuses on broad financial education, programs delivered in the workplace are often solely focused on retirement savings and portfolio allocation. To the best of our knowledge, no research has focused solely on connecting workplace financial education and emerging adults. However, some studies provided a few insights applicable to emerging adults. For instance, using an experimental design, Billari et al. (2023) found a persistent improvement in financial literacy and a shift to investing in higher-risk assets after financial education, particularly for younger workers who will benefit the most from a higher-risk, higher-return portfolio. Another example comes from Hasler et al. (2022) where young employees (ages 18–34) were less likely to engage in a 6-week financial challenge than older employees.

Financial Education in the Military

For emerging adults in the military with its guaranteed pay and other benefits, financial education may seem, at first, of less importance. However, those in the military often struggle to make good money management decisions and are more likely to fall prey to predatory lending (Duebner, 2022). As a response to these unmet needs, the U.S. federal government passed legislation in 2016 that mandated comprehensive financial education training to all members of the armed forces. Since this law was implemented, over half of members of the U.S. military have attended financial education, most of them emerging adults who joined recently. The aforementioned NFCS survey showed a very similar figure, where 52% of emerging adults in the U.S. military have received financial education. In addition to personal finance training, the American armed forces have been increasing their members' access to financial counseling.

While the spread of financial education in the military has been encouraging, positive financial behaviors (see Chapter 5) and financial knowledge (see Chapter 2) have not taken hold yet. Compared to civilians, young members of the military have more types of savings account in place but also more problematic credit behaviors and more use of alternative financial services (see Chapter 13; Wagner & Walstad, 2019). A 2016 study on financial education in the military found that positive effects on credit last only 1 year (Skimmyhorn, 2016). In the United Kingdom, the need for financial education in the military has also been recognized to improve financial stability (Slapakova et al., 2023).

Free-Access Financial Education for Emerging Adults

For those who need a refresher or those who have never taken financial education classes in high school, college, work, or the military, several free options are available. For emerging adults struggling with their finances, a lack of proper and actionable financial knowledge (see Chapter 2) might be one of the culprits that is easily fixed with proper training. Furthermore, some extra financial knowledge is especially valuable before making major financial decisions such as buying a car, taking out a mortgage, or choosing how to invest for retirement (see Chapters 5 and 6). Here are some free financial education options:

- *Better Money Habits*: a joint venture between Bank of America and Khan Academy in the format of a free financial education online platform providing information and resources in an easy-to-understand and practical manner. The platform is designed for all ages, based on their own financial situation, and is available in both English and Spanish. (https://bettermoneyhabits.bankofamerica.com/en)
- *VISA Practical Money Skills*: a free financial educational platform that includes articles, lesson plans, apps, and games, developed for people of all ages and available in 19 languages and 46 countries. Educators can also use this platform to deliver coursework from pre-K to college level. (https://www.practicalmoneyskills.com/en)
- *GLEC Fast Lane*: a research-based comprehensive website on financial literacy developed by the Global Financial Literacy Excellence Center (GFLEC) with tools, resources, and knowledge that can be used by teachers, parents, students, and policymakers. (https://fastlane-education.org)
- *Duke Behavioral Finance*: a course intended to guide participants toward better financial choices, focusing on decision-making and how to improve money management choices. The course consists of three modules that can be completed in 4 hours and offers a certificate of completion. It is a good option for understanding the financial mistakes we

make and how to avoid them. (https://www.coursera.org/learn/duke-behavioral-finance)

While all the free options listed here aim to help emerging adults make better financial decisions (see Chapters 5 and 6), seeking professional advice might be appropriate for some. Financial counseling is typically affordable and often includes components of financial education as part of the counseling sessions (Collins & O'Rourke, 2010). Emerging adults attending financial counseling might acquire relevant financial knowledge (see Chapter 2) while also receiving advice pertinent to their own situation.

Financial Education in Action

For emerging adults who choose to enroll in college (see Chapter 9), questions remain regarding their financial literacy and financial behaviors when they arrive on campus, as well as the ability of the college classroom to impact these factors. With at least 23 states now requiring coursework on personal finance prior to high school graduation (CEE, 2020), some emerging adults are arriving at college with prior financial education. In particular, Burke et al. (2020) suggested that state-mandated personal finance education may be associated with increased financial well-being (see Chapter 7) once students reach the college classroom. Kaiser et al. (2022) noted that financial education interventions have been found to have positive effects on both financial knowledge (see Chapter 2) and financial behaviors (see Chapter 5). Some may also be receiving prior financial education from parents or guardians, which LeBaron et al. (2020) suggested may positively impact financial behaviors in emerging adulthood (see Chapter 18). Prior financial education from one's workplace or the military is also possible.

To examine the relationship between prior financial education, literacy, and behaviors, in this section we will provide an example of financial education in action. The authors conducted a survey with emerging adults enrolled at a 4-year public university in the Southern United States. The sample consisted of 572 undergraduates (82% response rate) enrolled in a 15-week, three-credit general education personal finance course during 2019–2020, and who had not taken a prior college finance course. The course was designed using a curriculum following National Financial Educators Council Content Standards (NFEC, 2019). All course sections were taught by the same instructor, with an average of 26 students enrolled per section. Students who participated in the survey prior to the start of the course were also invited to participate again at the end of the semester, with a sample attrition rate of 5.4%.

These pre- and post-course surveys were administered 3.5 months apart and featured questions from the FINRA 2018 National Financial Capability Study, including subjective and objective financial literacy measures (see Chapter 2; FINRA IEF, 2019). Participants were asked to assess their overall financial knowledge on a 7-point scale for subjective literacy. For objective literacy, participants answered five financial knowledge quiz questions. These quiz questions covered financial content that was featured in the course curriculum. Although the objective literacy questions were identical pre-post, students did not receive feedback on their responses, and the answers were not disclosed. Additional questions included financial behavior measures (see Chapter 5), questions concerning prior financial education pre-college, and demographics. Similarly, the course content included material that directly related to the financial behaviors referenced in the survey.

The study protocol was reviewed and approved by the university's Institutional Review Board, with participants providing their informed consent. To limit response bias, the surveys were administered using an online survey software program outside of the course classroom. The survey invitation was not initiated by the instructor. Students were informed that their participation in the surveys would not influence their grades or academic or social standing in the course.

Participants were, on average, 23.5 years old, 63% were female, and 81% were upperclassmen (juniors or seniors). A portion of participants had also received prior financial education outside the college classroom: 43%ercent in high school, 60% from parents or guardians (see Chapter 18), and 33% from their workplace or the military. This allows us to examine differences between financial education groups—that is, those with and without prior financial education.

Differences in Financial Behaviors

Although our survey participants had not previously taken a college finance course, approximately 61% indicated receiving prior education from high school, their parents or guardians, their workplace, and/or the military. We observe differences then in the proportion of students who indicated several financial behaviors (see Chapter 5), for those with and without prior financial education; we will refer to these as our two "education groups."

These comparisons can be viewed in Table 19.1 and use chi-squared tests of proportions (tests of homogeneity).

Table 19.1 Pre- and Post-Course Financial Behaviors, by Prior Education

Financial Behaviors	Pre-Course			Post-Course		
	Prior Financial Education	No Prior Financial Education	P^1	Prior Financial Education	No Prior Financial Education	P^1
Percentage that indicated they have . . .						
set aside a 3-month emergency fund.	37.37 (48.46)	19.37 (39.62)	**0.009**	38.94 (48.88)	40.26 (49.20)	0.884
a checking account.	98.58 (11.87)	97.38 (16.01)	0.352	95.19 (21.44)	98.70 (11.36)	0.113
a savings account.	80.07 (40.02)	64.40 (48.01)	**0.048**	77.40 (41.92)	72.08 (45.01)	0.300
obtained their credit report.	41.99 (49.44)	38.22 (48.72)	0.413	81.25 (39.13)	84.42 (36.39)	0.521
paid off credit card balances.	58.72 (49.32)	37.70 (48.59)	**0.006**	60.58 (48.98)	59.74 (49.20)	0.957
occasionally overdrawn their checking account.	12.46 (33.08)	15.71 (36.48)	0.315	12.50 (33.15)	12.99 (33.73)	0.891
found it *very difficult* to cover expenses/pay bills.	27.76 (44.86)	43.46 (49.70)	**0.019**	29.41 (50.66)	45.16 (49.64)	**0.047**
frequently or *sometimes* used a mobile payment app.	49.11 (50.08)	47.12 (50.05)	0.671	58.40 (49.48)	56.21 (49.54)	0.658
certain or *could probably* come up with $2,000 if a need arose for it.	24.55 (43.12)	19.89 (40.03)	0.236	25.60 (49.74)	23.53 (43.35)	0.748
Observations	349	223		326	215	

[1]*p*-values are obtained from χ^2-tests of proportions (tests of homogeneity) and have been adjusted for multiple comparisons using Bonferroni correction. Values in bold are significant at the 10%*, 5%**, and 1%*** level.

Pre-course, significant differences are observed between our two education groups, for those indicating they have: set aside a 3-month emergency fund (p = 0.009), a savings account (p = 0.048), and paid off credit card balances (p = 0.006). For all three of these positive financial behaviors, a greater proportion of students are observed among those who received prior financial education. This seems to align with Shim et al. (2010) who suggest that early financial socialization (see Chapter 18) is associated with positive financial behaviors (see Chapter 5) in college. A significant difference is also observed pre-course where those without previous financial education experience are more likely to find it very difficult to cover their expenses and pay their bills (p = 0.019). Our results suggest that prior financial education may result in a greater proportion of emerging adults self-reporting healthy financial behaviors. In our study here, these behaviors consisted of savings and responsible credit card use. It could be that any prior education received may have focused on these two particular areas.

Post-course, a significant difference between the two education groups is only observed for one of the financial behaviors included in the survey. Similar to our pre-course finding, a greater proportion of students who did not have prior financial education indicated they found it very difficult to cover their expenses and pay their bills (p = 0.047). This suggests that resources beyond a single 15-week personal finance course, such as increased access to funds and time to readjust their budget, are likely needed to address the difficulties these students are having in covering their expenses and bills. This disparity between the two education groups may also be due to differences in financial situations (e.g., familial socioeconomic status; see Chapter 15) or financial capabilities.

Post-course, the significant differences that were earlier observed between education groups pre-course were no longer observed for the savings and responsible credit card use behaviors.

Differences in Subjective and Objective Financial Literacy

Differences between subjective and objective financial literacy rates, both between education groups and compared pre-post course, are displayed in Table 19.2. Pre-course, we found significant differences between education groups for the proportion of students rating their subjective (self-assessed) financial literacy as "slightly high" or better (p = 0.003). This finding aligns with Xiao and O'Neill (2016), who found higher subjective

Table 19.2 Survey Measures, Pre-Post Course and by Prior Education

	Pre-Course			**Post-Course**			**Pre-Post**
Survey Measures	**Prior Financial Education**	**No Prior Financial Education**	P^1	**Prior Financial Education**	**No Prior Financial Education**	P^1	P^1
Percentage that indicated they . . .							
agree or *strongly agree* they are good at dealing with day-to-day financial matters.	53.74 (49.95)	40.84 (49.28)	**0.084**	59.46 (49.32)	55.14 (49.97)	0.680	**0.028**
agree or *strongly agree* they are good at math.	50.53 (50.86)	43.46 (49.70)	0.131	54.71 (49.99)	50.63 (50.32)	0.246	0.481
are satisfied with their current personal financial condition, 7 or greater.	42.25 (41.64)	21.75 (20.71)	**0.006**	53.67 (50.64)	48.93 (47.29)	0.557	**0.046**
rate their subjective financial literacy as *slightly high* or better.	23.96 (19.25)	5.37 (4.20)	**0.003**	62.03 (61.05)	60.92 (59.04)	0.406	**0.006**
Percentage answering at least four objective financial literacy questions correctly.	44.14 (41.19)	43.19 (41.11)	0.709	58.55 (54.15)	53.38 (52.19)	0.100	**0.096**
Observations	349	223		326	215		

[1] *p*-values are obtained from χ^2 tests of proportions (tests of homogeneity) and have been adjusted for multiple comparisons using Bonferroni correction. Values in bold are significant at the 10%*, 5%**, and 1%*** level.

financial literacy rates among U.S. adults who had received prior financial education (see Chapter 2). However, no significant differences were observed between groups for subjective financial literacy post-course, suggesting our 15-week personal finance course may have successfully increased the financial confidence of those without prior education at the start of the semester.

We also found evidence of a significant pre-post course difference for overall subjective financial literacy rates, significant at the 10% level. The distribution of overall subjective financial literacy rates, pre- and post-course, can be viewed in Figure 19.1. The mean subjective financial literacy rate was 3.72 (*SD* = 1.09) pre-course and 5.41 (*SD* = 1.04) post-course.

For objective financial literacy scores (see Chapter 2), no differences are observed between education groups, but we found an overall difference pre- versus post-course. A modest increase in the number of questions that were correctly answered post-course was observed. The proportion of students correctly answering at least four questions correctly was 43.2% (*SD* = 41.17) pre-course and 56.9% (*SD* = 55.51) post-course, significant at the 10% level. The distribution of the number of objective financial literacy questions correctly answered, pre- and post-course, can be viewed in Figure 19.2.

Although our 15-week personal finance course covered content assessed in the five objective financial literacy questions, it may be that additional education is still needed. It may also be that other measures, such as the Consumer Financial Protection Bureau's Financial Well-Being Scale (CFPB, 2020), which focuses on one's financial security, may yield different results. Lee et al. (2020) noted the positive relationship between financial well-being (see Chapter 7) and financial knowledge (see Chapter 2), while acknowledging that financial well-being is a function, in part, of financial knowledge.

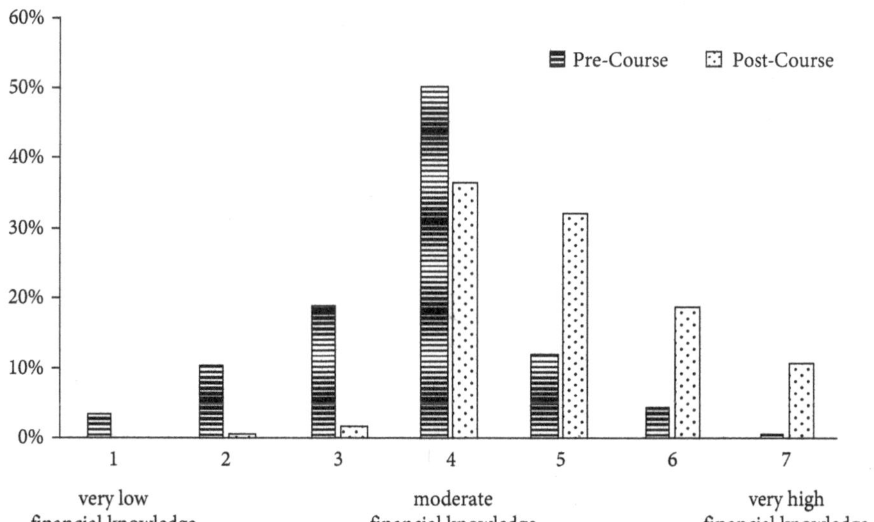

Figure 19.1 Subjective Financial Literacy, Pre- and Post-Course

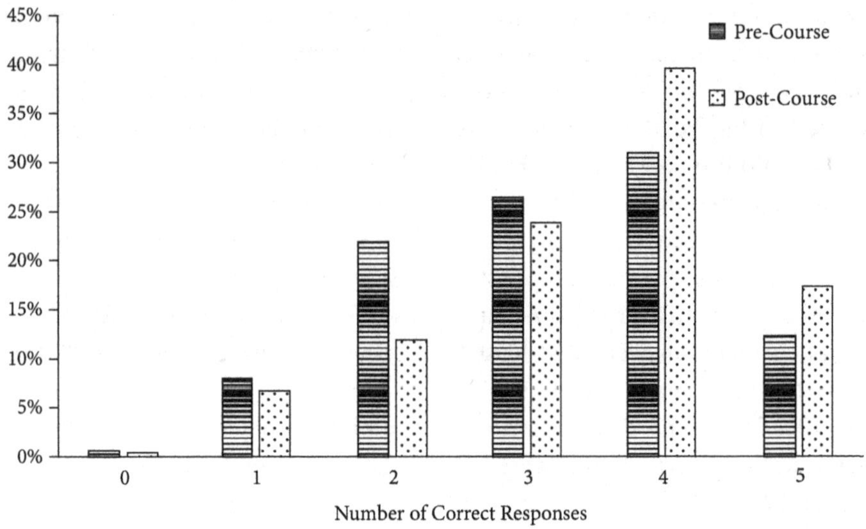

Figure 19.2 Objective Financial Literacy, Pre- and Post-Course

Thus, measuring financial well-being in future efforts may allow for a more complete understanding of potential differences between education groups pre- versus post-course.

Students were also asked to rate how satisfied they were with their current personal financial condition on a 10-point scale. Significant differences between education groups were observed pre-course (p = 0.006) but not post-course. Pre-course, 20.5% more students indicated they were satisfied with their personal financial condition in the prior financial education group compared to those without prior education. Post-course, there was no discernible difference between the two education groups. Yet there was an overall pre-post course difference (p = 0.046) in financial satisfaction. From Table 19.2, it appears that this significant difference may largely be attributed to a shift in financial satisfaction by the end of the 15-week course among those without prior financial education. The pre-post distribution of how satisfied students were with their current personal financial condition can be viewed in Figure 19.3.

Future Directions

The example of financial education in action presented here suggests that a general education college financial course may be one way to help address potential discrepancies between those with and without prior financial

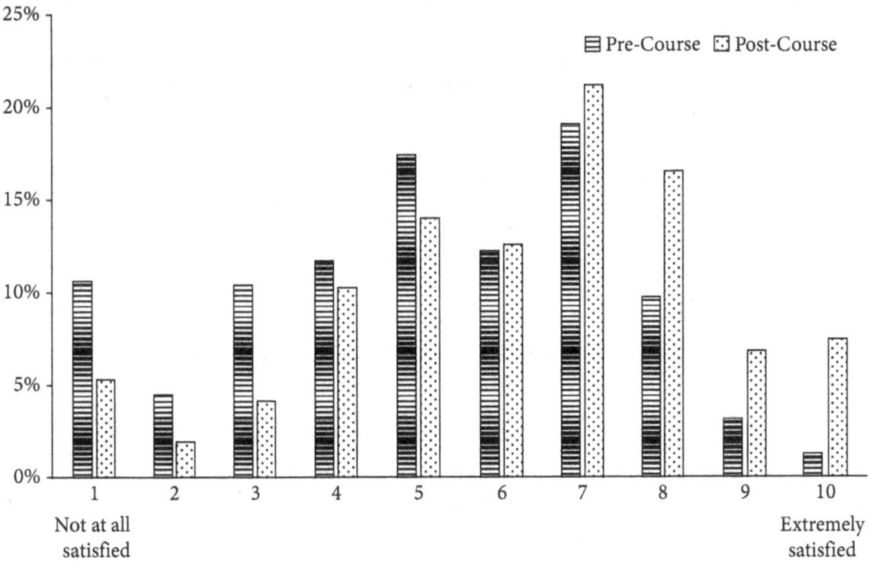

Figure 19.3 How Satisfied are You with Your Current Personal Financial Condition?

education. This may be particularly important for emerging adults who may not have had access to prior education at their high school or workplace or from their parents or guardians. We found that for the majority of financial behaviors surveyed, there were no differences between the two education groups at the end of our 15-week course.

We also found that for financial satisfaction, and for subjective and objective financial literacy, there were also no discernible differences post-course between groups. While much focus recently has been aimed at personal finance education in high schools, the example shared in this chapter suggests that for emerging adults, college financial education may also have a positive impact on subjective and objective financial literacy. Finally, the example shared in this section utilizes data collected prior to the impact of COVID-19. Future efforts may wish to utilize observed financial behaviors, particularly post-pandemic, as opposed to the self-reported measures collected in our survey.

Conclusion

Emerging adults are living in-between adolescence and full adulthood. Their lives are becoming more complex, moving away from the parental nest to college (see Chapter 9), work (see Chapter 10), or a mix of both. This life complexity involves managing their own finances as an independent household at a certain point (see Chapter 11). The right source(s) and quality of financial education will be needed to complement what they have learned from their families (see Chapter 18) and on their own. The final goal is their financial well-being (see Chapter 7), which can be achieved with a combination of many factors that include financial education, financial knowledge (see Chapter 2), and financial behaviors (see Chapter 5) (Sorgente & Lanz, 2017).

State mandates for personal finance classes in high school are a welcome trend in developing financial literacy across the United States. However, the timing between the training and when the knowledge needs to be employed might be problematic. A high school sophomore might not buy a car on their own for several years or apply for a mortgage for over a decade after taking the class. Knowledge is forgotten if not recent; knowledge fades if not activated regularly. As such, a continuum of financial education across the lifespan with boosters before making major financial decisions (i.e., "just-in-time" financial education) might be optimal.

Mandates to avoid the selection issues of participants are another important component of delivering effective financial education to emerging adults. In addition to the growing high school initiatives, colleges and workplaces have important roles to play in disseminating financial education. Colleges have added more personal finance as part of their curriculum, sometimes as a required course. In the workplace, when financial education is present, it often takes the form of retirement education before signing up for a 401(k) plan. Comprehensive workplace programs seem to be few and far between; the research done for this chapter found that there is mostly a vacuum for financial education in the workplace, severely limiting opportunities for emerging adults who do not attend college. When emerging adults are not given the opportunity to acquire financial education from high school, college, or workplace, they are left to seek this knowledge on their own, perhaps using one of the free programs listed in this chapter. However, this venue of access is dependent on their own initiative and information search with the potential for selection issues such as only those with more education are more likely to seek financial education (Zhang & Xiong, 2020). A widespread delivery of (or at least, access to) financial education to reach a majority of emerging adults could be achieved. One opportunity to disseminate financial education information is at tax time, either offered during the preparation process or as a link as part of communication materials such as emails. At the workplace, financial education programs could also be offered to new employees as part of the onboarding process, like OSHA requirements.

Financial knowledge (see Chapter 2) and financial literacy (see Chapter 1) are desirable outcomes of financial education but should not be considered the main units of success. Measurements of financial knowledge might not apprehend the full benefits of a financial education class or training. While more precise and comprehensive measurements of the effectiveness of financial education are indispensable to better understand what works and what does not, the current research evidence mounts that financial behaviors (see Chapter 5) and financial well-being (see Chapter 7) are often the main beneficiaries. For emerging adults, financial education should be taught as a life skill that can be used in the here and now and can advance their financial futures.

Chapter 20
Conclusion and Future Research Directions

Sharon M. Danes[1]

Introduction

The chapter authors, guided by this book's editors LeBaron-Black, Kelley, and Sorgente, have provided an evidence-based, application-centered handbook to help emerging adults flourish rather than flounder financially. Financial independence (see Chapter 11) and financial well-being (see Chapter 7) are goals of emerging adults. However, emerging adults are floundering in reaching those goals across the world due to a complex and uncertain economy (see Chapter 5), varied access to financial markets (see Chapter 15), lack of financial knowledge (see Chapter 2), and a work environment that is rapidly changing culturally, socially, and digitally (see Chapter 10). Yet, emerging adults often must make critical financial decisions that have consequences for their entire life (see Chapter 6). Chapter contents will be useful to emerging adults and their parents as well as educators, researchers, and clinicians who support the financial journey of emerging adults. The handbook also provides emerging adults with the tools to improve their financial situation.

Chapter authors have reflected on the multifaceted, multidisciplinary, and complex study of the financial literacy of emerging adults. This book consists of four parts. Each part discusses contributions that encourage financial flourishing or factors that lead to financial floundering. The chapters in Part I address major concepts within the current emerging adult financial literacy research base. Those in Part II focus on financial concerns that emerging adults are facing. The chapters in Part III express how socioeconomic vulnerability, gender, and cultural/racial orientation affect access and opportunity to financial markets. Those in Part IV focus on the improvement of financial literacy.

[1] Family Social Science Department, University of Minnesota, USA

Sharon M. Danes, *Conclusion and Future Research Directions*. In: *Flourishing and Floundering Financially in Emerging Adulthood*. Edited by: Ashley B. LeBaron-Black, Heather Kelley, and Angela Sorgente, Oxford University Press.
 DOI: 10.1093/9780197699157.003.0021

This final chapter's purpose is to provide a concluding statement on the current state of financial literacy research about emerging adults and to provide insight into future research directions. The chapter achieves this goal through a number of sections. The first, "State of Research about Financial Literacy of Emerging Adults," provides a summary of what we currently know about the financial literacy of emerging adults. The second section, "Methodological Research Gaps and Future Directions," addresses sampling, measurement, and data analysis concerns. The third section provides justification for "Why the Concept of Financial Capability Should Replace Financial Literacy." The fourth section, "Theoretical Research Gaps and Future Directions," includes an introduction to a new overarching theory: financial capability systems theory. The chapter then ends with concluding remarks.

State of Research about Financial Literacy of Emerging Adults

Here, the text aims to summarize the contents of this book, for each of its four parts, respectively.

Part I: Emerging Adults' Financial Literacy

Chapter 1 of this book presents OECD's (Organisation for Economic Co-operation and Development) definition of financial literacy—"a combination of financial awareness, knowledge, skills, attitudes, and behaviors necessary to make sound financial decisions and ultimately achieve individual well-being"—and discusses other definitions and models of financial literacy. Chapter 2 demonstrates how a lack of emerging adults' financial knowledge and overconfidence in their estimation of that knowledge have a detrimental impact on financial well-being. Chapter 3 states that numeracy, reading abilities, and executive functioning are critical skills in achieving financial well-being; cognitive flexibility is a particularly important skill because it is core to creative problem solving. Chapter 4 indicates that financial attitudes evolving during emerging adulthood have long-term effects on financial outcomes, such as credit scores, debt, savings, and wealth accumulation. Chapter 5 demonstrates that emerging adult behaviors set the tone for future decisions because they establish habits and carry consequences that persist for many years. Chapter 6 presents a neurocognitive perspective on decisions, indicating that financial mistakes and mismanagement by emerging adults occur through impulsive decisions, risk and sensation seeking, and present bias. Chapter 7 indicates that financial well-being is a complex, multidimensional condition that has both objective and subjective dimensions. In Chapter 8, it is proposed that understanding financial stress and anxiety status is important for promoting a flourishing state of mind, which is an essential component in building a more financially resilient emerging adult.

Part II: Financial Considerations in Emerging Adulthood

While Part I identifies the components of financial literacy, there are many other financial concerns influencing the nature and degree of flourishing or floundering experienced in any one emerging adult. Chapter 9 discusses problems created by student loan debt, especially in the United States. Chapter 10 explores the complex developmental trajectory of the education-to-work transition. Chapter 11 outlines issues in navigating financial self-sufficiency and emphasizes the centrality of that concept as a new worldwide social norm for emerging adults. Chapter 12 shows that a fully formed financial identity is a state where emerging adults make commitments to a personally meaningful set of values and beliefs that serve as the compass for their future decisions and behaviors. Chapter 13 indicates that sustainable consumption is a challenge for emerging adults who often meet that challenge by accumulating various types of debt. Chapter 14 presents a number of reciprocal and circular associations between finances and romantic relationships.

Part III: Sociodemographic Characteristics and Emerging Adults' Financial Literacy

Navigating financial barriers and facilitators in financial and economic systems differs by such characteristics as socioeconomic status (Chapter 15), gender (Chapter 16), and culture/race (Chapter 17). The chapter authors identify unique concerns that affect the nature and degree of floundering or flourishing for emerging adults with various characteristics. They illustrate that facilitators and barriers lie in two areas: ability-opportunity and access-opportunity. Ability-opportunity is internal to the emerging adult, reflected in their financial literacy state. Access-opportunity lies at the interface of emerging adults and other systems.

Part IV: How to Improve Emerging Adults' Financial Literacy

Chapter 18 indicates that parents are the most impactful financial socialization agent (through discussion, modeling, and experiential learning). Chapter 19 reviews various financial education environments—college, work, military, and self-education. Strengthening these two means of improving financial literacy contributes to the nature of how, and the degree to which, emerging adults financially flourish or flounder.

Methodological Research Gaps and Future Directions

There are a number of methodological research gaps in the current literature about the financial literacy of emerging adults. Those include: (1) a disconnect between conceptualization and measurement, (2) lack of diversity in sampling procedures, (3) lack of multiinformants when concepts vary among those involved, (4) lack of longitudinal data for capturing developmental concepts, and (5) lack of mixed research methods to capture underlying decision processes influencing behavioral outcomes or the verification process in the developing of a financial identity.

Chapter 1 highlights the existing disconnect between measurement and conceptualization among some concepts within the study of the financial literacy of emerging adults. This concern is voiced for both predictor variables and outcome variables. The need exists for an in-depth review of the conceptualization/measurement interface to align with this book's conceptual review. Such a review will set the stage for adjustments of current conceptualizations, construction of missing conceptualizations, and/or refinement of concept measurement.

Lack of diversity in sampling is a major concern. College students are the primary sample across current studies. The confirmation of research findings in Part I's chapters with more representative samples of the emerging adult population is essential to cement our understanding of financial literacy. Research resulting from such samples will address issues cited in Part III about the intersectionality of socioeconomic vulnerability, gender, and culture/race. Because of these sampling issues, the generalization of study findings is problematic. Several authors cited the knowledge gaps or inconsistency in findings that exist because of this sampling issue.

More multiinformant, quantitative research such as that of Lanz et al. (2020) would capture the underlying dynamics motivating financial behavior. Their family communication quality measure was composed of four latent variables evaluated by the emerging adult and each parent. Qualitative methodologies videotaping parents, the emerging adult, and other critical family members (per cultural norms) discussing a financial socialization issue could also provide deeper insights. Videotaping interactions captures nonverbal interaction subtleties underlying decision-making and behavior change (or stagnation) that would carry into emerging adulthood. Melby and Conger's (2001) Iowa Family Interaction Rating Scales provide a coding scheme to codify family interactions for such research.

The call for this sort of family interaction research is both theory- and practice-based. For example, when I conducted workshops on children and money, participants seemed to fall into two camps. Either they indicated that they would wholeheartedly repeat their parents' actions related to allowances, or the other camp would do just the opposite from their parents' actions. After experiencing this phenomenon repeatedly, I knew there was something underlying this trend that needed to be understood in the transfer of financial capability from one generation to another. The authors in Chapter 18 provide verification of this phenomenon.

Current data are primarily cross-sectional, but financial behavior and well-being are conditional on varied circumstances across time. The current research captures behavior at a set point in time. There is much yet to discover about conditions that influence behavior patterns over time. Conditions that initiate behavior change or that terminate or adjust such behavior as time progresses (e.g., turning and tipping points) are key. Those conditions may lie within the capabilities of the emerging adult or evolve from the socioeconomic environment. Each contributes a great deal to well-being status at any point in time and over time.

Longitudinal data would provide a lens into the variability in the progression of flourishing and floundering and the conditions of that variability. It is important to understand both the transition into emerging adulthood and the journey through emerging adulthood. For example, Chapter 9 indicates that when paying for their educational costs, the decision for most U.S. emerging adults is not about whether to take out a student loan, but rather about when and how much to borrow. Determining the effect of student loan debt on flourishing and floundering over time requires longitudinal data that follow the emerging adult throughout their emerging adult years and beyond. Chapter 8 indicates that simply being financially literate may not be sufficient to achieve financial well-being. Longitudinal data measuring stress and anxiety about finances over time would assess whether the level of stress and anxiety had reached such a level where it becomes so overwhelming that their emotional state compromises their ability to apply their own knowledge effectively.

Expansion of the types of analyses utilized within studies also needs attention. Applying recent advancements in qualitative methodologies and in the combination of quantitative and qualitative (i.e., mixed-method) analyses would facilitate examination of the complexities underlying financial decision-making and behavior. An example of the combining of quantitative and qualitative analyses is the use of SEM (structural equation modeling) and fsQCA (fuzzy set qualitative comparative analysis). SEM combines the econometric perspective focusing on prediction and the psychometric perspective target of measuring latent variables (Sartal et al., 2017). The fsQCA procedure investigates which concept combination better explains an outcome, rather than only explaining the isolated impact of each concept (Ragin, 2008). Using such a methodological combination captures underlying perceptions and comprehensions of emerging adults' financial decision and identity verification processes that stimulate their financial behavior. Understanding such complexity moves the research focus of emerging adults beyond that of financial literacy to financial capability.

Why the Concept of Financial Capability Should Replace Financial Literacy

The current financial literacy literature, because of lack of diversity in sampling, does not include the effect of cultural socialization on the development of the ability-opportunity aspects of financial literacy. And, that literature base has only recently begun to address the aspects of access-opportunity for many emerging adults, particularly those related to socioeconomic status (Chapter 15), gender (Chapter 16), and culture/race (Chapter 17).

OECD's definition of financial literacy (Chapter 1) focuses on behavior outcomes based on informed decisions. Let's think about emerging adult characteristics and the nature of "informed decisions." Chapter 2 indicates that that misalignment of actual and perceived financial knowledge is common among emerging adults. Chapter 7 further illustrates that financial well-being behaviors are rooted not just in financial facts such as income, consumption, credit, and debt. For instance, the primary currency in individualistic cultures is money, but in many collectivist cultures, relationships are another highly valued currency (Chapter 17). Thus, OECD's definition is not as good a fit with collectivist cultures as with individualistic cultures.

For Native Americans where family extends to the tribe, there is an obligatory belief that resources are to be shared with all family members (Danes et al., 2016b). Another example occurs in some African American families. When one child receives family support for their college education, they have an obligation after graduation to assist the next sibling in their educational endeavors (Danes et al., 2008). These family/cultural expectations are just as important as the emerging adult's financial literacy state in affecting their financial and overall well-being, yet these expectations receive little research attention.

The term "financial capability" better captures what emerging adults are able to do based on resources available, demands placed on those resources, and the constraints they face. These decision process assessments are based on emerging adults' perceptions and comprehensions. Changing behavior entails understanding motivations for behaviors and meanings people hold about things they value highly or that verify their identities (Danes et al., 2016a).

OECD's financial literacy definition is primarily about knowledge of financial decision content. It is about how emerging adults feel about the content (attitudes), the degree of proficiency in which they relate to that content (skills), and the resulting interaction with that content (behavior) (see Chapters 3–5). These factors are important. However, a more inclusive lens that recognizes the importance of social processes and personal perceptions and comprehensions (i.e., that interact with a person's knowledge base) opens the door to new insights into the financial capability of emerging adults and its effect on well-being (Sherraden, 2010).

Future research must delve to a greater degree into elements of the decision processes of emerging adults. Such a movement involves a call for the study of financial capability rather than financial literacy for several reasons. *First*, financial capability includes both the ability to act (i.e., knowledge, skills, confidence, and motivation to take action) and the opportunity to act (i.e., access to quality financial products and services) (Sherraden, 2013). Financial capability is a deeper concept that includes not only the multiple elements of the OECD definition but also takes into account the underlying, unseen emotion/behavior duality that composes the motivation for action (see Chapter 1). Shepherd (2009) described this emotion/behavior duality as sensemaking. Decision processes are a precursor to enactment of behavior, and sensemaking is central to those decision processes.

Sensemaking is an interpretive process where people assign meaning to occurrences that involve continuing interpretations over time (Gudmunson & Danes, 2013). Sensemaking includes felt expressions (i.e., perceptions) and cognitive interpretations (i.e., comprehensions) of those felt expressions. Perceptions and comprehensions are an essential part of an emerging adult's financial capability identity that has social, psychological, and cultural meanings (Chapter 12).

Identity is a process because the central proposition of identity theory is that people seek ways to establish and maintain behaviors and relationships that verify their identities. This verification process stimulates the reason for action. Identity verification occurs both internally in the mind and through interaction with the outside world (Landers et al., 2021). Thus, emotion-based felt perceptions and interpretative comprehensions are internal to the individual, as part of their decision process, until the individual interacts behaviorally with others in their contextual environment. The behavior can then become beneficial to the individual.

Second, financial capability recognizes the larger socioeconomic system in which emerging adults navigate as financial decision-makers. Access and opportunity to financial markets are beyond the emerging adult's circle of influence but are critical to the achievement of their financial goals. Capability better captures the emerging adult within societal structures that variously provide opportunities and constraints. Access and opportunity are of particular concern for those emerging adults who are socioeconomically vulnerable, those of various gender orientations, and those of various racial/cultural/religious orientations (Chapters 15–17).

Third, instead of financial literacy, which is a state of awareness and knowledge about financial decision content, financial capability captures the continually developing and lifelong decision process of financial management. Reflecting this variability over time, the authors of Chapter 10 indicated that lifelong learning is a concept recently introduced in career research due to the ever-changing demands of modern work.

Financial capability recognizes turning points between healthy and unhealthy decisions and the thresholds that mark the tipping point that creates change. Decision processes include assessing internal resources available to make the decision, such as the physical and mental health of the emerging adult, in addition to their state of financial literacy. Decision processes also include assessing resources in the external environment that affect the access-opportunity conditions for the emerging adult. Sustainable consumption behavior discussed in Chapter 13 reflects such a decision process.

Financial capability captures a greater depth of what is nested within the emerging adult by acknowledging the emotion-behavior duality of sense-making underlying financial decision processes. Financial capability also acknowledges that healthy decision-making is not a static event but an ongoing developmental, contextual navigation grounded in a financial capability identity verification meaning set that undergirds the motivation to take action.

Theoretical Research Gaps and Future Directions

The study of the financial journey of emerging adults is in its infancy. Thus far, there is a lack of an overarching theory to guide that study. Sherraden's (2013) financial capability framework combines individual and institutional features that address ability-opportunity and access-opportunity aspects of financial capability. Serido, Shim, and Tang's developmental model of financial capability addresses change in financial knowledge, self-beliefs, behavior, and well-being within the emerging adult.

However, there is no overarching theory that presents the underlying financial capability identity verification meanings considering the ability-opportunity, access-opportunity, and relational (e.g., familial, couplehood, and cultural socialization) aspects of healthy financial capability development. I would like to introduce a new theory, "financial capability systems theory (FCST)," that meets these criteria.

This theory's propositions would both guide research and act as a repository to integrate research findings that support or refute the theory's propositions. Without integrating findings across studies into a larger theoretical context, especially in a complex, multidisciplinary research focus such as this one, the full impact of the findings falls flat. The best approach involves grounding a study in an overarching theory while integrating it with another theory that specifically targets the unique content of the study's research question. This dual-pronged approach is about unification of theory that can be either upward or downward unification (Sztompka, 1974). With downward unification, the link is a common outcome or problem; with upward unification, the link is a common explanatory construct. An overarching theory also is a way to tackle the existing disparate conceptualizations that currently exist.

Financial Capability Systems Theory

A system is a complex set of interconnected things that work together as a whole (Von Bertalanffy, 1968). Just as the medical community views the body as a system, it is important in the financial literacy literature to view the emotion/behavior duality of emerging adults as a system. Underlying their financial behavior is a complex set of perceptions and comprehensions that motivate their decision processes, then resulting in their financial behavior. Understanding how those perceptions and comprehensions affect the development and verification of their financial identity is core to their ability-opportunity experience.

In addition, Von Bertalanffy (1968) indicated that to understand a complex system such as the emerging adult, one must not examine that system in isolation but must examine it in relation to systems in which it interacts to achieve its goals. Thus, to fully understand how emerging adults flourish or flounder financially, one must understand the dynamics among several systems. Doing so provides a lens into the access-opportunity experience of emerging adults.

FCST presents such a context. It contains four interrelated and interdependent systems. Those systems include: (1) the socioeconomic system containing facilitators and barriers that impact emerging adults' financial decisions; (2) the familial/cultural system where their primary financial socialization begins; (3) the couplehood system where they blend diverse personal and financial capability identities and decision patterns and socialize the next generation; and (4) the emerging adult system where they develop their unique financial capability identity that drives their financial behavior. The next section begins to outline the scope and properties of what each system within FCST brings to the study of the financial capability of emerging adults.

Socioeconomic System

The socioeconomic system consists of institutions (public or private) or environmental conditions in the community (local or national) that create facilitators or barriers for the goal pursuits of emerging adults. The interface between the emerging adult system and the socioeconomic system is critical to the development of financial capability. Barriers and facilitators at the crossroads of ability-opportunity and access-opportunity aspects of financial capability need consideration during the resource–demand assessment in financial decisions.

The institutions fall into three categories: (1) policy producing, (2) change generating, and (3) resource providing. Policy-producing institutions include government agencies and religious institutions. These groups set regulations or establish a belief foundation that emerging adults must follow, are expected to follow, or where it is assumed that they will follow them. In some cases, as is true for Native Americans, distinct federal policies affect access and use of resources.

Social norms, a part of the socioeconomic system, are an environmental condition that establishes an implicit belief foundation that emerging adults are expected to follow. These norms often are slow to change but have major effects on how people perceive things. An example is the introduction of the concept of "emerging adult" itself. Many conditions within the socioeconomic environment have changed, resulting in young people not following the customary progressive journey of educational graduation, job attainment, marriage, and raising children. Puzzlement and concern developed about the length of time it was taking many adult children to become financially independent. That length of time was exceeding social norms. Thus, the concept of "emerging adulthood" was born along with the study surrounding this new phenomenon.

The change-generating category includes economic conditions, employment potential, financial institutions, and technological advancements. This category carries the label of "change generating" because fluctuations in these institutions or conditions have ripple effects, influencing the creation of turning and tipping points in financial decisions and behavior. The inclusion of technological advancements in this category results from Twenge's (2023) research indicating that these advancements are the underlying driver of each generation's makeup. For example, with current emerging adults, the introduction of smartphones has had a profound effect on their mental health, on their perceptions and comprehensions underlying their financial capability identity verification, and on their decision process and resulting behavior (see Chapter 8).

Resource-providing institutions include educational institutions that provide financial knowledge, social support institutions that provide assistance, and medical institutions that provide physical and mental health-sustaining or recovery services. More research about what occurs at the intersection of the larger socioeconomic system and emerging adults as they pursue adult-like goals is in order across the many different organizations, institutions, and conditions of the socioeconomic system that create barriers to, or facilitate access to, financial resources.

Familial/Cultural System

Nuggets of financial capability first germinate in the family context through cultural values, beliefs, and expectations (Gudmunson & Danes, 2011). Family context is where imprinting of ethnicity occurs (Danes et al., 2008). Understanding of this imprinting is critical because demand–resource decisions depend on family values embedded in culture. These demand–resource decisions serve as fuel for the goals of emerging adults. Chapters 15–18 indicate that there is much yet to learn about the intersectionality of family, culture, gender, and SES prior to entering emerging adulthood. Since much change occurs through the emerging adulthood years, future research should extend through the entire journey of emerging adulthood.

Matters surrounding money resources vary across collectivist and individualist cultures (see Chapter 17; Danes et al., 2016b). Defining "family" in research studies needs consideration. The Vanier Institute of the Family is an organization dedicated to understanding the diversity and complexity of families. Their family definition allows for universal applicability. According to this institute, family consists of two or more people related by blood, marriage, or adoption, or who have a long-term commitment to each other and who share resources (financial, human, social, physical; Mirabelli, 2021). This definition does not require legal marriage. This definition goes beyond structure by including the sharing of resources. Sharing resources in this definition has no limits on when, how, or the form in which sharing occurs. Sharing resources accommodates varied currencies as culturally defined (see Chapter 17). Such a family definition sets the stage for a deeper understanding of the intergenerational transmission of financial flourishing and floundering, especially within and across cultural contexts.

Gudmunson and Danes introduced family financial socialization theory (FFST) in 2011 where they specified the properties and scope of family financial socialization by introducing components of family socialization processes and outcomes. Danes and Yang (2014) presented testable propositions for FFST. A literature review of studies testing FFST's propositions is needed to capture financial capability generated through family financial socialization. After such a review, additional propositions would extend and strengthen FFST.

The purpose of the current version of FFST was to delineate the role of family financial socialization in the development of financial literacy. It reflects a point-in-time snapshot. The theory's propositions need further development to depict the ongoing, life-course dynamics of financial socialization. A bidirectional influence between financial behavior and financial well-being over time is an example of one potential adjustment to reflect the developmental nature of financial socialization and the resulting financial capability.

Chapter 18 indicates that family financial socialization occurs through parental action such as financial discussions, modeling behavior, and creating experiential learning opportunities. We still know little, however, about emerging adults' decision-making perceptions about finances and how their normative comprehensions and activities are reinforced or are redirected to facilitate or create behavior change (Gudmunson & Danes, 2011). Further pursuit of these concepts and their measurement as a predictor versus a control variable in quantitative financial capability and couplehood research is important.

Couplehood System

McGovern (2011) coined the concept of "couplehood," which represents the relationship between two committed individuals who share a sense of identity and purpose. I would amend the concept's definition by adding that they share resources in addition to a sense of identity and purpose. This integrated couplehood definition allows for greater relevance across cultures by recognizing both relationship structure and interactions such as decision processes.

Chapter 14 indicates that a major dimension of romantic relationship development is the reciprocal and circular associations between finances and relationship issues. Couplehood relationships for emerging adults create a particularly complicated dynamic because each partner is pursuing verification of their financial capability identity at the same time that they are establishing a committed relationship. Each partner is floundering or flourishing at a different pace within that verification process. Thus, before jumping into this discussion, changing economic and social norms dictates a view into the decision criteria that emerging adults use in determining relationship status: living apart, co-habitation, or marriage.

The current generation of emerging adults are struggling to balance their work and relational goals (see Chapter 10; Rea et al., 2020). Rea and colleagues discovered that relationship choice may not be driven by financial resources, but rather more so by individual values. The study sample was college students. Their research question needs to be studied across a more representative sample. However, the trajectory of relationship status decision processes over the emerging adult journey and the turning and tipping points of value prioritization across that journey are avenues to pursue in future research.

Much is yet to be learned about the perceptions and comprehensions that underlie the financial decision processes within couplehood. When individuals in a committed relationship engage in managing their finances, they also engage in an ongoing comparison between what they do and what they perceive their partner does (Mao et al., 2018). In fact, Mao and his colleagues discovered that the sense of shared financial values and goals within couplehood (a dynamic association within financial decision processes) provides a stronger foundation for relationship satisfaction than financial management quality or perceived partner behavior.

This dynamic reflects a collective financial capability identity within the couple relationship. Collective identities represent a combination of individual-level affective factors that group members possess as well as relationship factors that shape the interactional experience. Collective identities are socially constructed, representing shared perceptions and comprehensions that members feel are central, enduring, and distinctive (Berscheid, 1994).

Emerging adults may have a financial socialization foundation resulting from their family and culture of origin and other socialization agents experienced in their emerging adulthood. Blending two distinct sets of financial socialization foundations is a huge challenge (see Chapter 14). Much of the data in this arena is cross-sectional. So even though the association between financial interactions and relationship quality is dynamic over time, little is known about the trajectory over time or the nature of the turning and tipping points under varying circumstances.

Related to this point, the study of couplehood financial conflict and its effect on relationship quality at one point in time may present a false picture. That conflict needs to be placed in context with the overall state of the relationship. Gottman and Levenson (2000) indicated that a positive/negative interaction ratio between the partners that favors positivity stimulates a couple's relational culture. This interaction ratio may temper any detrimental effect of financial conflict at any one point in time. However, to place the conflict within a positive/negative relationship ratio requires longitudinal data. Striving for data from each member of the couplehood is also a critical goal in capturing the essence of couplehood financial decision processes because partners may experience divergent perceptions and comprehensions.

Emerging Adult System

The grounding for the verification process that emerging adults experience as they develop their financial capability identity falls in an identity meaning set that is an integration of perceptions and comprehensions that are motivation for their decisions and actions (Van Campenhout, 2015). People make decisions that align with their identities. Understanding perceptions and comprehensions within this meaning set provides a lens into motivations for financial decisions and actions.

Decision processes underlying financial capability identity involve both cognitive-demanding and emotion-elicited processes (see Chapter 6). The cognitive-demanding process of problem solving occurs when emerging adults determine their resource–demand discrepancy and surrounding constraints (see Chapter 3; Rettig et al., 1997). For example, when an emerging adult is searching for an apartment, they consider their income as the initial resource. The demands the emerging adult faces include the rent amount and what utilities are included in that rent level. Addressing the discrepancy might include potential roommates to share the cost or some financial assistance from parents. Constraints may include any barriers or rules that prevent the emerging adult from living in that location. The location of mass transit to the apartment could also prove to be a constraint.

The emotion-elicited sensemaking process occurs when emerging adults engage the meanings, perceptions, and comprehensions of the emerging adult's financial capability identity verification meaning set (see Chapter 12; Rettig et al., 1999)—for example, when emerging adults reflect on their past financial mistakes and those mistakes motivate them to make healthier decisions (see "Hindsight" in Rea et al., 2019).

Achieving financial capability identity meaning set functions reduces anxiety so that emerging adults can better manage change within their financial journey and more likely flourish. Emerging adult perceptions and comprehensions center around five identity functions (see Table 20.1): (1) significance, (2) recognition, (3) expressive, (4) mediating change, and (5) defense against anxiety (Hauge, 2007). The composition of an identity verification meaning set contains an identity component for each identity function and its meaning, along with the perceptions and comprehensions experienced by the emerging adult related to each component.

The *significance* function of their financial capability identity is verified when the emerging adult believes they have integrated their family/cultural beliefs into their unique financial identity. The significance of this cultural socialization is not only the cultural roots of the family but also the specific manner in which the family system incorporates those cultural underpinnings with the family dynamics (Chapter 17). This identity function is verified when the emerging adult feels that they have been able to balance their family/cultural financial socialization with the other socialization agents that they have experienced in their emerging adulthood years.

The *recognition* identity function lies within the ability-opportunity dimension of financial capability. Verifying the recognition function is about how the emerging adult is able to recognize the ways in which application of their financial knowledge and skills is able to create opportunities. How they structure their problem solving and decision processes with their knowledge and skills to negotiate their resource–demand discrepancy is recognition of the ability-opportunity connection. That recognition affects the degree to which they believe they are able to execute healthy financial decisions.

The emerging adult verifies the *expressive* function when they enter a couple relationship. The expressive function is relational in that the emerging adult needs to communicate and share aspects of their financial capability identity with their relationship partner. Underlying healthy relationship development involves developing a couple relationship identity but also expressing and integrating aspects of their financial identities. In order to achieve a positive couple interaction ratio, blending diverse financial

Table 20.1 Financial Capability Identity Verification Meaning Set

Identity Component	Identity Function	Meaning	Perceptions (Felt Expressions)	Comprehensions (Interpretations)
Cultural socialization	Significance	Cultural (imprinting family/cultural values and beliefs)	Balancing family/cultural financial socialization with emerging adult socialization agents	Integrating family/cultural values/beliefs into their financial identity
Ability-opportunity	Recognition	Structural (applying financial literacy knowledge and skills)	Negotiating resource–demand discrepancy	Executing healthy adultlike financial decisions
Couplehood	Expressive	Relational (sharing relational/financial identities)	Blending diverse financial identities between partners	Establishing positive couplehood interaction ratio
Access-opportunity	Mediating change	Transitional (managing turning and tipping points)	Mediating ability-opportunity with access-opportunity	Striving for psychological and financial self-sufficiency
Family financial socialization	Defense against anxiety	Preservational (seeking info and financial or social support)	Renegotiating parent–adult-child relationship (fluctuating power dynamics)	Deciphering self-determination vs. help-seeking alternatives

identities between partners is essential (Mao et al., 2018; Rea et al., 2020). Achieving that positive interaction ratio and verifying the expressive function of financial capability identity involve a great deal of communication about finances as well as relationship issues among partners within the couplehood setting.

The *mediating* change identity function carries a transitional meaning that is composed of managing turning and tipping points. It is rooted in the access-opportunity dimension of financial capability (see Chapter 15).

Turning points (whether a change will occur) depend on the assessment of their resource–demand status. Tipping points rest on what the emerging adult perceives will maintain or improve their psychological and financial self-sufficiency (see Chapter 4).

Finally, the *defense against anxiety* identity function is about preservation of their identity as they experience the ever-changing conditions of their emerging adult years. The meaning of the defense function is about seeking information and financial and social support. Renegotiating the parent–adult-child relationship that involves fluctuating power dynamics is central to the emerging adult's perceptions as they maneuver to verify their developing adult identity (see Chapter 11). Their comprehensions about this newly forming parent–adult-child relationship involve deciphering self-determination (i.e., what is within their circle of influence) and when to elicit help-seeking alternatives in order to achieve their goals. An example of this defense against anxiety function is the following quote from an emerging adult who was attending a financial decision-making workshop as part of a pre-marital series: "My father was always my stopgap before making a final financial decision. I would consult with him, and if I could answer all his questions, I knew that I would be making the best decision in my current situation."

Decision execution, then, centers around ability-opportunity and access-opportunity realities (Rettig et al., 1999). These realities are the platforms that harbor the barriers or facilitators of decision execution. The financial capability identity verification meaning set, grounded in the decision-making process, serves as the motivator for financial behavior. Because perceptions and comprehensions of this meaning set are unseen, underlying decision-making phenomenon, measurable indicators will need to be determined for quantitative research, but qualitative methodologies will be more fruitful in pursuing this research direction.

Concluding Remarks

The important study of the financial journey of emerging adults and what results in a flourishing or floundering emerging adult is in its infancy. The authors of other chapters in this handbook captured what we currently know about financial literacy and how it relates to flourishing and floundering within emerging adults. This chapter's purpose was to provide a concluding statement on the current state of financial literacy research about emerging adults and to offer insight into future research directions.

The chapter also suggested questions, challenges, and ideas to consider in future research endeavors. Suggestions included: (1) developing more precise conceptual definitions, (2) collecting samples more representative of the emerging adult population, (3) collecting longitudinal data to reflect the fluctuating nature of financial decision-making and behavior over time (i.e., turning and tipping points), (4) utilizing qualitative methodologies to capture nuances of decision-making and financial capability, (5) transitioning from financial literacy to financial capability as a research focus, (6) introducing the financial capability systems theory (FCST), and (7) capturing perceptions and comprehensions underlying financial capability identity verification as motivators of the financial decision-making process.

Research about the financial journey of emerging adults needs to move from a focus on their financial literacy state to a focus on processes that create financial capability. Financial capability involves an understanding of the perceptions and comprehensions that interact with a person's knowledge base in serving as motivators for action. For example, an emerging adult may experience healthy family financial socialization (see Chapter 18) and have exposure to further financial education (see Chapter 19) but still exhibit risk-taking financial behaviors (see Chapters 5 and 6).

Seeking an understanding of the underlying decision processes of emerging adults as they verify their financial capability identity moves research beyond a behavior focus. What creates financial flourishing and floundering will become clearer as we delve to a greater degree into the meanings, perceptions, and comprehensions experienced by emerging adults as they seek to fulfill identity functions of their financial capability identity.

Directions forward include verifying the current research findings with greater sample inclusivity beyond college students. Incorporating indicators of the access-opportunity barriers and facilitators of the greater socioeconomic system provides the context that emerging adults face and over which they have little direct influence. Focusing on underlying perceptions and comprehensions of financial decision processes brings an understanding of influences that inform financial decisions and behavior beyond their financial literacy status.

Taking these actions will advance understanding of the development of financial capability identities in emerging adults and the floundering and flourishing dynamics as they progress through their financial journey. Next-step development of the FCST involves identifying testable propositions. Furthermore, combining the overarching FCST with a support-content theory targeted toward the specific research question would have a dramatic effect on understanding the financial flourishing and floundering of emerging adults.

References

Introduction

Aladangady. A., Chang, A. C., & Krimmel, J. (2023, October 18). Greater wealth, greater uncertainty: Changes in racial inequality in the Survey of Consumer Finances. Retrieved from https://www.federalreserve.gov/econres/notes/feds-notes/greater-wealth-greater-uncertainty-changes-in-racial-inequality-in-the-survey-of-consumer-finances-20231018.html

Angrisani, M., Burke, J., Lusardi, A., & Mottola, G. (2020). *The stability and predictive power of financial literacy: Evidence from longitudinal data* (Working Paper No. 28125). National Bureau of Economic Research. https://doi.org/10.3386/w28125

Angrisani, M., & Casanova, M. (2021). What you think you know can hurt you: Under/over confidence in financial knowledge and preparedness for retirement. *Journal of Pension Economics & Finance, 20*(4), 516–531. https://doi.org/10.1017/s1474747219000131

American Psychological Association. (2020, September 21). *What's the difference between stress and anxiety? Knowing the difference can ensure you get the help you need.* Retrieved from https://www.apa.org/topics/stress/anxiety-difference

Aristei, D., & Gallo, M. (2021). Financial knowledge, confidence, and sustainable financial behavior. *Sustainability, 13*(19), 10926. https://doi.org/10.3390/su131910926

Arnett, J. J. (2000). Emerging adulthood: A theory of development from the late teens through the twenties. *American Psychologist, 55*(5), 469–480. https://doi.org/10.1037//0003-066x.55.5.469

Babiarz, P., & Robb, C. A. (2014). Financial literacy and emergency saving. *Journal of Family and Economic Issues, 35*(1), 40–50. https://doi.org/10.1007/s10834-013-9369-9

Badger, S., Nelson, L. J., & Barry, C. M. (2006). Perceptions of the transition to adulthood among Chinese and American emerging adults. *International Journal of Behavioral Development, 30*(1), 84–93. https://doi.org/10.1177/0165025406062128

Bartholomae, S., & Fox, J. J. (2021). A decade review of research on college student financial behavior and well-being. *Journal of Family and Economic Issues, 42*(1), 154–177. https://doi.org/10.1007/s10834-021-09756-6

Billari, F. C., & Liefbroer, A. C. (2010). Towards a new pattern of transition to adulthood? *Advances in Life Course Research, 15*(2–3), 59–75. https://doi.org/10.1016/j.alcr.2010.10.003

Brüggen, E. C., Hogreve, J., Holmlund, M., Kabadayi, S., & Löfgren, M. (2017). Financial well-being: A conceptualization and research agenda. *Journal of Business Research, 79*, 228–237. https://doi.org/10.1016/j.jbusres.2017.03.013

Brzozowski, M., & Spotton Visano, B. (2020). "Havin' money's not everything, not havin' it is": The importance of financial satisfaction for life satisfaction in financially stressed households. *Journal of Happiness Studies, 21*(2), 573–591. https://doi.org/10.1007/s10902-019-00091-0

Carroll, J. S., Badger, S., Willoughby, B. J., Nelson, L. J., Madsen, S. D., & Barry, C. M. (2009). Ready or not? Criteria for marriage readiness among emerging adults. *Journal of Adolescent Research, 24*(3), 349–375. https://doi.org/10.1177/0743558409334253

Eisenberg, N., Losoya, S., Fabes, R. A., Guthrie, I. K., Reiser, M., Murphy, B., Shepard, S. A., Poulin, R., & Padgett, S. J. (2001). Parental socialization of children's dysregulated expression of emotion and externalizing problems. *Journal of Family Psychology, 15*, 183–205. https://doi.org/10.1037/0893-3200.15.2.183

Netemeyer, R. G., Warmath, D., Fernandes, D., & Lynch Jr., J. G. (2018). How am I doing? Perceived financial well-being, its potential antecedents, and its relation to overall well-being. *Journal of Consumer Research, 45*(1), 68–89. https://doi.org/10.1093/jcr/ucx109

Organisation for Economic Co-operation and Development. (2020a). OECD/INFE 2020 international survey of adult financial literacy. Retrieved from https://www.oecd.org/financial/education/launchoftheoecdinfeglobalfinancialliteracysurveyreport.htm

Organisation for Economic Co-operation and Development. (2020b). *Recommendation of the Council on Financial Literacy* [Legal instrument]. Retrieved from https://legalinstruments.oecd.org/en/instruments/OECD-LEGAL-0461

Pew Research Center. (2020). A majority of young adults in the U.S. live with their parents for the first time since the Great Depression. Retrieved from https://tinyurl.com/mnp62s24

Serido, J., & Deenanath, V. (2016). Financial parenting: Promoting financial self-reliance of young consumers. In J. J. Xiao (Ed.), *Handbook of consumer finance research* (pp. 291–300). Springer International. https://doi.org/10.1007/978-3-319-28887-1_24

Sinha, G., Tan, K., & Zhan, M. (2018). Patterns of financial attributes and behaviors of emerging adults in the United States. *Children and Youth Services Review, 93*, 178–185. https://doi.org/10.1016/j.childyouth.2018.07.023

Sorgente, A., & Lanz, M. (2017). Emerging adults' financial well-being: A scoping review. *Adolescent Research Review, 2*(4), 255–292. https://doi.org/10.1007/s40894-016-0052-x

Sorgente, A., & Lanz, M. (2019). The Multidimensional Subjective Financial Well-Being Scale for emerging adults: Development and validation studies. *International Journal of Behavioral Development, 43*(5), 466–478. https://doi.org/10.1177/0165025419851859

Sorgente, A., Zambelli, M., & Lanz, M. (2023). Are financial well-being and financial stress the same construct? insights from an intensive longitudinal study. *Social Indicators Research, 169*(1), 553–573. https://doi.org/10.1007/s11205-023-03171-0

Terriquez, V., & Gurantz, O. (2015). Financial challenges in emerging adulthood and students' decisions to stop out of college. *Emerging Adulthood, 3*(3), 204–214. https://doi.org/10.1177/2167696814550684

Chapter 1

Agarwalla, S. K., Barua, S. K., Jacob, J., & Varma, J. R. (2013). Financial literacy among working young in urban India (Working Paper No. 2013-10-02). Indian Institute of Management. https://doi.org/10.2139/ssrn.2338723

Ajzen, I. (2012). The theory of planned behavior. In P. A. M. Lange, A. W. Kruglanski, & E. T. Higgins (Eds.), *Handbook of theories of social psychology* (pp. 438–459). SAGE. https://doi.org/10.4135/9781446249215.n22

APEC (Asia-Pacific Economic Cooperation). (2014). *APEC guidebook on financial and economic literacy in basic education.* https://www.apec.org/docs/default-source/publications/2014/11/apec-guidebook-on-financial-and-economic-literacy-in-basic-education/apec-guidebook-on-financial-and-economic-literacy-final-formated_251114.pdf?sfvrsn=6ad1dea3_1

Aren, S., & Dinç Aydemir, S. (2014). A literature review on financial literacy. *Finansal Araştırmalar ve Çalışmalar Dergisi, 11*(6), 33–49. https://doi.org/10.14784/JFRS.2014117326

Arnett, J. J. (2015). *The winding road from the late teens through the twenties* (2nd ed.). Oxford University Press. https://doi.org/10.1093/acprof:oso/9780199929382.001.0001

Atkinson, A., & Messy, F. (2012). *Measuring financial literacy: Results of the OECD/International Network on Financial Education (INFE) pilot study* (Working Paper on Finance, Insurance and Private Pensions No. 15). OECD. https://doi.org/10.1787/5k9csfs90fr4-en

Bajaj, I., & Kaur, M. (2022). Validating multi-dimensional model of financial literacy using confirmatory factor analysis. *Managerial Finance, 48*(9/10), 1488–1512. https://doi.org/10.1108/MF-06-2021-0285

Bernheim, B. D., & Garrett, D. M. (2003). The effects of financial education in the workplace: Evidence from a survey of households. *Journal of Public Economics, 87*(7–8), 1487–1519. https://doi.org/10.1016/S0047-2727(01)00184-0

Breitbach, E., & Walstad, W. B. (2016). Financial literacy and financial behavior among young adults in the United States. In E. Wuttke, J. Seifried, & S. Schumann (Eds.), *Economic competence and financial literacy of young adults: Status and challenges* (Vol. 3, pp. 81–98). Verlag Barbara Budrich. https://doi.org/10.2307/j.ctvbkk29d.7

Danes, S. M., & Haberman, H. R. (2007). Teen financial knowledge, self-efficacy, and behavior: A gendered view. *Financial Counselling and Planning, 18*(2), 48–60.

Delgadillo, L. M. (2014). Financial clarity: Education, literacy, capability, counselling, planning, and coaching. *Family and Consumer Sciences Research Journal, 43*(1), 18–28. https://doi.org/10.1111/fcsr.12078

Dewi, V. I., Febrian, E., Effendi, N., Anwar, M., & Nidar, S. R. (2020). Financial literacy and its variables: The evidence from Indonesia. *Economics and Sociology, 13*(3), 133–154. https://doi.org/10.14254/2071-789X.2020/13-3/9

Fernandes, D., Lynch, J. G., Jr., & Netemeyer, R. G. (2014). Financial literacy, financial education, and downstream financial behaviors. *Management Science, 60*(8), 1861–1883. https://doi.org/10.1287/mnsc.2013.1849

Firli, A. (2017). Factors that influence financial literacy: A conceptual framework. *IOP Conference Series: Materials Science and Engineering, 180*, Article 012254. https://doiorg/10.1088/1757-899X/180/1/012254

Gale, W. G., & Levine, R. E. (2010). Financial literacy: What works? How could it be more effective? *SSRN eJournal*. https://doi.org/10.2139/ssrn.2316933

Garg, N., & Singh, S. (2018). Financial literacy among youth. *International Journal of Social Economics, 45*(1), 173–186. https://doi.org/10.1108/IJSE-11-2016-0303

Gudmunson, C. G., & Danes, S. M. (2011). Family financial socialization: Theory and critical review. *Journal of Family and Economic Issues, 32*(4), 644–667. https://doi.org/10.1007/s10834-011-9275-y

Guiso, L., & Viviano, E. (2015). How much can financial literacy help? *Review of Finance, 19*(4), 1347–1382. https://doi.org/10.1093/rof/rfu033

Hung, A. A., Parker, A. M., & Yoong, J. K. (2009). *Defining and measuring financial literacy* (Working Paper No. WR-708). RAND Corporation. https://doi.org/10.7249/wr708

Huston, S. J. (2010). Measuring financial literacy. *Journal of Consumer Affairs, 44*(2), 296–316. https://doi.org/10.1111/j.1745-6606.2010.01170.x

Jorgensen, B. L., & Savla, J. (2010). Financial literacy of young adults: The importance of parental socialization. *Family Relations: An Interdisciplinary Journal of Applied Family Studies, 59*(4), 465–478. https://doi.org/10.1111/j.1741-3729.2010.00616.x

Kartini, K., Fitri, F., Rabiyah, U., & Anggraeni, D. (2020). Analysis of the financial literacy behavior model. *Golden Ratio of Finance Management, 1*(2), 114–122. https://doi.org/10.52970/grfm.v1i2.69

Kempson, E., Finney, A., & Poppe, C. (2017). *Financial well-being: A conceptual model and preliminary analysis* (Project Note No. 3-2017). SIFO Consumption Research Norway. https://doi.org/10.13140/RG.2.2.18737.68961

Klontz, B. T., & Britt, S. L. (2012). How clients' money scripts predict their financial behaviors. *Journal of Financial Planning, 25*(11), 33–43.

Klontz, B., & Klontz, T. (2009). *Mind over money: Overcoming the money disorders that threaten our financial health.* Crown Business.

Kovács, L., & Terták, E. (2019). *Financial literacy:Theory and evidence.* Verlag Dashöfer.
Kunovskaya, I. A., Cude, B. J., & Alexeev, N. (2014). Evaluation of a financial literacy test using classical test theory and item response theory. *Journal of Family and Economic Issues, 35*(4), 516–531. https://doi.org/10.1007/s10834-013-9386-8
Lawson, D., Klontz, B. T., & Britt, S. L. (2015). Money scripts. In B. T. Klontz, S. L. Britt, & K. L. Archuleta (Eds.), *Financial therapy: Theory, research, and practice* (pp. 23–34). Springer International. https://doi.org/10.1007/978-3-319-08269-1_3
LeBaron, A. B., & Kelley, H. H. (2021). Financial socialization: A decade in review. *Journal of Family and Economic Issues, 42,* 195–206. https://doi.org/10.1007/s10834-020-09736-2
Lep, Ž., Zupančič, M., & Poredoš, M. (2021). Saving of freshmen and their parents in Slovenia: Saving motives and links to parental financial socialization. *Journal of Family and Economic Issues, 43*(4), 756–773. https://doi.org/10.1007/s10834-021-09789-x
Lusardi, A. (2015). Financial literacy skills for the 21st century: Evidence from PISA. *Journal of Consumer Affairs, 49*(3), 639–659. https://doi.org/10.1111/joca.12099
Lusardi, A., & Mitchell, O. S. (2011). Financial literacy around the world: An overview. *Journal of Pension Economics and Finance, 10*(4), 497–508. https://doi.org/10.1017/S1474747211000448
Lusardi, A., & Mitchell, O. S. (2014). The economic importance of financial literacy: Theory and evidence. *Journal of Economic Literature, 52*(1), 5–44. https://doi.org/10.1257/jel.52.1.5
Maio, G. R., Haddock, G., & Verplanken, B. (2018). *The psychology of attitudes and attitude change.* SAGE.
Mandell, L. (2008). Financial literacy of high school students. In J. J. Xiao (Ed.), *Handbook of consumer finance research* (pp. 163–183). Springer. https://doi.org/10.1007/978-0-387-75734-6_10
Mandell, L. (2009). The impact of financial education in high school and college on financial literacy and subsequent financial decision making. Meeting of American Economic Association, San Francisco, CA.
Moschis, G. P. (1987). *Consumer socialization: A life-cycle perspective.* Lexington Books.
Noctor, M., Stoney, S., & Stradling, R. (1992). *Financial literacy: A discussion of concepts and competences of financial literacy and opportunities for its introduction into young people's learning.* National Foundation for Educational Research.
Nolan, B., Richiardi, M. G., & Valenzuela, L. (2019). The drivers of income inequality in rich countries. *Journal of Economic Surveys, 33*(4), 1285–1324. https://doi.org/10.1111/joes.12328
OECD. (2019). *PISA 2021 financial literacy analytical and assessment framework.*
OECD/INFE. (2012). *High-level principles on national strategies for financial education.* https://doi.org/10.1787/12e3989f-en
Otto, A. (2013). Saving in childhood and adolescence: Insights from developmental psychology. *Economics of Education Review, 33,* 8–18. https://doi.org/10.1016/j.econedurev.2012.09.005
Özkale, A., & Özdemir Erdoğan, E. (2022). Review of financial literacy models for educational studies. *HAYEF: Journal of Education, 19*(1), 61–70. https://doi.org/10.5152/hayef.2022.21050
Potrich, A. C. G., & Vieira, K. M. (2018). Demystifying financial literacy: A behavioral perspective analysis. *Management Research Review, 41*(9), 1047–1068. https://doi.org/10.1108/MRR-08-2017-0263
Potrich, A. C. G., Vieira, K. M., & Mendes-Da-Silva, W. (2016). Development of a financial literacy model for university students. *Management Research Review, 39*(3), 356–376. https://doi.org/10.1108/MRR-06-2014-0143

Remund, D. L. (2010). Financial literacy explicated: The case for a clearer definition in an increasingly complex economy. *Journal of Consumer Affairs, 44*(2), 276–295. https://doi.org/10.1111/j.1745-6606.2010.01169.x

Shim, S., Barber, B. L., Card, N. A., Xiao, J. J., & Serido, J. (2010). Financial socialization of first-year college students: The roles of parents, work, and education. *Journal of Youth and Adolescence, 39*(12), 1457–1470. https://doi.org/10.1007/s10964-009-9432-x

Sirsch, U., Zupančič, M., Poredoš, M., Levec, K., & Friedlmeier, M. (2020). Does parental financial socialization for emerging adults matter? The case of Austrian and Slovene first-year university students. *Emerging Adulthood, 8*(6), 509–520. https://doi.org/10.1177/2167696819882178

Świecka, B. (2019). A theoretical framework for financial literacy and financial education. In B. Świecka, A. Grzesiuk, D. Korczak, & O. Wyszkowska-Kaniewska (Eds.), *Financial literacy and financial education: Theory and survey* (pp. 1–12). De Gruyter Oldenbourg. https://doi.org/10.1515/9783110636956-001

Thomas, A., & Spataro, L. (2018). Financial literacy, human capital and stock market participation in Europe. *Journal of Family and Economic Issues, 39*(4), 532–550. https://doi.org/10.1007/s10834-018-9576-5

Totenhagen, C. J., Casper, D. M., Faber, K. M., Bosch, L. A., Bracamonte Wiggs, C., & Borden, L. M. (2015). Youth financial literacy: A review of key considerations and promising delivery methods. *Journal of Family and Economic Issues, 36*(2), 167–191. https://doi.org/10.1007/s10834-014-9397-0

van Rooij, M., Lusardi, A., & Alessie, R. (2011). Financial literacy and stock market participation. *Journal of Financial Economics, 101*(2), 449–472. https://doi.org/10.1016/j.jfineco.2011.03.006

van Rooij, M. C., Lusardi, A., & Alessie, R. J. (2012). Financial literacy, retirement planning and household wealth. *The Economic Journal, 122*(560), 449–478. https://doi.org/10.1111/j.1468-0297.2012.02501.x

Vieira, K. M., Potrich, A. C. G., & Mendes-Da-Silva, W. (2019). A financial literacy model for university students. In W. Mendes-Da-Silva (Ed.), *Individual behaviors and technologies for financial innovations* (pp. 69–95). Springer. https://doi.org/10.1007/978-3-319-91911-9_4

Ward, S. (1974). Consumer socialization. *The Journal of Consumer Research, 1*(2), 1–14. https://doi.org/10.1086/208584

Warmath, D., & Zimmerman, D. (2019). Financial literacy as more than knowledge: The development of a formative scale through the lens of Bloom's domains of knowledge. *The Journal of Consumer Affairs, 53*(4), 1602–1629. https://doi.org/10.1111/joca.12286

Xiao, J. J., Chen, C., & Chen, F. (2014). Consumer financial capability and financial satisfaction. *Social Indicators Research, 118*(1), 415–432. https://doi.org/10.1007/s11205-013-0414-8

Zupančič, M., Poredoš, M., & Lep, Ž. (2023). Intergenerational model of financial satisfaction and parent-child financial relationship. *Journal of Social and Personal Relationships*, Advance online publication, *40*(8), 2568-2591. https://doi.org/10.1177/02654075231153352

Chapter 2

Agnew, J. R., Bateman, H., & Thorp, S. (2013). Financial literacy and retirement planning in Australia. *Numeracy, 6*(2), 1–25. https://doi.org/10.5038/1936-4660.6.2.7

Ali, S., & Talha, N. (2022). During COVID-19, impact of subjective and objective financial knowledge and economic insecurity on financial management behavior: Mediating role of financial wellbeing. *Journal of Public Affairs, 22*, e2789. https://doi.org/10.1002/pa.2789

Allgood, S., & Walstad, W. (2013). Financial literacy and credit card behaviors: A cross-sectional analysis by age. *Numeracy*, *6*(2), 3. https://doi.org/10.5038/1936-4660.6.2.3

Allgood, S., & Walstad, W. (2016). The effects of perceived and actual financial literacy on financial behaviors. *Economic Inquiry*, *54*(1), 675–697. https://doi.org/10.1111/ecin.12255

Arnett, J. J. (2014). *Emerging adulthood: The winding road from the late teens through the twenties.* Oxford University Press. https://doi.org/10.1093/acprof:oso/9780199929382.001.0001

Babiarz, P., & Robb, C. A. (2014). Financial literacy and emergency saving. *Journal of Family and Economic Issues*, *35*, 40–50. https://doi.org/10.1007/s10834-013-9369-9

Birmingham, W. C., Wadsworth, L. L., Lassetter, J. H., Graff, T. C., Lauren, E., & Hung, M. (2023). COVID-19 lockdown: Impact on college students' lives. *Journal of American College Health*, *71*(3), 879–893. https://doi.org/10.1080/07448481.2021.1909041

Boisclair, D., Lusardi, A., & Michaud, P. C. (2017). Financial literacy and retirement planning in Canada. *Journal of Pension Economics & Finance*, *16*(3), 277–296. https://doi.org/10.1017/S1474747215000311

Britt, S. L., Canale, A., Fernatt, F., Stutz, K., & Tibbetts, R. (2015). Financial stress and financial counseling: Helping college students. *Journal of Financial Counseling and Planning*, *26*(2), 172–186. https://doi.org/10.1891/1052-3073.26.2.172

Carlsson Hauff, J., & Nilsson, J. (2020). Determinants of indebtedness among young adults: Impacts of lender guidelines, explicit information and financial (over) confidence. *International Journal of Consumer Studies*, *44*(2), 89–98. https://doi.org/10.1111/ijcs.12549

Council for Economic Education. (2022). *Survey of the states: Economic and personal finance education in our nation's schools.* Retrieved from https://www.councilforeconed.org/wp-content/uploads/2022/03/2022-SURVEY-OF-THE-STATES.pdf

Cude, B. J., Chatterjee, S., & Tavosi, J. (2019). Financial knowledge among Iranian investors. *International Journal of Consumer Studies*, *43*(6), 503–513. https://doi.org/10.1111/ijcs.12535

de Bassa Scheresberg, C. (2013). Financial literacy and financial behavior among young adults: Evidence and implications. *Numeracy*, *6*(2), 5. https://doi.org/10.5038/1936-4660.6.2.5

Flynn, L. R., & Goldsmith, R. E. (1999). A short, reliable measure of subjective knowledge. *Journal of Business Research*, *46*(1), 57–66. https://doi.org/10.1016/S0148-2963(98)00057-5

García, J., Gómez, Y., & Vila, J. (2022). Financial overconfidence, promotion of financial advice, and aging. *Journal of Business Research*, *145*, 325–333. https://doi.org/10.1016/j.jbusres.2022.02.068

Gerrans, P. (2021). Undergraduate student financial education interventions: Medium term evidence of retention, decay, and confidence in financial literacy. *Pacific-Basin Finance Journal*, *67*, 101552. https://doi.org/10.1016/j.pacfin.2021.101552

Gerrans, P., & Heaney, R. (2019). The impact of undergraduate personal finance education on individual financial literacy, attitudes and intentions. *Accounting & Finance*, *59*(1), 177–217. https://doi.org/10.1111/acfi.12247

Goldsmith, R. E., & Goldsmith, E. B. (2006). The effects of investment education on gender differences in financial knowledge. *Journal of Personal Finance*, *5*(2), 55–69.

Hastings, J. S., Madrian, B. C., & Skimmyhorn, W. L. (2013). Financial literacy, financial education, and economic outcomes. *Annual Review of Economics*, *5*(1), 347–373. https://doi.org/10.1146/annurev-economics-082312-125807

Henager, R., & Cude, B. J. (2016). Financial literacy and long-and short-term financial behavior in different age groups. *Journal of Financial Counseling and Planning*, *27*(1), 3–19. https://doi.org/10.1891/1052-3073.27.1.3

Heo, W., Rabbani, A. G., & Lee, J. M. (2021). Mediation between financial risk tolerance and equity ownership: Assessing the role of financial knowledge underconfidence. *Journal of Financial Services Marketing*, *26*, 169–180. https://doi.org/10.1057/s41264-021-00088-y

Jacobs-Lawson, J. M., & Hershey, D. A. (2005). Influence of future time perspective, financial knowledge, and financial risk tolerance on retirement saving behaviors. *Financial Services Review, 14*(4), 331–344.

Jorgensen, B. L., & Savla, J. (2010). Financial literacy of young adults: The importance of parental socialization. *Family Relations, 59*(4), 465–478. https://doi.org/10.1111/j.1741-3729.2010.00616.x

Kadoya, Y., & Khan, M. S. R. (2020). What determines financial literacy in Japan? *Journal of Pension Economics & Finance, 19*(3), 353–371. https://doi.org/10.1017/S1474747218000379

Khan, M. N., Rothwell, D. W., Cherney, K., & Sussman, T. (2017). Understanding the financial knowledge gap: A new dimension of inequality in later life. *Journal of Gerontological Social Work, 60*(6-7), 487–503. https://doi.org/10.1080/01634372.2017.1317311

Kim, K. T., Anderson, S. G., & Seay, M. C. (2019). Financial knowledge and short-term and long-term financial behaviors of millennials in the United States. *Journal of Family and Economic Issues, 40*, 194–208. https://doi.org/10.1007/s10834-018-9595-2

Kim, K. T., Wilmarth, M. J., & Henager, R. (2017). Poverty levels and debt indicators among low-income households before and after the Great Recession. *Journal of Financial Counseling and Planning, 28*(2), 196–212. https://doi.org/10.1891/1052-3073.28.2.196

Kim, K. T., & Yuh, Y. (2018). Financial knowledge and household savings: Evidence from the survey of consumer finances. *Family & Consumer Sciences Research Journal, 47*(1), 5–24. https://doi.org/10.1111/fcsr.12270

Klapper, L., & Lusardi, A. (2019). Financial literacy and financial resilience: Evidence from around the world. *Financial Management, 49*(3), 1–26. https://doi.org/10.1111/fima.12283

Knoll, M. A. Z., & Houts, C. R. (2012). The financial knowledge scale: An application of item response theory to the assessment of financial literacy. *Journal of Consumer Affairs, 46*(3), 381–410. https://doi.org/10.1111/j.1745-6606.2012.01241.x

Kunovskaya, I. A., Cude, B. J., & Alexeev, N. (2014). Evaluation of a financial literacy test using classical test theory and item response theory. *Journal of Family and Economic Issues, 35*, 516–531. https://doi.org/10.1007/s10834-013-9386-8

Larson, L. R., Eastman, J. K., & Bock, D. E. (2016). A multi-method exploration of the relationship between knowledge and risk: The impact on millennials' retirement investment decisions. *Journal of Marketing Theory and Practice, 24*(1), 72–90. https://doi.org/10.1080/10696679.2016.1089765

LeBaron, A. B., & Kelley, H. H. (2021). Financial socialization: A decade in review. *Journal of Family and Economic Issues, 42*(Suppl. 1), 195–206. https://doi.org/10.1007/s10834-020-09736-2

LeBaron-Black, A. B., Yorgason, J. B., Curran, M. A., Saxey, M. T., & Okamoto, R. M. (2022). The ABC-X's of stress among US emerging adults during the COVID-19 pandemic: Relationship quality, financial distress, and mental health. *International Journal of Environmental Research and Public Health, 19*(20), 13125. https://doi.org/10.3390/ijerph192013125

Lee, S. T., & Hanna, S. D. (2022). What, me worry? Financial knowledge overconfidence and the perception of emergency fund needs. *Journal of Financial Counseling and Planning, 33*(1), 140–155. https://doi.org/10.1891/JFCP-2021-0045

Lee, S. T., & Kim, K. T. (2020). Propensity to plan, financial knowledge, overconfidence, and credit card management behaviors of millennials. *Family and Consumer Sciences Research Journal, 49*(2), 123–143. https://doi.org/10.1111/fcsr.12381

Lee, S. T., & Kim, K. T. (2022). A decomposition analysis of racial/ethnic differences in financial knowledge and overconfidence. *Journal of Family and Economic Issues, 43*(4), 815–831. https://doi.org/10.1007/s10834-021-09795-z

Letkiewicz, J. C., & Fox, J. J. (2014). Conscientiousness, financial literacy, and asset accumulation of young adults. *Journal of Consumer Affairs, 48*(2), 274–300. https://doi.org/10.1111/joca.12040

Li, X. (2020). When financial literacy meets textual analysis: A conceptual review. *Journal of Behavioral and Experimental Finance, 28*, 100402. https://doi.org/10.1016/j.jbef.2020.100402

Lim, T. S., Mail, R., Abd Karim, M. R., Ulum, Z. K. A. B., Jaidi, J., & Noordin, R. (2018). A serial mediation model of financial knowledge on the intention to invest: The central role of risk perception and attitude. *Journal of Behavioral and Experimental Finance, 20*, 74–79. https://doi.org/10.1016/j.jbef.2018.08.001

Liu, L., & Zhang, H. (2021). Financial literacy, self-efficacy and risky credit behavior among college students: Evidence from online consumer credit. *Journal of Behavioral and Experimental Finance, 32*, 100569. https://doi.org/10.1016/j.jbef.2021.100569

Lusardi, A. (2019). Financial literacy and the need for financial education: Evidence and implications. *Swiss Journal of Economics and Statistics, 155*(1), 1–8. https://doi.org/10.1186/s41937-019-0027-5

Lusardi, A., Michaud, P. C., & Mitchell, O. S. (2017). Optimal financial knowledge and wealth inequality. *Journal of Political Economy, 125*(2), 431–477. https://doi.org/10.1086/690950

Lusardi, A., & Mitchell, O. S. (2007). *Financial literacy and retirement planning: New evidence from the RAND American Life Panel* (Michigan Retirement Research Center Research Paper No. 157). https://doi.org/10.2139/ssrn.1095869

Lusardi, A., & Mitchell, O. S. (2011). *Financial literacy and planning: Implications for retirement wellbeing* (Publication No. w17078). National Bureau of Economic Research. https://doi.org/10.3386/w17078

Lusardi, A., & Mitchell, O. S. (2017). How ordinary consumers make complex economic decisions: Financial literacy and retirement readiness. *Quarterly Journal of Finance, 7*(03), 1750008. https://doi.org/10.1142/S2010139217500082

Lusardi, A., Mitchell, O. S., & Curto, V. (2010). Financial literacy among the young. *Journal of Consumer Affairs, 44*(2), 358–380. https://doi.org/10.1111/j.1745-6606.2010.01173.x

McCannon, B. C., Asaad, C. T., & Wilson, M. (2016). Financial competence, overconfidence, and trusting investments: Results from an experiment. *Journal of Economics and Finance, 40*, 590–606. https://doi.org/10.1007/s12197-015-9328-4

Mitchell, O. S., & Lusardi, A. (2015). Financial literacy and economic outcomes: Evidence and policy implications. *The Journal of Retirement, 3*(1), 107–114. https://doi.org/10.3905/jor.2015.3.1.107

Moher, D., Liberati, A., Tetzlaff, J., Altman, D. G., & Prisma Group. (2010). Preferred reporting items for systematic reviews and meta-analyses: The PRISMA statement. *International Journal of Surgery, 8*(5), 336–341. https://doi.org/10.1016/j.ijsu.2010.02.007

Moore, D. A., & Healy, P. J. (2008). The trouble with overconfidence. *Psychological Review, 115*(2), 502–517. https://doi.org/10.1037/0033-295X.115.2.502

Nejad, M. G., & Javid, K. (2018). Subjective and objective financial literacy, opinion leadership, and the use of retail banking services. *International Journal of Bank Marketing, 36*(4), 784–804. https://doi.org/10.1108/IJBM-07-2017-0153

Porto, N., & Xiao, J. J. (2016). Financial literacy overconfidence and financial advice seeking. *Journal of Financial Service Professionals, 70*(4), 78–88.

O'Connor, G. E. (2019). Exploring the interplay of cognitive style and demographics in consumers' financial knowledge. *Journal of Consumer Affairs, 53*(2), 382–423. https://doi.org/10.1111/joca.12195

OECD. (2020). *OECD/INFE 2020 international survey of adult financial literacy.* Retrieved from https://www.oecd.org/financial/education/oecd-infe-2020-international-survey-of-adult-financial-literacy.pdf

Perry, V. G., & Morris, M. D. (2005). Who is in control? The role of self-perception, knowledge, and income in explaining consumer financial behavior. *Journal of Consumer Affairs, 39*(2), 299–313. https://doi.org/10.1111/j.1745-6606.2005.00016.x

Rabbani, A. G., Heo, W., & Lee, J. M. (2022). A latent profile analysis of college students' financial knowledge: The role of financial education, financial well-being, and financial risk tolerance. *Journal of Education for Business, 97*(2), 112–118. https://doi.org/10.1080/08832323.2021.1895046

Reyes-Portillo, J. A., Masia Warner, C., Kline, E. A., Bixter, M. T., Chu, B. C., Miranda, R., ... Jeglic, E. L. (2022). The psychological, academic, and economic impact of COVID-19 on college students in the epicenter of the pandemic. *Emerging Adulthood, 10*(2), 473–490. https://doi.org/10.1177/21676968211066657

Richardson, J., Alpert, K., Tanner, M., & Birt, J. (2022). Financial literacy and retirement spending: A university student perspective. *Australian Accounting Review, 32*(3), 367–387. https://doi.org/10.1111/auar.12377

Robb, C. A. (2011). Financial knowledge and credit card behavior of college students. *Journal of Family and Economic Issues, 32*, 690–698. https://doi.org/10.1007/s10834-011-9259-y

Robb, C. A., Babiarz, P., Woodyard, A., & Seay, M. C. (2015). Bounded rationality and use of alternative financial services. *Journal of Consumer Affairs, 49*(2), 407–435. https://doi.org/10.1111/joca.12071

Rothwell, D. W., & Wu, S. (2019). Exploring the relationship between financial education and financial knowledge and efficacy: Evidence from the Canadian financial capability survey. *Journal of Consumer Affairs, 53*(4), 1725–1747. https://doi.org/10.1111/joca.12259

Salas-Velasco, M. (2022). Causal effects of financial education intervention aimed at university students on financial knowledge and financial self-efficacy. *Journal of Risk and Financial Management, 15*(7), 284. https://doi.org/10.3390/jrfm15070284

Sconti, A. (2022). Digital vs. in-person financial education: What works best for Generation Z? *Journal of Economic Behavior & Organization, 194*, 300–318. https://doi.org/10.1016/j.jebo.2021.12.001

Sironi, M. (2018). Economic conditions of young adults before and after the Great Recession. *Journal of Family and Economic Issues, 39*(1), 103–116. https://doi.org/10.1007/s10834-017-9554-3

Smith, C., & Barboza, G. (2014). The role of trans-generational financial knowledge and self-reported financial literacy on borrowing practices and debt accumulation of college students. *Journal of Personal Finance, 13*(2), 28–50. https://doi.org/10.2139/ssrn.2342168

Tang, N., & Baker, A. (2016). Self-esteem, financial knowledge and financial behavior. *Journal of Economic Psychology, 54*, 164–176. https://doi.org/10.1016/j.joep.2016.04.005

Tenney, J., Kalenkoski, C., & Serido, J. (2021). Where knowledge meets perceptions: Emerging adults and their perceptions of financial knowledge. *Journal of Personal Finance, 20*(2), 89–101.

Tokar Asaad, C. (2015). Financial literacy and financial behavior: Assessing knowledge and confidence. *Financial Services Review, 24*(2), 101–117. https://doi.org/10.61190/fsr.v24i2.3236

Totenhagen, C. J., Casper, D. M., Faber, K. M., Bosch, L. A., Wiggs, C. B., & Borden, L. M. (2015). Youth financial literacy: A review of key considerations and promising delivery methods. *Journal of Family and Economic Issues, 36*, 167–191. https://doi.org/10.1007/s10834-014-9397-0

Totenhagen, C. J., Wilmarth, M. J., Serido, J., Curran, M. A., & Shim, S. (2019). Pathways from financial knowledge to relationship satisfaction: The roles of financial behaviors, perceived shared financial values with the romantic partner, and debt. *Journal of Family and Economic Issues, 40*, 423–437. https://doi.org/10.1007/s10834-019-09611-9

Xiao, J. J., & Porto, N. (2017). Financial education and financial satisfaction: Financial literacy, behavior, and capability as mediators. *International Journal of Bank Marketing, 35*(5), 805–817. https://doi.org/10.1108/IJBM-01-2016-0009

Xiao, J. J., Tang, C., Serido, J., & Shim, S. (2011). Antecedents and consequences of risky credit behavior among college students: Application and extension of the theory of planned behavior. *Journal of Public Policy & Marketing, 30*(2), 239–245. https://doi.org/10.1509/jppm.30.2.239

Xiao, X., Li, X., & Zhou, Y. (2022). Financial literacy overconfidence and investment fraud victimization. *Economics Letters, 212*, 110308. https://doi.org/10.1016/j.econlet.2022.110308

Chapter 3

Almenberg, J., & Gerdes, C. (2012). Exponential growth bias and financial literacy. *Applied Economics Letters, 19*(17), 1693–1696. https://doi.org/10.1080/13504851.2011.652772

Asebedo, S. D., Wilmarth, M. J., Seay, M. C., Archuleta, K., Brase, G. L., & MacDonald, M. (2019). Personality and saving behavior among older adults. *Journal of Consumer Affairs, 53*(2), 488–519. https://doi.org/10.1111/joca.12199

Ashby, N. J. S. (2017). Numeracy predicts preference consistency: Deliberative search heuristics increase choice consistency for choices from description and experience. *Judgment and Decision Making, 12*(2), 128–139. https://doi.org/10.1017/S1930297500005672

Barton, D. (2006). Significance of a social practice view of language, literacy, and numeracy. In L. Tett, M. Hamilton, & Y. Hillier (Eds.), *Adult literacy, numeracy, and language: Policy, practice, and research* (pp. 21–30). Open University Press.

Bishop, J. P. (2012). "She's always been the smart one. I've always been the dumb one": Identities in the mathematics classroom. *Journal for Research in Mathematics Education, 43*(1), 34–74. https://doi.org/10.5951/jresematheduc.43.1.0034

Braze, D., Tabor, W., Shankweiler, D. P., & Mencl, W. E. (2007). Speaking up for vocabulary: Reading skill differences in young adults. *Journal of Learning Disabilities, 40*(3), 226–243. https://doi.org/10.1177/00222194070400030401

Brounen, D., Koedijk, K., & Pownall, R. A. J. (2015). Household financial planning and savings behavior. *Journal of International Money and Finance, 69*, 95–107. https://doi.org/10.1016/j.jimonfin.2016.06.011

Bucciol, A., & Luca, Z. (2019). Saving education received in early life and future orientation in adulthood. *Journal of Financial Counseling and Planning, 30*(1), 67–82. https://doi.org/10.1891/1052-3073.30.1.67

Butterfuss, R., & Kendeou, P. (2018). The role of executive functions in reading comprehension. *Educational Psychology Review, 30*, 801–826.

Bruin, W. B., & Slovic, P. (2021). Low numeracy is associated with poor financial well-being around the world. *PLOS ONE, 16*(11). https://doi.org/10.1371/journal.pone.0260378

Clark, L., Bechara, A., Damasio, H., Aitken, M. R. F., Sahakian, B. J., & Robbins, T. (2008). Differential effects of insular and ventromedial prefrontal cortex lesions on risky decision-making. *Brain, 131*(5), 1311–1322. https://doi.org/10.1093/brain/awn066

Dare, S. E., van Dijk, W. W., van Dijk, E., van Dillen, L. F., Gallucci, M., & Simonse, O. (2022). How executive functioning and financial self-efficacy predict subjective financial well-being via positive financial behaviors. *Journal of Family and Economic Issues*, 1–17. https://doi.org/10.1007/s10834-022-09845-0

Davis, O. S., Band, G., Pirinen, M., Haworth, C. M., Meaburn, E. L., Kovas, Y., . . . Spencer, C. C. (2014). The correlation between reading and mathematics ability at age twelve has a substantial genetic component. *Nature Communications, 5*(1), 4204. https://doi.org/10.1038/ncomms5204

Diamond, A., & Lee, K. (2011). Interventions shown to aid executive function development in children 4 to 12 years old. *Science, 333*(6045), 959–964. https://doi.org/10.1126/science.1204529

Drever, A. I., Odders-White, E., Kalish, C. W., Else-Quest, N. M., Hoagland, E. M., & Nelms, E. N. (2015). Foundations of financial well-being: Insights into the role of executive function, financial socialization, and experience-based learning in childhood and youth. *Journal of Consumer Affairs, 49*(1), 13–38. https://doi.org/10.1111/joca.12068

Elder, L., & Paul, R. (2004). Critical thinking . . . and the art of close reading (part II). *Journal of Developmental Education, 27*(3), 36–37.

Ersner-Hershfield, H., Wimmer, G. E., & Knutson, B. (2009). Saving for the future self: Neural measures of future self-continuity predict temporal discounting. *Social Cognitive and Affective Neuroscience, 4*(1), 85–92. https://doi.org/10.1093/scan/nsn042

Estrada-Mejia, C., de Vries, M., & Zeelenberg, M. (2016). Numeracy and wealth. *Journal of Economic Psychology, 54*, 53–63. https://doi.org/10.1016/j.joep.2016.02.011

Garcia-Retamero, R., Sobkow, A., Petrova, D., Garrido, D., & Traczyk, J. (2019). Numeracy and risk literacy: What have we learned so far? *The Spanish Journal of Psychology, 22*(e10), 1–11. https://doi.org/10.1017/sjp.2019.16

Goda, G. S., Levy, M., Manchester, C. F., Sojourner, A., & Tasoff, J. (2019). Predicting retirement savings using survey measures of exponential-growth bias and present bias. *Economic Inquiry, 57*(3), 1636–1658. https://doi.org/10.1111/ecin.12792

Grissom, N. M., & Reyes, T. M. (2019). Let's call the whole thing off: Evaluating gender and sex differences in executive function. *Neuropsychopharmacology, 44*(1), 86–96. https://doi.org/10.1038/s41386-018-0179-5

Guiney, H., & Machado, L. (2013). Benefits of regular aerobic exercise for executive functioning in healthy populations. *Psychonomic Bulletin & Review, 20*, 73–86.

Guo, G., & Harris, K. M. (2000). The mechanisms mediating the effects of poverty on children's intellectual development. *Demography, 37*, 431–447. https://doi.org/10.1353/dem.2000.0005

Harvard Business Publishing. (n.d.). *Simulations.* Retrieved from https://hbsp.harvard.edu/simulations

Lane, M., & Conlon, G. (2016), *The impact of literacy, numeracy and computer skills on earnings and employment outcomes* (Education Working Paper No. 129). OECD. https://doi.org/10.1787/5jm2cv4t4gzs-en

Johnson, E. D., & Tubau, E. (2013). Words, numbers, and numeracy: Diminishing individual differences in Bayesian reasoning. *Learning and Individual Differences, 28*, 34–40. https://doi.org/10.1016/j.lindif.2013.09.004

Johnson, S. B., Blum, R. W., & Giedd, J. N. (2009). Adolescent maturity and the brain: The promise and pitfalls of neuroscience research in adolescent health policy. *Journal of Adolescent Health, 45*(3), 216–221.

Jonas, N. (2018). *Numeracy practices and numeracy skills among adults* (Education Working Paper No. 177). OECD. https://doi.org/10.1787/8f19fc9f-en

Mania, E., & Tröster, M. (2017). *The financial literacy competence model.* Project CurVe. Retrieved from https://www.die-curve.de/content/pdf/DIE_Competence_Model-engl.pdf

Masarik, A. S., & Conger, R. D. (2017). Stress and child development: A review of the family stress model. *Current Opinion in Psychology, 13*, 85–90.

Moffitt, T. E., Arseneault, L., Belsky, D., Dickson, N., Hancox, R. J., Harrington, H., . . . Caspi, A. (2011). A gradient of childhood self-control predicts health, wealth, and public safety. *Proceedings of the National Academy of Sciences, 108*(7), 2693–2698.

Mol, S. E., & Bus, A. G. (2011). To read or not to read: A meta-analysis of print exposure from infancy to early adulthood. *Psychological Bulletin, 137*(2), 267.

Moretti, L., Dragone, D., & Di Pellegrino, G. (2009). Reward and social valuation deficits following ventromedial prefrontal damage. *Journal of Cognitive Neuroscience, 21*(1), 128–140.

Parkinson, J. (2015). The potential for school-based interventions that target executive function to improve academic achievement: A review. *Review of Educational Research, 85*(4), 512–552.

Raver, C. C., Blair, C., & Willoughby, M. (2013). Poverty as a predictor of 4-year-olds' executive function: New perspectives on models of differential susceptibility. *Developmental Psychology, 49*(2), 292.

Reardon, S. F., Valentino, R. A., & Shores, K. A. (2012). Patterns of literacy among US students. *The Future of Children, 22*(2), 17–37.

Roberts, S. O., Bareket-Shavit, C., Dollins, F. A., Goldie, P. D., & Mortenson, E. (2020). Racial inequality in psychological research: Trends of the past and recommendations for the future. *Perspectives on Psychological Science, 15*(6), 1295–1309.

Sages, R. A., & Grable, J. E. (2010). Financial numeracy, net worth, and financial management skills: Client characteristics that differ based on financial risk tolerance. *Journal of Financial Service Professionals, 64*(6), 57–65.

Sanfey, A. G., Rilling, J. K., Aronson, J. A., Nystrom, L. E., & Cohen, J. D. (2003). The neural basis of economic decision-making in the ultimatum game. *Science, 300*(5626), 1755–1758. https://doi.org/10.1126/science.1082976

Santos, J., Shapiro, T. M., & Stewart, S. H. (2019). *The black-white racial wealth gap*. Retrieved from https://scholar.google.com/scholar?hl=en&as_sdt=0%2C5&q=what+we+get+wrong+about+the+wealth+gap&btnG=

Schroeder, J. (2021). *Could reading literature make you better with money?* Retrieved from https://www.evidenceinvestor.com/literature-money

Singh, P., Hoon, T. S., Nasir, A., Ramly, A., Rasid, S., & Meng, C. C. (2021). Card game as a pedagogical tool for numeracy skills development. *International Journal of Evaluation and Research in Education, 10*(2), 693–705. https://doi.org/10.11591/ijere.v10i2.20722

Smits, W. (2007). Industry-specific or generic skills? Conflicting interests of firms and workers. *Labour Economics, 14*(3), 653–663. https://doi.org/10.1016/j.labeco.2006.09.002

Spinella, M., Yang, B., & Lester, D. (2007). Development of the executive personal finance scale. *International Journal of Neuroscience, 117*(3), 301–313. https://doi.org/10.1080/00207450500534043

Stango, V., & Zinman, J. (2009). Exponential growth bias and household finance. *The Journal of Finance, 64*(6), 2807–2849. https://doi.org/10.1111/j.1540-6261.2009.01518.x

Taylor, E. L., & Taylor, P. C. (2022). Introduction–transformative STEAM education for sustainable development: Beyond traditional STEM education. In *Transformative STEAM education for sustainable development* (pp. 3–19). Brill. https://doi.org/10.1163/9789004524705_001

Teravainen-Goff, A., & Clark, C. (2019). *Reading and financial capability: Exploring the relationships. A national literacy trust research report.* National Literacy Trust. https://eric.ed.gov/?id=ED603667

Thames, A. D. (2014). Toxic exposure: The impact of racial inequality on the brain. *Psychology Benefits Society, 2.* https://psychologybenefits.org/2014/09/02/toxic-exposure-the-impact-of-racial-inequality-on-the-brain/

Tout, D., & Gal, I. (2015). Perspectives on numeracy: Reflections from international assessments. *ZDM, 47*(4), 691–706. https://doi.org/10.1007/s11858-015-0672-9

U.S. Department of Education. (2019). *2019 Mathematics assessment.* Institute of Education Sciences, National Center for Education Statistics, National Assessment of Educational Progress. https://nces.ed.gov/pubsearch/pubsinfo.asp?pubid=2020012

Vernon-Feagans, L., Willoughby, M., & Garrett-Peters, P. (2016). Predictors of behavioral regulation in kindergarten: Household chaos, parenting, and early executive functions. *Developmental Psychology*, *52*(3), 430. https://doi.org/10.1037/dev0000087

Webley, P., & Nyhus, E. K. (2013). Economic socialization, saving and assets in European young adults. *Economics of Education Review*, *33*, 19–30. https://doi.org/10.1016/j.econedurev.2012.09.001

Windisch, H. (2015). *Adults with low literacy and numeracy skills: A literature review on policy intervention* (Education Working Paper No. 123). OECD. https://doi.org/10.1787/5jrxnjdd3r5k-en

Chapter 4

Almenberg, J., Lusardi, A., Säve-Söderbergh, J., & Vestman, R. (2021). Attitudes towards debt and debt behavior. *The Scandinavian Journal of Economics*, *123*(3), 780–809. https://doi.org/10.1111/sjoe.12419

American Psychological Association. (2022). *Stress in America: Money, inflation, war pile on to nation stuck in COVID-19 survival mode.* Retrieved from https://www.apa.org/news/press/releases/stress/2022/march-2022-survival-mode

Beutler, I. F., & Gudmunson, C. G. (2012). New adolescent money attitude scales: Entitlement and conscientiousness. *Journal of Financial Counseling and Planning*, *23*(2), 18–31. Retrieved from https://files.eric.ed.gov/fulltext/EJ996784.pdf

Borden, L. M., Lee, S., Serido, J., & Collins, D. (2008). Changing college students' financial knowledge, attitudes, and behavior through seminar participation. *Journal of Family and Economic Issues*, *29*(1), 23–40. https://doi.org/10.1007/s10834-007-9087-2

Britt, S. L., Ammerman, D. A., Barrett, S. F., & Jones, S. (2017). Student loans, financial stress, and college student retention. *Journal of Student Financial Aid*, *47*(1), 25–37. https://doi.org/10.55504/0884-9153.1605

Capital One. (2023). *What is the average credit card debt in America?* Retrieved from https://tinyurl.com/y4ekp3hj

Chen, H., & Volpe, R. P. (1998). An analysis of personal financial literacy among college students. *Financial Services Review*, *7*(2), 107–128. https://doi.org/10.1016/S1057-0810(99)80006-7

Cherry, K. (2023). *The components of attitudes: Definition, formation, and changes.* Retrieved from https://tinyurl.com/mrym6utx

Dew, J., Dean, L., Duncan, S. F., & Britt-Lutter, S. (2020). A review of effectiveness evidence in the financial-helping fields. *Family Relations*, *69*(3), 614–627. https://doi.org/10.1111/fare.12445

Farrell, L., Fry, T. R. L., & Risse, L. (2016). The significance of financial self-efficacy in explaining women's personal finance behaviour. *Journal of Economic Psychology*, *54*, 85–99. https://doi.org/10.1016/j.joep.2015.07.001

FDIC (Federal Deposit Insurance Corporation). (2021). *2021 FDIC national survey of unbanked and underbanked households.* Retrieved from https://www.fdic.gov/analysis/household-survey/index.html

Foster, S. (2022). *Nearly half of Gen Z, millennial social media users have felt negatively about their finances after seeing others' posts.* Retrieved from https://www.bankrate.com/f/102997/fe2d3d0c95/20220718-social-media-survey.pdf

Hanson, M. (2023). *Student loan debt statistics.* Education Data Initiative. Retrieved from https://educationdata.org/student-loan-debt-statistics

Jones, J., Shepard, D., & Martinez-White, X. (2023). *Average car payment and auto loan statistics 2023. LendingTree.* Retrieved from https://tinyurl.com/ysa5ts2u

Jorgensen, B. L., Foster, D., Jensen, J. F., & Vieira, E. (2017). Financial attitudes and responsible spending behavior of emerging adults: Does geographic location matter? *Journal of Family and Economic Issues, 38*(1), 70–83. https://doi.org/10.1007/s10834-016-9512-5

Klontz, B., Britt, S. L., Mentzer, J., & Klontz, T. (2011). Money beliefs and financial behaviors: Development of the Klontz Money Script Inventory. *Journal of Financial Therapy, 2*(1), 1–22. https://doi.org/10.4148/jft.v2i1.451

Klontz, B., & Klontz, T. (2009). *Mind over money: Overcoming the money disorders that threaten our financial health.* Broadway Books.

LeBaron, A. B., & Kelley, H. H. (2021). Financial socialization: A decade in review. *Journal of Family and Economic Issues, 42*(1), 195–206. https://doi.org/10.1007/s10834-020-09736-2

LeBaron-Black, A. B, Kelley, H. H., Hill, E. J., Jorgensen, B. L., & Jensen, J. F. (2023b). Financial socialization agents and spending behavior of emerging adults: Do parents, peers, employment, and media matter? *Journal of Financial Counseling and Planning, 34*(1), 6–19. https://doi.org/10.1891/JFCP-2021-0036

Lusardi, A., Mitchell, O. S., & Curto, V. (2010). Financial literacy among the young. *The Journal of Consumer Affairs, 44*(2), 358–380. https://doi.org/10.1111/j.1745-6606.2010.01173.x

Morris, T., Maillet, S., & Koffi, V. (2022). Financial knowledge, financial confidence and learning capacity on financial behavior: A Canadian study. *Cogent Social Sciences, 8*(1), Article 1996919. https://doi.org/10.1080/23311886.2021.1996919

National Center for Education Statistics. (2023). *Annual earnings by educational attainment.* Retrieved from https://nces.ed.gov/programs/coe/indicator/cba/annual-earnings

Okamoto, R. M., Saxey, M. T., Wikle, J. S., & LeBaron-Black, A. B. (2024). Confident commitment: Financial self-efficacy's indirect association with romantic relationship flourishing through financial behaviors. *Journal of Family and Economic Issues, 45*(1), 35-44. Advance online publication. https://doi.org/10.1007/s10834-023-09903-1

Riaz, S., Khan, H. H., Sarwar, B., Ahmed, W., Muhammad, N., Reza, S., & Ul Haq, S. M. N. (2022). Influence of financial social agents and attitude toward money on financial literacy: The mediating role of financial self-efficacy and moderating role of mindfulness. *SAGE Open, 12*(3), 1–16. https://doi.org/10.1177/21582440221117140

Robson, J., & Peetz, J. (2020). Gender differences in financial knowledge, attitudes, and behaviors: Accounting for socioeconomic disparities and psychological traits. *The Journal of Consumer Affairs, 54*(3), 813–835. https://doi.org/10.1111/joca.12304

Saxey, M. T., LeBaron-Black, A. B., Totenhagen, C. J., & Curran, M. A. (2023). More than a score? Indirect associations between credit score and romantic relationship quality in emerging adulthood. *Journal of Financial Counseling and Planning, 34*(1), 55–67. https://doi.org/10.1891/JFCP-2022-0018

Serido, J., Curran, M. J., Wilmarth, M., Young Ahn, S., Shim, S., & Ballard, J. (2015). The unique role of parents and romantic partners on college students' financial attitudes and behaviors. *Family Relations, 64*(5), 696–710. https://doi.org/10.1111/fare.12164

Shim, S., Serido, J., Tang, C., & Card, N. (2015). Socialization processes and pathways to healthy financial development for emerging young adults. *Journal of Applied Developmental Psychology, 38*(1), 29–38. https://doi.org/10.1016/j.appdev.2015.01.002

Tang, N. (2017). Like father like son: How does parents' financial behavior affect their children's financial behavior? *Journal of Consumer Affairs, 51*(2), 284–311. https://doi.org/10.1111/joca.12122

Tang, N. (2022). *Building women's financial confidence to improve their financial wellness.* TIAA Institute. Retrieved from https://tinyurl.com/msc54b9r

Yanto, H., Ismail, N., Kiswanto, K., Mat Rahim, N., & Baroroh, N. (2021). The roles of peers and social media in building financial literacy among the millennial generation: A case of Indonesian economics and business students. *Cogent Social Sciences, 7*(1), Article 1947579. https://doi.org/10.1080/23311886.2021.1947579

Chapter 5

Addo, F. R. (2014). Debt, cohabitation, and marriage in young adulthood. *Demography, 51*(5), 1677–1701. https://doi.org/10.1007/s13524-014-0333-6

Ando, A., & Modigliani, F. (1963). The "life-cycle" hypothesis of saving: Aggregate implications and tests. *American Economic Review, 53*(1), 55–84.

Arnett, J. J. (2004). *Emerging adulthood: The winding road from the late teens through the twenties.* Oxford University Press.

Barber, B. M., Huang, X., Odean, T., & Schwarz, C. G. (2021). Attention induced trading and returns: Evidence from Robinhood users. *The Journal of Finance, 77*(6), 3141–3190. https://doi.org/10.1111/jofi.13183

BEA (U.S. Bureau of Economic Analysis). (2023, September). *Personal income and outlays.* Retrieved from https://www.bea.gov/data/income-saving/personal-income

Bleemer, Z., Brown, M., Lee, D., Strair, K., & van der Klaauw, W. (2017). *Echoes of rising tuition in student's borrowing, educational attainment, and homeownership in post-recession America.* Federal Reserve Bank of New York. Retrieved from https://www.newyorkfed.org/medialibrary/media/research/staff_reports/sr820.pdf

de Bassa Scheresberg, C. (2013). Financial literacy and financial behavior among young adults: Evidence and implications. *Numeracy, 6*(2): Article 5. https://doi.org/10.5038/1936-4660.6.2.5

Durkin, T. A. (2000). Credit cards: Use and consumer attitudes, 1970–2000. *Federal Reserve Bulletin*, pp. 623–634. Retrieved from https://www.federalreserve.gov/pubs/bulletin/2000/0900lead.pdf

Durkin, T. A., Elliehausen, G., Staten, M. E., & Zywicki, T. J. (2014). *Consumer credit and the American economy.* Oxford University Press.

Federal Reserve. (2020). *Report on the economic well-being of U.S. households in 2019, featuring supplemental data from April 2020.* Retrieved from https://www.federalreserve.gov/publications/files/2019-report-economic-well-being-us-households-202005.pdf

Federal Reserve Bank of New York. (2018). *Quarterly report on household debt and credit.* Retrieved from https://www.newyorkfed.org/medialibrary/interactives/householdcredit/data/pdf/HHDC_2018Q2.pdf

Federal Reserve Bank of New York. (2020). *Quarterly report on household debt and credit.* Retrieved from https://www.newyorkfed.org/medialibrary/interactives/householdcredit/data/pdf/HHDC_2020Q3.pdf

Fernando, J. (2023, March 24). *What are index funds, and how do they work?* Investopedia. Retrieved from https://www.investopedia.com/terms/i/indexfund.asp

Greenwood, R., & Nagel, S. (2009). Inexperienced investors and bubbles. *Journal of Financial Economics, 93*(2), 239–258. https://doi.org/10.1016/j.jfineco.2008.08.004

Hahn, A. (2023, February 22). *2023 student loan debt statistics: Average student loan debt.* Forbes Advisor. Retrieved from https://www.forbes.com/advisor/student-loans/average-student-loan-statistics/#:~:text=The%20federal%20student%20loan%20portfolio,breaks%20down%20by%20loan%20type

Hanson, M. (2023, January 22). *Average student loan debt [2023]: By year, age & more.* Education Data Initiative. Retrieved from https://educationdata.org/average-student-loan-debt#:~:text=The%20average%20student%20loan%20debt,debt%20averages%20%2454%2C921%20per%20borrower

Haughwout, A., Lee, D., Scally, J., & van der Klaauw, W. (2015). *Student loan borrowing and repayment trends, 2015.* Federal Reserve Bank of New York. Retrieved from https://www.newyorkfed.org/medialibrary/media/newsevents/mediaadvisory/2015/Student-Loan-PressBriefing-Presentation.pdf

Lin, J. T., Bumcrot, C., Mottola, G., Valdes, O., & Walsh, G. (2022). *The changing landscape of investors in the United States: A report of the National Financial Capability Study.* FINRA Investor Education Foundation. Retrieved from https://www.FINRAFoundation.org/Investor-Report2021

Loibl, C., Kraybill, D. S., & DeMay, S. W. (2011). Accounting for the role of habit in regular saving. *Journal of Economic Psychology, 32*(4), 581–592. https://doi.org/10.1016/j.joep.2011.04.004

Lowe, K., & Arnett, J. J. (2020). Failure to grow up, failure to pay? Parents' views of conflict over money with their emerging adults. *Journal of Family Issues, 41*(3), 359–382. https://doi.org/10.1177/0192513x19876061

Modigliani, F. (1986). Life cycle, individual thrift and the wealth of nations. *The American Economic Review, 76*(3), 297–313. Retrieved from https://econpapers.repec.org/RePEc:aea:aecrev:v:76:y:1986:i:3:p:297-313

Nkoutchou, H., & Eiselen, R. (2012). Retirement saving behaviour of young adults in the financial services sector. *Journal of Economic and Financial Sciences, 5*(1), 31–48. https://doi.org/10.4102/jef.v5i1.304

OECD. (2020). *OECD/INFE 2020 international survey of adult financial literacy.* Retrieved from http://www.oecd.org/financial/education/launchoftheoecdinfeglobalfinancialliteracysurveyreport.htm

Pew Research Center. (2012, February 9). *Young, underemployed and optimistic: Coming of age, slowly, in a tough economy.* Retrieved from https://www.pewsocialtrends.org/2012/02/09/young-underemployed-and-optimistic/4

Robb, C. A. (2017). College student financial stress: Are the kids alright? *Journal of Family and Economic Issues, 38*(4), 514–527. https://doi.org/10.1007/s10834-017-9527-6

Robb, C. A. (2022). The use of credit in the consumer marketplace. In J. Grable & S. Chatterjee (Eds.), *Handbook of personal finance.* De Gruyter. https://doi.org/10.1515/9783110727692-013

Robb, C. A., Moody, B., & Abdel-Ghany, M. (2011). College student persistence to degree: The burden of debt. *Journal of College Student Retention: Research, Theory, and Practice, 13*(4), 431–456. https://doi.org/10.2190/cs.13.4.b

Robb, C. A., Schreiber, S. L., & Heckman, S. J. (2020). The role of federal and private student loans in homeownership decisions. *Journal of Consumer Affairs, 54*(1), 43–69. https://doi.org/10.1111/joca.12248

Shanmugham, R., & Ramya, K. (2012). Impact of social factors on individual investors' trading behaviour. *Procedia Economics and Finance, 2*, 237–246. https://doi.org/10.1016/s2212-5671(12)00084-6

Sherraden, M. S. (2013). Building blocks of financial capability. In J. M. Birkenmaier, M. S. Sherraden, & J. C. Curley, J. (Eds.), *Financial capability and asset building: Research, education, policy, and practice* (pp. 1–43). New York and Oxford: Oxford University Press. https://doi.org/10.1093/acprof:oso/9780199755950.003.0012

Thaler, R. H., & Benartzi, S. (2004). Save More Tomorrow^{TM}: Using behavioral economics to increase employee saving. *Journal of Political Economy, 112*(S1), S164–S187. https://doi.org/10.1086/380085

U.S. Census Bureau. (2022, February 24). *Census Bureau releases new educational attainment data.* Retrieved from https://www.census.gov/newsroom/press-releases/2022/educational-attainment.html

Zhang, C. Y., Sussman, A. B., Wang-Ly, N., & Lyu, J. K. (2022). How consumers budget. *Journal of Economic Behavior and Organization, 204*, 69–88. https://doi.org/10.1016/j.jebo.2022.09.025

Chapter 6

Achtziger, A., Hubert, M., Kenning, P., Raab, G., & Reisch, L. (2015). Debt out of control: The links between self-control, compulsive buying, and real debts. *Journal of Economic Psychology, 49*, 141–149. https://doi.org/10.1016/j.joep.2015.04.003

Antonietti, A., Borsetto, A., & Iannello, P. (2016). A metacognitive approach to financial literacy. In C. Aprea, E. Wuttke, K. Breuer, N. K. Koh, P. Davies, B. Fuhrmann, & J. S. Lopus (Eds.), *International handbook of financial literacy* (pp. 57–68). Springer. https://doi.org/10.1007/978-981-10-0360-8_5

Antonietti, A., Cancer, A., Colautti, L., & Iannello, P. (2023). Livelli di inibizione della risposta e comportamenti funzionali nella vita quotidiana [Levels of response inhibition and functional behaviours in daily life]. *Giornale Italiano di Psicologia, 50*(1), 37–144. https://doi.org/10.1421/106926

Bandura, A. (1977). Self-efficacy: Toward a unifying theory of behavioral change. *Psychological Review, 84*(2), 191–215. https://doi.org/10.1016/0146-6402(78)90002-4

Bandura, A. (1982). Self-efficacy mechanism in human agency. *American Psychologist, 37*(2), 122–147. https://doi.org/10.1037/0003-066X.37.2.122

Barrault, S., & Varescon, I. (2013). Impulsive sensation seeking and gambling practice among a sample of online poker players: Comparison between non pathological, problem and pathological gamblers. *Personality and Individual Differences, 55*(5), 502–507. https://doi.org/10.1016/j.paid.2013.04.022

Bloom, D. E., Canning, D., Mansfield, R. K., & Moore, M. (2007). Demographic change, social security systems, and savings. *Journal of Monetary Economics, 54*(1), 92–114. https://doi.org/10.1016/j.jmoneco.2006.12.004

Boettiger, C. A., Mitchell, J. M., Tavares, V. C., Robertson, M., Joslyn, G., D'Esposito, M., & Fields, H. L. (2007). Immediate reward bias in humans: Fronto-parietal networks and a role for the catechol-O-methyltransferase 158Val/Val genotype. *Journal of Neuroscience, 27*(52), 14383–14391. https://doi.org/10.1523/JNEUROSCI.2551-07.2007

Broekema, S., & Kramer, M. G. (2021). Overconfidence, financial advice seeking and household portfolio under-diversification. *Journal of Risk and Financial Management, 14*(11), 553. https://doi.org/10.3390/jrfm14110553

Brown, S., & Taylor, K. (2014). Household finances and the "Big Five" personality traits. *Journal of Economic Psychology, 45*, 197–212. https://doi.org/10.1016/j.joep.2014.10.006

Cai, H., & Liu, C. (2004). Anterior cingulate cortex and executive function. *Advances in Psychological Science, 12*(5), 643.

Casey, B. J., Getz, S., & Galvan, A. (2008). The adolescent brain. *Developmental Review, 28*(1), 62–77. https://doi.org/10.1016/j.dr.2007.08.003

Choi, J. J., Laibson, D., & Madrian, B. C. (2011). $100 bills on the sidewalk: Suboptimal investment in 401(k) plans. *Review of Economics and Statistics*, *93*(3), 748–763. https://doi.org/10.1162/REST_a_00100

Colautti, L., Antonietti, A., & Iannello, P. (2022). Executive functions in decision-making under ambiguity and risk in healthy adults: A scoping review adopting the hot and cold executive functions perspective. *Brain Sciences*, *12*(10), 1335. https://doi.org/10.3390/brainsci12101335

Colautti, L., Iannello, P., Silveri, M. C., & Antonietti, A. (2023). Decision-making under ambiguity and risk and executive functions in Parkinson's disease patients: A scoping review of the existing studies investigating the Iowa gambling task and the game of dice. *Cognitive, Affective, and Behavioral Neuroscience*, *23*, 1225–1243. https://doi.org/10.3758/s13415-023-01106-3

Colombo, B., Iannello, P., Puglisi, G., & Antonietti, A. (2020). Personal impulsivity mediates the effects of neuromodulation in economic intertemporal choices: A pilot study. *Studia Psychologica*, *63*(2), 123–137. https://doi.org/10.31577/sp.2020.02.795

Cooper, N., Kable, J. W., Kim, B. K., & Zauberman, G. (2013). Brain activity in valuation regions while thinking about the future predicts individual discount rates. *Journal of Neuroscience*, *33*(32), 13150–13156. https://doi.org/10.1523/JNEUROSCI.0400-13.2013

Cristofori, I., Cohen-Zimerman, S., & Grafman, J. (2019). Executive functions. *Elsevier EBooks*, 197–219. https://doi.org/10.1016/b978-0-12-804281-6.00011-2

Cyders, M. A., & Coskunpinar, A. (2011). Measurement of constructs using self-report and behavioral lab tasks: Is there overlap in nomothetic span and construct representation for impulsivity? *Clinical Psychology Review*, *31*(6), 965–982. https://doi.org/10.1016/j.cpr.2011.06.001

Dang, J., King, K. M., & Inzlicht, M. (2020). Why are self-report and behavioral measures weakly correlated? *Trends in Cognitive Sciences*, *24*(4), 267–269. https://doi.org/10.1016/j.tics.2020.01.007

Deaves, R., Lüders, E., & Luo, G. Q. (2009). An experimental test of the impact of overconfidence and gender on trading activity. *European Finance Review*, *13*(3), 555–575. https://doi.org/10.1093/rof/rfn023

Duckworth, A. L., & Kern, M. L. (2011). A meta-analysis of the convergent validity of self-control measures. *Journal of Research in Personality*, *45*, 259–268. https://doi.org/10.1016/j.jrp.2011.02.004

Fernandez-Vargas, J., Tremmel, C., Valeriani, D., Bhattacharyya, S., Cinel, C., Citi, L., & Poli, R. (2021). Subject-and task-independent neural correlates and prediction of decision confidence in perceptual decision-making. *Journal of Neural Engineering*, *18*(4), 046055. https://doi.org/10.1088/1741-2552/abf2e4

Fischhoff, B., Slovic, P., & Lichtenstein, S. (1977). Knowing with certainty: The appropriateness of extreme confidence. *Journal of Experimental Psychology: Human Perception and Performance*, *3*(4), 552–564. https://doi.org/10.1037/0096-1523.3.4.552

Fisher, P. J., & Yao, R. (2017). Gender differences in financial risk tolerance. *Journal of Economic Psychology*, *61*, 191–202. https://doi.org/10.1016/j.joep.2017.03.006

Fleming, S. M., & Dolan, R. J. (2012). The neural basis of metacognitive ability. *Philosophical Transactions of the Royal Society B*, *367*(1594), 1338–1349. https://doi.org/10.1098/rstb.2011.0417

Frigerio, M., Ottaviani, C., & Vandone, D. (2020). A meta-analytic investigation of consumer over-indebtedness: The role of impulsivity. *International Journal of Consumer Studies*, *44*(4), 328–342. https://doi.org/10.1111/ijcs.12570

Gathergood, J. (2012). Self-control, financial literacy and consumer over-indebtedness. *Journal of Economic Psychology*, *33*(3), 590–602. https://doi.org/10.1016/j.joep.2011.11.006

Gehring, W. J., & Willoughby, A. R. (2002). The medial frontal cortex and the rapid processing of monetary gains and losses. *Science*, *295*(5563), 2279–2282. https://doi.org/10.1126/science.1066893

Gillebaart, M., & de Ridder, D. (2018). Positioning self-control in a dual-systems framework. In D. de Ridder, M. Adriaanse, & K. Fujita (Eds.), *The Routledge international handbook of self-control in health and well-being* (pp. 35–46). Routledge/Taylor & Francis Group. https://doi.org/10.4324/9781315648576-4

Grinblatt, M., & Keloharju, M. (2009). Sensation seeking, overconfidence, and trading activity. *The Journal of Finance*, *64*(2), 549–578. https://doi.org/10.1111/j.1540-6261.2009.01443.x

Haber, S. N. (2016). Corticostriatal circuitry. *Dialogues in Clinical Neuroscience*, *18*(1), 7–21. https://doi.org/10.31887/dcns.2016.18.1/shaber

Haruno, M., & Kawato, M. (2006). Different neural correlates of reward expectation and reward expectation error in the putamen and caudate nucleus during stimulus-action-reward association learning. *Journal of Neurophysiology*, *95*(2), 948–959. https://doi.org/10.1152/jn.00382.2005

Hoffman, W. F., Schwartz, D. L., Huckans, M. S., McFarland, B. H., Meiri, G., Stevens, A. A., & Mitchell, S. H. (2008). Cortical activation during delay discounting in abstinent methamphetamine dependent individuals. *Psychopharmacology*, *201*, 183–193. https://doi.org/10.1007/s00213-008-1261-1

Hoffmann, A. O. I., Post, T., & Pennings, J. M. E. (2015). How investor perceptions drive actual trading and risk-taking behavior. *Journal of Behavioral Finance*, *16*(1), 94–103. https://doi.org/10.1080/15427560.2015.1000332

Iannello, P., & Colautti, L. (2023). Metacognitive decision-making scenarios (MDMS): Proposta di uno strumento per valutare la consapevolezza nei processi decisionali. *Ricerche Di Psicologia*, *3*, 1–43. https://doi.org/10.3280/rip2022oa15308

Josef, A. K., Richter, D., Samanez-Larkin, G. R., Wagner, G. G., Hertwig, R., & Mata, R. (2016). Stability and change in risk-taking propensity across the adult life span. *Journal of Personality and Social Psychology*, *111*(3), 430–450. https://doi.org/10.1037/pspp0000090

Joseph, J. E., Liu, X., Jiang, Y., Lynam, D., & Kelly, T. H. (2009). Neural correlates of emotional reactivity in sensation seeking. *Psychological Science*, *20*(2), 215–223.

Kalenscher, T., Ohmann, T., & Güntürkün, O. (2006). The neuroscience of impulsive and self-controlled decisions. *International Journal of Psychophysiology*, *62*(2), 203–211. https://doi.org/10.1016/j.ijpsycho.2006.05.010

Keller, C., & Siegrist, M. (2006). Investing in stocks: The influence of financial risk attitude and values-related money and stock market attitudes. *Journal of Economic Psychology*, *27*, 285–303. https://doi.org/10.1016/j.joep.2005.07.002

Kim, K. H., Anderson, S. G., & Seay, M. C. (2019). Financial knowledge and short-term and long-term financial behaviors of millennials in the United States. *Journal of Family and Economic Issues*, *40*(2), 194–208. https://doi.org/10.1007/s10834-018-9595-2

Korreck, S. L., Feltz, D. L., & Albrecht, R. R. (2013). Overconfidence in emerging adulthood: Evidence from judgments of confidence for self-performances. *Journal of Adult Development*, *20*(2), 93–100.

Kraemer, P. M., Weilbächer, R. A., Fontanesi, L., & Gluth, S. (2020). Neural bases of financial decision-making: From spikes to large-scale brain connectivity. *Psychological Perspectives on Financial Decision-Making*, 3–19. https://doi.org/10.1007/978-3-030-45500-2_1

Kramer, M. M. (2016). Financial literacy, confidence and financial advice seeking. *Journal of Economic Behavior & Organization, 131*, 198–217. https://doi.org/10.1016/j.jebo.2016.08.016

Kringelbach, M. L., & Rolls, E. T. (2004). The functional neuroanatomy of the human orbitofrontal cortex: Evidence from neuroimaging and neuropsychology. *Progress in Neurobiology, 72*(5), 341–372. https://doi.org/10.1016/j.pneurobio.2004.03.006

Lee, S., & Hanna, S. D. (2020). Financial knowledge overconfidence and early withdrawals from retirement accounts. *Financial Planning Review, 3*(2). https://doi.org/10.1002/cfp2.1091

Lee, S., & Hanna, S. D. (2022). What, me worry? Financial knowledge overconfidence and the perception of emergency fund needs. *Journal of Financial Counseling and Planning, 33*(1), 140–155. https://doi.org/10.1891/jfcp-2021-0045

Lee, S., Pantzalis, C., & Park, J. C. (2019). Does local culture trigger speculative investment behavior? *Journal of Business Research, 103*, 71–88. https://doi.org/10.1016/j.jbusres.2019.06.011

Levenson, M. R. (1990). Risk taking and personality. *Journal of Personality and Social Psychology, 58*, 1073–1080.

Li, N., Ma, N., Liu, Y., He, X., Sun, D. S., Fu, X.,... Zhang, D. (2013). Resting-state functional connectivity predicts impulsivity in economic decision-making. *The Journal of Neuroscience, 33*(11), 4886–4895. https://doi.org/10.1523/jneurosci.1342-12.2013

Liu, F., Yilmazer, T., Loibl, C., & Montalto, C. (2019). Professional financial advice, self-control and saving behavior. *International Journal of Consumer Studies, 43*(1), 23–34. https://doi.org/10.1111/ijcs.12480

Luck, S. J. (2014). *An introduction to the event-related potential technique*. MIT Press.

Ma, L., & Yao, K. (2023). Investigating young adults' use of internet credit services: A reflective-impulsive dual-process model. *International Journal of Consumer Studies, 47*(4), 1434–1448. https://doi.org/10.1111/ijcs.12918

Mata, R., Josef, A. K., & Hertwig, R. (2016). Propensity for risk taking across the life span and around the globe. *Psychological Science, 27*(2), 231–243. https://doi.org/10.1177/0956797615617811

McClure, S. M., Laibson, D. I., Loewenstein, G., & Cohen, J. D. (2004). Separate neural systems value immediate and delayed monetary rewards. *Science, 306*(5695), 503–507. https://doi.org/10.1126/science.1100907

Menon, V., & D'Esposito, M. (2022). The role of PFC networks in cognitive control and executive function. *Neuropsychopharmacology, 47*(1), 90–103. https://doi.org/10.1038/s41386-021-01152-w

Moeller, F. G., Barratt, E. S., Dougherty, D. M., Schmitz, J. M., & Swann, A. C. (2001). Psychiatric aspects of impulsivity. *American Journal of Psychiatry, 158*(11), 1783–1793. https://doi.org/10.1176/appi.ajp.158.11.1783

Molenberghs, P., Trautwein, F. M., Böckler, A., Singer, T., & Kanske, P. (2016). Neural correlates of metacognitive ability and of feeling confident: A large-scale fMRI study. *Social Cognitive and Affective Neuroscience, 11*(12), 1942–1951. https://doi.org/10.1093/scan/nsw093

Moreira, D., & Barbosa, F. (2019). Delay discounting in impulsive behavior. *European Psychologist, 24*(4), 312–321. https://doi.org/10.1027/1016-9040/a000360

Muller, A., Sirianni, L. A., & Addante, R. J. (2020). Neural correlates of the Dunning–Kruger effect. *European Journal of Neuroscience, 53*(2), 460–484. https://doi.org/10.1111/ejn.14935

Netter, P., Hennig, J., & Roed, I. S. (1996). Serotonin and dopamine as mediators of sensation seeking behavior. *Neuropsychobiology, 34*(3), 155–165. https://doi.org/10.1159/000119318

Nguyen, L., Gallery, G., & Newton, C. (2017). The joint influence of financial risk perception and risk tolerance on individual investment decision-making. *Accounting & Finance, 59*(S1), 747–771. https://doi.org/10.1111/acfi.12295

OECD. (2019). *Fiscal challenges and inclusive growth in ageing societies*.https://doi.org/10.1787/2226583X

Oehler, A., Horn, M., & Wedlich, F. (2018). Young adults' subjective and objective risk attitude in financial decision making: Evidence from the lab and the field. *Review of Behavioral Finance, 10*(3), 274–294. https://doi.org/10.1108/rbf-07-2017-0069

Oliva, A., Antolín-Suárez, L., & Rodríguez-Meirinhos, A. (2019). Uncovering the link between self-control, age, and psychological maladjustment among Spanish adolescents and young adults. *Psychosocial Intervention, 28*(1), 49–55. https://doi.org/10.5093/pi2019a1

Ott, T., & Nieder, A. (2019). Dopamine and cognitive control in prefrontal cortex. *Trends in Cognitive Sciences, 23*(3), 213–234. https://doi.org/10.1016/j.tics.2018.12.006

Ottaviani, C., & Vandone, D. (2011). Impulsivity and household indebtedness: Evidence from real life. *Journal of Economic Psychology, 32*, 754–761. https://doi.org/10.1016/j.joep.2011.05.002

Panikratova, Y. R., Vlasova, R. M., Akhutina, T. V., Korneev, A. A., Sinitsyn, V. E., & Pechenkova, E. V. (2020). Functional connectivity of the dorsolateral prefrontal cortex contributes to different components of executive functions. *International Journal of Psychophysiology, 151*, 70–79. https://doi.org/10.1016/j.ijpsycho.2020.02.013

Parker, A. M., De Bruin, W. B., Yoong, J. K., & Willis, R. (2012). Inappropriate confidence and retirement planning: Four studies with a national sample. *Journal of Behavioral Decision-Making, 25*(4), 382–389. https://doi.org/10.1002/bdm.745

Peltier, J. W., Dahl, A. J., & Schibrowsky, J. E. (2016). Sequential loss of self-control: Exploring the antecedents and consequences of student credit card debt. *Journal of Financial Services Marketing, 21*(3), 167–181. https://doi.org/10.1057/s41264-016-0002-5

Pennycook, G., Ross, R. M., Koehler, D. J., & Fugelsang, J. A. (2017). Dunning–Kruger effects in reasoning: Theoretical implications of the failure to recognize incompetence. *Psychonomic Bulletin & Review, 24*, 1774–1784. https://doi.org/10.3758/s13423-017-1242-7

Peters, J., & Büchel, C. (2011). The neural mechanisms of inter-temporal decision-making: Understanding variability. *Trends in Cognitive Sciences, 15*(5), 227–239. https://doi.org/10.1016/j.tics.2011.03.002

Pharo, H., Sim, C., Graham, M., Gross, J., & Hayne, H. (2011). Risky business: Executive function, personality, and reckless behavior during adolescence and emerging adulthood. *Behavioral Neuroscience, 125*(6), 970. https://doi.org/10.1037/a0025768

Piazza, P. V., Deroche, V., Deminiere, J. M., Maccari, S., Le Moal, M., & Simon, H. E. R. V. (1993). Corticosterone in the range of stress-induced levels possesses reinforcing properties: Implications for sensation-seeking behaviors. *Proceedings of the National Academy of Sciences, 90*(24), 11738–11742. https://doi.org/10.1073/pnas.90.24.11738

Rabbani, A. G., Yao, Z., Wang, C., & Grable, J. E. (2020). Financial risk tolerance, sensation seeking, and locus of control among pre-retiree Baby Boomers. *Journal of Financial Counseling and Planning, 32*(1), 146–157. https://doi.org/10.1891/jfcp-18-00072

Rangel, A., Camerer, C., & Montague, P. R. (2008). A framework for studying the neurobiology of value-based decision-making. *Nature Reviews Neuroscience, 9*(7), 545–556. https://doi.org/10.1038/nrn2357

Reardon, K. W., Wang, M., Neighbors, C., & Tackett, J. L. (2018). The personality context of adolescent gambling: Better explained by the Big Five or sensation-seeking? *Journal of Psychopathology and Behavioral Assessment, 41*(1), 69–80. https://doi.org/10.1007/s10862-018-9690-6

Rey-Ares, L., Fernández-López, S., Castro-González, S., & Rodeiro-Pazos, D. (2021). Does self-control constitute a driver of millennials' financial behaviors and attitudes? *Journal of Behavioral and Experimental Economics, 93*, 101702. https://doi.org/10.1016/j.socec.2021.101702

Robba, M., Sorgente, A., & Iannello, P. (2024a). In search of socially responsible investors: A latent profile analysis. *Frontiers in Behavioral Economics, 3*, 1369261. https://doi.org/10.3389/frbhe.2024.1369261

Robba, M. P., Sorgente, A., Miccoli, M. R., & Iannello, P. (2024b). *Is financial literacy enough to explain investment decisions? Understanding the role of psychological characteristics.* [Preprint]. *PsyArXiv*. https://doi.org/10.31234/osf.io/yd8u3

Robba, M., Sorgente, A., & Iannello, P. (2024c). Disentangling the "crypto fever": An exploratory study of the psychological characteristics of cryptocurrency owners. *Current Research in Behavioral Sciences*, 6, 100151. https://doi.org/10.1016/j.crbeha.2024.100151

Roberti, J. W. (2004). A review of behavioral and biological correlates of sensation seeking. *Journal of Research in Personality, 38*(34), 256–279. https://doi.org/10.1016/S0092-6566(03)00067-9

Rolls, E. T. (2019). The orbitofrontal cortex and emotion in health and disease, including depression. *Neuropsychologia, 128*, 14–43. https://doi.org/10.1016/j.neuropsychologia.2017.09.021

Roth, M., Schumacher, J., & Brähler, E. (2005). Sensation seeking in the community: Sex, age, and sociodemographic comparisons on a representative German population sample. *Personality and Individual Differences, 39*(7), 1261–1271. https://doi.org/10.1016/j.paid.2005.05.003

Schultz, W., Preuschoff, K., Camerer, C., Hsu, M., Fiorillo, C. D., Tobler, P. N., & Bossaerts, P. (2008). Explicit neural signals reflecting reward uncertainty. *Philosophical Transactions of the Royal Society B, 363*(1511), 3801–3811. https://doi.org/10.1098/rstb.2008.0152

Sekścińska, K., & Rudzinska-Wojciechowska, J. (2020). Individual differences in dark triad traits and risky financial choices. *Personality and Individual Differences, 152*, 109598. https://doi.org/10.1016/j.paid.2019.109598

Sekścińska, K., Rudzinska-Wojciechowska, J., & Jaworska, D. (2021). Self-control and investment choices. *Journal of Behavioral Decision-Making, 34*(5), 691–705. https://doi.org/10.1002/bdm.2236

Steinberg, L., Albert, D., Cauffman, E., Banich, M., Graham, S., & Woolard, J. (2008). Age differences in sensation seeking and impulsivity as indexed by behavior and self-report: Evidence for a dual systems model. *Developmental Psychology, 44*(6), 1764–1778. https://doi.org/10.1037/a0012955

Steinberg, L., Graham, S., O'Brien, L. M., Woolard, J. L., Cauffman, E., & Banich, M. T. (2009). Age differences in future orientation and delay discounting. *Child Development, 80*(1), 28–44. https://doi.org/10.1111/j.1467-8624.2008.01244.x

Strömbäck, C., Lind, T., Skagerlund, K., Västfjäll, D., & Tinghög, G. (2017). Does self-control predict financial behavior and financial well-being? *Journal of Behavioral and Experimental Finance, 14*, 30–38. https://doi.org/10.1016/j.jbef.2017.04.002

Tanner, J. (2006). Recentering during emerging adulthood: A critical turning point in life span human development. In J. Arnett & J. Tanner (Eds.), *Emerging adults in America: Coming of age in the 21st century* (pp. 21–55). American Psychological Association. https://doi.org/10.1037/11381-002

Tervo-Clemmens, B., Calabro, F. J., Parr, A. C., Fedor, J., Foran, W., & Luna, B. (2022). *A canonical trajectory of executive function maturation during the transition from adolescence to adulthood* [Preprint]. PsyArXiv. https://doi.org/10.31234/osf.io/73yfv

Toga, A. W., Thompson, P. M., & Sowell, E. R. (2006). Mapping brain maturation. *Focus, 29*(3), 148–390. https://doi.org/10.1016/j.tins.2006.01.007

Worthy, S. L., Jonkman, J., & Blinn-Pike, L. (2010). Sensation-seeking, risk-taking, and problematic financial behaviors of college students. *Journal of Family and Economic Issues, 31*(2), 161–170. https://doi.org/10.1007/s10834-010-9183-6

Xia, T., Wang, Z., & Li, K. (2014). Financial literacy, overconfidence and stock market participation. *Social Indicators Research, 119*(3), 1233–1245. https://doi.org/10.1007/s11205-013-0555-9

Xiao, J. J., & Porto, N. (2019). Present bias and financial behavior. *Financial Planning Review, 2*, e1048.

Xu, S., Luo, L., Xiao, Z., Zhao, K., Wang, H., Wang, C., & Rao, H. (2019). High sensation seeking is associated with behavioral and neural insensitivity to increased negative outcomes during decision-making under uncertainty. *Cognitive, Affective, & Behavioral Neuroscience, 19*, 1352–1363. https://doi.org/10.3758/s13415-019-00751-x

Yeh, T., & Ling, Y. (2022). Confidence in financial literacy, stock market participation, and retirement planning. *Journal of Family and Economic Issues, 43*, 169–186. https://doi.org/10.1007/s10834-021-09769-1

Yuki, S., Nakatani, H., Nakai, T., Okanoya, K., & Tachibana, R. O. (2019). Regulation of action selection based on metacognition in humans via a ventral and dorsal medial prefrontal cortical network. *Cortex, 119*, 336–349. https://doi.org/10.1016/j.cortex.2019.05.001

Zabel, K. L., Christopher, A. N., Marek, P., Wieth, M. B., & Carlson, J. J. (2009). Mediational effects of sensation seeking on the age and financial risk-taking relationship. *Personality and Individual Differences, 47*(8), 917–921. https://doi.org/10.1016/j.paid.2009.07.016

Zhang, Q., Wang, S., Zhu, Q., Yan, J., Zhang, T., Zhang, J., . . . Li, L. (2022). The brain stimulation of DLPFC regulates choice preference in intertemporal choice self-other differences. *Behavioural Brain Research, 440*, 114265. https://doi.org/10.1016/j.bbr.2022.114265

Zuckerman, M. (1979). *Sensation-seeking: Beyond the optimal level of arousal.* Erlbaum.

Zuckerman, M. (2005). The neurobiology of impulsive sensation seeking: Genetics, brain physiology, biochemistry, and neurology. *Neurobiology of Exceptionality*, 31–52.

Zuckerman, M., Eysenck, S. B., & Eysenck, H. J. (1978). Sensation seeking in England and America: Cross-cultural, age, and sex comparisons. *Journal of Consulting and Clinical Psychology, 46*(1), 139–149. https://doi.org/10.1037/0022-006x.46.1.139

Chapter 7

Arnett, J. J. (2001). Conceptions of the transition to adulthood: Perspectives from adolescence through midlife. *Journal of Adult Development, 8*(2), 133–143. https://doi.org/10.1023/A:1026450103225

Aubrey, M., Morin, A. J., Fernet, C., & Carbonneau, N. (2022). Financial well-being: Capturing an elusive construct with an optimized measure. *Frontiers in Psychology*, 13. https://doi.org/10.3389/fpsyg.2022.935284

Bashir, I., & Qureshi, I. H. (2023a). A systematic literature review on personal financial well-being: The link to key sustainable development goals 2030. *FIIB Business Review, 12*(1) 31–48. https://doi.org/10.1177/23197145221106862

Bashir, I., & Qureshi, I. H. (2023b). Examining theories, mediators and moderators in financial well-being literature: A systematic review and future research agenda. *Qualitative Research in Organizations and Management: An International Journal, 18*(4), 265-290. Advance online publication. https://doi.org/10.1108/QROM-04-2022-2314

Brüggen, E. C., Hogreve, J., Holmlund, M., Kabadayi, S., & Löfgren, M. (2017). Financial well-being: A conceptualization and research agenda. *Journal of Business Research, 79*, 228–237. https://doi.org/10.1016/j.jbusres.2017.03.013

CFPB (Consumer Financial Protection Bureau). (2015). *Financial well-being: The goal of financial education.* Retrieved from https://files.consumerfinance.gov/f/201501_cfpb_report_financial-well-being.pdf

Chadda, R. K., & Deb, K. S. (2013). Indian family systems, collectivistic society and psychotherapy. *Indian Journal of Psychiatry, 55*(2), S299–S309. https://doi.org/10.4103/0019-5545.105555

Chan, S. F., Chau, A. W. L., & Chan, K. Y. K. (2012). Financial knowledge and aptitudes: Impacts on college students' financial well-being. *College Student Journal, 46*(1), 114–132

Clarkberg, M. (1999). The price of partnering: The role of economic well-being in young adults' first union experiences. *Social Forces, 77*(3), 945–968.

Comerton-Forde, C., de New, J., Salamanca, N., Ribar, D. C., Nicastro, A., & Ross, J. (2020). *Measuring financial wellbeing with self-reported and bank-record data* (Working Paper No. 26/20). Melbourne Institute. https://doi.org/10.2139/ssrn.3737273

Delaney, L., Newman, C., & Nolan, B. (2006). Reference dependent financial satisfaction over the course of the Celtic tiger: A panel analysis utilising the living in Ireland survey 1994–2001 (Trinity Economics Paper No. TEP200611). Trinity College Dublin, Department of Economics.

Diener, E., & Biswas-Diener, R. (2002). Will money increase subjective well-being? *Social Indicators Research, 57*, 119–169. https://doi.org/10.1023/A:1014411319119

Easterlin, R. A. (1973). Does money buy happiness? *The Public Interest, 30*, 3–10.

Easterlin, R. A. (1974). Does economic growth improve the human lot? Some empirical evidence. In P. A. David & M. W. Reder (Eds.), *Nations and households in economic growth* (pp. 89–125). Academic Press.

Friedline, T., Nam, I., & Loke, V. (2014). Households' net worth accumulation patterns and young adults' financial health: Ripple effects of the great recession? *Journal of Family and Economic Issues, 35*(3), 390–410. https://doi.org/10.1007/s10834-013-9379-7

George, L. K. (1992). Economic status and subjective well-being: A review of literature and an agenda for future research. In N. E. Cutler, D. W. Gregg, & M. P. Lawton (Eds.), *Aging, money, and life satisfaction: Aspects of financial gerontology* (pp. 69–99). Springer.

Ghazali, M. S., Alwi, S. F. S., Abd Aziz, N. N., & Hazudin, S. F. (2020). Pathway to financial well-being: A review on the role of psychological factors. *Environment-Behaviour Proceedings Journal, 5*(13), 55–61. https://doi.org/10.21834/e-bpj.v5i13.2063

Gonçalves, V. N., Ponchio, M. C., & Basílio, R. G. (2021). Women's financial well-being: A systematic literature review and directions for future research. *International Journal of Consumer Studies, 45*(4), 824–843. https://doi.org/10.1111/ijcs.12673

Guille, M. (2002). Student loans: A solution for Europe? *European Journal of Education, 37*(4), 417–431. https://doi.org/10.1111/1467-3435.00119

Hansen, T., Slagsvold, B., & Moum, T. (2008). Financial satisfaction in old age: A satisfaction paradox or a result of accumulated wealth? *Social Indicators Research, 89*(2), 323–347. https://doi.org/10.1007/s11205-007-9234-z

Iannello, P., Sorgente, A., Lanz, M., & Antonietti, A. (2021). Financial well-being and its relationship with subjective and psychological well-being among emerging adults: Testing the moderating effect of individual differences. *Journal of Happiness Studies, 22*, 1385–1411. https://doi.org/10.1007/s10902-020-00277-x

Kabadayi, S., & O'Connor, G. E. (2019). Exploring the antecedents of financial well-being: Where we are and where we go from here. *International Journal of Bank Marketing, 37*(4), 930–933. https://doi.org/10.1108/IJBM-06-2019-338

Kaur, G., & Singh, M. (2024). Pathways to individual financial well-being: Conceptual framework and future research agenda. *FIIB Business Review, 13*(1), 27–41. https://doi.org/10.1177/23197145221105947

Kaur, G., Singh, M., & Singh, S. (2021). Mapping the literature on financial well-being: A systematic literature review and bibliometric analysis. *International Social Science Journal, 71*(241–242), 217–241. https://doi.org/10.1111/issj.12278

Kempson, E., & Poppe, C. (2018). Understanding financial well-being and capability: A revised model and comprehensive analysis. *SIFO Consumption Research Norway.*

Professional Report No. 3. Oslo: Consumption Research Norway—SIFO.

Keyes, C. L., Shmotkin, D., & Ryff, C. D. (2002). Optimizing well-being: The empirical encounter of two traditions. *Journal of Personality and Social Psychology, 82*(6), 1007–1022. https://doi.org/10.1037/0022-3514.82.6.1007

Killingsworth, M. A., Kahneman, D., & Mellers, B. (2023). Income and emotional well-being: A conflict resolved. *Proceedings of the National Academy of Sciences, 120*(10), e2208661120. https://doi.org/10.1073/pnas.2208661120

Lanz, M., & Serido, J. (2020). Introduction to special issue financial and life instability: Obstacles to and opportunities for emerging adult development and future well-being. *Emerging Adulthood, 8*(6), 439–442. https://doi.org/10.1177/2167696820951042

Mahendru, M. (2021). Financial well-being for a sustainable society: A road less travelled. *Qualitative Research in Organizations and Management: An International Journal, 16*(3/4), 572–593. https://doi.org/10.1108/QROM-03-2020-1910

Mahendru, M., Sharma, G. D., & Hawkins, M. (2022a). Toward a new conceptualization of financial well-being. *Journal of Public Affairs*, 22(e2505), 1–15. https://doi.org/10.1002/pa.2505

Mahendru, M., Sharma, G. D., Pereira, V., Gupta, M., & Mundi, H. S. (2022b). Is it all about money honey? Analyzing and mapping financial well-being research and identifying future research agenda. *Journal of Business Research, 150*, 417–436. https://doi.org/10.1016/j.jbusres.2022.06.034

Money and Pensions Service. (2019). *Transforming customer wellbeing. What can retail banking do to build financial capability?* Retrieved from https://maps.org.uk/wp-content/uploads/2019/06/Transforming-customer-wellbeing-1.pdf

Muir, K., Hamilton, M., Noone, J. H., Marjolin, A., Salignac, F., & Saunders, P. (2017). *Exploring financial wellbeing in the Australian context.* Centre for Social Impact. Retrieved from www.csi.edu.au/media/Exploring_Financial_Wellbeing_in_the_Australian_Context_Final_Report.pdf

Nanda, A. P., & Banerjee, R. (2021). Consumer's subjective financial well-being: A systematic review and research agenda. *International Journal of Consumer Studies, 45*(4), 750–776. https://doi.org/10.1111/ijcs.12668

Nelson, L. J., Badger, S., & Wu, B. (2004). The influence of culture in emerging adulthood: Perspectives of Chinese college students. *International Journal of Behavioral Development, 28*(1), 26–36. https://doi.org/10.1080/01650250344000244

Ng, W., & Diener, E. (2014). What matters to the rich and the poor? Subjective well-being, financial satisfaction, and postmaterialist needs across the world. *Journal of Personality and Social Psychology, 107*(2), 326–338. https://doi.org/10.1037/a0036856

Norvilitis, J. M., Szablicki, P. B., & Wilson, S. D. (2003). Factors influencing levels of credit-card debt in college students. *Journal of Applied Social Psychology, 33*(5), 935–947. https://doi.org/10.1111/j.1559-1816.2003.tb01932.x

OECD. (2020). *Recommendation of the Council on Financial Literacy* [Legal instrument]. Retrieved from https://legalinstruments.oecd.org/en/instruments/OECD-LEGAL-0461

OECD. (2021). *Financial education responses to COVID-19*. Retrieved from https://www.oecd.org/financial/education/financialeducation-responses-to-covid-19.htm

Plagnol, A. C., & Easterlin, R. A. (2008). Aspirations, attainments, and satisfaction: Life cycle differences between American women and men. *Journal of Happiness Studies*, *9*(4), 601–619. https://doi.org/10.1007/s10902-008-9106-5

Prawitz, A., Garman, E. T., Sorhaindo, B., O'Neill, B., Kim, J., & Drentea, P. (2006). InCharge financial distress/financial well-being scale: Development, administration, and score interpretation. *Journal of Financial Counseling and Planning*, *17*(1), 34–50.

Ramlee, R., Zain, S. R. S. M., & Husain, W. R. W. (2019). Are Muslims practising moderation in their financial decisions? *Asian Academy of Management Journal*, *24*, 157–170. https://doi.org/10.21315/AAMJ2019.24.S1.11

Rea, J. K., Danes, S. M., Serido, J., Borden, L. M., & Shim, S. (2019). "Being able to support yourself": Young adults' meaning of financial well-being through family financial socialization. *Journal of Family and Economic Issues*, *40*(2), 250–268. https://doi.org/10.1007/s10834-018-9602-7

Riitsalu, L., Sulg, R., Lindal, H., Remmik, M., & Vain, K. (2023). From security to freedom—The meaning of financial well-being changes with age. *Journal of Family and Economic Issues*, 1–14. https://doi.org/10.1007/s10834-023-09886-z

Riitsalu, L., & van Raaij, W. F. (2022). Current and future financial well-being in 16 countries. *Journal of International Marketing*, *30*(3), 35–56. https://doi.org/10.1177/1069031X221095076

Salignac, F., Hamilton, M., Noone, J., Marjolin, A., & Muir, K. (2020). Conceptualizing financial wellbeing: An ecological life-course approach. *Journal of Happiness Studies*, *21*(5), 1581–1602. https://doi.org/10.1007/s10902-019-00145-3

Seiter, L. N., & Nelson, L. J. (2011). An examination of emerging adulthood in college students and nonstudents in India. *Journal of Adolescent Research*, *26*(4), 506–536. https://doi.org/10.1177/0743558410391262

Sharma, G. D., Tiwari, A. K., Zutshi, A., & Singh, K. (Eds.). (2023). *The psychological underpinnings of financial well-being* (Vol. 16648714). Frontiers Media SA. https://doi.org/10.3389/978-2-83251-448-1

She, L., Waheed, H., Lim, W. M., & E-Vahdati, S. (2023). Young adults' financial well-being: Current insights and future directions. *International Journal of Bank Marketing*, *41*(2), 333–368. https://doi.org/10.1108/IJBM-04-2022-0147

Shim, S., Xiao, J. J., Barber, B. L., & Lyons, A. C. (2009). Pathways to life success: A conceptual model of financial well-being for young adults. *Journal of Applied Developmental Psychology*, *30*(6), 708–723. https://doi.org/10.1016/j.appdev.2009.02.003

Solis, O., & Durband, D. B. (2015). Financial support and its impact on undergraduate student financial satisfaction. *College Student Journal*, *49*(1), 93–105.

Sorgente, A., Atay, B., Aubrey, M., Bhatia, S., Crespo, C., Fonseca, G., . . . Lanz, M. (2024). One (financial well-being) model fits all? Testing the multidimensional subjective financial well-being scale across nine countries. *Journal of Happiness Studies*, *25*(1), 13. https://doi.org/10.1007/s10902-024-00708-z

Sorgente, A., & Lanz, M. (2017). Emerging adults' financial well-being: A scoping review. *Adolescent Research Review*, *2*(4), 255–292. https://doi.org/10.1007/s40894-016-0052-x

Sorgente, A., Totenhagen, C. J., & Lanz, M. (2022). The use of the intensive longitudinal methods to study financial well-being: A scoping review and future research agenda. *Journal of Happiness Studies*, *23*, 333–358. https://doi.org/10.1007/s10902-021-00381-6

Taylor, N., & Davies, W. (2021). The financialization of anti-capitalism? The case of the "financial independence retire early" community. *Journal of Cultural Economy, 14*(6), 694–710. https://doi.org/10.1080/17530350.2021.1891951

Telzer, E. H., Masten, C. L., Berkman, E. T., Lieberman, M. D., & Fuligni, A. J. (2010). Gaining while giving: An fMRI study of the rewards of family assistance among White and Latino youth. *Social Neuroscience, 5*(5–6), 508–516. https://doi.org/10.1080/17470911003687913

UNCDF (United Nations Capital Development Fund). (2021). *Delivering financial health globally: A collection of insights, approaches and recommendations.* Retrieved from https://www.uncdf.org/article/7008/delivering-financial-health-globally-a-collection-of-insightsapproaches-and-recommendations

United Nations. (2014). *Country classification.* Retrieved from https://www.un.org/en/development/desa/policy/wesp/wesp_current/2014wesp_country_classification.pdf

UNSGSA (UN Secretary-General's Special Advocate for Inclusive Finance for Development). (2021). *Financial health: An introduction for financial sector policymakers.* Retrieved from https://www.unsgsa.org/publications/financial-health-introduction-financial-sector-policymakers

Vera-Toscano, E., Ateca-Amestoy, V., & Serrano-Del-Rosal, R. (2006). Building financial satisfaction. *Social Indicators Research, 77*, 211–243. https://doi.org/10.1007/s11205-005-2614-3

Wilmarth, M. J. (2021). Financial and economic well-being: A decade review from *Journal of Family and Economic Issues. Journal of Family and Economic Issues, 42*(1), 124–130. https://doi.org/10.1007/s10834-020-09730-8

Chapter 8

American Psychological Association. (2015). *Stress in America: Paying with our health.* Retrieved from https://www.apa.org/news/press/releases/stress/2014/stress-report.pdf

Andrews, B., & Wilding, J. M. (2004). The relation of depression and anxiety to life-stress and achievement in students. *British Journal of Psychology, 95*(4), 509–521. https://doi.org/10.1348/0007126042369802

Archuleta, K. L., Dale, A., & Spann, S. M. (2013). College students and financial distress: Exploring debt, financial satisfaction, and financial anxiety. *Journal of Financial Counseling and Planning, 24*(2), 50–62.

Arnett, J. J. (2000). Emerging adulthood: A theory of development from the late teens through the twenties. *American Psychologist, 55*(5), 469. https://doi.org/10.1037//0003-066x.55.5.469

Asebedo, S. D., & Wilmarth, M. J. (2017). Does how we feel about financial strain matter for mental health? *Journal of Financial Therapy, 8*(1), 5. https://doi.org/10.4148/1944-9771.1130

Bandura, A. (1977). Self-efficacy: Toward a unifying theory of behavioral change. *Psychological Review, 84*(2), 191. https://doi.org/10.1037//0033-295x.84.2.191

Bandura, A. (2006). Toward a psychology of human agency. *Perspectives on Psychological Science, 1*(2), 164–180.

Beck, J. S. (2011). Cognitive-behavioral therapy. In *Clinical textbook of addictive disorders* (pp. 474–501). Guilford Press.

Bialik, K., & Fry, R. (2019). *Millennial life: How young adulthood today compares with prior generations.* Retrieved from. https://www.pewsocialtrends.org/essay/millennial-life-how-young-adulthood-today-compares-with-prior-generations/

Bøe, T., Balaj, M., Eikemo, T. A., McNamara, C. L., & Solheim, E. F. (2017). Financial difficulties in childhood and adult depression in Europe. *European Journal of Public Health, 27*(Suppl.1), 96–101. https://doi.org/10.1093/eurpub/ckw253

Borden, L. M., Lee, S. A., Serido, J., & Collins, D. (2008). Changing college students' financial knowledge, attitudes, and behavior through seminar participation. *Journal of Family and Economic Issues, 29*, 23–40. https://doi.org/10.1007/s10834-007-9087-2

Bridges, S., & Disney, R. (2010). Debt and depression. *Journal of Health Economics, 29*(3), 388–403. https://doi.org/10.1016/j.jhealeco.2010.02.003

Brulé, G., & Suter, C. (2019). Why wealth matters more than income for subjective well-being? In G. Brulé & C. Suter (Eds.), *Wealth(s) and subjective well-being* (pp. 1–13). Springer International. https://doi.org/10.1007/978-3-030-05535-6_1

Callender, C., & de Gayardon, A. (2021). *Hidden voices: graduates' perspectives on the student loan system in England.* Higher Education Policy Institute.

Cannon, W. B. (1932). *The wisdom of the body.* Norton.

Chatterjee, S., Finke, M., & Harness, N. (2011). The impact of self-efficacy on wealth accumulation and portfolio choice. *Applied Economics Letters, 18*(7), 627–631. https://doi.org/10.1080/13504851003761830

Chatterjee, S., Kim, J., & Chung, S. (2021a). Emerging adulthood milestones, perceived capability, and psychological well-being while transitioning to adulthood: Evidence from a national study. *Financial Planning Review, 4*(4), e1132. https://doi.org/10.1002/cfp2.1132

Chatterjee, S., Kim, J., & Chung, S. R. (2021b). Financial strain, non-marital relationship satisfaction, and psychological well-being of emerging adults: Evidence from a national study. In *Consumer Interests Annual* (Vol. 67). American Council on Consumer Interests.

Chen, Z., Fedina, L., DeVylder, J., Lemieux, C. M., King, C., & Abbott, K. (2022). Pandemic financial hardships and suicide risk in a nationally representative sample of young adults. *Social Work in Mental Health*, 1–15. https://doi.org/10.1080/15332985.2022.2161861

Choung, Y., Chatterjee, S., & Pak, T. Y. (2022). Depression and financial planning horizon. *Journal of Behavioral and Experimental Economics, 98*, 101877. https://doi.org/10.1016/j.socec.2022.101877

Cobb, S. (1976). Social support as a moderator of life stress. *Psychosomatic Medicine, 38*(5), 300–314. https://doi.org/10.1097/00006842-197609000-00003

Cooke, R., Barkham, M., Audin, K., Bradley, M., & Davy, J. (2004). Student debt and its relation to student mental health. *Journal of Further and Higher Education, 28*(1), 53–66. https://doi.org/10.1080/0309877032000161814

Dew, J., LeBaron, A., & Allsop, D. (2018). Can stress build relationships? Predictors of increased marital commitment resulting from the 2007–2009 recession. *Journal of Family and Economic Issues, 39*(3), 405–421. https://doi.org/10.1007/s10834-018-9566-7

Drentea, P., & Reynolds, J. R. (2012). Neither a borrower nor a lender be: The relative importance of debt and SES for mental health among older adults. *Journal of Aging and Health, 24*(4), 673–695. https://doi.org/10.1177/0898264311431304

Drentea, P., & Lavrakas, P. J. (2000). Over the limit: The association among health, race and debt. *Social Science & Medicine, 50*(4), 517–529. https://doi.org/10.1016/s0277-9536(99)00298-1

Dvořáková, K., Kishida, M., Li, J., Elavsky, S., Broderick, P. C., Agrusti, M. R., & Greenberg, M. T. (2017). Promoting healthy transition to college through mindfulness training with first-year college students: Pilot randomized controlled trial. *Journal of American College Health, 65*(4), 259–267. https://doi.org/10.1080/07448481.2017.1278605

Eagan, K., Stolzenberg, E. B., Ramirez, J. J., Aragon, M. C., Suchard, M. R., & Rios-Agulair, C. R. (2016). *The American freshman: Fifty-year trends 1966–2015.* Higher Education Research Institute, UCLA.

Falconier, M. K., & Epstein, N. B. (2011). Couples experiencing financial strain: What we know and what we can do. *Family Relations, 60*(3), 303–317. https://doi.org/10.1111/j.1741-3729.2011.00650.x

Falconier, M. K., Nussbeck, F., Bodenmann, G., Schneider, H., & Bradbury, T. (2015). Stress from daily hassles in couples: Its effects on intradyadic stress, relationship satisfaction, and physical and psychological well-being. *Journal of Marital and Family Therapy, 41*(2), 221–235. https://doi.org/10.1111/jmft.12073

Fan, L., Chatterjee, S., & Kim, J. (2022). Young adults' personality traits and subjective well-being: The role of perceived money management capability. *Journal of Behavioral and Experimental Finance, 35*, 100689. https://doi.org/10.1016/j.jbef.2022.100689

Ferraro, K. F., & Shippee, T. P. (2009). Aging and cumulative inequality: How does inequality get under the skin? *The Gerontologist, 49*, 333–343. https://doi.org/10.1093/geront/gnp034

Ferrer-i-carbonell, A. (2005). Income and well-being: An empirical analysis of the comparison income effect. *Journal of Public Economics, 89*(5–6), 997–1019. https://doi.org/10.1016/j.jpubeco.2004.06.003

Friedline, T., West, S., Rosell, N., Serido, J., & Shim, S. (2017). Do community characteristics relate to young adult college students' credit card debt? The hypothesized role of collective institutional efficacy. *American Journal of Community Psychology, 59*(1–2), 80–93. https://doi.org/10.1002/ajcp.12116

Fry, R. (2014). *Young adults, student debt and economic well-being.* Retrieved from https://www.pewresearch.org/social-trends/wp-content/uploads/sites/3/2014/05/ST_2014.05.14_student-debt_complete-report.pdf

Goetz, J., Cude, B. J., Nielsen, R. B., Chatterjee, S., & Mimura, Y. (2011). College-based personal finance education: Student interest in three delivery methods. *Journal of Financial Counseling and Planning, 22*(1), 28.

Greenglass, E., & Mara, C. A. (2012). Self-efficacy as a psychological resource in difficult economic times. In K. A. Moore, K. Kaniasty, & P. Buchwald (Eds.), *Stress and anxiety: Application to economic hardship, occupational demands, and developmental challenges* (pp. 29–38). Logos Verlag Berlin.

Guan, N., Guariglia, A., Moore, P., Xu, F., & Al-Janabi, H. (2022). Financial stress and depression in adults: A systematic review. *PLOS ONE, 17*(2), e0264041. https://doi.org/10.1371/journal.pone.0264041

Gudmunson, C. G., & Danes, S. M. (2011). Family financial socialization: Theory and critical review. *Journal of Family and Economic Issues, 32*, 644–667. https://doi.org/10.1007/s10834-011-9275-y

Hall, M. H., Matthews, K. A., Kravitz, H. M., Gold, E. B., Buysse, D. J., Bromberger, J. T., . . . Sowers, M. (2009). Race and financial strain are independent correlates of sleep in midlife women: The SWAN sleep study. *Sleep, 32*(1), 73–82. https://doi.org/10.5665/sleep/32.1.73

Heckman, S., Lim, H., & Montalto, C. (2014). Factors related to financial stress among college students. *Journal of Financial Therapy, 5*(1), 19–39. https://doi.org/10.4148/1944-9771.1063

Herman-Stabl, M. A., Stemmler, M., & Petersen, A. C. (1995). Approach and avoidant coping: Implications for adolescent mental health. *Journal of Youth and Adolescence, 24*(6), 649–665. https://doi.org/10.1007/bf01536949

Hilbert, L. P., Noordewier, M. K., & van Dijk, W. W. (2022). The prospective associations between financial scarcity and financial avoidance. *Journal of Economic Psychology, 88*, 102459. https://doi.org/10.1016/j.joep.2021.102459

Hira, T. K., & Mugenda, O. M. (1999). The relationship between personal financial wellness and selected mental health variables. *Journal of Financial Counseling and Planning, 10*(1), 73–87.

Holzer, H. J., & Baum, S. (2017). *Making college work: Pathways to success for disadvantaged students*. Brookings Institution Press.

Ismail, N., & Zaki, N. D. A. (2019). Does financial literacy and financial stress affect the financial wellness. *International Journal of Modern Trends in Social Sciences, 2*(8), 1–11. https://doi.org/10.35631/ijmtss.28001

Jenzer, T., Read, J. P., Naragon-Gainey, K., & Prince, M. A. (2019). Coping trajectories in emerging adulthood: The influence of temperament and gender. *Journal of Personality, 87*(3), 607–619. https://doi.org/10.1111/jopy.12419

Jessop, D. C., Herberts, C., & Solomon, L. (2005). The impact of financial circumstances on student health. *British Journal of Health Psychology, 10*(3), 421–439. https://doi.org/10.1348/135910705X25480

Kelley, H. H., Lee, Y., LeBaron-Black, A., Dollahite, D. C., James, S., Marks, L. D., & Hall, T. (2023). Change in financial stress and relational wellbeing during COVID-19: Exacerbating and alleviating influences. *Journal of Family and Economic Issues, 44*, 34–52. https://doi.org/10.1007/s10834-022-09822-7

Kim, J. (2004). Impact of a workplace financial education program on financial attitude, financial behavior, financial well-being, and financial knowledge. *Proceedings of the Association for Financial Counseling and Planning Education, 22*(1), 82–89.

Kim, J., & Chatterjee, S. (2013). Childhood financial socialization and young adults' financial management. *Journal of Financial Counseling and Planning, 24*(1), 61–92.

Kim, J., & Chatterjee, S. (2021). Financial debt and mental health of young adults. *Journal of Financial Counseling and Planning, 32*(2), 187–201. https://doi.org/10.1891/jfcp-18-00048

Kim, J., Chatterjee, S., & Kim, J. (2012). Debt burden of young adults in the United States. *Journal of Financial Counseling and Planning, 23*(2), 55–67.

Kim, J., Chatterjee, S., Young, J., & Moon, U. J. (2017). The cost of access: Racial disparities in student loan burdens of young adults. *College Student Journal, 51*(1), 99–114.

Kim, J., & Garman, E. T. (2004). Financial stress, pay satisfaction and workplace performance. *Compensation & Benefits Review, 36*(1), 69–76. https://doi.org/10.1177/0886368703261215

Kim, J., Gutter, M. S., & Spangler, T. (2017). Review of family financial decision making: Suggestions for future research and implications for financial education. *Journal of Financial Counseling and Planning, 28*(2), 253–267. https://doi.org/10.1891/1052-3073.28.2.253

Kim, J., Sorhaindo, B., & Garman, E. T. (2006). Relationship between financial stress and workplace absenteeism of credit counseling clients. *Journal of Family and Economic Issues, 27*, 458–478. https://doi.org/10.1007/s10834-006-9024-9

Kim, W., Kim, T. H., Lee, T. H., Ju, Y. J., & Park, E. C. (2016). The effect of childhood and current economic status on depressive symptoms in South Korean individuals: A longitudinal study. *International Journal for Equity in Health, 15*, 1–7. https://doi.org/10.1186/s12939-016-0402-0

Klontz, B., Britt, S. L., Archuleta, K. L., & Klontz, T. (2012). Disordered money behaviors: Development of the Klontz Money Behavior Inventory. *Journal of Financial Therapy, 3*(1), 2. https://doi.org/10.4148/jft.v3i1.1485

Knoesen, R., & Naudé, L. (2018). Experiences of flourishing and languishing during the first year at university. *Journal of Mental Health, 27*(3), 269–278. https://doi.org/10.1080/09638237.2017.1370635

Lazarus, R. S., & Folkman, S. (1984). *Stress, appraisal, and coping*. Springer.

LeBaron, A. B., Curran, M. A., Li, X., Dew, J. P., Sharp, T. K., & Barnett, M. A. (2020). Financial stressors as catalysts for relational growth: Bonadaptation among lower-income, unmarried couples. *Journal of Family and Economic Issues, 41*(3), 424–441. https://doi.org/10.1007/s10834-020-09666-z

LeBaron-Black, A. B., Curran, M. A., Hill, E. J., Toomey, R. B., Speirs, K. E., & Freeh, M. E. (2022a). Talk is cheap: Parent financial socialization and emerging adult financial well-being. *Family Relations, 72*(3), 1201–1219. https://doi.org/10.1111/fare.12751

LeBaron-Black, A. B., Li, X., Okamoto, R. M., Saxey, M. T., & Driggs, T. M. (2022b). Finances and fate: Parent financial socialization, locus of control, and mental health in emerging adulthood. *Emerging Adulthood, 10*(6), 1484–1496. https://doi.org/10.1177/21676968221111054

LeBaron-Black, A. B., Yorgason, J. B., Curran, M. A., Saxey, M. T., & Okamoto, R. M. (2022c). The ABC-X's of stress among US emerging adults during the COVID-19 pandemic: Relationship quality, financial distress, and mental health. *International Journal of Environmental Research and Public Health, 19*(20), 13125. https://doi.org/10.3390/ijerph192013125

Lee, Y. G., Kelley, H. H., & Lee, J. (2023). Untying financial stress and financial anxiety: Implications for research and financial practitioners. *Journal of Financial Therapy, 14*(1), 4. https://doi.org/10.4148/1944-9771.1293

Liu, Y., Zhang, Y., & Chatterjee, S. (2023). Financial hardship and depression experienced by pre-retirees during the COVID-19 pandemic: The mitigating role of stimulus payments. *Applied Economics Letters, 30*(3), 391–396. https://doi.org/10.1080/13504851.2021.1989364

Lown, J. M., Kim, J., Gutter, M. S., & Hunt, A. T. (2015). Self-efficacy and savings among middle and low income households. *Journal of Family and Economic Issues, 36*, 491–502. https://doi.org/10.1007/s10834-014-9419-y

Lund, C., Breen, A., Flisher, A. J., Kakuma, R., Corrigall, J., Joska, J. A., . . . Patel, V. (2010). Poverty and common mental disorders in low and middle income countries: A systematic review. *Social Science & Medicine, 71*(3), 517–528. https://doi.org/10.1016/j.socscimed.2010.04.027

Lund, C., & Cois, A. (2018). Simultaneous social causation and social drift: Longitudinal analysis of depression and poverty in South Africa. *Journal of Affective Disorders, 229*, 396–402. https://doi.org/10.1016/j.jad.2017.12.050

Lyons, A. C., Palmer, L., Jayaratne, K. S., & Scherpf, E. (2006). Are we making the grade? A national overview of financial education and program evaluation. *Journal of Consumer Affairs, 40*(2), 208–235. https://doi.org/10.1111/j.1745-6606.2006.00056.x

Mandell, L., & Klein, L. S. (2009). The impact of financial education in high school and college on financial literacy and subsequent financial decision making. *Journal of Consumer Affairs, 43*(2), 249–284.

Matud, M. P., Díaz, A., Bethencourt, J. M., & Ibáñez, I. (2020). Stress and psychological distress in emerging adulthood: A gender analysis. *Journal of Clinical Medicine, 9*(9), 2859. https://doi.org/10.3390/jcm9092859

McCloud, T., & Bann, D. (2019). Financial stress and mental health among higher education students in the UK up to 2018: Rapid review of evidence. *Journal of Epidemiological Community Health, 73*(10), 977–984. https://doi.org/10.1136/jech-2019-212154

Narendorf, S. C., & Palmer, A. (2016). Perception of need and receipt of mental health treatment: A three-group comparison of young adults with psychological distress. *Psychiatric Services, 67*(8), 924–927. https://doi.org/10.1176/appi.ps.201500230

Northern, J. J., O'Brien, W. H., & Goetz, P. W. (2010). The development, evaluation, and validation of a financial stress scale for undergraduate students. *Journal of College Student Development, 51*(1), 79–92. https://doi.org/10.1353/csd.0.0108

Paul, K. I., & Moser, K. (2009). Unemployment impairs mental health: Meta-analyses. *Journal of Vocational Behavior, 74*(3), 264–282. https://doi.org/10.1016/j.jvb.2009.01.001

Perreault, M., Touré, E. H., Perreault, N., & Caron, J. (2017). Employment status and mental health: Mediating roles of social support and coping strategies. *Psychiatric Quarterly*, *88*, 501–514. https://doi.org/10.1007/s11126-016-9460-0

Pollack, C. E., & Lynch, J. (2009). Health status of people undergoing foreclosure in the Philadelphia region. *American Journal of Public Health*, *99*(10), 1833–1839. https://doi.org/10.2105/AJPH.2009.161380

Prawitz, A. D., Garman, E. T., Sorhaindo, B., O'Neill, B., Kim, J., & Drentea, P. (2006). The incharge financial distress/financial well-being scale: Establishing validity and reliability. *Journal of Financial Counseling Planning*, *17*, 34–50.

Qian, Y., & Fan, W. (2021). Student loans, mental health, and substance use: A gender comparison among US young adults. *Journal of American College Health*, 1–12. https://doi.org/10.1080/07448481.2021.1909046

Rahman, M., Isa, C. R., Masud, M. M., & Moniruzzaman, S. (2021). The role of financial behaviour, financial literacy, and financial stress in explaining the financial well-being of B40 group in Malaysia. *Future Business Journal*, *7*, 52. https://doi.org/10.1186/s43093-021-00099-0

Reading, R., & Reynolds, S. (2001). Debt, social disadvantage and maternal depression. *Social Science & Medicine*, *53*(4), 441–453. https://doi.org/10.1016/s0277-9536(00)00347-6

Regehr, C., Glancy, D., & Pitts, A. (2013). Interventions to reduce stress in university students: A review and meta-analysis. *Journal of Affective Disorders*, *148*(1), 1–11. https://doi.org/10.1016/j.jad.2012.11.026

Richardson, T., Elliott, P., & Roberts, R. (2013). The relationship between personal unsecured debt and mental and physical health: A systematic review and meta-analysis. *Clinical Psychology Review*, *33*(8), 1148–1162. https://doi.org/10.1016/j.cpr.2013.08.009

Riggs, S. A., & Han, G. (2009). Predictors of anxiety and depression in emerging adulthood. *Journal of Adult Development*, *16*, 39–52. https://doi.org/10.1007/s10804-009-9051-5

Robb, C. A., & Chy, S. (2023). Undergraduate financial knowledge, attitudes, and behaviors: The impact of financial life skills course on college students. *Financial Planning Review*, *6*(1), e1155. https://doi.org/10.1002/cfp2.1155

Roberts, R., Golding, J., Towell, T., & Weinreb, I. (1999). The effects of students' economic circumstances on British students' mental and physical health. *Journal of American College Health*, *48*(3), 103–109. https://doi.org/10.1080/07448489909595681

Roth, S., & Cohen, L. J. (1986). Approach, avoidance, and coping with stress. *American Psychologist*, *41*(7), 813–819. https://doi.org/10.1037//0003-066x.41.7.813

Roy, C., & Andrews, H. A. (2008). *The Roy adaptation model*: Pearson Prentice Hall.

Serido, J., Lawry, C., Li, G., Conger, K. J., & Russell, S. T. (2014). The associations of financial stress and parenting support factors with alcohol behaviors during young adulthood. *Journal of Family and Economic Issues*, *35*, 339–350. https://doi.org/10.1007/s10834-013-9376-x

Serido, J., Tang, C., Ahn, S. Y., & Shim, S. (2020). Financial behavior change and progress toward self-sufficiency: A goal-framing theory application. *Emerging Adulthood*, *8*(6), 521–529. https://doi.org/10.1177/2167696819861467

Shahidi, S., Akbari, H., & Zargar, F. (2017). Effectiveness of mindfulness-based stress reduction on emotion regulation and test anxiety in female high school students. *Journal of Education and Health Promotion*, *6*, 87. https://doi.org/10.4103/jehp.jehp_98_16

Shapiro, G. K., & Burchell, B. J. (2012). Measuring financial anxiety. *Journal of Neuroscience, Psychology, and Economics*, *5*(2), 92–103. https://doi.org/10.1037/a0027647

Shim, S., Serido, J., & Lee, S. K. (2019). Problem-solving orientations, financial self-efficacy, and student-loan repayment stress. *Journal of Consumer Affairs*, *53*(3), 1273–1296. https://doi.org/10.1111/joca.12228

Short, K., Goetz, J., Cude, B., Sperling, L., Welch-Devine, M., & Chstterjee, S. (2019). A case for graduate student financial education. *College Student Journal, 53*(1), 47–55.

Stein, C. H., Hoffmann, E., Bonar, E. E., Leith, J. E., Abraham, K. M., Hamill, A. C., . . . Fogo, W. R. (2013). The United States economic crisis: Young adults' reports of economic pressures, financial and religious coping and psychological well-being. *Journal of Family and Economic Issues, 34*, 200–210. https://doi.org/10.1007/s10834-012-9328-x

Sweet, E., Nandi, A., Adam, E. K., & McDade, T. W. (2013). The high price of debt: Household financial debt and its impact on mental and physical health. *Social Science & Medicine, 91*, 94–100. https://doi.org/10.1016/j.socscimed.2013.05.009

Tran, A. G., Mintert, J. S., Llamas, J. D., & Lam, C. K. (2018). At what costs? Student loan debt, debt stress, and racially/ethnically diverse college students' perceived health. *Cultural Diversity and Ethnic Minority Psychology, 24*(4), 459. https://doi.org/10.1037/cdp0000207

Wikle, J. S., Leavitt, C. E., Yorgason, J. B., Dew, J. P., & Johnson, H. M. (2021). The protective role of couple communication in moderating negative associations between financial stress and sexual outcomes for newlyweds. *Journal of Family and Economic Issues, 42*(2), 282–299. https://doi.org/10.1007/s10834-020-09728-2

Williams, D. R., Yu, Y., Jackson, J. S., & Anderson, N. B. (1997). Racial differences in physical and mental health: Socio-economic status, stress and discrimination. *Journal of Health Psychology, 2*(3), 335–351. https://doi.org/10.1177/135910539700200305

Woolf, S. H., Aron, L. Y., Dubay, L., Simon, S. M., Zimmerman, E., & Luk, K. (2015). *How are income and wealth linked to health and longevity?* Virginia Commonwealth University Center on Society and Health, Urban Institute.

Xiao, J. J., Chatterjee, S., & Kim, J. (2014). Factors associated with financial independence of young adults. *International Journal of Consumer Studies, 38*(4), 394–403. https://doi.org/10.1111/ijcs.12106

Zhang, Y., & Chatterjee, S. (2023). Financial well-being in the United States: The roles of financial literacy and financial stress. *Sustainability, 15*(5), 4505.

Chapter 9

Aboagye, J., & Jung, J. Y. (2018). Debt holding, financial behavior, and financial satisfaction. *Journal of Financial Counseling and Planning, 29*(2), 208–218. https://doi.org/10.1891/1052-3073.29.2.208

Addo, F. R., Houle, J. N., & Simon, D. (2016). Young, Black, and (still) in the red: Paternal wealth, race, and student loan debt. *Race and Social Problems, 8*(1), 64–76. https://doi.org/10.1007/s12552-016-9162-0

Akers, B., & Chingos, M. M. (2014). *Is a student loan crisis on the horizon?* Brown Center on Education Policy at the Brookings Institution. Retrieved from https://www.issuelab.org/resources/18380/18380.pdf

Andruska, E. A., Hogarth, J. M., Fletcher, C. N., Forbes, G. R., & Wohlgemuth, D. R. (2014). Do you know what you owe? Students' understanding of their student loans. *Journal of Student Financial Aid, 44*(2), 125–148. https://doi.org/10.55504/0884-9153.1222

Association of Public Land-Grant Universities. (2023). *How does a college degree improve graduates' employment and earnings potential?* Retrieved from https://www.aplu.org/our-work/4-policy-and-advocacy/publicuvalues/employment-earnings

Austin, D. A. (2013). The indentured generation: Bankruptcy and student loan debt. *Santa Clara Law Review, 53*(2), 329–420.

Avard, S., Manton, E., English, D., & Walker, J. (2005). The financial knowledge of college freshmen. *College Student Journal, 39*(2), 321–340.

Baggett, C. B., & Cole, C. R. (2022). Student loans, financial well-being, and the role of the financial planner. *Journal of Financial Service Professionals, 76*(1), 27–40.

Baker, A. R., Andrews, B. D., & McDaniel, A. (2017). The impact of student loans on college access, completion, and returns. *Sociology Compass, 11*(6), 1–11. https://doi.org/10.1111/soc4.12480

Baker, A. R., & Montalto, C. P. (2019). Student loan debt and financial stress: Implications for academic performance. *Journal of College Student Development, 60*(1), 120–155. https://doi.org/10.1353/csd.2019.0008

Bartholomae, S., Kiss, D. E., Jurgenson, J. B., O'Neill, B., Worthy, S. L., & Kim, J. (2019). Framing the human capital investment decision: Examining gender bias in student loan borrowing. *Journal of Financial and Economic Issues, 40*(1), 132–145. https://doi.org/10.1007/s10834-018-9603-6

Becker, G. S. (1993). *Human capital: A theoretical and empirical analysis, with special reference to education.* University of Chicago Press.

Beiser, M. (2003). Why should researchers care about culture? *The Canadian Journal of Psychiatry, 48*(3), 154–160. https://doi.org/10.1177/070674370304800303

Bolton, P. (2023). *Student loan statistics.* UK Parliament House of Commons Library. Retrieved from https://commonslibrary.parliament.uk/research-briefings/sn01079

Booij, A. S., Leuven, E., & Oosterbeek, H. (2012). The role of information in the take-up of student loans. *Economics of Education Review, 31*(1), 33–44. https://doi.org/10.1016/j.econedurev.2011.08.009

Bouchrika, I. (2023, June 28). *College dropout rates: 2023 Statistics by race, gender & income.* Retrieved from https://research.com/universities-colleges/college-dropout-rates

Bowen, C. F. (2002). Financial knowledge of teens and their parents. *Journal of Financial Counseling and Planning, 13*(2), 93–102.

Britt, S. L., Ammerman, D. A., Barrett, S. F., & Jones, S. (2017). Student loans, financial stress, and college student retention. *Journal of Student Financial Aid, 47*(1), 25–37. Retrieved from https://publications.nasfaa.org/jsfa/vol47/iss1/3

Bustamante, J. (2019). *Percentage of high school graduates that got to college.* Education Data Initiative. Retrieved from https://educationdata.org/high-school-graduates-who-go-to-college

Carneiro, P., Heckman, J. J., & Vytlacil, E. (2010). Estimating marginal returns to education. *American Economic Review, 101*(6), 2754–2781. http://doi:10.1257/aer.101.6.2754

Cherney, K., Rothwell, D., Serido, J., & Shim, S. (2020). Subjective financial well-being during emerging adulthood: The role of student debt. *Emerging Adulthood, 8*(6), 485–495. https://doi.org/10.1177/2167696819879252

Cho, S. H., Xu, Y. & Kiss, D. E. (2015). Understanding student loan decisions: A literature review. *Family and Consumer Sciences Research Journal, 43*(3), 229–243. https://doi.org/10.1111/fcsr.12099

Christie, H., & Munro, M. (2003). The logic of loans: Students' perceptions of the costs and benefits of the student loan. *British Journal of Sociology of Education, 24*(5), 621–636. https://doi.org/10.1080/0142569032000127170

Consumer Financial Protection Bureau. (2023). *Student loan forgiveness.* Retrieved from https://www.consumerfinance.gov/paying-for-college/student-loan-forgiveness/#:~:text=If%20you%20have%20loans%20that,loans%20forgiven%20in%20Spring%202023

Cordero, J. M., Gil-Izquierdo, M., & Pedraja-Chaparro, F. (2020). Financial education and student financial literacy: A cross-country analysis using PISA 2012 data. *The Social Science Journal, 59*(1), 1–19. https://doi.org/10.1016/j.soscij.2019.07.011

Cronin, J. M., & Simmons, S. Q. (1987). *Student loans: Risks and realities.* Auburn House.

Crook, T. R., Todd, S. Y., Combs, J. G., Woehr, D. J., & Ketchen Jr., D. J. (2011). Does human capital matter? A meta-analysis of the relationship between human capital and firm performance. *Journal of Applied Psychology*, *96*(3), 443–456. https://doi.org/10.1037/a0022147

Darolia, R. (2016). *An experiment on information use in college loan decisions* (Working Paper No. 16-18). Federal Reserve Bank of Philadelphia. Retrieved from https://www.philadelphiafed.org/-/media/frbp/assets/working-papers/2016/wp16-18.pdf

Deckard, F. M., Goosby, B. J., & Cheadle, J. E. (2022). Debt stress, college stress: Implications for Black and Latinx students' mental health. *Race and Social Problems*, *14*(3), 238–253. https://doi.org/10.1007/s12552-021-09346-z

Delisle, J., & Holt, A. (2015). *Why student loans are different: Findings from six focus groups of student loan borrowers.* New America. Retrieved from https://www.newamerica.org

Department of Financial Protection and Innovation. (2023). *Student loan debt: A disproportionate burden on Black and Latino borrowers.* DFPI. Retrieved from https://dfpi.ca.gov/2023/02/13/student-loan-debt-a-disproportionate-burden-on-black-and-latino-borrowers

Dickler, J. (2018, July 10). *Here's how US college costs stack up to the rest of the world.* CNBC. Retrieved from https://www.cnbc.com/2018/07/09/heres-how-us-college-costs-stack-up-to-the-world.html

Dillon, E., & Carey, K. (2009). *Drowning in debt: The emerging student loan crisis.* Charts You Can Trust. Retrieved from https://www.researchgate.net/publication/265178874_Drowning_in_Debt_The_Emerging_Student_Loan_Crisis

Draut, T., & Silva, J. (2004). *Generation broke: The growth of debt among young Americans.* Borrowing to Make Ends Meet. Retrieved from https://www.campusactivism.org/server-new/uploads/generation_broke.pdf

Dynarski, M. (1994). Who defaults on student loans? Findings from the national postsecondary student aid study. *Economics of Education Review*, *13*(1), 55–68. https://doi.org/10.1016/0272-7757(94)90023-X

Dynarski, S. M. (2016). The dividing line between haves and have-nots in home ownership: Education, not student debt. *Evidence Speaks Reports*, *1*(17). Retrieved from https://www.brookings.edu/wp-content/uploads/2016/07/home-ownership-FINAL2b.pdf

Elliott, W., & Lewis, M. (2015). Student debt effects on financial well-being: Research and policy implications. *Journal of Economic Surveys*, *29*(4), 614–636. https://doi.org/10.1111/joes.12124

Ey, C. (2023, June 9). *HELP Debt—The evolution of higher education contributions.* Parliament of Australia Library. Retrieved from https://www.aph.gov.au/About_Parliament/Parliamentarydepartments/Parliamentary_Library/FlagPost/2023/June/HELP-debt

Federal Reserve Bank of New York. (2023, August 31). *Student loan balances decline to $1.57 trillion in Q2 2023.* Retrieved from https://www.newyorkfed.org/microeconomics/topics/student-debt

Federal Student Aid. (2024a). Income-driven repayment plans. Retrieved from https://studentaid.gov/manageloans/repayment/plans/income-driven

Federal Student Aid. (2024b). Federal student loans Retrieved from https://studentaid.gov/understand-aid/types/loans

Federal Student Aid. (2024c). Student loan repayment. Retrieved from https://studentaid.gov/manage-loans/ repayment

Federal Student Aid. (2024d). Federal student loan repayment plans. Retrieved from https://studentaid.gov/manage-loans/repayment/plans

Federal Student Aid. (2024e). Student loan delinquency and default. Retrieved from https://studentaid.gov/manage-loans/default

Federal Student Aid. (2024f). Complete your student loan entrance counseling requirement. Retrieved from https://studentaid.gov/entrance-counseling

Fernandes, D., Lynch Jr., J. G., & Netemeyer, R. G. (2014). Financial literacy, financial education, and downstream financial behaviors. *Management Science*, *60*(8), 1861–1883. https://doi.org/10.1287/mnsc.2013.1849

Fox, J. J., Bartholomae, S., Letkiewicz, J. C., & Montalto, C. P. (2017). College student debt and anticipated repayment difficulty. *Journal of Student Financial Aid*, *47*(2), 111–135. Retrieved from https://files.eric.ed.gov/fulltext/EJ1151786.pdf

Fry, R. (2012, September 26). A record one-in-five households now owe student loan debt. Pew Research Center. Retrieved from https://www.pewresearch.org/social-trends/2012/09/26/a-record-one-in-five-households-now-owe-student-loan-debt/

Fry, R. (2014, May 14). Young adults, student debt and economic well-being. Pew Research Center. Retrieved from https://www.pewresearch.org/social-trends/2014/05/14/young-adults-student-debt-and-economic-well-being

Fry, R. (2020, April 28). Millennials overtake Baby Boomers as America's largest generation. Pew Research Center. Retrieved from https://www.pewresearch.org/short-reads/2020/04/28/millennials-overtake-baby-boomers-as-americas-largest-generation

Gladieux, L. & Perna, L. (2005). Borrowers who drop out: A neglected aspect of the college student loan trend. National Center Report #05-2. National Center for Public Policy and Higher Education. Retrieved from https://files.eric.ed.gov/fulltext/ED508094.pdf

Griffiths, L. E. (2022). University student descriptions of their financial knowledge of student loan debt [doctoral dissertation]. Walden University. Retrieved from https://scholarworks.waldenu.edu/cgi/viewcontent.cgi?article=13946&context=dissertations

Gordon, T. (2022). First-generation academically at-risk black college students' perceptions of borrowing and repayment of student loans [doctoral dissertation]/ Walden University. Retrieved from https://www.proquest.com/docview/2753998780?pq-origsite=gscholar&fromopenview=true&sourcetype=Dissertations%20&%20Theses

Goyal, K., & Kumar, S. (2020). Financial literacy: A systematic review and bibliometric analysis. *International Journal of Consumer Studies*, *45*(1), 80–105. https://doi.org/10.1011/ijcs.12605

Greenberg, J. (2022, September 13). *40% of Student borrowers lack a four-year degree.* PolitiFact. Retrieved from https://www.politifact.com/factchecks/2022/sep/13/elizabeth-warren/40-student-borrowers-lack 4 year degree

Greene, L. L. (1989). An economic analysis of student loan default. *Educational Evaluation and Policy Analysis*, *11*(1), 61–68. https://doi.org/10.3102/01623737011001061

Grohmann, A. (2018). Financial literacy and financial behavior: Evidence from the emerging Asian middle class. *Pacific-Basin Finance Journal*, *48*, 129–143. https://doi.org/10.1016/j.pacfin.2018.01.007

Gutter, M., & Copur, Z. (2011). Financial behaviors and financial well-being of college students: Evidence from a national survey. *Journal of Family and Economic Issues*, *32*(4), 699–714. https://doi.org/10.1007/s10834-011-9255-2

Hahn, A., & Tarver, J. (2023). *2023 Student loan debt statistics: Average student loan debt.* Retrieved from https://www.forbes.com/advisor/student-loans/average-student-loan-statistics

Hales, E. S. (2021). *Determinants of the student loan decision and financial well-being: The role of financial education, financial literacy, and student loan characteristics* [doctoral dussertation]. Utah State University. Retrieved from https://www.proquest.com/docview/2609694811?pqorigsite=gscholar&fromopenview=true&sourcetype=Dissertations%20&%20Theses

Hansen, J. S. (1987). *Student loans: Are they overburdening a generation?* Joint Economic Committee, U.S. Congress.

Hansen, W. L., & Rhodes, M. S. (1988). Student debt crisis: Are students incurring excessive debt? *Economics of Education Review*, *7*(1), 101–112.

Hanson, M. (2023, September 24). Student loan debt by generation. Education Data Initiative. Retrieved from https://educationdata.org/student-loan-debt-by-generation

Hanson, M. (2024a, May 11). Average cost of college by country. Education Data Initiative. Retrieved from https://educationdata.org/average-cost-of-college-by-country

Hanson, M. (2024b, May 28). Average cost of college & tuition. Education Data Initiative. Retrieved from https://educationdata.org/average-cost-of-college

Hanson, M. (2024c, June 20). Student loan debt by gender. Education Data Initiative. Retrieved from https://educationdata.org/student-loan-debt-by-gender

Hanson, M. (2024d, July 15). Student loan debt statistics. Education Data Initiative. Retrieved from https://educationdata.org/student-loan-debt-statistics

Hanson, M. (2024e, August 16). College dropout rates. Education Data Initiative. Retrieved from https://educationdata.org/college-dropout-rates

Hanson, M. (2024f, August 28). Student loan default rate. Education Data Initiative. Retrieved from https://educationdata.org/student-loan-default-rate

Hanson, M. (2024g, August 31). Percentage of high school graduates that got to college. Education Data Initiative. Retrieved from https://educationdata.org/college-enrollment-statistics/#high-school-to-college

Hawkins, W. N. (2017). Does looking for help matter? The relationship between information sources and borrowing decision factors in student loan decisions [doctoral dissertation]. Ohio State University. Retrieved from https://rave.ohiolink.edu/etdc/view?acc_num=osu1492421762767966

Henager, R., & Wilmarth, M. J. (2018). The relationship between student loan debt and financial wellness. *Family and Consumer Sciences Research Journal*, *46*(4), 381–395. https://doi.org/10.1111/fcsr.12263

Hess, L. E., Petersen, A. C., & Mortimer, J. T. (1994). Youth, unemployment, and marginality: The problem and the solution. *Youth Unemployment and Society*, 3–33. https://doi.org/10.1017/CBO9780511664021.003

Hillman, N. W. (2014). College on credit: A multi-level analysis of student loan default. *The Review of Higher Education*, *37*(2), 169–195. https://doi.org/10.1353/rhe.2014.0011

Jackson, B. A., & Reynolds, J. R. (2013). The price of opportunity: Race, student loan debt, and college achievement. *Sociological Inquiry*, *83*(3), 335–368. https://doi.org/10.1111/soin.12012

Johnson, C. L., O'Neill, B., Worthy, S. L., Lown, J. M., & Bowen, C. F. (2016). What are student loan borrowers thinking? Insights from focus groups on college selection and student loan decision making. *Journal of Financial Counseling and Planning*, *27*(2), 184–198. https://doi.org/10.1891/1052-3073.27.2.184

Kaiser, T., & Menkhoff, L. (2017). Does financial education impact financial literacy and financial behaviors, and if so, when? *The World Bank Economic Review*, *31*(3), 611–630. https://doi.org/10.1093/wber/lhx018

Karolyi, G. A. (2016). The gravity of culture for finance. *Journal of Corporate Finance*, *41*, 610–625. https://doi.org/10.1016/j.jcorpfin.2016.07.003

Kenton, W. (2023). *Human capital definition: Types, examples, and relationship to the economy.* Investopedia. Retrieved from https://www.investopedia.com/terms/h/humancapital.asp

Kim, J., & Chatterjee, S. (2019). Student loans, health, and life satisfaction of US households: Evidence from a panel study. *Journal of Family and Economic Issues*, *40*, 36–50. https://doi.org/10.1007/s10834-018-9594-3

Kim, J., Chatterjee, S., & Kim, J. (2012). Outstanding AFCPE® conference paper: Debt burden of young adults in the United States. *Journal for Financial Counseling and Planning, 23*(2), 55–67. Retrieved from https://files.eric.ed.gov/fulltext/EJ996782.pdf

Kim, K. T., Lee, J. M., & Lee, J. (2021). Student loans and financial satisfaction: The moderating role of financial education. *Journal of Financial Counseling and Planning, 32*(2), 266–279. https://doi.org/10.1891/JFCP-19-00002

Kirkham, E. (2018, October 8). Is income-based student loan repayment a good idea? Student Loan Hero. Retrieved from https://studentloanhero.com/featured/income-based-repayment-plan

Kirkpatrick, J. I. (1968). A study of federal student loan programs. Retrieved from https://files.eric.ed.gov/fulltext/ED125397.pdf

Kyaw, M. (2020). Financial literacy and student loan debt [thesis]. California State University. Retrieved from https://scholarworks.calstate.edu/downloads/jm214w031

Lee, J. M., Kim, K. T., & Hong, E. J. (2018). Exploring financial burdens of student loan holders in the United States. *Family and Consumer Sciences Research Journal, 46*(4), 347–362. doi:10.1111/fcsr.12261.

Lochner, L., Stinebrickner, T., & Suleymanoglu, U. (2013). *The importance of financial resources for student loan repayment.* National Bureau of Economic Research. https://doi.org/10.3386/w19716

Looney, A. (2021). The student debt burden and its impact on racial justice, borrowers, and the economy. Brookings. Retrieved from https://www.brookings.edu/articles/the-student-debt-burden-and-its-impact-on-racial-justice-borrowers-and-the-economy

Looney, A., & Yannelis, C. (2015). A crisis in student loans? How changes in the characteristics of borrowers and in the institutions they attend contributed to rising loan defaults. *Brookings Papers on Economic Activity*, Vol. 2, pp. 1–89. https://doi.org/10.1353/eca.2015.0003

Luna-Torres, M., McKinney, L., Horn, C., & Jones, S. (2018). Understanding loan use and debt burden among low-income and minority students at a large urban community college. *Journal of Student Financial Aid, 48*(1), 2–28. https://doi.org/10.1177/0895904818773902

Luong, M. (2010). The financial impact of student loans. Retrieved from https://citeseerx.ist.psu.edu/document?repid=rep1&type=pdf&doi=74466c5178b5ee0aab3b8a5f6648419dec8e0ea5

Lusardi, A. (2008). Financial literacy: An essential tool for informed consumer choice? (Working Paper No. 14084). National Bureau of Economic Research. https://doi.org/10.3386/w14084

Lusardi, A., & Mitchell, O. S. (2007). Financial literacy and retirement planning: New evidence from the RAND American Life Panel (Working Paper No. 157). Michigan Retirement Research Center. https://doi.org/10.2139/ssrn.1095869

Lusardi, A., Mitchell, O. S., & Curto, V. (2010). Financial literacy among the young. *The Journal of Consumer Affairs, 44*(2), 358–380. https://doi.org/10.1111/j.1745-6606.2010.01173.x

Mandell, L. (2008). Financial education in high school. In *Overcoming the savings slump: How to increase the effectiveness of financial education and saving programs* (pp. 257–279). University of Chicago Press.

Mangrum, D. (2022). Personal finance education mandates and student loan repayment. *Journal of Financial Economics, 146*(1), 1–26. https://doi.org/10.1016/j.jfineco.2022.06.006

Markle, G. (2019). Crushing debt or savvy strategy? Financial literacy and student perception of their student loan debt. *Journal of Student Financial Aid, 49*(1), 1–20. https://doi.org/10.55504/0884-9153.1651

Miller, B. (2019). The continued student loan crisis for Black borrowers. Retrieved from https://hdl.handle.net/10919/97814

Miller, K. (2017). *Deeper in debt: Women and student loans.* American Association of University Women. Retrieved from https://files.eric.ed.gov/fulltext/ED580345.pdf

Min, S., & Taylor, M. G. (2018). Racial and ethnic variation in the relationship between student loan debt and the transition of first birth. *Demography, 55*(1), 165–188. https://doi.org/10.1007/s13524-017-0643-6

Mincer, J. (1958). Investment in human capital and personal income distribution. *Journal of Political Economy, 66*(4), 281–302. https://doi.org/10.1086/258055

Montalto, C. P., Phillips, E. L., McDaniel, A., & Baker, A. R. (2019). College student financial wellness: Student loans and beyond. *Journal of Family and Economic Issues, 40*(1), 3–21. https://doi.org/10.1007/s10834-018-9593-4

Mountain, T., Cao, X., Kim, N., & Gutter, M. (2020). Millennials' future homeownership and the role of student loan debt. *Family and Consumer Sciences Research Journal, 49*(1), 5–23. https://doi.org/10.1111/fcsr.12374

Mueller, H. M., & Yannelis, C. (2019). The rise in student loan defaults. *Journal of Financial Economics, 131*(1), 1–19. https://doi.org/10.1016/j.jfineco.2018.07.013

National Center for Education Statistics. (2023, May). Undergraduate enrollment. Institute of Education Sciences. Retrieved from https://nces.ed.gov/programs/coe/indicator/cha.

National Consumer Law Center (2023). Surviving debt: Expert advice for getting out of financial trouble. Boston, MA: National Consumer Law Center.

New America. (2020). *Education policy: Student loan history.* Retrieved from https://www.newamerica.org/education-policy/topics/higher-education-funding-and-financial-aid/federal-student-aid/federal-student-loans/federal-student-loan-history

Overs, R. P. (1957). A house is not a home; Neither is a student! *Vocational Guidance Quarterly, 5*(4), 157–160. https://doi.org/10.1002/j.2164-585X.1957.tb01753.x

Redd, K. E. (2001). Why do students borrow so much? Recent national trends in student loan debt. *ERIC Digest*, pp. 1–7. Retrieved from https://files.eric.ed.gov/fulltext/ED451759.pdf

Rothstein, J., & Rouse, C. E. (2011). Constrained after college: Student loans and early-career occupational choices. *Journal of Public Economics, 95*(1), 149–163. https://doi.org/10.1016/j.jpubeco.2010.09.015

Sabri, M. F. (2011). *Pathways to financial success: Determinants of financial literacy and financial well-being among young adults* [graduate thesis]. Iowa State University. Retrieved from https://www.proquest.com/docview/876180733?pq-origsite=gscholar&fromopenview=true&sourcetype=Dissertations%20&%20Theses

Schultz, T. W. (1961). Investment in human capital. *The American Economic Review, 51*(1), 1–17. Retrieved from https://www.jstor.org/stable/1818907

Scott-Clayton, J. (2018). The looming student loan default crisis is worse than we thought. *Evidence Speaks Reports, 2*(34), 1–10. Retrieved from https://hdl.handle.net/10919/96125

Scott-Clayton, J., & Li, J. (2016). Black-white disparity in student loan debt more than triples after graduation. *Evidence Speaks Reports*, 2(3), 2–9. Retrieved from https://vtechworks.lib.vt.edu/server/api/core/bitstreams/c610f39b-87df-4ba8-ae7c-15dcb4910bbb/content

Stark, E., & Poppler, P. (2016). What are they thinking? Employers requiring college degrees for low-skilled jobs. *SAM Advancement Management Journal, 81*(3), 17–21. Retrieved from https://www.researchgate.net/profile/ErnieStark/publication/306444567_What_Are_They_Thinking_Employers_Requiring_College_Degrees_For_Low-Skilled_Jobs/links

Ueda, K. (2019). How do local labor markets and human capital affect employment outcomes after job loss? *Southern Economic Journal, 86*(2), 548–572. https://doi.org/10.1002/soej.12353

U.S. Bureau of Labor Statistics. (2020). *College enrollment and work activity of recent high school and college graduates summary.* Retrieved from https://www.bls.gov/news.release/hsgec.nr0.htm

Value Colleges. (2020). *College access and affordability: USA vs. the World.* Retrieved from https://www.valuecolleges.com/collegecosts/

Walsemann, K. M., Gee, G. C., & Gentile, D. (2015). Sick of out loans: Student borrowing and mental health of young adults in the United States. *Social Sciences and Medicine, 124*, 85–93. https://doi.org/10.1016/j.socscimed.2014.11.027

Welding, L. (2023). *Average student loan debt: 2023 Statistics.* Best Colleges. Retrieved from https://www.bestcolleges.com/research/average-student-loan-debt

Welding, L. (2024). *Student loan debt over the years: 2000s to 2024.* Best Colleges. Retrieved from https://www.bestcolleges.com/research/student-loan-debt-by-year

Wilkerson, I. (1987, January 29). Heavy burden of college debt raises anxiety for young families' future. *The New York Times.* Retrieved from https://www.nytimes.com/1987/01/29/us/heavy-burden-of-college-debt-raises-anxiety-for-young-families-future.html

Williamson, R. (2010). *The role of culture in finance. Behavioral finance: Investors, corporations, and markets*, 629–645. Retrieved from https://randallmorck.ca/wp-content/uploads/2020/02/23 loyalty-agency-conflicts-and-corporate-governance.pdf#page=620

Wong, A. (2023, June 18). *How student loans keep some people trapped in debt. Expert says student loans are a "gateway debt" that perpetuate inequality.* CBC News. Retrieved from https://www.cbc.ca/news/business/student-loans-debt-trap-1.6877888

Xiao, J. J., Porto, N., & Mason, I. M. (2020). Financial capability of student loan holders who are college students, graduates, or dropouts. *The Journal of Consumer Affairs, 54*(4), 1383–1401. https://doi.org/10.1111/joca.12336

Chapter 10

Aassve, A., Cottini, E., & Vitali, A. (2013). Youth prospects in a time of economic recession. *Demographic Research, 29*, 949–962. Retrieved from https://www.jstor.org/stable/26348180

Akkermans, J., Blokker, R., Buers, C., Van der Heijden, B., & De Vos, A. (2021). Ready, set, go! In E. A. Marshall & J. E. Symonds (Eds.), *Young adult development at the school-to-work transition* (pp. 77–103). Oxford University Press. https://doi.org/10.1093/oso/9780190941512.003.0004

Alpaydın, Y., & Kültür, K. (2022). Improving the transition from higher education to employment: A review of current policies. In *Education policies in the 21st century: Comparative perspectives* (pp. 103–129). Palgrave Macmillan. https://doi.org/10.1007/978-981-19-1604-5_5

American College Health Association. (2014). *National college health assessment: Fall 2014 reference group executive summary.* Retrieved from https://www.acha.org/documents/ncha/NCHA-II_FALL_2014_REFERENCE_GROUP_EXECUTIVE_SUMMARY.pdf

Antenucci, D., Cafarella, M., Levenstein, M., Ré, C., & Shapiro, M. D. (2014). *Using social media to measure labor market flows* (Working Paper No. w20010). National Bureau of Economic Research. https://doi.org/10.3386/w20010

Arnett, J. J. (2015). *Emerging adulthood: The winding road from the late teens through the twenties* (2nd ed.). Oxford University Press. https://doi.org/10.1093/oxfordhb/9780199795574.013.9

Asonitou, S. (2015). Employability skills in higher education and the case of Greece. *Procedia: Social and Behavioral Sciences, 175*, 283–290. https://doi.org/10.1016/j.sbspro.2015.01.1202

Beiter, R., Nash, R., McCrady, M., Rhoades, D., Linscomb, M., Clarahan, M., & Sammut, S. (2015). The prevalence and correlates of depression, anxiety, and stress in a sample of college students. *Journal of Affective Disorders, 173*, 90–96. https://doi.org/10.1016/j.jad.2014.10.054

Bennett, S., & Maton, K. (2010). Beyond the "digital natives" debate: Towards a more nuanced understanding of students' technology experiences. *Journal of Computer Assisted Learning, 26*(5), 321–331. https://doi.org/10.1111/j.1365-2729.2010.00360.x

Braghieri, L., Levy, R. E., & Makarin, A. (2022). Social media and mental health. *American Economic Review, 112*(11), 3660–3693. https://doi.org/10.1257/aer.20211218

Brandenberg, G., Ozimek, P., Bierhoff, H. W., & Janker, C. (2019). The relation between use intensity of private and professional SNS, social comparison, self-esteem, and depressive tendencies in the light of self-regulation. *Behaviour & Information Technology, 38*(6), 578–591. https://doi.org/10.1080/0144929X.2018.1545049

Burcher, S. A. (2017). *Using the expectancy-value theory to understand young adults' financial behavior and financial well-being* [doctoral dissertation]. University of Minnesota. https://conservancy.umn.edu/items/a3f05808-42ff-41ef-9407-4507fab09b1b

Carnevale, A. P., & Hanson, A. (2015). Learn and earn: Career pathways for youth in the 21st century. *E-Journal of International and Comparative Labour Studies, 4*(1). Retrieved from https://ejcls.adapt.it/index.php/ejcls_adapt/article/download/253/323

Chevalier, A. (2011). Subject choice and earnings of UK graduates. *Economics of Education Review, 30*(6), 1187–1201. https://doi.org/10.1016/j.econedurev.2011.04.007

Correa, T. (2016). Digital skills and social media use: How Internet skills are related to different types of Facebook use among "digital natives." *Information, Communication & Society, 19*(8), 1095–1107. https://doi.org/10.1080/1369118X.2015.1084023

Davis, J., Wolff, H. G., Forret, M. L., & Sullivan, S. E. (2020). Networking via LinkedIn: An examination of usage and career benefits. *Journal of Vocational Behavior, 118*, 103396. https://doi.org/10.1016/j.jvb.2020.103396

De Hauw, S., & De Vos, A. (2010). Millennials' career perspective and psychological contract expectations: Does the recession lead to lowered expectations? *Journal of Business and Psychology, 25*, 293–302. https://doi.org/10.1007/s10869-010-9162-9

Dogruer, N., Eyyam, R., & Menevis, I. (2011). The use of the internet for educational purposes. *Procedia: Social and Behavioral Sciences, 28*, 606–611. https://doi.org/10.1016/j.sbspro.2011.11.115

Doherty, J. (2021). *College as a pressure cooker: Relationships between the pressure to succeed, mental health distress, and coping in college students.* Retrieved from https://digitalcommons.assumption.edu/cgi/viewcontent.cgi?article=1092&context=honorstheses

Eurofound, Sándor, E., Patrini, V., Mascherini, M., et al., (2021). *Impact of COVID-19 on young people in the EU.* European Union. Retrieved from https://data.europa.eu/doi/10.2806/361465

Fang, R. T., & Saks, A. M. (2022). A self-regulatory model of how future work selves change during job search and the school-to-work transition. *Journal of Vocational Behavior, 138*, 103783. https://doi.org/10.1016/j.jvb.2022.103783

Flatt, A. (2013). A suffering generation: Six factors contributing to the mental health crisis in North American higher education. *College Quarterly, 16*(1), n1.

Fowle, M. (2019). The entrepreneurial dream: Happiness, depression and freedom. *International Review of Entrepreneurship, 17*(3), 305–322.

Gallagher, R. P. (2015). *2014 National survey of college counseling centers.* Retrieved from https://d-scholarship.pitt.edu/id/eprint/28178

Garcia-Aracil, A., Monteiro, S., & Almeida, L. S. (2021). Students' perceptions of their preparedness for transition to work after graduation. *Active Learning in Higher Education, 22*(1), 49–62. https://doi.org/10.1177/1469787418791026

Hakkarainen, K., Hietajärvi, L., Alho, K., Lonka, K., & Salmela-Aro, K. (2015). Sociodigital revolution: Digital natives vs. digital immigrants. In J. D. Wright (Ed.), *International encyclopedia of the social and behavioral sciences* (pp. 918–923). Elsevier. https://doi-org.ezproxy.jyu.fi/10.1016/B978-0-08-097086-8.26094-7

Harrington, B., & Hall, D. T. (2007). *Career management & work-life integration: Using self assessment to navigate contemporary careers*. SAGE.

Harrington, B., Van Deusen, F., Fraone, J. S., & Morelock, J. (2015). *How millennials navigate their careers. Young adult views on work, life and success*. Boston College Center for Work and Family. Retrieved from https://www.bc.edu/content/dam/files/centers/cwf/research/publications/researchreports/how-millennials-navigate-their-careers.pdf

Helsper, E. (2008). Digital natives and ostrich tactics?: The possible implications of labelling young people as digital experts. *The New York Times*. Retrieved from https://www.nytimes.com/2022/09/16/business/linkedin-overshare.html

Helsper, E. J., & Smahel, D. (2020). Excessive internet use by young Europeans: Psychological vulnerability and digital literacy? *Information, Communication & Society*, *23*(9), 1255–1273. https://doi.org/10.1080/1369118X.2018.1563203

Holm, J. R., & Lorenz, E. (2022). The impact of artificial intelligence on skills at work in Denmark. *New Technology, Work and Employment*, *37*(1), 79–101. https://doi.org/10.1111/ntwe.12215

Humburg, M., Van der Velden, R., & Verhagen, A. (2013). *The employability of higher education graduates*. Publications Office of the European Union. Retrieved from https://www.bruegel.org/sites/default/files/wp-content/uploads/imported/events/Graduate_Employability_study.pdf

Hussong, A. M., Benner, A. D., Erdem, G., Lansford, J. E., Makila, L. M., Petrie, R. C., & SRA COVID-19 Response Team. (2021). Adolescence amid a pandemic: Short-and long-term implications. *Journal of Research on Adolescence*, *31*(3), 820–835. https://doi.org/10.1111/jora.12671

Icha, O. (2015). Effectiveness of social media networks as a strategic tool for organizational marketing management. *Journal of Internet Banking and Commerce*, 01(S2). https://doi.org/10.4172/1204-5357.S2-006

Jacob, M., & Klein, M. (2019). Social origin, field of study and graduates' career progression: Does social inequality vary across fields? *The British Journal of Sociology*, *70*(5), 1850–1873. https://doi.org/10.1111/1468-4446.12696

Kelley, L. (2022). How LinkedIn became a place to overshare. *The New York Times*. Retrieved from https://www.nytimes.com/2022/09/16/business/linkedin-overshare.html

Kennedy, G., Dalgarno, B., Bennett, S., Gray, K., Waycott, J., Judd, T., . . . Chang, R. (2009). *Educating the net generation: A handbook of findings for practice and policy*. University of Melbourne Press. Retrieved from https://researchoutput.csu.edu.au/files/9390003/59277_Report

Kross, E., Verduyn, P., Sheppes, G., Costello, C. K., Jonides, J., & Ybarra, O. (2021). Social media and well-being: Pitfalls, progress, and next steps. *Trends in Cognitive Sciences*, *25*(1), 55–66. https://doi.org/10.1016/j.tics.2020.10.005

Kuhn, M., & Ploj, G. (2020). *Job stability, earnings dynamics, and life-cycle savings* (CERP Discussion Paper No. DP15460). Retrieved from https://ssrn.com/abstract=3737593

Lent, R. W., & Brown, S. D. (2020). Career decision making, fast and slow: Toward an integrative model of intervention for sustainable career choice. *Journal of Vocational Behavior*, *120*, 103448. https://doi.org/10.1016/j.jvb.2020.103448

Lent, R. W., Hackett, G., & Brown, S. D. (1999). A social cognitive view of school-to-work transition. *The Career Development Quarterly*, *47*(4), 297–311. https://doi.org/10.1002/j.2161-0045.1999.tb00739.x

Li, L., Serido, J., Vosylis, R., Sorgente, A., Lep, Z., Zhang, Y., . . . Lanz, M. (2023). Employment disruption and wellbeing among young adults: A cross-national study of perceived impact of the COVID-19 lockdown. *Journal of Happiness Studies, 24*(3), 991–1012. https://doi.org/10.1007/s10902-023-00629-3

Livingstone, S., Mascheroni, G., & Stoilova, M. (2023). The outcomes of gaining digital skills for young people's lives and wellbeing: A systematic evidence review. *New Media & Society, 25*(5), 1176–1202. https://doi.org/10.1177/14614448211043189

Mahmoud, J. S. R., Staten, R. T., Hall, L. A., & Lennie, T. A. (2012). The relationship among young adult college students' depression, anxiety, stress, demographics, life satisfaction, and coping styles. *Issues in Mental Health Nursing, 33*(3), 149–156. https://doi.org/10.3109/01612840.2011.632708

Mañé, F., & Corbella, T. (2017). Developing and running an establishment skills survey. In *Compendium on anticipation and matching of skills:/ETF, CEDEFOP, European Centre for the Development of Vocational Training, ILO, International Labour Office, Geneva* (Vol. 5). European Union. Retrieved from https://www.ilo.org/wcmsp5/groups/public/—ed_emp/—ifp_skills/documents/publication/wcms_548324.pdf

Marsh, E., Vallejos, E. P., & Spence, A. (2022). The digital workplace and its dark side: An integrative review. *Computers in Human Behavior, 128*, 107118. https://doi.org/10.1016/j.chb.2021.107118

Masten, A. S., & Powell, J. L. (2003). A resilience framework for research, policy, and practice. In S. S. Luthar (Ed.), *Resilience and vulnerability, adaptation in the context of childhood adversities* (pp. 1–25). Cambridge University Press.

McIlveen, P., Beccaria, G., &Burton, L. J. (2013). Beyond conscientiousness: Career optimism and satisfaction with academic major. *Journal of Vocational Behavior, 83*(3), 229–236. https://doi.org/10.1016/j.jvb.2013.05.005

Minor-Cooley, D., & Parks-Yancy, R. (2020). The power of the brand: Personal branding and its effect on job seeking attributes. *Journal of Internet Commerce, 19*(3), 241–261. https://doi.org/10.1080/15332861.2020.1777028

Nuckols, J. A., Silinskas, G., Ranta, M., & Wilska, T. A. (2023a). Income and career concerns among emerging adults from Finland, Sweden, and the United Kingdom during COVID-19. *Emerging Adulthood, 11*(3), 721–734. https://doi.org/10.1177/21676968231153691

Nuckols, J. A., Sirola, A., Ylilahti, M., & Wilska, T. A. (2023b). Life course challenges in crises: Transition from higher education to work during COVID-19 in Finland and Sweden. *Journal of Education and Work, 36*(7–8), 576–591, 1–16. https://doi.org/10.1080/13639080.2023.2292155

Patel, A. K., Tiwari, S. K., Singh, S., & Lindinger-Sternart, S. (2018). Self-esteem and life satisfaction among university students of Eastern Uttar Pradesh of India: A demographical perspective. *Indian Journal of Positive Psychology, 9*(3), 382–386. https://doi.org/10.5281/zenodo.7062925

Pisarik, C. T., Rowell, P. C., & Thompson, L. K. (2017). A phenomenological study of career anxiety among college students. *The Career Development Quarterly, 65*(4), 339–352. https://doi.org/10.1002/cdq.12112

Ranta, M., Chow, A., & Salmela-Aro, K. (2013). Trajectories of life satisfaction and the financial situation in the transition to adulthood. *Longitudinal and Life Course Studies, 4*(1), 57–77. https://doi.org/10.14301/llcs.v4i1.216

Ranta, M., Silinskas, G., & Wilska, T. A. (2020). Young adults' personal concerns during the COVID-19 pandemic in Finland: An issue for social concern. *International Journal of Sociology and Social Policy, 40*(9/10), 1201–1219. https://doi.org/10.1108/IJSSP-07-2020-0267

Recksiedler, C., & Landberg, M. (2021). Emerging adults' self-efficacy as a resource for coping with the COVID-19 pandemic. *Emerging Adulthood, 9*(5), 576–582. https://doi.org/10.1177/21676968211019287

Reid, A., Ronda-Perez, E., & Schenker, M. B. (2021). Migrant workers, essential work, and COVID-19. *American Journal of Industrial Medicine, 64*(2), 73–77. https://doi.org/10.1002/ajim.23209

Říhová, H. (2016). *Using labour market information: Compendium on anticipation and matching of skills* (Vol. 1). European Centre for the Development of Vocational Training and ILO, European Union. Retrieved from https://www.ilo.org/wcmsp5/groups/public/—ed_emp/—ifp_skills/documents/publication/wcms_534314.pdf

Saks, A. M. (2018). Job search and the school-to-work transition. In U.-C. Klehe & E. A. J. van Hooft (Eds.), *The Oxford handbook of job loss and job search* (pp. 379–400). Oxford University Press. https://doi.org/10.1093/oxfordhb/9780199764921.013.008

Salmela-Aro, K., & Nurmi, J. E. (2007). Self-esteem during university studies predicts career characteristics 10 years later. *Journal of Vocational Behavior, 70*(3), 463–477. https://doi.org/10.1016/j.jvb.2007.01.006

Sharma, I., & Sudhesh, N. T. (2018). Social media and work-life balance among corporate employees. *International Journal of Education and Management Studies, 8*(1), 65–70.

She, L., Waheed, H., Lim, W. M., & E-Vahdati, S. (2022). Young adults' financial well-being: Current insights and future directions. *International Journal of Bank Marketing, 41*(2), 333–368. https://doi.org/10.1108/IJBM-04-2022-0147

Sibide, N. (2015, June 11). *Millennials aren't as tech savvy as people think.* CNBC. Retrieved from https://www.cnbc.com/2015/06/10/millennials-arent-as-tech-savvy-as-people-think.html

Steffy, B. D., Shaw, K. N., & Noe, A. W. (1989). Antecedents and consequences of job search behaviors. *Journal of Vocational Behavior, 35*(3), 254–269. https://doi.org/10.1016/0001-8791(89)90029-8

Steiner, R., Hirschi, A., & Akkermans, J. (2022). Many roads lead to Rome: Researching antecedents and outcomes of contemporary school-to-work transitions. *Journal of Career Development, 49*, 3–17. https://doi.org/10.1177/08948453211063580

Suorsa, O., & Sainio, J. (2020). *Osaamisesta yliopistojen maisteriseurantakyselyiden 2017–2019 pohjalta* [On competence based on the universities' master's follow-up surveys 2017–2019]. *Aarresaari. Yliopistojen Työelämä- ja Urapalveluiden Verkosto*/Aarresaari Network, Career Services Network of Universities in Finland. Retrieved from https://www.aarresaari.net/wp-content/uploads/2020/12/Uraseurantaraportti-osaamisesta-2020.pdf

Tanzi, A. (2023). *Most US college grads say that trade skills bring better job security.* Bloomberg. Retrieved from https://www.bloomberg.com/news/articles/2023-08-24/most-us-college-grads-say-trade-skills-bring-better-job-security#xj4y7vzkg

Thrupp, R. M. (2008). *A Study of ICT-associated identities of primary-aged learners.* CQ University. Retrieved from https://hdl.handle.net/10018/25930

Tynjälä, P., Slotte, V., Nieminen, J., Lonka, K., & Olkinuora, E. (2006). From university to working life: Graduates' workplace skills in practice. In P. Tynjälä, J. Välimaa, & G. Boulton-Lewis (Eds.), *Higher education and working life: Collaborations, confrontations and challenges* (pp. 73–88). Elsevier. Retrieved from https://www.academia.edu/download/39832077/From_university_to_working_life_Graduate20151109-1039-1211gt2.pdf

Van Dijck, J. (2013). "You have one identity": Performing the self on Facebook and LinkedIn. *Media, Culture & Society, 35*(2), 199–215. https://doi.org/10.1177/0163443712468605

Wilska, T. A. (2004). Oman elämänsä yrittäjät? Nuorisobarometri 2004. Opetusministeriö. Helsinki. Nuorisoasiainneuvottelukunta. Julkaisuja, 28.

Whitmer, J. M. (2019). You are your brand: Self-branding and the marketization of self. *Sociology Compass, 13*(3), e12662. https://doi.org/10.1111/soc4.12662

Yorke, M., & Harvey, L. (2005). Graduate attributes and their development. *New Directions for Institutional Research* (128), 41–58. https://doi.org/10.1002/ir.162

Zimmermann, K. F., Biavaschi, C., Eichhorst, W., Giulietti, C., Kendzia, M. J., Muravyev, A., . . . Schmidl, R. (2013). Youth unemployment and vocational training. *Foundations and Trends® in Microeconomics*, 9(1–2), 1–157. https://doi.org/10.1561/0700000058

Chapter 11

Arnett, J. J. (1994). Are college students adults? Their conceptions of the transition to adulthood. *Journal of Adult Development*, *1*(4), 213–224. https://doi.org/10.1007/BF02277582

Arnett, J. J. (1997). Young people's conceptions of the transition to adulthood. *Youth & Society*, *29*(1), 3–23. https://doi.org/10.1177/0044118X97029001001

Arnett, J. J. (1998). Learning to stand alone: The contemporary American transition to adulthood in cultural and historical context. *Human Development*, *41*, 295–315. https://doi.org/10.1159/000022591

Arnett, J. J. (2003). Conceptions of the transition to adulthood among emerging adults in American ethnic groups. *New Directions for Child and Adolescent Development* (100), 63–76. https://doi.org/10.1002/cd.75

Arnett, J. J. (2014). *Emerging adulthood: The winding road from the late teens through the twenties* (2nd ed.). Oxford University Press. https://doi.org/10.1093/acprof:oso/9780199929382.001.0001

Bartoszuk, K., Deal, J. E., & Yerhot, M. (2021). Parents' and college students' perceptions of support and family environment. *Emerging Adulthood*, *9*(1), 76–87. https://doi.org/10.1177/2167696818823947

Bea, M. D., & Yi, Y. (2019). Leaving the financial nest: Connecting young adults' financial independence to financial security. *Journal of Marriage and Family*, *81*(2), 397–414. https://doi.org/10.1111/JOMF.12553

Benson, J. E., & Furstenberg Jr., F. F. (2006). Entry into adulthood: Are adult role transitions meaningful markers of adult identity? *Advances in Life Course Research*, *11*, 199–224. https://doi.org/10.1016/S1040-2608(06)11008-4

Cobb-Clark, D. A., & Gørgens, T. (2014). Parents' economic support of young-adult children: Do socioeconomic circumstances matter? *Journal of Population Economics*, *27*(2), 447–471. https://doi.org/10.1007/S00148-013-0484-6

Corijn, M., & Klijzing, E. (2001). Transitions to adulthood in Europe: Conclusions and discussion. In M. Corijn & E. Klijzing (Eds.), *Transitions to adulthood in Europe* (pp. 313–340). Springer Netherlands. https://doi.org/10.1007/978-94-015-9717-3_13

Costa, S., Soenens, B., Gugliandolo, M. C., Cuzzocrea, F., & Larcan, R. (2015). The mediating role of experiences of need satisfaction in associations between parental psychological control and internalizing problems: A study among Italian college students. *Journal of Child and Family Studies*, *24*(4), 1106–1116. https://doi.org/10.1007/S10826-014-9919-2

Fingerman, K. L., Cheng, Y.-P., Kim, K., Fung, H. H., Han, G., Lang, F. R., . . . Wagner, J. (2016). Parental involvement with college students in Germany, Hong Kong, Korea, and the United States. *Journal of Family Issues*, *37*(10), 1384–1411. https://doi.org/10.1177/0192513X14541444

Fingerman, K. L., Miller, L., Birditt, K., & Zarit, S. (2009). Giving to the good and the needy: Parental support of grown children. *Journal of Marriage and Family*, *71*(5), 1220–1233. https://doi.org/10.1111/j.1741-3737.2009.00665.x

Fletcher, A. C., & Alligood, B. N. (2022). "I definitely wouldn't have been able to make it through college without my dad's money": American college students' reflections regarding caregiver financial support. *Emerging Adulthood, 10*(6), 1497–1510. https://doi.org/10.1177/21676968211066157

Fussell, E., & Furstenberg Jr., F. F. (2005). The transition to adulthood during the twentieth century: race, nativity, gender. In R. A. Settersten Jr., F. F. Furstenberg, & R. G. Rumbaut (Eds.), *On the frontier of adulthood: Theory, research, and public policy* (pp. 29–59). University of Chicago Press. https://doi.org/10.7208/chicago/9780226748924.003.0002

Hamilton, L. T. (2013). More is more or more is less? Parental financial investments during college. *American Sociological Review, 78*(1), 70–95. https://doi.org/10.1177/0003122412472680

Hill, J. M., van der Geest, V. R., & Blokland, A. A. J. (2017). Leaving the bank of mum and dad: Financial independence and delinquency desistance in emerging adulthood. *Journal of Developmental and Life-Course Criminology, 3*(4), 419–439. https://doi.org/10.1007/S40865-017-0058-5

Houle, J. N. (2014). Disparities in debt: Parents' socioeconomic resources and young adult student loan debt. *Sociology of Education, 87*(1), 53–69. https://doi.org/10.1177/0038040713512213

Johnson, M. K. (2013). Parental financial assistance and young adults' relationships with parents and well-being. *Journal of Marriage and Family, 75*(3), 713–733. https://doi.org/10.1111/jomf.12029

Johnson, M. K., & Ridgeway, S. (2023). Becoming independent and responsible adults: Does parental financial help interfere? *Journal of Family Issues, 45*(3), 571–591. https://doi.org/10.1177/0192513X231155600

Lowe, K., Dotterer, A. M., & Francisco, J. (2015). "If I pay, I have a say!": Parental payment of college education and its association with helicopter parenting. *Emerging Adulthood, 3*(4), 286–290. https://doi.org/10.1177/2167696815579831

Majamaa, K. (2013). The effect of socioeconomic factors on parental financial support from the perspectives of the givers and the receivers. *European Societies, 15*(1), 57–81, https://doi.org/10.1080/14616696.2012.721891

Manzoni, A. (2018). Parental support and youth occupational attainment: Help or hindrance? *Journal of Youth and Adolescence, 47*, 1580–1594. https://doi.org/10.1007/s10964-018-0856-z

Mortimer, J. T., Kim, M., Staff, J., & Vuolo, M. (2016). Unemployment, parental help, and self-efficacy during the transition to adulthood. *Work and Occupations, 43*(4), 434–465. https://doi.org/10.1177/0730888416656904

Mudrazija, S. (2014). The balance of intergenerational family transfers: A life-cycle perspective. *European Journal of Ageing, 11*, 249–259. https://doi.org/10.1007/s10433-013-0302-8

Nelson, L. J., & Luster, S. S. (2015). "Adulthood" by whose definition? The complexity of emerging adults' conceptions of adulthood. In J. J. Arnett (Ed.), *The Oxford handbook of emerging adulthood* (pp. 421–437). Oxford University Press. https://doi.org/10.1093/oxfordhb/9780199795574.013.24

Oh, S., & Lee, J. (2023). Parental financial assistance and psychological well-being among Korean emerging adults: Pressure from and fulfillment of parental career expectations as mediators. *Emerging Adulthood, 11*(5), 1119–1130. https://doi.org/10.1177/21676968231172550

Oliveira, C., Fonseca, G., Sotero, L., Crespo, C., & Relvas, A.P. (2020). Family dynamics during emerging adulthood: Reviewing, integrating, and challenging the field. *Journal of Family Theory & Review, 12*, 350–367. https://doi.org/10.1111/jftr.12386

Padilla-Walker, L., Nelson, L., & Carroll, J. (2012). Affording emerging adulthood: Parental financial assistance of their college-aged children. *Journal of Adult Development, 19*, 50–58. https://doi.org/10.1007/s10804-011-9134-y

Quintini, G., Martin, J. P., & Martin, S. (2007). *The changing nature of the school-to-work transition process in OECD countries* (SSRN Paper No. 1884070). Social Science Research Network. Retrieved from https://papers.ssrn.com/abstract=1884070

Schoeni, R. F., & Ross, K. E. (2013). Material assistance from families during the transition to adulthood. In R. A. Settersten Jr., F. F. Furstenberg, & R. G. Rumbaut (Eds.), *On the frontier of adulthood* (pp. 396–416). University of Chicago Press. https://doi.org/10.7208/CHICAGO/9780226748924.003.0012

Seiffge-Krenke, I. (2013). "She's leaving home . . ." Antecedents, consequences, and cultural patterns in the leaving home process. *Emerging Adulthood, 1*(2), 114–124. https://doi.org/10.1177/2167696813479783

Serido, J., Pollitt, A. M., Muraco, J. A., Conger, K. J., & Russell, S. T. (2018). Financial stress and drinking during the transition to adulthood: The role of parental financial support. *Emerging Adulthood, 7*(6), 490–500. https://doi.org/10.1177/2167696818785555

Shanahan, M. J., Porfeli, E., & Mortimer, J. (2005). Subjective age identity and the transition to adulthood: When does one become an adult? In R. A. Settersten Jr., F. F. Furstenberg, & R. G. Rumbaut (Eds.), *On the frontier of adulthood: Theory, research, and public policy.* University of Chicago Press. https://doi/10.7208/chicago/9780226748924.003.0007

Shin, D. C., & Johnson, D. M. (1978). Avowed happiness as an overall assessment of the quality of life. *Social Indicators Research, 5*, 475–492. https://doi.org/10.1007/BF00352944

Soenens, B., Vansteenkiste, M., Luyten, P., Duriez, B., & Goossens, L. (2005). Maladaptive perfectionistic self-representations: The mediational link between psychological control and adjustment. *Personality and Individual Differences, 38*(2), 487–498. https://doi.org/10.1016/J.PAID.2004.05.008

Swartz, T. T. (2008). Family capital and the invisible transfer of privilege: Intergenerational support and social class in early adulthood. *New Directions for Child and Adolescent Development* (119), 11–24. https://doi.org/10.1002/cd.206

Swartz, T. T., Kim, M., Uno, M., Mortimer, J., & O'Brien, K. B. (2011). Safety nets and scaffolds: Parental support in the transition to adulthood. *Journal of Marriage and the Family, 73*(2), 411–429. https://doi.org/10.1111/J.1741-3737.2010.00815.X

Swartz, T. T., & O'Brien, K. B. (2016). Intergenerational support during the transition to adulthood. In A. Furlong (Ed.), *Routledge handbook of youth and young adulthood* (pp. 221–228). Routledge. https://doi.org/10.4324/9781315753058-36

Tanner, J. L. (2006). Recentering during emerging adulthood: A critical turning point in life span human development. In *Emerging adults in America: Coming of age in the 21st century.* (pp. 21–55). American Psychological Association. https://doi.org/10.1037/11381-002

Van Herreweghe, L., & Van Lancker, W. (2021). *The accumulation of (dis)advantages: downward parent-child financial transfers across European countries* (Working Paper No. CeSO/SPSW/2021-03). SPSW. https://lirias.kuleuven.be/retrieve/628288

Vosylis, R., & Klimstra, T. (2022). How does financial life shape emerging adulthood? Short-term longitudinal associations between emerging adulthood features, financial behaviors, and financial well-being in college freshmen. *Emerging Adulthood, 10*, 90–108. https://doi.org/10.1177/2167696820908970

Webber, K. L., & Burns, R. (2021). Increases in graduate student debt in the U.S.: 2000 to 2016. *Research in Higher Education, 62*, 709–732. https://doi.org/10.1007/s11162-020-09611-x

Wightman, P. H., Patrick, M. E., Schoeni, R. F., & Schulenberg, J. E. (2013). Historical trends in parental financial support of young adults. *PSC Research Reports*, 1–33. Retrieved from https://shorturl.at/gnxK3

Chapter 12

Adams, G. R., & Marshall, S. K. (1996). A developmental social psychology of identity: Understanding the person-in-context. *Jounal of Adolescence, 19*, 429–442. https://doi.org/10.1006/jado.1996.0041

Adams, G. R., Shea, J., & Fitch, S. A. (1979). Toward the development of an objective assessment of ego-identity status. *Journal of Youth and Adolescence, 8*, 223–237. https://doi.org/10.1007/BF02087622

Arnett, J. J. (1998). Learning to stand alone: The contemporary American transition to adulthood in cultural and historical context. *Human Development, 41*(5–6), 295–315. https://doi.org/10.1159/000022591

Arnett, J. J. (2000). Emerging adulthood. A theory of development from the late teens through the twenties. *American Psychologist, 55*(5), 469–480. PMID: 10842426.

Aronson, P., Callahan, T., & Davis, T. (2015). The transition from college to work during the great recession: Employment, financial, and identity challenges. *Journal of Youth Studies, 18*(9), 1097–1118. https://doi.org/10.1080/13676261.2015.1020931

Baltes, P. B., & Baltes, M. M. (1990). Psychological perspectives on successful aging: The model of selective optimization with compensation. In P. B. Baltes & M. M. Baltes (Eds.), *Successful aging: Perspectives from the behavioral sciences* (pp. 1–34). Cambridge University Press. https://doi.org/10.1017/CBO9780511665684

Barber, B. L., Card, N. A., Serido, J., & Shim, S. (2011, November). *Financial identity of United States and Australian college students* [Paper presentation]. 2011 National Council of Family Relations Conference, Orlando, FL.

Barry, C. M., Madsen, S. D., Nelson, L. J., Carroll, J. S., & Badger, S. (2009). Friendship and romantic relationship qualities in emerging adulthood: Differential associations with identity development and achieved adulthood criteria. *Journal of Adult Development, 16*(4), 209–222. https://doi.org/10.1007/s10804-009-9067-x

Berzonsky, M. D. (1989). Identity style: Conceptualization and measurement. *Journal of Adolescent Research, 4*(3), 268–282. https://doi.org/10.1177/074355488943002

Bosch, L. A., Serido, J., Card, N., Shim, S., & Barber, B. L. (2016). Predictors of financial identity development in emerging adulthood. *Emerging Adulthood, 4*(6), 417–426. https://doi.org/10.1177/2167696816631845

British Academy. (2021). *The COVID decade: Understanding the long-term societal impacts of COVID-19*. https://doi.org/10.5871/bac19stf/9780856726583.001

Butterbaugh, S. M., Ross, D. B., & Campbell, A. (2020). My money and me: Attaining financial independence in emerging adulthood through a conceptual model of identity capital theory. *Contemporary Family Therapy: An International Journal, 42*(1), 33–45. https://doi.org/10.1007/s10591-019-09515-8

Côté, J. E., & Levine, C. (2002). *Identity formation, agency, and culture*. Erlbaum.

Crocetti, E., Klimstra, T. A., Hale III, W. W., Koot, H. M., & Meeus, W. (2013). Impact of early adolescent externalizing problem behaviors on identity development in middle to late adolescence: A prospective 7-year longitudinal study. *Journal of Youth and Adolescence, 42(11)*, 1–14. https://doi.org/10.1007/s10964-013-9924-6

Crocetti, E., Prati, F., & Rubini, M. (2018). The interplay of personal and social identity. *European Psychologist, 23*(4), 300–310. https://doi.org/10.1027/1016-9040/a000336

Crocetti, E., Rubini, M., & Meeus, W. (2008). Capturing the dynamics of identity formation in various ethnic groups: Development and validation of a three-dimensional model. *Journal of Adolescence, 31*(2), 207–222. https://doi.org/10.1016/j.adolescence.2007.09.002

Erikson, E. H. (1950). *Childhood and society*. Norton.

Erikson, E. H. (1968). *Identity: Youth and crisis*. Norton.

Galambos, N. L., Turner, P. K., & Tilton-Weaver, L. C. (2005). Chronological and subjective age in emerging adulthood: The crossover effect. *Journal of Adolescent Research, 20*(5), 538–556. https://doi.org/10.1177/0743558405274876

Galliher, R. V., McLean, K. C., & Syed, M. (2017). An integrated developmental model for studying identity content in context. *Developmental Psychology, 53*(11), 2011–2022. https://doi.org/10.1037/dev0000299

Kalleberg, A. L. (2020). Labor market uncertainties and youth labor force experiences: Lessons learned. *The Annals of the American Academy of Political and Social Science, 688*(1), 258–270. https://doi.org/10.1177/0002716220913861

Kirkpatrick Johnson, M. (2013). Parental financial assistance and young adults' relationships with parents and well-being. *Journal of Marriage and Family, 75*(3), 713–733. https://doi.org/10.1111/jomf.12029

Kroger, J., & Marcia, J. E. (2011). The identity statuses: Origins, meanings, and interpretations. In S. J. Schwartz, K. Luyckx, & V. L. Vignoles (Eds.), *Handbook of identity theory and research* (Vol. 1, pp. 31–53). Springer. https://doi.org/10.1007/978-1-4419-7988-9_2

Lauer, J. (2010). The good consumer: Credit reporting and the invention of financial identity in the United States, 1840–1940. *Enterprise & Society, 11*(4), 688–696. https://www.jstor.org/stable/23701244

Laughland-Booy, J., Newcombe, P., Skrbiš, Z. (2017). Looking forward: Career identity formation and the temporal orientations of young Australians. *Journal of Vocational Behavior, 101*, 43–56. https://doi.org/10.1016/j.jvb.2017.04.005

LeBaron, A. B., & Kelley, H. H. (2021). Financial socialization: A decade in review. *Journal of Family and Economic Issues*, 42 (Suppl 1), 195–206. https://doi.org/10.1007/s10834-020-09736-2

Lowe, S. R., Dillon, C. O., Rhodes, J. E., & Zwiebach, L. (2013). Defining adult experiences: Perspectives of a diverse sample of young adults. *Journal of Adolescent Research, 28*(1), 31–68. https://doi.org/10.1177/0743558411435854

Luyckx, K., Goossens, L., & Soenens, B. (2006). A developmental contextual perspective on identity construction in emerging adulthood: Change dynamics in commitment formation and commitment evaluation. *Developmental Psychology, 42*(2), 366–380. https://doi.org/10.1037/0012-1649.42.2.366

Luyckx, K., Schwartz, S. J., Goossens, L., & Pollock, S. (2008). Employment, sense of coherence, and identity formation: Contextual and psychological processes on the pathway to sense of adulthood. *Journal of Adolescent Research, 23*(5), 566–591. https://doi.org/10.1177/0743558408322146

Luyckx, K., Seiffge-Krenke, I., Schwartz, S. j., Crocetti, E., & Klimstra, T. A. (2014). Identity configurations across love and work in emerging adults in romantic relationships. *Journal of Applied Developmental Psychology, 35*(3), 192–203. https://doi.org/10.1016/j.appdev.2014.03.007

Mancini, T., Caricati, L., Panari, C., & Tonarelli, A. (2015). Personal and social aspects of professional identity: An extension of Marcia's identity status model applied to a sample of university students. *Journal of Vocational Behavior, 89*, 140–150. https://doi.org/10.1016/j.jvb.2015.06.002.

Marcia, J. E. (1966). Development and validation of egoidentity status. *Journal of Personality and Social Psychology, 3*(5), 551–558. https://doi.org/10.1037/h0023281

McLean, K. C., Syed, M., & Shucard, H. (2016). Bringing identity content to the fore: Links to identity development processes. *Emerging Adulthood, 4*(5), 356–364. https://doi.org/10.1177/2167696815626820

Negru-Subtirica, O., Pop, E. I., & Crocetti, E. (2017). A longitudinal integration of identity styles and educational identity processes in adolescence. *Developmental Psychology, 53*, 2127–2138. https://doi.org/10.1037/dev0000325

Padilla-Walker, L. M., Barry, C. M., Carroll, J. S., Madsen, S. D., & Nelson, L. J. (2008). Looking on the bright side: The role of identity status and gender on positive orientations during emerging adulthood. *Journal of Adolescence, 31*(4), 451–467. https://doi.org/10.1016/j.adolescence.2007.09.001

Padilla-Walker, L. M., Nelson, L. J., & Carroll, J. S. (2012). Affording emerging adulthood: Parental financial assistance of their college-aged children. *Journal of Adult Development, 19*, 50–58. https://doi.org/10.1007/s10804-011-9134-y

Ranta, M., Punamäki, R.-L., Tolvanen, A., & Salmela-Aro, K. (2012). The role of financial resources and agency in success and satisfaction regarding developmental tasks in early adulthood. In S. Lee Blair (Ed.), *Economic stress and the family: Contemporary perspectives in family research* (Vol. 6, pp. 187–233). Emerald Group. https://doi.org/10.1108/S1530-3535(2012)0000006011

Ritchie, R. A., Meca, A., Madrazo, V. L., Schwartz, S. J., Hardy, S. A., Zamboanga, B. L., . . . Lee, R. M. (2013). Identity dimensions and related processes in emerging adulthood: Helpful or harmful? *Journal of Clinical Psychology, 69*(4), 415–432. https://doi.org/10.1002/jclp.21960

Serido, J. (2021). Financial literacy among young adults. In G. Nicolini & B. Cude (Eds.), *The Routledge handbook of financial literacy* (pp. 31–47). Routledge.

Serido, J., Sorgente, A., Lanz, M., & Shim, S. (2022). A longitudinal person-centered examination of financial identity formation and adult status during the transition to adulthood. *Applied Developmental Science, 27*(2), 99–114. https://doi.org/10.1080/10888691.2022.2035224

Serido, J., Tang, C., Ahn, S. Y., & Shim, S. (2020). Financial behaviors as pathways to self-sufficiency: A goal-framing theory application [Special issue]. *Emerging Adulthood, 8*(6), 521–529. https://doi.org/10.1177/2167696819861467

Settersten, R. A., Jr., & Ray, B. (2010). What's going on with young people today? The long and twisting path to adulthood. *The Future of Children, 20*(1), 19–41. https://doi.org/10.1353/foc.0.0044

Shim, S., Serido, J., Bosch, L. & Tang, C. (2013). Financial identity-processing styles among young adults: A longitudinal study of socialization factors and consequences for financial capabilities. *Journal of Consumer Affairs, 47*(1), 128–152. https://doi.org/10.1111/joca.12002

Sorgente, A., Vosylis, R., Lanz, M., Serido, J., & Shim, S. (2020). The Financial Identity Scale (FIS): A multinational validation and measurement invariance study among emerging adults. *International Journal of Behavioral Development, 44*(6), 565–574. https://doi.org/10.1177/0165025420914986

Stringer, K. J., & Kerpelman, J. L. (2010). Career identity development in college students: Decision making, parental support, and work experience. *Identity, 10*(3), 181–200. https://doi.org/10.1080/15283488.2010.496102

Syed, M., & McLean, K. C. (2015). The future of identity development research: Reflections, tensions, and challenges. In K. C. McLean & M. Syed (Eds.), *The Oxford handbook of identity development* (pp. 562–574). Oxford University Press. https://doi.org/10.1093/oxfordhb/9780199936564.013.011

Vosylis, R., & Erentaitė, R. (2020). Linking family financial socialization with its proximal and distal outcomes: Which socialization dimensions matter most for emerging adults' financial identity, financial behaviors, and financial anxiety? [Special issue]. *Emerging Adulthood, 8*(6), 464–475. https://doi.org/10.1177/2167696819856763

Vosylis, R., Erentaitė, R., & Crocetti, E. (2018). Global versus domain-specific identity processes: Which domains are more relevant for emerging adults? *Emerging Adulthood*, *6*(1), 32–41. https://doi.org/10.1177/2167696817694698

Vosylis, R., Sorgente, A., & Lanz, M. (2022). The role of financial identity processes in financial behaviors and financial well-being. *Emerging Adulthood*, *10*(5), 1132–1145. https://doi.org/10.1177/21676968211016142

Waterman, A. S. (1999). Identity, the identity statuses, and identity status development: A contemporary statement. *Developmental Review*, *19*, 591–621. https://doi.org/10.1006/drev.1999.0493

Chapter 13

Addo, F. R., Houle, J. N., & Sassler, S. (2019). The changing nature of the association between student loan debt and marital behavior in young adulthood. *Journal of Family and Economic Issues*, *40*, 86–101. https://doi.org/10.1007/s10834-018-9591-6

Addo, F. R., Houle, J. N., & Simon, D. (2016). Young, black, and (still) in the red: Parental wealth, race, and student loan debt. *Race and Social Problems*, *8*, 64–76. https://doi.org/10.1007/s12552-016-9162-0

Annunziata, A., Mariani, A., & Vecchio, R. (2019). Effectiveness of sustainability labels in guiding food choices: Analysis of visibility and understanding among young adults. *Sustainable Production and Consumption*, *17*, 108–115. https://doi.org/10.1016/j.spc.2018.09.005

Artavanis, N., & Karra, S. (2020). Financial literacy and student debt. *The European Journal of Finance*, *26*(4–5), 382–401. https://doi.org/10.1080/1351847X.2019.1711435

Barrera, G. A., & Ponce, H. R. (2021). Personality traits influencing young adults' conspicuous consumption. *International Journal of Consumer Studies*, *45*(3), 335–349. https://doi.org/10.1111/ijcs.12623

Bolognesi, A., Hasier, A., & Lusardi, A. (2022). *Millennials and money: The state of their financial management and how workplaces can help them.* TIAA Institute.

Bureau of Labor Statistics. (2022). *Consumer expenditures—2021* [News release]. https://www.bls.gov/opub/reports/consumer-expenditures/2021/

Bureau of Labor Statistics. (2023, January 25). *Employment status of the civilian noninstitutional population by age, sex, and race.* Retrieved from https://www.bls.gov/cps/cpsaat03.htm

Carlsson-Hauff, J., & Nilsson, J. (2020). Determinants of indebtedness among young adults: Impacts of lender guidelines, explicit information and financial (over) confidence. *International Journal of Consumer Studies*, *44*(2), 89–98. https://doi.org/10.1111/ijcs.12549

Cui, X., Xiao, J. J., Yi, J., Porto, N., & Cai, Y. (2019). Impact of family income in early life on the financial independence of young adults: Evidence from a matched panel data. *International Journal of Consumer Studies*, *43*(6), 514–527. https://doi.org/10.1111/ijcs.12536

Cwynar, A., Cwynar, W., Baryła-Matejczuk, M., & Betancort, M. (2019). Sustainable debt behaviour and well-being of young adults: The role of parental financial socialisation process. *Sustainability*, *11*(24), 7210. https://doi.org/10.3390/SU11247210

Darrat, A. A., Darrat, M. A., & Darrat, M. A. (2023). Does wanting more lead to losing control? Examining the psychological drivers of compulsive buying. *Young Consumers*, *24*(1), 56–73. https://doi.org/10.1108/YC-01-2022-1453

Dettling, L. J., & Hsu, J. W. (2018). Returning to the nest: Debt and parental co-residence among young adults. *Labour Economics*, *54*, 225–236. https://doi.org/10.2139/ssrn.2511411

Fan, F., & Chan, K. (2019). Young adults' perceptions of personal loan commercials. *Young Consumers, 20*(2), 109–120. https://doi.org/10.1108/YC-10-2018-0854

Faschan, M., Chailan, C., & Huaman-Ramirez, R. (2020). Emerging adults' luxury fashion brand value perceptions: A cross-cultural comparison between Germany and China. *Journal of Global Fashion Marketing, 11*(3), 207–231. https://doi.org/10.1080/20932685.2020.1761422

Fernández-Villaverde, J., & Krueger, D. (2007). Consumption over the life cycle: Facts from consumer expenditure survey data. *The Review of Economics and Statistics, 89*(3), 552–565. https://doi.org/10.1162/rest.89.3.552

Gärling, T., Michaelsen, P., & Gamble, A. (2020). Young adults' borrowing to purchases of desired consumer products related to present-biased temporal discounting, attitude towards borrowing and financial involvement and knowledge. *International Journal of Consumer Studies, 44*(2), 131–139. https://doi.org/10.1111/ijcs.12552

Geiger, S. M., Fischer, D., & Schrader, U. (2018). Measuring what matters in sustainable consumption: An integrative framework for the selection of relevant behaviors. *Sustainable development, 26*(1), 18–33. https://doi.org/10.1002/sd.1688

Helhoski, A., Lane, R., & Haverstock, E. (2023, January 31). *Student loan debt statistics: 2023.* NerdWallet. Retrieved from https://www.nerdwallet.com/article/loans/student-loans/student-loan-debt

Helm, S., Serido, J., Ahn, S. Y., Ligon, V., & Shim, S. (2019). Materialist values, financial and pro-environmental behaviors, and well-being. *Young Consumers, 20*(4), 264–284. https://doi.org/10.1108/YC-10-2018-0867

Hohnen, P., Gram, M., & Jakobsen, T. B. (2020). Debt as the new credit or credit as the new debt? A cultural analysis of credit consumption among Danish young adults. *Journal of Youth Studies, 23*(3), 356–370. https://doi.org/10.1080/13676261.2019.1609660

Houle, J. N. (2014a). A generation indebted. *Social Problems, 61*(3), 448–465. https://doi.org/10.1525/sp.2014.12110

Houle, J. N. (2014b). Disparities in debt: Parents' socioeconomic resources and young adult student loan debt. *Sociology of Education, 87*(1), 53–69. https://doi.org/10.1177/0038040713512213

Houle, J. N., & Berger, L. (2015). Is student loan debt discouraging homeownership among young adults? *Social Service Review, 89*(4), 589–621. https://doi.org/10.1086/684587

Houle, J. N., & Warner, C. (2017). Into the red and back to the nest? Student debt, college completion, and returning to the parental home among young adults. *Sociology of Education, 90*(1), 89–108. https://doi.org/10.1177/0038040716685873

Jones, J. (2022, December 14). *Average car payment and auto loan statistics 2023.* Lending Tree. Retrieved from https://www.lendingtree.com/auto/debt-statistics

Kadic-Maglajlic, S., Arslanagic-Kalajdzic, M., Micevski, M., Dlacic, J., & Zabkar, V. (2019). Being engaged is a good thing: Understanding sustainable consumption behavior among young adults. *Journal of Business Research, 104*, 644–654. https://doi.org/10.1016/j.jbusres.2019.02.040

Kim, J., & Chatterjee, S. (2021). Financial debt and mental health of young adults. *Journal of Financial Counseling and Planning, 32*(2), 187–201. https://doi.org/10.1891/JFCP-18-00048

Kim, J., Chatterjee, S., & Kim, J. (2012). Debt burden of young adults in the United States. *Journal of Financial Counseling and Planning, 23*(2), 55–67.

Kreuzer, C., Weber, S., Off, M., Hackenberg, T., & Birk, C. (2019). Shedding light on realized sustainable consumption behavior and perceived barriers of young adults for creating stimulating teaching–learning situations. *Sustainability, 11*(9), 2587. https://doi.org/10.3390/su11092587

Maccarrone-Eaglen, A., & Schofield, P. (2020). Compulsive buying among young adults: A behavioural segmentation. *Young Consumers, 21*(1), 57–76. https://doi.org/10.1108/YC-02-2019-0958

Majamaa, K., & Rantala, K. (2019). Parental financial support: A safety net for young adults with debt problems. *International Journal of Consumer Studies, 43*(4), 379–389. https://doi.org/10.1111/ijcs.12517

Martinchek, K., Andre, J., & Santillo, M. (2022). *What can policymakers do to help young adults cope with debt? Credit health among adults ages 18–24.* Urban Institute. Retrieved from https://www.urban.org/sites/default/files/2022-12/What%20Can%20Policymakers%20Do%20to%20Help%20Young%20Adults%20Cope%20with%20Debt.pdf

Napolitano, L., Tevington, P., Carr, P. J., & Kefalas, M. (2022). "Longer than I would've originally liked and originally thought": Postsecondary debt and marriage plans for young adults coming of age in the Great Recession. *Sociological Perspectives, 65*(4), 684–701. https://doi.org/10.1177/07311214211052019

National Center for Education Statistics. (n.d.). *Percentage of 18- to 24-year-olds enrolled in college, by level of institution and sex and race/ethnicity of student: 1970 through 2020.* Retrieved from https://nces.ed.gov/programs/digest/d21/tables/dt21_302.60.asp

Nie, J., & Gautam, A. S. (2020). Spending patterns and cost of living for younger versus older households. *The Federal Reserve Bank of Kansas City Economic Review, QIV*, 5–21. https://doi.org/10.18651/ER/4q19

Niesiobędzka, M., & Konaszewski, K. (2022). Narcissism, activity on Facebook, and conspicuous consumption among young adults. *Current Issues in Personality Psychology, 9*(1), 21–31. https://doi.org/10.5114/CIPP.2021.108751

O'Guinn, T. C., & Faber, R. J. (1989). Compulsive buying: A phenomenological exploration. *Journal of Consumer Research, 16*, 147–157. https://doi.org/10.1086/209204

Oksanen, A., Aaltonen, M., & Rantala, K. (2016). Debt problems and life transitions: A register-based panel study of Finnish young people. *Journal of Youth Studies, 19*(9), 1184–1203. https://doi.org/10.1080/13676261.2016.1145638

Oksanen, A., Savolainen, I., Sirola, A., & Kaakinen, M. (2018). Problem gambling and psychological distress: A cross-national perspective on the mediating effect of consumer debt and debt problems among emerging adults. *Harm Reduction Journal, 15*(1), 1–11. https://doi.org/10.1186/s12954-018-0251-9

Ong, Z., Lau, J., & Zainudin, N. (2021). Money attitude, materialism and compulsive buying among Malaysian young adults. *Management Science Letters, 11*(1), 281–290. https://doi.org/10.5267/j.msl.2020.8.005

Pahlevan Sharif, S., She, L., Yeoh, K. K., & Naghavi, N. (2022). Heavy social networking and online compulsive buying: The mediating role of financial social comparison and materialism. *Journal of Marketing Theory and Practice, 30*(2), 213–225. https://doi.org/10.1080/10696679.2021.1909425

Qian, Y., & Fan, W. (2021). Student loans, mental health, and substance use: A gender comparison among US young adults. *Journal of American College Health, 71*(3), 930–941. https://doi.org/10.1080/07448481.2021.1909046

She, L., Rasiah, R., Waheed, H., & Sharif, S. P. (2021). Excessive use of social networking sites and financial well-being among young adults: The mediating role of online compulsive buying. *Young Consumers, 22*(2), 272–289. https://doi.org/10.1108/YC-11-2020-1252

Shim, S., Barber, B., Card, N., Xiao, J. J., & Serido, J. (2010). Financial socialization of first-year college students: The roles of parents, work, and education. *Journal of Youth and Adolescence, 39*, 1457–1470. https://doi.org/10.1007/s10964-009-9432-x

Shim, S., Xiao, J. J., Barber, B., & Lyons, A. (2009). Pathway to life success: A conceptual model of financial well-being for young adults. *Journal of Applied Developmental Psychology, 30*, 708–723. https://doi.org/10.1016/j.appdev.2009.02.003

Sun, F., Xiao, J. J., & Zhang, Y. X. (2012). Social stratification and status consumption in China. *American Review of China Studies, 13*(1), 1–16.

UNDP (United Nations Development Programme). (2022). *Human development report 2021/2022.* Retrieved from https://hdr.undp.org/system/files/documents/global-report-document/hdr2021-22pdf_1.pdf

Veblen, T. B. (1899). *The theory of the leisure class.* Houghton Mifflin.

Wang, J., & Xiao, J. J. (2009). Buying behavior, social support, and credit card indebtedness of college students. *International Journal of Consumer Studies, 33*, 2–10. https://doi.org/10.1111/j.1470-6431.2008.00719.

Xiao, J. J. (2015). *Consumer economic wellbeing.* Springer.

Xiao, J. J. (2021). Life satisfaction and sustainable consumption. In F. Maggino (Ed.), *Encyclopedia of quality of life and well-being research* (2nd ed.) (pp. 1-4). Springer. https://doi.org/10.1007/978-3-319-69909-7_3698-2

Xiao, J. J. (2022). Consumer capability and sustainable consumer behavior: Applying the transtheoretical model of behavior change (TTM). *Yamaguchi Journal of Economics, Business Administration & Laws, 70*(6), 33–56. Retrieved from https://petit.lib.yamaguchi-u.ac.jp/journals/yunoca000041/v/70/i/6/item/29088

Xiao, J. J., Chatterjee, S., & Kim, J. (2014). Factors associated with financial independence of young adults. *International Journal of Consumer Studies, 38*, 394–403. https://doi.org/10.1111/ijcs.12106

Xiao, J. J., Huang, J., Goyal, K., & Kumar, S. (2022). Financial capability: A systematic conceptual review, extension, and synthesis. *International Journal of Bank Marketing, 40*(7), 1680–1717. https://doi.org/10.1108/IJBM-05-2022-0185

Xiao, J. J., & Li, H. (2011). Sustainable consumption and life satisfaction. *Social Indicators Research, 104*(2), 323–329. https://doi.org/10.1007/s11205-010-9746-9

Xiao, J. J., Tang, C., & Shim, S. (2009). Acting for happiness: Financial behavior and life satisfaction of college students. *Social Indicator Research, 92*(1), 53–68. https://doi.org/10.1007/s11205-008-9288-6

Xiao, J. J., & Yao, R. (2022). Good debt, bad debt: Family debt portfolios and financial burdens. *International Journal of Bank Marketing, 40*(4), 659–678. https://doi.org/10.1108/IJBM-06-2021-0243

Zhan, M. (2022). Financial stress and hardship among young adults: The role of student loan debt. *Journal of Sociology & Social Welfare, 49*(3), 84–111. https://doi.org/10.15453/0191 5096.4541

Zhang, Q., & Kim, H. (2019). American young adults' debt and psychological distress. *Journal of Family and Economic Issues, 40*, 22–35. https://doi.org/10.1007/s10834-018-9605-4

Zhu, X., Geng, Y., Pan, Y., & Shi, L. (2022). Conspicuous consumption in Chinese young adults: The role of dark tetrad and gender. *Current Psychology*, 1–13. https://doi.org/10.1007/s12144-022-03129-4

Chapter 14

Addo, F. R. (2014). Debt, cohabitation, and marriage in young adulthood. *Demography, 51*(5), 1677–1701. https://doi.org/10.1007/s13524-014-0333-6

Archuleta, K. L., & Burr, E. A. (2015). Systemic financial therapy. In B. T. Klontz, S. L. Britt, & K. L. Archuleta (Eds.), *Financial therapy: Theory, research, and practice* (pp. 217–234). Springer. https://doi.org/10.1007/978-3-319-08269-1_13

Arnett, J. J. (2007). Emerging adulthood: What is it, and what is it good for? *Child Development Perspectives, 1*(2), 68–73. https://doi.org/10.1111/j.1750-8606.2007.00016.x

Bowlby, J. (1973). *Separation: Anxiety and anger*. Basic Books.

Britt, S. L., Hill, E. J., LeBaron, A. B., Lawson, D. R., & Bean, R. A. (2017). Tightwads and spenders: Predicting financial conflict in couple relationships. *Journal of Financial Planning, 30*(5), 36–42.

Christy, K., Welter, T., Dundon, K., Valandra, & Bruce, A. (2022). Economic abuse: A subtle but common form of power and control. *Journal of Interpersonal Violence, 37*(1–2), 473–499. https://doi.org/10.1177/0886260520916264

Clarke, M., Heaton, M., Israelsen, C., & Eggett, D. (2005). The acquisition of family financial roles and responsibilities. *Family and Consumer Sciences Research Journal, 33*(4), 321–340. https://doi.org/10.1177/1077727x04274117

Conger, R. D., Conger, K. J., & Martin, M. J. (2010). Socioeconomic status, family processes, and individual development. *Journal of Marriage and Family, 72*(3), 685–704. https://doi.org/10.1111/j.1741-3737.2010.00725.x

Cooper, A., Totenhagen, C. J., Curran, M. A., Randall, A. K., & Smith, N. E. (2017). Daily relationship quality in same-sex couples: Attachment and sacrifice motives. *Evolutionary Behavioral Sciences, 11*(2), 146–160. https://doi.org/10.1037/ebs0000089

Dew, J., Barham, C., & Hill, E. J. (2021). The longitudinal associations of sound financial behaviors and marital quality. *Journal of Family & Economic Issues, 42*(1), 1–12. https://doi.org/10.1007/s10834-020-09701-z

Dew, J., Trujillo, S., & Saxey, M. (2022). Predicting marital financial deception in a national sample: A person-centered approach. *Family Relations, 71*(4), 1497–1514. https://doi.org/10.1111/fare.12654

Eickmeyer, K. J., Manning, W. D., Longmore, M. A., & Giordano, P. C. (2023). Exploring the married-cohabiting income pooling gap among young adults. *Journal of Family and Economic Issues*, 44, 990–1006, Advanced online publication. https://doi.org/10.1007/s10834-023-09885-0

ESDlife. (2022, November). *ESDlife announces 2022 Hong Kong wedding spending survey results*. Retrieved from https://corporate.esdlife.com/esdlife-announces-2022-hong-kong-wedding-spending-survey-results-2

Fincham, F. D., & Bradbury, T. N. (1987). The assessment of marital quality: A reevaluation. *Journal of Marriage and the Family,49*(4), 797–809. https://doi.org/10.2307/351973

Hardie, H. J., & Lucas, A. (2010). Economic factors and relationship quality among young couples: Comparing cohabitation and marriage. *Journal of Marriage and Family, 72*(5), 1141–1154. https://doi.org/10.1111/j.1741-3737.2010.00755.x

Hiekel, N., Liefbroer, A. C., & Poortman, A. R. (2014). Income pooling strategies among cohabiting and married couples: A comparative perspective. *Demographic Research, 30*, 1527–1560. https://doi.org/10.4054/DemRes.2014.30.55

Hoff, T., & Lee, D. R. (2021). The gender pay gap in medicine: A systematic review. *Health Care Management Review, 46*(3), E37–E49. https://doi.org/10.1097/HMR.0000000000000290

James, S. L., Yorgason, J. B., Holmes, E. K., Johnson, D. R., & Busby, D. M. (2022). Is it still possible to collect nationally representative marriage data in the United States? A case study from the CREATE project. *Family Relations, 71*(4), 1428–1443. https://doi.org/10.1111/fare.12577

Kelley, H., Chandler, A., LeBaron-Black, A., Li, X., Curran, M., Yorgason, J., & James, S. (2022). Spenders and tightwads among newlywed heterosexual couples: Perceptions of partner financial management behaviors and relational well-being. *Journal of Financial Therapy, 13*(1), 20–38. https://doi.org/10.4148/1944-9771.1288

Kutin, J. J., Reid, M., & Russell, R. (2019). Special WSMC edition paper. *Journal of Social Marketing, 9*(1), 111–128. https://doi.org/10.1108/JSOCM-03-2018-0028

Kutin, J. J., Russell, R., & Reid, M. (2022). "I didn't even know it was a thing": Australian young adults' experience of economic abuse. *Health Promotion International, 37*(6), 1–11. https://doi.org/10.1093/heapro/daac152

LeBaron, A. B., Holmes, E. K., Yorgason, J. B., Hill, E. J., & Allsop, D. B. (2019). Feminism and couple finance: Power as a mediator between financial processes and relationship outcomes. *Sex Roles, 81*(3), 140–156. https://doi.org/10.1007/s11199-018-0986-5

LeBaron-Black, A. B., Yorgason, J. B., Curran, M. A., Saxey, M. T., & Okamoto, R. M. (2022). The ABC-X's of stress among U.S. emerging adults during the COVID-19 pandemic: Relationship quality, financial distress, and mental health. *International Journal of Environmental Research and Public Health, 19*(20), Article 13125. https://doi.org/10.3390/ijerph192013125

Li, X., Curran, M. A., LeBaron, A. B., Serido, J., & Shim, S. (2020). Romantic attachment orientations, financial behaviors, and life outcomes among young adults: A mediating analysis of a college cohort. *Journal of Family and Economic Issues, 41*, 658–671. https://doi.org/10.1007/s10834-020-09664-1

Li, X., Curran, M. A., LeBaron, A. B., Yorgason, J., Jorgensen, B., & Wilmarth, M. J. (2023a). Couple-level attachment styles, finances, and marital satisfaction: Mediational analyses among young adult newlywed couples. *Journal of Family and Economic Issues, 44*, 125–142. https://doi.org/10.1007/s10834-021-09808-x

Li, X., Curran, M. A., Serido, J., LeBaron-Black, A., Shim, S., & Zhou. N. (2022). Financial behaviors, financial satisfaction, and goal attainment among college-educated emerging adults: A mediating analysis with latent change scores. *Applied Developmental Science, 26*(3), 603–617. https://doi.org/10.1080/10888691.2021.1976182

Li, X., Curran, M. A., Zhou, N., Serido, J., Shim, S., & Cao, H. (2019). Financial behaviors and adult identity: Mediating analyses of a college cohort. *Journal of Applied Developmental Psychology, 64*, Article 101419. https://doi.org/10.1016/j.appdev.2019.101049

Li, X., Wheeler, B., James, S., LeBaron-Black, A. B., Holmes, E. K., & Yorgason, J. (2024). For richer, for poorer: Financial behaviors, power (im)balance, and relational aggression among U.S. newlyweds. *Family Process*, 63, 176-191. Advanced online publication. https://doi.org/10.1111/famp.12886

Mallory, A. B., Dharnidharka, P., Deitz, S. L., Barros-Gomes, P., Cafferky, B., Stith, S. M., & Van, K. (2016). A meta-analysis of cross cultural risk markers for intimate partner violence. *Aggression and Violent Behavior, 31*, 116–126. https://doi.org/10.1016/j.avb.2016.08.004

Mikulincer, M., & Shaver, P. R. (2008). "Can't buy me love": An attachment perspective on social support and money as psychological buffers. *Psychological Inquiry, 19*(3–4), 167–173. https://doi.org/10.1080/10478400802631295.

Mikulincer, M., & Shaver, P. R. (2009). An attachment and behavioral systems perspective on social support. *Journal of Social and Personal Relationships, 26*, 7–19. https://doi.org/10.1177/0265407509105518.

Mikulincer, M., & Shaver, P. R. (2012). Adult attachment orientations and relationship processes. *Journal of Family Theory & Review, 4*, 259–274. https://doi.org/10.1111/j.1756-2589.2012.00142.x

Miller, R. B., Dyer, W. J., & Day, R. D. (2022). Development and initial validation of the Perceived Power Imbalance Scale. *Contemporary Family Therapy, 44*(3), 210–221. https://doi.org/10.1007/s10591-021-09618-1

Nerdwallet. (2023 March). *How much does the average wedding cost.* Bankrate. Retrieved from https://www.nerdwallet.com/article/finance/how-much-does-average-wedding-cost

Papp, L. M. (2018). Topics of marital conflict in the everyday lives of empty nest couples and their implications for conflict resolution. *Journal of Couple & Relationship Therapy, 17*(1), 7–24. https://doi.org/10.1080/15332691.2017.1302377

Papp, L. M., Cummings, E. M., & Goeke-Morey, M. C. (2009). For richer, for poorer: Money as a topic of marital conflict in the home. *Family Relations, 58*(1), 91–103. https://doi.org/10.1111/j.1741-3729.2008.00537.x

Präg, P., Begall, K., & Treas, J. (2019, April). *Understanding the marriage–cohabitation gap in income pooling: Evidence from 29 European countries.* Retrieved from https://doi.org/10.31235/osf.io/rqzj3

Rea, J. K., Zuiker, V. S., & Mendenhall, T. J. (2016). Money and emerging adults: A glimpse into the lives of college couples' financial management practices. *Journal of Financial Therapy, 7*(2), 16–40. https://doi.org/10.4148/1944-9771.1110

Rick, S. I., Cryder, C. E., & Loewenstein, G. (2008). Tightwads and spendthrifts. *Journal of Consumer Research, 34*(6), 767–782. https://doi.org/10.1086/523285

Rick, S. I., Small, D. A., & Finkel, E. J. (2011). Fatal (fiscal) attraction: Spendthrifts and tightwads in marriage. *Journal of Marketing Research, 48*(6), 228–237. https://doi.org/10.1509/jmkr.48.2.228

Romo, L. K. (2011). Money talks: Revealing and concealing financial information in families. *Journal of Family Communication, 11*(4), 264–281. https://doi.org/10.1080/15267431.2010.544634

Saxey, M. T., LeBaron-Black, A. B., & Curran, M. A. (2022a). The sooner, the better? Couples' first financial discussion, relationship quality, and financial conflict in emerging adulthood. *Journal of Financial Therapy, 13*(1), 20–18. https://doi.org/10.4148/1944-9771.1299

Saxey, M. T., LeBaron-Black, A. B., Dew, J. P., & Curran, M. A. (2022b). Less than fully honest: Financial deception in emerging adult romantic relationships. *Emerging Adulthood, 10*(6), 1529–1542. https://doi.org/10.1177/21676968221089190

Saxey, M. T., LeBaron-Black, A. B., Dew, J. P., Yorgason, J. B., James, S. L., & Holmes, E. K. (2023a). Money to marriage, or marriage to money? Examining the directionality between financial processes and marital processes among newlywed couples. *Journal of Social and Personal Relationships*, 40(8), 2445-2465. https://doi.org/10.1177/02654075221149967

Saxey, M. T., LeBaron-Black, A. B., Totenhagen, C. J., & Curran, M. A. (2023b). More than a score? Indirect associations between credit score and romantic relationship quality in emerging adulthood. *Journal of Financial Counseling and Planning, 34*(1), 55–67. https://doi.org/10.1891/JFCP-2022-0018

Saxey, M. T., Li, X., Wikle, J. S., Hill, E. J., LeBaron-Black, A. B., James, S. L., Yorgason, J. B. (2022c). Latent profiles of sleep quality, financial management behaviors, and sexual satisfaction in emerging adult newlywed couples and longitudinal connections with marital satisfaction. *Frontiers in Psychology, 13*, Article 883352. https://doi.org/10.3389/fpsyg.2022.883352

Serido, J., Curran, M. J., Wilmarth, M., Ahn, S. Y., Shim, S., & Ballard, J. (2015). The unique role of parents and romantic partners on college students' financial attitudes and behaviors. *Family Relations, 64*(5), 696–710. https://doi.org/10.1111/fare.12164

Shapiro, M. (2007). Money: A therapeutic tool for couples therapy. *Family Process, 46*(3), 279–291. https://doi.org/10.1111/j.1545-5300.2007.00211.x.

Shrum, L. J., Chaplin, L. N., & Lowrey, T. M. (2022). Psychological causes, correlates, and consequences of materialism. *Consumer Psychology Review, 5*(1), 69–86. https://doi.org/10.1002/arcp.1077

Smock, P. J., Manning, W. D., & Porter, M. (2005). "Everything's there except money": How money shapes decisions to marry among cohabitors. *Journal of Marriage and Family, 67*(3), 680–696. https://doi.org/10.1111/j.1741-3737.2005.00162.x

Tang, T. L. P. (2010). Money, the meaning of money, management, spirituality, and religion. *Journal of Management, Spirituality, and Religion, 7*(2), 173–189. https://doi.org/10.1080/14766081003746448

Totenhagen, C. J., Curran, M. A., Serido, J., & Butler, E. A. (2013). Good days, bad days: Do sacrifices improve relationship quality? *Journal of Social and Personal Relationships*, *30*(7), 881–900. https://doi.org/10.1177/0265407512472475

Totenhagen, C. J., Li, X., Wilmarth, M. J., Aruchuleta, K. L., & Yorgason, J. (2023). Do couples who play together stay together? A longitudinal dyadic examination of shared leisure, financial distress, and relationship outcomes? *Family Process*, 2024, 63, 210-227. Advanced online publication. https://doi.org/10.1111/famp.12869

Widiss, D. A. (2016). Legal recognition of same-sex relationships: New possibilities for research on the role of marriage law in household labor allocation. *Journal of Family Theory & Review*, *8*(1), 10–29. https://doi.org/10.1111/jftr.12123

Williams, K. C., & Page, R. A. (2011). Marketing to the generations. *Journal of Behavioral Studies in Business*, *3*(1), 37–53.

Xu, J., Ellington, L., Heyman, R. E., Vadaparampil, S. T., & Reblin, M. (2020). Money matters: An analysis of advanced cancer couples' communication about financial concerns. *Supportive Care in Cancer*, *28*(5), 2239–2246. https://doi.org/10.1007/s00520-019-05045-z

Zagorsky, J. L. (2005). Marriage and divorce's impact on wealth. *Journal of Sociology*, *41*(4), 406–424. https://doi.org/10.1177/1440783305058478

Chapter 15

Ajunwa, I. (2020, August 10). Race, labor, and the future of work. In E. Houh, K. Bridges, & D. Carbado (Eds.), *Oxford handbook of race and law*. https://doi.org/10.2139/ssrn.3670785
(It is 18 pages total, but I am unsure how to find the page range).

Al-Bahrani, A., Weathers, J., & Patel, D. (2019). Racial differences in the returns to financial literacy education. *Journal of Consumer Affairs*, *53*(2), 572–599. https://doi.org/10.1111.joca.12205

Aliprantis, D., Carroll, D., & Young, E. R. (2022, November). *The dynamics of the racial wealth gap* (Report No. 19-18R). Federal Reserve Bank of Cleveland. https://doi.org/10.26509/frbc-wp-201918r

Arnett, J. J. (2003). Conceptions of the transition to adulthood among emerging adults in American ethnic groups. *New Directions for Child and Adolescent Development*, *2003*(100), 63–76. https://doi.org/10.1002/cd.75

Bhutta, N., Chang, A. C., Dettling, L. J., & Joanne W. Hsu, with assistance from Julia Hewitt. (2020). *Disparities in wealth by race and ethnicity in the 2019 survey of consumer finances*. Board of Governors of the Federal Reserve System. Retrieved from https://www.federalreserve.gov/econres/notes/feds-notes/disparities-in-wealth-by-race-and-ethnicity-in-the-2019-survey-of-consumer-finances-20200928.html

Board of Governors of the Federal Reserve System. (2023). *Economic well-being of U.S. households*. Retrieved from https://www.federalreserve.gov/publications/2022-economic-well-being-of-us-households-in-2021-student-loans.htm

Boen, C., Keister, L., & Aronson, B. (2020). Beyond net worth: Racial differences in wealth portfolios and Black-White health inequality across the life course. *Journal of Health and Social Behavior*, *61*(2), 153–169. https://doi.org/10.1177/0022146520924811

Bonnie, R., Stroud, C. & Breiner, H. (2017). *Investing in the health and well-being of young adults*. National Academies Press. https://doi.org/10.17226/18869

Brown, M., Biu, O, Harvey, C., & Shanks, T. (2023). *The state of baby bonds*. Urban Institute, pp. 1–31. Retrieved from https://www.urban.org/sites/default/files/2023-02/The%20State%20of%20Baby%20Bonds.pdf

Buckland, J. (2010). Are low-income Canadians financially literate? Placing financial literacy in the context of personal and structural constraints. *Adult Education Quarterly*, *60*(4), 357–376. https://doi.org/10.1177/0741713609358449

Campbell, C. (2018). *The forgotten faces of student loan default.* Center for American Progress. Retrieved from https://vetsedsuccess.org/wp-content/uploads/2019/08/CAP-report-Veteran-Default-Rates-1.pdf

Cheng, P., Lin, Z., & Liu, Y. (2015). Racial discrepancy in mortgage interest rates. *The Journal of Real Estate Finance and Economics*, *51*, 101–120. Retrieved from https://ssrn.com/abstract=2443694

Choi, J. (2023, March). *Unmasking the real gender homeownership gap.* Urban Institute. Retrieved from https://www.urban.org/urban-wire/unmasking-real-gender-homeownership-gap

Crenshaw, K. W. (2017). *On intersectionality: Essential writings.* The New Press.

Crenshaw, K., & Harris, L. (2021). *The unequal opportunity race.* African American Policy Forum. Retrieved from https://youtube/EMS_fF0pFzQ https://www.youtube.com/watch?v=vX_Vzl-r8NY

Daniels, C., McCalman, J., & Bainbridge, R. (2021). Meeting people where they're at: A systematic review of financial counseling for Indigenous peoples. *Journal of Financial Counseling and Planning.* https://doi.org/10.1891/JFCP-19-00065

Darity, W., & Hamilton, D. (2012). Bold policies for economic justice. *The Review of Black Political Economy*, *39*(1), 79–85. https://doi.org/10.1007/s12114-011-9129-8

Emmons, W. R., & Noeth, B. J. (2013). Economic vulnerability and financial fragility. *Federal Reserve Bank of St. Louis Review*, *95*(5), 361–388. Retrieved from https://ideas.repec.org/a/fip/fedlrv/y2013iseptemberp361-388nv.95no.5.html

Fisher, O., O'Donnell, S. C., & Oyserman, D. (2017). Social class and identity-based motivation. *Current Opinion in Psychology*, *18*, 61–66. https://doi.org/10.1016/j.copsyc.2017.07.035

Flynn, K., Catalano, T. & Logan, M. (2023, September). *Paying for college as an LGBTQ+ student.* Investopedia. Retrieved from https://www.investopedia.com/paying-for-college-as-an-lgbtq-student-5176574

Friedline, T., Steward, K., Bolinger, C., & Wood, A. K. (2024). Credit scoring as a carceral practice: An abolitionist framework. *Race and Social Problems*, *16*, 230–248 https://doi.org/10.1007/s12552-023-09406-6

Fuligni, A. J., Tseng, V., & Lam, M. (1999). Attitudes toward family obligations among American adolescents with Asian, Latin American, and European backgrounds. *Child Development*, *70*(4), 1030–1044. https://doi.org/10.1111/1467-8624.00075

Gemelas, J., Davison, J., Keltner, C., & Ing, S. (2021). Inequities in employment by race, ethnicity, and sector during COVID-19. *Journal of Racial and Ethnic Health Disparities*, 1–6. https://doi.org/10.1007/s40615-021-00963-3

Geron, T., Cohen, C., Henriquez, K., Fowler, M., & Lykes., J. (2020). *Race, ethnicity, and the financial lives of young adults exploring disparities in financial health outcomes.* Financial Health Network. Retrieved from https://finhealthnetwork.org/research/race-ethnicity-and-the-financial-lives-of-young-adults

Hamilton, D., & Darity, Jr., W. (2010). Can "baby bonds" eliminate the racial wealth gap in putative post-racial America? *The Review of Black Political Economy*, *37*(3-4), 207–216. https://doi.org/10.1007/s12114-010-90

Hamilton, D., & Darity Jr., W. A. (2017). The political economy of education, financial literacy, and the racial wealth gap. *Federal Reserve Bank of St. Louis Review*, *99*(1), 59–76. https://doi.org/10.20955/r.2017.59-76

Hanks, A., Solomon, D., & Weller, C. E. (2018). *Systematic inequality: How America's structural racism helped create the Black-white wealth gap*. Center for American Progress, Vol. 21, pp. 3–12. Retrieved from https://www.americanprogress.org/article/systematic-inequality

Havens, T. (2021). Educational redlining: The disproportionate effects of the student loan crisis on Black and Latinx graduates. *The Vermont Connection*, *42*(1). Retrieved from https://scholarworks.uvm.edu/tvc/vol42/iss1/11

Hong, P. Y. P., Choi, S., & Key. W. (2018). Psychological self-sufficiency: A bottom-up theory of change in workforce development. *Social Work Research*, *42*(1), 22–32. https://doi.org/10.1093/swr/svx025

Hong, P. Y. P., Wathen, M. V., Shin, A. J., Yoon, I., & Park, J. H. (2022). Psychological self-sufficiency and financial literacy among low-income participants: An empowerment-based approach to financial capability. *Journal of Family and Economic Issues*, *43*, 690–702. https://doi.org/10.1007/s10834-022-09865-w

Hsueh, L., Werntz, A., Hobaica, S., Owens, S., Lumley, M., & Washburn, J. (2020). Clinical psychology PhD students' admission experiences: Implications for recruiting racial/ethnic minority and LGBTQ students. *Journal of Clinical Psychology*, *77*(1), 105–120. https://doi-org.ezp3.lib.umn.edu/10.1002/jclp.23074

Jones, M. (2015, November 29). Why so many minority millennials can't get ahead. *The Atlantic*. Retrieved from https://www.theatlantic.com/business/archive/2015/11/gifts-debts-inheritances/417423/

Kempson, E., Atkinson, A., & Pilley, O. (2004). *Policy level response to financial exclusion in developed economies: Lessons for developing countries*. Personal Finance Research Centre, University of Bristol. https://www.findevgateway.org/sites/default/files/publications/files/mfg-en-paper-policy-level-response-to-financial-exclusion-in-developed-economies-lessons-for-developing-countries-2004.pdf

Kim, K. T., & Xiao, J. J. (2021). Racial/ethnic differences in consumer financial capability: The role of financial education. *International Journal of Consumer Studies*, *45*, 379–395. https://doi.org/10.1111/ijcs.12628

Kochhar, R., Taylor, P., & Fry, R. (2011). *Wealth gaps rise to record highs between Whites, Blacks and Hispanics*. Pew Research Center, Vol. 26. Retrieved from https://dsodown.mywebtext.org/pdf/s06-Wealth_Gaps.pdf

Levine, P., & Ritter, D. (2022). *The racial wealth gap, financial aid, and college access*. Brookings Institution. Retrieved from https://www.brookings.edu/blog/up-front/2022/09/27/the-racial-wealth-gap-financial-aid-and-college-access

Levy, B. L. (2022). Wealth, race, and place: How neighborhood (dis)advantage from emerging to middle adulthood affects wealth inequality and the racial wealth gap. *Demography*, *59*(1), 293–320. https://doi.org/10.1215/00703370-9710284

Long, M. G. (2022). The relationship between debt aversion and college enrollment by gender, race, and ethnicity: A propensity scoring approach. *Studies in Higher Education*, *47*(9), 1808–1826. https://doi.org/10.1080/03075079.2021.1968367

Looney, A. (2022). *Student loan forgiveness is regressive whether measured by income, education, or wealth: Why only targeted debt relief policies can reduce injustices in student loans* (Working Paper No. 75). Brookings Institution, Hutchins Center. Retrieved from https://www.brookings.edu/wp-content/uploads/2022/01/WP75-Looney_updated_1.pdf

Lusardi, A., & Mitchell, O. S. (2023). *The importance of financial literacy: Opening a new field* (Working Paper No. 31145). National Bureau of Economic Research. Retrieved from https://www.nber.org/papers/w31145

Markle, G. (2019). Crushing debt or savvy strategy? Financial literacy and student perceptions of their student loan debt. *Journal of Student Financial Aid*, *49*(1), 4. https://doi.org/10.55504/0884-9153.1651

Markoff, S., Ain, J., Celwa, G., & Hamilton, D. (2022). *A brighter future with baby bonds-How states and cities should invest in our kids.* Institute on Race, Power and Political Economy and ProsperityNow. Retrieved from https://prosperitynow.org/sites/default/files/resources/A-Brighter-Future-With-Baby-Bonds_2.pdf

Martinchek, K., Andre, J., & Santillo, M. (2022). *What can policymakers do to help young adults cope with debt?* Urban Institute, Vol. 10, pp. 42–57. Retrieved from https://www.urban.org/sites/default/files/2022-12/What%20Can%20Policymakers%20Do%20to%20Help%20Young%20Adults%20Cope%20with%20Debt.pdf

Mehrotra, A., Bealore, L., & Montoya-Boyer, A. (2022). *Zoning in: How inclusionary zoning increases affordable housing for communities of color to build wealth.* ProsperityNow Scorecard. Retrieved from https://prosperitynow.org/sites/default/files/PDFs/Scorecard%202022/Scorecard-Policy-Report-Zoning-In.pdf

National Center for Education Statistics (NCES). (2017). *The condition of education.* U.S. Department of Education, Office of Educational Research and Improvement. Retrieved from https://nces.ed.gov/pubs2017/2017144.pdf

National Community Reinvestment Coalition (NCRC). (2019, May). *A review of the state of barriers to minority homeownership.* Retrieved from https://ncrc.org/a-review-of-the-state-of-barriers-to-minority-homeownership

Perry, A. M., Steinbaum, M., & Romer, C. (2021). *Student loans, the racial wealth divide, and why we need full student debt cancellation.* Brookings Institution. https://www.brookings.edu/articles/student-loans-the-racial-wealth-divide-and-why-we-need-full-student-debt-cancellation/

Phinney, J. S. (2000). Identity formation across cultures: The interaction of personal, societal, and historical change. *Human Development, 43*(1), 27–31. https://doi.org/10.1159/000022653

Rathner, S. (2023). *Buy now, pay later isn't bad-but be careful.* Nerd Wallet. Retrieved from https://www.nerdwallet.com/article/credit-cards/buy-now-pay-later-isnt-bad-but-be-careful

Robles, B. J. (2014). Economic inclusion and financial education in culturally diverse communities: Leveraging cultural capital and whole-family learning. In K. S. Forte, E. W. Taylor, & E. J. Tisdell (Eds.), *Financial literacy and adult education: New directions for adult and continuing education,* Vol. 141, pp. 57–65. https://doi.org/10.1002/ace.20085

Saunders, K. M., Williams, K. L., & Smith, C. L. (2016). *Fewer resources, more debt: Loan debt burdens students at historically black colleges and universities.* UNCF Frederick D. Patterson Research Institute. Retrieved from https://files.eric.ed.gov/fulltext/ED573646.pdf

Shapiro, T., Meschede, T., & Osoro, S. (2013). *The roots of the widening racial wealth gap: Explaining the black-white economic divide.* Institute on Assets and Social Policy. Retrieved from https://hdl.handle.net/1903/24590

Sherraden, M. (1991). *Assets and the poor: A new American welfare policy.* M.E. Sharpe.

Sherraden, M. S. (2010). *Financial capability: What is it, and how can it be created?* (CSD Working Paper No. 10-17). Washington University, Center for Social Development. https://doi.org/10.7936/K7SX6CQX

Shierholz, H. (2014). *Low wages and few benefits mean many restaurant workers can't make ends meet.* Economy Policy Institute. Retrieved from https://www.epi.org/publication/restaurant-workers

Shupe, C., Li, G., & Fulford, S. (2023). *Consumer use of buy now, pay later: Insights from the CFPB making ends meet survey.* Consumer Protection Finance Board. Retrieved from https://files.consumerfinance.gov/f/documents/cfpb_consumer-use-of-buy-now-pay-later_2023-03.pdf

Smeeding, T. M. (2016). Multiple barriers to economic opportunity for the "truly" disadvantaged and vulnerable. *RSF: The Russell Sage Foundation Journal of the Social Sciences, 2*(2), 98–122. https://doi.org/10.7758/RSF.2016.2.2.04

Solheim, C. A., Quiñones, M., Ballard, J., & Marsalis, S. (2021). Integrating community cultural wealth in financial education design and practice with immigrant families. In A. Betz-Hamilton (Ed.), *2021 AFCPE Symposium Proceedings* (pp. 206–216). The Association of Financial Counseling and Planning Education.

Sullivan, L., Meschede, T., Dietrich, L., & Shapiro, T. (2015). *The racial wealth gap.* Institute for Assets and Social Policy, Brandeis University. DEMOS. Retrieved from https://static1.squarespace.com/static/6201784fcd12fa2baee377b0/t/625ecb561b173761b3a3b929/1650379606773/Demos+RacialWealthGap.pdf

Sun, S., Chen, Y.-C., Ansong, D., Huang, J., & Sherraden, M. S. (2022). Household financial capability and economic hardship: An empirical examination of the financial capability framework. *Journal of Family and Economic Issues, 43*, 716–729. https://doi.org/10.1007/s10834-022-09816-S

Taylor, B. J., & Cantwell, B. (2019). *Unequal higher education: Wealth, status, and student opportunity.* Rutgers University Press.

Thiemann, E. (2021, March 16). *2020 state of the children's savings field—resilience despite challenges.* ProsperityNow. Retrieved from https://prosperitynow.org/blog/2020-state-childrens-savings-field-resilience-despite-challenges

U.S. Bureau of Labor Statistics. (2019). *Labor force characteristics by race and ethnicity, 2018* (Report No. 1082). Retrieved from https://www.bls.gov/opub/reports/race-and-ethnicity/2017/home.htm#:~:text=By%20race%2C%20Whites%20made%20up,of%20less%20than%201%20percent

van Meeter, M., Curry, S. R., Tully, B. A., Ault, S., Nesmith, A., & White, J. (2022). The costs of caring: Navigating material challenges when adults informally host youth facing homelessness. *Youth & Society*, 1–18. https://doi.org/10.1177/0044118X221099992

van Rooij, M. C. J., Lusardi, A., & Alessie, R. J. M. (2012). Financial literacy, retirement planning and household wealth. *The Economic Journal, 122*(560), 449–478. https://doi.org/10.1111/j.1468-0297.2012.02501.x

Visalli, K., Mehrotra, A., Hill, T. & Pruitt, M. (2023, August). *Three trends in LGBTQ+ homeownership gaps underscore research and policy needs.* Urban Institute. Retrieved from https://www.urban.org/urban-wire/three-trends-lgbtq-homeownership-gaps-underscore-research-and-policy-needs

Wanberg, C. (2012). The individual experience of unemployment. *Annual Review of Psychology, 63*(1), 369–396. https://doi.org/10.1146/annurev-psych-120710-100500

Welbeck, K., & Kaufman, B. (2020). *Fintech lenders' responses to Senate probe heighten fears of educational redlining.* Student Borrower Protection Center. https://doi.org/10.2139/ssrn.3757054

Wheeler, C. H., & Olson, L. M. (2015). Racial differences in mortgage denials over the housing cycle: Evidence from U.S. metropolitan areas. *Journal of Housing Economics, 30*, 33–49. https://doi.org/10.1016/j.jhe.2015.10.004

Williams, D. R., Priest, N., & Anderson, N. B. (2016). Understanding associations among race, socioeconomic status, and health: Patterns and prospects. *Health Psychology, 35*(4), 407–411. https://doi.org/10.1037/hea0000242

Williams, W., Catalano, T., & Ma, J. (2023, August). *Student loan debt by gender.* Investopedia. Retrieved from https://www.investopedia.com/student-loan-debt-by-gender-5194243

Yosso, T. J. (2005). Whose culture has capital? A critical race theory discussion of community cultural wealth. *Race Ethnicity and Education, 8*(1), 69–91. https://doi.org/10.1080/1361332052000341006

Chapter 16

Aarntzen, L., Derks, B., van Steenbergen, E., & van der Lippe, T. (2023). When work–family guilt becomes a women's issue: Internalized gender stereotypes predict high guilt in working mothers but low guilt in working fathers. *British Journal of Social Psychology, 62*(1), 12–29. https://doi.org/10.1111/bjso.12575

Agarwalla, S. K., Barua, S. K., Jacob, J., & Varma, J. R. (2015). Financial literacy among working young in urban India. *World Development, 67*, 101–109. https://doi.org/10.1016/j.worlddev.2014.10.004

Agasisti, T., Barucci, E., Cannistrà, M., Marazzina, D., & Soncin, M. (2023). Online or on-campus? Analysing the effects of financial education on student knowledge gain. *Evaluation and Program Planning, 98*, 102273. https://doi.org/10.1016/j.evalprogplan.2023.102273

Agnew, S., & Cameron-Agnew, T. (2015). The influence of consumer socialisation in the home on gender differences in financial literacy. *International Journal of Consumer Studies, 39*(6), 630–638. https://doi.org/10.1111/ijcs.12179

Agnew, S., Maras, P., & Moon, A. (2018). Gender differences in financial socialization in the home—An exploratory study. *International journal of consumer studies, 42*(3), 275–282.

Ali, M., Ali, I., Badghish, S., & Soomro, Y. A. (2021). Determinants of financial empowerment among women in Saudi Arabia. *Frontiers in Psychology, 12*, 747255. https://doi.org/10.3389/fpsyg.2021.747255

Amagir, A., Groot, W., van den Brink, H. M., & Wilschut, A. (2020). Financial literacy of high school students in the Netherlands: Knowledge, attitudes, self-efficacy, and behavior. *International Review of Economics Education, 34*, 100185. https://doi.org/10.1016/j.iree.2020.100185

Arellano, A., Cámara, N., & Tuesta, D. (2018). Explaining the gender gap in financial literacy: The role of non-cognitive skills. *Economic Notes: Review of Banking, Finance and Monetary Economics, 47*(2-3), 495–518. https://doi.org/10.1111/ecno.12113

Ashmore, R. D., Del Boca, F. K., & Hamilton, D. L. (1981). Cognitive processes in stereotyping and intergroup behavior. In *Conceptual approaches to stereotypes and stereotyping*. Erlbaum.

Atkinson, A., & Messy, F. A. (2012). *Measuring financial literacy: Results of the OECD/International Network on Financial Education (INFE) Pilot Study.* OECD Working Papers on Finance, Insurance and Private Pensions, Vol. 15. https://doi.org/10.1787/5k9csfs90fr4-en

Bandelj, N., Lanuza, Y. R., & Kim, J. J. (2021). Gendered relational work: How gender shapes money attitudes and expectations of young adults. *Journal of Cultural Economy, 14*(6), 765–784. https://doi.org/10.1080/17530350.2021.1952098

Bandelj, N., Wherry, F. F., & Zelizer, V. A. (Eds.). (2017). *Money talks: Explaining how money really works.* Princeton University Press. https://doi.org/10.23943/princeton/9780691168685.001.0001

Bapat, D. (2020). Antecedents to responsible financial management behavior among young adults: Moderating role of financial risk tolerance. *International Journal of Bank Marketing, 38*(5), 1177–1194. https://doi.org/10.1108/IJBM-10-2019-0356

Barboza, G., Smith, C., & Pesek, J. G. (2016). Assessing financial literacy, gender gap and cognitive differences. *Journal of Financial Education, 42*(3–4), 205–242.

Bennedsen, M., Larsen, B., & Wei, J. (2023). Gender wage transparency and the gender pay gap: A survey. *Journal of Economic Surveys, 37*(5), 1529–1533. https://doi.org/10.1111/joes.12545

Blossfeld, H. P., Skopek, J., Triventi, M., & Buchholz, S. (Eds.). (2015). *Gender, education and employment: An international comparison of school-to-work transitions.* Edward Elgar. https://doi.org/10.4337/9781784715038

Boggio, C., Fornero, E., Prast, H. M., & Sanders, J. (2015). *Seven ways to knit your portfolio: Is investor communication neutral?* Netspar Discussion Papers, Vol. 10. https://doi.org/10.2139/ssrn.2668579

Bongini, P., Trivellato, P., & Zenga, M. (2015). Business students and financial literacy: When will the gender gap fade away? *Journal of Financial Management, Markets and Institutions, 3*(1), 13–30. https://doi.org/10.12831/80528

Bottazzi, L., & Lusardi, A. (2020). Stereotypes in financial literacy: Evidence from PISA. *Journal of Corporate Finance, 71*, 101831. https://doi.org/10.1016/j.jcorpfin.2020.101831

Bucher-Koenen, T., Lusardi, A., Alessie, R., & van Rooij, M. (2017). How financially literate are women? An overview and new insights. *Journal of Consumer Affairs, 51*(2), 255–283. https://doi.org/10.1111/joca.12121

Campbell, C. (2009). Distinguishing the power of agency from agentic power: A note on Weber and the "black box" of personal agency. *Sociological Theory, 27*(4), 407–418. https://doi.org/10.1111/j.1467-9558.2009.01355.x

Capelle-Blancard, G., & Reberioux, A. (2021). Women and finance. *SSRN Electronic Journal.* https://doi.org/10.2139/ssrn.3802724

Chancel, L., Piketty, T., Saez, E., & Zucman, G. (Eds.). (2022). *World inequality report 2022.* Harvard University Press. https://doi.org/10.2307/j.ctv3006zpt

Charness, G., & Gneezy, U. (2012). Strong evidence for gender differences in risk taking. *Journal of Economic Behavior & Organization, 83*(1), 50–58. https://doi.org/10.1016/j.jebo.2011.06.007

Chen, H., & Volpe, R. P. (2002). Gender differences in personal financial literacy among college students. *Financial Services Review, 11*(3), 289–307.

Chobhthaigh, N.B. (2019). *Understanding the gender gap in financial well-being evidence of a gender gap in financial well-being in EU member states.* European Economy Discussion Papers, Vol. 121, pp. 1–35. https://doi.org/10.2765/394693

Cialdini, R. B., & Trost, M. R. (1998). Social influence: Social norms, conformity and compliance. In D. T. Gilbert, S. T. Fiske, & G. Lindzey (Eds.), *The handbook of social psychology* (4th ed., Vol. 2, pp. 151–192). McGraw-Hill.

Coffman, K. B. (2014). Evidence on self-stereotyping and the contribution of ideas. *The Quarterly Journal of Economics, 129*(4), 1625–1660. https://doi.org/10.1093/qje/qju023

Crocetti, E., Tagliabue, S., Sugimura, K., Nelson, L. J., Takahashi, A., Niwa, T., . . . Jinno, M. (2015). Perceptions of emerging adulthood: A study with Italian and Japanese university students and young workers. *Emerging Adulthood, 3*(4), 229–243. https://doi.org/10.1177/2167696815569848

Cupák, A., Fessler, P., & Schneebaum, A. (2021). Gender differences in risky asset behavior: The importance of self-confidence and financial literacy. *Finance Research Letters, 42*, 101880. https://doi.org/10.1016/j.frl.2020.101880

Cupák, A., Fessler, P., Schneebaum, A., & Silgoner, M. (2018). Decomposing gender gaps in financial literacy: New international evidence. *Economics Letters, 168*, 102–106. https://doi.org/10.1016/j.econlet.2018.04.004

Danes, S. M., & Haberman, H. (2007). Teen financial knowledge, self-efficacy, and behavior: A gendered view. *Journal of Financial Counseling and Planning, 18*(2). Retrieved from https://ssrn.com/abstract=2228406

Davoli, M., & Rodríguez-Planas, N. (2022). *Culture, gender, and financial literacy* (Discussion Paper No. 15054). IZA. https://doi.org/10.2139/ssrn.4114598

Demirgüç-Kunt, A., Klapper, L., Singer, D., Ansar, S., & Hess, J. (2020). The Global Findex Database 2017: Measuring financial inclusion and opportunities to expand access to and use of financial services. *The World Bank Economic Review, 34*(Suppl. 1), S2–S8. https://doi.org/10.1093/wber/lhz013

Deutsch, F. M., Roksa, J., & Meeske, C. (2003). How gender counts when couples count their money. *Sex Roles, 48*(7), 291–304. https://doi.org/10.1023/a:1022982328840

Dittmar, H. (1989). Gender identity-related meanings of personal possessions. *British Journal of Social Psychology, 28*(2), 159–171. https://doi.org/10.1111/j.2044-8309.1989.tb00857.x

Driva, A., Lührmann, M., & Winter, J. (2016). Gender differences and stereotypes in financial literacy: Off to an early start. *Economics Letters, 146*, 143–146. https://doi.org/10.1016/j.econlet.2016.07.029

Dwyer, R. E., Hodson, R., & McCloud, L. (2013). Gender, debt, and dropping out of college. *Gender & Society, 27*(1), 30–55. https://doi.org/10.1177/0891243212464906

Edwards, R., Allen, M. W., & Hayhoe, C. R. (2007). Financial attitudes and family communication about students' finances: The role of sex differences. *Communication Reports, 20*(2), 90–100. https://doi.org/10.1080/08934210701643719

Ellemers, N. (2018). Gender stereotypes. *Annual Review of Psychology, 69*, 275–298. https://doi.org/10.1146/annurev-psych-122216-011719

Falahati, L., & Paim, L. H. (2011). Gender differences in financial literacy among college students. *Journal of American Science, 7*(6), 1180–1183.

Filipiak, U., & Walle, Y. M. (2015). *The financial literacy gender gap: A question of nature or nurture?* Discussion Papers, Vol. 176. Georg-August-Universität Göttingen. https://www.econstor.eu/bitstream/10419/111350/1/CRC-PEG_DP_176_1.pdf

Fiske, S. T., Cuddy, A. J., Glick, P., & Xu, J. (2002). A model of (often mixed) stereotype content: Competence and warmth respectively follow from perceived status and competition. *Journal of Personality and Social Psychology, 82*, 878–902. https://doi.org/10.1037//0022-3514.82.6.878

Fonseca, R., Mullen, K. J., Zamarro, G., & Zissimopoulos, J. (2012). What explains the gender gap in financial literacy? The role of household decision making. *The Journal of Consumer Affairs, 46*(1), 90–106. https://doi.org/10.1111/j.1745-6606.2011.01221.x

García Mata, O. (2021). The effect of financial literacy and gender on retirement planning among young adults. *International Journal of Bank Marketing, 39*(7), 1068–1090. https://doi.org/10.1108/IJBM-10-2020-0518

García-Mendoza, M. D. C., Parra, A., Sánchez-Queija, I., Oliveira, J. E., & Coimbra, S. (2022). Gender differences in perceived family involvement and perceived family control during emerging adulthood: A cross-country comparison in Southern Europe. *Journal of Child and Family Studies, 31*, 1007–1018. https://doi.org/10.1007/s10826-021-02122-y

Goyal, K., & Kumar, S. (2021). Financial literacy: A systematic review and bibliometric analysis. *International Journal of Consumer Studies, 45*(1), 80–105. https://doi.org/10.1111/ijcs.12605

Graeber, D. (2012). *Debt: The first 5000 years.* Penguin UK.

The Guardian. (n.d.). Women's rights and their money: A timeline from Cleopatra to Lilly Ledbetter. Retrieved from https://www.theguardian.com/money/us-money-blog/2014/aug/11/women-rights-money-timeline-history

Gudjonsson, S., Minelgaite, I., Kristinsson, K., & Pálsdóttir, S. (2022). Financial literacy and gender differences: Women choose people while men choose things? *Administrative Sciences, 12*(4), 179. https://doi.org/10.3390/admsci12040179

Harvey, M. (2019). Impact of financial education mandates on younger consumers' use of alternative financial services. *Journal of Consumer Affairs, 53*(3), 731–769. https://doi.org/10.1111/joca.12242

Hasler, A., & Lusardi, A. (2017). *Understanding the gender gap in financial well-being evidence of a gender gap in financial well-being in EU member states.* The George Washington University School of Business. Retrieved from https://gflec.org/wp-content/uploads/2017/05/The-Gender-Gap-in-Financial-Literacy-A-Global-Perspective-Report.pdf

Hayhoe, C. R., Leach, L. J., Turner, P. R., Bruin, M. J., & Lawrence, F. C. (2000). Differences in spending habits and credit use of college students. *Journal of Consumer Affairs, 34*(1), 113–133. https://doi.org/10.1111/j.1745-6606.2000.tb00087.x

Henry, R. A., Weber, J. G., & Yarbrough, D. (2001). Money management practices of college students. *College Student Journal, 35*(2), 244–244. Retrieved from https://projectinnovation.biz/csj_2006.html

Hentschel, T., Heilman, M. E., & Peus, C. V. (2019). The multiple dimensions of gender stereotypes: A current look at men's and women's characterizations of others and themselves. *Frontiers in Psychology, 11.* https://doi.org/10.3389/fpsyg.2019.00011

Hollander, J. A. (2013). "I demand more of people": Accountability, interaction, and gender change. *Gender & Society, 27*(1), 5–29. https://doi.org/10.1177/0891243212464301

ISTAT (Istituto Nazionale di Statistica). (2011). *Infanzia e vita quotidiana.* Rapporto annuale. https://www.istat.it/it/files/2011/11/report-infanzia-2011.pdf

Jacobson, G. C. (1980). *Money in congressional elections.* Yale University Press.

Johnson, J. H. (1994). "Annuity contracts" and marriage. In D. P. Silverman (Ed.), *For his Ka. Essays in memory of Klaus Baer. Studies in ancient oriental civilization*, Vol. 55, pp. 113–132.

Judd, C. M., & Park, B. (1993). Definition and assessment of accuracy in social stereotypes. *Psychological Review, 100*(1), 109. https://doi.org/10.1037/0033-295X.100.1.109

Kaiser, T., Lusardi, A., Menkhoff, L., & Urban, C. (2022). Financial education affects financial knowledge and downstream behaviors. *Journal of Financial Economics, 145*(2), 255–272. https://doi.org/10.1016/j.jfineco.2021.09.022

Kalmi, P., & Ruuskanen, O. P. (2017). Financial literacy and retirement planning in Finland. *Journal of Pension Economics & Finance, 17*(3), 1–28. https://doi.org/10.1017/S1474747217000270

Knight, J. A. (1968). *For the love of money: Human behavior & money.* Lippincott.

Kosakowska-Berezecka, N., Bosson, J. K., Jurek, P., Besta, T., Olech, M., Vandello, J. A., . . . van der Noll, J. (2023). Gendered self-views across 62 countries: A test of competing models. *Social Psychological and Personality Science, 14*(7), 808–824. https://doi.org/10.1177/19485506221129687

Kutin, J. J., Reid, M., & Russell, R. (2019). Special WSMC edition paper: What is this thing called money? Economic abuse in young adult relationships. *Journal of Social Marketing, 9*(1), 111–128. https://doi.org/10.1108/JSOCM-03-2018-0028

LeBaron, A. B., & Kelley, H. H. (2021). Financial socialization: A decade in review. *Journal of family and economic issues, 42*(Suppl 1), 195–206.

Leccardi, C. (2007). Stereotipi di genere [Gender stereotypes]. In C. Buzzi, A. Cavalli, & A. de Lillo (Eds.), *Rapporto giovani: Sesta indagine dell'Istituto IARD sulla condizione giovanile in Italia* (pp. 233–247). Il Mulino.

Lindgren, H. C. (1980). *Great expectations: The psychology of money.* W. Kaufmann.

Lusardi, A., & Mitchell, O. S. (2006). *Planning and financial literacy: How do women fare?* Michigan Retirement Research Center. https://doi.org/10.2139/ssrn.1094097

Lyons, A. C. (2008). Risky credit card behavior of college students. In J. J. Xiao (Ed.), *Handbook of consumer finance research* (pp. 185–207). Springer New York. https://doi.org/10.1007/978-0-387-75734-6_11

Makarova, E., Aeschlimann, B., & Herzog, W. (2019). The gender gap in STEM fields: The impact of the gender stereotype of math and science on secondary students' career aspirations. *Frontiers in Education*, 4(60). https://doi.org/10.3389/feduc.2019.00060

Manzi, C., Giannella, V. A., & Crapolicchio, E. (under review). Gender differences in attitudes towards money: An analysis of the Italian population.

Marinucci, M., Stacchini, M., & Travaglino, F. (2024). *Indagini sull'alfabetizzazione finanziaria e le competenze di finanza digitale in Italia: Giovani* (Surveys on financial literacy and digital finance skills in Italy: Youth). Statistiche. Banca d'Italia. Retrieved from https://www.bancaditalia.it/media/notizia/indagini-sull-alfabetizzazione-finanziaria-e-le-competenze-di-finanza-digitale-in-italia-giovani-2023/?dotcache=refresh

Matsumoto, M., & Elder, S. (2010). *Characterizing the school-to-work transitions of young men and women: Evidence from the ILO school-to-work transition surveys* (Employment Working Paper No. 51). International Labour Organization. https://www.ilo.org/publications/characterizing-school-work-transitions-young-men-and-women-evidence-ilo

McKenzie, C. (2023, February 27). *Part one: The myth of the financial personality defect.* NEFE. https://www.nefe.org/news/2023/02/part-one-the-myth-of-the-financial-personality-defect.aspx

Morsy, H., & Youssef, H. (2017). *Access to finance—Mind the gender gap* (EBRD Working Paper No. 202). https://doi.org/10.2139/ssrn.3092974

Niederle, M., & Vesterlund, L. (2010). Explaining the gender gap in math test scores: The role of competition. *Journal of Economic Perspectives, 24*(2), 129–144. https://doi.org/10.1257/jep.24.2.129

OECD. (2014). *PISA 2012 results: Students and money: Financial literacy skills for the 21st century* (Vol. 6). https://doi.org/10.1787/9789264208094-en

OECD. (2019). *Society at a glance 2019: OECD social indicators.* Retrieved from https://www.oecd.org/en/publications/2019/03/society-at-a-glance-2019_g1g9f661.html

OECD. (2020). *OECD/INFE 2020 international survey of adult financial literacy.* https://www.oecd-ilibrary.org/finance-and-investment/oecd-infe-2020-international-survey-of-adult-financial-literacy_145f5607-en

OECD. (2022). *Same skills, different pay: Tackling gender inequalities at firm level.* Retrieved from https://www.oecd.org/gender/same-skills-different-pay-2022.pdf

Pahlevan Sharif, S., Ahadzadeh, A. S., & Turner, J. J. (2020). Gender differences in financial literacy and financial behaviour among young adults: The role of parents and information seeking. *Journal of Family and Economic Issues, 41*(4), 672–690. https://doi.org/10.1007/s10834-020-09674-z

Palladino, G. (2022). *Ask a question, get an answer. A study of the framing effect on financial literacy in Italy* (Publication No. 112168). MPRA. Retrieved from https://mpra.ub.uni-muenchen.de/id/eprint/112168

Prast, H., Sanders, J., & Leonhard, O. (2018). *Can words breed or kill investment? Metaphors, imagery, affect and investor behaviour* (Discussion Paper, Vol. 2018-014). CentER (Center for Economic Research). https://research.tilburguniversity.edu/en/publications/can-words-breed-or-kill-investment-metaphors-imagery-affect-and-i

Preston, A. C., & Wright, R. E. (2019). Understanding the gender gap in financial literacy: Evidence from Australia. *Economic Record, 95*(S1), 1–29. https://doi.org/10.1111/1475-4932.12472

PWC. (2023). *Women in work 2023: Closing the gender pay gap for good: A focus on the motherhood penalty.* Retrieved from https://www.pwc.co.uk/economic-services/WIWI/pwc-women-in-work-index-2023.pdf

Richards, C. L., Bouman, W. P., & Barker, M. (2017). *Genderqueer and non-binary genders.* Palgrave Macmillan. https://doi.org/10.1057/978-1-137-51053-2

Rinaldi, E. E., Salmieri, L., & Vera, J. (2022). Gender differences in financial literacy and socialization: Comparing Italy to Spain. *Italian Journal of Sociology of Education, 14*(2), 121–149. https://doi.org/10.14658/PUPJ-IJSE-2022-2-7

Rossi, A. (2018). *Gender and the life course.* Routledge. https://doi.org/10.4324/9781351329040

Rudmin, F. W. (1990). The economic psychology of Leon Litwinski (1887–1969): A program of cognitive research on possession and property. *Journal of Economic Psychology, 11*(3), 307–339. https://doi.org/10.1016/0167-4870(90)90016-3

Scott, C. A. (1976). The effects of trial and incentives on repeat purchase behavior. *Journal of Marketing Research, 13*(3), 263–269. https://doi.org/10.1177/002224377601300307

Serido, J., Shim, S., & Tang, C. (2013). A developmental model of financial capability: A framework for promoting a successful transition to adulthood. *International Journal of Behavioral Development, 37*(4), 287–297. https://doi.org/10.1177/0165025413479476

Sesini, G., Manzi, C., & Lozza, E. (2023). Is psychology of money a gendered affair? A scoping review and research agenda. *International Journal of Consumer Studies*, 47(6), 2701–2723. https://doi.org/10.1111/ijcs.12975

Simmel, G. (1900/1989). *Philosophie des Geldes.* Suhrkamp.

Simon, R. M., Wagner, A., & Killion, B. (2017). Gender and choosing a STEM major in college: Femininity, masculinity, chilly climate, and occupational values. *Journal of Research in Science Teaching, 54*(3), 299–323. https://doi.org/10.1002/tea.21345

Streeter, J. L. (2020). Gender differences in widowhood in the short-run and long-run: Financial, emotional, and mental wellbeing. *The Journal of the Economics of Ageing, 17*, 100258. https://doi.org/10.1016/j.jeoa.2020.100258

Tang, T. L. P. (1992). The meaning of money revisited. *Journal of Organizational Behaviour, 13*(2), 197–202. https://doi.org/10.1002/job.4030130209

Tinghög, G., Ahmed, A., Barrafrem, K., Lind, T., Skagerlund, K., & Västfjäll, D. (2021). Gender differences in financial literacy: The role of stereotype threat. *Journal of Economic Behavior & Organization, 192*, 405–416. https://doi.org/10.1016/j.jebo.2021.10.015

UN Women (United Nations Entity for Gender Equality and the Empowerment of Women). (2019). *Progress on the sustainable development goals. The gender snapshot 2019.* DESA (Department of Economic and Social Affairs). Retrieved from https://www.unwomen.org/en/digital-library/publications/2019/09/progress-on-the-sustainable-development-goals-the-gender-snapshot-2019

Walther, A., & Plug, W. (2006). Transitions from school to work in Europe: Destandardization and policy trends. *New Directions for Child and Adolescent Development* (113), 77–90. https://doi.org/10.1002/cd.170

West, C., & Zimmerman, D. H. (1987). Doing gender. *Gender & Society, 1*(2), 125–151.

West, C., & Zimmerman, D. H. (2009). Accounting for doing gender. *Gender & Society, 23*(1), 112–122. https://doi.org/10.1177/0891243208326529

Williams, M. J., Elizabeth, L. P., & Spencer-Rodgers, J. (2010). The masculinity of money: Automatic stereotypes predict gender differences in estimated salaries. *Psychology of Women Quarterly, 34*(1), 7–20. https://doi.org/10.1111/j.1471-6402.2009.01537.x

Wilson, G. (2022, October 19). *The gender pay gap starts early: Girls get less pocket money and pay higher prices than boys.* Starling Bank. Retrieved from https://www.starlingbank.com/news/gender-pay-gap-starts-early

World Economic Forum. (2022). *Global gender gap report 2022: Insight report.* Retrieved from https://www3.weforum.org/docs/WEF_GGGR_2022.pdf

World Health Organization. (n.d.). *Gender.* Retrieved from https://www.euro.who.int/en/health-topics/health-determinants/gender/gender-definitions

World Health Organization. (2006). *Gender equality, work and health: A review of the evidence.* https://www.who.int/publications/i/item/gender-equality-work-and-health-a-review-of-the-evidence

Yamauchi, K. T., & Templer, D. J. (1982). The development of a money attitude scale. *Journal of Personality Assessment, 46*(5), 522–528. https://doi.org/10.1207/s15327752jpa4605_14
Zelizer, V. A. (1994). *Pricing the priceless child: The changing social value of children.* Princeton University Press.
Zelizer, V.A. (1997). *The social meaning of money: Pin money, paychecks, poor relief and other currencies.* Princeton University Press.
Zelizer, V. A. (2005). *The purchase of intimacy.* Princeton University Press.

Chapter 17

Ahunov, M., & Van Hove, L. (2020). National culture and financial literacy: International evidence. *Applied Economics, 52*(21), 2261–2279. http://doi.org/10.1080/00036846.2019.1688241
Al-Bahrani, A., Weathers, J., & Patel, D. (2019). Racial differences in the returns to financial Literacy education. *Journal of Consumer Affairs, 53*(2), 572–599. https://doi.org/10.1111/joca.12205
Anong, S. T. (2016). Financial issues of African Americans. In J. J. Xiao (Ed.), *Handbook of consumer finance research* (pp. 215–224). Springer. https://doi.org/10.1007/978-3-319-28887-1_18
Anong, S. T., Aboagye, J., & Yoo, J. (2021). Financial literacy and financial education in Africa. In *The Routledge handbook of financial literacy* (pp. 420–437). Routledge. https://doi.org/10.4324/9781003025221-32
ANZ. (2015). *ANZ survey of adult financial literacy in Australia.* Retrieved from https://www.anz.com/resources/3/1/31cbc1fd-9491-4a22-91dc-4c803e4c34ab/adult-financial-literacy-survey-full-results.pdf
Arnett, J. J. (2015). Identity development from adolescence to emerging adulthood: What we know and (especially) don't know. *The Oxford handbook of identity development,* 53–64. Oxford University Press. https://doi.org/10.1093/oxfordhb/9780199936564.013.009
Arnett, J. J. (2016). Does emerging adulthood theory apply across social classes? National data on a persistent question. *Emerging Adulthood, 4,* 227–235. https://doi.org/10.1177/2167696815613000
Australian Security and Investments Commission. (2011). *National financial literacy strategy* (Report No. 229). Retrieved from https://files.moneysmart.gov.au/media/tsrhiihv/rep229-national-financial-literacy-strategy-2011.pdf
Australian Security and Investments Commission. (2014). *National financial literacy strategy 2014–17* (Report No. 403). Retrieved from https://asic.gov.au/regulatory-resources/find-a-document/reports/rep-403-national-financial-literacy-strategy-2014-17/
Baluja, G. (2016). Financial literacy among women in India: A review. *Pacific Business Review International, 9*(4), 82–88. Retrieved from https://www.pbr.co.in/2016/2016_month/October/11.pdf
Banfield, E. C. (1958). *The moral basis of a backward society.* Free Press.
Batsaikhan, U., & Demertzis, M. (2018). *Financial literacy and inclusive growth in the European Union* (Publication No. 2018/08). Bruegel Policy Contribution. https://www.bruegel.org/sites/default/files/wp-content/uploads/2018/05/PC-08_2018.pdf
Beckmann, E. (2013). Financial literacy and household savings in Romania. *Numeracy, 6*(2), 9. https://doi.org/10.5038/1936-4660.6.2.9
Bel, S., & Eberlein, J. (2015). Why financial literacy matters for development. *Organization for Economic Cooperation and Development. The OECD Observer, 303,* 28–29.

Bernheim, B. D., Garrett, D. M., & Maki, D. M. (2001). Education and saving: The long-term effects of high school financial curriculum mandates. *Journal of Public Economics, 80*(3), 435–465. https://doi.org/10.1016/s0047-2727(00)00120-1

Bove, V., & Elia, L. (2017). Migration, diversity, and economic growth. *World Development, 89*, 227–239. https://doi.org/10.1016/j.worlddev.2016.08.012

Brounen, D., Koedijk, K. G., & Pownall, R. A. (2016). Household financial planning and savings behavior. *Journal of International Money and Finance, 69*, 95–107. https://doi.org/10.1016/j.jimonfin.2016.06.011

Brown, M., Grigsby, J., Van Der Klaauw, W., Wen, J., & Zafar, B. (2016). Financial education and the debt behavior of the young. *The Review of Financial Studies, 29*(9), 2490–2522. https://doi.org/10.1093/rfs/hhw006

Brown, M., Henchoz, C., & Spycher, T. (2018). Culture and financial literacy: Evidence from a within-country language border. *Journal of Economic Behavior & Organization, 150*, 62–85. https://doi.org/10.1016/j.jebo.2018.03.011

Bucher-Koenen, T., Lusardi, A., Alessie, R., & Van Rooij, M. (2017). How financially literate are women? An overview and new insights. *Journal of Consumer Affairs, 51*(2), 255–283. https://doi.org/10.1111/joca.12121

Budiman, A., & Ruiz, N. G. (2021). *Key facts about Asian Americans, a diverse and growing population.* Pew Research Center. https://www.pewresearch.org/short-reads/2021/04/29/key-facts-about-asian-americans/

Campbell, L. A., & Kaufman, R. L. (2006). Racial differences in household wealth: Beyond Black and White. *Research in Social Stratification and Mobility, 24*(2), 131–152. https://doi.org/10.1016/j.rssm.2005.06.001

Commission for Financial Capability. (2015). *National strategy for financial capability.* Retrieved from https://assets.retirement.govt.nz/public/Uploads/National-Strategy/PDFs/92262d1e19/National-Strategy-for-Financial-Capability-June-2015.pdf

Council for Economic Education. (2018). *Economic and personal finance education in our nation's schools.* Retrieved from https://www.councilforeconed.org/wp-content/uploads/2018/02/2018-SOS-Layout-18.pdf

Cwynar, A. (2021). Financial literacy and financial education in Eastern Europe. In *The Routledge handbook of financial literacy* (pp. 400–419). Routledge. https://doi.org/10.4324/9781003025221-31

Damian, L. E., Negru-Subtirica, O., Domocus, I. M., & Friedlmeier, M. (2020). Healthy financial behaviors and financial satisfaction in emerging adulthood: A parental socialization perspective. *Emerging Adulthood, 8*(6), 548–554. https://doi.org/10.1177/2167696819841952

Danes, S. M. (1994). Parental perceptions of children's financial socialization. *Journal of Financial Counseling and Planning, 5*, 127–149.

Davoli, M., & Rodríguez-Planas, N. (2020). Culture and adult financial literacy: Evidence from the United States. *Economics of Education Review, 78*, 102013. https://doi.org/10.1016/j.econedurev.2020.102013

De Beckker, K., De Witte, K., & Van Campenhout, G. (2020). The role of national culture in financial literacy: Cross-country evidence. *Journal of Consumer Affairs, 54*(3), 912–930. https://doi.org/10.1111/joca.12306

Demirgüç-Kunt, A., & Klapper, L. (2012). *Financial inclusion in Africa: An overview.* The World Bank Development Research Group. https://doi.org/10.1596/1813-9450-6088

Federal Deposit Insurance Corporation. (2016). *2016 annual report.* Retrieved from https://archive.fdic.gov/view/fdic/182

Fernandez, R. (2008). Culture and economics. In *The new Palgrave dictionary of economics*(Vol. 1–8, 1229–1236. https://doi.org/10.1057/978-1-349-95121-5_2192-1

FinMark Trust. (2021). *FinMark trust data portal.* Retrieved from https://finmark.org.za/data-portal

Fonseca, R., Mullen, K. J., Zamarro, G., & Zissimopoulos, J. (2012). What explains the gender gap in financial literacy? The role of household decision making. *Journal of Consumer Affairs, 46*(1), 90–106. https://doi.org/10.1111/j.1745-6606.2011.01221.x

Gallo, L. C., Penedo, F. J., Espinosa de Los Monteros, K., & Arguelles, W. (2009). Resiliency in the face of disadvantage: Do Hispanic cultural characteristics protect health outcomes? *Journal of Personality, 77*(6), 1707–1746. https://doi.org/10.1111/j.1467-6494.2009.00598.x

Guiso, L., Sapienza, P., & Zingales, L. (2016). Long-term persistence. *Journal of the European Economic Association, 14*(6), 1401–1436. https://doi.org/10.1111/jeea.12177

Gutter, M. S., Copur, Z., & Blanco, A. (2014). Racial differences in financial socialization and financial behaviors of U.S. college students. In H. Dinçer & Ü. Hacioğlu (Eds.), *Global strategies in banking and finance* (pp. 272–292). IGI Global. https://doi.org/10.4018/978-1-4666-4635-3.ch018

Haliassos, M., Jansson, T., & Karabulut, Y. (2017). Incompatible European partners? Cultural predispositions and household financial behavior. *Management Science, 63*(11), 3780–3808. https://doi.org/10.1287/mnsc.2016.2538

Hofstede, G. (2011). Dimensionalizing cultures: The Hofstede model in context. *Online Readings in Psychology and Culture, 2*(1), 8. https://doi.org/10.9707/2307-0919.1014

Houkamau, C., & Sibley, C. (2017). Cultural connection predicts perceptions of financial security for Māori. *Social Indicators Research, 133*(1), 395–412. https://doi.org/10.1007/s11205-016-1367-5

Houkamau, C., Stevens, A., Oakes, D., & Blank, M. (2019, April 30). *Ngā whakautu a Te Māori mō Te Whakahaeretanga o te pūtea, Te Whairawatanga me Te Penapena Pūtea* [Taking control: Māori responses to money management, wealth and saving]. ResearchSpace Home. Retrieved from https://researchspace.auckland.ac.nz/handle/2292/46503

Hunter, M. A. (2019). *22 million reasons black America doesn't trust banks.* PRI. Retrieved from https://www.pri.org/stories/2018-02-02/22-million-reasons-black-america-doesn-t-trust-banks

Huston, S. J. (2012). Financial literacy and the cost of borrowing. *International Journal of Consumer Studies, 36*, 566–572. https://doi.org/10.1111/j.1470-6431.2012.01122.x

Hsu, J. W. (2016). Aging and strategic learning: The impact of spousal incentives on financial literacy. *Journal of Human Resources, 51*(4), 1036–1067. DOI: https://doi.org/10.3368/jhr.51.4.1014-6712R

Karakurum-Ozdemir, K., Kokkizil, M., & Uysal, G. (2019). Financial literacy in developing countries. *Social Indicators Research, 143*(1), 325–353. https://doi.org/10.1007/s11205-018-1952-x

Kim, K. T., Lee, J., & Lee, J. M. (2019). Exploring racial/ethnic disparities in the use of alternative financial services: The moderating role of financial knowledge. *Race and Social Problems, 11*(2), 149–160. https://doi.org/10.1007/s12552-019-09259-y

Kim, K. T., & Xiao, J. J. (2021). Racial/ethnic differences in consumer financial capability: The role of financial education. *International Journal of Consumer Studies, 45*(3), 379–395. https://doi.org/10.1111/ijcs.12628

Klapper, L., & Lusardi, A. (2019). Financial literacy and financial resilience: Evidence from around the world. *Financial Management, 49*(3), 589–614. https://doi.org/10.1111/fima.12283

Klapper, L., Lusardi, A., & van Oudheudsen, P. (2015). *Financial literacy around the world: Insights from the S&P global financial literacy survey.* Global Financial Literacy Excellence Center. Retrieved from https://gflec.org/wp-content/uploads/2015/11/Finlit_paper_16_F2_singles.pdf

Kochhar, R., & Fry, R. (2014). Wealth inequality has widened along racial, ethnic lines since end of Great Recession. *Pew Research Center, 12*(104), 121–145.

Kroeber, A. L., & Kluckhohn, C. (1952). *Culture: A critical review of concepts and definitions.* Peabody Museum of Archaeology and Ethnology, Harvard University.

Lee, J., & Hanna, S. D. (2012). Limitations of combining Hispanics and African Americans for analysis of credit problems. *Journal of Consumer Affairs, 46*(3), 506–536. https://doi.org/10.1111/j.1745-6606.2012.01237.x

Lehtinen, A. R. (2017). *Nuorten asuntolainojen takaisinmaksu ja talousosaaminen* [Adolescent mortgage repayment and financial literacy]. In M.-L. Niemi (Ed.), *Nuoret ja velka—Akatemiahankkeen tutkimuskoosteita. Nuorten velkaongelmat—Velkatyypit, selviytyminen ja vastuukysymykset* [Research papers from the Academy Project Youth and Debt. Youth debt problems—debt types, survival and responsibility issues] (pp. 55–71). Retrieved from https://urn.fi/URN:ISBN:978-952-484-972-2

Li, Y., Zuiker, V. S., Mendenhall, T. J., & Montalto, C. P. (2021). Parental financial socialization, financial experiences, and financial behaviors: Comparing Asian American and international Asian college students. *Journal of Financial Counseling & Planning, 32*(1), 68–85. https://doi.org/10.1891/JFCP-19-00008

Licht, A. N., Goldschmidt, C., & Schwartz, S. H. (2007). Culture rules: The foundations of the rule of law and other norms of governance. *Journal of Comparative Economics, 35*(4), 659–688. https://doi.org/10.1016/j.jce.2007.09.001

Lusardi, A. (2010, April 25). Compound interest 101. *The New York Times.* Retrieved from https://www.nytimes.com/2010/04/25/weekinreview/25chan.html?pagewanted=1&sq=They%20have%20got%20it:%20fixes%20for%20the%20financial%20system&st=cse&scp=1

Lusardi, A. (2012). *Numeracy, financial literacy, and financial decision-making* (Publication No. w17821). National Bureau of Economic Research.

Lusardi, A., & Mitchell, O. S. (2014). The economic importance of financial literacy. Theory and evidence. *Journal of Economic Literacy, 52*(1), 5–44. https://doi.org/10.1257/jel.52.1.5

Mandell, L. (2008). Financial literacy of high school students. In J. J. Xiao (Ed.), *Handbook of consumer finance research* (pp. 163–183). Springer New York. https://doi.org/10.1007/978-0-387-75734-6_10

McKernan, S. M., Ratcliffe, C., Simms, M., & Zhang, S. (2014). Do racial disparities in private transfers help explain the racial wealth gap? New evidence from longitudinal data. *Demography, 51*(3), 949–974. https://doi.org/10.1007/s13524-014-0296-7

Naidu, J. G. (2017). Financial literacy in India: A review of literature. *International Journal of Research in Business Studies and Management, 4*(6), 30–32. Retrieved from https://www.ijrbsm.org/papers/v4-i6/4.pdf

Nanziri, E. L., & Leibbrandt, M. (2018). Measuring and profiling financial literacy in South Africa. *South African Journal of Economic and Management Sciences, 21*(1), a1645. https://doi.org/10.4102/sajems.v21i1.1645

Norvilitis, J. M., & MacLean, M. G. (2010). The role of parents in college students' financial behaviors and attitudes. *Journal of Economic Psychology, 31*(1), 55–63. https://doi.org/10.1016/j.joep.2009.10.003

Norvilitis, J. M., Merwin, M. M., Osberg, T. M., Roehling, P. V., Young, P., & Kamas, M. M. (2006). Personality factors, money attitudes, financial knowledge, and credit-card debt in college students. *Journal of Applied Social Psychology, 36*(6), 1395–1413. https://doi.org/10.1111/j.0021-9029.2006.00065.x

Organisation for Economic Co-operation and Development. (2016). *OECD/INFE international survey of adult financial literacy competencies.* Retrieved from https://www.oecd.

org/daf/fin/financial-education/OECD-INFE-International-Survey-of-Adult-Financial-Literacy-Competencies.pdf

Organisation for Economic Co-operation and Development. (2017). *PISA 2015 results (Vol. IV): Students' financial literacy*. Retrieved from https://www.oecd.org/education/pisa-2015-results-volume-iv-9789264270282-en.htm

Organisation for Economic Co-operation and Development. (2018). OECD/ INFE toolkit for measuring financial literacy and financial inclusion. www.oecd.org/daf/fin/financial-education/2018-INFE-FinLit-Measurement-Toolkit.pdf

Organisation for Economic Co-operation and Development. (2019). *OECD/INFE report on financial education in APEC economies*. Retrieved from https://www.oecd.org/financial/education/2019-financial-education-in-apec-economies.pdf

Organisation for Economic Co-operation and Development. (2020). *PISA 2018 results (Vol. IV): Are students smart about money?* https://doi.org/10.1787/48ebd1ba-en

Porto N. (2016). Financial issues of Hispanic Americans. In J. J. Xiao (Ed.), *Handbook of consumer finance research* (pp. 205–214). Springer International. https://doi.org/10.1007/978-3-319-28887-1_17

Putnam, R. D. (1993). What makes democracy work? *National Civic Review*, *82*(2), 101–107. https://doi.org/10.1002/ncr.4100820204

Rafinda, A., & Gal, T. (2020). *Financial literacy of economics and non-economics student*. SHS Web Conference, Vol. 86. https://doi.org/10.1051/shsconf/20208601018

Raijas, A. (2021). Financial literacy and financial education in Northern Europe. In *The Routledge handbook of financial literacy* (pp. 382–399). Routledge. https://doi.org/10.4324/9781003025221-30

Ranta, M., Punamäki, R.- L., Chow, A., & Salmela- Aro, K. (2019). The economic stress model in emerging adulthood: The role of social relationships and financial capability. *Emerging Adulthood*, *8*(6), 496–508. https://doi.org/10.1177/2167696819893574

Ranta, M., & Salmela-Aro, K. (2018). Subjective financial situation and financial capability of young adults in Finland. *International Journal of Behavioral Development*, *42*(6), 525–534. https://doi.org/10.1177%2F0165025417745382

Rivero, C. C. (2021). Financial literacy and financial education in South America. In *The Routledge handbook of financial literacy* (pp. 344–362). Routledge. https://doi.org/10.4324/9781003025221-28

Robb, C. A., & James III, R. N. (2009). Associations between individual characteristics and financial knowledge among college students. *Journal of Personal Finance*, 8.

Schoeni, R. F., & Ross, K. E. (2005). Material assistance from families during the transition to adulthood. In R. A. Settersten Jr., F. F. Furstenberg Jr., & R. G. Rumbaut (Eds.), *On the frontier of adulthood: Theory, research, and public policy* (pp. 396–416). University of Chicago Press. https://doi.org/10.7208/chicago/9780226748924.003.0012

Schularick, M., Kuhn, M., & Steins, U. (2018). Income and wealth inequality in America, 1949–2016. *Centre for Economic Policy Research-Discussion Paper*, *128*(9), 3469–3519.

Schwartz, S. H. (2012). An overview of the Schwartz theory of basic values. *Online Readings in Psychology and Culture*, *2*(1). https://doi.org/10.9707/2307-0919.1116

Shapiro, T., Meschede, T., & Osoro, S. (2014). The widening racial wealth gap: Why wealth is not color blind. In R. Cramer & T. R. W. Shanks (Eds.), *The assets perspective: The rise of asset building and its impact on social policy* (pp. 99–122). Palgrave Macmillan USA. https://doi.org/10.1057/9781137384881_5

Sharpe, D. L., & Abdel-Ghany, M. (2006). Determinants of income differentials: Comparing Asians with Whites and Blacks. *Journal of Family and Economic Issues*, *27*(4), 588–600. https://doi.org/10.1007/s10834-006-9034-7

Sherraden, M. S. (2013). Building blocks of financial capability. In J. Birkenmaier, J. Curley, & M. Sherraden (Eds.), *Financial capability and asset development: Research, education, policy, and practice* (pp. 3–43). Oxford University Press. https://doi.org/10.1093/acprof:oso/9780199755950.003.0012

Standard & Poor's. (2015). *Financial literacy around the world: Insights from the Standard & Poor's ratings services global financial literacy survey.* Retrieved from https://media.mhfi.com/documents/2015-Finlit_paper_17_F3_SINGLES.pdf

Triandis, H. C. (1995). *Individualism and collectivism.* Westview.

US Census Bureau. (November 21, 2022). Number of households in the United States in 2022, by ethnic group (in millions) [Graph]. In Statista. Retrieved October 24, 2024, from https://www.statista.com/statistics/242027/number-of-households-in-the-us-by-ethnic-group/

White, K., Watkins, K., McCoy, M., Muruthi, B., & Byram, J. L. (2021). How financial socialization messages relate to financial management, optimism and stress: Variations by race. *Journal of Family and Economic Issues, 42,* 237–250. https://doi.org/10.1007/s10834-020-09704-w

Wolff, E. N. (2017). *Household wealth trends in the United States, 1962 to 2016: Has middle class wealth recovered?* (Publication No. w24085). National Bureau of Economic Research.

World Bank. (2018). *The little data book on financial inclusion.* Retrieved from https://data.worldbank.org/products/data-books/little-data-book-on-financial-inclusion

World Bank. (2020). *Migration and remittances database.* Retrieved from www.worldbank.org/en/topic/labormarkets/brief/migration-and-remittances

Xiao, J. J. (2021). Financial literacy and financial education in Asia. In *The Routledge handbook of financial literacy* (pp. 438–453). Routledge. https://doi.org/10.4324/9781003025221-33

Xiao, J. J., Chen, C., & Sun, L. (2015). Age differences in consumer financial capability. *International Journal of Consumer Studies, 39*(4), 387–395. https://doi.org/10.1111/ijcs.12205

Yakoboski, P. J., Lusardi, A., Hasler, A., & Center, E. (2019). *Financial literacy in the United States and its link to financial wellness.* The George Washington University School of Business and Global Financial Literacy Excellence Center (GFLEC).

Yao, R. (2016). Financial well-being of Asian Americans. In J. J. Xiao (Ed.), *Handbook of consumer finance research* (pp. 225–238). Springer International. https://doi.org/10.1007/978-3-319-28887-1_17

Yew, S. Y., Yong, C. C., Cheong, K. C., & Tey, N. P. (2017). Does financial education matter? Education literacy among undergraduates in Malaysia. *Institutions and Economies,* 43–60.

Chapter 18

Allsop, D. B., Boyack, M. N., Hill, E. J., Loderup, C. L., & Timmons, J. E. (2021). When parenting pays off: Influences of parental financial socialization on children's outcomes in emerging adulthood. *Journal of Family and Economic Issues, 42*(3), 545–560. https://doi.org/10.1007/s10834-020-09716-6

Clarke, M. C., Heaton, M. B., Israelsen, C. L., & Eggett, D. L. (2005). The acquisition of family financial roles and responsibilities. *Family and Consumer Sciences Research Journal, 33*(4), 321–340. https://doi.org/10.1177/1077727X04274117

Curran, M. A., Parrott, E., Ahn, S. Y., Serido, J., & Shim, S. (2018). Young adults' life outcomes and well-being: Perceived financial socialization from parents, the romantic partner, and young adults' own financial behaviors. *Journal of Family and Economic Issues, 39*(3), 445–456. https://doi.org/10.1007/s10834-018-9572-9

Danes, S. M. (1994). Parental perceptions of children's financial socialization. *Financial Counseling and Planning, 5*(1), 127–149.

Hancock, A. M., Jorgensen, B. L., & Swanson, M. S. (2013). College students and credit card use: The role of parents, work experience, financial knowledge, and credit card attitudes. *Journal of Family and Economic Issues, 34*(4), 369–381. https://doi.org/10.1007/s10834-012-9338-8

Hira, T. K. (2012). Promoting sustainable financial behaviour: Implications for education and research. *International Journal of Consumer Studies, 36*, 502–507. https://doi.org/10.1111/j.1470-6431.2012.01115.x

Gudmunson, C. G., Ray, S. K., & Xiao, J. J. (2016). Financial socialization. In J. J. Xiao, (Ed.), *Handbook of consumer finance research*, (pp. 61–72). Springer. https://doi.org/10.1007/978-3-319-28887-1_5

Jorgensen, B. L., Allsop, D. B., Runyan, S. D., Wheeler, B. E., Evans, D. A., & Marks, L. D. (2019). Forming financial vision: How parents prepare young adults for financial success. *Journal of Family and Economic Issues, 40*(3), 553–563. https://doi.org/10.1007/s10834-019-09624-4

Jorgensen, B. L., Rappleyea, D. L., Schweichler, J. T., Fang, X., & Moran, M. E. (2017). The financial behavior of emerging adults: A family financial socialization approach. *Journal of Family and Economic Issues, 38*(1), 57–69. https://doi.org/10.1007/s10834-015-9481-0

Jorgensen, B. L., & Savla, J. (2010). Financial literacy of young adults. *Family Relations, 59*(4), 465–478. https://doi.org/10.1111/j.1741-3729.2010.00616.x

Kim, J., & Chatterjee, S. (2013). Childhood financial socialization and young adults' financial management. *Journal of Financial Counseling & Planning, 24*(1), 61–79.

Kim, J., LaTaillade, J., & Kim, H. (2011). Family processes and adolescents' financial behaviors. *Journal of Family and Economic Issues, 32*(4), 668–679. https://doi.org/10.1007/s10834-011-9270-3

LeBaron, A. B. (2019). The socialization of financial giving: A multigenerational exploration. *Journal of Family and Economic Issues, 40*(4), 633–646. https://doi.org/10.1007/s10834-019-09629-z

LeBaron, A. B., Hill, E. J., Rosa, C. M., & Marks, L. D. (2018a). Whats and hows of family financial socialization: Retrospective reports of emerging adults, parents, and grandparents. *Family Relations, 67*(4), 497–509. https://doi.org/10.1111/fare.12335

LeBaron, A. B., Hill, E. J., Rosa, C. M., Spencer, T. J., Marks, L. D., & Powell, J. T. (2018b). I wish: Multigenerational regrets and reflections on teaching children about money. *Journal of Family and Economic Issues, 39*(2), 220–232. https://doi.org/10.1007/s10834-017-9556-1

LeBaron, A. B., Holmes, E. K., Jorgensen, B. L., & Bean, R. A. (2020a). Parental financial education during childhood and financial behaviors of emerging adults. *Journal of Financial Counseling and Planning, 31*(1), 42–54. https://doi.org/10.1891/JFCP-18-00021

LeBaron, A. B., Marks, L. D., Rosa, C. M., & Hill, E. J. (2020b). Can we talk about money? Financial socialization through parent–child financial discussion. *Emerging Adulthood, 8*(6), 453–463. https://doi.org/10.1177/2167696820902673

LeBaron, A. B., Rosa, C. M., Mork, L. A., Hill, E. J., & Marks, L. D. (2018c). Teaching children about money: Prospective parenting ideas from undergraduate students. *Journal of Financial Counseling and Planning, 29*(2), 259–271. https://doi.org/10.1891/1052-3073.29.2.259

LeBaron, A. B., Runyan, S. D., Jorgensen, B. L., Marks, L. D., Li, X., & Hill, E. J. (2019). Practice makes perfect: Experiential learning as a method for financial socialization. *Journal of Family Issues, 40*(4), 435–463. https://doi.org/10.1177/0192513X18812917

LeBaron-Black, A. B., Curran, M. A., Hill, E. J., Freeh, M. E., Toomey, R. B., & Speirs, K. E. (2022). Parent Financial Socialization Scale: Development and preliminary validation. *Journal of Family Psychology, 36*(6), 943–953. https://doi.org/10.1037/fam0000927

LeBaron-Black, A. B., Curran, M. A., Hill, E. J., Toomey, R. B., Speirs, K. E., & Freeh, M. E. (2023a). Talk is cheap: Parent financial socialization and emerging adult financial well-being. *Family Relations, 72*(3), 1201–1219. Advance online publication. https://doi.org/10.1111/fare.12751

LeBaron-Black, A. B., Saxey, M. T., McRae, K., Pistritto, M. M., Barros, J. D., Lindman, M. V., . . . Cavalcante, I. (2024a). Rise from the ashes: The modeling-compensation hypothesis applied to parent financial socialization. *Journal of Financial Counseling and Planning.* https://doi.org/10.1891/JFCP-2023-0044

LeBaron-Black, A. B., Saxey, M. T., Okamoto, R. M., Leonhardt, N. D., Rogers, A. A., & Curran, M. A. (2024b). Nine versions of the Parent Financial Socialization Scale: Full, short, and minimal versions for emerging adults, adolescents, and parents. *Journal of Family.* https://doi.org/10.1007/s10834-024-09966-8

Lep, Ž., Zupančič, M., & Poredoš, M. (2022). Saving of freshmen and their parents in Slovenia: saving motives and links to parental financial socialization. *Journal of Family and Economic Issues, 43*(4), 756–773. https://doi.org/10.1007/s10834-021-09789-x

Loderup, C. L., Timmons, J. E., Kimball, E. R., Hill, E. J., Marks, L. D., & LeBaron, A. B. (2021). How do parents teach their children about work? A qualitative exploration of household chores, employment, and entrepreneurial experiences. *Journal of Family and Economic Issues, 42*(1), 73–89. https://doi.org/10.1007/s10834-020-09709-5

Marks, L. D. (2015). A pragmatic, step-by-step guide for qualitative methods: Capturing the disaster and long-term recovery stories of Katrina and Rita. *Current Psychology, 34*(3), 494–505. https://doi.org/10.1007/s12144-015-9342-x

Pinto, M. B., Parente, D. H., & Mansfield, P. M. (2005). Information learned from socialization agents: Its relationship to credit card use. *Family and Consumer Sciences Research Journal, 33*(4), 357–367. https://doi.org/10.1177/1077727X04274113

Programme for International Student Assessment. (2018). *Are students smart about money?* Organisation for Economic Co-operation and Development. Retrieved from https://www.oecd.org/education/pisa-2018-results-volume-iv-48ebd1ba-en.htm

Rosa, C. M., Marks, L. D., LeBaron, A. B., & Hill, E. J. (2018). Multigenerational modeling of money management. *Journal of Financial Therapy, 9*(2), 54–74. https://doi.org/10.4148/1944-9771.1164

Serido, J., & Deenanath, V. (2016). Financial parenting: Promoting financial self-reliance of young consumers. In J. J. Xiao (Ed.), *Handbook of consumer finance research* (pp. 291–300). Springer. https://doi.org/10.1007/978-3-319-28887-1_24

Serido, J., LeBaron, A. B., Li, L., Parrott, E., & Shim, S. (2020a). The lengthening transition to adulthood: Financial parenting and recentering during the college-to-career transition. *Journal of Family Issues, 41*(9), 1626–1648. https://doi.org/10.1177/0192513X19894662

Serido, J., Shim, S., Mishra, A., & Tang, C. (2010). Financial parenting, financial coping behaviors, and well-being of emerging adults. *Family Relations, 59*(4), 453–464. https://doi.org/10.1111/j.1741-3729.2010.00615.x

Serido, J., Tang, C., Ahn, S. Y., & Shim, S. (2020b). Financial behavior change and progress toward self-sufficiency: A goal-framing theory application. *Emerging Adulthood, 8*(6), 521–529. https://doi.org/10.1177%2F2167696819861467

Sohn, S. H., Joo, S. H., Grable, J. E., Lee, S., & Kim, M. (2012). Adolescents' financial literacy: The role of financial socialization agents, financial experiences, and money attitudes in shaping financial literacy among South Korean youth. *Journal of Adolescence, 35*(4), 969–980. https://doi.org/10.1016/j.adolescence.2012.02.002

Solheim, C. A., Zuiker, V. S., & Levchenko, P. (2011). Financial socialization family pathways: Reflections from college students' narratives. *Family Science Review, 16*(2), 97–112.

Sorgente, A., Serido, J., Lanz, M., & Shim, S. (2024). Family financial socialization during emerging adulthood: Insights from a cross-lagged panel model. *Journal of Family Psychology, 38*(1), 161–173. https://doi.org/10.1037/fam0001139

Vosylis, R., & Erentaitė, R. (2020). Linking family financial socialization with its proximal and distal outcomes: Which socialization dimensions matter most for emerging adults' financial identity, financial behaviors, and financial anxiety? *Emerging Adulthood, 8*(6), 464–475. https://doi.org/10.1177/2167696819856763

White, K. J., Love, K., McCoy, M., Reiter, M., Seponski, D. M., Koposko, J., & Regan, E. (2022). Factors associated with the financial strain of transgender and gender diverse college students. *Journal of Consumer Affairs, 56*(4), 1617–1637. https://doi.org/10.1111/joca.12483

White, K. J., McCoy, M., Watkins, K., Chen, X., Koposko, J., & Mizuta, M. (2021a). "We don't talk about that": Exploring money conversations of Black, Hispanic, and White households. *Family and Consumer Sciences Research Journal, 49*(4), 328–343. https://doi.org/10.1111/fcsr.12397

White, K., Watkins, K., McCoy, M., Muruthi, B., & Byram, J. L. (2021b). How financial socialization messages relate to financial management, optimism and stress: Variations by race. *Journal of Family and Economic Issues, 42*(2), 237–250. https://doi.org/10.1007/s10834-020-09704-w

Chapter 19

Atkinson, A., & Messy, F. (2012). *Measuring financial literacy: Results of the OECD/International Network on Financial Education (INFE) pilot study*. OECD Working Papers on Finance, Insurance and Private Pensions, Vol. 15. OECD. https://doi.org/10.1787/20797117

Atlas, S., Nilton P., & Xiao, J. J. (2018). Financial education and confidence in financial knowledge. In A. Gershoff, R. Kozinets, & T. White (Eds.), *NA: Advances in consumer research* (Vol. 46, pp. 23–27). Association for Consumer Research. Retrieved from https://www.researchgate.net/profile/Stephen-Atlas/publication/327920889_Financial_Education_and_Confidence_in_Financial_Knowledge/links/5bad729b92851ca9ed2b8044/Financial-Education-and-Confidence-in-Financial-Knowledge.pdf

Bayer, P. J., Bernheim, B. D., & Scholz, J. K. (2009). The effects of financial education in the workplace: Evidence from a survey of employers. *Economic Inquiry, 47*(4), 605–624. https://doi.org/10.1111/j.1465-7295.2008.00156.x

Billari, F. C., Favero, C. A., & Saita, F. (2023). Online financial and demographic education for workers: Experimental evidence from an Italian pension fund. *Journal of Banking & Finance, 151*, 106849. https://doi.org/10.1016/j.jbankfin.2023.106849

Brugiavini, A., Cavapozzi, D., Padula, M., & Pettinicchi, Y. (2020). On the effect of financial education on financial literacy: Evidence from a sample of college students. *Journal of Pension Economics & Finance, 19*(3), 344–352. https://doi.org/10.1017/S1474747218000276

Burcher, S. A., Serido, J., Danes, S., Rudi, J., & Shim, S. (2021). Using the expectancy-value theory to understand emerging adult's financial behavior and financial well-being. *Emerging Adulthood, 9*(1), 66–75. https://doi.org/10.1177/2167696818815387

Burke, J., Collins, J. M., & Urban, C. (2020). *Does state-mandated financial education affect financial well-being?* Global Financial Literacy Excellence Center. Retrieved from https://gflec.org/wp-content/uploads/2023/04/Burke-Collins-Urban-Does-State-mandated-Financial-Education-CB2023-.pdf

Clark, R. L. (2023). Effectiveness of employer-provided financial education programs. *Journal of Financial Literacy and Wellbeing, 1*, 154–168. https://doi.org/10.1017/flw.2023.1

Collins, J. M., & O'Rourke, C. M. (2010). Financial education and counseling—Still holding promise. *Journal of Consumer Affairs, 44*(3), 483–498. https://doi.org/10.1111/j.1745-6606.2010.01179.x

Consumer Financial Protection Bureau (CFPB). (2015). *Measuring financial well-being: A guide to using the CFPB Financial Well-Being Scale.* Retrieved from https://www.consumerfinance.gov/data-research/research-reports/financial-well-being-scale

Cordero, J. M., Gil-Izquierdo, M., & Pedraja-Chaparro, F. (2022). Financial education and student financial literacy: A cross-country analysis using PISA 2012 data. *The Social Science Journal, 59*(1), 15–33. https://doi.org/10.1016/j.soscij.2019.07.011

Council for Economic Education (CEE). (2020). *Survey of the states: Economic and personal finance education in our nation's schools.* Retrieved from https://www.councilforeconed.org/wp-content/uploads/2020/02/2020-Survey-of-the-States.pdf

Duebner, B. (2022). A military solution to a military problem. *Military Review, 1.* Retrieved from https://www.armyupress.army.mil/Portals/7/military-review/Archives/English/Online-Exclusive/2022/Duebner/Duebner-v1.pdf

Edmiston, K. D., & Fisher, M. G. (2006). *Financial education at the workplace: Evidence from a survey of Federal Reserve Bank employees* (Community Affairs Research Working Paper No. 2006-02). Federal Reserve Bank of Kansas City. Retrieved from https://fedinprint.org/item/fedkcw/29904/original

FINRA IEF (Investment Education Foundation). (2019). *The state of U.S. financial capability: The 2018 national financial capability study.* Retrieved from https://finrafoundation.org/sites/finrafoundation/files/NFCS-2018-Report-Natl-Findings.pdf

Garman, E. T., Kim, J., Kratzer, C. Y., Brunson, B. H., & Joo, S. H. (1999). Workplace financial education improves personal financial wellness. *Financial Counseling and Planning, 10*(1), 79–88. Retrieved from https://uri.idm.oclc.org/login?url=https://www.proquest.com/scholarly-journals/workplace-financial-education-improves-personal/docview/1355870052/se-2?accountid=28991

Hanson, M. (2022, July 26). *College enrollment and student demographic statistics.* Retrieved from https://educationdata.org/college-enrollment-statistics

Hasler, A., Lusardi, A., Orellana, N., & Sconti, A. (2022). *Financial wellness programs in the workplace: Evidence from a Fortune 25 company development and testing of a comprehensive financial well-being measure.* Global Financial Literacy Excellence. Retrieved from https://gflec.org/wp-content/uploads/2022/12/EFE_report_2-FINAL.pdf

Johan, I., Rowlingson, K., & Appleyard, L. (2021). The effect of personal finance education on the financial knowledge, attitudes and behaviour of university students in Indonesia. *Journal of Family and Economic Issues, 42*, 351–367. https://doi.org/10.1007/s10834-020-09721-9

LeBaron, A. B., Holmes, E. K., Jorgensen, B. L., & Bean, R. A. (2020). Parental financial education during childhood and financial behaviors of emerging adults. *Journal of Financial Counseling and Planning, 31*(1), 42–54. https://doi.org/10.1891/JFCP-18-00021

Lee, J. M., Lee, J., & Kim, K. T. (2020). Consumer financial well-being: Knowledge is not enough. *Journal of Family and Economic Issues, 41*(2), 218–228. https://doi.org/10.1007/s10834-019-09649-9

National Financial Educators Council (NFEC). (2019). *Financial literacy standards and framework for learners.* Retrieved from https://www.financialeducatorscouncil.org

OECD. (2005). *Recommendation on principles and good practices for financial education and awareness.* Directorate for Financial and Enterprise Affairs. Recommendation of the Council. Retrieved from https://www.oecd.org/finance/financial-education/35108560.pdf

OECD. (2019). Policy handbook on financial education for young people in the Commonwealth of Independent States. Retrieved from https://www.oecd.org/daf/fin/financial-education/financial-education.htm

Philippas, N. D., & Avdoulas, C. (2020). Financial literacy and financial well-being among Generation Z university students: Evidence from Greece. *The European Journal of Finance, 26*(4–5), 360–381. https://doi.org/10.1080/1351847X.2019.1701512

Porto, N., & Xiao, J. J. (2021). The effectiveness of financial education on emerging adults. *Journal of Financial Service Professionals, 75*(5).

Skimmyhorn, W. L. (2016). Comparing military and civilian household finances: Descriptive evidence from recent surveys. *Journal of Consumer Affairs, 50*(2), 471–483. https://doi.org/10.1111/joca.12109

Slapakova, L., Thue, K., & Huxtable, L. (2023). *Understanding and supporting the financial stability of UK military families: Summary of findings and recommendations for policy and practice.* RAND Corporation. https://doi.org/10.7249/RBA2514-1

Stoddard, C., & Urban, C. (2020). The effects of state-mandated financial education on college financing behaviors. *Journal of Money, Credit and Banking, 52*(4), 747–776. https://doi.org/10.1111/jmcb.12624

Tan, X., Li, X., Hu, Z., Niu, Y., Ying, Q., Lu, Y., & Xu, J. (2022). Is it necessary to launch a school-based financial literacy curriculum? Evidence from China. *Frontiers in Psychology, 13*, 846382. https://doi.org/10.3389/fpsyg.2022.846382

Toosi, N. R., Voegeli, E. N., Antolin, A., Babbitt, L. G., & Brown, D. K. (2020). Do financial literacy training and clarifying pay calculations reduce abuse at work? *Journal of Social Issues, 76*(3), 681–720. https://doi.org/10.1111/josi.12388

Urban, C., Schmeiser, M., Collins, J. M., & Brown, A. (2020). The effects of high school personal financial education policies on financial behavior. *Economics of Education Review, 78*, 101786. https://doi.org/10.1016/j.econedurev.2018.03.006

Wagner, J., & Walstad, W. B. (2019). The effects of financial education on short-term and long-term financial behaviors. *Journal of Consumer Affairs, 53*(1), 234–259. https://doi.org/10.1111/joca.12210

Xiao, J. J. (2022). Personal finance research: An editor's perspective. In J. Grable & S. Chatterjee (Eds.), *De Gruyter handbook of personal finance* (pp. 585–598). De Gruyter. https://doi.org/10.1515/9783110727692

Xiao, J. J., & O'Neill, B. (2016). Consumer financial education and financial capability. *International Journal of Consumer Studies, 40*(6), 712–721. https://doi.org/10.1111/ijcs.12285

Zhang, H., & Xiong, X. (2020). Is financial education an effective means to improve financial literacy? Evidence from rural China. *Agricultural Finance Review, 80*(3), 305–320. https://doi.org/10.1108/AFR-03-2019-0027

Chapter 20

Berscheid, E. (1994). Interpersonal relationships. *Annual Review of Psychology, 45*(5), 79–129. https://doi.org/10.1146/annurev.psych.45.1.79

Danes, S. M., Alba, A., & Landers, A. (2016a). Cultural meanings of resource management for Mexican Americans. *Journal of Family and Economic Issues, 37*(4), 607–623. https://doi.org/10.1007/s10834-015-9476-x

Danes, S. M., Garbow, J., & Hagen-Jokela, R. (2016b). Financial management and culture: The American Indian case. *Journal of Financial Counseling and Planning, 27*(1), 61–79. https://doi.org/10.1891/1052-3073.27.1.61

Danes, S. M., Lee, J., Stafford, K., & Heck, R. K. Z. (2008). The effects of ethnicity, families and culture on entrepreneurial experience: An extension of sustainable family business theory. *Journal of Developmental Entrepreneurship, 13*(3), 229–268. https://doi.org/10.1142/S1084946708001010

Danes, S. M., & Yang, Y. (2014). Assessment of the use of theory within the *Journal of Financial Counseling and Planning* and contribution of the family socialization conceptual model. *Journal of Financial Counseling and Planning Education, 25*(1), 53–68.

Gottman, J. M., & Levenson, R. W. (2000). The timing of divorce: Predicting when a couple will divorce over a 14-year period. *Journal of Marriage and the Family, 62*, 737–745. https://doi.org/10.1111/j.1741-3737.2000.00737.x

Gudmunson, C. G., & Danes, S. M. (2013). Family social capital in family businesses: A stocks and flows investigation. *Family Relation, 62*, 399–414. https://doi.org/10.1111.fare.12017

Hauge, A. L. (2007). Identity and place: A critical comparison of three identity theories. *Architectural Science Review, 50*(1), 44–51. https://doi.org/10.3763/asre.2007.5007

Landers, A. L., Danes, S. M., Morgan, A. A., Merritt, S., & White Hawk, S. (2021). My relatives are waiting: Barriers to tribal enrollment of fostered/adopted American Indians. *Journal of Marriage and Family, 83*(5), 1373–1400. https://doi.org/10.1111/jomf.12797

Lanz, M., Sorgente, A., Tagliabue, S., & Danes, S. M. (2020). Implicit family financial socialization and emerging adults' financial well-being: A multiple informant approach. *Emerging Adulthood, 8*(6), 443–452. https://doi.org/10.1177/2167696819876752

Mao, D., Serido, J., & Danes, S.M. (2018). Financial influences impacting young adult's relationship satisfaction: Personal management quality, perceived partner behavior, and perceived financial mutuality. *Financial Therapy, 8*(2), 24–41. https://doi.org/10.4148/1944-9771.1151

McGovern, J. (2011). Couple meaning-making and dementia: Challenges to the deficit model. *Journal of Gerontological Social Work, 54*, 678–690. https://doi.org/10.1080/01634372.2011.593021

Melby, J., & Conger, R. (2001). The Iowa Family Interaction Rating Scales: Instrument summary. In P. Kerig & K. Lindahl (Eds.), *Family observational coding systems: Resources for systematic research* (pp. 33–58). Erlbaum.

Mirabelli, A. (2021). *What's in a name? Defining family in a diverse society. Transition.* The Vanier Institute of the Family. Retrieved from https://vanierinstitute.ca/definition-of-family

Ragin, C. C. (2008). *Redesigning social inquiry: Fuzzy sets and beyond.* University of Chicago Press. https://doi.org/10.7208/chicago/9780226702797.001.0001

Rea, J. K., Serido, J., Borden, L. M., Danes, S. M., & Shim, S. (2019). "Being able to support yourself": Young adults' meaning of financial well-being through family financial socialization. *Journal of Family and Economic Issues, 40*(2), 250–268. https://doi.org/10.1007/s10834-018-9602-7

Rea, J. K., Serido, J., Borden, L. M., Danes, S. M., & Shim, S. (2020). Before I say I do: The roles of finances, individual values, and personal and background factors on emerging adults' relationship choices. *Journal of Financial Counseling and Planning, 31*(1), 28–41. https://doi.org/10.1891/jfcp-19-00016

Rettig, K., Danes, S., & Leichtentritt, R. (1997). Affective, cognitive, and behavioral responses to economic stress. *Family and Consumer Sciences Research Journal, 26*, 3–28. https://doi.org/10.1177/1077727x970261001

Rettig, K. D., Leichentritt, R. D., & Danes, S. M. (1999). The effects of resources, decision making and decision implementing on perceived family well-being in adjusting to an economic stressor. *Journal of Family and Economic Issues, 20*(1), 5–34. https://doi.org/10.1023/A:1022163729635

Sartal, A., Llach, J., Vazquez, X. H., & de Castro, R. (2017). How much does lean manufacturing need environmental and information technologies? *Journal of Manufacturing Systems, 45*(1), 260–272. https://doi.org/10.1016/j.jmsy.2017.10.005

Shepherd, D. A. (2009). Grief recovery from the loss of family business: A multi- and meso-level theory. *Journal of Business Venturing, 24*, 81–97. https://doi.org/10.1016/j.jbusvent.2007.09.003

Sherraden, M. S. (2010). Financial capability: What is it, and how can it be created? (Working Paper No. 10-17). Washington University, Center for Social Development. https://doi.org/10.7936/K7SX6CQX

Sherraden, M. S. (2013). Building blocks of financial capability. In J. M. Birkenmaier, M. S. Sherraden, & J. C. Curly (Eds.), *Financial capability and asset building: Research education, policy, and practice* (pp. 1–43). Oxford University Press. https://doi.org/10.1093/acprof:oso/9780199755950.003.0012

Sztompka, P. (1974). *System and function: Toward a theory of society*. Academic Press.

Twenge, J. M. (2023). *The real differences between Gen Z, millenials, Gen X, boomers, and silents—and what they mean for America's future*. Atria Books.

Van Campenhout, G. (2015). Revaluing the role of parents as financial socialization agents in youth financial literacy programs. *Journal of Consumer Affairs, 49*(1), 186–222. https://doi.org/10.1111/joca.12064.

Von Bertalanffy, L. (1968). *General system theory: Foundations, development, applications*. George Braziller.

Index

For the benefit of digital users, indexed terms that span two pages (e.g., 52–53) may, on occasion, appear on only one of those pages.

Note: Tables, figures, and boxes are indicated by an italic t, f, and b following the page/paragraph number